PARKMAN

THE
OREGON
TRAIL

EDITED BY

E. N. Feltskog

University of Nebraska Press
Lincoln and London

First Bison Book printing: 1994
Most recent printing indicated by the last digit below:
10   9   8   7   6   5   4   3   2   1

Library of Congress Cataloging-in-Publication Data
Parkman, Francis, 1823–1893.
The Oregon Trail / Parkman; edited by E.N. Feltskog.
p.   cm.
Originally published: Madison: University of Wisconsin Press, 1969.
Includes bibliographical references and index.
ISBN 0-8032-8739-9
1. West (U.S.)—Description and travel.   2. Indians of North America—West
(U.S.)   3. Frontier and pioneer life—West (U.S.)   4. Oregon Trail.   5. Cali-
fornia Trail.   6. West—History—To 1848.
I. Feltskog, E. N.   II. Title.
F592.P284   1994
978'.02—dc20
94-19303
CIP

Reprinted by arrangement with E. N. Feltskog

∞

THE OREGON TRAIL

Introduction to the Bison Book Edition

The present edition of Francis Parkman's classic narrative of far western travel and adventure in 1846 began as a doctoral dissertation at the University of Illinois in 1963–65 under the wise guidance of Professor Edward H. Davidson. He had even then begun the tedious analyses of the various "editions" and revisions of Parkman's texts from its initial serial-publication in *The Knickerbocker Magazine* in 1846–48 down to the "Illustrated Edition" of 1893. The latter was very nearly a "death-bed edition" and contained no important or even meaningful textual changes or developments; its greater value, in Davidson's view and my own, lay in Frederic Remington's reconstructive illustrations and particularly in Parkman's own careful and elaborate responses to Remington's letters of inquiry — a correspondence in part copied here. Of course, my own "edition" of *The Oregon Trail* — primarily a textual study — in no way represented the best methods of textual analysis and copy-text theory in scholarly practice even then, though the final dissertation may be called accurate in the listing of variant readings of every sort. Practically, these variants from Parkman's final text, many reported here, allow the reconstruction of any true edition of *The Oregon Trail* before 1893, the year of Parkman's death.

Though my own original manuscript was almost immediately accepted for scholarly publication, I soon recognized that the few and paltry historical and biographical notes I had included for the "Illustrated Edition" as copy-text were neither comprehensive nor often very sensible; whether by luck or design I must have decided early on, in my *own* revisions, that Bernard DeVoto and his *The Year of Decision: 1846* provided the best immediate historiographic models and methods for a younger scholar with nothing but literary credentials. More than that, I soon discovered that my edition must inevitably appear as a companion-piece to DeVoto rather than (as I had hoped) the reverse. Depending thus on De-

Voto even at *this* distance, I can say that most of the physical geography, the popular science, and the military, emigrant, fur-trade, and Native American identifications, biographies, and history still hold up. Parkman's own letters and journals from 1846 remain always the first source for what he saw and *felt* in that year of his own and America's decision. There are, however, some details I might have further clarified or gotten right in the first place: I misplaced the mouth of the Colorado River; Deslauriers' "charette" might have been different in make and purpose from what I thought was a "Red River Cart" (though Remington's illustrations looked that way); and *someone* named or *dit* "Lee Bontee the guide" was killed at the Fetterman Fight in 1866.

Parkman scholarship has always been an active and expansive endeavor; I'm glad to recommend three or four exceptional titles out of the ten or fifteen recent studies in Parkman biography and western history, a field as constantly interesting and generous as the scholars engaged in it. For Parkman himself, Wilbur R. Jacobs' *Francis Parkman, Historian as Hero: The Formative Years* (1991) and Robert L. Gale's *Francis Parkman* (1974) present a strenuous advocacy for the historian's greatness. Of more general and cross-disciplinary or cross-cultural studies, Roderick Nash's *Wilderness and the American Mind* (1982) and Robert C. Vitzthum's *The American Compromise: Theme and Method in the Histories of Bancroft, Parkman and Adams* (1974) are exceptionally useful. I wish I had had all of them twenty-five years ago.

—This again looks to Mark, Ellen, Barbara.

E. N. Feltskog
Madison, Wisconsin
April 1994

Editor's Preface

FRANCIS Parkman's *The Oregon Trail* has long been accepted as a classic account of western adventure. It has been read primarily as a narrative of a summer's romantic rambles "out of bounds"; for half a century it has remained the perennial favorite of high-school reading lists. Yet the book has escaped much searching critical analysis, perhaps because it seems so deceptively clear, so free from the intellectual and emotional tensions of Parkman's great histories.

The present text of *The Oregon Trail* is the first edition to demonstrate in detail how carefully Parkman prepared himself for his journey to the Far West and how fully his experience of the wilderness justified his suffering along the Oregon and Santa Fe trails. It is the first to identify positively many of the persons he met in the West in 1846, and the first to place Parkman's narrative of western life and adventure in its appropriate literary context. Finally, this edition rests upon a complete collation of the various "editions" of *The Oregon Trail* published during Parkman's lifetime, from its serialization in the *Knickerbocker Magazine* in 1847–1849, through its first book publication in 1849, and through all the subsequent "editions" until Parkman established his final text in the "Illustrated Edition" of 1892, the text for this facsimile edition. Of major interest in this connection is his consistent and careful editing of the text of *The Oregon Trail* through four distinct versions, a fact which puts to rest the legend of authorial carelessness and indifference.

This edition also demonstrates, quite contrary to accepted

biographical opinion, that Parkman alone was responsible for most of those textual changes and expurgations which have hitherto been charged to his friend Charles Eliot Norton. The original collations of the texts of *The Oregon Trail* and many of the excisions and variant readings restored in the textual notes in this edition show conclusively that Parkman was a literary stylist of considerable ability at the very beginning of his career and that he strove, then and afterwards, for clarity of detail and stylistic refinement in his several major revisions of the book.

The inspiration for this edition of *The Oregon Trail* came from the director of my doctoral dissertation, Professor Edward H. Davidson of the University of Illinois, without whose constant interest and encouragement it would never have been completed. Professor Robert M. McColley of the University of Illinois Department of History gave largely of his knowledge and friendship during every step of the preparation of the original manuscript. I am also indebted to Professor G. Blakemore Evans of the Department of English of Harvard University and to Professors Walter B. Rideout, Merton M. Sealts, Jr., and Herbert F. Smith, all of the University of Wisconsin Department of English, for scholarly criticism and counsel. Professor Robert W. Rogers and the Research Council of the University of Illinois made it possible for me to examine manuscript collections at Cambridge and Boston; the University of Wisconsin Graduate School materially assisted me in the revision of my original manuscript with a summer research grant in 1966.

The staffs of the Massachusetts Historical Society in Boston and the Houghton Library of Harvard University placed at my disposal Parkman's Oregon Trail notebooks and letters and the Charles Eliot Norton Letterbooks; I acknowledge with thanks the permissions of both institutions to quote from published and unpublished Parkman and Norton materials. The libraries of the University of California at Berkeley, the University of Chicago, the University of Wisconsin, and Ohio State University, and the Library of Congress, the Newberry Library, and the State Historical Society of Wisconsin have provided me with various editions of *The Oregon Trail.* I wish also to thank Miss Alma DeJordy of the University of Illinois Library for securing those editions for me. Mrs. Mary Kay Peer of the University of Illinois Department of English has helped me in innumerable professional and personal ways. Miss Joan Krager and Mrs. Margaret B. Hickey of the University of Wisconsin Press have been of considerable and conscientious help to me in the preparation of this edition for publication. I am indebted to the University of Wisconsin Cartographic Laboratory for the preparation of the map of Parkman's western travels in 1846. My wife and my parents know how greatly they too have helped.

I am glad to acknowledge not only the scholarly productions but, more importantly, the example of men like Bernard DeVoto, Donald Jackson, LeRoy R. Hafen, Dale L. Morgan, and George R. Stewart, all of whom are frequently cited in the notes accompanying this edition. Any scholar at work on the history of the American West knows the intelligence and imagination which these men have brought to their discipline, and I can only say that their work and their methods of research and inquiry have served me well. I am greatly in their debt.

E. N. Feltskog

Madison, Wisconsin
September 1, 1968

Contents

Editor's Introduction

THIRTY miles west of Westport, Missouri, a solitary fingerpost marked the separation of the Oregon and Santa Fe trails. "Road to Oregon" was the short and uncompromising message it bore,[1] and past that last symbol of civilization streamed many of the thousands of emigrants, traders, and soldiers who made 1846 the year of decision in the history of the Westward Movement and who changed Manifest Destiny from newspaper rhetoric to hard-won reality in California and Oregon and New Mexico.[2]

Down emigrant road and trader's trace there passed, this same year, men and women whose subsequent accounts of their adventures make 1846 the best-documented year in the early history of western exploration, travel, and settlement. Philip St. George Cooke and J. W. Abert, William H. Emory and John T. Hughes and other soldiers described the march of the Army of the West and Doniphan's expedition. Edwin Bryant and Jesse Quinn Thornton and Heinrich Lienhard and many other emigrants kept diaries on the long roads to Oregon and California; George Frederick Ruxton, the English soldier, recorded scenes of trapper life in the Rocky Moun-

---

[1] F. A. Wislizenus, *Memoir of a Tour to Northern Mexico, Connected with Col. Doniphan's Expedition, in 1846 and 1847* (Washington, D.C. 1848), p. 6.

[2] *The Year of Decision 1846* (Boston, 1943) is, of course, Bernard DeVoto's masterful re-creation and recapitulation of the events of 1846.

tains; James Clyman, a retired mountain man and California pioneer, set down the harrowing account of his trip eastward along the backtrail from California to Missouri; Susan Shelby Magoffin kept a log of her travels down the Santa Fe Trail; and Lewis H. Garrard and Francis Parkman turned rough journal notes into classic narratives of western adventure.[3]

In all these accounts and in other more obscure journals and diaries there runs a predominant symbol of civilization and security. That symbol is the road, but only Francis Parkman called his book *The Oregon Trail*, and Parkman seems particularly to have sensed the importance of that symbol, to have understood how the road, stretching westward in vast isolation and terrifying loneliness, dominated the imaginations of those who traveled it. The roads westward from Independence and Westport and St. Joseph to Sutter's Fort, Oregon City, and Santa Fe were the only links between widely separated frontiers; 10 feet from the wagon traces the wilderness began and civilization died.

In May, 1846, when Parkman turned his horse's head west-

---

[3] Mason Wade discovered Parkman's "Oregon Trail" Journals and a great many other important notebooks and diaries in 1940 and published most of them in a two-volume edition of *The Journals of Francis Parkman* in 1947. I have compared microfilms of Parkman's three original Oregon Trail notebooks (now owned by the Massachusetts Historical Society) with Wade's transcription of them in the second volume of *The Journals of Francis Parkman* and am satisfied that Wade copied them carefully and completely. All subsequent references to Parkman's Oregon Trail notebooks will therefore be to vol. II of Wade's edition, hereafter cited as *Journals*.

All students of Parkman's life and career owe an immense debt of gratitude to Wade for his indefatigable research; his life of Parkman, *Francis Parkman: Heroic Historian* (New York, 1942), is probably still the standard biography. From time to time in this Introduction I shall be obliged to argue strongly against some of Wade's ideas, but I am aware of the lucidity and the stimulation of his arguments, even when I most disagree with them.

ward down the Mission Road out of Westport, he knew only that he hoped to strike the "course of the traders," the combined Oregon and Santa Fe trails bearing southwestward across the prairies to approximately the present site of Gardner, Kansas. But his English companions, for reasons of their own, had determined to visit Fort Leavenworth, and so Parkman left the emigrants' and the traders' trace almost as soon as he found it. When he crossed the Kansas River at the Grinter Ferry and rode northeastward toward Fort Leavenworth, he left behind him the bawling confusion of the emigrant wagons and the sure landmarks of a traveled road.

The first significant fact about Parkman's experience with the western wilderness in 1846 is that he was lost almost immediately after he and his companions rode out of Fort Leavenworth on the morning of May 13. Had he remained with the Oregon and California companies moving along the established routes, his early impressions of the wilderness might have been a great deal more prosaic, even tedious, but his first emotion of wonder, of "admiration" at the rough scenes of frontier life in Independence and Westport, might not so soon have been transformed into a darker sense of loneliness and dread. From Fort Leavenworth to the Big Blue River, Parkman was alone and lost on the illimitable prairies of eastern Kansas, though he knew that south and west of him the wagon trains were measuring the first hundred miles of the roads to Oregon and California.

The Oregon and California Trails: Emigration

The emigrants themselves had not yet lost the sense of community; they had organized themselves, in their camps around Westport and Independence and St. Joseph, by the tested methods of frontier democracy, stump oratory and judicious flattery, and for the first few weeks the companies were town meetings on wheels. Household remedies and rumors passed from wagon to wagon, and couriers from the settlements rode up with the latest newspapers and "camp reports." Both the enthusiasm and the cohesiveness of the wagon trains began to crumble, however, soon after they turned northwestward along the Oregon Trail, and by the time they reached the crossing of the Wakarusa River, a few miles south of modern Lawrence, Kansas, fatigue and the obstinacy of men and oxen had begun a slow and sure dissolution of morale and mutual trust.

The emigrant wagons dragged on toward Coon Hollow and the crossing of the Kansas River near modern Topeka. Bearing west and then northwest they forded Cross Creek, the Red Vermillion River, and Rock Creek and then turned almost due north toward the Black Vermillion and the Independence Crossing of the Big Blue River south of modern Marysville. By this time many of the simmering feuds had grown into outright rupture; Parkman, riding westward along the St. Joseph Road to its junction with the Oregon Trail north of the Independence Crossing, saw the collapse of one emigrant company and for a while traveled with one of the "go-ahead" sections. From the Independence Crossing the increasingly divided trains drove across the prairies to the north bank of the Little Blue River, a well-timbered stream pointing them west and northwest toward the Platte.

And here Parkman and the emigrants found themselves in true "Indian Country"—in the territory of the roving Pawnees, who had not yet succumbed to civilization and whiskey like the Kaws and the reservation Indians from the East. "Pawnee Trails" ran south from Grand Island, and the emigrants took care not to wander too far from the trail; the Pawnees had a bad name for robbing stragglers and stampeding draft animals.

The country, too, had begun to change when the emigrants struck the south bank of the Platte near Grand Island. The forests and prairies of "the States" had given way to what the nineteenth century called a "desert"—a vast treeless plain cut by a wide, silt-laden river. As the wagons pushed westward, the atmosphere became ever drier, the landscape more broken, the forage harder and harder to find, and only buffalo and antelope moved along the profiles of the barren hills along the riverbank. Children and old people had begun to die by the time the wagons reached the forks of the river and forded the South Platte; collapsing wagons and dying oxen and the fantastic scenery from the Courthouse and Chimney Rock westward to Fort Laramie changed the joyous wonder of the first weeks of the trail into a sense of fear and brutal isolation; Parkman and the emigrants had begun to *learn* the wilderness.

At Fort Bernard and Fort Laramie the wagons paused long enough to refit and reprovision before the long miles of deserts and mountains to Fort Bridger and Fort Hall, to Sutter's Fort and Oregon City and the end of the trail. The most difficult three-fifths of their journey still lay before the emigrants after they left Fort Laramie, and Parkman himself never got more than 70 or 80 miles west of the post. From Fort Laramie to the Sweetwater River the westward tilt of the continent grew constantly steeper until the wagons crossed the Continental Divide at South Pass. Here the waters ran east and west to the Missouri and the Columbia, and from South Pass the main Oregon Trail pointed southwestward toward Fort Bridger and then northwestward down the valley of the Bear River to Soda Springs and Fort Hall on the Snake River of Idaho. The emigrant wagons then followed the Snake on its long bend to the southwest, crossed over to the north bank of the river near modern Glenns Ferry, and came down the Boise River to Fort Boise. Crossing the Snake River again and the Malheur and the Burnt rivers, the trail descended into the Grande Ronde Valley of eastern Oregon and then made a difficult crossing of the Blue Mountains. Two alternate roads came down to the Columbia along the Umatilla and Walla Walla rivers, and the emigrants then followed the Columbia westward through the perilous gorges at The

Parkman's route from Westport to Fort Laramie along the Oregon Trail and return along the Santa Fe Trail in 1846. His voyage upriver from St. Louis to

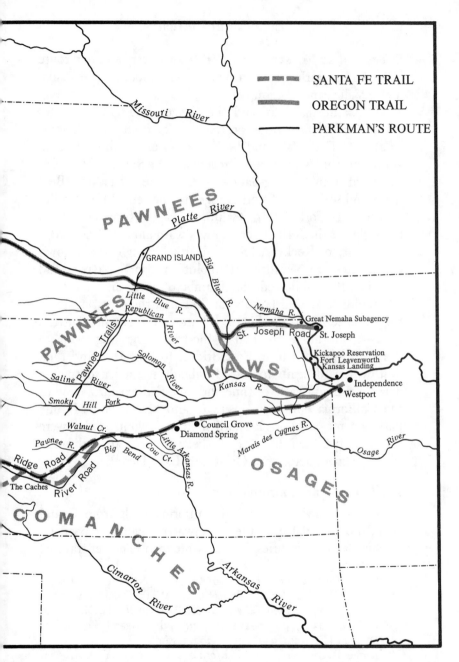

Kansas Landing has been purposely omitted so as to include important subsequent details. Map: UW Cartographic Lab.

Dalles and still westward to Fort Vancouver; another route followed the Barlow Road around Mount Hood to the Willamette Valley and Oregon City.[4]

The California Trail and the Oregon Trail ran west together for the first 1,000 or 1,200 miles from the Missouri frontier to Fort Hall, and both Oregon and California emigrant companies used the Greenwood, or Sublette, Cut-Off westward from the Big Sandy River to the Green and Bear rivers and so bypassed Fort Bridger to the south. Forty miles southwest of Fort Hall the California wagons turned south up the valley of the Raft River and westward along Cassia Creek to the City of Rocks. A long, dull drive brought them down Goose Creek to Nevada's Humboldt (or Mary's) River, and the trail then followed the Humboldt west and south to Humboldt Lake and Humboldt Sink and then west again to the Truckee River, the Sierra, Johnson's Ranch, and Sutter's Fort—California at the end of the trail.[5] The long swing to the northwestward from Fort Bridger to Fort Hall and then southwestward again to the Humboldt seemed a desperate delay, a ruinous waste of time and men and oxen, to some of the California emigrants in 1846, and at the end of June Parkman met at Fort Bernard men and women who were about to bet their lives on a "better route" to California southwestward across the Great Salt Lake Desert.

The Oregon and California Trails: History

The combined Oregon and California trails from Grand Island up the Platte to the Sweetwater River had been an Indian road for centuries, but no white men had ever traveled

[4] W. J. Ghent, *The Road to Oregon* (New York, 1929), pp. 121–148; Federal Writers' Project of the Works Progress Administration, *The Oregon Trail: The Missouri River to the Pacific Ocean* (New York, 1939), pp. 37–161 *passim;* and Margaret Long, *The Oregon Trail* (Denver, 1954), pp. 3–272 *passim.*

[5] George R. Stewart, *The California Trail* (New York, 1962), pp. 127–141.

that route before a party of eastward-bound Astorians under Robert Stuart discovered South Pass in October, 1812.[6] After the failure of William H. Ashley's second expedition up the Missouri River in 1823, Jedediah S. Smith, Thomas Fitzpatrick, James Clyman, and other mountain men rediscovered South Pass in the spring of 1824, and, as Charles Camp notes, "The discoveries made by these scouts led almost immediately to American control of the Rocky Mountain beaver trade and to explorations of the great unknown districts lying between the Rockies and the Sierra Nevada. Thus were trails opened for the westward rush by trapper-guided settlers who saved Oregon for America and stimulated the early conquest of California."[7]

South Pass was the great natural gateway for the penetration of the central mountain region by American trappers and traders, and in the late winter of 1826–1827 William L. Sublette and Moses "Black" Harris came down to St. Louis from the mountains by way of the Platte, the Little Blue, and the Kansas rivers—a route first known as "Sublette's Trace" and finally as the first half of the Oregon Trail. In the spring of 1827 Sublette and his trading caravan retraced his new route westward up the Platte and over South Pass to the trappers' rendezvous at Bear Lake. With the pack train rolled a four-pounder cannon mounted on a mule-drawn cart—the first wheels to cross the Continental Divide.[8]

---

[6] Robert Stuart, *The Discovery of the Oregon Trail: Robert Stuart's Narratives of His Overland Trip Eastward from Astoria in 1812–1813*, ed. Philip Ashton Rollins (New York, 1935), pp. lxv–lxxi, 163–165, 181–183.

[7] James Clyman, *James Clyman, Frontiersman: The Adventures of a Trapper and Covered-Wagon Emigrant as Told in His Own Reminiscences and Diaries*, ed. Charles L. Camp (Portland, 1960), p. 5.

[8] Louise A. Barry, "Kansas before 1854: A Revised Annals," *Kansas Historical Quarterly*, XXVIII (Spring, 1962), 33; Dale L. Morgan and Eleanor Towles Harris, eds. *The Rocky Mountain Journals of William Marshall Anderson: The West in 1834* (San Marino, 1967), pp. 7–11;

By the spring of 1830 Sublette and his partners, David Jackson and Jedediah Smith, had determined to experiment with wagons in the supply train to that year's rendezvous, held east of the mountains at the junction of the Wind and Popo Agie rivers near modern Riverton, Wyoming. Sublette drove two dearborn carriages, 10 large freight wagons, and a small herd of cattle all the way up the Platte Valley to the turnoff toward the Popo Agie; the Oregon Trail was now a proven wagon road to the foot of the mountains. When Captain Benjamin Bonneville and his 20 wagons crossed South Pass on the way to the Green River rendezvous of 1832, the great Oregon and California overland emigrations of the 1840's and 1850's were only a matter of the proper application of forces already stirring.[9]

"Oregon" by this time had become not only a sonorous name in nature poetry but a place, a more or less definite land of supposed milk and honey, and in 1829 Hall Kelley of Boston organized the American Society for Encouraging the Settlement of Oregon Territory and began to sign up recruits for a wildly visionary march of 3,000 colonists overland from St. Louis. Kelley's enthusiasm and the synopsis of all known information about the Northwest Coast which he published in 1830 had an initially strong effect on such men as the Massachusetts merchant Nathaniel Jarvis Wyeth, but for the next several years the East sent no one but missionaries to California. In 1834 Jason and Daniel Lee and Cyrus Shepherd traveled the whole length of what would become the Oregon

---

and David Lavender, *Westward Vision: The Story of the Oregon Trail* (New York, 1963), pp. 210–211.

[9] Lavender, *Westward Vision*, pp. 223–243 *passim*; LeRoy R. Hafen, ed. *The Mountain Men and the Fur Trade of the Far West*, 1 (Glendale, Calif., 1965), 90–123 *passim*; Washington Irving, *The Adventures of Captain Bonneville*, ed. Edgeley W. Todd (Norman, 1961), pp. 3–51 *passim*; and John E. Sunder, *Bill Sublette: Mountain Man* (Norman, 1959), pp. 68–89 *passim*.

Trail in response to the "Macedonian cry" from the Far West, driving with them a herd of cows and calves as far westward as Fort Walla Walla; in 1836 the famous medical missionary Dr. Marcus Whitman brought a wagon as far as Fort Hall, and its fragments, in the form of a cart, to Fort Boise.[10]

Missionaries continued to travel to Oregon throughout the rest of the 1830's, and in 1839 several members of a party from Peoria, Illinois, had managed by a roundabout route to get to Oregon, but most historians of the Westward Movement agree with Dale L. Morgan[11] in considering 1840 the crucial first year in the history of overland emigration to California and Oregon. On April 30, 1840, Joel P. Walker (the brother of the famous mountain man Joseph Reddeford Walker), his wife and five children, three Protestant missionary couples, and Father Pierre-Jean De Smet of the Jesuits left Westport with the trading caravan for the last trappers' rendezvous on the Green River. Walker and the missionaries left their four wagons at Fort Hall, but in the spring or summer of 1841 Robert "Doc" Newell, a retired mountain man, managed to bring the running gear of one wagon from Fort Walla Walla down to the Columbia and by portage all the way to the Willamette Valley.[12]

In that spring of 1841 the small Bartleson party jumped off for California from the Missouri frontier, in company with

[10] Lavender, *Westward Vision*, pp. 222–265 *passim;* Ghent, *Road to Oregon*, pp. 25–47 *passim;* and Bernard DeVoto, *Across the Wide Missouri* (Boston, 1947), pp. 178–278 *passim.*

[11] Dale L. Morgan, ed. *Overland in 1846: Letters and Diaries of the California-Oregon Trail* (Georgetown, Calif., 1963), I, 14–15.

[12] Lavender, *Westward Vision*, pp. 340–343; Ghent, *Road to Oregon*, pp. 45–46; Hafen, ed. *Mountain Men and the Fur Trade*, I, 163–165; and Robert Newell, *Robert Newell's Memoranda . . .* , ed. Dorothy O. Johansen (Portland, 1959), pp. 22–23, 38–39: "this is to be remembered that I Robert Newell was the first who brought waggons across the rocky mountains. . . ."

Father De Smet, an Englishman named Romaine (Parkman's companion in 1846), and the famous mountain man, Thomas Fitzpatrick, the Catholic party's guide. At Soda Springs the Bartleson party divided; some of the emigrants kept on for Oregon, but 31 men, one woman, and her baby were in the company that turned down the Bear River for California, which they reached in the fall by way of the Humboldt and Walker rivers and Sonora Pass. These California pioneers had abandoned their wagons at the foot of the Pequop Mountains, and, as Morgan notes, "After a fashion the Bartleson party had proved that it was possible to reach California overland."[13]

There was no organized emigration to California in 1842, but in the spring of that year Dr. Elijah White, the newly appointed subagent for the Indians of Oregon, was elected captain of an Oregon-bound company of more than 100 persons and 18 or 20 wagons. After a good many quarrels and regroupings, most of the White party got through to Oregon City, though all their wagons had had to be abandoned by the time the emigrants reached Fort Hall.

The "Great Emigration" of 1843 to Oregon, led in part by Marcus Whitman, numbered more than 800 persons; many of the wagons went all the way through to Oregon City. Only a few pioneers got to California in 1843, under the divided leadership of Joseph Chiles and the famous mountain man Joseph Reddeford Walker, and their wagons were abandoned east of the summit of Walker Pass. There was another very large emigration to Oregon in 1844, but that year is memorable in the history of overland travel because the Stephens-Townsend-Murphy company, bound for California, first used the Greenwood Cut-Off north of Fort Bridger and then followed the Humboldt-Truckee route over what came to be known as Donner Pass. The California Trail was now open

[13] Morgan, ed. *Overland in 1846*, I, 16. See also Stewart, *California Trail*, pp. 7–29.

from end to end, and in 1845 both Oregon and California received larger emigrations than ever before.[14]

The Santa Fe Trail: History

Trading wagons had rolled over the Santa Fe Trail, the third of the great highways of the West, fully 20 years before the first emigrant parties brought their wagons through to Oregon City and Sutter's Fort. Jean Baptise LaLande had reached Santa Fe with a pack train by way of the headwaters of the South Platte River as early as 1804, and when Zebulon M. Pike arrived in New Mexico in 1806 he discovered James Purcell of Kentucky, who in 1805 had also come down to Sante Fe from the South Platte. In his explorations up the Arkansas River, Pike had pioneered a long stretch of what would eventually be known as the Mountain Route of the Santa Fe Trail. In 1812 Robert McKnight, James Baird, and Samuel Chambers led a small party overland to New Mexico, where they were seized by the authorities and imprisoned for the best part of the next nine years for their violation of Spanish territory.

After the winning of Mexican Independence, three American trading parties fitted out for New Mexico in 1821. In 1822 William Becknell opened the first wagon road to Santa Fe by way of the Arkansas and Cimarron rivers, and in 1825 the United States government undertook a survey of the whole route.[15]

The Mountain Route of the Santa Fe Trail in 1846 ran

[14] Morgan, ed. *Overland in 1846*, I, 16–18; Lavender, *Westward Vision*, pp. 325–382 *passim*; Stewart, *California Trail*, pp. 30–105 *passim*; and Ghent, *Road to Oregon*, pp. 48–85 *passim*.

[15] Hafen, ed. *Mountain Men and the Fur Trade*, I, 59–65; Dean Earl Wood, *The Old Santa Fe Trail from the Missouri River* (Kansas City, Mo., 1951), pp. 1–25 *passim*; and Josiah Gregg, *The Commerce of the Prairies*, in R. G. Thwaites, ed. *Early Western Travels*, XIX (Cleveland, 1905), 173–187; and Margaret Long, *The Santa Fe Trail* (Denver, 1954), pp. 3–28 *passim*.

southwestward across the prairies from Independence to the Big Bend of the Arkansas River and then followed the river upstream to Bent's Fort, near modern La Junta, Colorado. The trail then turned southwestward up Timpas Creek to the Purgatoire River and entered New Mexico over Raton Pass. The Desert Route left the Arkansas at several crossings west of the Big Bend and turned southwestward over the barren prairies to the Cimarron River, which it ascended southwestward toward the Canadian River and New Mexico. There was never any organized emigration along the Santa Fe Trail, though in 1846 a number of Americans were already living and trading in Taos and Santa Fe.

The Trails in 1846

Thus, the three great highways of the West stretched across the continent to California and Oregon and New Mexico, westward to Manifest Destiny, in the lengthening spring of 1846. By the end of April most of the passes were clear of snow, the trails dry enough to bear wagons and herds. The fur posts began equipping the trappers for their spring beaver hunts in the mountains; the Indians were breaking up their winter lodges and moving toward the buffalo plains along the Platte and the Arkansas. In Missouri and Illinois, Indiana and Kentucky, and all along the advancing agricultural frontier people like the Donners and the Thorntons, Edwin Bryant and William H. Russell and Lillburn Boggs and Alphonso Boone were laying in cornmeal and salt pork, lead and percussion caps and powder, and mirrors and plugs of cheap tobacco for the Indians they expected to meet on the road to California or Oregon. Many of the "movers" had purchased copies of Frémont's *Report* or Lansford W. Hastings' *Emigrants' Guide to Oregon and California* and had tried to puzzle out the deserts and mountains from the printed pages before them. Rumors of the "burnings" at Nauvoo and of Mormon armies marching westward agitated the whole frontier, and at

Fort Leavenworth the First Dragoons, Colonel Stephen W. Kearny's crack regiment, exercised remounts and polished equipment, waiting for the war with Mexico over Texas or with England over Oregon that newspapers across the country were calling for. President Polk, the patient and devious diplomatist, confided to his diary his contempt for James Buchanan, his Secretary of State, and hoped that Taylor's army at Corpus Christi would persuade what momentarily passed for a government in Mexico to accept Ambassador Slidell and a compromise on Texas.

Thus the season opened in 1846, and before winter closed the mountains the year had produced its prodigies, great and small. Perhaps a dozen trappers and hunters fell in fights with Blackfeet or Arapahoes or Snakes. Fort Laramie and Fort Bridger saw more than 2,700 emigrants pause and pass on to Oregon and California. The long caravans of trading wagons rolled into Taos and Santa Fe, but Kearny's Army of the West was right behind them, and New Mexico dropped easily into American hands. Kearny and Kit Carson joined Frémont in California, where the Bear Flag Republic alternated between farce and tragedy, and the Mormon Battalion plodded into history, seeing military action only against wild cattle and wild dogs.

The Oregon and California trails live in the American imagination through the enduring symbol of white-topped wagons beating westward through the high sun of a mountain summer. In May, 1846, when the emigrant parties began to rendezvous near Independence and Westport, California and Oregon were still controlled or contested by Mexico and Great Britain, but by the end of the season the pioneers found themselves at last in American territory. In the emigration of 1846 Parkman saw but could not appreciate men of profound moral and physical courage, men like William H. Russell and Lillburn Boggs and some members at least of the doomed Donner party, whose "Cannibal Camp" at Donner Lake was the site of the first great disaster ever to strike an overland emigrant party.

Francis Parkman: The East

The West Parkman went to see was not the emigrants' or the soldiers' West or even the trappers' and hunters' West. In one sense his whole life had been a partial preparation for his Oregon Trail summer in 1846. The son of an old New England family of churchmen, merchants, and soldiers, Parkman was born in Boston in 1823 into a comfortable fortune and an assured social position, but, as Russel B. Nye justly observes, he "could not exactly remember when his interest in Indians first began."[16] As Parkman later wrote in a long third-person autobiographical letter, "The age of fifteen or sixteen produced a revolution. . . . A new passion seized him, which, but half gratified, still holds its force. He became enamoured of the woods, a fancy which soon gained full control over the course of the literary pursuits to which he was also addicted. . . . At the age of eighteen, the plan which he is still attempting to execute was, in its most essential features, formed."[17]

By his sophomore year at Harvard, then, Parkman had determined to write the history of "the old French War,"[18] a task which, as he thought, "would require about twenty years. . . . His reliance, however, was less on books than on such personal experience as should, in some sense, identify him with his theme. His natural inclinations urged him in the same direction, for his thoughts were always in the forest,

---

[16] "Parkman, Red Fate, and White Civilization," in *Essays on American Literature in Honor of Jay B. Hubbell*, ed. Clarence Gohdes (Durham, N.C., 1967), p. 152. This article is an important survey of Parkman's attitudes toward the Indian.

[17] Parkman to George E. Ellis, 1864, in *Letters of Francis Parkman*, ed. Wilbur R. Jacobs (Norman, 1960), I, 176—hereafter cited as *Letters*.

[18] *Letters*, I, 184 n.

whose features, not unmixed with softer images, possessed his waking and sleeping dreams, filling him with vague cravings impossible to satisfy."[19]

Parkman attempted to satisfy those "cravings" with three summer excursions in 1841–1843 among the mountains and forests of New England and New York (and with a side trip to Montreal and Quebec), a walking tour of the Berkshires in 1844, and a two months' trip to the Old Northwest in July and August, 1845 (when he met Robert Stuart at Mackinac Island), in search of material for his projected history of the conspiracy of Pontiac.[20] The better effects of these rambles are perhaps best expressed in this paean to the wilderness:

To him who has once tasted the reckless independence, the haughty self-reliance, the sense of irresponsible freedom, which the forest life engenders, civilization thenceforth seems flat and stale. . . . The wilderness, rough, harsh, and inexorable, has charms more potent in their seductive influence than all the lures of luxury and sloth. And often he on whom it has cast its magic finds no heart to dissolve the spell, and remains a wanderer and an Ishmaelite to the hour of his death.

There is a chord, in the breasts of most men, prompt to answer loudly or faintly, as the case may be, to such rude appeals. But there is influence of another sort, strongest with minds of the finest texture, yet sometimes holding a controlling power over those who neither acknowledge nor suspect its workings. There are few so imbruted by vice, so perverted by art and luxury, as to dwell in the closest presence of Nature, deaf to her voice of melody and power, untouched by the ennobling influences which mould and penetrate the heart that has not hardened himself against them. Into the spirit of such an [sic] one the mountain wind breathes its own freshness, and the midsummer tempest, as it rends the forest, pours its own fierce energy. His thoughts flow with

[19] Parkman to George E. Ellis, 1864, in *Letters*, I, 176–177.
[20] Parkman's notebooks for these excursions will be found in *Journals*, I. See also Mason Wade, *Francis Parkman*, pp. 23–215 *passim*.

the placid stream of the broad, deep river, or dance in light with the sparkling current of the mountain brook. No passing mood or fancy of his mind but has its image and echo in the wild world around him. There is softness in the mellow air, the warm sunshine, and the budding leaves of spring; and in the forest flower which, more delicate than the pampered offspring of gardens, lifts its tender head through the refuse and decay of the wilderness. But it is the grand and the heroic in the hearts of men which finds its worthiest symbol and noblest inspiration amid these desert realms, —in the mountain, rearing its savage head through clouds and sleet, or basking its majestic strength in the radiance of the sinking sun; in the interminable forest, the thunder booming over its lonely waste, the whirlwind tearing through its inmost depths, or the sun at length setting in gorgeous majesty beyond its waves of verdure. To the sick, the wearied, or the sated spirit, nature opens a theatre of boundless life, and holds forth a cup brimming with redundant pleasure. In the other joys of existence, fear is balanced against hope, and satiety against delight; but here one may fearlessly drink, gaining, with every draught, new vigor and a heightened zest, and finding no dregs of bitterness at the bottom.[21]

The experience of the wilderness was crucial to the kind of history Parkman hoped to write, and all of his backwoods outings before his Oregon Trail summer in 1846 were made both to steel himself against hardship and to "imbue himself with the life and spirit of the time. [The historian] must study events in their bearings near and remote; in the character, habits and manners of those who took part in them. He must himself be, as it were, a sharer or spectator of the action he describes."[22] Thus, Parkman's earliest expeditions to the wil-

[21] *The Conspiracy of Pontiac and the Indian War after the Conquest of Canada* (Boston, 1901), II, 253–256 vol. xv of *Francis Parkman's Works*. All subsequent references to Parkman's histories after their first citation are by short title (e.g., *Pontiac*) and to volumes in the Frontenac Edition of *Francis Parkman's Works*.

[22] *Pioneers of France in the New World* (Boston, 1901), I, c, vol. I of *Works*.

derness of Maine and New Hampshire were very much in the nature of field trips to the scenes which would figure so largely in the history he hoped to write, and his visits to the surviving remnants of the Indian tribes of the East reflected in part his reading at Harvard in Joseph François Lafitau's *Moeurs des Sauvages*. Lafitau, an early Jesuit, argued that the culture of the American Indian was comparatively stable and that earlier stages of that culture might be inferred, at least in broad outline, from that of his own day.[23]

But Parkman's health had always been delicate, and his double labors as a Harvard undergraduate (and, later, law student) and researcher in colonial history brought on various alarming symptoms of a general collapse.[24] Considerably later in his life he was to recall that his feats of wilderness endurance in the East were in part sheer bravado: "As fond of hardships as he was vain of enduring them, cherishing a sovereign scorn for every physical weakness or defect, deceived, moreover, by a rapid development of frame and sinews, which flattered him with the belief that discipline, sufficiently unsparing, would harden him into an athlete, he slighted the precautions of a more reasonable woodcraft, tired old foresters with long marches, stopped neither for heat nor rain, and slept on the earth without a blanket."[25]

This "discipline" had its inevitable effects, and after a breakdown during his senior year at Harvard, Parkman made

[23] Jacobs points out Parkman's reading in Lafitau in *Letters*, I, xxxvi.

[24] See Jacobs' discussion of Parkman's various illnesses in *Letters*, I, xlv–xlvi. Jacobs argues persuasively that an underlying neuroticism, an obsessional drive toward perfectionism, and hypochondria all help to explain Parkman's lifelong struggles with his "Enemy," palpitations of the heart, "nervousness," weak eyesight, and severe headaches (apparently with migraine symptoms), not to speak of swellings in his knees and insomnia, all of which culminated, Jacobs believes, in a "struggle situation": "Struggle became the keynote of his life, and through adherence to it he maintained his self-respect."

[25] Parkman to George E. Ellis, 1864, in *Letters*, I, 177.

the required European tour in 1843–1844. But even after his return to the United States and other wilderness rambles, his health, particularly his "nervousness" and what seems to have been a persistent if undiagnosable case of eye trouble,[26] continued to plague him, and, even as he determined to pursue his Indian researches in the West, he hoped, ironically enough, to cure his eyes: "A specific sign of the mischief [earlier described as a "highly irritable organism" seemingly accompanied by heart spasms] soon appeared in a weakness of sight, increasing with an ominous rapidity. Doubtless to study with the eyes of another is practicable, yet the expedient is not an eligible one, and the writer bethought him of an alternative. It was essential to his plans to gain an inside view of Indian life. This then was the time at once to accomplish the object and rest his failing vision. Accordingly he went to the Rocky Mountains, but he reckoned without his host."[27]

Francis Parkman: The West

The original idea for the Oregon Trail summer may, as Mason Wade argues, have come from Quincy Adams Shaw, Parkman's first cousin,[28] but it is perfectly clear from his own letters that Parkman eagerly embraced the proposal and went west in 1846 specifically to gather firsthand experience and knowledge for the ethnological notes which would become the extended introduction to the first of his histories, *The*

---

[26] DeVoto, *Year of Decision*, p. 511, came to the conclusion that Parkman suffered from aniseikonia and rejected the contention of George M. Gould, *Biographic Clinics*, ii (Philadelphia, 1904), 131–193 *passim*, that Parkman had asymmetrical compound astigmatism. Jacobs, *Letters*, i, xlvi, finds a "neurotic element" in Parkman's weak eyes or eyestrain, but it is certain that Parkman did himself no good by riding for six months in the glaring sun and choking dust of the West.

[27] Parkman to George E. Ellis, 1864, in *Letters*, i, 178.

[28] *Francis Parkman*, p. 225.

Conspiracy of Pontiac and the Indian War after the Conquest of Canada. In a letter written from Boston on March 28, 1846, to the American bookseller and bibliographer, Henry Stevens in London,[29] Parkman specifically stated that "I set out tomorrow for the far West, to see the Indians, glean their traditions, and study their character, for the benefit of 'Pontiac,' " even though he must have known that the Plains Indians of the trans-Mississippi West were very different in the material aspects of their culture from the forest tribes of the East, the central figures in his planned history of Pontiac's conspiracy.

Parkman left Boston in the spring of 1846 in search of Indians and wilderness adventure and a rest from the fatigues of historical scholarship. It is one of the great ironies of Parkman's life and career that, seeking "wildness" and perhaps a belated but not impossible confirmation of the idea of the Noble Savage, he arrived at Westport on the very edge of the frontier in the spring of that year that saw all the energies of Manifest Destiny at last in vigorous motion—energies which, before the year was out, would capture Oregon and California and the Mexican Southwest and make the final destruction of the Plains Indians inevitable. Parkman, had he known it, was almost uniquely fortunate in appearing on the frontier at the critical history of the American West, fortunate, too, because he met at one time or another almost all the people who bent the wilderness to the design of the American Empire in 1846.

Parkman's notebooks and canceled passages in *The Oregon Trail* itself show how, even before he left Boston, he had sought out Nathaniel Jarvis Wyeth, a well-known Cambridge businessman but once a leader of Rocky Mountain trapping

[29] "The Correspondence of Francis Parkman and Henry Stevens, 1845–1885," ed. John Buechler, *Transactions of the American Philosophical Society*, N.S., LVII, pt. 6 (1967), 16.

parties and the first *bourgeois* of Fort Hall.[30] Parkman may also have called on Ramsay Crooks in New York City, for his address appears in Parkman's "1846 Account Book."[31] Crooks had been one of the original Astorians on the overland march across the continent to the mouth of the Columbia and knew more about the beginnings of the American penetration of the mountains than almost anyone else Parkman could have found in the East. By the time Parkman was ready to set out from New York for the West, he had complemented his extensive reading in the literature of prairie and mountain life[32] and his earlier backwoods adventures with firsthand accounts of the West from men with long and thorough experience in the country he was about to visit.

At St. Louis Parkman planned not only to purchase equipment and hire a guide for his Oregon Trail trip, but, more important, to gather material from the old French settlers for the history of Pontiac's last days and death. On April 19 he met Pascal Cerré, a member of one of the pioneer St. Louis families,[33] and on April 27 he talked with old Pierre Chouteau, the half brother of that Auguste Chouteau who had helped found St. Louis in November, 1763.[34] From Pierre Chouteau he learned invaluable information about the circumstances of Pontiac's murder; much of what the old man told him appears in the last chapter of *The Conspiracy of Pontiac*.[35] Though Parkman found much that appealed to his romantic sensibilities in the picturesque old French towns near St. Louis, the modern city and its boisterous democracy

[30] See note 7 for p. 308 of the present edition.

[31] In *Journals*, II, 486.

[32] The notes to the present edition draw a number of obvious literary parallels between *The Oregon Trail* and other books of western travel and adventure which Parkman might have read.

[33] *Journals*, II, 411.

[34] *Journals*, II, 415.

[35] See also *Pontiac*, II, 273–275, Vol. xv of *Works*.

was not much to his taste. He saw Henry Clay, the paladin of the West, making a speech in front of the Planters' House and mixed his admiration for Clay with a Bostonian distaste for the arts of the demagogue: "As he [Clay] passed away, he asked an old man for a pinch of snuff, at which the mob was gratified, and the old man, striking his cane on the bricks, declared emphatically that Clay was the greatest man in the nation, and that it was a burning shame he was not in the presidential chair. So much for the arts by which politicians —even the best of them—thrive."[36]

Parkman's Oregon Trail notebooks and canceled passages in the *Knickerbocker Magazine* serial version of *The Oregon Trail* and in the first two Putnam "editions" of the book in 1849 and 1852 show that while he was in St. Louis Parkman also met men whose names had been synonymous with western adventure and exploration since the 1820's. Though the evidence from Parkman's notebooks is not conclusive, it appears that he interviewed Thomas Fitzpatrick about the Indians of the West. Fitzpatrick (1799–1854), otherwise known in the mountains as "Broken Hand" or "White Head," had first gone into the fur trade in 1823 as a member of William H. Ashley's second expedition.[37] In St. Louis Parkman also met Kenneth McKenzie, once the "King of the Missouri" and the "Emperor of the West" at his great Fort Union; McKenzie seems to have given Parkman valuable advice about the

[36] *Journals*, II, 410.

[37] *Journals*, II, 412–415. It seems to me impossible to say whether he did in fact speak with Fitzpatrick or whether in the notebook entries he was merely quoting from a letter or letters which Fitzpatrick wrote to Lieutenant Abert of the Topographical Engineers. See Morgan and Harris, eds. *Rocky Mountain Journals of W. M. Anderson*, pp. 300–307, and LeRoy R. Hafen and W. J. Ghent, *Broken Hand: The Life Story of Thomas Fitzpatrick, Chief of the Mountain Men* (Denver, 1931). Morgan and Harris place Fitzpatrick in St. Louis in February and May, 1846, but not in April.

country he was about to visit, advice which Parkman later chose to disregard.[38]

Thus, by the time he arrived at Westport, Parkman had learned a good deal about the country he was to cross and the tribesmen who inhabited it. Westport continued his frontier initiation, for there he saw the wagon trains massing for Oregon and California, and there, too, he found the Santa Fe trading caravans and their motley contingents of Mexican drovers and French hunters. He talked to Passed Midshipman Selim E. Woodworth, a visionary aflame with dreams of conquest in New Mexico and a coward who left the Donner party starving in the snow.[39] At Westport he heard rumors of war with Mexico; at Fort Leavenworth he met Stephen Watts Kearny and some of the men who would fight the war.

From the Big Blue River westward Parkman was in almost daily contact with the emigrant trains; the vast panorama of the West stretched before him, and he met Pierre D. Papin and boatloads of mountain men struggling over the shoals of the Platte. One hundred and fifty miles east of Fort Laramie he began to see buffalo, and soon afterwards he began to feel the power of the wilderness in his own body; the choking and blinding dust, the bad water, the glaring sun, and the increasing altitude gave him a bad case of "mountain fever," or lingering and painful dysentery, cramps, and dizziness. He was not well when he reached Fort Laramie, the gateway to the mountain West, but he had come too far to turn back.

At Fort Laramie, then, he paused before leaving behind him the last vestiges of civilization for the isolation and danger of the Oglala village. He stood on the ramparts of Fort Laramie and watched the emigrant wagons plunge through the Laramie River, and on June 26 he rode down to Fort Bernard, eight miles distant, and met Colonel William H.

---

[38] See note 7 for p. 308 of the present edition.
[39] *Journals*, II, 411, and see note 26 for p. 8 of the present edition.

Russell, "drunk as a pigeon," and Robert Ewing and his friend R. T. Jacobs and, very probably, some members of what became the doomed Donner party.[40]

At Fort Laramie Parkman met Louis Vasquez, "old Vaskiss," Jim Bridger's partner at Fort Bridger and a preeminent mountain man, and heard how the *bourgeois* Henry Fraeb had been killed at Battle Creek by a large band of Arapahoes, Cheyennes, and Sioux in August, 1841. Henry Chatillon, Parkman's guide and hunter, introduced him into the suspicious society of an Oglala village, and it was with The Whirlwind's band that Parkman found all the savage adventure he had long looked for. Though the Oglalas were not Cooper Indians, they were both wildly romantic and brutally real as they sat around the evening fires in camp or chased the buffalo over the desolate plains of the Laramie Basin.

During his two weeks' visit to the Oglala village, Parkman completed his wilderness education; he was both desperately ill and deeply disillusioned when he returned to Fort Laramie on August 3. The rest of his trip was almost anticlimactic as he rode down from Fort Laramie to the Pueblo, where he completed the second leg of his long triangulation of the West.

At the Pueblo he heard of Zachary Taylor's victories in Mexico and saw the only Mormon emigrants to reach the West in 1846. His trip from the Pueblo to Bent's Fort and thence down the Arkansas River along the Mountain Route of the Santa Fe Trail brought Parkman no insight into the meaning of the life he saw along the road—the dusty concourse of traders, volunteer cavalry, provision wagons, and the Mormon Battalion—and only the exhausting joy of the buffalo chase. But at Bent's Fort he had come upon the dispirited fragments of the glory that was the Army of the West, for there he found the sick troopers whom Kearny had left behind

[40] *Journals*, II, 447–448, and see note 32 for p. 135.

on his march to New Mexico, the Tête Rouges of Manifest Destiny. The month it took Parkman to descend the Arkansas and to return to Westport along the Santa Fe Trail is summarized with comparative brevity in *The Oregon Trail*, and Parkman's mountain fever curtailed his notebook entries for the last part of his trip.

The Oregon Trail: *The Narrative*

When Parkman reached Westport toward the end of September in 1846, he had ridden over more than 2,000 miles of prairies, deserts, and mountains and had seen or heard of almost all the heroic figures in the year that made the Great West at last and forever American. But little of this hard-won experience appears in *The Oregon Trail*; the book is notably lacking in analysis, and Parkman's own fastidious disdain at clumsy emigrants and ragged volunteers goes far to justify Bernard DeVoto's exasperated despair at Parkman's apparent obtuseness:

It was Parkman's fortune to witness and take part in one of the greatest national experiences, at the moment and site of its occurrence. It is our misfortune that he did not understand the smallest part of it. No other historian, not even Xenophon, has ever had so magnificent an opportunity: Parkman did not even know it was there, and if his trip to the prairies produced one of the exuberant masterpieces of American literature, it ought instead to have produced a key work of American history. But the other half of his inheritance forbade. It was the Puritan virtues that held him to the ideal of labor and achievement and kept him faithful to his goal in spite of suffering all but unparalleled in literary history. And likewise it was the narrowness, prejudice, and mere snobbery of the Brahmins that insulated him from the coarse, crude folk who were the movement he traveled with, turned him shuddering away from them to rejoice in the ineffabilities of Beacon Hill, and denied our culture a history of the American empire at the moment of its birth. Much may be rightly regretted, therefore. But set it down also that, though the Brahmin was indifferent to Manifest Destiny, the Puritan took with him a quiet valor which has not been outmatched among literary folk or in the history of the West.[41]

DeVoto's judgment, barring some exaggeration, is ex post facto just. Where in *The Oregon Trail* or in Parkman's notebooks is there any indication that he saw the California and Oregon emigrants as much more than ignorant, even faintly ridiculous malcontents whom "the States" were well rid of? Though he noted approvingly Colonel Kearny's gentlemanly bearing, where has Parkman shown that he recognized Kearny and the Army of the West as one of the principal agents of Manifest Destiny in 1846 or that he saw the Mexican War as anything more than an occasion for heroic postures? Again, how did Parkman, who met the very men who opened the West to America—Wyeth, Fitzpatrick, McKenzie, Vasquez, and the nameless trappers he met at Fort Laramie—fail to appreciate the boundless daring of men who confronted the wilderness as many as 30 years before John Charles Frémont earned the dubious title of "Pathfinder"? Why did he spend more than a third of his book in presenting not very perceptive pictures of life in an Oglala village when he might, instead, have described the wild romance of the lives of men like Henry Chatillon, his guide and hunter, or Paul Dorion or Bill May?

These obvious questions seem to lend support to DeVoto's sweeping criticism of Parkman's faulty vision of the West. They suggest the basis, too, for the strictures of Mason Wade, who blames Parkman's aristocratic Bostonian prejudices for the failures of insight in *The Oregon Trail*: "By force of environment and heredity he was blind to the profound social forces at work in the West; by tradition and taste he was

[41] *Year of Decision*, p. 115.

contemptuous of the masses, and so he found the company of foreigners more congenial than that of men who were making America out of the wilderness."[42] Wade also argues that the immediacy and the power of Parkman's original experience in the West, especially as that experience is to be found in the Oregon Trail notebooks, have been replaced in the book with hackneyed set-piece descriptions of the scenery and a merely "literary" approach to the Indians and the pioneers. Indeed, Wade seems to regard Parkman's notebooks as a kind of instant history, the raw material out of which an epic history of 1846 might have been made had Parkman had the imagination and the insight. Instead, Parkman bowed to the gentility of the age and produced what Wade considers mere "literature," only another book of western travels: "But more serious than this bowdlerizing [of the notebooks] was the attempt to make literature out of history, at the expense of the latter, for which Parkman himself must bear the ultimate blame."[43]

Such comments, it seems to me, represent a kind of critical wishful thinking, a refusal to respect an author's intention and a misguided effort to impose upon a given work of art a totally specious set of altogether irrelevant criteria. Parkman himself was perfectly clear about the significance of his first book, for, as he noted in the "Preface to the Fourth Edition" of *The Oregon Trail*, "My business was observation, and I was willing to pay dearly for the opportunity of exercising it."[44] The operative word in this sentence is "observation," not analysis, and DeVoto and Wade and others certainly err in considering that, since Parkman spent most of his life as a historian, his first book should also have been a history, particularly because 1846 was a year that, with a longer and different perspective, later seemed crucial to other historians.

[42] *Journals*, II, 403.
[43] *Journals*, II, 387–388.
[44] See p. xiii of the present edition.

Moreover, while Parkman took considerable liberties with the day-to-day chronology of his Oregon Trail trip in order to heighten suspense and to exaggerate the dangers he had faced in the Oglala village, *The Oregon Trail* does not greatly differ in content and in emphasis from the notebooks. Howard Doughty is certainly correct when he dismisses the claim that the notebooks contain an impressive amount of the history of 1846 and that they should thus have inspired a book radically different in theme and development from *The Oregon Trail*: "Impressive as the journals are, they hardly support such a claim, and there is no evidence that Parkman had any intention of writing a book different in kind from the book he actually did write: of a kind, that is to say, in which, for good reasons, the age particularly abounded, and of which Melville's *Typee* and *Omoo* are specimens. . . . Whether or not Parkman should have written a different kind of book is another question, but the journals, to repeat, can hardly be said to reveal any major distortion of emphasis between the day-to-day records of his experiences and their final reworking in the shape of a narrative of travel."[45]

As the extracts from Parkman's Oregon Trail notebooks which accompany the notes to the present edition clearly show, Doughty's judgment of their value as source material for *The Oregon Trail* is entirely justified. Furthermore, any criticism which argues for the superiority of the notebooks to *The Oregon Trail* has to take into account the generally unrecognized fact that Parkman clearly kept those notebooks with an eye to his family in Boston, which is to say that, like most young men of his period on their travels, he was expected to bring home a tangible record of his experiences and adventures for the judgment of his parents and the improvement of himself. That Parkman's notebooks were written (at least in part) for the Boston family circle may be inferred, first

[45] *Francis Parkman* (New York, 1962), pp. 150–151.

of all, from the fact that Wade discovered Parkman's letters from the West to his parents _and_ the Oregon Trail notebooks together in Parkman's desk. In the second place, Wade reprints in the first volume of his edition of the _Journals_ an "Appendix [to the] European Notebook" of 1843–1844, which seems to be a fragment of Parkman's rough daily notes during his European tour, notes which he later turned into the polished, formal narrative which Wade calls the "European Journal 1843–1844."

As part of the literature of western travel and adventure, then, _The Oregon Trail_ must stand or fall. That Parkman missed the significance of a great deal of what he saw in the West in 1846 may, from a longer historical perspective, be unfortunate, but it certainly is not tragic, and, as Samuel Eliot Morison argues, there is a certain danger in _a posteriori_ arguments: "It is true that Parkman was not interested in the westward movement; it was simply not his dish. He went west to hunt buffalo, view the scenery, and study the Indians— which is what he did. Everyone praises Parkman for seeing through the eighteenth-century myth of the Noble Savage; why, then, scold him for not supporting the nineteenth-century myth of the Noble Democrat, or the twentieth-century myth of the Noble Western Pioneer?"[46] Even the rhetorical patterns of _The Oregon Trail_ show that one of Parkman's principal aims in the book was to show action and motion. Parkman is not here interested in the interaction of men and society; rather, as Otis A. Pease suggests, much of the emphasis in _The Oregon Trail_ falls upon the relationship of the plainsman to weather and landscape.[47]

Thus, it seems intellectually more honest to judge Parkman

[46] _The Parkman Reader_, ed. Samuel Eliot Morison (Boston, 1955), p. 16.
[47] _Parkman's History: The Historian as Literary Artist_ (New Haven, 1953), pp. 8–10.

on what he did see and what he did achieve with his wilderness education than to blame him for errors of judgment and perspective which only time would disclose. Parkman's attitude toward the emigrants he would meet in the wagon trains is foreshadowed by an entry he made in his notebooks while he was still on his way to St. Louis: "Man lounging by the river bank. Is it not true, that the lower you descend in education and social position, the more vicious men become?"[48] Though such an expression of class prejudice might seem to reflect the basis of Parkman's disdain for the emigrants, it is only a part of a whole series of attitudes toward the agricultural frontier that Parkman shared with many other nineteenth-century observers of the Westward Movement.

The process of frontier settlement (and, by extension, overland emigration to the Pacific Coast) represented, from the point of view of the exponents of Manifest Destiny, the triumph of America's civilizing spirit over the wilderness. The pioneer and the yeoman farmer together mastered the forests and broke the prairies to the plow, and behind them followed all the virtues of an enlightened democratic civilization based firmly on an agrarian system of freehold farmers. Thus, the advancing agricultural frontier was both challenge and fulfillment, the challenge of subduing a rude wilderness and the fulfillment of a national destiny.

From this point of view, the axmen at work in the American forests and the backwoods farmer scratching a scanty harvest among the stumps of his clearing were the real builders of the American system, and Jefferson was right in calling the small farmer the foundation of American democracy. But, as Henry Nash Smith has brilliantly demonstrated, it was quite commonly believed in the later eighteenth century and through much of the nineteenth century that the western farmer was not, in fact, a noble pioneer selflessly exposing

[48] *Journals*, ii, 406.

himself to the perils of the wilderness for the benefit of succeeding generations, but rather an outcast, an Ishmael, an
"anarch" who restlessly chafed under the compulsions of civilization and law and fled to the woods in search of a wild
freedom from civilized restraints.[49]

As Smith shows, these opposing views of the frontiersman
as civilization's pioneer or civilization's outcast especially informed the nineteenth century's judgments of Daniel Boone
and certainly were reflected in Cooper's most important character, Leatherstocking, or Natty Bumppo. Boone appeared in
both contemporary history and fiction as a paradigm of the
noble western pioneer, never happier than when leading
happy settlers to Kentucky or preparing the foundations of a
new commonwealth in the western wilderness. But other accounts portrayed Boone as a solitary misanthrope, even an
outlaw, never happy while the sound of axes was in his ears.[50]
The last chapter of Cooper's *The Pioneers* reflects the same
cultural double image of the frontiersman in Leatherstocking
who, hating the life of the settlements, yet retires to the
western wilderness as "the foremost in that band of pioneers
who are opening the way for the march of the nation across
the continent."[51]

[49] *Virgin Land: The American West as Symbol and Myth* (Cambridge, Mass., 1950), pp. 210–223.

[50] *Virgin Land*, pp. 51–58.

[51] For some nineteenth-century observers of the frontier there was,
of course, a real distinction between the solitary hunter, trapper, or
scout, like Leatherstocking, and the backwoods settler at the very
farthest verge of the frontier. Cooper, for example, clearly draws a line
in *The Prairie* between Leatherstocking, who has passed far beyond the
frontier in his solitary beaver hunts, and the Bush family who, for all
their excesses, still clearly belong inside the tenuous boundaries of
civilization. But a good many other contemporary writers were content
to lump the solitary hunters and the frontier farmers together, both as
outcasts from society and as pioneers in the western wilderness, and
the same kinds of rhetoric, damning or praising, were often applied to
both.

Behind these contrasted views of the frontiersman and pioneer and in part explaining them is a theory of civilization deriving from the French eighteenth-century *philosophes* and perhaps most clearly expressed in the *Esquisse d'un tableau historique des progrès de l'esprit humain* of Marie Jean Antoine Nicolas Caritat, Marquis de Condorcet. Smith argues convincingly that "The most influential aspect of Condorcet's theory of civilization was the notion that all human societies pass through the same series of social stages in the course of their evolution upward from barbarism toward the goal of universal enlightenment. He divided the history of the human race into ten epochs. . . . The most important of these epochs for social theory were the earliest, which comprised the union of autonomous families who subsisted mainly by hunting, into 'hordes'; the domestication of animals, inaugurating the pastoral stage of society; and the transition from a pastoral to an agricultural stage."[52]

That Parkman recognized the importance of these stages is obvious from *The Oregon Trail*, and it is equally clear that the theory of the stages of civilization meant that the "pastoral" emigrants and the frontier farmers represented less progressive stages of development than did the complex culture of the East.[53] Thus, Parkman had sound contemporary opinion on his side when he pictured the emigrants as a crowd of gaping yokels; his disdain was as much "philosophical" as personal and derived as much from the established attitudes of his time toward the frontier as from the "ineffabilities" of Boston.

For much the same reasons his attitudes toward the Indians

[52] *Virgin Land*, p. 218.

[53] Compare Parkman's *Montcalm and Wolfe* (Boston, 1901), ii, 19–20, Vol. xii of *Works:* "Along the skirts of the southern and middle colonies [in the 1750's] ran for six or seven hundred miles a loose, thin, dishevelled fringe of population, the half-barbarous pioneers of advancing civilization. . . . It was the repulsive transition from savagery to civilization, from the forest to the farm."

in *The Oregon Trail,* however objectionable they may have been to some of his contemporaries,[54] very clearly reflect common nineteenth-century viewpoints toward civilization and the idea of progress and toward "savagism." Though in the composition of the book Parkman had occasionally tried to make the Indian seem heroic by wrapping him in the panoply of epic glory, his disgust at Indian life and customs shows through the Homeric descriptions of weapons and battle dress, through the stories of battles fought by men with such resounding names as The Whirlwind or the Eagle-Feather. Though the Indian might look like the Pythian Apollo and though he rode his war horse like a chivalric hero, he was for Parkman still a naked savage, and "To make an Indian a hero of romance is mere nonsense."[55]

Parkman came to see the mind of the Indian as shapeless and fatally dangerous in its blind acceptance of a hideous tradition and a bloody amorality, and in a number of canceled passages in earlier versions of *The Oregon Trail* he came very close to regarding the Indian simply as a wild beast worthy of speedy destruction. An excised passage shows Parkman thinking how gladly he would have shot an old medicine man, "to see how ugly he would look when he was dead."[56] In *A Half-Century of Conflict,* published the year before he died, Parkman gave his final judgment of the Indians: "The English

[54] See Melville's attack on Parkman's pictures of the Indians in his unsigned review of *The California and Oregon Trail* in the *Literary World,* IV, 113 (March 31, 1849), 291. Compare also Theodore Parker's letter of December 22, 1851, to Parkman, complaining of the "Sentiments & Ideas" expressed toward the Indians in *Pontiac.* Parker's letter is reprinted in Wade, *Francis Parkman,* pp. 311–314.

[55] *The Jesuits in North America in the Seventeenth Century* (Boston, 1901), I, 21 n., Vol. III of *Works.*

[56] See note 3 for p. 180 of this edition. Nye, "Parkman, Red Fate, and White Civilization," p. 161 n., notes that by 1875 Parkman had come "perilously close to the 'good Indian is a dead Indian' theory. . . ."

borderers, on their part, regarded the Indians less as men than as vicious and dangerous wild animals. In fact, the benevolent and philanthropic view of the American savage is for those who are beyond his reach; it has never yet been held by any whose wives and children have lived in danger of his scalping-knife"[57]—though this statement rather begs the question of whether the "English borderers" were finally justified in their "Indian hating."

Such a statement, however, shows perfectly well how Parkman rejected the ideal of the Noble Savage, that optimistic construct of ideas which presented the Indians (and, for that matter, any primitive people untouched by European civilization) as the innocent inhabitants of a wilderness Eden, living in simple harmony and unaffected sensibility in the midst of a beneficent nature and drawing counsels of moral perfectability from it. That the concept of the Noble Savage engaged the imaginations of Cooper, Irving, and Melville among other nineteenth-century American writers needs no demonstration here, but each author expressed serious reservations about this aspect of primitivism, if for no other reason than that the Noble Savage represented a prelapsarian innocence and an intellectual and moral equilibrium and stasis from which no development, no intellectual or moral progress, could be expected.

Furthermore, the realities of the American wilderness and the Indians themselves continually undercut efforts to find a placid paradise and a Noble Savage in the Western world, and, as Nye observes, "The idea of the Indian as irremediably primitive was the commonly accepted basis for thinking about him for the first half of the nineteenth century; he was assumed to be inherently different from and inferior to civilized peoples, incapable of any betterment."[58] Accepting this inter-

[57] Boston, 1901, I, 223, Vol. ix of *Works*.
[58] "Parkman, Red Fate, and White Civilization," p. 154.

pretation of Indian character and potentiality, Parkman constantly refers to them in his histories as the children of the human race, culturally a case of arrested development: "Unstable as water, capricious as the winds, they seem in some of their moods like ungoverned children fired with the instincts of devils."[59]

In discussing the roots of the "Indian Problem" in its cross-cultural aspects, Roy Harvey Pearce suggests that the twentieth century has a distinct advantage over Parkman's nineteenth century, "For we may work with hypotheses which do not press us to see primitive cultures as at once historically anterior and morally inferior to ours."[60] Nor are we obliged to test every culture by the touchstones of progress, of growth, evolution, and development. But Parkman saw the Indians as static, unchanging, "impracticable conservatists of barbarism"[61] who would not change, who could not adapt, and who were, therefore, doomed:

Some races of men seem moulded in wax, soft and melting, at once plastic and feeble. Some races, like some metals, combine the greatest flexibility with the greatest strength. But the Indian is hewn out of a rock. You can rarely change the form without destruction of the substance. Races of inferior energy have possessed a power of expansion and assimilation to which he is a stranger; and it is this fixed and rigid quality which has proved his ruin. He will not learn the arts of civilization, and he and his forest must perish together. The stern, unchanging features of his mind excite our admiration from their very immutability; and we look with deep interest on the fate of this irreclaimable son of the wilderness,

[59] *Pontiac*, ii, 306, Vol. xv of *Works*.

[60] *The Savages of America: A Study of the Indian and the Idea of Civilization* (Baltimore, 1965), p. 105.

[61] *Jesuits*, i, 59, Vol. iii of *Works*. Parkman's reference is specifically, in this quoted passage, to the Iroquois, who were advanced "beyond most other American tribes."

the child who will not be weaned from the breast of his rugged mother. . . .[62]

Or, as Parkman rephrased the Indian's devotion to savagery, "His haughty mind is imbued with the spirit of the wilderness, and the light of civilization falls on him with a blighting power."[63]

Thus, nineteenth-century historians could look with a certain equanimity on the extinction of the aboriginal populations of America, and David Levin justly observes that, "Despite the sadness with which he [Parkman] viewed the passing of the forest and of the Indian's highest virtues, he considered it inevitable and proper that an energetic race colonizing according to natural law would cover the continent and use it more effectively."[64] For Parkman and many other nineteenth-century Americans, the "Indian Problem" could be and frequently was reduced to the simple either/or of progressive white civilization overspreading the entire continent or the abandonment of North America to the Indians: "To reclaim the Indians from their savage state has again and again been attempted, and each attempt has failed. Their intractable, unchanging character leaves no other alternative than their gradual extinction or the abandonment of the western world to eternal barbarism. . . ."[65]

As Levin demonstrates, this contrast between progressive civilization and torpid savagery bore its own implicit resolution, for natural law and history both showed that progress was a constant factor in human life, that progress was identi-

---

[62] *Pontiac*, I, 48, Vol. xiv of *Works*.

[63] *Ibid.*, I, 3.

[64] *History as Romantic Art: Bancroft, Prescott, Motley, and Parkman* (Stanford, 1959), p. 138.

[65] *Pontiac*, II, 170, Vol. xv of *Works*.

cal to natural law, and that savagery *must* sink before the progressive principle embodied in some conquering race.[66] Perhaps Pearce provides the best summary of the nineteenth century's ideal of progress and its absolutely predetermined victory over "savagism," the existence of primitive, static cultures standing in the way of growth and development:

The American solution was worked out as an element in an idea of progress, American progress. Cultures are good, it was held, as they allow for full realization of man's essential and absolute moral nature; and man realizes this nature as he progresses historically from a lesser to a greater good, from the simple to the complex, from savagism to civilization. Westward American progress would, in fact, be understood to be reproducing this historical progression; and the savage would be understood as one who had not and somehow could not progress into the civilized, who would inevitably be destroyed by the civilized, the lesser good necessarily giving way to the greater. Civilized men who gave in to the temptations of savagism and its simplicities would likewise be destroyed. For the Indian was the remnant of a savage past away from which civilized men had struggled to grow. To study him was to study the past. To civilize him was to triumph over the past. To kill him was to kill the past. History would thus be the key to the moral worth of cultures; the history of American civilization would thus be conceived of as three-dimensional, progressing from past to present, from east to west, from lower to higher.[67]

These ideas—they reach the intensity of metaphors in his histories—Parkman bore with him to the West in 1846, and they underlie many of Parkman's formally expressed attitudes toward the emigrants and the Indians in *The Oregon Trail*. They help to explain, too, the obsessive contrasts (especially evident in passages which Parkman later excised during one or another of his revisions of the book) between East and West,

---

[66] *History as Romantic Art*, pp. 133–141.
[67] *Savages of America*, pp. 48–49.

civilization and the wilderness, and innocence and experience throughout *The Oregon Trail*. They also suggest the reasons for Parkman's determination to endure everything that the wilderness could thrust upon him, and serve to explain if not to justify the conscious Byronism of many of Parkman's attitudes toward his experiences in the West, the bravado of his visit to the Oglala village, and the neurotic sensibility that Parkman later was to call "the most miserable of all conflicts, the battle of the eager spirit against the treacherous and failing flesh."[68]

Throughout *The Oregon Trail* and especially in the earlier chapters of the book there are numerous indications that Parkman first saw his Oregon Trail trip as simply a summer's outing, a holiday jaunt undertaken in something of the same spirit that led other young men in the 1840's to sign up for a cruise to California or the Marquesas. Parkman later deleted a number of passages which too greatly emphasized the bravura attitude which he and Shaw assumed toward their tour of the prairies. Though the initial bravado with which he began his trip survives in the high spirits of his ridicule of Romaine and the Chandlers, in the mechanical picturesqueness of his descriptions of the prairies of eastern Kansas, and in the comic accounts of the misadventures of Raymond and Tête Rouge, Parkman also later excised a number of passages like the following one, which seemed perhaps to express too emphatic a preference for the free life of the wilderness: "Our idea of what is indispensable to human existence and enjoyment had been wonderfully curtailed; and a horse, a rifle and a knife seemed to make up the whole of life's necessaries. For these once obtained, together with the skill to use them, all else that is essential would follow in their train, and a host of luxuries besides. One other lesson our short prairie experience had

[68] *Pioneers of France in the New World* (Boston, 1901), II, 179–180, Vol. II of *Works*.

taught us; that of profound contentment in the present, and utter contempt for what the future might bring forth."[69]

Such passages become increasingly rare, however, as the narrative penetrates ever more deeply into the heart of the wilderness. As Parkman encounters the wild country and the wilder men who inhabit it, his descriptions become darker and more sombre; his own illness, more clearly shown in canceled passages than in the present text of *The Oregon Trail*, makes him aware that he might be reduced in a day to the same passive helplessness and fatalistic acceptance of death which the Indians showed when they believed themselves possessed by an evil spirit. Moreover, as Parkman rode farther westward, he came closer and closer to doubting the values of the civilization which had produced him and Shaw. Canceled passages in earlier versions of the book frequently contrast the virile West and the effeminate East. Parkman's "visions" of New England and civilization, if at first they seem merely self-consciously Byronic, become at last indistinct and melancholy, the desolate memories of an irretrievably lost sanctuary where Nature was far kinder and softer than the empty plains and dark mountains he crossed with the Oglala village.

The excised passages emphasize even more strongly a number of unresolved paradoxes which the present text of *The Oregon Trail* still clearly shows. The East—and especially New England—is a haven of peace and rest; there Nature is beneficent and healing, and civilization holds men in its firm support. The West is destructive; it brutalizes white men and Indians alike and reduces civilization to a mocking memory. Yet the West tests a man's endurance and proves his courage and strength; the East saps moral and physical energy by offering him safety without effort, experience without pain.

With this tension between East and West, between inno-

[69] See note 7 for p. 308 of the present edition.

cence and hard-won maturity, *The Oregon Trail* assumes a deeper meaning. Especially in the earlier versions of the book the narrative shows a terrible struggle with sickness and death; the Oregon Trail becomes not only the solitary link with civilization but also an intellectual backtrail by which Parkman, growing steadily weaker as he moved westward in space and backward in time, came steadily closer to an understanding of the mind of an Indian, closer, that is, to a comprehension of a mind almost timeless in its nameless fears and superstition. Parkman's prairie and mountain education along the Oregon Trail was, in one sense at least, the history of his reversion to the terrors of the strange and forbiddingly vacant mind of the primeval world. As he sat in front of the buffalo lodges in the Oglala village, himself the victim of a mysterious and painful disease, he began to to realize that he was as helpless as any naked Indian and that, in the fancied security of civilization, modern man is simply primitive man in another guise.

In this respect it is significant that Parkman was sickest when he was in the Oglala village; both his notebooks and *The Oregon Trail* itself show that his health began to mend after he left Fort Laramie for the Pueblo, Bent's Fort, and civilization. Moreover, when Parkman revised the book most extensively in 1872, he had already lived a quarter of a century with pain, and thus he deleted many of the passages dealing with his illness in 1846. By 1872 suffering had become his constant companion, the fear of death had grown familiar, and Parkman could perhaps no longer see the meaning of the agony he had endured during his Oregon Trail trip. But traces of that suffering appear in Parkman's histories; his typical heroes are men like La Salle, Champlain, Marquette, the Jesuit Father Isaac Jogues, or General Wolfe, men of culture and education who, racked by disease or weakness, still dauntlessly confront the inexorable wilderness. For these men, as for Parkman himself, "the wilderness is a rude touchstone, which often reveals traits that would have lain buried and unsuspected in civilized life."[70]

The wilderness, then, was as much Parkman's Yale College and Harvard as a whaleship was Melville's. The West, especially in the earlier chapters of The Oregon Trail, is a region of wonder; one of the key words in the book is "admiration," especially in the sense of astonishment or surprise. Parkman seems to have been singularly impressed by a sense of the transience of the scenes he had witnessed; he knew that the Indians would be corrupted by whiskey and overawed by military posts, and he knew, too, that the emigrants would drive off the buffalo and reduce the wilderness to "irresistible commonplace." Parkman knew that civilization would conquer at last and that the price to be paid for its victory would be terrible.

For Parkman as for Melville, a season among the savages was one way of getting out of the nineteenth century in order to gain a new perspective toward it. The wilderness is thus potentially a morally neutral ground, a testing place for manhood and energy, and finally almost an extension of mind: "Where the moral instincts are originally strong, they may find nutriment and growth among the rude scenes and grand associations of the wilderness."[71] At the end of The Oregon Trail Parkman contrasts his innocence at the beginning of his prairie and mountain summer with his hard-won experience at its end through the linked analogies of spring and fall, "tokens of maturity and decay where all had before been fresh with opening life."[72] The present text of The Oregon Trail, extensively revised from earlier versions of the book according to

[70] La Salle and the Discovery of the Great West (Boston, 1901), p. 421, vol. v of Works.

[71] "The Works of James Fenimore Cooper," North American Review, LXXIV (January, 1852), 151.

[72] See p. 409 of the present text.

the canons of realistic writing of the early 1870's, is still the record of a deeply divided personality seeking in the wilderness a point of integration, a common ground of civilized refinement and natural strength. Perhaps a lifetime of suffering was the answer the wilderness gave him.

THE TEXTS OF *The Oregon Trail*

The Nine "Editions"

The Oregon Trail appeared in a number of "editions" between its first serial publication in 1847–1849 and the "Illustrated Edition" of 1892, a year before Parkman's death. The *Knickerbocker Magazine* of New York City printed 21 installments which were entitled "The Oregon Trail. Or A Summer's Journey Out of Bounds. By A Bostonian." from February, 1847, through February, 1849; Chapter x, "The War Parties," was not printed in the *Knickerbocker Magazine*, for reasons which are not clear, and no installments were printed in March and November, 1847, and in September and November, 1848.[73]

---

[73] See Parkman's letter of September 12, 1848, to Charles Eliot Norton in *Letters*, I, 56: "This month I sent no chapter to the *Knickerbocker*, because I want the book to be out before the appearance of the last chapter, for fear of piracy."

The Oregon Trail appeared in the *Knickerbocker Magazine* in the following installments: "The Oregon Trail. Or A Summer's Journey Out of Bounds. By A Bostonian," xxix (February, 1847), 160–165. (This version of Chapter I, "The Frontier," was otherwise untitled. "The Oregon Trail" was the running head for all subsequent installments in the *Knickerbocker Magazine*.) "Breaking the Ice," xxix (April, 1847), 310–316. "Fort Leavenworth" and " 'Jumping Off,' " xxix (May, 1847), 389–398. " 'The Big Blue,' " xxix (June, 1847), 499–510. "The Platte and the Desert," xxx (July, 1847), 19–28. "The Buffalo," xxx (August, 1847), 126–136. "Taking French Leave," xxx (September, 1847), 227–237. "Scenes at Fort Laramie," xxx (Octo-

The first edition of *The Oregon Trail*, somewhat revised from the *Knickerbocker* installments, was published on or about March 10, 1849, by George P. Putnam, as *The California and Oregon Trail: Being Sketches of Prairie and Rocky Mountain Life*, an edition which, as James E. Walsh[74] has demonstrated, consisted of some 2,500 copies. There was no second edition of *The Oregon Trail*. In 1852 Putnam published a "Third Edition"[75] of *The Oregon Trail* as *Prairie and*

---

ber, 1847), 283–292. "Scenes at the Camp," xxx (December, 1847), 475–488. (Material which in 1849 became Chapter xii, "Ill-Luck," is printed in this *K* installment as an untitled, continuous part of "Scenes at the Camp," pp. 488–492.) "Hunting Indians," xxxi (January, 1848), 1–15. "The Ogillallah Village," xxxi (February, 1848), 111–124. "The Hunting Camp," xxxi (March, 1848), 189–203. "The Trappers" and "The Black Hills," xxxi (April, 1848), 326–335. "A Mountain Hunt," xxxi (May, 1848), 398–406. "Passage of the Mountains," xxxi (June, 1848), 482–493. "The Lonely Journey," xxxii (July, 1848), 42–55. "The Pueblo and Bent's Fort" and "Tête Rouge, the Volunteer," xxxii (August, 1848), 95–102. "Indian Alarms," xxxii (October, 1848), 310–317. (Chapter xxiv, "The Chase," was not printed separately in the *Knickerbocker Magazine*; it first appears in the Putnam first edition of 1849 as a combination of material originally found on pp. 507–508 of the *Knickerbocker* version of Chapter xxv, "The Buffalo Camp," and on pp. 317–321 of the *Knickerbocker* version of Chapter xxiii, "Indian Alarms"; see note 1 for p. 356 for additional details.) "The Buffalo Camp," xxxii (December, 1848), 504–515. "Down the Arkansas," xxxiii (January, 1849), 1–12. "The Settlement," xxxiii (February, 1849), 108–115.

[74] *"The California and Oregon Trail*: A Bibliographical Study," *New Colophon*, iii, 9 (December, 1950), 279–285.

[75] Strictly speaking, the Putnam "Third Edition" was not an edition at all but rather a new impression from the same stereotyped plates used for *The California and Oregon Trail* in 1849. Writing to Parkman on March 30, 1849 ("Letters Received" Folders, Parkman Papers, Massachusetts Historical Society, and reprinted in part in Walsh, *"California and Oregon Trail,"* p. 283), Putnam clearly shows what both he and Parkman meant by "edition":

The 1ˢᵗ ed.ⁿ (1000) of the Trail is now all sold—*including* paper covers— The second ed.ⁿ (500) will be ready tomorrow—and will be *all* in cloth,

Rocky Mountain Life; Or, The California and Oregon Trail, from the rather battered stereotyped plates used for the first edition.

Parkman extensively revised the book in 1872 for a "Fourth Edition" published by Little, Brown and Company as *The Oregon Trail;* a "Fifth Edition" of 1873, a "Sixth Edition" of 1877, a "Seventh Edition" of 1880, and an "Eighth Edition" of 1883 were all printed from the plates used for the "Fourth Edition" of 1872. By 1883 these plates had begun to show signs of wear, and my original collations[76] of the texts of *The Oregon Trail* show a progressive degeneration of type faces, especially at the ends of lines, in the "editions" of 1877, 1880, and 1883. The fiction of a new "edition" for each new impression of *The Oregon Trail* was abandoned after 1883, and in a number of impressions of the "Eighth Edition" published between 1883 and 1891, Little, Brown and Company changed only the dates on the title pages.

Thus, before 1892 Parkman had revised *The Oregon Trail* for the Putnam first edition of 1849 and for the Little, Brown "Fourth Edition" of 1872. When Little, Brown and Company decided in 1891 to produce a deluxe "Illustrated Edition" of *The Oregon Trail* and commissioned Frederic Remington to illustrate it, the book was again reset, and Parkman

---

with the plates. I think with you that the cloth copies are much preferable & that it is unnecessary to do any more in paper.— The paper books are fast going out of favor—& I dislike them particularly. I have printed but 500 of 2.[d] ed.[n] simply on a/c of shortage of time & paper—but I hope to print another ed.[n] of 1000 in a very short time. The book has so far "sold" even better than I had hoped or anticipated.

Although Walsh describes three "printings" of *The California and Oregon Trail* in 1849, I find no real distinctions for issue or state in this Putnam first edition. Putnam may have regarded one of these three 1849 impressions as a "second edition."

[76] For a full collation of all the "editions" of *The Oregon Trail* through 1892 see my unpublished doctoral dissertation (University of Illinois, 1966), "Francis Parkman's *The Oregon Trail:* A Textual Edition and Critical Study."

took this opportunity to revise it once more. Although there is no positive evidence on this point, it seems probable that Parkman had already seen some of Remington's sketches for the "Illustrated Edition" before he revised the text of *The Oregon Trail* for the last time. One sentence in the 1892 text (see note 7 for p. 235) seems to have been added to this edition to conform to Remington's picture of a wounded buffalo pursued by wolves (see p. 229 of the present edition).

Thus, *The Oregon Trail* exists in four separate and distinct versions: the *Knickerbocker* serial installments (hereafter cited as *K*); the two Putnam "editions" of 1849 and 1852 (hereafter 49–52); the five Little, Brown "editions" of 1872–1883 (hereafter 72–83); and the "Illustrated Edition" of 1892 (hereafter 92).

That Parkman revised the book three times is not particularly surprising, for his usual practice was to edit and in some cases almost to rewrite his books as new materials or new interpretations came to light. The only exceptions to this rule are *Vassall Morton*, Parkman's one novel, which he seems to have regarded as better forgotten, and *A Half-Century of Conflict*, first published in 1892. The very last extended historical writing that Parkman did before his death was the section entitled "The Feudal Chiefs of Acadia," in effect a new introduction for the first volume of *The Old Régime in Canada*, first published in 1874. *The Oregon Trail* received perhaps only half the editing that Parkman gave such a book as his *La Salle*, but even the last revisions of *The Oregon Trail* in 1891 or 1892 are significant, for they show him continuing those processes of stylistic refinement and clarification of detail which are so large and important a part of the major revision of the book which he performed in 1871 or 1872. Because the "Illustrated Edition" does in fact represent the last text of *The Oregon Trail* to pass under Parkman's hand and because the revisions which he made for that edition are not inconsiderable, it has seemed to me best to use that edition as my text for the present facsimile edition.[77] Marginal numbers have been added to facilitate reference to the textual notes, which begin on page 415.

The Knickerbocker *Version and Its Revision*

The most difficult problem in any discussion of the texts of *The Oregon Trail* is to determine how the K version of the book was originally written and how it was thereafter prepared for the press as *The California and Oregon Trail* in 1849. As my notes to the present edition show, Parkman's Oregon Trail notebooks are clearly the primary source for the structure and incidents of the narrative, though Parkman occasionally took artistic liberties with the actual chronology and events of the trip, at least so far as they can be determined from his notebooks.

An introductory note to the 72–83 "editions" points out that "The book was written from dictation," and a canceled passage in K–52 is even more explicit: "Besides other formidable inconveniences, I owe it in great measure to the remote effects of that unlucky disorder [his prolonged dysentery or "mountain fever"], that from deficient eyesight I am compelled to employ the pen of another in taking down this narrative from my lips. . . ."[78] Precisely who Parkman's amanuensis was in 1847 and 1848 I have been unable to determine; the original K holograph has not survived, nor, after extensive search, have I found any evidence to support Mason Wade's undocumented assertion that Parkman dictated the K install-

---

[77] Objections to this decision can easily be made. Both K and 49–52 present special problems. K is both incomplete and textually corrupt, and 49–52, as Walsh, *"California and Oregon Trail,"* p. 282, notes, contain "an astonishing number of typographical errors." Textually the 72–83 "editions" have nothing to recommend them, and thus by a partial process of elimination there remains the "Illustrated Edition," the text for the collations upon which these and succeeding comments rest.

[78] See note 38 for p. 166.

ments to Quincy Adams Shaw, his cousin and companion in the West in 1846. Wade's supporting argument that Shaw's influence, at the very moment of the creation of *The Oregon Trail*, kept the book from becoming an epic chronicle of the West is also, I believe, unproven.[79] What does seem possible, on the evidence of Parkman's contemporary letters, is that he *may* have dictated parts of the book to some member of his family, to his mother, perhaps, or to one of his aunts, or even to a hired secretary while at intervals during 1847–1848 he underwent treatment for his eyes at Doctor Samuel M. Elliott's clinic on Staten Island.[80]

Wade's account of the revision of the K installments of *The Oregon Trail* has been generally accepted without question.[81] On the authority of several of Charles Eliot Norton's letters in 1848–1849 to Parkman (now in the Parkman Papers, Massachusetts Historical Society), Wade assumed that Norton volunteered to revise *The Oregon Trail* before its first Putnam publication. Wade argues that, in the process of revision, Norton effectually bowdlerized the book and reduced it to a genteel account of a summer's romantic rambles in the West by stripping from the serial version almost everything that made it a really important and historically realistic narrative of western life and adventure in 1846. Wade suggests that Norton not only schoolmastered the grammar and syntax of *The Oregon Trail* but also and more heinously excised almost all the raw life and excitement in the book, all the emphasis

[79] *Francis Parkman*, pp. 221–222. See also *Journals*, II, 386.

[80] Walsh, "*California and Oregon Trail*," p. 281, reprints part of a letter of February 4, 1848, to Parkman from his aunt, Miss Mary Brooks Hall, who seems to have helped to prepare printer's copy for at least some of the K installments.

[81] See, for example, Robert Edson Lee, *From West to East: Studies in the Literature of the American West* (Urbana, 1966), pp. 73–74, although Lee does undertake a rather inconclusive comparison of the K installments with the "Fourth Edition" of 1872.

on physical suffering, brutality, drunkenness, sexuality, and savagery that Parkman's first exuberant response to the wilderness had made an integral part of the *K* installments: "Still more of the original quality [of *The Oregon Trail*] was lost by the editing of Charles Eliot Norton, who revised the *Knickerbocker* version for book publication in accordance with the literary amenities as then understood by right-thinking Bostonians."[82]

However convincingly Wade has constructed his thesis of Norton's destructive gentility, the facts of Norton's and Parkman's own contemporary letters and my original collations of all the "editions" of *The Oregon Trail* published during Parkman's lifetime show that Wade's interpretation of the process of revision of the *K* installments for the Putnam first edition of 1849 rests upon a serious misreading of the evidence. In the first place, the *K* version of the book, filled as it is with gross typographical errors, numerous misspellings, erratic and even eccentric punctuation, and occasionally absurd word choices and scrambled syntax, seems to suggest that the serial installments may have been dictated to one or more not very attentive and perhaps even ill-educated amanuenses. What is certain, however, is that the *K* installments saw no proofreading by the author before they appeared in print. Although Parkman had published five narratives of frontier adventure in the magazine in 1845, Lewis Gaylord Clark, the owner and editor of the *Knickerbocker Magazine*, apparently made no effort to see that *The Oregon Trail* would receive even rudimentary editing in manuscript or in proof before its appearance in the monthly parts.[83]

[82] *Journals*, ii, 387. See also Wade, *Francis Parkman*, pp. 286–287. Does Wade mean that Norton "edited" or "revised" the *K* serial version of *The Oregon Trail*?

[83] For the literary history of Clark and the *Knickerbocker Magazine*, see Perry Miller, *The Raven and the Whale: The War of Words and Wits in the Era of Poe and Melville* (New York, 1956), pp. 11–344

Norton seems to have kept up with the *K* installments of *The Oregon Trail* quite carefully; on August 3, 1848, he wrote to Parkman (again undergoing treatment for his eyes at Doctor Elliott's clinic) to complain that no waterfalls had been described in any of the chapters so far published. On September 4, 1848, Norton wrote again to discover why "the worthless number of the Knickerbocker for this month" did not contain an installment of *The Oregon Trail*.[84] In the same letter he offered to help Parkman find a Boston publisher for the book; he also suggested that he would be glad to read the *proofs* for the first book publication of *The Oregon Trail*. Since this generous offer is the basis upon which Wade postulates Norton's drastic revision of *The Oregon Trail*, the relevant passage in Norton's letter deserves quotation: "At any rate let me do as much for you in looking over the proofs, or in any other way as I can."[85]

Writing from New York City on September 12, 1848, Parkman told Norton that he had already made arrangements with Putnam to bring out *The Oregon Trail*, with illustrations by Felix Darley, in the spring of 1849.[86] He accepted "thankfully" Norton's "very friendly offers to read the proofs of the *Oregon Trail*," very clearly an indication that Parkman did not mean to give his friend absolute freedom to *revise* the

---

passim. The *Literary World* of New York City published in its third number (on February 20, 1847) a short version of Chapter ix, "Scenes at Fort Laramie" (see note 1 for p. 104), which is notably free from the errors which so disfigure the *K* installments.

[84] Both of Norton's holograph letters are in the "Letters Received" folders, Parkman Papers, Massachusetts Historical Society.

[85] Whether Norton meant to revise page or galley proofs remains unclear, though the distinction is crucial for the argument that Norton was primarily responsible for the revision of the *K* serial version of *The Oregon Trail*.

[86] Parkman's letter is in the Norton Letterbooks, Houghton Library of Harvard University, and is reprinted in *Letters*, 1, 55–56.

book. On September 15, 1848, Norton acknowledged Parkman's letter and promised to go over the proofs with great care: "If there should occur any difficult or doubtful points Mr. Folsom [Charles Folsom, librarian of the Boston Athenaeum] will be at hand, to whom I can apply for assistance; & if any considerable alterations should occur to me I will write to you at once, & leave you to make it or not as you like."[87] This letter would seem to show, almost conclusively, that Norton was authorized simply to correct the proofs for the Putnam first edition and not to revise the K installments of *The Oregon Trail*. In an autobiographical letter written toward the end of his life, however, Norton claimed to have undertaken a complete revision of the K serial at Parkman's express request and with his assistance: "During my years in the counting-house a casual acquaintance with Frank Parkman developed into a friendship which lasted through life. He was then printing in the 'Knickerbocker Magazine,' if I remember rightly, his first book, 'The Oregon Trail,' and when it was to be published as a volume he asked me to revise the numbers, and many an evening, when there was not other work to be done, was spent by me and him in the solitary counting-room in going over his work."[88]

---

[87] "Letters Received" folders, Parkman Papers, Massachusetts Historical Society, and partially reprinted in Walsh, *"California and Oregon Trail,"* p. 282. Norton had written to Parkman in New York to send him the proofs in Boston "by the afternoon boat, [and] I shall receive them the next morning, & can read & return them by the mail of the same day."

[88] *Letters of Charles Eliot Norton, with Biographical Comment*, eds. Sarah Norton and M. A. DeWolfe Howe (Boston, 1913), I, 27–28. This letter has been generally accepted as a reliable account of Parkman's and Norton's collaboration on the revision of the K installments, but the ascertainable chronology of Parkman's activities in 1848 leaves little time available for "many an evening . . . spent . . . in going over his work," particularly since Parkman's and Norton's letters during the same period mention no such sessions.

This comparatively late account of the revision of the *K* installments, however, differs in striking detail from Norton's letters to Parkman in 1848–1849. Norton offered to revise the proofs of *The Oregon Trail* for the Putnam first edition, not the *K* serial version of the book. Parkman never asked Norton to undertake the correction of page or galley proofs, though he was glad enough to accept his friend's offer when he made it. Norton was several years younger than Parkman and in 1848 had given little real promise of the brilliant academic and literary career that lay before him; it would therefore seem highly unlikely that Parkman would have given him carte blanche in the revision of his first book.

Norton's last connection with *The Oregon Trail* is to be found in his letter of February 25, 1849, to Parkman in Boston, written while Norton was in New York City. Norton wrote: "I found Putnam, and learned from him that 'Oregon & California Trail' [*sic*] would be out in about ten days,— sometime in next week [*sic*]. He said that so far as he knew there had not been the least difficulty in making out the corrections in the copy you had sent him, that he received the last proof that morng. . . ."[89] This letter demonstrates that Parkman had done at least some revision of the proofs of *The Oregon Trail* during Parkman's absence from Boston. Moreover, many of the corrections in the Putnam first edition could have been made only by Parkman himself; for example, the frequent misspelling of "Mahto-Tatouka" in *K* for "Mahto-Tatonka" in 49 and subsequent editions could only have been changed by Parkman himself, since Norton would not have known the correct spelling of the name of an obscure Oglala chieftain.

Thus, Wade's carefully constructed thesis that the ultrare-

---

[89] "Letters Received" folders, Parkman Papers, Massachusetts Historical Society, and partially reprinted in Walsh, *"California and Oregon Trail,"* p. 282.

fined Norton was responsible for the bowdlerizing and school-mastering of Parkman's spontaneous and uninhibited descriptions of the West in 1846 gains little support from an analysis of Norton's and Parkman's contemporary letters or from my original collations of the texts of *The Oregon Trail* itself. Moreover, much the largest number of revisions of the book were made in 1871–1872 by Parkman himself for the Little, Brown "Fourth Edition." Parkman made the heaviest excisions from the text and the most extensive recastings of the grammar and syntax of the book almost 25 years after the Putnam first edition was published in 1849. While there are a good many substantive variants between K and 49–52, the process of revision which the K installments underwent sometime in 1848 is hardly as extensive or as thorough as has been generally thought.

In the first place, Parkman and whoever may have helped him revise the K installments for the press almost certainly did not prepare a new manuscript of *The Oregon Trail* for the Putnam compositors. As my original collation of K and 49–52 showed and as the summary of substantive variants given below will indicate, *The California and Oregon Trail* was probably set in type from the K installments themselves, which, with only three significant interpolated additions and a fair amount of judicious cutting and pasting (a common method in the nineteenth century for preparing serially published material for book publication), very easily served as printer's copy for the Putnam first edition. Almost all the significant changes between K and 49 could have been made on the margins of the K installments and probably were.

The changes made in *The Oregon Trail* in the Putnam first edition extended even to the title of the book, which appeared as *The California and Oregon Trail*, perhaps to appeal to the contemporary excitement over the California Gold Rush, although Parkman never mentioned the California Trail in the K serial version and in 1872 blamed the publishers for changing the title of the book without his permission.[90] Though the Putnam first and "third" editions are not free from errors of various kinds, Parkman and whoever helped him revise the *K* installments were more scrupulous in correcting the serial version of *The Oregon Trail* than has been generally supposed, although a number of new errors crept into the 49–52 text. It is probably for this reason that Walsh remarks: "As for the proofreading [of the Putnam first edition] (though it appears not to have been done entirely by Norton), one cannot help wondering whether Norton himself was not afflicted with some sort of eye trouble, for the book in its final form contains an astonishing number of typographical errors."[91]

As a matter of fact, almost every typographical error in the very careless *K* version was corrected in 49; such gross misreadings of the original manuscript as "seen" in *K* for "sun" in 49, and "precious" in *K* for "precocious" in 49 are corrected (cf. pp. 97:7 and 250:1).[92] Other corrections of probable printer's errors include the reading of "deposits" in 49 for "deposites" in *K* and "Mr. R. an English gentleman" in 49 for "Mr. R., and an English gentleman" in *K* (cf. pp. 3:5 and 5:7). It is hard, however, to decide in such cases whether the given typographical error in *K* was due to a printer's carelessness or to the possible spelling practices and even misapprehensions of Parkman's amanuenses in 1847 and 1848.

The same doubt would seem to apply to certain orthographic changes made in 1849, particularly the spelling of proper names. "Sorel" and "Mahto-Tatonka" almost always appear in *K* as "Lorel" and "Mahto-Tatouka"; it seems improbable that Parkman's amanuensis could consistently have misheard the difference between "Sorel" and "Lorel" or

---

[90] See the introductory note to 72–83 on p. 416 of this edition.

[91] Walsh, *"California and Oregon Trail,"* p. 282.

[92] Parenthetical citations refer to page and line numbers of the facsimile "Illustrated Edition," which is typographically uncorrected from the original impression.

"Mahto-Tatonka" and "Mahto-Tatouka" or that the printers could have made the same errors in more than 30 instances, and perhaps Parkman himself is responsible for these later changes. Other orthographic changes in 49 include "canvas" for "canvass" in *K*, "gully" for "gulley" in *K*, and "galloped" for "gallopped" in *K* (cf. pp. 47:31, 9:24, and 7:29). These changes presumably reflect Parkman's own spelling practices as against those of his amanuensis, as do "reïnforcement" in 49 for "reinforcement" in *K*, and "connection" in 49 for "connexion" in *K* (cf. pp. 5:12 and 5:16). Finally, 49 makes much less use of hyphenated spellings than does *K*, which divides words like "school-boys" and "foot-prints" (cf. pp. 115:3 and 192:31).

In punctuation, grammar, and syntax 49 makes a very considerable number of improvements over the mechanically careless *K* version of *The Oregon Trail*. First of all, 49 uses comma punctuation much more carefully and consistently than does *K*; 49 supplies necessary emphasis in series and conjunctive adverb constructions like "plain, black saddle" and "had, moreover," for "plain black saddle" and "had moreover" in *K* (cf. pp. 12:4 and 14:31). Some substantive changes are also accomplished by improved comma punctuation in 49: "He gave me the pipe, confidently expecting" clearly differs from "He gave me the pipe confidently, expecting" in *K* (cf. p. 162:2). Commas in 49 replace many semicolons in *K*, thereby avoiding numerous fragmentary constructions; 49 also changes case punctuation in such instances as "horses' necks" for "horse's necks" in *K* (cf. p. 68:11).

Occasionally 49 also adjusts Parkman's faulty grammar in *K* in such passages as "The buffalo began" for "The buffalo begun" in *K*, or "the hide and the tongue of the buffalo belong" for "the hide and the tongue of the buffalo belongs" in *K* (cf. pp. 362:30 and 263:20–21).

The 49 text also makes complete sentences of occasionally fragmentary constructions in *K* and corrects some unidiomatic phrasing. Stylistically 49 shows distinct improvements over *K*.

Almost all of Parkman's minor changes and deletions in individual phrases and clauses lead to a greater simplicity and clarity of language. The most obvious single rhetorical change in the Putnam first edition is the excision of adjectives before nouns; for example, "the pool" in 49 replaces "the pellucid pool" in K, "a conflict" in 49 stands in place of "a sanguinary conflict" in K, and "low sound" in 49 has been changed from "low gurgling sound" in K (cf. pp. 195:32, 197:8, and 195:25). A number of obvious redundancies are excised in 49, as, for example, "had consciousness" in 49 for "had life and consciousness" in K (cf. p. 62:22). A good deal of simple wordiness is also eliminated in 49, as in "as usual" for "as I commonly did" in K or "he" for "the cowardly ruffian" in K (cf. pp. 243:33 and 272:17).

Again, 49 often softens unpleasant details, as, for example, when "Having killed him" replaces "Having hammered him on the head with a stone mallet" in K (see note 11 for p. 211), and 49 also drops a reference to Raymond's having vomited (see note 12 for p. 186). A number of apparent improprieties are excised in 49, where "little log-house" replaces "little old log-house" in K, an expression which Parkman may have regarded as too colloquial (cf. p. 18:21–22). The 49 revisions also include a number of changes essential for clarity of meaning, as, for example, "Eleven" in 49 for "Almost a dozen" in K, or "encamped, they told us, near" in 49 for "encamped near" in K (cf. pp. 253:7 and 87:7). This process, however, is more often reversed, as when a particular name or number in K is replaced by a more general term in 49: "He" stands in place of "Jack" in K, and "Several" has replaced "About a dozen" in K (cf. pp. 164:13 and 205:25).

Almost all of Parkman's direct addresses to the reader in K are deleted in 49, as are most of his rather more obvious attempts at humor; "assume the scanty costume of an Indian" in 49 replaces "assume the costume of an Indian, which closely resembles that adopted by Father Adam" in K (see note 16 for p. 300).

Parkman seems to have been content not to make many extensive substantive changes in 49. Chapter x, "The War Parties," makes its first appearance, however, and 49 takes sections from the K versions of Chapters xxiii and xxv and rearranges them to form a new Chapter xxiv. The epigraphs (excised in 72) for a number of chapters in 49 are either slightly altered in phrasing from their K counterparts (i.e., quoted exactly rather than approximately, in K) or else changed completely. There is one quite long footnote addition describing the further adventures of Romaine and the Chandlers after Parkman saw the last of them at Fort Laramie (see note 32 for p. 120). Parkman also added a new sentence showing how his party had discovered more strayed cavalry horses (see note 25 for p. 396), but there are otherwise no substantive additions of any importance in 49.

As he did far more extensively in 1871–1872, Parkman made extensive excisions in 1848 from the K version of *The Oregon Trail* for the Putnam first edition. All the end-of-chapter "teasers" in the K serial version are dropped in 49. More important, Parkman has deleted in 49 one extremely interesting paragraph in K which compared, perhaps too vividly, the evils of both civilization and the wilderness (see note 26 for p. 161). A number of too explicit references to Parkman's mountain fever are excised in 49 (see note 8 for p. 293 and note 31 for p. 400), and Parkman's forcefully stated disgust at Mormonism (a "horde of fanatics" in K) is considerably toned down in 49 (see note 3 for p. 42). The only other significant excision has to do with Parkman's contempt for the high-handed exactions of the American Fur Company at Fort Laramie, a contempt freely expressed in K but perhaps more prudently deleted in 49 (see notes 19 and 20 for p. 114).

Edition of 1872

Thus, 49 shows significant changes from K and is in every respect an important though not major revision of the book. The "Fourth Edition" of *The Oregon Trail*, published by

Little, Brown and Company in 1872, shows the most comprehensive changes that Parkman made in the book; fully 60 percent of the variant readings listed in my original collations of the texts represent changes which Parkman made for the 72 edition.

Corrections of typographical errors are less numerous in 72 than in the earlier revision of the K installments for 49, although 72 does supply "deep" for "deed" and "short" for "sbout" in 49–52 (cf. pp. 53:16 and 170:1). More significant are Parkman's changes in the spellings of proper names; "Bridger's" now replaces "Bridge's" in K–52 (cf. p. 336:6), an indication that Parkman had finally, perhaps, learned the correct name of the great mountain man. Parkman's French seems to have improved a great deal since the publications of K–52, and a number of French names now appear in more familiar forms; "Deslauriers" in 72, the usual spelling for this quite common French name, now replaces "Delorier" in K–52, and "Gingras" appears in 72 for "Jean Gras" in K–52, although "Jean Gras" may have been correct for this apparent nickname. A number of French phrases are now spelled correctly, as "*Sacré enfant de garce!*" in 72 for "*sacre enfan de garce*," in K–52 (cf. p. 390:11). Other variant spellings are now regularized, as "moccasins" in 72 for "moccasons" in 49–52 and "grizzly" for "grisly" in K–52, though the latter spelling in "grisly bear" was not unknown in the 1840's (cf. pp. 11:1 and 21:32).

Extensive changes in punctuation, grammar, and syntax appear in 72. As in 49–52, comma usage is made clearer and more consistent in such constructions as "such, for instance," in 72 for "such for instance" in 49–52, and "charger, Pontiac," in 72 for "charger Pontiac" in K–52 (cf. pp. 133:24 and 33:8). A number of semicolon fragments are corrected in 72; many exclamation marks are also excised. Needed quotation marks have been added in several places, and one or two gross errors in punctuation (which entered the text in 49–52) are corrected in 72. Several borrowed words now appear in italics, as "*pukwi*" in 72 for "pukwi" in K–52 (cf. p. 27:8).

Other 72 changes include some obvious schoolmastering of Parkman's grammar; thus, 72 uses "which" to refer to animals rather than the "who" of K–52 (cf. p. 341:6). Terminal prepositions in a number of K–52 sentences demand that a certain number of sentences be recast in 72, as in "with which he was acquainted" for "which he was acquainted with" in K–52 (cf. p. 339:6–7). Faulty verbs are corrected in 72, as in "lay down" for "laid down" in K–52 (cf. p. 8:3–4). The "Fourth Edition" also shows very considerable changes in syntactical patterns, and many of these changes are clearly the result of Parkman's efforts to achieve a simpler, clearer, and more direct style. A number of participial constructions are eliminated in 72, and very often the past progressive verbs of the earlier "editions" are reduced to simple past tenses, as "ran" in 72 for "was running" in K–52 (cf. p. 113:17). Some transpositions are evident in 72, as "now asked only" for "now only asked" in K–52 (cf. p. 14:23), and 72 continues the practice of the first revision for 49 in reducing subordinate clauses to appositive or participial phrases, as in "a blacksmith attached" for "a blacksmith who was attached" in K–52 (cf. p. 58:26). Finally, 72 shows some combining of separate sentences into compound clause constructions.

The alterations which Parkman made in the punctuation, grammar, and syntax of *The Oregon Trail* for the "Fourth Edition" are, however, of much less importance than are the changes which he made in diction, usage, and style, almost all of which resulted in greater sharpness of detail and clearer emphasis. In 72 almost every vestige of slang and colloquialism has at last been eliminated; "puppies" has replaced "pups" in K–52, and "hindmost" stands in place of "hindermost" in K–52 (cf. pp. 99:31 and 67:26). A certain amount of obsolete word choice has now been brought up to date, as "trousers" in 72 for "pantaloons" in K–52, or "concert" in 72 for "concerto" in K–52 (cf. pp. 5:3 and 36:1–2). Redundancy has been almost entirely eliminated; 72 now reads "tripod of poles" for "tripod of three poles" in K–52 (cf. p. 97:13). In 72 Parkman was careful to excise a good deal of poetic diction and sheer wordiness, as "scarcely" in 72 for "scarce" in K–52, and "Hundreds of others" in 72 for "Multitudes besides" in K–52 (cf. pp. 88:17 and 47:2–3). Parkman in 72 also continued to excise unnecessary adjectives, though at times with some loss of rhetorical force. A reference to the Oregon and California emigrants now appears as "this migration" instead of "this strange migration" in K–52 (cf. p. 7:4); the alteration is an important one, showing Parkman's later changed point of view toward the frontiersmen whom he had seen at Westport in 1846.

Other more colorful or explicit details are lost in 72, as when "The Hog" appears as "a bloated savage" instead of "a huge bloated savage" in K–52 (cf. p. 97:31–32). If a number of these adjectival decisions show a certain weakening of descriptive force, the changes on the whole are beneficial insofar as they present in 72 a simpler, less cluttered style.

Most of the other minor stylistic changes in 72 show that almost always Parkman strove for the clearer, more exact word and phrase in this revision of the text. For example, "skulls" in 72 is much more explicit than the vague "heavy loads" in K–52, and "war-party" in 72 is an obvious improvement over "warlike expedition" in K–52 (cf. pp. 251:21 and 244:29). In 72 "hill" almost always replaces "declivity" in K–52 (cf. p. 59:4); other examples of the excision of latinate diction might be shown. Frequently the 72 changes make for distinctly clearer images, as when "crouched" replaces "seated ourselves" in K–52, or when "was less tender" stands for "was somewhat less exemplary" in K–52 (cf. pp. 188:24 and 250:2–3). A decided improvement in nuance appears in "notion" for "theory" in K–52 in a reference to the widespread nineteenth-century belief that the Indians were descendants of the Lost Ten Tribes of Israel (cf. p. 145:20).

Other alterations are perhaps less successful; 72 provides the vaguer "overwhelm" for "break to pieces" in K–52, and the less precise "a group" for "half a dozen" in K–52 (cf. pp. 88:18 and 172:13). Wright, who is simply "an American" in K–52, appears as "an American ruffian" in 72 (cf. p. 6:1–2), but there is scarcely another significant minor addition to the 72 text.

The major changes in the 72 text of *The Oregon Trail* include only a very small number of additions, among them the new dedication of the book to Quincy Adams Shaw and a new prefatory note and introduction. A paragraph describing an Indian's quarrel with his squaw, perhaps inserted for comic relief, has been added at pp. 174:24–175:20, and a new sentence appears at p. 205:8–11, but, in 72 as in 49, these changes are insignificant in comparison with the number of excisions Parkman made from the text, and all the evidence of my collations of K, 49–52, and 72 seems to indicate that Parkman revised for 72 from the Putnam editions of 49–52.

All the epigraphs and almost all the other poetry have been excised from the 72 text. Taken in conjunction with the excision of a good deal more that may be loosely called "romantic" in K–52, these deletions of the poetry would seem to indicate that Parkman wished the 72 text of *The Oregon Trail* to appear less as a Byronic account of romantic rambles among wilderness scenes than as a serious and reliable account of Indian life and customs. Thus, almost all of the traditional "visions" of the East and of civilization are eliminated in 72, doubtless because they now seemed irrelevant to the comparatively straightforward descriptions of Parkman's adventures among the Oglalas (cf. note 7 for p. 183 and note 32 for p. 200). Again, Parkman deleted a number of the too elaborate and mechanically picturesque descriptions of the moun-

tains and forests he saw when he visited the Oglala village
(see note 29 for p. 196). Almost all the pointed contrasts
between the effeminate East and the robust West are deleted
in 72 (see note 14 for p. 213), and material consciously ro-
manticizing the Indian has also been rather heavily cut in 72
(see note 20 for p. 156, for a passage very reminiscent of
Cooper). From K–52 Parkman also deleted a number of passages of biographical interest, especially those dealing too
explicitly with his "mountain fever" (see note 11 for p. 124
and notes 36–39 for p. 166), perhaps because such references
seemed unimportant and even trivial to a man who had lived
for more than a quarter of a century with racking physical
pain and the daily fear that he was losing his mind. Less
understandable is his excision of a passage explaining his early
interest in the ethnology of the American Indian and his
reasons for going west in 1846 (see note 6 for p. 122).

Perhaps in the interest of narrative unity and coherence,
Parkman cut heavily from K–52 passages dealing with the
Chandlers and Romaine. Gone now is Parkman's account of
the Captain's ludicrous failure to "run" a buffalo (see note 10
for p. 74) and even longer sections describing the back-
grounds of Parkman's British companions and their reasons
for undertaking a hunting trip across the continent (see note
13 for p. 51), as well as the footnote describing Shaw's later
meeting with the Captain in New York City (see note 32 for
p. 120). Again, Parkman seems to have recognized that his
ridicule of the Chandlers after he left them along the Platte
rang rather hollow, and thus a number of sentences have been
canceled in 72 (see notes 9–11 for p. 90), as is one scurrilous
reference to Jack (see note 13 for p. 90).

For probably the same considerations of unity and coherence, almost all of Tête Rouge's misadventures are deleted in
72; Parkman must have regarded his earlier description of
Tête Rouge's buffalo hunt or of his sprees at Fort Leavenworth as too frivolous for inclusion in the more serious and

restrained 72 text (see note 10 for p. 347, note 17 for p. 394, and note 33 for p. 410). Less understandable is Parkman's deletion of the long paragraph of praise for Henry Chatillon at the conclusion of K–52 (see note 34 for p. 411); this prose poem is reduced to the single sentence of admiration at p. 411:13–14. The only other significant excisions show some softening of Parkman's earlier mocking references to Raymond and Deslauriers (see, e.g., note 28 for p. 221).

Edition of 1892

The 92 or "Illustrated Edition" text of *The Oregon Trail* was, as I have noted, the last to pass directly under Parkman's hand and thus represents his final intentions toward the book. Many of the changes made in 92 are those which might have been made by any good publisher's proofreader; comparatively few of the alterations in 92 are substantive ones. This text is a remarkably clean one; there are but two or three minor errors in omitted quotation marks and only one uncorrected misprint (see note 29 for p. 318), an error which first appears in 72, though there are several instances of obsolete spelling which might pass at first glance for misprints. A number of typographical errors have been corrected in 92, as "cavalcade" for "calvacade" in 72–83, and "it's" for "its" in 72–83 (cf. pp. 270:18 and 58:15). A certain amount of old-fashioned spelling is regularized in 92, as "anything" for "any thing" in K–83, and "schoolhouses" for "school-houses" in K–83 (cf. pp. 18:28 and 18:1). Capitals frequently replace lower-case usages in 92, as "Captain" for "captain" in K–83, and "East" in 92 for "east" in K–83 (cf. pp. 5:9 and 21:8), and several proper names now appear in more familiar forms, as "Dakota" in 92 for "Dahcotah" in K–83 (cf. p. 94:8).

Punctuation, grammar, and syntax again receive considerable attention in 92, generally to the improvement of rhetorical force and clarity. Comma punctuation conforms to the usual conventions in series and appositive constructions, and a good many unnecessary commas have been deleted. Semicolons now usually replace colons in appositive clauses, and dashes have replaced semicolons in a number of incomplete constructions. A few faulty possessives are corrected in 92, as are a number of instances of faulty usage and idiom, for example, "further" in 92 for "farther" in K–83, or "intrusted it to" in 92 for "intrusted it with" in K–83 (cf. pp. 120:17 and 8:27). Several new paragraph divisions appear in the "Illustrated Edition."

Minor stylistic changes occur from time to time in 92; an occasional adjective or adverb is excised, as "desperate" in 92 for "most desperate" in K–83 (cf. p. 133:23). A more colloquial style reappears in 92, as "I'll" for "I will" in K–83 (cf. p. 33:28), but the only stylistic alterations of any significance have to do with minor changes in word choice, as "strap" in 92 for "thong" in K–83, "disappointment" for "mortification" in K–83, or "green belt" for "verdant line" in K–83 (cf. pp. 22:1, 319:32–33, and 199:20–21). Oddly enough, 92 also changes the sex of Reynal's horse from "her" and "she" in K–83 to "him" and "he" in 92 (cf. p. 274:24), and a phrase is also added in 92 to explain how a rifle ball is often spat into the barrel of a rifle during the chase (cf. "or . . . barrel," p. 357:12–13). A sentence is added at p. 235:25–26 to conform to one of Remington's illustrations, but, except for a new introduction, nothing else of substance has been added to the "Illustrated Edition" of *The Oregon Trail.*

This discussion of Parkman's three revisions of the book would be incomplete unless some attention is drawn to the fact that many of the citations in my original collations of the texts show Parkman revising given passages more than once and in a number of instances through all three versions of the text after K. Other citations show Parkman making a minor change in 49 and then in 72 changing the 49 reading back to the original K reading. These citations are always revisions of punctuation; nevertheless they show Parkman constantly involved in perfecting his text even to the smallest accidental. *The Oregon Trail* received only about half the editing which Parkman gave to his *La Salle*, a work which needs serious textual criticism. The present edition of *The Oregon Trail* will have served one of its purposes if it stimulates the searching textual study which Parkman's histories demand and which they will certainly repay.[93]

[93] The only extended discussion of the revisions of Parkman's histories that I have seen is Howard H. Peckham, "The Sources and Revisions of Parkman's *Pontiac*," *Papers of the Bibliographical Society of America*, xxxvii (1943), 1–15.

THE OREGON TRAIL

THE

OREGON TRAIL

SKETCHES

OF

PRAIRIE AND ROCKY-MOUNTAIN LIFE

BY

FRANCIS PARKMAN

Illustrated by Frederic Remington

BOSTON
LITTLE, BROWN, AND COMPANY
1892

University Press:
JOHN WILSON AND SON, CAMBRIDGE.

PREFACE

———•———

IN the preface to the fourth edition of this book, printed in 1872, I spoke of the changes that had already come over the Far West. Since that time change has grown to metamorphosis. For Indian teepees, with their trophies of bow, lance, shield, and dangling scalplocks, we have towns and cities, resorts of health and pleasure seekers, with an agreeable society, Paris fashions, the magazines, the latest poem, and the last new novel. The sons of civilization, drawn by the fascinations of a fresher and bolder life, thronged to the western wilds in multitudes which blighted the charm that had lured them.

The buffalo is gone, and of all his millions nothing is left but bones. Tame cattle and fences of barbed wire have supplanted his vast herds and boundless grazing grounds. Those discordant serenaders, the wolves that howled at evening about the traveller's camp-fire have succumbed to arsenic and hushed their savage music. The wild Indian is turned into an ugly caricature of his conqueror; and that which made him romantic, terrible, and hateful, is in large measure scourged out of him. The slow cavalcade of horsemen armed to the teeth has disappeared before parlor cars and the effeminate comforts of modern travel.

5   The rattlesnakes have grown bashful and retiring. The mountain lion shrinks from the face of man, and
6   even grim " Old Ephraim," [1] the grizzly bear, seeks the seclusion of his dens and caverns. It is said that he is no longer his former self, having found by an intelligence not hitherto set to his credit, that his ferocious strength is no match for a repeating rifle; with which discovery he is reported to have grown diffident, and abated the truculence of his more prosperous days. One may be permitted to doubt if the blood-thirsty old savage has really experienced a change of heart; and before inviting him to single combat, the ambitious tenderfoot, though the proud possessor of a Winchester with sixteen cartridges in the magazine, would do well to consider not only the quality of his weapon, but also that of his own nerves.

He who feared neither bear, Indian, nor devil, the all-daring and all-enduring trapper, belongs to the

---

[1] Alias " Old Caleb " and " Old Enoch."

past, or lives only in a few gray-bearded survivals. In his stead we have the cowboy, and even his star begins to wane. 7

The Wild West is tamed, and its savage charms have withered. If this book can help to keep their memory alive, it will have done its part. It has found a powerful helper in the pencil of Mr. Rem- 8 ington, whose pictures are as full of truth as of spirit, for they are the work of one who knew the prairies and the mountains before irresistible commonplace had subdued them.

BOSTON, 16 September, 1892.

PREFACE

———•———

THE following sketches first appeared in 1847. A sum- 10
mer's adventures of two youths just out of college might
well enough be allowed to fall into oblivion, were it not that
a certain interest will always attach to the record of that
which has passed away never to return. This book is the
reflection of forms and conditions of life which have ceased,
in great measure, to exist. It reflects the image of an irrevocable past.

I remember that, as we rode by the foot of Pike's Peak,
when for a fortnight we had met no face of man, my companion remarked, in a tone anything but complacent, that a time
would come when those plains would be a grazing country,
the buffalo give place to tame cattle, farm-houses be scattered
along the water-courses, and wolves, bears, and Indians be
numbered among the things that were. We condoled with
each other on so melancholy a prospect, but we little thought
what the future had in store. We knew that there was more
or less gold in the seams of those untrodden mountains; but
we did not foresee that it would build cities in the waste, and
plant hotels and gambling-houses among the haunts of the
grizzly bear. We knew that a few fanatical outcasts were 11
groping their way across the plains to seek an asylum from
gentile persecution; but we did not imagine that the polyga-

mous hordes of Mormon would rear a swarming Jerusalem in the bosom of solitude itself. We knew that, more and more, year after year, the trains of emigrant wagons would creep in slow procession towards barbarous Oregon or wild and distant California; but we did not dream how Commerce and Gold would breed nations along the Pacific, the disenchanting screech of the locomotive break the spell of weird, mysterious mountains, woman's rights invade the fastnesses of the Arapahoes, and despairing savagery, assailed in front and rear, vail its scalplocks and feathers before triumphant commonplace. We were no prophets to foresee all this; and, had we foreseen it, perhaps some perverse regrets might have tempered the ardor of our rejoicing.

The wild cavalcade that defiled with me down the gorges of the Black Hills, with its paint and war-plumes, fluttering trophies and savage embroidery, bows, arrows, lances, and shields, will never be seen again. Those who formed it have found bloody graves, or a ghastlier burial in the maws of wolves. The Indian of to-day, armed with a revolver and crowned with an old hat, cased, possibly, in trousers or muffled in a tawdry shirt, is an Indian still, but an Indian shorn of the picturesqueness which was his most conspicuous merit.

The mountain trapper is no more, and the grim romance of his wild, hard life is a memory of the past.

As regards the motives which sent us to the mountains, our liking for them would have sufficed; but, in my case, another incentive was added. I went in great measure as a student, to prepare for a literary undertaking of which the plan was already formed, but which, from the force of inexorable circumstances, is still but half accomplished. It was this that prompted some proceedings on my part which, without a fixed purpose in view, might be charged with youthful rashness. My business was observation, and I was willing to pay dearly for the opportunity of exercising it.

Two or three years ago I made a visit to our guide, the brave and true-hearted Henry Chatillon, at the town of Caron- 16 delet, near St. Louis. It was more than twenty years since we had met. Time hung heavy on his hands, as usual with old mountain-men married and established; his hair was touched with gray, and his face and figure showed tokens of early hardship; but the manly simplicity of his character was unchanged. He told me that the Indians with whom I had been domesticated, a band of the hated Sioux, had nearly all been killed in fights with the white men.

The faithful Deslauriers is, I believe, still living on the frontier of Missouri. The hunter Raymond perished in the 17 snow during Fremont's disastrous passage of the mountains in the winter of 1848.

BOSTON, March 30, 1872.

CONTENTS.

———◆———

LIST OF ILLUSTRATIONS.

Full-page Illustrations.

Illustrations in Text.

CHAPTER I.

THE FRONTIER.

L AST spring, 1846, was a busy season in the city of 1
St. Louis.   Not only were emigrants from every part
of the country preparing for the journey to Oregon and
California, but an unusual number of traders were making ready their wagons and outfits for Santa Fé.   The 2
hotels were crowded, and the gunsmiths and saddlers were
kept constantly at work in providing arms and equipments
for the different parties of travellers.   Steamboats were
leaving the levee and passing up the Missouri, crowded
with passengers on their way to the frontier.

In one of these, the "Radnor," since snagged and lost, 3
my friend and relative Quincy Adams Shaw, and myself
left St. Louis on the 28th of April, on a tour of curiosity

and amusement to the Rocky Mountains. The boat was loaded until the water broke alternately over her guards. Her upper-deck was covered with large wagons of a peculiar form, for the Santa Fé trade, and her hold was crammed with goods for the same destination. There were also the equipments and provisions of a party of Oregon emigrants, a band of mules and horses, piles of saddles and harness, and a multitude of nondescript articles, indispensable on the prairies. Almost hidden in this medley was a small French cart, of the sort very appropriately called a "mule-killer" beyond the frontiers, and not far distant a tent, together with a miscellaneous assortment of boxes and barrels. The whole equipage was far from prepossessing in its appearance; yet, such as it was, it was destined to a long and arduous journey, on which the persevering reader will accompany it.

The passengers on board the "Radnor" corresponded with her freight. In her cabin were Santa Fé traders, gamblers, speculators, and adventurers of various descriptions, and her steerage was crowded with Oregon emigrants, "mountain men," negroes, and a party of Kanzas Indians, who had been on a visit to St. Louis.

Thus laden the boat struggled upward for seven or eight days against the rapid current of the Missouri, grating upon snags, and hanging for two or three hours at a time upon sand-bars. We entered the mouth of the Missouri in a drizzling rain, but the weather soon became clear, and showed distinctly the broad and turbid river, with its eddies, its sand-bars, its ragged islands, and forest-covered shores. The Missouri is constantly changing its course,— wearing away its banks on one side, while it forms new ones on the other. Its channel is continually shifting. Islands are formed, and then washed away; and while the

old forests on one side are undermined and swept off, a
young growth springs up from the new soil upon the other.
With all these changes the water is so charged with mud
and sand that, in spring, it is perfectly opaque, and in a
few minutes deposits a sediment an inch thick in the bot- 8
tom of a tumbler. The river was now high; but when we
descended in the autumn it was fallen very low, and all the
secrets of its treacherous shallows were exposed to view.
It was frightful to see the dead and broken trees, thick-set
as a military abattis, firmly imbedded in the sand, and all
pointing down stream, ready to impale any unhappy steamboat that at high water should pass over them.

In five or six days we began to see signs of the great
western movement that was taking place. Parties of emigrants, with their tents and wagons, were encamped on
open spots near the bank, on their way to the common
rendezvous at Independence. On a rainy day, near sunset,
we reached the landing of this place, which is some miles 9
from the river, on the extreme frontier of Missouri. The
scene was characteristic, for here were represented at one
view the most remarkable features of this wild and enterprising region. On the muddy shore stood some thirty or
forty dark, slavish-looking Spaniards, gazing stupidly out 10
from beneath their broad hats. They were attached to
one of the Santa Fé companies, whose wagons were
crowded together on the banks above. In the midst of
these, crouching over a smouldering fire, was a group of
Indians, belonging to a remote Mexican tribe. One or
two French hunters from the mountains, with their long 11
hair and buckskin dresses, were looking at the boat; and
seated on a log close at hand were three men, with rifles
lying across their knees. The foremost of these, a tall,
strong figure, with a clear blue eye and an open, intelli-

gent face, might very well represent that race of restless and intrepid pioneers whose axes and rifles have opened a path from the Alleghanies to the western prairies. He was on his way to Oregon, probably a more congenial field to him than any that now remained on this side of the great plains.

Early on the next morning we reached Kanzas, about five hundred miles from the mouth of the Missouri. Here we landed, and leaving our equipments in charge of Colonel Chick, whose log-house was the substitute for a tavern, we set out in a wagon for Westport, where we hoped to procure mules and horses for the journey.

It was a remarkably fresh and beautiful May morning. The woods, through which the miserable road conducted us, were lighted by the bright sunshine and enlivened by a multitude of birds. We overtook on the way our late fellow-travellers, the Kanzas Indians, who adorned with all their finery were proceeding homeward at a round pace; and whatever they might have seemed on board the boat, they made a very striking and picturesque feature in the forest landscape.

Westport was full of Indians, whose little shaggy ponies were tied by dozens along the houses and fences. Sacs and Foxes, with shaved heads and painted faces, Shawanoes and Delawares, fluttering in calico frocks and turbans, Wyandots dressed like white men, and a few wretched Kanzas wrapped in old blankets, were strolling about the streets or lounging in and out of the shops and houses.

As I stood at the door of the tavern I saw a remarkable-looking personage coming up the street. He had a ruddy face, garnished with the stumps of a bristly red beard and moustache; on one side of his head was a round cap with a knob at the top, such as Scottish laborers sometimes wear; his coat was of a nondescript form, and made of a gray Scotch plaid, with the fringes hanging all about it; he wore trousers of coarse homespun, and hobnailed shoes; and to complete his equipment, a little black pipe was stuck in one corner of his mouth. In this curious attire, I recognized Captain C——, of the British army, who, with his brother, and Mr. R——, an English gentleman, was bound on a hunting expedition across the continent. I had seen the Captain and his companions at St. Louis. They had now been for some time at Westport, making preparations for their departure, and waiting for a reinforcement, since they were too few in number to attempt it alone. They might, it is true, have joined some of the parties of emigrants who were on the point of setting out for Oregon and California; but they professed great disinclination to have any connection with the "Kentucky fellows."

The Captain now urged it upon us that we should join forces and proceed to the mountains in company. Feeling no greater partiality for the society of the emigrants than they did, we thought the arrangement a good one, and consented to it. Our future fellow-travellers had installed themselves in a little log-house, where we found them surrounded by saddles, harness, guns, pistols, telescopes, knives, and in short their complete appointments for the prairie. R——, who had a taste for natural history, sat at a table stuffing a woodpecker; the brother of the Captain, who was an Irishman, was splicing a trail-rope on the floor. The Captain pointed out, with much complacency, the different articles of their outfit. "You see," said he, "that we are all old travellers. I am convinced that no party ever went upon the prairie better provided." The hunter whom they had employed, a surly-

17

18 looking Canadian, named Sorel, and their muleteer, an American ruffian from St. Louis, were lounging about the building. In a little log stable close at hand were their horses and mules, selected with excellent judgment by the Captain.

We left them to complete their arrangements, while we pushed our own to all convenient speed. The emigrants, for whom our friends professed such contempt were encamped on the prairie about eight or ten miles distant, to the number of a thousand or more, and new parties were constantly passing out from Independence to join them. They were in great confusion, holding meetings, passing resolutions, and drawing up regulations, but unable to unite in the choice of leaders to conduct them across the prairie. Being at leisure one day, I rode over

19 to Independence. The town was crowded. A multitude of shops had sprung up to furnish the emigrants and Santa Fé traders with necessaries for their journey; and there was an incessant hammering and banging from a dozen blacksmiths' sheds, where the heavy wagons were being repaired, and the horses and oxen shod. The streets were thronged with men, horses, and mules. While I was in the town, a train of emigrant wagons from Illinois passed through, to join the camp on the prairie, and stopped in the principal street. A multitude of healthy children's faces were peeping out from under the covers of the wagons. Here and there a buxom damsel was seated on horseback, holding over her sunburnt face an old umbrella or a parasol, once gaudy enough, but now miserably faded. The men, very sober-looking countrymen, stood about their oxen; and as I passed I noticed three old fellows, who, with their long whips in their hands, were zealously

20 discussing the doctrine of regeneration. The emigrants,

however, are not all of this stamp. Among them are some of the vilest outcasts in the country. I have often perplexed myself to divine the various motives that give impulse to this migration; but whatever they may be, whether an insane hope of a better condition in life, or a desire of shaking off restraints of law and society, or mere restlessness, certain it is that multitudes bitterly repent the journey, and, after they have reached the land of promise, are happy enough to escape from it. 21

In the course of seven or eight days we had brought our preparations nearly to a close. Meanwhile our friends had completed theirs, and, becoming tired of Westport, they told us that they would set out in advance, and wait at the crossing of the Kanzas till we should come up. Accordingly R—— and the muleteer went forward with the wagon and tent, while the Captain and his brother, together with Sorel and a trapper named Boisverd, who 22 had joined them, followed with the band of horses. The commencement of the journey was ominous, for the captain was scarcely a mile from Westport, riding along in state at the head of his party, leading his intended buffalo horse by a rope, when a tremendous thunder-storm came on and drenched them all to the skin. They hurried on to reach the place, about seven miles off, where R—— was to have had the camp in readiness to receive them. 23 But this prudent person, when he saw the storm approaching, had selected a sheltered glade in the woods, where he pitched his tent, and was sipping a comfortable cup of coffee while the Captain galloped for miles beyond through the rain to look for him. At length the storm cleared away, and the sharp-eyed trapper succeeded in discovering his tent. R—— had by this time finished his coffee, and was seated on a buffalo-robe smoking his pipe.

The Captain was one of the most easy-tempered men in existence, so he bore his ill-luck with great composure, shared the dregs of the coffee with his brother, and lay down to sleep in his wet clothes.

24   We ourselves had our share of the deluge. We were leading a pair of mules to Kanzas when the storm broke. Such sharp and incessant flashes of lightning, such stunning and continuous thunder I had never known before. The woods were completely obscured by the diagonal sheets of rain that fell with a heavy roar, and rose in spray from the ground, and the streams swelled so rapidly that we could hardly ford them. At length, looming through the rain, we saw the log-house of Colonel Chick, who received us with his usual bland hospitality; while his wife, who, though a little soured and stiffened by a long course of camp-meetings, was not behind him in good-will, supplied us with the means of bettering our drenched and bedraggled condition. The storm clearing away at about sunset opened a noble prospect from the porch of the Colonel's house which stands upon a high hill. The sun streamed from the breaking clouds upon the swift and angry Missouri, and on the vast expanse of forest that stretched from its banks back to the distant bluffs.

25   Returning on the next day to Westport we received a message from the Captain, who had ridden back to deliver it in person, but finding that we were in Kanzas, had intrusted it to an acquaintance of his, named Vogel, who kept a small grocery and liquor shop. Whiskey, by the way, circulates more freely in Westport than is altogether safe in a place where every man carries a loaded
26   pistol in his pocket. As we passed this establishment
27   we saw Vogel's broad German face thrust from his door. He said he had something to tell us, and invited us **to**

take a dram. Neither his liquor nor his message was very palatable. The Captain had returned to give us notice that R——, who assumed the direction of his party had determined upon another route from that agreed upon between us; and instead of taking the course of the traders, had resolved to pass northward by Fort Leavenworth, and follow the path marked out by the dragoons in their expedition of last summer. To adopt such a plan without consulting us, we looked upon as a high-handed proceeding; but suppressing our dissatisfaction as well as   28
we could, we made up our minds to join them at Fort Leavenworth, where they were to wait for us.

Accordingly, our preparation being now complete, we attempted one fine morning to begin our journey. The   29
first step was an unfortunate one. No sooner were our animals put in harness than the shaft-mule reared and plunged, burst ropes and straps, and nearly flung the cart into the Missouri. Finding her wholly uncontrollable, we   30
exchanged her for another, with which we were furnished by our friend Mr. Boone, of Westport, a grandson of   31
Daniel Boone, the pioneer. This foretaste of prairie experience was very soon followed by another. Westport was scarcely out of sight when we encountered a deep muddy gully, of a species that afterward became but too familiar to us, and here for the space of an hour or more the cart stuck fast.

CHAPTER II.

BREAKING THE ICE.

1 EMERGING from the mud-holes of Westport, we pursued our way for some time along the narrow track, in the checkered sunshine and shadow of the woods, till at length, issuing into the broad light, we left behind us the farthest outskirts of the great forest that once spread from the western plains to the shore of the Atlantic. Looking over an intervening belt of bushes, we saw the green, ocean-like expanse of prairie, stretching swell beyond swell to the horizon.

It was a mild, calm spring day,— a day when one is more disposed to musing and reverie than to action, and the softest part of his nature is apt to gain the upper hand.
2 I rode in advance of the party as we passed through the bushes, and as a nook of green grass offered a strong temptation, I dismounted and lay down there. All the trees and saplings were in flower, or budding into fresh leaf; the red clusters of the maple-blossoms and the rich
3 flowers of the Indian apple were there in profusion; and I was half inclined to regret leaving behind the land of gardens, for the rude and stern scenes of the prairie and the mountains.

Meanwhile the party came in sight out of the bushes. Foremost rode Henry Chatillon, our guide and hunter, a fine athletic figure, mounted on a hardy gray Wyandot pony. He wore a white blanket-coat, a broad hat of felt,

moccasins, and trousers of deer-skin, ornamented along the seams with rows of long fringes. His knife was stuck in his belt; his bullet-pouch and powder-horn hung at his side, and his rifle lay before him, resting against the high pommel of his saddle, which like all his equipments had seen hard service and was much the worse for wear. Shaw   4

followed close, mounted on a little sorrel horse and leading a larger animal by a rope. His outfit, which resembled mine, had been provided with a view to use rather
than ornament.   It consisted of a plain, black Spanish
saddle, with holsters of heavy pistols, a blanket rolled up
behind, and the trail-rope attached to his horse's neck
hanging coiled in front. He carried a double-barrelled
smooth-bore, while I had a rifle of some fifteen pounds'
weight.   At that time our attire, though far from elegant,
bore some marks of civilization, and offered a very favorable contrast to the inimitable shabbiness of our appearance on the return journey. A red flannel shirt, belted
around the waist like a frock, then constituted our upper
garment; moccasins had supplanted our failing boots; and
the remaining essential portion of our attire consisted of
an extraordinary article manufactured by a squaw out of
smoked buckskin. Our muleteer, Deslauriers, brought up
the rear with his cart, wading ankle-deep in the mud,
alternately puffing at his pipe and ejaculating, in his
prairie patois, "*Sacré enfant de garce!*" as one of the mules
would seem to recoil before some abyss of unusual profund-
ity.   The cart was of the kind that one may see by scores
around the market-place at Quebec, and had a white covering to protect the articles within. These were our provisions and a tent, with ammunition, blankets, and presents
for the Indians.

We were in all four men with eight animals; for besides
the spare horses led by Shaw and myself, an additional
mule was driven along with us as a reserve in case of
accident.

After this summing up of our forces it may not be amiss
to glance at the characters of the two men who accompanied us.

8   Deslauriers was a Canadian, with all the characteristics of the true Jean Baptiste. Neither fatigue, exposure, nor hard labor could ever impair his cheerfulness and gayety, 9 or his politeness to his *bourgeois;* and when night came he would sit down by the fire, smoke his pipe, and tell stories with the utmost contentment. The prairie was his element. Henry Chatillon was of a different stamp. When we were at St. Louis, several gentlemen of the Fur 10 Company had kindly offered to procure for us a hunter and guide suited for our purposes; and on coming one afternoon to the office, we found there a tall and exceedingly well-dressed man, with a face so open and frank that it attracted our notice at once. We were surprised at being told that it was he who wished to guide us to the mountains. He was born in a little French town near St. Louis, and from the age of fifteen years had been constantly in the neighborhood of the Rocky Mountains, employed for the most part by the company, to supply their forts with buffalo meat. As a hunter, he had but one rival in the whole region, a 11 man named Simoneau, with whom, to the honor of both of them, he was on terms of the closest friendship. He had arrived at St. Louis the day before, from the mountains, where he had been for four years; and he now asked only to go and spend a day with his mother, before setting out on another expedition. His age was about thirty; he was six feet high, and very powerfully and gracefully moulded. The prairies had been his school; he could neither read nor write, but he had a natural refinement and delicacy of mind, such as is rare even in women. His manly face was a mirror of uprightness, simplicity, and kindness of heart; he had, moreover, a keen perception of character, and a tact that would preserve him from flagrant error in 12 any society. Henry had not the restless energy of an

Anglo-American. He was content to take things as he found them; and his chief fault arose from an excess of easy generosity, not conducive to thriving in the world. 13 Yet it was commonly remarked of him that, whatever he

might choose to do with what belonged to himself, the property of others was always safe in his hands. His bravery was as much celebrated in the mountains as his skill in hunting; but it is characteristic of him that, in a country where the rifle is the chief arbiter between man and man, he was very seldom involved in quarrels. Once or twice, indeed, his quiet good-nature had been mistaken and presumed upon, but the consequences of the error were such that no one was ever known to repeat it. No better evidence of the intrepidity of his temper could be asked than the common report that he had killed more than thirty grizzly bears. He was a proof of what unaided nature will sometimes do. I have never, in the city or in the wilderness, met a better man than my true-hearted friend, Henry Chatillon.

We were soon free of the woods and bushes, and fairly upon the broad prairie. Now and then a Shawanoe passed us, riding his little shaggy pony at a "lope," his calico shirt, his gaudy sash, and the gay handkerchief bound around his snaky hair, fluttering in the wind. At noon we stopped to rest not far from a little creek, replete with frogs and young turtles. There had been an Indian encampment at the place, and the framework of the lodges still remained, enabling us very easily to gain a shelter from the sun, by merely spreading one or two blankets over them. Thus shaded, we sat upon our saddles, and Shaw for the first time lighted his favorite Indian pipe, while Deslauriers was squatted over a hot bed of coals, shading his eyes with one hand, and holding a little stick in the other, with which he regulated the hissing contents of the frying-pan. The horses were turned to feed among the scattered bushes of a low, oozy meadow. A drowsy spring-like sultriness pervaded the air, and the voices of ten thousand young frogs and insects, just awakened into life, rose in varied chorus from the creek and the meadows.

Scarcely were we seated when a visitor approached. This was an old Kanzas Indian,—a man of distinction, if one might judge from his dress. His head was shaved and painted red, and from the tuft of hair remaining on the crown dangled several eagle's-feathers, and the tails of two or three rattlesnakes. His cheeks, too, were daubed with vermilion; his ears were adorned with green glass pendants; a collar of grizzly bears' claws surrounded his neck, and several large necklaces of wampum hung on his breast. Having shaken us by the hand with a grunt of salutation, the old man, dropping his red blanket from his shoulders, sat down cross-legged on the ground. We offered him a cup of sweetened water, at which he ejaculated, "Good!" and was beginning to tell us how great a man he was, and how many Pawnees he had killed, when suddenly a motley concourse appeared wading across the creek toward us. They filed past in rapid succession, men, women and children: some were on horseback, some on foot, but all were alike squalid and wretched. Old squaws, mounted astride of shaggy, meagre, little ponies, with perhaps one or two snake-eyed children seated behind them, clinging to their tattered blankets; tall, lank young men on foot, with bows and arrows in their hands; and girls whose native ugliness not all the charms of glass beads and scarlet cloth could disguise, made up the procession; although here and there was a man who, like our visitor, seemed to hold some rank in this respectable community. They were the dregs of the Kanzas nation, who, while their betters were gone to hunt the buffalo, had left the village on a begging expedition to Westport.

When this ragamuffin horde had passed, we caught our horses, saddled, harnessed, and resumed our journey. Fording the creek, the low roofs of a number of rude buildings appeared, rising from a cluster of groves and woods on the left; and riding up through a long lane amid a profusion of wild roses and early spring flowers,

2

we found the log-church and schoolhouses belonging to
19 the Methodist Shawanoe Mission.   The Indians were on
the point of gathering to a religious meeting.   Some scores
of them, tall men in half-civilized dress, were seated
on wooden benches under the trees, while their horses
20 were tied to the sheds and fences.   Their chief, Parks, a
remarkably large and athletic man, had just arrived from
Westport, where he owns a trading establishment.   Besides this, he has a large farm and a considerable number
of slaves.   Indeed the Shawanoes have made greater progress in agriculture than any other tribe on the Missouri
frontier; and both in appearance and in character form a
marked contrast to our late acquaintance the Kanzas.

A few hours' ride brought us to the banks of the river
Kanzas.   Traversing the woods that lined it, and ploughing
through the deep sand, we encamped not far from the
21 bank, at the Lower Delaware crossing.   Our tent was
erected for the first time, on a meadow close to the
woods, and the camp preparations being complete, we
began to think of supper.   An old Delaware woman, of
some three hundred pounds' weight, sat in the porch of a little log-house, close to the water, and a very pretty half-breed
girl was engaged, under her superintendence, in feeding
a large flock of turkeys that were fluttering and gobbling
about the door.   But no offers of money, or even of tobacco,
could induce her to part with one of her favorites; so I
took my rifle, to see if the woods or the river could furnish
us anything.   A multitude of quails were plaintively whistling in the meadows; but nothing appropriate to the rifle
was to be seen, except three buzzards, seated on the spec-
tral limbs of an old dead sycamore, that thrust itself out
over the river from the dense sunny wall of fresh foliage.
Their ugly heads were drawn down between their shoul-

ders, and they seemed to luxuriate in the soft sunshine that was pouring from the west. As they offered no epicurean temptations, I refrained from disturbing their enjoyment; but contented myself with admiring the calm beauty of the sunset, — for the river, eddying swiftly in deep purple shadows between the impending woods, formed a wild but tranquillizing scene.

When I returned to the camp I found Shaw and an old Indian seated on the ground in close conference, passing the pipe between them. The old man was explaining that he loved the whites and had an especial partiality for tobacco. Deslauriers was arranging upon the ground our service of tin cups and plates; and as other viands were not to be had, he set before us a repast of biscuit and bacon, and a large pot of coffee. Unsheathing our knives, we attacked it, disposed of the greater part, and tossed the residue to the Indian. Meanwhile our horses, now hobbled for the first time, stood among the trees with their fore-legs tied together, in great disgust and astonishment. They seemed by no means to relish this foretaste of what awaited them. Mine, in particular, had conceived a mortal aversion to the prairie life. One of them, christened Hendrick, an animal whose strength and hardihood were his only merits, and who yielded to nothing but the cogent arguments of the whip, looked toward us with an indignant countenance, as if he meditated avenging his wrongs with a kick. The other, Pontiac, a good horse, 22 though of plebeian lineage, stood with his head drooping and his mane hanging about his eyes, with the grieved and sulky air of a lubberly boy sent off to school. His forebodings were but too just; for when I last heard from him, he was under the lash of an Ogillallah brave, on a war 23 party against the Crows.

As it grew dark and the voices of the whippoorwills succeeded the whistle of the quails, we removed our saddles to the tent to serve as pillows, spread our blankets upon the ground, and prepared to bivouac for the first time that season. Each man selected the place in the tent which he was to occupy for the journey. To Deslauriers, however, was assigned the cart, into which he could creep in wet weather, and find a much better shelter than his *bourgeois* enjoyed in the tent.

The river Kanzas at this point forms the boundary line between the country of the Shawanoes and that of the Delawares. We crossed it on the following day, rafting over our horses and equipments with much difficulty, and unlading our cart in order to make our way up the steep ascent on the farther bank. It was a Sunday morning; warm, tranquil, and bright; and a perfect stillness reigned over the rough inclosures and neglected fields of the Delawares, except the ceaseless hum and chirruping of myriads of insects. Now and then an Indian rode past on his way to the meeting-house, or, through the dilapidated entrance of some shattered log-house, an old woman might be discerned enjoying all the luxury of idleness. There was no village bell, for the Delawares have none; and yet upon that forlorn and rude settlement was the same spirit of Sabbath repose and tranquillity as in some New England village among the mountains of New Hampshire, or the Vermont woods.

A military road led from this point to Fort Leavenworth, and for many miles the farms and cabins of the Delawares were scattered at short intervals on either hand. The little rude structures of logs, erected usually on the borders of a tract of woods, made a picturesque feature in the landscape. But the scenery needed no foreign aid.

Nature had done enough for it; and the alternation of rich green prairies, and groves that stood in clusters, or lined the banks of the numerous little streams, had all the softened and polished beauty of a region that has been for centuries under the hand of man.   At that early season, too, it was in the height of its freshness.   The woods were flushed with the red buds of the maple; there were frequent flowering shrubs unknown in the East; and the green swells of the prairie were thickly studded with blossoms.

Encamping near a spring, by the side of a hill, we re- 26 sumed our journey in the morning, and early in the afternoon were within a few miles of Fort Leavenworth.   The road crossed a stream densely bordered with trees, and running in the bottom of a deep woody hollow.   We were about to descend into it when a wild and confused procession appeared, passing through the water below and coming up the steep ascent toward us.   We stopped to let them pass.   They were Delawares, just returned from a hunting expedition.   All, both men and women, were mounted on horseback, and drove along with them a considerable number of pack-mules, laden with the furs they had taken, together with the buffalo-robes, kettles, and other articles of their travelling equipment, which, as well as their clothing and their weapons, had a worn and dingy look, as if they had seen hard service of late.   At the rear of the party was an old man, who, as he came up, stopped his horse to speak to us.   He rode a tough, shaggy pony, with mane and tail well knotted with burs, and a rusty Spanish bit in its mouth, to which, by way of reins, 27 was attached a string of raw hide.   His saddle, robbed probably from a Mexican, had no covering, being merely a tree of the Spanish form, with a piece of grizzly bear's skin laid over it, a pair of rude wooden stirrups attached,

and, in the absence of girth, a strap of hide passing around
the horse's belly. The rider's dark features and keen snaky
eye were unequivocally Indian.   He wore a buckskin frock,
which, like his fringed leggings, was well polished and
blackened by grease and long service, and an old handkerchief was tied around his head.   Resting on the saddle
before him lay his rifle, a weapon in the use of which the
Delawares are skilful, though, from its weight, the distant
28   prairie Indians are too lazy to carry it.

"Who's your chief?" he immediately inquired.

Henry Chatillon pointed to us. The old Delaware fixed his eyes intently upon us for a moment, and then sententiously remarked,—

"No good! Too young!" With this flattering comment he left us and rode after his people.

This tribe, the Delawares, once the peaceful allies of William Penn, the tributaries of the conquering Iroquois, are now the most adventurous and dreaded warriors upon the prairies. They make war upon remote tribes, the very names of which were unknown to their fathers in their ancient seats in Pennsylvania, and they push these new quarrels with true Indian rancor, sending out their war-parties as far as the Rocky Mountains, and into the Mexican territories. Their neighbors and former confederates, the Shawanoes, who are tolerable farmers, are in a prosperous condition; but the Delawares dwindle every year, from the number of men lost in their warlike expeditions.

Soon after leaving this party we saw, stretching on the right, the forests that follow the course of the Missouri, and the deep woody channel through which at this point it runs. At a distance in front were the white barracks of Fort Leavenworth, just visible through the trees upon an eminence above a bend of the river. A wide green meadow, as level as a lake, lay between us and the Missouri, and upon this, close to a line of trees that bordered a little brook, stood the tent of the Captain and his companions, with their horses feeding around it; but they themselves were invisible. Wright, their muleteer, was there, seated on the tongue of the wagon, repairing his harness. Boisverd stood cleaning his rifle at the door of the tent, and Sorel lounged idly about. On closer examination, however, we discovered the Captain's brother, Jack, sitting in the tent, at his old occupation of splicing trail-ropes. He welcomed us in his broad Irish brogue, and said that his brother was fishing in the river, and R—— gone to the garrison. They returned before sunset. Meanwhile we pitched our own tent not far off, and after supper a council was held, in which it was resolved to remain one day at Fort Leavenworth, and on the next to bid a final adieu to the frontier, or, in the phraseology of the region, to "jump off." Our deliberations were conducted by the ruddy light from a distant swell of the prairie, where the long dry grass of last summer was on fire.

CHAPTER III.

FORT LEAVENWORTH.

ON the next morning we rode to Fort Leavenworth. Colonel, now General Kearney, to whom I had had the honor of an introduction when at St. Louis, was just arrived, and received us at his quarters with the courtesy habitual to him. Fort Leavenworth is in fact no fort, being without defensive works, except two block-houses. No rumors of war had as yet disturbed its tranquillity. In the square grassy area, surrounded by barracks and the quarters of the officers, the men were passing and repassing, or lounging among the trees; although not many weeks afterwards it presented a different scene; for here the off-scourings of the frontier were congregated for the expedition against Santa Fé.

Passing through the garrison, we rode toward the Kickapoo village, five or six miles beyond. The path, a rather dubious and uncertain one, led us along the ridge of high bluffs that border the Missouri; and, by looking to the right or to the left, we could enjoy a strange contrast of scenery. On the left stretched the prairie, rising into swells and undulations, thickly sprinkled with groves, or gracefully expanding into wide grassy basins, of miles in extent, while its curvatures, swelling against the horizon, were often surmounted by lines of sunny woods, — a scene to which the freshness of the season and the peculiar mellowness of the atmosphere gave additional softness. Below

us, on the right, was a tract of ragged and broken woods.
We could look down on the tops of the trees, some living
and some dead; some erect, others leaning at every angle,
and others piled in masses together by the passage of a
hurricane.   Beyond their extreme verge the turbid waters
of the Missouri were discernible through the boughs, rolling powerfully along at the foot of the woody declivities
on its farther bank.

   The path soon after led inland; and as we crossed an open
meadow we saw a cluster of buildings on a rising ground
before us, with a crowd of people surrounding them.   They
were the storehouse, cottage, and stables of the Kickapoo
4 trader's establishment.   Just at that moment, as it chanced,
he was beset with half the Indians of the settlement.
They had tied their wretched, neglected little ponies by
dozens along the fences and out-houses, and were either
lounging about the place, or crowding into the trading-
house.   Here were faces of various colors, — red, green,
white, and black,— curiously intermingled and disposed over
the visage in a variety of patterns.   Calico shirts, red
and blue blankets, brass ear-rings, wampum necklaces,
appeared in profusion.   The trader was a blue-eyed, open-
faced man, who neither in his manners nor his appearance
betrayed any of the roughness of the frontier; though just
at present he was obliged to keep a lynx eye on his customers, who, men and women, were climbing on his coun-
ter, and seating themselves among his boxes and bales.

   The village itself was not far off, and sufficiently illustrated the condition of its unfortunate and self-abandoned
5 occupants.   Fancy to yourself a little swift stream working its devious way down a woody valley; sometimes wholly
hidden under logs and fallen trees, sometimes spreading
into a broad, clear pool; and on its banks, in little nooks

cleared away among the trees, miniature log-houses, in utter ruin and neglect. A labyrinth of narrow, obstructed paths connected these habitations one with another. Sometimes we met a stray calf, a pig, or a pony, belonging to some of the villagers, who usually lay in the sun in front of their dwellings, and looked on us with cold, suspicious eyes as we approached. Farther on, in place of the log- 6 huts of the Kickapoos, we found the *pukwi* lodges of their 7 neighbors, the Pottawattamies, whose condition seemed no better than theirs.

Growing tired at last, and exhausted by the excessive heat and sultriness of the day, we returned to our friend, the trader. By this time the crowd around him had dispersed, and left him at leisure. He invited us to his cottage, — a little white-and-green building, in the style of the old French settlements,— and ushered us into a neat, well-furnished room. The blinds were closed, and the heat and glare of the sun excluded; the room was as cool as a cavern. It was neatly carpeted, too, and furnished in a manner that we hardly expected on the frontier. The sofas, chairs, tables, and a well-filled bookcase, would not have disgraced an eastern city; though there were one or two little tokens that indicated the rather questionable civilization of the region. A pistol, loaded and capped, 8 lay on the mantel-piece; and through the glass of the bookcase, peeping above the works of John Milton, glittered the handle of a very mischievous-looking knife.

Our host went out, and returned with iced water, glasses, and a bottle of excellent claret,— a refreshment most welcome in the extreme heat of the day; and soon after appeared a merry, laughing woman, who must have been, a year or two before, a very rich specimen of creole beauty. She came to say that lunch was ready in the next room. Our

hostess evidently lived on the sunny side of life, and troubled
herself with none of its cares.   She sat down and entertained us while we were at table with anecdotes of fishing parties, frolics, and the officers at the fort.   Taking
9   leave at length of the hospitable trader and his friend, we
rode back to the garrison.

Shaw passed on to the camp, while I remained to call
upon Colonel Kearney.   I found him still at table.   There
sat our friend the Captain, in the same remarkable habiliments in which we saw him at Westport; the black pipe,
however, being for the present laid aside.   He dangled
his little cap in his hand and talked of steeple-chases,
touching occasionally upon his anticipated exploits in
buffalo-hunting.   There, too, was R——, somewhat more
elegantly attired.   For the last time we tasted the luxuries
of civilization, and drank adieus to it in wine good enough
to make us regret the leave-taking.   Then, mounting, we
rode together to the camp, where everything was
10   in readiness for departure on the morrow.

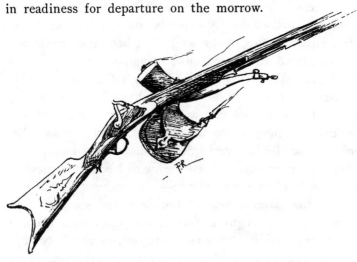

CHAPTER IV.

"JUMPING OFF."

OUR transatlantic companions were well equipped for the journey. They had a wagon drawn by six mules, and crammed with provisions for six months, besides ammunition enough for a regiment, spare rifles and fowling-pieces, ropes and harness, personal baggage, and a miscellaneous assortment of articles, which produced infinite embarrassment. They had also decorated their persons with telescopes and portable compasses, and carried English double-barrelled rifles of sixteen to the pound calibre, slung to their saddles in dragoon fashion.

By sunrise on the twenty-third of May we had breakfasted; the tents were levelled, the animals saddled and harnessed, and all was prepared. "*Avance donc!* get up!" cried Deslauriers to his mule. Wright, our friends' muleteer, after some swearing and lashing, got his insubordinate train into motion, and then the whole party filed from the ground. Thus we bade a long adieu to bed and board, and the principles of Blackstone's Commentaries. The day was a most auspicious one; and yet Shaw and I felt certain misgivings, which in the sequel proved but too well founded. We had just learned that though R—— had taken it upon him to adopt this course without consulting us, not a single man in the party knew the way; and the absurdity of the proceeding soon became manifest. His plan was to strike the trail of several companies of

dragoons, who last summer had made an expedition under
3   Colonel Kearney to Fort Laramie, and by this means to
reach the grand trail of the Oregon emigrants up the
Platte.

We rode for an hour or two, when a familiar cluster
of buildings appeared on a little hill. "Hallo!" shouted
the Kickapoo trader from over his fence, "where are you
going?" A few rather emphatic exclamations might have
been heard among us, when we found that we had gone
miles out of our way, and were not advanced an inch
toward the Rocky Mountains. So we turned in the direction the trader indicated; and with the sun for a guide,
4   began to trace a "bee-line" across the prairies. We struggled through copses and lines of wood; we waded brooks
and pools of water; we traversed prairies as green as an
emerald expanding before us mile after mile, wider and
more wild than the wastes Mazeppa rode over.

> " Man nor brute,
> Nor dint of hoof, nor print of foot,
> Lay in the wild luxuriant soil;
> No sign of travel; none of toil;
> The very air was mute."

5

Riding in advance, as we passed over one of these great
plains, we looked back and saw the line of scattered horsemen stretching for a mile or more; and far in the rear,
against the horizon, the white wagons creeping slowly
6   along. "Here we are at last!" shouted the Captain.
And, in truth, we had struck upon the traces of a large
7   body of horse. We turned joyfully and followed this
new course, with tempers somewhat improved, and towards
sunset encamped on a high swell of the prairie, at the
8   foot of which a lazy stream soaked along through clumps
of rank grass. It was getting dark. We turned the horses

loose to feed. "Drive down the tent-pickets hard," said Henry Chatillon, "it is going to blow." We did so, and secured the tent as well as we could; for the sky had changed totally, and a fresh, damp smell in the wind warned us that a stormy night was likely to succeed the hot, clear day. The prairie also wore a new aspect, and its vast swells had grown black and sombre under the shadow of the clouds. The thunder soon began to growl at a distance. Picketing and hobbling the horses among the rich grass at the foot of the slope where we encamped, we gained a shelter just as the rain began to fall; and sat at 9 the opening of the tent, watching the proceedings of the Captain. In defiance of the rain, he was stalking among the horses, wrapped in an old Scotch plaid. An extreme solicitude tormented him, lest some of his favorites should escape, or some accident should befall them; and he cast an anxious eye towards three wolves who were sneaking along over the dreary surface of the plain, as if he dreaded some hostile demonstration on their part.

On the next morning we had gone but a mile or two when we came to an extensive belt of woods, through the midst of which ran a stream, wide, deep, and of an appearance particularly muddy and treacherous. Deslauriers was 10 in advance with his cart; he jerked his pipe from his mouth, lashed his mules, and poured forth a volley of Canadian ejaculations. In plunged the cart, but midway it stuck fast. He leaped out knee-deep in water, and by dint of *sacrés* and a vigorous application of the whip, urged the mules out of the slough. Then approached the long team and heavy wagon of our friends; but it paused on the brink.

"Now my advice is," — began the Captain, who had been anxiously contemplating the muddy gulf.

"Drive on!" cried R——.

But Wright, the muleteer, apparently had not as yet decided the point in his own mind; and he sat still in his seat, on one of the shaft-mules, whistling in a low, contemplative strain to himself.

"My advice is," resumed the Captain, "that we unload; for I'll bet any man five pounds that if we try to go through we shall stick fast."

"By the powers, we shall stick fast!" echoed Jack, the Captain's brother, shaking his large head with an air of firm conviction.

"Drive on! drive on!" cried R——, petulantly.

"Well," observed the Captain, turning to us as we sat looking on, much edified by this by-play among our confederates, "I can only give my advice, and if people won't be reasonable, why, they won't, that's all!"

Meanwhile Wright had apparently made up his mind; for he suddenly began to shout forth a volley of oaths and curses, that, compared with the French imprecations of Deslauriers, sounded like the roaring of heavy cannon after the popping and sputtering of a bunch of Chinese crackers. At the same time he discharged a shower of blows upon his mules, who hastily dived into the mud, and drew the wagon lumbering after them. For a moment the issue was doubtful. Wright writhed about in his saddle, and swore and lashed like a madman; but who can count on a team of half-broken mules? At the most critical point, when all should have been harmony and combined effort, the perverse brutes fell into disorder, and huddled together in confusion on the farther bank. There was the wagon up to the hub in mud, and visibly settling every instant. There was nothing for it but to unload; then to dig away the mud from before the wheels with a spade, and lay a causeway of bushes and branches. This agreeable labor accomplished, the wagon at length emerged; but as some interruption of this sort occurred at least four or five times a day for a fortnight, our progress towards the Platte was not without its obstacles.

We travelled six or seven miles farther, and "nooned" near a brook. On the point of resuming our journey, 11 when the horses were all driven down to water, my home-sick charger, Pontiac, made a sudden leap across, and set off at a round trot for the settlements. I mounted my remaining horse and started in pursuit. Making a cir-cuit, I headed the runaway, hoping to drive him back to camp, but he instantly broke into a gallop, made a wide tour on the prairie, and got by me again. I tried this plan repeatedly with the same result,— Pontiac was evi-dently disgusted with the prairie; so I abandoned it and tried another, trotting along gently behind him, in hopes that I might quietly get near enough to seize the trail-rope which was fastened to his neck, and dragged about a dozen feet behind him. The chase grew interesting. For mile after mile I followed the rascal with the utmost care not to alarm him, and gradually got nearer, until at length old Hendrick's nose was fairly brushed by the whisk-ing tail of the unsuspecting Pontiac. Without drawing rein I slid softly to the ground; but my long, heavy rifle encumbered me, and the low sound it made in striking the horn of the saddle startled him, he pricked up his ears and sprang off at a run. "My friend," thought I, re-mounting, "do that again and I 'll shoot you!"

Fort Leavenworth was about forty miles distant, and 12 thither I determined to follow him. I made up my mind to spend a solitary and supperless night, and then set out again in the morning. One hope, however, remained. The creek where the wagon had stuck was just before

us; Pontiac might be thirsty with his run and stop there
to drink. I kept as near him as possible, taking every
precaution not to alarm him again; and the result proved
as I had hoped, for he walked deliberately among the
trees and stooped down to the water. I alighted, dragged
old Hendrick through the mud, and with a feeling of infinite satisfaction picked up the slimy trail-rope, and twisted
it three times round my hand. "Now let me see you get
away again!" I thought as I remounted. But Pontiac was
exceedingly reluctant to turn back; Hendrick, too, who had
evidently flattered himself with vain hopes, showed the utmost repugnance, and grumbled in a manner peculiar to
himself at being compelled to face about. A smart cut
of the whip restored his cheerfulness; and, dragging the
recovered truant behind, I set out in search of the camp.
An hour or two elapsed, when, near sunset, I saw the
tents, standing on a swell of the prairie, beyond a line of
woods, while the bands of horses were feeding in a low
meadow close at hand. There sat Jack C——, cross-legged
in the sun, splicing a trail-rope; and the rest were lying
on the grass, smoking and telling stories. That night we
enjoyed a serenade from the wolves, more lively than any
with which they had yet favored us; and in the morning
one of the musicians appeared, not many rods from the
tents, quietly seated among the horses, looking at us with
a pair of large gray eyes; but perceiving a rifle levelled
at him, he leaped up and made off in hot haste.

I pass by the following day or two of our journey, for
13 nothing occurred worthy of record. Should any one of my
readers ever be impelled to visit the prairies, and should
14 he choose the route of the Platte (the best, perhaps, that
can be adopted), I can assure him that he need not think
to enter at once upon the paradise of his imagination. A

dreary preliminary, a protracted crossing of the threshold,
awaits him before he finds himself fairly upon the verge
of the "great American desert," — those barren wastes, the   15
haunts of the buffalo and the Indian, where the very shadow
of civilization lies a hundred leagues behind him. The intervening country, the wide and fertile belt that extends for
several hundred miles beyond the extreme frontier, will
probably answer tolerably well to his preconceived ideas of
the prairie; for this it is from which picturesque tourists,
painters, poets, and novelists, who have seldom penetrated   16
farther, have derived their conceptions of the whole region.
If he has a painter's eye, he may find his period of proba-
tion not wholly void of interest. The scenery, though
tame, is graceful and pleasing. Here are level plains
too wide for the eye to measure; green undulations, like
motionless swells of the ocean; abundance of streams, followed through all their windings by lines of woods and
scattered groves. But let him be as enthusiastic as he
may, he will find enough to damp his ardor. His wagons
will stick in the mud; his horses will break loose; harness
will give way; and axle-trees prove unsound. His bed will
be a soft one, consisting often of black mud of the richest
consistency. As for food, he must content himself with
biscuit and salt provisions; for strange as it may seem, this
tract of country produces very little game. As he advances,   17
indeed, he will see, mouldering in the grass by his path, the
vast antlers of the elk, and farther on the whitened skulls   18
of the buffalo, once swarming over this now deserted region.
Perhaps, like us, he may journey for a fortnight, and see
not so much as the hoof-print of a deer; in the spring, not
even a prairie-hen is to be had.   19

Yet, to compensate him for this unlooked-for deficiency
of game, he will find himself beset with "varmints" in-

numerable. The wolves will entertain him with a concert at night, and skulk around him by day just beyond rifle-shot; his horse will step into badger-holes; from every marsh and mud-puddle will arise the bellowing, croaking and trilling of legions of frogs, infinitely various in color, shape, and dimensions. A profusion of snakes will glide away from under his horse's feet, or quietly visit him in his tent at night; while the pertinacious humming of unnumbered mosquitoes will banish sleep from his eyelids. When, thirsty with a long ride in the scorching sun over some boundless reach of prairie, he comes at length to a pool of water and alights to drink, he discovers a troop of young tadpoles sporting in the bottom of his cup. Add to this that, all the morning, the sun beats upon him with a sultry, penetrating heat, and that, with provoking regularity, at about four o'clock in the afternoon a thunder-storm rises and drenches him to the skin.

One day, after a protracted morning's ride, we stopped to rest at noon upon the open prairie. No trees were in sight; but close at hand a little dribbling brook was twisting from side to side through a hollow; now forming holes of stagnant water, and now gliding over the mud in a scarcely perceptible current, among a growth of sickly bushes, and great clumps of tall, rank grass. The day was excessively hot and oppressive. The horses and mules were rolling on the prairie to refresh themselves, or feeding among the bushes in the hollow. We had dined; and Deslauriers, puffing at his pipe, knelt on the grass, scrubbing our service of tin-plate. Shaw lay in the shade, under the cart, to rest for a while, before the word should be given to "catch up." Henry Chatillon, before lying down, was looking about for signs of snakes, the only living things that he feared, and uttering various ejaculations of disgust at finding several suspicious-looking holes close to the cart. I sat leaning against the wheel in a scanty strip of shade, making a pair of hobbles to replace those which my contumacious steed Pontiac had broken the night before. The camp of our friends, a rod or two distant, presented the same scene of lazy tranquillity.

"Hallo!" cried Henry, looking up from his inspection of the snake-holes, "here comes the old Captain."

The Captain approached, and stood for a moment contemplating us in silence.

"I say, Parkman," he began, "look at Shaw there, asleep under the cart, with the tar dripping off the hub of the wheel on his shoulder."

At this Shaw got up, with his eyes half opened, and feeling the part indicated, found his hand glued fast to his red flannel shirt.

"He 'll look well, when he gets among the squaws, won't he?" observed the captain, with a grin.

He then crawled under the cart, and began to tell stories, of which his stock was inexhaustible. Yet every moment he would glance nervously at the horses. At last he jumped up in great excitement. "See that horse! There — that fellow just walking over the hill! By Jove! he 's off. It 's your big horse, Shaw; no it is n't, it 's Jack's. Jack! Jack! hallo, Jack!" Jack, thus invoked, jumped up and stared vacantly at us.

"Go and catch your horse, if you don't want to lose him," roared the Captain.

Jack instantly set off at a run through the grass, his broad trousers flapping about his feet. The Captain gazed anxiously till he saw that the horse was caught; then he sat down, with a countenance of thoughtfulness and care.

"I tell you what it is," he said, "this will never do at all.

We shall lose every horse in the band some day or other, and then a pretty plight we should be in! Now I am convinced that the only way for us is to have every man in the camp stand horse-guard in rotation whenever we stop. Supposing a hundred Pawnees should jump up out of that ravine, all yelling and flapping their buffalo robes, in the way they do! Why, in two minutes, not a hoof would be in sight." We reminded the Captain that a hundred Pawnees would probably demolish the horse-guard if he were to resist their depredations.

"At any rate," pursued the Captain, evading the point, "our whole system is wrong; I'm convinced of it; it is totally unmilitary. Why, the way we travel, strung out over the prairie for a mile, an enemy might attack the foremost men, and cut them off before the rest could come up."

"We are not in an enemy's country yet," said Shaw; "when we are we'll travel together."

"Then," said the Captain, "we might be attacked in camp. We've no sentinels; we camp in disorder; no precautions at all to guard against surprise. My own convictions are, that we ought to camp in a hollow-square, with the fires in the centre; and have sentinels, and a regular password appointed for every night. Beside, there should be vedettes riding in advance, to find a place for the camp and give warning of an enemy. These are my convictions. I don't want to dictate to any man. I give advice to the best of my judgment, that's all,— and then let people do as they please."

23   His plan of sending out vedettes seemed particularly dear to him; and as no one else was disposed to second his views on this point, he took it into his head to ride forward that afternoon himself.

"Come, Parkman," said he, "will you go with me?"

We set out together, and rode a mile or two in advance. The Captain, in the course of twenty years' service in the British army, had seen something of life; and being naturally a pleasant fellow, he was a very entertaining companion. He cracked jokes and told stories for an hour or two; until, looking back, we saw the prairie behind us stretching away to the horizon, without a horseman or a wagon in sight.

"Now," said the Captain, "I think the vedettes had better stop till the main body comes up."

I was of the same opinion. There was a thick growth of woods just before us, with a stream running through them. Having crossed this, we found on the other side a level meadow, half encircled by the trees; and, fastening our horses to some bushes, we sat down on the grass, while with an old stump of a tree for a target, I began to display the superiority of the renowned rifle of the backwoods over the foreign innovation borne by the Captain. At length voices could be heard in the distance, behind the trees.

"There they come," said the Captain; "let's go and see how they get through the creek."

We mounted and rode to the bank of the stream, where the trail crossed it. It ran in a deep hollow, full of trees. As we looked down we saw a confused crowd of horsemen riding through the water; and among the dingy habiliments of our party glittered the uniforms of four dragoons.

Shaw came whipping his horse up the bank, in advance of the rest, with a somewhat indignant countenance. The first word he spoke was a blessing fervently invoked on the head of R——, who was riding, with a crest-fallen air, in the rear. Thanks to the ingenious devices of this gentleman,

we had missed the track entirely, and wandered, not towards
25   the Platte, but to the village of the Iowa Indians.   This we
learned from the dragoons, who had lately deserted from Fort
Leavenworth.   They told us that our best plan now was
to keep to the northward until we should strike the trail

formed by several parties of Oregon emigrants, who had
26   that season set out from St. Joseph, in Missouri.
    In extremely bad temper, we encamped on this ill-starred
spot, while the deserters, whose case admitted of no delay,
rode rapidly forward.   On the day following, striking the
27   St. Joseph trail, we turned our horses' heads towards Fort
Laramie, then about seven hundred miles to the westward.

CHAPTER V.

THE great medley of Oregon and California emigrants at their camps around Independence had heard reports that several additional parties were on the point of setting out from St. Joseph farther to the northward. The prevailing impression was that these were Mormons, twenty-three hundred in number; and a great alarm was excited in consequence. The people of Illinois and Missouri, who composed by far the greater part of the emigrants, have never been on the best terms with the "Latter Day Saints;" and it is notorious throughout the country how much blood has been spilt in their feuds, even far within the limits of the settlements. No one could predict what would be the result when large armed bodies of these fanatics should encounter the most impetuous and reckless of their old enemies on the broad prairie, far beyond the reach of law or military force. The women and children at Independence raised a great outcry; the men themselves were seriously alarmed; and as I learned, they sent to Colonel Kearney, requesting an escort of dragoons as far as the Platte. This was refused; and, as the sequel proved, there was no occasion for it. The St. Joseph emigrants were as good Christians and as zealous Mormon-haters as the rest; and the very few families of the "Saints" who passed out this season by the route of the Platte remained behind until the great tide of emigra-

1

tion had gone by, — standing in quite as much awe of the "gentiles" as the latter did of them.

We were now upon this St. Joseph trail. It was evident, by the traces, that large parties were a few days in advance of us; and as we too supposed them to be Mormons, we had some apprehension of interruption.

The journey was monotonous. One day we rode on for hours, without seeing a tree or a bush: before, behind, and on either side, stretched the vast expanse, rolling in a succession of graceful swells, covered with the unbroken carpet of fresh green grass. Here and there a crow, a raven, or a turkey-buzzard, relieved the uniformity.

"What shall we do to-night for wood and water?" we began to ask of each other; for the sun was within an hour of setting. At length a dark green speck appeared, far off on the right: it was the top of a tree, peering over a swell of the prairie; and, leaving the trail, we made all haste towards it. It proved to be the vanguard of a cluster of bushes and low trees, that surrounded some pools of water in an extensive hollow; so we encamped on the rising ground near it.

Shaw and I were sitting in the tent, when Deslauriers thrust his brown face and old felt hat into the opening, and, dilating his eyes to their utmost extent, announced supper. There were the tin cups and the iron spoons, arranged in order on the grass, and the coffee-pot predominant in the midst. The meal was soon dispatched, but Henry Chatillon still sat cross-legged, dallying with the remnant of his coffee, the beverage in universal use upon the prairie, and an especial favorite with him. He preferred it in its virgin flavor, unimpaired by sugar or cream; and on the present occasion it met his entire approval, being exceedingly strong, or, as he expressed it, "right black."

It was a gorgeous sunset; and the ruddy glow of the sky was reflected from some extensive pools of water among the shadowy copses in the meadow below.

"I must have a bath to-night," said Shaw. "How is it, Deslauriers? Any chance for a swim down there?"

"Ah! I cannot tell; just as you please, Monsieur," replied Deslauriers, shrugging his shoulders, perplexed by his ignorance of English, and extremely anxious to conform in all respects to the opinions and wishes of his *bourgeois*.

"Look at his moccasin," said I. It had evidently been lately immersed in a profound abyss of black mud.

"Come," said Shaw; "at any rate we can see for ourselves."

We set out together; and as we approached the bushes, which were at some distance, we found the ground becoming rather treacherous. We could only get along by stepping upon large clumps of tall rank grass, with fathomless gulfs between, like innumerable little quaking islands in an ocean of mud, where a false step would have involved our boots in a catastrophe like that which had befallen Deslauriers's moccasins. The thing looked desperate; we separated, to search in different directions, Shaw going off to the right, while I kept straight forward. At last I came to the edge of the bushes, — they were young water-willows covered with their caterpillar-like blossoms, but intervening between them and the last grass clump was a black and deep slough, over which, by a vigorous exertion, I contrived to jump. Then I shouldered my way through the willows, trampling them down by main force, till I came to a wide stream of water, three inches deep, languidly creeping along over a bottom of sleek mud. My arrival produced a great commotion. A huge green bull-frog uttered an indignant croak, and jumped off the bank with a loud splash; his webbed feet twinkled above the surface, as he jerked them energetically upward, and I could see him ensconcing himself in the unresisting slime at the bottom, whence several large air-bubbles struggled lazily to the top. Some little spotted frogs followed the patriarch's example; and then three turtles, not larger than a dollar, tumbled themselves off a broad "lily pad," where they had been reposing.   At the same time a snake, gayly striped with 6   black and yellow, glided out from the bank, and writhed across to the other side; and a small stagnant pool into which my foot had inadvertently pushed a stone was instantly alive with a congregation of black tadpoles.

"Any chance for a bath where you are?" called out Shaw, from a distance.

The answer was not encouraging.   I retreated through the willows, and rejoining my companion, we proceeded to push our researches in company.   Not far on the right, a rising ground, covered with trees and bushes, seemed to sink down abruptly to the water, and give hope of better success; so towards this we directed our steps.   When we reached the place we found it no easy matter to get along between the hill and the water, impeded as we were by a growth of stiff, obstinate young birch-trees, laced together by grape-vines.   In the twilight we now and then, to support ourselves, snatched at the touch-me-not stem of some ancient sweetbrier.   Shaw, who was in advance, suddenly uttered an emphatic monosyllable; and, looking up, I saw him with one hand grasping a sapling, and one foot immersed in the water, from which he had forgotten to withdraw it, his whole attention being engaged in con- 7   templating the movements of a water-snake, about five feet long, curiously checkered with black and green, who

was deliberately swimming across the pool. There being
no stick or stone at hand to pelt him with, we looked at him
for a time in silent disgust, and then pushed forward. Our
perseverance was at last rewarded; for several rods farther
on, we emerged upon a little level grassy nook among the
brushwood, and by an extraordinary dispensation of fortune, the weeds and floating sticks, which elsewhere covered the pool, seemed to have drawn apart, and left a few
yards of clear water just in front of this favored spot. We
sounded it with a stick; it was four feet deep: we lifted a
specimen in our closed hands; it seemed reasonably transparent, so we decided that the time for action was arrived.
But our ablutions were suddenly interrupted by ten thousand punctures, like poisoned needles, and the humming of
myriads of overgrown mosquitoes, rising in all directions
from their native mud and swarming to the feast. We were
fain to beat a retreat with all possible speed.   8

We made towards the tents, much refreshed by the bath,
which the heat of the weather, joined to our prejudices, had
rendered very desirable.

"What 's the matter with the Captain? look at him!" said
Shaw. The Captain stood alone on the prairie, swinging
his hat violently around his head, and lifting first one foot
and then the other, without moving from the spot. First
he looked down to the ground with an air of supreme abhorrence; then he gazed upward with a perplexed and indignant countenance, as if trying to trace the flight of an
unseen enemy. We called to know what was the matter;
but he replied only by execrations directed against some
unknown object. We approached, when our ears were
saluted by a droning sound, as if twenty bee-hives
had been overturned at once. The air above was full of
large, black insects, in a state of great commotion, and

multitudes were flying about just above the tops of the grass-blades.

"Don't be afraid," called the Captain, observing us recoil. "The brutes won't sting."

At this I knocked one down with my hat, and discovered him to be no other than a "dor-bug;" and, looking closer, we found the ground thickly perforated with their holes.

We took a hasty leave of this flourishing colony, and walking up the rising ground to the tents, found Deslauriers's fire still glowing brightly. We sat down around it, and Shaw began to expatiate on the admirable facilities for bathing that we had discovered, recommending the Captain by all means to go down there before breakfast in the morning. The Captain was in the act of remarking that he couldn't have believed it possible, when he suddenly interrupted himself, and clapped his hand to his cheek, exclaiming that "those infernal humbugs were at him again." In fact, we began to hear sounds as if bullets were humming over our heads. In a moment something rapped me sharply on the forehead, then upon the neck, and immediately I felt an indefinite number of sharp, wiry claws in active motion, as if their owner were bent on pushing his explorations farther. I seized him, and dropped him into the fire. Our party speedily broke up, and we adjourned to our respective tents, where, closing the opening fast, we hoped to be exempt from invasion. But all precaution was fruitless. The dor-bugs hummed through the tent, and marched over our faces until daylight; when, opening our blankets, we found several dozen clinging there with the utmost tenacity. The first object that met our eyes in the morning was Deslauriers, who seemed to be apostrophizing his frying-pan, which he held by the handle at arm's length. It appeared

that he had left it at night by the fire; and the bottom
was now covered with dor-bugs, firmly imbedded. Hun
dreds of others, curiously parched and shrivelled, lay scat
tered among the ashes.

The horses and mules were turned loose to feed. We
had just taken our seats at breakfast, or rather reclined
in the classic mode, when an exclamation from Henry
Chatillon, and a shout of alarm from the Captain, gave
warning of some casualty, and looking up, we saw the
whole band of animals, twenty-three in number, filing off
for the settlements, the incorrigible Pontiac at their head,
jumping along with hobbled feet, at a gait much more rapid
than graceful. Three or four of us ran to cut them off,
dashing as best we might through the tall grass, which
was glittering with dew-drops. After a race of a mile or
more, Shaw caught a horse. Tying the trail-rope by way
of bridle round the animal's jaw, and leaping upon his
back, he got in advance of the remaining fugitives, while
we, soon bringing them together, drove them in a crowd
up to the tents, where each man caught and saddled his
own. Then were heard lamentations and curses; for half
the horses had broke their hobbles, and many were seriously galled by attempting to run in fetters.   10

It was late that morning before we were on the march;
and early in the afternoon we were compelled to encamp,
for a thunder-gust came up and suddenly enveloped us in
whirling sheets of rain. With much ado we pitched our
tents amid the tempest, and all night long the thunder
bellowed and growled over our heads. In the morning
light peaceful showers succeeded the cataracts of rain that
had been drenching us through the canvas of our tents.
About noon, when there were some treacherous indications
of fair weather, we got in motion again.

Not a breath of air stirred over the free and open prairie; the clouds were like light piles of cotton; and where the blue sky was visible, it wore a hazy and languid aspect. The sun beat down upon us with a sultry, penetrating heat almost insupportable, and as our party crept slowly along over the interminable level, the horses hung their heads as they waded fetlock deep through the mud, and the men slouched into the easiest position upon the saddle. At last, towards evening, the old familiar black heads of thunder-clouds rose fast above the horizon, and the same deep muttering of distant thunder that had become the ordinary accompaniment of our afternoon's journey began to roll hoarsely over the prairie. Only a few minutes elapsed before the whole sky was densely shrouded, and the prairie and some clusters of woods in front assumed a purple hue beneath the inky shadows. Suddenly from the densest fold of the cloud the flash leaped out, quivering again and again down to the edge of the prairie; and at the same instant came the sharp burst and the long rolling peal of the thunder. A cool wind, filled with the smell of rain, just then overtook us, levelling the tall grass by the side of the path.

"Come on; we must ride for it!" shouted Shaw, rushing by at full speed, his led horse snorting at his side. The whole party broke into full gallop, and made for the trees in front. Passing these, we found beyond them a meadow which they half inclosed. We rode pell-mell upon the ground, leaped from horseback, tore off our saddles, and in a moment each man was kneeling at his horse's feet. The hobbles were adjusted, and the animals turned loose; then as the wagons came wheeling rapidly to the spot, we seized upon the tent-poles, and just as the storm broke we were prepared to receive it. It came upon us almost with the darkness of night: the trees, which were close at hand, were completely shrouded by the roaring torrents of rain.

We were sitting in the tent when Deslauriers, with his broad felt hat hanging about his ears, and his shoulders glistening with rain, thrust in his head.

"Voulez vous du souper, tout de suite? I can make fire, sous la charette — I b'lieve so — I try." 11

"Never mind supper, man; come in out of the rain."

Deslauriers accordingly crouched in the entrance, for modesty would not permit him to intrude farther.

Our tent was none of the best defence against such a cataract. The rain could not enter bodily, but it beat through the canvas in a fine drizzle, that wetted us just as effectually. We sat upon our saddles with faces of the utmost surliness, while the water dropped from the visors of our caps and trickled down our cheeks. My india-rubber cloak conducted twenty little rapid streamlets to the ground; and Shaw's blanket coat was saturated like a sponge. But what most concerned us was the sight of several puddles of water rapidly accumulating; one, in particular, that was gathering around the tent-pole, threatened to overspread the whole area within the tent, holding forth but an indifferent promise of a comfortable night's rest. Towards sunset, however, the storm ceased as suddenly as it began. A bright streak of clear red sky appeared above the western verge of the prairie; the horizontal rays of the sinking sun streamed through it, and glittered in a thousand prismatic colors upon the dripping groves and the prostrate grass. The pools in the tent dwindled and sunk into the saturated soil.

But all our hopes were delusive. Scarcely had night set in when the tumult broke forth anew. The thunder here is not like the tame thunder of the Atlantic coast. Burst-

ing with a terrific crash directly above our heads, it roared
over the boundless waste of prairie, seeming to roll around
the whole circle of the firmament with a peculiar and awful
reverberation. The lightning flashed all night, playing with
its livid glare upon the neighboring trees, revealing the vast
expanse of the plain, and then leaving us shut in as if by a
palpable wall of darkness.

It did not disturb us much. Now and then a peal awakened us, and made us conscious of the electric battle that
was raging, and of the floods that dashed upon the stanch
canvas over our heads. We lay upon india-rubber cloths,
placed between our blankets and the soil. For a while they
excluded the water to admiration; but when at length it
accumulated and began to run over the edges, they served
equally well to retain it, so that towards the end of the
night we were unconsciously reposing in small pools of
rain.

On finally awaking in the morning the prospect was not
a cheerful one. The rain no longer poured in torrents;
but it pattered with a quiet pertinacity upon the strained
and saturated canvas. We disengaged ourselves from our
blankets, every fibre of which glistened with little bead-
like drops of water, and looked out in the vain hope of
discovering some token of fair weather. The clouds, in
lead-colored volumes, rested upon the dismal verge of the
prairie, or hung sluggishly overhead, while the earth wore
an aspect no more attractive than the heavens, exhibiting
nothing but pools of water, grass beaten down, and mud
well trampled by our mules and horses. Our companions'
tent, with an air of forlorn and passive misery, and their
wagons in like manner drenched and woe-begone, stood
not far off. The Captain was just returning from his
morning's inspection of the horses. He stalked through

the mist and rain with his plaid around his shoulders, his little pipe, dingy as an antiquarian relic, projecting from beneath his moustache, and his brother Jack at his heels.   13

At noon the sky was clear, and we set out, trailing through mud and slime six inches deep. That night we were spared the customary infliction of the shower-bath.   14

On the next afternoon we were moving slowly along, not far from a patch of woods which lay on the right. Jack C—— rode a little in advance, —

> "The livelong day he had not spoke;"   15

when suddenly he faced about, pointed to the woods, and roared out to his brother, —

"O Bill! here's a cow."

The Captain instantly galloped forward, and he and Jack made a vain attempt to capture the prize; but the cow, with a well-grounded distrust of their intentions, took refuge among the trees. R—— joined them, and they soon drove her out. We watched their evolutions as they galloped around her, trying in vain to noose her with their trail-ropes, which they had converted into *lariettes* for the occasion. At length they resorted to milder measures, and the cow was driven along with the party. Soon after the usual thunder-storm came up, the wind blowing with such fury that the streams of rain flew almost horizontally along the prairie, roaring like a cataract. The horses turned tail to the storm, and stood hanging their heads, bearing the infliction with an air of meekness and resignation; while we drew our heads between our shoulders, and crouched forward, so as to make our backs serve as a pent-house for the rest of our persons. Meanwhile the cow taking advantage of the tumult, ran off, to the great discomfiture of the Captain. In defiance of the storm, he pulled his cap   16 tight over his brows, jerked a huge buffalo-pistol from his holster, and set out at full speed after her. This was the last we saw of them for some time, the mist and rain making an impenetrable veil; but at length we heard the Captain's shout, and saw him looming through the tempest, the picture of a Hibernian cavalier, with his cocked pistol held aloft for safety's sake, and a countenance of anxiety and excitement. The cow trotted before him, but exhibited evident signs of an intention to run off again, and the Captain was roaring to us to head her. But the rain had got in behind our coat collars, and was travelling over our necks in numerous little streamlets, and being afraid to move our heads, for fear of admitting more, we sat stiff and immovable, looking at the Captain askance, and laughing at his frantic movements. At last the cow made a sudden plunge and ran off; the Captain grasped his pistol firmly, spurred his horse, and galloped after, with evident designs of mischief. In a moment we heard the faint report, deadened by the rain, and then the conqueror and his victim reappeared, the latter shot through the body, and quite helpless. Not long after, the storm moderated, and we advanced again. The cow walked painfully along under the charge of Jack, to whom the Captain had committed her, while he himself rode forward in his old capacity of vedette. We were approaching a long line of trees, that followed a stream stretching across our path far in front, when we beheld the vedette galloping towards us apparently much excited, but with a broad grin on his face.

"Let that cow drop behind!" he shouted to us; "here's her owners."

And, in fact, as we approached the line of trees, a large white object like a tent was visible behind them. On approaching, however, we found, instead of the expected Mormon camp, nothing but the lonely prairie, and a large white rock standing by the path.   The cow, therefore, resumed her place in our procession.   She walked on until we encamped, when R——, approaching with his English double-barrelled rifle took aim at her heart, and discharged into it first one bullet and then the other.   She was then butchered on the most approved principles of woodcraft, and furnished a very welcome item to our somewhat limited bill of fare.   17

In a day or two more we reached the river called the "Big Blue."   By titles equally elegant, almost all the   18 streams of this region are designated.   We had struggled through ditches and little brooks all that morning; but on traversing the dense woods that lined the banks of the Blue, we found that more formidable difficulties awaited us, for the stream, swollen by the rains, was wide, deep, and rapid.

No sooner were we on the spot than R—— flung off his clothes, and swam across, or splashed through the shallows, with the end of a rope between his teeth.   We all looked on in admiration, wondering what might be the object of this energetic preparation; but soon we heard him shouting: "Give that rope a turn round that stump.   You, Sorel; do you hear?   Look sharp, now, Boisverd.   Come over to this side, some of you, and help me."   The men to whom these orders were directed paid not the least attention to them, though they were poured out without pause or intermission.   Henry Chatillon directed the work, and it proceeded quietly and rapidly.   R——'s sharp, brattling voice might have been heard incessantly; and he was leaping about with the utmost activity.   His commands were   19 rather amusingly inconsistent; for when he saw that the men would not do as he told them he accommodated him-

self to circumstances, and with the utmost vehemence ordered them to do precisely that which they were at the
time engaged upon, no doubt recollecting the story of
Mahomet and the refractory mountain. Shaw smiled;
R—— observed it, and, approaching with a countenance
of indignation, began to vapor a little, but was instantly
20 reduced to silence.

The raft was at length complete. We piled our goods
upon it, with the exception of our guns, which each man
chose to retain in his own keeping. Sorel, Boisverd,
Wright, and Deslauriers took their stations at the four
corners, to hold it together, and swim across with it; and
in a moment more all our earthly possessions were floating on the turbid waters of the Big Blue. We sat on
the bank, anxiously watching the result, until we saw the
raft safe landed in a little cove far down on the opposite bank. The empty wagons were easily passed across;
and then, each man mounting a horse, we rode through
the stream, the stray animals following of their own
accord.

CHAPTER VI.

THE PLATTE AND THE DESERT

WE were now at the end of our solitary journeyings along the St. Joseph trail. On the evening of the twenty-third of May we encamped near its junction with the old legitimate trail of the Oregon emigrants. We had ridden long that afternoon, trying in vain to find wood and water, until at length we saw the sunset sky reflected from a pool encircled by bushes and rocks. The water lay in the bottom of a hollow, the smooth prairie gracefully rising in ocean-like swells on every side. We pitched our tents by it; not however before the keen eye of Henry Chatillon had discerned some unusual object upon the faintly defined outline of the distant swell. But in the moist, hazy atmosphere of the evening, nothing could be clearly distinguished. As we lay around the fire after supper, a low and distant sound, strange enough amid the loneliness of the prairie, reached our ears, — peals of laughter, and the faint voices of men and women. For eight days we had not encountered a human being, and this singular warning of their vicinity had an effect extremely impressive.

About dark a sallow-faced fellow descended the hill on horseback, and splashing through the pool, rode up to the tents. He was enveloped in a huge cloak, and his broad felt hat was weeping about his ears with the drizzling moisture of the evening. Another followed, a stout, square-built, intelligent-looking man, who announced himself as leader

of an emigrant party, encamped a mile in advance of us.
About twenty wagons, he said, were with him; the rest of
his party were on the other side of the Big Blue, waiting
for a woman who was in the pains of childbirth, and quar-
3 relling meanwhile among themselves.

These were the first emigrants that we had overtaken, although we had found abundant and melancholy traces of their

progress throughout the
course of the journey.
Sometimes we passed
the grave of one who
had sickened and died
on the way. The earth
was usually torn up, and
covered thickly with
wolf-tracks. Some had
escaped this violation.

One morning, a piece of plank, standing upright on the
summit of a grassy hill, attracted our notice, and riding
up to it, we found the following words very roughly traced
upon it, apparently with a red-hot iron: —

MARY ELLIS.

DIED MAY 7TH, 1845.

AGED TWO MONTHS.

4   Such tokens were of common occurrence.

We were late in breaking up our camp on the following
morning, and scarcely had we ridden a mile when we saw,
far in advance of us, drawn against the horizon, a line of
objects stretching at regular intervals along the level edge
of the prairie. An intervening swell soon hid them from
sight, until, ascending it a quarter of an hour after, we saw
close before us the emigrant caravan, with its heavy white

wagons creeping on in slow procession, and a large drove
of cattle following behind.   Half a dozen yellow-visaged   5
Missourians, mounted on horseback, were cursing and shouting among them, their lank, angular proportions enveloped
in brown homespun, evidently cut and adjusted by the hands
of a domestic female tailor.   As we approached, they called
out to us: "How are ye, boys?   Are ye for Oregon or
California?"

As we pushed rapidly by the wagons, children's faces
were thrust out from the white coverings to look at us;
while the care-worn, thin-featured matron, or the buxom
girl, seated in front, suspended the knitting on which most
of them were engaged, to stare at us with wondering curiosity.   By the side of each wagon stalked the proprietor,   6
urging on his patient oxen, who shouldered heavily along,
inch by inch, on their interminable journey.   It was easy
to see that fear and dissension prevailed among them; some
of the men — but these, with one exception, were bachelors,
— looked wistfully upon us as we rode lightly and swiftly
by, and then impatiently at their own lumbering wagons and
heavy-gaited oxen.   Others were unwilling to advance at all,
until the party they had left behind should have rejoined
them.   Many were murmuring against the leader they had
chosen, and wished to depose him; and this discontent was
fomented by some ambitious spirits, who had hopes of succeeding in his place.   The women were divided between
regrets for the homes they had left and fear of the deserts
and savages before them.   7

We soon left them far behind, and hoped that we had
taken a final leave; but our companions' wagon stuck so
long in a deep muddy ditch, that before it was extricated   8
the van of the emigrant caravan appeared again descending a ridge close at hand. Wagon after wagon plunged

through the mud; and as it was nearly noon, and the place promised shade and water, we saw with satisfaction that they were resolved to encamp. Soon the wagons were wheeled into a circle; the cattle were grazing over the meadow, and the men, with sour, sullen faces, were look-

ing about for wood and water. They seemed to meet but indifferent success. As we left the ground, I saw a tall, slouching fellow, with the nasal accent of "down east," contemplating the contents of his tin cup, which he had just filled with water.

"Look here, you," said he; "it's chock-full of animals!"

The cup, as he held it out, exhibited in fact an extraordinary variety and profusion of animal and vegetable life.

Riding up the little hill and looking back on the meadow, we could easily see that all was not right in the camp of the emigrants. The men were crowded together, and an angry discussion seemed to be going forward. R—— was missing from his wonted place in the line, and the Captain told us that he had remained behind to get his horse shod by a blacksmith attached to the emigrant party. Something whispered in our ears that mischief was on foot; we kept on, however, and coming soon to a stream of tolerable water, we stopped to rest and dine. Still the absentee lingered behind. At last, at the distance of a mile, he and his horse suddenly appeared, sharply defined against the sky on the summit of a hill; and close behind, a huge white object rose slowly into view.

"What is that blockhead bringing with him now?"

A moment dispelled the mystery. Slowly and solemnly, one behind the other, four long trains of oxen and four emigrant wagons rolled over the crest of the hill and gravely descended, while R—— rode in state in the van. It seems that, during the process of shoeing the horse, the smothered dissensions among the emigrants suddenly broke into open rupture. Some insisted on pushing forward, some on remaining where they were, and some on going back. Kearsley, their captain, threw up his command in disgust. "And now, boys," said he, "if any of you are for going ahead, just you come along with me." 9

Four wagons, with ten men, one woman, and one small child, made up the force of the "go-ahead" faction, and R——, with his usual proclivity toward mischief, invited them to join our party. Fear of the Indians — for I can conceive no other motive — must have induced him to court so burdensome an alliance. At all events the proceeding was a cool one. The men who joined us, it is true, were 10 all that could be desired,— rude indeed in manners, but frank, manly, and intelligent. To tell them we could not travel with them was out of the question. I merely reminded Kearsley that if his oxen could not keep up with our mules he must expect to be left behind, as we could not consent to be farther delayed on the journey; but he immediately replied that his oxen "*should* keep up; and if they could n't, why, he allowed, he'd find out how to make 'em." 11

On the next day, as it chanced, our English companions broke the axle-tree of their wagon, and down came the whole cumbrous machine lumbering into the bed of a brook. Here was a day's work cut out for us. Meanwhile 12 our emigrant associates kept on their way, and so vigorously did they urge forward their powerful oxen that, what with the broken axle-tree and other mishaps, it was full a week before we overtook them; when at length we discovered them, one afternoon, crawling quietly along the sandy brink of the Platte.   But meanwhile various incidents occurred to ourselves.

It was probable that at this stage of our journey the Pawnees would attempt to rob us.   We began, therefore, to stand guard in turn, dividing the night into three watches, and appointing two men for each.   Deslauriers and I held guard together.   We did not march with military precision to and fro before the tents; our discipline was by no means so strict.   We wrapped ourselves in our blankets and sat down by the fire; and Deslauriers, combining his culinary functions with his duties as sentinel, employed himself in boiling the head of an antelope for our breakfast.   Yet we were models of vigilance in comparison with some of the party; for the ordinary practice of the guard was to lay his rifle on the ground, and, enveloping his nose in his blanket, meditate on his mistress, or whatever subject best pleased him.   This is all well enough when among Indians who do not habitually proceed further in their hostility than robbing travellers of their horses and mules, though, indeed, a Pawnee's forbearance is not always to be trusted; but in certain regions farther to the west, the guard must beware how he exposes his person to the light of the fire, lest some keen-eyed skulking marksman should let fly a bullet or an arrow from the darkness.

Among various tales that circulated around our camp-fire was one told by Boisverd, and not inappropriate here.   He was trapping with several companions on the skirts of the Blackfoot country.   The man on guard, knowing that it behooved him to put forth his utmost precaution, kept aloof from the fire-light, and sat watching intently on all sides. At length he was aware of a dark, crouching figure, stealing noiselessly into the circle of the light. He hastily cocked his rifle, but the sharp click of the lock caught the ear of the Blackfoot, whose senses were all on the alert. Raising his arrow, already fitted to the string he shot it in the direction of the sound. So sure was his aim that he drove it through the throat of the unfortunate guard, and then, with a loud yell, bounded from the camp. 15

As I looked at the partner of my watch, puffing and blowing over his fire, it occurred to me that he might not prove the most efficient auxiliary in time of trouble.

"Deslauriers," said I, "would you run away if the Paw nees should fire at us?"

"Ah! oui, oui, Monsieur!" he replied very decisively. 16

At this instant a whimsical variety of voices,— barks, howls, yelps, and whines, all mingled together,— sounded from the prairie, not far off, as if a conclave of wolves of every age and sex were assembled there. Deslauriers looked up from his work with a laugh, and began to imitate this medley of sounds with a ludicrous accuracy. At this they were repeated with redoubled emphasis, the musician being apparently indignant at the successful efforts of a rival. They all proceeded from the throat of one little wolf, not larger than a spaniel, seated by himself at some distance. He was of the species called the prairie-wolf,— a grim-visaged, but 17 harmless little brute, whose worst propensity is creeping among horses and gnawing the ropes of raw hide by which they are picketed around the camp. Other beasts roam the prairies far more formidable in aspect and in character. These are the large white and gray wolves, whose deep howl we heard at intervals from far and near.

At last I fell into a doze, and awaking from it found Des-lauriers fast asleep. Scandalized by this breach of discipline, I was about to stimulate his vigilance by stirring him with the stock of my rifle; but compassion prevailing, I determined to let him sleep a while, and then arouse him to administer a suitable reproof for such forgetfulness of duty. Now and then I walked the rounds among the silent horses, to see that all was right. The night was chill, damp, and dark, the dank grass bending under the icy dew-drops. At the distance of a rod or two the tents were invisible, and nothing could be seen but the obscure figures of the horses deeply breathing, and restlessly starting as they slept, or still slowly champing the grass. Far off, beyond the black outline of the prairie, there was a ruddy light, gradually increasing, like the glow of a conflagration; until at length the broad disk of the moon, blood-red, and vastly magnified by the vapors, rose slowly upon the darkness, flecked by one or two little clouds, and as the light poured over the gloomy plain, a fierce and stern howl, close at hand, seemed to greet it as an unwelcome intruder. There was something impressive and awful in the place and the hour; for I and the beasts were all that had consciousness for many a league around.

Some days elapsed, and brought us near the Platte. Two men on horseback approached us one morning, and we watched them with the curiosity and interest that, upon the solitude of the plains, such an encounter always excites. They were evidently whites, from their mode of riding, though, contrary to the usage of that region, neither of them carried a rifle.

"Fools!" remarked Henry Chatillon, "to ride that way on the prairie; Pawnee find them — then they catch it."

Pawnee *had* found them, and they had come very near

"catching it;" indeed nothing saved them but the approach of our party. Shaw and I knew one of them,—a man named Turner whom we had seen at Westport. He and his companion belonged to an emigrant party encamped a few miles in advance, and had returned to look for some stray oxen, leaving their rifles, with characteristic rashness or ignorance, behind them. Their neglect had nearly cost them dear; for, just before we came up, half a dozen Indians approached, and seeing them apparently defenceless, one of the rascals seized the bridle of Turner's horse and ordered him to dismount. Turner was wholly unarmed; but the other jerked a pistol out of his pocket, at which the Pawnee recoiled; and just then some of our men appearing in the distance, the whole party whipped their rugged little horses and made off. In no way daunted, Turner foolishly persisted in going forward.   18

Long after leaving him, and late that afternoon, in the midst of a gloomy and barren prairie, we came suddenly upon the great trail of the Pawnees, leading from their villages on the Platte to their war and hunting grounds to the southward. Here every summer passes the motley concourse: thousands of savages, men, women, and children, horses and mules, laden with their weapons and implements, and an innumerable multitude of unruly wolfish dogs, who have not acquired the civilized accomplishment of barking, but howl like their wild cousins of the prairie.   19

The permanent winter villages of the Pawnees stand on the lower Platte, but throughout the summer the greater part of the inhabitants are wandering over the plains,—a treacherous, cowardly banditti, who, by a thousand acts of pillage and murder, have deserved chastisement at the hands of government. Last year a Dakota warrior performed a notable exploit at one of these villages. He

approached it alone, in the middle of a dark night, and clambering up the outside of one of the lodges, which are in the form of a half-sphere, looked in at the round hole made at the top for the escape of smoke. The dusky light from the embers showed him the forms of the sleeping inmates; and dropping lightly through the opening, he unsheathed his knife, and stirring the fire, coolly selected his victims. One by one he stabbed and scalped them; when a child suddenly awoke and screamed. He rushed from the lodge, yelled a Sioux war-cry, shouted his name in triumph and defiance, and darted out upon the dark prairie, leaving the whole village behind him in a tumult, with the howling and baying of dogs, the screams of women, and the
20 yells of the enraged warriors.

Our friend Kearsley, as we learned on rejoining him, signalized himself by a less bloody achievement. He and his men were good woodsmen, well skilled in the use of the rifle, but found themselves wholly out of their element on the prairie. None of them had ever seen a buffalo; and they had very vague conceptions of his nature and appearance. On the day after they reached the Platte, looking towards a distant swell they beheld a multitude of little black specks in motion upon its surface.

"Take your rifles, boys," said Kearsley, "and we'll have fresh meat for supper." This inducement was quite sufficient. The ten men left their wagons, and set out in hot haste, some on horseback and some on foot, in pursuit of the supposed buffalo. Meanwhile a high grassy ridge shut the game from view; but mounting it after half an hour's running and riding, they found themselves suddenly confronted by about thirty mounted Pawnees. Amazement and consternation were mutual. Having nothing but their bows and arrows, the Indians thought their hour was come, and the fate that they were conscious of richly deserving about to overtake them. So they began, one and all, to shout forth the most cordial salutations, running up with extreme earnestness to shake hands with the Missourians, who were as much rejoiced as they were to escape the expected conflict.

A low, undulating line of sand-hills bounded the horizon before us. That day we rode ten hours, and it was dusk before we entered the hollows and gorges of these gloomy little hills. At length we gained the summit, and the long-expected valley of the Platte lay before us. We all drew rein, and sat joyfully looking down upon the prospect. It was right welcome,—strange, too, and striking to the imagination; and yet it had not one picturesque or beautiful feature; nor had it any of the features of grandeur, other than its vast extent, its solitude, and its wildness. For league after league, a plain as level as a lake was outspread beneath us; here and there the Platte, divided into a dozen thread-like sluices, was traversing it, and an occasional clump of wood, rising in the midst like a shadowy island, relieved the monotony of the waste. No living thing was moving throughout the vast landscape, except the lizards that darted over the sand and through the rank grass and prickly pears at our feet.

We had passed the more tedious part of the journey; but four hundred miles still intervened between us and Fort Laramie; and to reach that point cost us the travel of three more weeks. During the whole of this time we were passing up the middle of a long, narrow, sandy plain, reaching like an outstretched belt nearly to the Rocky Mountains. Two lines of sandhills, broken often into the wildest and most fantastic forms, flanked the valley at the distance of a mile or two on the right and left; while beyond them lay

21

22

23

24

a barren trackless waste, extending for hundreds of miles to the Arkansas on the one side and the Missouri on the other. Before and behind us the level monotony of the plain was unbroken as far as the eye could reach. Sometimes it glared in the sun, an expanse of hot, bare sand; sometimes it was veiled by long coarse grass. Skulls and whitening bones of buffalo were scat-

tered everywhere; the ground was tracked by myriads of them, and often covered with the circular indenta-tions where the bulls had wallowed in the hot weather. From every gorge and ra-vine opening from the hills, descended deep, well-worn paths, where the buffalo is-sue twice a day in regular procession to drink in the Platte. The river itself runs through the midst, a thin sheet of rapid, turbid water, half a mile wide, and scarcely two feet deep. Its low banks, for the most part without a bush or a tree, are of loose sand, with which the stream is so charged that it grates on the teeth in drinking. The naked landscape is, of itself, dreary and monotonous enough; and yet the wild beasts and wild men that frequent the valley of the Platte make it a scene of interest and excitement to the traveller. Of those who have journeyed there, scarcely one, perhaps, fails to look back with fond regret to his horse and his rifle.

Early in the morning after we reached the Platte, a long procession of squalid savages approached our camp. Each was on foot, leading his horse by a rope of bull-hide. His attire consisted merely of a scanty cincture, and an old buffalo robe, tattered and begrimed by use, which hung over his shoulders. His head was close shaven, except a ridge of hair reaching over the crown from the middle of the forehead, very much like the long bristles on the back of a hyena, and he carried his bow and arrows in his hand, while his meagre little horse was laden with dried buffalo meat, the produce of his hunting. Such were the first specimens that we met — and very indifferent ones they were — of the genuine savages of the plains.   27

They were the Pawnees whom Kearsley had encountered the day before, and belonged to a large hunting party, known to be ranging the prairie in the vicinity. They strode rapidly by, within a furlong of our tents, not pausing or looking towards us, after the manner of Indians when meditating mischief or conscious of ill desert. I went out to meet them, and had an amicable conference with the chief, presenting him with half a pound of tobacco, at which unmerited bounty he expressed much gratification. These fellows, or some of their companions, had committed a dastardly outrage upon an emigrant party in advance of   28 us. Two men, at a distance from the rest, were seized by them, but, lashing their horses, they broke away and fled. At this the Pawnees raised the yell and shot at them, transfixing the hindmost through the back with several arrows, while his companion galloped away and brought in the news to his party. The panic-stricken emigrants remained for several days in camp, not daring even to go out in quest of the dead body.   29

Our New England climate is mild and equable compared with that of the Platte. This very morning, for instance, was close and sultry, the sun rising with a faint oppressive

heat; when suddenly darkness gathered in the west, and a
furious blast of sleet and hail drove full in our faces, icy
cold, and urged with such demoniac vehemence that it felt
like a storm of needles.   It was curious to see the horses;
they faced about in extreme displeasure, holding their tails
like whipped dogs, and shivering as the angry gusts, howling louder than a concert of wolves, swept over us. Wright's
long train of mules came sweepng round before the storm,
like a flight of snow-birds driven by a winter tempest.   Thus
we all remained stationary for some minutes, crouching close
to our horses' necks, much too surly to speak, though once
the Captain looked up from between the collars of his coat,
his face blood-red, and the muscles of his mouth contracted
by the cold into a most ludicrous grin of agony.   He grumbled something that sounded like a curse, directed, as we believed, against the unhappy hour when he had first thought of
leaving home.   The thing was too good to last long; and the
instant the puffs of wind subsided we pitched our tents, and
remained in camp for the rest of a gloomy and lowering
30   day.   The emigrants also encamped near at hand.   We
being first on the ground, had appropriated all the wood
within reach; so that our fire alone blazed cheerily.   Around
it soon gathered a group of uncouth figures, shivering in
the drizzling rain.   Conspicuous among them were two or
three of the half-savage men who spend their reckless lives
in trapping among the Rocky Mountains, or in trading for
the Fur Company in the Indian villages.   They were all
of Canadian extraction; their hard, weather-beaten faces
and bushy moustaches looked out from beneath the hoods
of their white capotes with a bad and brutish expression,
as if their owners might be the willing agents of any
villany.   And such in fact is the character of many of
31   these men.

On the day following we overtook Kearsley's wagons, and thenceforward for a week or two, we were fellow-travellers. One good effect, at least, resulted from the alliance; it materially diminished the fatigues of standing guard; for the party being now more numerous, there were longer intervals between each man's turns of duty. 32

CHAPTER VII.

THE BUFFALO.

FOUR days on the Platte, and yet no buffalo! Last year's signs of them were provokingly abundant; and wood being extremely scarce, we found an admirable substitute in the *bois de vache*, which burns like peat, producing no unpleasant effects. The wagons one morning had left the camp; Shaw and I were already on horseback, but Henry Chatillon still sat cross-legged by the dead embers of the fire, playing pensively with the lock of his rifle, while his sturdy Wyandot pony stood quietly behind him, looking over his head. At last he got up, patted the neck of the pony (which, from an exaggerated appreciation of his value, he had christened "Five Hundred Dollar"), and then mounted, with a melancholy air.

"What is it, Henry?"

"Ah, I feel lonesome; I never been here before but I see away yonder over the buttes, and down there on the prairie, black — all black with buffalo."

In the afternoon he and I left the party in search of an antelope, until, at the distance of a mile or two on the right, the tall white wagons and the little black specks of horsemen were just visible, so slowly advancing that they seemed motionless; and far on the left rose the broken line of scorched, desolate sand-hills. The vast plain waved with tall rank grass, that swept our horses' bellies; it swayed to and fro in billows with the light breeze, and far and near antelope and wolves were moving through it, the hairy backs of the latter alternately appearing and disappearing, as they bounded awkwardly along; while the antelope,   4 with the simple curiosity peculiar to them, would often approach us closely, their little horns and white throats just visible above the grass tops, as they gazed eagerly at us with their round black eyes.

I dismounted, and amused myself with firing at the wolves. Henry attentively scrutinized the surrounding landscape; at length he gave a shout, and called on me to mount again, pointing in the direction of the sand-hills. A mile and a half from us two black specks slowly traversed the bare, glaring face of one of them, and disappeared behind the summit. "Let us go!" cried Henry, belabor-   5 ing the sides of "Five Hundred Dollar;" and I following in his wake, we galloped rapidly through the rank grass toward the base of the hills.

From one of their openings descended a deep ravine, widening as it issued on the prairie. We entered it, and galloping up, in a moment were surrounded by the bleak sand-hills. Half of their steep sides were bare; the rest were scantily clothed with clumps of grass, and various uncouth plants, conspicuous among which appeared the reptile-like prickly-pear. They were gashed with number-   6 less ravines; and as the sky had suddenly darkened, and a cold, gusty wind arisen, the strange shrubs and the dreary hills looked doubly wild and desolate. But Henry's face was all eagerness. He tore off a little hair from the piece of buffalo-robe under his saddle, and threw it up, to show the course of the wind. It blew directly before us. The game was therefore to leeward, and it was necessary to make our best speed to get round them.

We scrambled from this ravine, and galloping away

through the hollows soon found another, winding like a snake among the hills, and so deep that it completely concealed us. We rode up the bottom of it, glancing through the bushes at its edge, till Henry abruptly jerked his rein and slid out of his saddle. Full a quarter of a mile distant, on the outline of the farthest hill, a long procession of buffalo were walking, in Indian file, with the utmost gravity and deliberation; then more appeared, clambering from a hollow not far off, and ascending, one behind the other, the grassy slope of another hill; then a shaggy head and a pair of short broken horns issued out of a ravine close at hand, and with a slow, stately step, one by one, the enormous brutes came into view, taking their way across the valley, wholly unconscious of an enemy. In a moment Henry was worming his way, lying flat on the ground, through grass and prickly-pears, towards his unsuspecting victims. He had with him both my rifle and his own. He was soon out of sight, and still the buffalo kept issuing into the valley. For a long time all was silent; I sat holding his horse, and wondering what he was about, when suddenly in rapid succession, came the sharp reports of the two rifles, and the whole line of buffalo, quickening their pace into a clumsy trot, gradually disappeared over the ridge of the hill. Henry rose to his feet, and stood looking after them.

"You have missed them," said I.

"Yes," said Henry; "let us go." He descended into the ravine, loaded the rifles, and mounted his horse.

We rode up the hill after the buffalo. The herd was out of sight when we reached the top, but lying on the grass, not far off, was one quite lifeless, and another violently struggling in the death agony.

"You see I miss him!" remarked Henry. He had fired

from a distance of more than a hundred and fifty yards, and both balls had passed through the lungs, the true mark in shooting buffalo. 7

The darkness increased, and a driving storm came on. Tying our horses to the horns of the victims, Henry began the bloody work of dissection, slashing away with the science of a connoisseur, while I vainly tried to imitate 8 him. Old Hendrick recoiled with horror and indignation when I endeavored to tie the meat to the strings of raw hide, always carried for this purpose, dangling at the back of the saddle. After some difficulty we overcame his scruples; and, heavily burdened with the more eligible portions of the buffalo, we set out on our return. Scarcely had we emerged from the labyrinth of gorges and ravines, and issued upon the open prairie, when the prickling sleet came driving, gust upon gust, directly in our faces. It was strangely dark, though wanting still an hour of sunset. The freezing storm soon penetrated to the skin, but the uneasy trot of our heavy-gaited horses kept us warm enough, as we forced them unwillingly in the teeth of the sleet and rain by the powerful suasion of our Indian whips. The prairie in this place was hard and level. A flourishing colony of prairie-dogs had burrowed into it in every direc- 9 tion, and the little mounds of fresh earth around their holes were about as numerous as the hills in a corn-field; but not a yelp was to be heard; not the nose of a single citizen was visible; all had retired to the depths of their burrows, and we envied them their dry and comfortable habitations. An hour's hard riding showed us our tent dimly looming through the storm, one side puffed out by the force of the wind, and the other collapsed in proportion, while the disconsolate horses stood shivering close around, and the wind kept up a dismal whistling in the boughs of three old half-dead trees above.   Shaw, like a patriarch, sat on his saddle in the entrance, with a pipe in his mouth and his arms folded, contemplating with cool satisfaction the piles of meat that we flung on the ground before him.   A dark and dreary night succeeded; but the sun rose with a heat so sultry and languid that the Captain excused himself on that account from waylaying an old buffalo bull, who with stupid gravity was walking over the prairie to drink at the river.   So much for the climate of the Platte.

But it was not the weather alone that had produced this sudden abatement of the sportsman-like zeal which the Captain had always professed.   He had been out on the afternoon before, together with several members of his party; but their hunting was attended with no other result than the loss of one of their best horses, severely injured by Sorel, in vainly chasing a wounded bull.   The Captain, whose ideas of hard riding were all derived from transatlantic sources, expressed the utmost amazement at the feats of Sorel, who went leaping ravines, and dashing at full speed up and down the sides of precipitous hills, lashing his horse with the recklessness of a Rocky Mountain rider.   Unfortunately for the poor animal, he was the property of R ——, against whom Sorel entertained an unbounded aversion.   The Captain himself, it seemed, had also attempted to "run" a buffalo, but though a good and practised horseman, he had soon given over the attempt, being astonished and utterly disgusted at the nature of the ground he was required to ride over.

"Here's old Papin and Frederic, down from Fort Laramie," shouted Henry, as we returned from a reconnoitring tour on the next morning.   We had for some days expected this encounter.   Papin was the *bourgeois*, or "boss," of Fort

Laramie. He had come down the river with the buffalo-robes and the beaver, the produce of the last winter's trading. I had among our baggage a letter which I wished to commit to his hands; so requesting Henry to detain the boats if he could until my return, I set out after the wagons. They were about four miles in advance. In half an hour I overtook them, got the letter, trotted back upon the trail, and looking carefully, as I rode, saw a patch of broken storm-blasted trees, and moving near them, some little black specks like men and horses. Arriving at the place, I found a strange assembly. The boats, eleven in

number, deep-laden with the skins, hugged close to the shore, to escape being borne down by the swift current. The rowers, swarthy, ignoble Mexicans, turned up their brutish faces to look, as I reached the bank. Papin sat in the middle of one of the boats, upon the canvas covering that protected the cargo. He was a stout, robust fellow, with a little gray eye that had a peculiarly sly twinkle. "Frederic," also, stretched his tall, raw-boned proportions close by the *bourgeois*, and "mountain men" completed the group: some lounging in the boats, some strolling on shore; some attired in gayly painted buffalo robes, like Indian dandies; some with hair saturated with red paint, and plastered with glue to their temples; and one bedaubed with vermilion upon the forehead and each cheek. They were a mongrel race; yet the French blood seemed to predominate; in a few, indeed, might be seen the black, snaky eye of the Indian half-breed, and one and all, they seemed

11 to aim at assimilating themselves to their red associates.

12   I shook hands with the *bourgeois*, and delivered the letter; then the boats swung round into the stream and floated away. They had reason for haste, for already the voyage from Fort Laramie had occupied a full month, and the river was growing daily more shallow. Fifty times a day the boats had been aground; indeed, those who navigate the Platte invariably spend half their time upon sand-bars. Two of these boats, the property of private traders, afterwards separating from the rest, got hopelessly involved in the shallows not very far from the Pawnee villages, and were soon surrounded by a swarm of the inhabitants. They carried off everything that they thought valuable, including most of the robes; and amused themselves by tying up the

13 men left on guard, and soundly whipping them with sticks.

We encamped that night upon the bank of the river. Among the emigrants was an overgrown boy, some eighteen years old, with a head as round and about as large as a pumpkin, and fever-and-ague fits had dyed his face to a corresponding color. He wore an old white hat, tied under his chin with a handkerchief; his body was short and stout, but his legs were of disproportioned and appalling length. I observed him at sunset, breasting the hill with gigantic strides, and standing against the sky on the summit, like a colossal pair of tongs. In a moment after we heard him screaming frantically behind the ridge, and nothing doubting that he was in the clutches of Indians or grizzly bears, some of the party caught up their rifles and ran to the rescue. His outcries, however, were but an ebullition of joyous excitement; he had chased two wolf pups to their burrow, and was on his knees, grubbing away like a dog at the mouth of the hole to get at them.

Before morning he caused more serious disquiet in the camp. It was his turn to hold the middle-guard; but no sooner was he called up than he coolly arranged a pair of saddle-bags under a wagon, laid his head upon them, closed his eyes, opened his mouth, and fell asleep. The guard on our side of the camp, thinking it no part of his duty to look after the cattle of the emigrants, contented himself with watching our own horses and mules; the wolves, he said, were unusually noisy; still no mischief was foreboded, but when the sun rose not a hoof or horn was in sight. The cattle were gone. While Tom was quietly slumbering, the wolves had driven them away.

Then we reaped the fruits of R——'s precious plan of travelling in company with emigrants. To leave them in their distress was not to be thought of, and we felt bound to wait until the cattle could be searched for, and if possible, recovered. But the reader may be curious to know what punishment awaited the faithless Tom. By the wholesome law of the prairie, he who falls asleep on guard is condemned to walk all day, leading his horse by the bridle; and we found much fault with our companions for not enforcing such a sentence on the offender. Nevertheless, had he been of our own party, I have no doubt that he would in like manner have escaped scot-free. But the emigrants went farther than mere forbearance; they decreed that since Tom couldn't stand guard without falling asleep, he shouldn't stand guard at all, and henceforward his slumbers were unbroken. Establishing such a premium on drowsiness could have no very beneficial effect upon the vigilance of our sentinels; for it is far from agreeable, after riding

from sunrise to sunset, to feel your slumbers interrupted by
the but of a rifle nudging your side, and a sleepy voice
growling in your ear that you must get up, to shiver and
freeze for three weary hours at midnight.

"Buffalo! buffalo!" It was but a grim old bull, roaming
the prairie by himself in misanthropic seclusion; but there
might be more behind the hills. Dreading the monotony
and languor of the camp, Shaw and I saddled our horses,
buckled our holsters in their places, and set out with Henry
Chatillon in search of the game. Henry, not intending to
take part in the chase, but merely conducting us, carried his
rifle with him while we left ours behind as incumbrances.
We rode for some five or six miles, and saw no living thing
but wolves, snakes, and prairie-dogs.

"This won't do at all," said Shaw.

"What won't do?"

"There's no wood about here to make a litter for the
wounded man; I have an idea that one of us will need
something of the sort before the day is over."

There was some foundation for such an idea, for the
ground was none of the best for a race, and grew worse
continually as we proceeded; indeed, it soon became desperately bad, consisting of abrupt hills and deep hollows,
cut by frequent ravines not easy to pass. At length, a mile
in advance, we saw a band of bulls. Some were scattered
grazing over a green declivity, while the rest were crowded
together in the wide hollow below. Making a circuit, to
keep out of sight, we rode towards them, until we ascended
a hill within a furlong of them, beyond which nothing intervened that could possibly screen us from their view. We
dismounted behind the ridge, just out of sight, drew our
saddle-girths, examined our pistols, and mounting again,
rode over the hill, and descended at a canter towards them,

bending close to our horses' necks. Instantly they took the alarm; those on the hill descended, those below gathered into a mass, and the whole got into motion, shouldering each other along at a clumsy gallop. We followed, spurring our horses to full speed; and as the herd rushed, crowding and trampling in terror through an opening in the hills, we were close at their heels, half suffocated by the clouds of dust. But as we drew near, their alarm and speed increased; our horses, being new to the work, showed signs of the utmost fear, bounding violently aside as we approached, and refusing to enter among the herd. The buffalo now broke into several small bodies, scampering over the hills in different directions, and I lost sight of Shaw; neither of us knew where the other had gone. Old Pontiac ran like a frantic elephant up hill and down hill, his ponderous hoofs striking the prairie like sledge-hammers. He showed a curious mixture of eagerness and terror, straining to overtake the panic-stricken herd, but constantly recoiling in dismay as we drew near. The fugitives, indeed, offered no very attractive spectacle, with their shaggy manes and the tattered remnants of their last winter's hair covering their backs in irregular shreds and patches, and flying off in the wind as they ran. At length I urged my horse close behind a bull, and after trying in vain, by blows and spurring to bring him alongside, I fired from this disadvantageous position. At the report Pontiac swerved so much that I was again thrown a little behind the game. The bullet, entering too much in the rear, failed to disable the bull; for a buffalo requires to be shot at particular points, or he will certainly escape. The herd ran up a hill, and I followed in pursuit. As Pontiac rushed headlong down on the other side, I saw Shaw and Henry descending the hollow on the right, at a leisurely gallop; and in front, the buffalo were

16

just disappearing behind the crest of the next hill, their
short tails erect, and their hoofs twinkling through a cloud
of dust.

At that moment I heard Shaw and Henry shouting to me;
but the muscles of a stronger arm than mine could not have
checked at once the furious course of Pontiac, whose mouth
was as insensible as leather.   Added to this, I rode him
that morning with a snaffle, having the day before, for the
benefit of my other horse, unbuckled from my bridle the curb
which I commonly used.   A stronger and hardier brute
never trod the prairie; but the novel sight of the buffalo
filled him with terror, and when at full speed he was almost
incontrollable.   Gaining the top of the ridge, I saw nothing
of the buffalo; they had all vanished amid the intricacies
of the hills and hollows.   Reloading my pistols in the best
way I could, I galloped on until I saw them again scuttling
along at the base of the hill, their panic somewhat abated.
Down went old Pontiac among them, scattering them to the
right and left; and then we had another long chase.   About
a dozen bulls were before us, scouring over the hills, rushing down the declivities with tremendous weight and im-
petuosity, and then laboring with a weary gallop upward.
Still Pontiac, in spite of spurring and beating, would not
close with them.   One bull at length fell a little behind
the rest, and by dint of much effort, I urged my horse
within six or eight yards of his side.   His back was darkened with sweat; he was panting heavily, while his tongue
lolled out a foot from his jaws.   Gradually I came up abreast
of him, urging Pontiac with leg and rein nearer to his side,
when suddenly he did what buffalo in such circumstances
will always do: he slackened his gallop, and turning towards
us, with an aspect of mingled rage and distress, lowered
his huge, shaggy head for a charge.   Pontiac, with a snort,

leaped aside in terror, nearly throwing me to the ground, as I was wholly unprepared for such an evolution. I raised my pistol in a passion to strike him on the head, but thinking better of it, fired the bullet after the bull, who had resumed his flight; then drew rein and determined to rejoin my companions. It was high time. The breath blew hard from Pontiac's nostrils, and the sweat rolled in big drops down his sides; I myself felt as if drenched in warm water. Pledging myself to take my revenge at a future opportunity, I looked about for some indications to show me where I was, and what course I ought to pursue; I might as well have looked for landmarks in the midst of the ocean. How many miles I had run, or in what direction, I had no idea; and around me the prairie was rolling in steep swells and pitches, without a single distinctive feature to guide me. I had a little compass hung at my neck; and ignorant that the Platte at this point diverged considerably from its easterly course, I thought that by keeping to the northward I should certainly reach it. So I turned and rode about two hours in that direction. The prairie changed as I advanced, softening away into easier undulations, but nothing like the Platte appeared, nor any sign of a human being: the same wild, endless expanse lay around me still; and to all appearance I was as far from my object as ever. I began now to think myself in danger of being lost, and, reining in my horse, summoned the scanty share of woodcraft that I possessed (if that term be applicable on the prairie) to extricate me. It occurred to me that the buffalo might prove my best guides. I soon found one of the paths made by them in their passage to the river: it ran nearly at right angles to my course; but turning my horse's head in the direction it indicated, his freer gait and erected ears assured me that I was right.

But in the mean time my ride had been by no means a
solitary one. The face of the country was dotted far and
wide with countless hundreds of buffalo. They trooped
along in files and columns, bulls, cows, and calves, on the
green faces of the declivities in front. They scrambled
away over the hills to the right and left; and far off, the
pale blue swells in the extreme distance were dotted with
innumerable specks. Sometimes I surprised shaggy old
bulls grazing alone, or sleeping behind the ridges I ascended. They would leap up at my approach, stare stupidly at me through their tangled manes, and then gallop
heavily away. The antelope were very numerous; and as
they are always bold when in the neighborhood of buffalo,
they would approach to look at me, gaze intently with
their great round eyes, then suddenly leap aside, and
stretch lightly away over the prairie, swift as a race-horse.
Squalid, ruffian-like wolves sneaked through the hollows
and sandy ravines. Several times I passed through villages of prairie-dogs, who sat, each at the mouth of his
burrow, holding his paws before him in a supplicating attitude, and yelping away most vehemently, whisking his
little tail with every squeaking cry he uttered. Prairie-
dogs are not fastidious in their choice of companions; various long, checkered snakes were sunning themselves in the
midst of the village, and demure little gray owls, with a
large white ring round each eye, were perched side by
21   side with the rightful inhabitants. The prairie teemed
with life. Again and again I looked toward the crowded
hill-sides, and was sure I saw horsemen; and riding near,
with a mixture of hope and dread, for Indians were abroad,
I found them transformed into a group of buffalo. There
was nothing in human shape amid all this vast congregation of brute forms.

When I turned down the buffalo path, the prairie seemed changed; only a wolf or two glided by at intervals, like conscious felons, never looking to the right or left. Being now free from anxiety, I was at leisure to observe minutely the objects around me; and here, for the first time, I noticed insects wholly different from any of the varieties found farther eastward. Gaudy butterflies fluttered about my horse's head; strangely formed beetles, glittering with metallic lustre, were crawling upon plants that I had never seen before; multitudes of lizards, too, were darting like lightning over the sand.

I had run to a great distance from the river. It cost me a long ride on the buffalo path before I saw, from the ridge of a sand-hill, the pale surface of the Platte glistening in the midst of its desert valley, and the faint outline of the hills beyond waving along the sky. From where I stood, not a tree nor a bush nor a living thing was visible throughout the whole extent of the sun-scorched landscape. In half an hour I came upon the trail, not far from the river; and seeing that the party had not yet passed, I turned eastward to meet them, old Pontiac's long swinging trot again assuring me that I was right in doing so. Having been slightly ill on leaving camp in the morning, six or seven hours of rough riding had fatigued me extremely. I soon stopped, therefore, flung my saddle on the ground, and with my head resting on it, and my horse's trail-rope tied loosely to my arm, lay waiting the arrival of the party, speculating meanwhile on the extent of the injuries Pontiac had received.

At length the white wagon-coverings rose from the verge of the plain. By a singular coincidence, almost at the same moment two horsemen appeared coming down from the hills. They were Shaw and Henry, who had searched for me awhile in the morning, but well knowing the futility of the attempt in such a broken country, had placed themselves on the top of the highest hill they could find, and picketing their horses near them, as a signal to me, had lain down and fallen asleep. The stray cattle had been recovered, as the emigrants told us, about noon. Before sunset we pushed forward eight miles farther.

"JUNE 7, 1846. Four men are missing: R——, Sorel, and two emigrants. They set out this morning after buffalo, and have not yet made their appearance; whether killed or lost, we cannot tell."

I find the above in my note-book, and well remember the council held on the occasion. Our fire was the scene of it; for the superiority of Henry Chatillon's experience and skill made him the resort of the whole camp upon every question of difficulty. He was moulding bullets at the fire, when the Captain drew near, with a perturbed and careworn expression of countenance, faithfully reflected on the heavy features of Jack, who followed close behind. Then the emigrants came straggling from their wagons towards the common centre. Various suggestions were made to account for the absence of the four men, and one or two of the emigrants declared that, when out after the cattle, they had seen Indians dogging them, and crawling like wolves along the ridges of the hills. At this the Captain slowly shook his head with double gravity, and solemnly remarked,—

"It's a serious thing to be travelling through this cursed wilderness;" an opinion in which Jack immediately expressed a thorough coincidence. Henry would not commit himself by declaring any positive opinion.

"Maybe he only followed the buffalo too far; maybe Indian kill him; maybe he got lost; I cannot tell."

With this the auditors were obliged to rest content; the emigrants, not in the least alarmed, though curious to know what had become of their comrades, walked back to their wagons, and the Captain betook himself pensively to his tent. Shaw and I followed his example.

CHAPTER VIII.

ON the eighth of June, at eleven o'clock, we reached the South Fork of the Platte, at the usual fording-place. For league upon league the desert uniformity of the prospect was almost unbroken; the hills were dotted with little tufts of shrivelled grass, but betwixt these the white sand was glaring in the sun; and the channel of the river, almost on a level with the plain, was but one great sand-bed, about half a mile wide. It was covered with water, but so scantily that the bottom was scarcely hidden; for, wide as it is, the average depth of the Platte does not at this point exceed a foot and a half. Stopping near its bank, we gathered *bois de vache*, and made a meal of buffalo-meat. Far off, on the other side, was a green meadow, where we could see the white tents and wagons of an emigrant camp; and just opposite to us we could discern a group of men and animals at the water's edge. Four or five horsemen soon entered the river, and in ten minutes had waded across and clambered up the loose sand-bank. They were ill-looking fellows, thin and swarthy, with care-worn, anxious faces, and lips rigidly compressed. They had good cause for anxiety; it was three days since they first encamped here, and on the night of their arrival they had lost a hundred and twenty-three of their best cattle, driven off by the wolves, through the neglect of the man on guard. This discouraging and alarming calamity was not the first that had overtaken

them. Since leaving the settlements they had met with
nothing but misfortune. Some of their party had died;
one man had been killed by the Pawnees; and about a 3
week before, they had been plundered by the Dakota of
all their best horses, the wretched animals on which our
visitors were mounted being the only ones that were left.
They had encamped, they told us, near sunset, by the side
of the Platte, and their oxen were scattered over the meadow,
while the horses were feeding a little farther off. Suddenly
the ridges of the hills were alive with a swarm of mounted
Indians, at least six hundred in number, who came pouring
with a yell down towards the camp, rushing up within a few
rods, to the great terror of the emigrants; when suddenly
wheeling, they swept around the band of horses, and in five
minutes disappeared with their prey through the openings
of the hills. 4

As these emigrants were telling their story, we saw four
other men approaching. They proved to be R—— and his
companions, who had encountered no mischance of any kind,
but had only wandered too far in pursuit of the game. They
said they had seen no Indians, but only "millions of buffalo;" and both R—— and Sorel had meat dangling behind their saddles.

The emigrants recrossed the river, and we prepared to
follow. First the heavy ox-wagons plunged down the bank
and dragged slowly over the sand-beds; sometimes the hoofs
of the oxen were scarcely wet by the thin sheet of water;
and the next moment the river would be boiling against
their sides, and eddying around the wheels. Inch by inch
they receded from the shore, dwindling every moment, until
at length they seemed to be floating far out in the middle
of the river. A more critical experiment awaited us; for
our little mule-cart was ill-fitted for the passage of so swift

a stream. We watched it with anxiety, till it seemed a
motionless white speck in the midst of the waters; and it
was motionless, for it had stuck fast in a quicksand. The
mules were losing their footing, the wheels were sinking
deeper and deeper, and the water began to rise through
the bottom and drench the goods within. All of us who
had remained on the hither bank galloped to the rescue;
the men jumped into the water, adding their strength to
that of the mules, until by much effort the cart was extricated, and conveyed in safety across.

As we gained the other bank a rough group of men surrounded us. They were not robust, nor large of frame, yet
they had an aspect of hardy endurance. Finding at home
no scope for their energies, they had betaken themselves
to the prairie; and in them seemed to be revived, with redoubled force, that fierce spirit which impelled their an-
cestors, scarcely more lawless than themselves, from the
German forests, to inundate Europe, and overwhelm the
Roman empire. A fortnight afterwards this unfortunate
party passed Fort Laramie, while we were there. Not
one of their missing oxen had been recovered, though they
had remained encamped a week in search of them; and
they had been compelled to abandon a great part of their
baggage and provisions, and yoke cows and heifers to their
wagons to carry them forward upon their journey, the most
toilsome and hazardous part of which lay still before them.

It is worth noticing that on the Platte one may sometimes
see the shattered wrecks of ancient claw-footed tables,
well waxed and rubbed, or massive bureaus of carved
oak. These, some of them no doubt the relics of ancestral
prosperity in the colonial time, must have encountered
strange vicissitudes. Brought, perhaps, originally from England; then, with the declining fortunes of their owners,

borne across the Alleghanies to the wilderness of Ohio
or Kentucky; then to Illinois or Missouri; and now at last
fondly stowed away in the family wagon for the interminable journey to Oregon.   But the stern privations of the
way are little anticipated.   The cherished relic is soon
flung out to scorch and crack upon the hot prairie.   7

We resumed our journey; but we had gone scarcely a
mile, when R—— called out from the rear,—

"We'll 'camp here."

"Why do you want to 'camp?   Look at the sun.   It is
not three o'clock yet."

"We'll 'camp here!"

This was the only reply vouchsafed.   Deslauriers was
in advance with his cart.   Seeing the mule-wagon wheeling
from the track, he began to turn his own team in the same
direction.

"Go on, Deslauriers;" and the little cart advanced again.
As we rode on, we soon heard the wagon of our confederates creaking and jolting behind us, and the driver, Wright,
discharging a furious volley of oaths against his mules; no
doubt venting upon them the wrath which he dared not
direct against a more appropriate object.

Something of this sort had frequently occurred.   Our
English companion was by no means partial to us, and
we thought we discovered in his conduct an intention to
thwart and annoy us, especially by retarding the movements of the party, which he knew that we were anxious
to quicken.   Therefore he would insist on encamping at
all unseasonable hours, saying that fifteen miles was a sufficient day's journey.   Finding our wishes disregarded, we   8
took the direction of affairs into our own hands.   Keeping
always in advance, to the inexpressible indignation of R——,
we encamped at what time and place we thought proper, not

much caring whether the rest chose to follow or not. They always did so, however, pitching their tent near ours, with sullen and wrathful countenances.

9   Travelling together on these terms did not suit our tastes, and for some time we had meditated a separation. We resolved to leave camp early in the morning, and push forward as rapidly as possible for Fort Laramie, which we hoped to reach, by hard travelling, in four or five days. The Captain soon trotted up between us, and we explained our intentions.

10   "A very extraordinary proceeding, upon my word!" he remarked. The most prominent impression in his mind evidently was that we were deserting his party, in what he regarded as a very dangerous stage of the journey. We ventured to suggest that we were only four in number, while his party still included sixteen men; and as we were to go forward and they were to follow, a full proportion of

11   the perils he apprehended would fall upon us. But the austerity of the Captain's features would not relax. "A very extraordinary proceeding, gentlemen!" and repeating

12   this, he rode off to confer with his principal.

Before sunrise on the next morning our tent was down, we harnessed our best horses to the cart, and left the camp. But first we shook hands with our friends the emigrants, who sincerely wished us a safe journey, though some others of the party might easily have been consoled had we encountered an Indian war-party on the way. The Captain and his brother were standing on the top of a hill, wrapped in their plaids, like spirits of the mist, keeping an anxious eye on the band of horses below. We waved adieu to them as we rode off the ground. The Captain replied with a salutation of the utmost dignity, which Jack tried to imi-

13   tate, though not with perfect success.

In five minutes we had gained the foot of the hills, but here we came to a stop. Hendrick was in the shafts, and being the incarnation of perverse and brutish obstinacy, he utterly refused to move. Deslauriers lashed and swore till he was tired, but Hendrick stood like a rock, grumbling to himself and looking askance at his enemy, until he saw a favorable opportunity to take his revenge, when he struck out under the shaft with such cool malignity of intention that Deslauriers only escaped the blow by a sudden skip into the air, such as no one but a Frenchman could achieve. Shaw and he then joined forces, and lashed on both sides at once. The brute stood still for a while, till he could bear it no longer, when he began to kick and plunge till he threatened the utter demolition of the cart and harness. We glanced back at the camp, which was in full sight. Our companions, inspired by emulation, were levelling their tents and driving in their cattle and horses.

"Take the horse out," said I.

I took the saddle from Pontiac and put it upon Hendrick; the former was harnessed to the cart in an instant. "*Avance donc!*" cried Deslauriers. Pontiac strode up the hill, twitching the little cart after him as if it were a feather's weight; and though, as we gained the top we saw the wagons of our deserted comrades just getting into motion, we had little fear that they could overtake us.

Leaving the trail, we struck directly across the country, and took the shortest cut to reach the main stream of the Platte. A deep ravine suddenly intercepted us. We followed its sides until we found them less abrupt, and then plunged through in the best way we could. Passing behind the sandy ravines called "Ash Hollow," we stopped for a short nooning at the side of a pool of rain-water; but soon resumed our journey, and some hours before sunset descended the ravines and gorges opening downward upon the Platte west of Ash Hollow. Our horses waded to the fetlock in sand; the sun scorched like fire, and the air swarmed with sand-flies and mosquitoes.

At last we gained the Platte. Following it for about five miles we saw, just as the sun was sinking, a great meadow, dotted with hundreds of cattle, and beyond them an encampment of emigrants. A party of them came out to meet us, looking upon us at first with cold and suspicious faces. Seeing four men, different in appearance and equipment from themselves, emerging from the hills, they had taken us for the van of the much-dreaded Mormons, whom they were very apprehensive of encountering. We made known our true character, and then they greeted us cordially. They expressed much surprise that so small a party should venture to traverse that region, though in fact such attempts are often made by trappers and Indian traders. We rode with them to their camp. The wagons, some fifty in number, with here and there a tent intervening, were arranged as usual in a circle; the best horses were picketed in the area within, and the whole circumference was glowing with the dusky light of fires, displaying the forms of the women and children who were crowded around them. This patriarchal scene was curious and striking enough; but we made our escape from the place with all possible dispatch, being tormented by the intrusive questioning of the men who thronged about us. Yankee curiosity was nothing to theirs. They demanded our names, whence we came, whither we were going, and what was our business. The last query was particularly embarrassing; since travelling in that country, or indeed anywhere, from any other motive than gain, was an idea of which they took no cognizance. Yet they were fine-looking fellows, with an air of frankness, generosity, and even courtesy, having come from one of the least barbarous of the frontier counties. 16

We passed about a mile beyond them, and encamped. Being too few in number to stand guard without excessive fatigue, we extinguished our fire, lest it should attract the notice of wandering Indians; and, picketing our horses close around us, slept undisturbed till morning. For three days we travelled without interruption, and on the evening of the third encamped by the well-known spring on Scott's Bluff. 17

Henry Chatillon and I rode out in the morning, and, descending the western side of the Bluff, were crossing 18 the plain beyond. Something that seemed to me a file of buffalo came into view, descending the hills several miles before us. But Henry reined in his horse, and peering across the prairie with a better and more practised eye, soon discovered its real nature. "Indians!" he said. "Old Smoke's lodges, I b'lieve. Come; let us go! Wah! get up, now, ' Five Hundred Dollar.'" And laying on the lash with good will, he galloped forward, and I rode by his side. Not long after, a black speck became visible on the prairie full two miles off. It grew larger and larger; it assumed the form of a man and horse; and soon we could discern a naked Indian, careering at full gallop towards us. When within a furlong he wheeled his horse in a wide circle, and made him describe various mystic figures upon the prairie; Henry immediately compelled "Five Hundred Dollar" to execute similar evolutions. "It *is* Old Smoke's village," said he, interpreting 19 these signals; "did n't I say so?"

As the Indian approached we stopped to wait for him, when suddenly he vanished, sinking, as it were, into the earth. He had come upon one of the deep ravines that everywhere intersect these prairies.   In an instant the rough head of his horse stretched upward from the edge, and rider and steed came scrambling out, and bounded up to us; a sudden jerk of the rein brought the wild, panting horse to a full stop.   Then followed the needful formality of shaking hands.   I forget our visitor's name.   He was a young fellow, of no note in his nation; yet in his person and equipments he was a good specimen of a Dakota warrior in his ordinary travelling dress.   Like most of his people he was nearly six feet high; lithely and gracefully, yet strongly proportioned; and with a skin singularly clear and delicate.   He wore no paint; his head was bare; and his long hair was gathered in a clump behind, to the top of which was attached transversely, both by way of ornament and of talisman, the mystic whistle, made of the wing-bone of the war-eagle, and endowed with various magic virtues.   From the back of his head descended a line of glittering brass plates, tapering from the size of a doubloon to that of a half-dime, a cumbrous ornament, in high vogue among the Dakota, and for which they pay the traders a most extravagant price.   His chest and arms were naked; the buffalo robe, worn over them when at rest, had fallen about his waist, and was confined there by a belt. This, with the gay moccasins on his feet, completed his attire.   For arms he carried a quiver of dog-skin at his back, and a rude but powerful bow in his hand.   His horse had no bridle; a cord of hair, lashed around his jaw, served in place of one.   The saddle was made of wood covered with raw hide, and both pommel and cantle rose perpendicularly full eighteen inches, so that the warrior was wedged firmly in his seat, whence nothing could dislodge him but the bursting of the girths.

Advancing with our new companion, we found more of

his people, seated in a circle on the top of a hill; while a
rude procession came straggling down the neighboring hollow, men, women, and children, with horses dragging the
lodge-poles behind them. All that morning, as we moved
forward, tall savages were stalking silently about us. At

22   noon we reached Horse Creek. The main body of the Indians had arrived before us. On the farther bank stood a large and strong man, nearly naked, holding a white horse by a long cord, and eying us as we approached. This was the chief, whom Henry called "Old Smoke." Just behind him, his youngest and favorite squaw sat astride a fine mule, covered with caparisons of whitened skins, garnished with blue and white beads, and fringed with little ornaments of metal that tinkled with every movement of the animal. The girl had a light clear complexion, enlivened by a spot of vermilion on each cheek; she smiled, not to say grinned, upon us, showing two gleaming rows of white teeth. In her hand she carried the tall lance of her unchivalrous lord, fluttering with feathers; his round white shield hung at the side of her mule; and his pipe was slung at her back. Her dress was a tunic of deer-skin, made beautifully white by means of a species of clay found on the prairie, ornamented with beads, arranged in figures more gay than tasteful, and with long fringes at all the seams. Not far from the chief stood a group of stately figures, their white buffalo-robes thrown over their shoulders, gazing coldly upon us; and in the rear for several acres, the ground was covered with a temporary encampment. Warriors, women, and children swarmed like bees; hundreds of dogs, of all sizes and colors, ran restlessly about; and, close at hand, the wide shallow stream was alive with boys, girls, and young squaws, splashing, screaming, and laughing in the water. At the same time a long train of emigrants with their heavy wagons was crossing the creek, and dragging on in slow procession by the encampment of the people whom they and their descendants, in the space of a century, are to sweep from the face of

23   the earth.

The encampment itself was merely a temporary bivouac during the heat of the day. None of the lodges were pitched; but their heavy leather coverings, and the long poles used to support them, were scattered everywhere, among weapons, domestic utensils, and the rude harness of mules and horses. The squaws of each lazy warrior had made him a shelter from the sun, by stretching a few buffalo-robes, or the corner of a lodge-covering, upon poles; and here he sat in the shade, with a favorite young squaw, perhaps, at his side, glittering with all imaginable trinkets. Before him stood the insignia of his rank as a warrior, his white shield of bull-hide, his medicine-bag, his bow and quiver, his lance and his pipe, raised aloft on a tripod of poles. Except the dogs, the most active and noisy tenants of the camp were the old women, ugly as Macbeth's witches, with hair streaming loose in the wind, and nothing but the tattered fragment of an old buffalo-robe to hide their shrivelled limbs. The day of their favoritism passed two generations ago; now, the heaviest labors of the camp devolved upon them; they must harness the horses, pitch the lodges, dress the buffalo-robes, and bring in meat for the hunters. With the cracked voices of these hags, the clamor of dogs, the shouting and laughing of children and girls, and the listless tranquillity of the warriors, the whole scene had an effect too lively and picturesque to be forgotten. 24

We stopped not far from the Indian camp, and having invited some of the chiefs and warriors to dinner, placed before them a repast of biscuit and coffee. Squatted in a half-circle on the ground, they soon disposed of it. As we rode forward on the afternoon journey, several of our late guests accompanied us. Among the rest was a bloated savage, of more than three hundred pounds' weight, christened, *Le Cochon* in consideration of his preposterous dimensions, 25 26 and certain corresponding traits of his character. "The Hog" bestrode a little white pony, scarcely able to bear up under the enormous burden, though, by way of keeping up the necessary stimulus, the rider kept both feet in constant motion, playing alternately against his ribs. The old man was not a chief; he never had ambition enough to become one; he was not a warrior nor a hunter, for he was too fat and lazy; but he was the richest man in the village. Riches among the Dakota consist in horses, and of these "The Hog" had accumulated more than thirty. He had already ten times as many as he wanted, yet still his appetite for horses was insatiable. Trotting up to me, he shook me by the hand and gave me to understand that he was my devoted friend; then he began a series of signs and gesticulation, his oily countenance radiant with smiles, and his little eyes peeping out with a cunning twinkle from between the masses of flesh that almost obscured them. Knowing nothing at that time of the sign-language of the Indians, I could only guess at his meaning. So I called on Henry to explain it.

27

"The Hog," it seems, was anxious to conclude a matrimonial bargain, and barter one of his daughters for my horse. These overtures I chose to reject; at which "The Hog," still laughing with undiminished good humor, gathered his robe about his shoulders, and rode away.

28

Where we encamped that night, an arm of the Platte ran between high bluffs; it was turbid and swift as heretofore, but trees were growing on its crumbling banks, and there was a nook of grass between the water and the hill. Just before entering this place, we saw the emigrants encamping two or three miles distant on the right; while the whole Indian rabble were pouring down the neighboring hill in hope of the same sort of entertainment which they had experi-

29

enced from us. In the savage landscape before our camp,
nothing but the rushing of the Platte broke the silence.
Through the ragged boughs of the trees, dilapidated and
half dead, we saw the sun setting in crimson behind the
peaks of the Black Hills; the restless bosom of the river   30
was suffused with red; our white tent was tinged with it,
and the sterile bluffs, up to the rocks that crowned them,
partook of the same fiery hue. It soon passed away; no
light remained but that from our fire, blazing high among
the dusky trees and bushes, while we lay around it wrapped
in our blankets, smoking and conversing through half the
night.

We crossed a sun-scorched plain on the next morning;
the line of old cotton-wood trees that fringed the bank of
the Platte forming its extreme verge. Nestled close beneath them, we could discern in the distance something
like a building. As we came nearer, it assumed form and   31
dimensions, and proved to be a rough structure of logs. It
was a little trading fort, belonging to two private traders;
and originally intended, like all the forts of the country, to
form a hollow square, with rooms for lodging and storage
opening upon the area within. Only two sides of it had
been completed; the place was now as ill-fitted for the
purposes of defence as any of those little log-houses which
upon our constantly shifting frontier have been so often
successfully held against overwhelming odds of Indians.
Two lodges were pitched close to the fort; the sun beat
scorching upon the logs; no living thing was stirring except one old squaw, who thrust her round head from the
opening of the nearest lodge, and three or four stout
young puppies, who were peeping with looks of eager inquiry from under the covering. In a moment a door
opened, and a little, swarthy, black-eyed Frenchman came

out. His dress was rather singular; his black curling hair was parted in the middle of his head, and fell below his shoulders; he wore a tight frock of smoked deer-skin, gayly ornamented with figures worked in dyed porcupine-quills. His moccasins and leggings were also gaudily adorned in the same manner; and the latter had in addition a line of long fringes, reaching down the seams. The small frame of Richard, for by this name Henry made him known to us,

32 was in the highest degree athletic and vigorous. There was no superfluity, and indeed there seldom is among the white men of this country, but every limb was compact and hard; every sinew had its full tone and elasticity, and the whole man wore an air of mingled hardihood and buoyancy.

33 Richard committed our horses to a Navaho slave, a mean-looking fellow, taken prisoner on the Mexican frontier; and, relieving us of our rifles with ready politeness, led the way into the principal apartment of his establishment. This was a room ten feet square. The walls and floor were of black mud, and the roof of rough timber; there was a huge fire-place made of four flat rocks, picked up on the prairie. An Indian bow and otter-skin quiver, several gaudy articles of Rocky Mountain finery, an Indian medicine-bag, and a pipe and tobacco-pouch garnished the walls, and rifles rested in a corner. There was no furniture except a sort of rough settle, covered with buffalo-robes, upon which lolled a tall half-breed with his hair glued in masses upon each temple, and saturated with vermilion. Two or three more "mountain

34 men" sat cross-legged on the floor. Their attire was not unlike that of Richard himself; but the most striking figure of the group was a naked Indian boy of sixteen, with a handsome face, and light, active proportions, who sat in an easy posture in the corner near the door. Not one of his limbs

moved the breadth of a hair; his eye was fixed immovably, not on any person present, but, as it appeared, on the projecting corner of the fireplace opposite to him.   35

On the prairie the custom of smoking with friends is seldom omitted whether among Indians or whites. The pipe, therefore, was taken from the wall, and its red bowl crammed with the tobacco and *shongsasha*, mixed in suitable   36 proportions. Then it passed round the circle, each man inhaling a few whiffs and handing it to his neighbor. Having spent half an hour here we took our leave; first inviting our new friends to drink a cup of coffee with us at our camp a mile farther up the river.

By this time we had grown rather shabby; our clothes had burst into rags and tatters; and, what was worse, we had little means of renovation. Fort Laramie was but seven miles before us. Being averse to appearing in such a plight among any society that could boast an approximation to the civilized, we stopped by the river to make our toilet in the best way we could. We hung up small looking-glasses   37 against the trees and shaved, an operation neglected for six weeks; we performed our ablutions in the Platte, though the utility of such a proceeding was questionable, the water looking exactly like a cup of chocolate, and the banks consisting of the softest and richest yellow mud, so that we were obliged, as a preliminary, to build a causeway of branches and twigs. Having also put on radiant moccasins, procured from a squaw of Richard's establishment, and made what other improvements our narrow circumstances allowed, we took our seats on the grass with a feeling of greatly increased respectability, to await the arrival of our guests. They came; the banquet was concluded, and the pipe smoked. Bidding them adieu, we turned our horses' heads towards the fort.

An hour elapsed. The barren hills closed across our front, and we could see no farther; until, having surmounted them, a rapid stream appeared at the foot of the descent, running into the Platte; beyond was a green meadow, dotted with bushes, and in the midst of these, at the point where the two rivers joined, were the low

38 clay walls of a fort. This was not Fort Laramie, but another post, of less recent date, which having sunk before its successful competitor, was now deserted and ruinous. A moment after, the hills seeming to draw apart as we

39 advanced, disclosed Fort Laramie itself, its high bastions and perpendicular walls of clay crowning an eminence on the left beyond the stream, while behind stretched a line of arid and desolate ridges, and behind these again, towering seven thousand feet aloft, rose the grim Black Hills.

We tried to ford Laramie Creek at a point nearly opposite the fort, but the stream, swollen with rains, was too rapid. We passed up along its bank to find a better crossing-place. Men gathered on the wall to look at us. "There's Bordeaux!" called Henry, his face brightening as he recognized his acquaintance; "him there with the spy-glass; and there's old Vaskiss, and Tucker, and May;

40 and, by George! there's Simoneau." This Simoneau was Henry's fast friend, and the only man in the country who could rival him in hunting.

We soon found a ford. Henry led the way, the pony approaching the bank with a countenance of cool indifference, bracing his feet and sliding into the stream with the most unmoved composure. We followed; the water boiled against our saddles, but our horses bore us easily through. The unfortunate little mules were near going down with the current, cart and all; and we watched them with some solicitude scrambling over the loose round stones at the bottom, and bracing stoutly against the stream. All landed safely at last; we crossed a little plain, descended a hollow, and riding up a steep bank, found ourselves before the gateway of Fort Laramie, under the impending blockhouse erected above it to defend the entrance.

CHAPTER IX.

SCENES AT FORT LARAMIE.

2 LOOKING back, after the expiration of a year, upon Fort Laramie and its inmates, they seem less like a reality than like some fanciful picture of the olden time; so different was the scene from any which this tamer side of the world can present. Tall Indians, enveloped in their white buffalo-robes, were striding across the area or reclining at full length on the low roofs of the buildings which enclosed it. Numerous squaws, gayly bedizened, sat grouped in front of the rooms they occupied; their mongrel offspring, restless and vociferous, rambled in every direction through the fort; and 3 the trappers, traders, and *engagés* of the establishment were busy at their labor or their amusements.

We were met at the gate, but by no means cordially welcomed. Indeed we seemed objects of some distrust and suspicion, until Henry Chatillon explained that we were not traders, and we, in confirmation, handed to the *bour-* 4 *geois* a letter of introduction from his principals. He took it, turned it upside down, and tried hard to read it; but his literary attainments not being adequate to the task, he applied for relief to the clerk, a sleek, smiling French- 5 man, named Monthalon. The letter read, Bordeaux (the *bourgeois*) seemed gradually to awaken to a sense of what was expected of him. Though not deficient in hospitable intentions, he was wholly unaccustomed to act as master of ceremonies. Discarding all formalities of reception, he

did not honor us with a single word, but walked swiftly across the area, while we followed in some admiration to a railing and a flight of steps opposite the entrance. He signed to us that we had better fasten our horses to the railing; then he walked up the steps, tramped along a rude balcony, and, kicking open a door, displayed a large room, rather more elaborately furnished than a barn. For furniture it had a rough bedstead, but no bed, two chairs, a chest of drawers, a tin pail to hold water, and a board to cut tobacco upon. A brass crucifix hung on the wall, and close at hand a recent scalp, with hair full a yard long, was suspended from a nail. I shall again have occasion to mention this dismal trophy, its history being connected with that of our subsequent proceedings.

6

This apartment, the best in Fort Laramie, was that usually occupied by the legitimate *bourgeois*, Papin, in whose absence the command devolved upon Bordeaux. The latter, a stout, bluff little fellow, much inflated by a sense of his new authority, began to roar for buffalo-robes. These being brought and spread upon the floor formed our beds, — much better ones than we had of late been accustomed to. Our arrangements made, we stepped out to the balcony to take a more leisurely survey of the long looked-for haven at which we had arrived at last. Beneath us was the square area surrounded by little rooms, or rather cells, which opened upon it. These were devoted to various purposes, but served chiefly for the accommodation of the men employed at the fort, or of the equally numerous squaws whom they were allowed to maintain in it. Opposite to us rose the blockhouse above the gateway; it was adorned with the figure of a horse at full speed, daubed upon the boards with red paint, and exhibiting a degree of skill which might rival that displayed by the Indians in executing similar designs upon their robes and lodges. A busy scene was enacting in the area. The wagons of Vaskiss, an old trader, were about to set out for a remote post in the mountains, and the Canadians were going through their preparations with all

possible bustle, while here and there an Indian stood looking on with imperturbable gravity.

Fort Laramie is one of the posts established by the "American Fur Company," which well-nigh monopolizes the Indian trade of this region. Here its officials rule with an absolute sway; the arm of the United States has little force; for when we were there, the extreme outposts of her troops were about seven hundred miles to the eastward. The little fort is built of bricks dried in the sun, and externally is of an oblong form, with bastions of clay, in the form of ordinary blockhouses, at two of the corners. The walls are about fifteen feet high, and surmounted by a slender palisade. The roofs of the apartments within, which are built close against the walls, serve the purpose of a banquette. Within, the fort is divided by a partition: on one side is the square area, surrounded by the store-rooms, offices, and apartments of the inmates; on the other is the *corral*, a narrow place, encompassed by the high clay walls, where at night, or in presence of dangerous Indians, the horses and mules of the fort are crowded for safe keeping. The main entrance has two gates, with an arched passage intervening. A little square

window, high above the ground, opens laterally from an
adjoining chamber into this passage; so that when the inner
gate is closed and barred, a person without may still hold
communication with those within, through this narrow aperture.   This obviates the necessity of admitting suspicious
Indians, for purposes of trading, into the body of the
fort; for when danger is apprehended, the inner gate is shut
fast, and all traffic is carried on by means of the window.
This precaution, though necessary at some of the Company's
posts, is seldom resorted to at Fort Laramie; where, though
men are frequently killed in the neighborhood, no apprehensions are felt of any general designs of hostility from
the Indians.

We did not long enjoy our new quarters undisturbed.
The door was silently pushed open, and two eyeballs and
a visage as black as night looked in upon us; then a red
arm and shoulder intruded themselves, and a tall Indian,
gliding in, shook us by the hand, grunted his salutation,
and sat down on the floor.   Others followed, with faces
of the natural hue, and letting fall their heavy robes from
their shoulders, took their seats, quite at ease, in a semi-
circle before us.   The pipe was now to be lighted and
passed from one to another; and this was the only entertainment that at present they expected from us.   These
visitors were fathers, brothers, or other relatives of the
squaws in the fort, where they were permitted to remain,
loitering about in perfect idleness.   All those who smoked
with us were men of standing and repute.   Two or three
others dropped in also; young fellows who neither by their
years nor their exploits were entitled to rank with the old
men and warriors, and who, abashed in the presence of
their superiors, stood aloof, never withdrawing their eyes
from us.   Their cheeks were adorned with vermilion, their

ears with pendants of shell, and their necks with beads. Never yet having signalized themselves as hunters, or performed the honorable exploit of killing a man, they were held in slight esteem, and were diffident and bashful in proportion. Certain formidable inconveniences attended this influx of visitors. They were bent on inspecting everything in the room; our equipments and our dress alike underwent their scrutiny, for though the contrary has been asserted, few beings have more curiosity than Indians in regard to subjects within their ordinary range of thought. As to other matters, indeed, they seem utterly indifferent. They will not trouble themselves to inquire into what they cannot comprehend, but are quite contented to place their hands over their mouths in token of wonder, and exclaim that it is "great medicine." With this comprehensive solution, an Indian never is at a loss. He never launches into speculation and conjecture; his reason moves in its beaten track. His soul is dormant; and no exertions of the missionaries, Jesuit or Puritan, of the old world or of the new, have as yet availed to arouse it.

As we were looking, at sunset, from the wall, upon the desolate plains that surround the fort, we observed a cluster of strange objects like scaffolds, rising in the distance against the red western sky. They bore aloft some singular-looking burdens; and at their foot glimmered something white, like bones. This was the place of sepulture of some Dakota chiefs, whose remains their people are fond of placing in the vicinity of the fort, in the hope that they may thus be protected from violation at the hands of their enemies. Yet it has happened more than once, and quite recently, that war parties of the Crow Indians, ranging through the country, have thrown the bodies from the scaffolds, and broken them to pieces, amid the yells of the

Dakota, who remained pent up in the fort, too few to defend the honored relics from insult. The white objects upon the ground were buffalo skulls, arranged in the mystic circle commonly seen at Indian places of sepulture upon the prairie.

13

We soon discovered, in the twilight, a band of fifty or sixty horses approaching the fort. These were the animals belonging to the establishment; who, having been sent out to feed, under the care of armed guards, in the meadows below, were now being driven into the *corral* for the night. A gate opened into this inclosure; by the side of it stood one of the guards, an old Canadian, with gray bushy eyebrows, and a dragoon pistol stuck into his belt; while his comrade, mounted on horseback, his rifle laid across the saddle in front, and his long hair blowing before his swarthy face, rode

at the rear of the disorderly troop, urging them up the ascent. In a moment the narrow *corral* was thronged with the half-wild horses, kicking, biting, and crowding restlessly together.

The discordant jingling of a bell, rung by a Canadian in the area, summoned us to supper. The repast was served on a rough table in one of the lower apartments of the fort, and consisted of cakes of bread and dried buffalo meat, an excellent thing for strengthening the teeth. At this meal were seated the *bourgeois* and superior dignitaries of the establishment, among whom Henry Chatillon was worthily included. No sooner was it finished than the table was spread a second time (the luxury of bread being now, however, omitted), for the benefit of certain hunters and trappers of an inferior standing; while the ordinary Canadian *engagés* were regaled on dried meat in one of their lodging rooms. By way of illustrating the domestic economy of Fort Laramie, it may not be amiss to introduce in this place a story current among the men when we were there.

There was an old man named Pierre, whose duty it was to bring the meat from the store-room for the men. Old Pierre, in the kindness of his heart, used to select the fattest and the best pieces for his companions. This did not long escape the keen-eyed *bourgeois*, who was greatly disturbed at such improvidence, and cast about for some means to stop it. At last he hit on a plan that exactly suited him. At the side of the meat-room, and separated from it by a clay partition, was another apartment, used for the storage of furs. It had no communication with the fort, except through a square hole in the partition; and of course it was perfectly dark. One evening the *bourgeois*, watching for a moment when no one observed him, dodged into the meat-room, clambered through the hole, and ensconced himself among the furs and buffalo-robes. Soon after, old Pierre came in with his lantern, and muttering to himself, began to pull over the bales of meat and select the best pieces, as usual. But suddenly a hollow and sepulchral voice proceeded from the inner room: "Pierre, Pierre! Let that fat meat alone. Take nothing but lean." Pierre dropped his lantern, and bolted out into the fort, screaming, in an agony of terror, that the devil was in the store-room; but tripping on the threshold, he pitched over upon the gravel, and lay senseless, stunned by the fall. The Canadians ran out to the rescue. Some lifted the unlucky Pierre; and others, making an extempore crucifix of two sticks, were proceeding to attack the devil in his stronghold, when the *bourgeois*, with a crestfallen countenance, appeared at the door. To add to his mortification, he was obliged to explain the whole stratagem to Pierre, in order to bring him to his senses.

We were sitting, on the following morning, in the passage-way between the gates, conversing with the traders Vaskiss and May. These two men, together with our sleek friend, the clerk Monthalon, were, I believe, the only persons then in the fort who could read and write. May was telling a curious story about the traveller Catlin, when an ugly, diminutive Indian, wretchedly mounted, came up at a gallop, and rode by us into the fort. On being questioned, he said that Smoke's village was close at hand. Accordingly only a few minutes elapsed before the hills beyond the river were covered with a disorderly swarm of savages, on horseback and on foot. May finished his story; and by that time the whole array had descended to Laramie Creek, and begun to cross it in a mass. I walked down to the bank. The stream is wide, and was then between three and four feet deep, with a swift current. For several rods the water was alive with dogs, horses, and Indians. The long poles used in pitching the lodges are carried by the horses, fastened by the heavier end, two or three on each side, to a rude sort of pack-saddle, while the other end drags on the ground. About a foot behind the horse, a kind of large basket or pannier is suspended between the poles, and firmly lashed in its place. On the back of the horse are piled various articles of luggage; the basket also is well filled with domestic utensils, or, quite as often, with a litter of puppies, a brood of small children, or a superannuated old man.   Numbers of these curious vehicles, *traineaux*, or, as the Canadians called them, *travois*, were now splashing together through the stream.   Among them swam countless dogs, often burdened with miniature *traineaux;* and dashing forward on h o r s e b a c k through the throng came the warriors, the slender figure of some lynx-eyed boy clinging fast behind them.   The women sat perched on the pack-saddles, adding not a little to the load of the already over-burdened horses. The confusion was prodigious.   T h e dogs yelled a n d howled in chorus; the puppies in the *travois* set up a dismal whine as the water invaded their comfortable re-treat; the little black-eyed children, from one year of age upward, clung fast with both hands to the edge of their basket, and looked over in alarm at the water rushing so near them, sputtering and making wry mouths as it splashed against their faces.   Some of the dogs, encumbered by their load, were carried down by the current, yelping piteously; and the old squaws would rush into the water, seize their favorites by the neck, and drag them out.   As each horse gained the bank, he scrambled up as he could.   Stray horses and colts came among the rest, often breaking away at full speed through the crowd, followed by the old hags, screaming after their fashion on all occasions of excitement.   Buxom young squaws, blooming in all the charms of vermilion, stood here and there on the bank, holding aloft their master's lance, as a signal to collect the scattered portions of his household.   In a few moments the crowd melted away; each family with its horses and equipage, filing off to the plain at the rear of the fort; and here, in the space of half an hour, arose sixty or seventy of their tapering lodges. Their horses were feeding by hundreds over the surrounding prairie, and their dogs were roaming everywhere.   The fort was full of warriors, and the children were whooping and yelling incessantly under the walls.

These new-comers were scarcely arrived, when Bordeaux ran across the fort, shouting to his squaw to bring him his spy-glass.   The obedient Marie, the very model of a squaw, produced the instrument, and Bordeaux hurried with it to the wall.   Pointing it eastward, he exclaimed, with an oath, that the families were coming.   But a few moments elapsed before the heavy caravan of the emigrant wagons could be seen, steadily advancing from the hills.   They gained the   17 river, and, without turning or pausing, plunged in, passed through, and slowly ascending the opposing bank, kept directly on their way by the fort and the Indian village, until, gaining a spot a quarter of a mile distant, they wheeled into a circle.   For some time our tranquillity was undisturbed.   The emigrants were preparing their encampment; but no sooner was this accomplished than Fort Laramie was taken by storm.   A crowd of broad-brimmed hats, thin visages, and staring eyes, appeared suddenly at the gate.   Tall, awkward men, in brown home-

8

spun, women, with cadaverous faces and long lank figures, came thronging in together, and, as if inspired by the very demon of curiosity, ransacked every nook and corner of the fort.   Dismayed at this invasion we withdrew in all

speed to our chamber, vainly hoping that it might prove a sanctuary.   The emigrants prosecuted their investigations with untiring vigor.   They penetrated the rooms, or rather dens, inhabited by the astonished squaws.   Resolved to search every mystery to the bottom, they explored the apartments of the men, and even that of Marie and the *bourgeois*.   At last a

18

numerous deputation appeared at our door, but found no encouragement to remain.

Having at length satisfied their curiosity, they next proceeded to business.   The men occupied themselves in procuring supplies for their onward journey,— either buying them,

19   or giving in exchange superfluous articles of their own.

The emigrants felt a violent prejudice against the French

20   Indians, as they called the trappers and traders.   They thought, and with some reason, that these men bore them no good-will.   Many of them were firmly persuaded that the French were instigating the Indians to attack and cut them off.   On visiting the encampment we were at once struck with the extraordinary perplexity and indecision that

prevailed among them.   They seemed like men totally out
of their element,— bewildered and amazed, like a troop of
schoolboys lost in the woods.   It was impossible to be
long among them without being conscious of the bold
spirit with which most of them were animated.   But the
forest is the home of the backwoodsman.   On the remote
prairie he is totally at a loss.   He differs as much from
the genuine "mountain-man" as a Canadian voyageur, pad-
dling his canoe on the rapids of the Ottawa, differs from
an American sailor among the storms of Cape Horn.   Still
my companion and I were somewhat at a loss to account
for this perturbed state of mind.   It could not be cowardice; these men were of the same stock with the volunteers
of Monterey and Buena Vista.   Yet, for the most part, they   21
were the rudest and most ignorant of the frontier population; they knew absolutely nothing of the country and its
inhabitants; they had already experienced much misfortune,
and apprehended more; they had seen nothing of mankind,
and had never put their own resources to the test.

   A full share of suspicion fell upon us.   Being strangers,
we were looked upon as enemies.   Having occasion for a
supply of lead and a few other necessary articles, we used
to go over to the emigrant camps to obtain them.   After
some hesitation, some dubious glances, and fumbling of
the hands in the pockets, the terms would be agreed upon,
the price tendered, and the emigrant would go off to bring
the article in question.   After waiting until our patience
gave out, we would go in search of him, and find him seated
on the tongue of his wagon.

   "Well, stranger," he would observe, as he saw us approach, "I reckon I won't trade."

   Some friend of his had followed him from the scene of
the bargain, and whispered in his ear that clearly we

22   meant to cheat him, and he had better have nothing to do with us.

This timorous mood of the emigrants was doubly unfortunate, as it exposed them to real danger. Assume, in the presence of Indians, a bold bearing, self-confident yet vigilant, and you will find them tolerably safe neighbors. But your safety depends on the respect and fear you are able to inspire. If you betray timidity or indecision, you convert them from that moment into insidious and dangerous enemies. The Dakota saw clearly enough the perturbation of the emigrants, and instantly availed themselves of it. They became extremely insolent and exacting in their demands. It has become an established custom with them to go to the camp of every party, as it arrives in succession at the fort, and demand a feast. Smoke's village had come with this express design, having made several days' journey with no other object than that of enjoying a cup of coffee and two or three biscuit. So the "feast" was demanded, and the emigrants dared not refuse it.

One evening about sunset the village was deserted. We met old men, warriors, squaws, and children in gay attire, trooping off to the encampment with faces of anticipation; and, arriving here, they seated themselves in a semi-circle. Smoke occupied the centre, with his warriors on either hand; the young men and boys came next, and the squaws and children formed the horns of the crescent. The biscuit and coffee were promptly despatched, the emigrants staring open-mouthed at their savage guests.   With each emigrant party that arrived at Fort Laramie this scene was renewed; and every day the Indians grew more rapacious and presumptuous. One evening they broke in pieces, out of mere wantonness, the cups from which they had been feasted; and this so exasperated the emigrants that many of them seized their rifles and could scarcely be restrained from firing on the insolent mob of Indians. Before we left the country this dangerous spirit on the part of the Dakota had mounted to a yet higher pitch. They began openly to threaten the emigrants with destruction, and actually fired upon one or two parties of them. A military force and military law are urgently called for in that perilous region; and unless troops are speedily stationed at Fort Laramie, or elsewhere in the neighborhood, both emigrants and other travellers will be exposed to most imminent risks.

The Ogillallah, the Brulé, and the other western bands of the Dakota or Sioux, are thorough savages, unchanged by any contact with civilization. Not one of them can speak a European tongue, or has ever visited an American settlement. Until within a year or two, when the emigrants began to pass through their country on the way to Oregon, they had seen no whites, except the few employed about the Fur Company's posts. They thought them a wise people, inferior only to themselves, living in leather lodges, like their own, and subsisting on buffalo. But when the swarm of *Meneaska*, with their oxen and wagons, began to invade them, their astonishment was unbounded. They could scarcely believe that the earth contained such a multitude of white men. Their wonder is now giving way to indignation; and the result, unless vigilantly guarded against, may be lamentable in the extreme.

But to glance at the interior of a lodge. Shaw and I used often to visit them. Indeed we spent most of our evenings in the Indian village, Shaw's assumption of the medical character giving us a fair pretext. As a sample of the rest I will describe one of these visits. The sun had just set, and the horses were driven into the *corral*.

The Prairie Cock, a noted beau, came in at the gate with a bevy of young girls, with whom he began a dance in the area, leading them round and round in a circle, while he jerked up from his chest a succession of monotonous

28 sounds, to which they kept time in a rueful chant.

Outside the gate boys and young men were idly frolicking; and close by, looking grimly upon them, stood a warrior in his robe, with his face painted jet-black, in token that he had lately taken a Pawnee scalp. Passing these, the tall dark lodges rose between us and the red western sky. We repaired at once to the lodge of Old Smoke himself. It was by no means better than the others; indeed, it was rather shabby; for in this democratic community the chief never assumes superior state. Smoke sat cross-legged on a buffalo-robe, and his grunt of salutation as we entered was unusually cordial, out of respect, no doubt, to Shaw's medical character. Seated around the lodge were several squaws, and an abundance of children. The complaint of Shaw's patients was, for the most part, a severe inflamma-

29 tion of the eyes, occasioned by exposure to the sun, a species of disorder which he treated with some success.

30 He had brought with him a homœopathic medicine-chest, and was, I presume, the first who introduced that harmless system of treatment among the Ogillallah. No sooner had a robe been spread at the head of the lodge for our accommodation, and we had seated ourselves upon it, than a patient made her appearance,—the chief's daughter herself, who, to do her justice, was the best-looking girl in the village.

Being on excellent terms with the physician, she placed herself readily under his hands, and submitted with a good grace to his applications, laughing in his face during the whole process, for a squaw hardly knows how to smile. This case despatched, another of a different kind succeeded. A hideous, emaciated old woman sat in the darkest corner of the lodge, rocking to and fro with pain, and hiding her eyes from the light by pressing the palms of both hands against her face. At Smoke's command she came forward, very unwillingly, and exhibited a pair of eyes that had nearly disappeared from excess of inflammation. No sooner had the doctor fastened his grip upon her, than she set up a dismal moaning, and writhed so in his grasp that he lost all patience; but being resolved to carry his point, he succeeded at last in applying his favorite remedies.

"It is strange," he said when the operation was finished, "that I forgot to bring any Spanish flies with me; we must have something here to answer for a counter-irritant."

So, in the absence of better, he seized upon a red-hot brand from the fire, and clapped it against the temple of the old squaw, who set up an unearthly howl, at which the rest of the family broke into a laugh.

During these medical operations Smoke's eldest squaw entered the lodge, with a mallet in her hand, the stone head of which, precisely like those sometimes ploughed up in the fields of New England, was made fast to the handle by a covering of raw hide. I had observed some time before a litter of well-grown black puppies, comfortably nestled among some buffalo-robes at one side; but this new-comer speedily disturbed their enjoyment; for seizing one of them by the hind paw, she dragged him out and carrying him to the entrance of the lodge, hammered him on the head till she killed him. Aware to what this preparation tended, I looked through a hole in the back of the lodge to see the next steps of the process. The squaw, holding the puppy by the legs, was swinging him to and fro through the blaze of a fire, until the hair was singed off. This done, she unsheathed her knife and cut him into small pieces, which she dropped into a kettle to boil. In a few moments a large wooden dish was set before us filled with this delicate preparation. A dog-feast is the greatest compliment a Dakota can offer to his guest; and, knowing that to refuse eating would be an affront, we attacked the little dog, and devoured him 31 before the eyes of his unconscious parent. Smoke in the mean time was preparing his great pipe. It was lighted when we had finished our repast, and we passed it from one to another till the bowl was empty. This done, we took our leave without further ceremony, knocked at the gate of the fort, and after making ourselves known, were 32 admitted.

CHAPTER X.

THE summer of 1846 was a season of warlike excitement among all the western bands of the Dakota. In 1845 they encountered great reverses. Many war parties had been sent out; some of them had been cut off, and others had returned broken and disheartened; so that the whole nation was in mourning. Among the rest, ten warriors had gone to the Snake country, led by the son of a prominent Ogillallah chief, called the Whirlwind. In passing over Laramie Plains they encountered a superior number of their enemies, were surrounded, and killed to a man. Having performed this exploit, the Snakes became alarmed, dreading the resentment of the Dakota, and they hastened therefore to signify their wish for peace by sending the scalp of the slain partisan, with a small parcel of tobacco attached, to his tribesmen and relations. They had employed old Vaskiss, the trader, as their messenger, and the scalp was the same that hung in our room at the fort. But the Whirlwind proved inexorable. Though his character hardly corresponds with his name, he is nevertheless an Indian, and hates the

Snakes with his whole soul.   Long before the scalp arrived
he had made his preparations for revenge.   He sent messengers with presents and tobacco to all the Dakota within
three hundred miles, proposing a grand combination to
chastise the Snakes, and naming a place and time of ren-
4   dezvous.   The plan was readily adopted, and at this moment
many villages, probably embracing in the whole five or six
thousand souls, were slowly creeping over the prairies and
5   tending toward the common centre at "La Bonté's camp"
on the Platte.   Here their warlike rites were to be celebrated with more than ordinary solemnity, and a thousand
warriors, as it was said, were to set out for the enemy's
country.   The characteristic result of this preparation will
appear in the sequel.

I was greatly rejoiced to hear of it.   I had come into
the country chiefly with a view of observing the Indian
6   character.   To accomplish my purpose it was necessary to
live in the midst of them, and become, as it were, one of
them.   I proposed to join a village, and make myself an
inmate of one of their lodges; and henceforward this narrative, so far as I am concerned, will be chiefly a record of
the progress of this design, and the unexpected impedi-
ments that opposed it.

We resolved on no account to miss the rendezvous at
"La Bonté's camp."   Our plan was to leave Deslauriers
at the fort, in charge of our equipage and the better part
of our horses, while we took with us nothing but our
weapons and the worst animals we had.   In all probability, jealousies and quarrels would arise among so many
hordes of fierce, impulsive savages, congregated together
under no common head, and many of them strangers from
7   remote prairies and mountains.   We were bound in common prudence to be cautious how we excited any feeling

of cupidity. This was our plan; but unhappily we were not destined to visit "La Bonté's camp" in this manner, for one morning a young Indian came to the fort and brought us evil tidings. The new-comer was an arrant dandy. His ugly face was painted with vermilion; on his head fluttered the tail of a prairie-cock (a large species of 8 pheasant, not found, as I have heard, eastward of the Rocky Mountains); in his ears were hung pendants of shell, and a flaming red blanket was wrapped around him. He carried a dragoon-sword in his hand, solely for display, since the knife, the arrow, and the rifle are the arbiters of every prairie fight; but as no one in this country goes abroad unarmed, the dandy carried a bow and arrows in an otter-skin quiver at his back. In this guise, and bestriding his yellow horse with an air of extreme dignity, "The Horse," 9 for that was his name, rode in at the gate, turning neither to the right nor the left, but casting glances askance at the groups of squaws who, with their mongrel progeny, were sitting in the sun before their doors. The evil tidings brought by "The Horse" were of the following import: The squaw of Henry Chatillon, a woman with whom he had been connected for years by the strongest ties which in that country exist between the sexes, was dangerously ill. She and her children were in the village of The Whirlwind, at the distance of a few days' journey. Henry was anxious to see the woman before she died, and provide for the safety and support of his children, of whom he was extremely fond. To have refused him this would have been inhumanity. We abandoned our plan of joining Smoke's village and proceeding with it to the rendezvous, and determined to meet The Whirlwind, and go in his company.

I had been slightly ill for several weeks, but on the third night after reaching Fort Laramie a violent pain awoke me,

and I found myself attacked by the same disorder that occa-
10 sioned such heavy losses to the army on the Rio Grande.
In a day and a half I was reduced to extreme weakness, so
that I could not walk without pain and effort.   Having no

medical   adviser,
nor any choice of
diet, I resolved to
throw myself up-
on Providence for
recovery,   using,
without regard to
the disorder, any
portion of strength
that might remain
11   to me.   So on the
twentieth of June
we set out from

Fort Laramie to meet The Whirlwind's village.   Though
aided by the high-bowed "mountain-saddle," I could scarcely
keep my seat on horseback.   Before we left the fort we hired
12 another man, a long-haired Canadian, named Raymond, with
a face like an owl's, contrasting oddly enough with Deslauriers's mercurial countenance.   This was not the only
reinforcement to our party.   A vagrant Indian trader,
13 named Reynal, joined us, together with his squaw Margot, and her two nephews, our dandy friend, "The Horse,"
and his younger brother, "The Hail Storm."   Thus accompanied we betook ourselves to the prairie, leaving the beaten
trail, and passing over the desolate hills that flank the valley of Laramie Creek.   In all, Indians and whites, we
counted eight men and one woman.

Reynal, the trader, the image of sleek and selfish complacency, carried "The Horse's" dragoon-sword in his

hand, delighting apparently in this useless parade; for, from spending half his life among Indians, he had caught not only their habits but their ideas. Margot, a female 14 animal of more than two hundred pounds' weight, was crouched in the basket of a *travois*, such as I have before described; besides her ponderous bulk, various domestic utensils were attached to the vehicle, and she led by a trail-rope a packhorse, which carried the covering of Reynal's lodge. Deslauriers walked briskly by the side of the cart, and Raymond came behind, swearing at the spare horses which it was his business to drive. The restless young Indians, their quivers at their backs and their bows in their hands, galloped over the hills, often starting a wolf or an antelope from the thick growth of wild-sage bushes. Shaw and I were in keeping with the rest of the rude cavalcade, having, in the failure of other clothing, adopted the buckskin attire of the trappers. Henry Chatillon rode in advance of the whole. Thus we passed hill after hill and hollow after hollow, a country arid, broken, and so parched by the sun that none of the plants familiar to our more favored soil would flourish upon it, though there were multitudes of strange medicinal herbs, more especially the wild sage, which covered every declivity, 15 while cacti were hanging like reptiles at the edges of every ravine. At length we ascended a high hill, our horses treading upon pebbles of flint, agate, and rough jasper, until, gaining the top, we looked down on the wild bottoms of Laramie Creek, which far below us wound like a writhing snake from side to side of the narrow interval, amid a growth of shattered cotton-wood and ash trees. Lines of tall cliffs, white as chalk, shut in this green strip of woods and meadow-land, into which we descended and encamped for the night. In the morning we passed 16 a wide grassy plain by the river; there was a grove in front, and beneath its shadows the ruins of an old trading fort of logs. The grove bloomed with myriads of wild roses, with their sweet perfume fraught with recollections of home. As we emerged from the trees, a rattlesnake, as large as a man's arm, and more than four feet long, lay coiled on a rock, fiercely rattling and hissing at us; a gray hare, twice as large as those of New England, leaped up from the tall ferns; curlew flew screaming over our heads, and a host of little prairie-dogs sat yelping at us at the mouths of their burrows on the dry plain beyond. Suddenly an antelope leaped up from the wild-sage bushes, gazed eagerly at us, and then, erecting his white tail, stretched away like a greyhound. The two Indian boys found a white wolf, as large as a calf, in a hollow, and giving a sharp yell, they galloped after him; but the wolf leaped into the stream and swam across. Then came the crack of a rifle, the bullet whistling harmlessly over his head, as he scrambled up the steep declivity, rattling down stones and earth into the water below. Advancing a little, we beheld, on the farther bank of the stream, a spectacle not common even in that region; for, emerging from among the trees, a herd of some two hundred elk came out upon the meadow, their antlers clattering as they walked forward in a dense throng. Seeing us, they broke into a run, rushing across the opening and disappearing among the trees and scattered groves. On our left was a barren prairie, stretching to the horizon; on our right, a deep gulf, with Laramie Creek at the bottom. We found ourselves at length at the edge of a steep descent, — a narrow valley, with long rank grass and scattered trees, stretching before us for a mile or more along the course of the stream. Reaching the farther end, we stopped and encamped. A huge old cotton-wood tree spread its branches horizontally over our tent. Laramie Creek, circling before our camp, half inclosed us; it swept along the bottom of a line of tall white cliffs that looked down on us from the farther bank. There were dense copses on our right; the cliffs, too, were half hidden by bushes, though behind us a few cotton-wood trees, dotting the green prairie, alone impeded the view, and friend or enemy could be discerned in that direction at a mile's distance. Here we resolved to remain and await the arrival of The Whirlwind, who would certainly pass this way in his progress towards La Bonté's camp. To go in search of him was not expedient, both on account of the broken and impracticable nature of the country, and the uncertainty of his position and movements; besides, our horses were almost worn out, and I was in no condition to travel. We had good grass, good water, tolerable fish from the stream, and plenty of small game, such as antelope and deer, though no buffalo. There was one little drawback to our satisfaction,—a certain extensive tract of bushes and dried grass, just behind us, which it was by no means advisable to enter, since it sheltered a numerous brood of rattlesnakes. Henry Chatillon again despatched "The Horse" to the village, with a message to his squaw that she and her relatives should leave the rest and push on as rapidly as possible to our camp.

Our daily routine soon became as regular as that of a well-ordered household. The weather-beaten old tree was in the centre; our rifles generally rested against its vast trunk, and our saddles were flung on the ground around it; its distorted roots were so twisted as to form one or two convenient arm-chairs, where we could sit in the shade and read or smoke; but meal-times became, on the whole,

the most interesting hours of the day and a bountiful provision was made for them.   An antelope or a deer usually
swung from a bough, and haunches were suspended against
the trunk.   That camp is daguerrotyped on my memory,—
the old tree, the white tent, with Shaw sleeping in the
shadow of it, and Reynal's miserable lodge close by the
bank of the stream.   It was a wretched oven-shaped structure, made of begrimed and tattered buffalo-hides stretched
over a frame of poles; one side was open, and at the side
of the opening hung the powder-horn and bullet-pouch of
the owner, together with his long red pipe, and a rich
quiver of otter-skin, with a bow and arrows; for Reynal,
an Indian in most things but color, chose to hunt buffalo
with these primitive weapons.   In the darkness of this
cavern-like habitation might be discerned Madame Margot, her overgrown bulk stowed away among her domestic
implements, furs, robes, blankets, and painted cases of
raw hide, in which dried meat is kept.   Here she sat
from sunrise to sunset, an impersonation of gluttony and
laziness, while her affectionate proprietor was smoking,
or begging petty gifts from us, or telling lies concerning his
own achievements, or perchance engaged in the more profit-
able occupation of cooking some preparation of prairie
delicacies.   Reynal was an adept at this work; he and
Deslauriers have joined forces, and are hard at work together over the fire, while Raymond spreads, by way of
table-cloth, a buffalo-hide carefully whitened with pipe-clay,
on the grass before the tent.   Here he arranges the teacups
and plates; and then creeping on all fours, like a dog,
thrusts his head in at the opening of the tent.   For a
moment we see his round, owlish eyes rolling wildly, as
if the idea he came to communicate had suddenly escaped
him; then collecting his scattered thoughts, as if by an

effort, he informs us that supper is ready, and instantly
withdraws.

When sunset came, and at that hour the wild and desolate scene would assume a new aspect, the horses were
driven in.   They had been grazing all day in the neighboring meadow, but now they were picketed close about
the camp.   As the prairie darkened we sat and conversed
around the fire, until, becoming drowsy, we spread our
saddles on the ground, wrapped our blankets around us,
and lay down.   We never placed a guard, having by this
time become too indolent; but Henry Chatillon folded
his loaded rifle in the same blanket with himself, observing that he always took it to bed with him when he
'camped in that place.   Henry was too bold a man to
use such a precaution without good cause.   We had a hint
now and then that our situation was none of the safest;
several Crow war-parties were known to be in the vicinity,
and one of them, that passed here some time before, had
peeled the bark from a neighboring tree, and engraved upon
the white wood certain hieroglyphics to signify that they   24
had invaded the territories of their enemies, the Dakota,
and set them at defiance.   One morning a thick mist covered the whole country.   Shaw and Henry went out to
ride, and soon came back with a startling piece of intelligence; they had found within rifle-shot of our camp the recent trail of about thirty horsemen.   They could not be
whites, and they could not be Dakota, since we knew no
such parties to be in the neighborhood; therefore they must
be Crows.   Thanks to that friendly mist, we had escaped
a hard battle; they would inevitably have attacked us and
our Indian companions had they seen our camp.   Whatever doubts we might have entertained were removed a
day or two after by two or three Dakota, who came

to us with an account of having hidden in a ravine on that very morning, from whence they saw and counted the Crows; they said that they followed them, carefully keeping out of sight, as they passed up Chugwater; that here the Crows discovered five dead bodies of Dakota, placed according to custom in trees, and flinging them to the ground, held their guns against them and blew them to atoms.

If our camp was not altogether safe, still it was comfortable enough; at least it was so to Shaw, for I was tormented with illness and vexed by the delay in the accomplishment of my designs. When a respite in my disorder gave me some returning strength, I rode out well armed upon the prairie, or bathed with Shaw in the stream, or waged a petty warfare with the inhabitants of a neighboring prairie-dog village. Around our fire at night we employed ourselves in inveighing against the fickleness and inconstancy of Indians, and execrating The Whirlwind and all his crew. At last the thing grew insufferable.

"To-morrow morning," said I, "I will start for the fort, and see if I can hear any news there." Late that evening, when the fire had sunk low and all the camp were asleep, a loud cry sounded from the darkness. Henry leaped up, recognized the voice, replied to it, and our dandy friend, "The Horse," rode in among us, just returned from his mission to the village. He coolly picketed his mare without saying a word, sat down by the fire, and began to eat; but his imperturbable philosophy was too much for our patience. Where was the village? — about fifty miles south of us; it was moving slowly, and would not arrive in less than a week. And where was Henry's squaw? — coming as fast as she could, with Mahto-Tatonka and the rest of her brothers, but she would never reach us, for she was dying, and asking every moment for Henry. Henry's manly face became clouded and downcast; he said that if we were willing he would go in the morning to find her, at which Shaw offered to accompany him.

26

We saddled our horses at sunrise. Reynal protested vehemently against being left alone, with nobody but the two Canadians and the young Indians, when enemies were in the neighborhood. Disregarding his complaints, we left him, and, coming to the mouth of Chugwater, separated, Shaw and Henry turning to the right, up the bank of the stream, while I made for the fort.

27

Taking leave for a while of my friend and the unfortunate squaw, I will relate by way of episode what I saw and did at Fort Laramie. It was not more than eighteen miles distant, and I reached it in three hours. A shrivelled little figure, wrapped from head to foot in a dingy white Canadian capote, stood in the gateway, holding by a cord of bull-hide a shaggy wild-horse, which he had lately caught. His sharp prominent features, and his keen, snake-like eyes, looked out from beneath the shadowy hood of the capote, which was drawn over his head like the cowl of a Capuchin friar. His face was like an old piece of leather, and his mouth spread from ear to ear. Extending his long, wiry hand, he welcomed me with something more cordial than the ordinary cold salute of an Indian, for we were excellent friends. We had made an exchange of horses to our mutual advantage; and Paul, thinking himself well treated, had declared everywhere that the white man had a good heart. He was a Dakota from the Missouri, a reputed son of the half-breed interpreter,

28 Pierre Dorion, so often mentioned in Irving's "Astoria." He said that he was going to Richard's trading-house to sell his horse to some emigrants who were encamped there, and asked me to go with him. We forded the stream together, Paul dragging his wild charge behind him. As we passed over the sandy plains beyond, he grew communicative. Paul was a cosmopolitan in his way; he had been to the settlements of the whites, and visited in peace and war most of the tribes within the range of a thousand miles. He spoke a jargon of French and another of English, yet nevertheless he was a thorough Indian; and as he told of the bloody deeds of his own people against their enemies, his little eyes would glitter with a fierce lustre. He told how the Dakota extermi-

29 nated a village of the Hohays on the Upper Missouri, slaughtering men, women, and children; and how, in overwhelming force, they cut off sixteen of the brave Delawares, who fought like wolves to the last, amid the throng of their enemies. He told me also another story, which I did not believe until I had heard it confirmed from so

many independent sources
that my skepticism was
almost overcome.

Six years ago, a fellow
named Jim Beckworth, a
mongrel of French, Amer-
ican, and negro blood, was
trading for the Fur Com-
pany, in a large village of
the Crows. Jim Beck-
worth was last summer at
St. Louis. He is a ruf-
fian of the worst stamp;
bloody and treacherous,
without honor or honesty;
such at least is the character he bears upon the
prairie. Yet in his case
the standard rules of character fail, for though he
will stab a man in his
sleep, he will also perform
desperate acts of daring;
such, for instance, as the
following: While he was
in the Crow village, a
Blackfoot war-party, be-
tween thirty and forty in
number, came stealing
through the country, killing stragglers and carry-
ing off horses. The Crow
warriors got upon their

30

trail and pressed them so closely that they could not escape; at which the Blackfeet, throwing up a semi-circular breastwork of logs at the foot of a precipice, coolly awaited their approach. The logs and sticks, piled four or five feet high, protected them in front. The Crows might have swept over the breastwork and exterminated their enemies; but though outnumbering them tenfold, they did not dream of storming the little fortification. Such a proceeding would be altogether repugnant to their notions of warfare. Whooping and yelling, and jumping from side to side like devils incarnate, they showered bullets and arrows upon the logs; not a Blackfoot was hurt, but several Crows, in spite of their leaping and dodging, were shot down. In this childish manner the fight went on for an hour or two. Now and then a Crow warrior in an ecstasy of valor and vainglory would scream out his war-song, boast himself the bravest and greatest of mankind, grasp his hatchet, rush up, strike it upon the breastwork, and then as he retreated to his companions, fall dead under a shower of arrows; yet no combined attack was made. The Blackfeet remained secure in their intrenchment. At last Jim Beckworth lost patience.

"You are all fools and old women," he said to the Crows; "come with me, if any of you are brave enough, and I will show you how to fight."

He threw off his trapper's frock of buckskin and stripped himself naked, like the Indians themselves. He left his rifle on the ground, took in his hand a small light hatchet, and ran over the prairie to the right, concealed by a hollow from the eyes of the Blackfeet. Then climbing up the rocks, he gained the top of the precipice behind them. Forty or fifty young Crow warriors followed him. By the cries and whoops that rose from below he knew that the

Blackfeet were just beneath him; and running forward he leaped down the rock into the midst of them. As he fell he caught one by the long loose hair, and dragging him down tomahawked him; then grasping another by the belt at his waist, he struck him also a stunning blow, and gaining his feet, shouted the Crow war-cry. He swung his hatchet so fiercely around him that the astonished Blackfeet bore back and gave him room. He might, had he chosen, have leaped over the breastwork and escaped; but this was not necessary, for with devilish yells the Crow warriors came dropping in quick succession over the rock among their enemies. The main body of the Crows, too, answered the cry from the front, and rushed up simultaneously. The convulsive struggle within the breastwork was frightful; for an instant the Blackfeet fought and yelled like pent-up tigers; but the butchery was soon complete, and the mangled bodies lay piled together under the precipice. Not a Blackfoot made his escape.

As Paul finished his story we came in sight of Richard's Fort, a disorderly crowd of men around it, and an emigrant camp a little in front.

"Now, Paul," said I, "where are your Minneconjou lodges?"

"Not come yet," said Paul; "maybe come to-morrow."

Two large villages of a band of Dakota had come three hundred miles from the Missouri, to join in the war, and they were expected to reach Richard's that morning. There was as yet no sign of their approach; so pushing through a noisy, drunken crowd, I entered an apartment of logs and mud, the largest in the fort; it was full of men of various races and complexions, all more or less drunk. A company of California emigrants, it seemed, had made the discovery at this late day that they had encumbered themselves with too many supplies for their journey. A part, therefore, they had thrown away, or sold at great loss to the traders; but had determined to get rid of their very copious stock of Missouri whiskey, by drinking it on the spot. Here were maudlin squaws stretched on piles of buffalo-robes; squalid Mexicans, armed with bows and arrows; Indians sedately drunk; long-haired Canadians and trappers, and American backwoodsmen in brown homespun, the well-beloved pistol and bowie-knife displayed openly at their sides. In the middle of the room a tall, lank man, with a dingy broadcloth coat, was haranguing the company in the style of the stump orator. With one hand he sawed the air, and with the other clutched firmly a brown whiskey-jug, which he applied every moment to his lips, forgetting that he had drained the contents long ago. Richard formally introduced me to this personage, who was no less a

33 man than Colonel R——, once the leader of the party. Instantly the Colonel, seizing me, in the absence of buttons, by the leather fringes of my frock, began to define his position. His men, he said, had mutinied and deposed him; but still he exercised over them the influence of a superior mind; in all but the name he was yet their chief. As the Colonel spoke I looked round on the wild assemblage, and could not help thinking that he was but ill-fitted to conduct such men across the deserts to California. Conspicuous among the rest stood three tall young men, grandsons

34 of Daniel Boone. They had clearly inherited the adventurous character of that prince of pioneers; but I saw no

signs of the quiet and tranquil spirit that so remarkably distinguished him.

Fearful was the fate that, months after, overtook some of the members of that party. General Kearney, on his late return from California, brought back their story. They were interrupted by the deep snows among the mountains, and, maddened by cold and hunger, fed upon each other's flesh!

I got tired of the confusion. "Come, Paul," said I, "we will be off." Paul sat in the sun, under the wall of the fort. He jumped up, mounted, and we rode towards Fort Laramie. When we reached it, a man came out of the gate with a pack at his back and a rifle on his shoulder; others were gathering about him, shaking him by the hand, as if taking leave. I thought it a strange thing that a man should set out alone and on foot for the prairie. I soon got an explanation. Perrault — this, if I recollect right, was the Canadian's name — had quarrelled with the *bourgeois*, and the fort was too hot to hold him. Bordeaux, inflated with his transient authority, had abused him, and received a blow in return. The men then sprang at each other, and grappled in the middle of the fort. Bordeaux was down in an instant, at the mercy of the incensed Canadian; had not an old Indian, the brother of his squaw, seized hold of his antagonist, it would have fared ill with him. Perrault broke loose from the old Indian, and both the white men ran to their rooms for their guns; but when Bordeaux, looking from his door, saw the Canadian, gun in hand, standing in the area and calling on him to come out and fight, his heart failed him; he chose to remain where he was. In vain the old Indian, scandalized by his brother-in-law's cowardice, called upon him to go to the prairie and fight it out in the white man's manner; and Bordeaux's own squaw, equally incensed, screamed to her lord and master that he was a dog and an old woman. It all availed nothing. Bordeaux's prudence got the better of his valor, and he would not stir. Perrault stood showering opprobrious epithets at the recreant *bourgeois*, till, growing tired of this, he made up a pack of dried meat, and slinging it at his back, set out alone for Fort Pierre, on the Missouri, a distance of three hundred miles, over a desert country, full of hostile Indians.

I remained in the fort that night. In the morning, as I was coming out from breakfast, talking with a trader named McCluskey, I saw a strange Indian leaning against the side of the gate. He was a tall, strong man, with heavy features.

"Who is he?" I asked.

"That's The Whirlwind," said McCluskey. "He is the fellow that made all this stir about the war. It's always the way with the Sioux; they never stop cutting each other's throats, — it's all they are fit for, — instead of sitting in their lodges, and getting robes to trade with us in the winter. If this war goes on, we'll make a poor trade of it next season, I reckon."

And this was the opinion of all the traders, who were vehemently opposed to the war, from the injury that it must occasion to their interests. The Whirlwind left his village the day before to make a visit to the fort. His warlike ardor had abated not a little since he first conceived the design of avenging his son's death. The long and complicated preparations for the expedition were too much for his fickle disposition. That morning Bordeaux fastened upon him, made him presents, and told him that if he went to war he would destroy his horses and kill no buffalo to trade with the white men; in short, that he was a fool to think of such a thing, and had better make up his mind to sit quietly in his lodge and smoke his pipe, like a wise man. The Whirlwind's purpose was evidently shaken; he had become tired, like a child, of his favorite plan. Bordeaux exultingly predicted that he would not go to war. My philanthropy was no match for my curiosity, and I was vexed at the possibility that after all I might lose the rare opportunity of seeing the ceremonies of war. The Whirlwind, however, had merely thrown the firebrand; the conflagration was become general. All the western bands of the Dakota were bent on war; and, as I heard from McCluskey, six large villages were already gathered on a little stream, forty miles distant, and were daily calling to the Great Spirit to aid them in their enterprise. McCluskey had just left them, and represented them as on their way to La Bonté's camp, which they would reach in a week, *unless they should learn that there were no buffalo there.* I did not like this condition, for buffalo this season were rare in the neighborhood. There were also the two Minneconjou villages that I mentioned before; but about noon an Indian came from Richard's Fort with the news that they were quarrelling, breaking up, and dispersing. So much for the whiskey of the emigrants! Finding themselves unable to drink the whole,

they had sold the residue to these Indians, and it needed
no prophet to foretell the result; a spark dropped into a
powder-magazine would not have produced a quicker effect.
Instantly the old jealousies and rivalries and smothered
feuds that exist in an Indian village broke out into furious quarrels. They forgot the warlike enterprise that had
already brought them three hundred miles. They seemed
like ungoverned children inflamed with the fiercest passions
of men. Several of them were stabbed in the drunken
tumult; and in the morning they scattered and moved back
towards the Missouri in small parties. I feared that, after
all, the long-projected meeting and the ceremonies that
were to attend it might never take place, and I should lose
so admirable an opportunity of seeing the Indian under his
most fearful and characteristic aspect; however, in foregoing
this, I should avoid a very fair probability of being plundered
and stripped, and it might be, stabbed or shot into the bargain. Consoling myself with this reflection, I prepared
to carry the news, such as it was, to the camp.

I caught my horse, and to my vexation found that he had
lost a shoe and broken his hoof against the rocks. Horses
are shod at Fort Laramie at the moderate rate of three
dollars a foot; so I tied Hendrick to a beam in the *corral*,
and summoned Roubidou the blacksmith. Roubidou, with
the hoof between his knees, was at work with hammer
and file, and I was inspecting the process, when a strange
voice addressed me.

"Two more gone under! Well, there's more of us left
yet. Here's Gingras and me off to the mountains to-
morrow. Our turn will come next, I suppose. It's a
hard life, anyhow!"

I looked up and saw a man, not much more than five feet
high, but of very square and strong proportions. In appear-

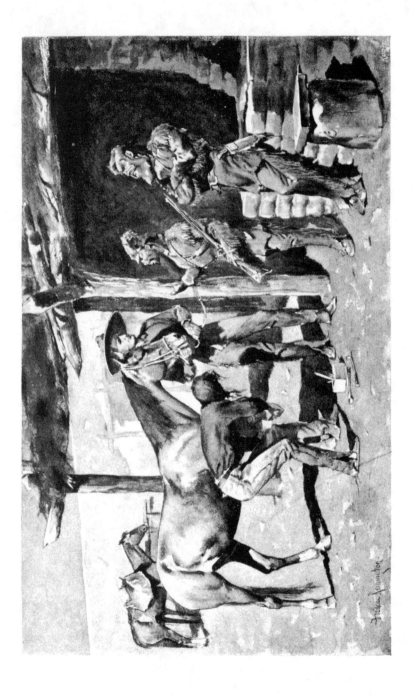

ance he was particularly dingy; for his old buck-skin frock
was black and polished with time and grease, and his belt,
knife, pouch, and powder-horn appeared to have seen the
roughest service. The first joint of each foot was entirely
gone, having been frozen off several winters before, and
his moccasins were curtailed in proportion. His whole
appearance and equipment bespoke the "free trapper."   45
He had a round, ruddy face, animated with a spirit of
carelessness and gayety not at all in accordance with the
words he had just spoken.

"'Two more gone,'" said I; "what do you mean by that?"

"Oh, the Arapahoes have just killed two of us in the
mountains. Old Bull-Tail has come to tell us. They   46
stabbed one behind his back, and shot the other with his
own rifle. That's the way we live here! I mean to give
up trapping after this year. My squaw says she wants a
pacing horse and some red ribbons; I'll make enough
beaver to get them for her, and then I'm done! I'll go   47
below and live on a farm."

"Your bones will dry on the prairie, Rouleau!" said
another trapper, who was standing by,—a strong, brutal-
looking fellow, with a face as surly as a bull-dog's.

Rouleau only laughed, and began to hum a tune, and
shuffle a dance on his stumps of feet.

"You'll see us, before long, passing up your way," said
the other man.

"Well," said I, "stop and take a cup of coffee with us;"
and, as it was late in the afternoon, I prepared to leave the
fort at once.

As I rode out, a train of emigrant wagons was passing   48
across the stream. "Whar are ye goin', stranger?" Thus
I was saluted by two or three voices at once.

"About eighteen miles up the creek."

"It's mighty late to be going that far! Make haste, ye 'd better, and keep a bright look-out for Indians!"

I thought the advice too good to be neglected. Fording the stream, I passed at a round trot over the plains beyond. But "the more haste, the worse speed." I proved the truth of the proverb by the time I reached the hills three miles from the fort. The trail was faintly marked, and, riding forward with more rapidity than caution, I lost sight of it. I kept on in a direct line, guided by Laramie Creek, which I could see at intervals darkly glistening in the evening sun, at the bottom of the woody gulf on my right. Half an hour before sunset I came upon its banks. There was something exciting in the wild solitude of the place. An antelope sprang suddenly from the sage-bushes before me. As he leaped gracefully not thirty yards before my horse, I fired, and instantly he spun round and fell. Quite sure of him, I walked my horse towards him, leisurely reloading my rifle, when to my surprise he sprang up and trotted rapidly away on three legs into the dark recesses of the hills, whither I had no time to follow. Ten minutes after, I was passing along the bottom of a deep valley, and, chancing to look behind me, I saw in the dim light that something was following. Supposing it to be a wolf, I slid from my seat and sat down behind my horse to shoot it; but as it came up, I saw by its motions that it was another antelope. It approached within a hundred yards, arched its neck, and gazed intently. I levelled at the white spot on its breast, and was about to fire when it started off, ran first to one side and then to the other, like a vessel tacking against the wind, and at last stretched away at full speed. Then it stopped again, 49 looked curiously behind it, and trotted up as before; but not so boldly, for it soon paused and stood gazing at me.

I fired; it leaped upward and fell upon its tracks. Measuring the distance, I found it two hundred and four paces. When I stood by his side, the antelope turned his expiring eye upward. It was like a beautiful woman's, dark and bright. "Fortunate that I am in a hurry," thought I; "I might be troubled with remorse if I had time for it."

Cutting the animal up, not in the most skilful manner, I hung the meat at the back of my saddle, and rode on again. The hills (I could not remember one of them) closed around me. "It is too late," thought I, "to go forward. I will stay here to-night, and look for the path in the morning." As a last effort, however, I ascended a high hill, from which, to my great satisfaction, I could see Laramie Creek stretching before me, twisting from side to side amid ragged patches of timber; and far off, close beneath the shadows of the trees, the ruins of the old trading-fort were visible. I reached them at twilight. It was far from pleasant, in that uncertain light, to be pushing through the dense trees and bushes of the grove beyond. I listened anxiously for the foot-fall of man or beast. Nothing was stirring but one harmless brown bird, chirping among the branches. I was glad when I gained the open prairie once more, where I could see if anything approached. When I came to the mouth of Chugwater, it was totally dark. Slackening the reins, I let my horse take his own course. He trotted on with unerring instinct, and by nine o'clock was scrambling down the steep descent into the meadows where we were encamped. While I was looking in vain for the light of the fire, Hendrick, with keener perceptions, gave a loud neigh, which was immediately answered by another neigh from the distance. In a moment I was hailed from the darkness by the voice of Reynal, who had come out, rifle in hand, to see who was approaching.

He, with his squaw, the two Canadians and the Indian boys, were the sole inmates of the camp, Shaw and Henry Chatillon being still absent. At noon of the following day they came back, their horses looking none the better for the journey. Henry seemed dejected. The woman was dead, and his children must henceforward be exposed, without a protector, to the hardships and vicissitudes of Indian life. Even in the midst of his grief he had not forgotten his attachment to his *bourgeois*, for he had procured among his Indian relatives two beautifully ornamented buffalo-robes, which he spread on the ground as a present to us.

Shaw lighted his pipe, and told me in a few words the history of his journey. When I went to the fort they left me as I mentioned, at the mouth of Chugwater. They followed the course of the little stream all day, traversing a desolate and barren country. Several times they came upon the fresh traces of a large war-party, the same, no doubt, from whom we had so narrowly escaped an attack. At an hour before sunset, without encountering a human being by the way, they came upon the lodges of the squaw and her brothers, who, in compliance with Henry's message, had left the Indian village in order to join us at our camp. The lodges were already pitched, five in number, by the side of the stream. The woman lay in one of them, reduced to a mere skeleton. For some time she had been unable to move or speak. Indeed, nothing had kept her alive but the hope of seeing Henry, to whom she was strongly and faithfully attached. No sooner did he enter the lodge than she revived, and she talked with him the greater part of the night. Early in the morning she was lifted into a *travois*, and the whole party set out towards our camp. There were but five warriors; the rest

were women and children. They were all in great alarm
at the proximity of the Crow war-party, who would certainly have killed them without mercy had they met.
They had advanced only a mile or two when they discerned a horseman, far off, on the edge of the horizon.
They all stopped, gathering together in the greatest anxiety, from which they did not recover until long after the
horseman disappeared; then they set out again. Henry was
riding with Shaw a few rods in advance of the Indians,
when Mahto-Tatonka, a younger brother of the woman,
hastily called after them. Turning back, they found all
the Indians crowded around the *travois* in which the
woman was lying. They reached her just in time to hear
the death-rattle in her throat. In a moment she lay dead
in the basket of the vehicle. A complete stillness succeeded; then the Indians raised in concert their cries of
lamentation over the corpse, and among them Shaw clearly
distinguished those strange sounds resembling the word
"Halleluyah," which, together with some other accidental
coincidences, has given rise to the absurd notion that the
Indians are descended from the ten lost tribes of Israel.   51

The Indian usage required that Henry, as well as the
other relatives of the woman, should make valuable presents, to be placed by the side of the body at its last resting-place. Leaving the Indians, he and Shaw set out for
the camp, and reached it, as we have seen, by hard pushing, at about noon. Having obtained the necessary arti-   52
cles, they immediately returned. It was very late and
quite dark when they again reached the lodges. They
were all placed in a deep hollow among dreary hills.
Four of them were just visible through the gloom, but
the fifth and largest was illumined by the blaze of a fire
within, glowing through the half-transparent covering of

raw hides. There was a perfect stillness as they approached. The lodges seemed without a tenant. Not a living thing was stirring; there was something awful in the scene. They rode up to the entrance of the lodge, and there was no sound but the tramp of their horses. A squaw came out and took charge of the animals, without speaking a word. Entering, they found the lodge crowded with Indians; a fire was burning in the middle, and the mourners encircled it in a triple row. Room was made for the new-comers at the head of the lodge, a robe spread for them to sit upon, and a pipe lighted and handed to them in perfect silence. Thus they passed the greater part of the night. At times the fire would subside into a heap of embers, until the dark figures seated around it were scarcely visible; then a squaw would drop upon it a piece of buffalo-fat, and a bright flame instantly springing up would reveal the crowd of wild faces, motionless as bronze. The silence continued unbroken. It was a relief to Shaw when daylight returned and he could escape from this house of mourning. He and Henry prepared to return homeward; first, however, they placed the presents they had brought near the body of the squaw, which, gaudily attired, remained in a sitting posture in one of the lodges. A fine horse was picketed not far off, destined to be killed that morning for the service of her spirit; for the woman was lame, and could not travel on foot over the dismal prairies to the villages of the dead. Food, too, was provided, and household implements, for her use upon this last journey.

Henry left her to the care of her relatives, and came immediately with Shaw to the camp. It was some time before he entirely recovered from his dejection.

FREDERIC REMINGTON

CHAPTER XI.

SCENES AT THE CAMP.

REYNAL heard guns fired one day at the distance of a mile or two from the camp. He grew nervous instantly. Visions of Crow war-parties began to haunt his imagination; and when we returned (for we were all absent) he renewed his complaints about being left alone with the Canadians and the squaw. The day after, the cause of the alarm appeared. Four trappers, called Morin, Saraphin, Rouleau, and Gingras, came to our camp and joined us. They it was who fired the guns, and disturbed the dreams of our confederate Reynal. They soon encamped by our side. Their rifles, dingy and battered with hard service, rested with ours against the old tree; their strong rude saddles, their buffalo-robes, their traps, and a few rough and simple articles of their travelling equipment were piled near our tent. Their mountain-horses were turned out to graze in the meadow among our own; and the men themselves, no less rough and hardy, used to lie half the day in the shade of our tree, lolling on the grass, lazily smoking, and telling stories of their adventures; and I defy the annals of chivalry to furnish the record of a life more wild and perilous than that of a Rocky Mountain trapper.

With this efficient reinforcement the agitation of Reynal's nerves subsided. We began to conceive a sort of attachment to our old camping ground; yet it was time to change our quarters, since remaining too long on one spot must lead to unpleasant results, not to be borne unless in case of dire necessity. The grass no longer presented a smooth surface of turf; it was trampled into mud and clay. So we removed to another old tree, larger yet, that grew by the side of the river a furlong distant. Its trunk was full six feet in diameter; on one side it was marked by a party of Indians with various inexplicable hieroglyphics, commemorating some warlike enterprise, and aloft among the branches were the remains of a scaffold, where dead bodies had once been deposited, after the Indian manner.

"There comes Bull-Bear," said Henry Chatillon, as we sat on the grass at dinner. Looking up, we saw several horsemen coming over the neighboring hill, and in a moment four stately young men rode up and dismounted. One of them was Bull-Bear, or Mahto-Tatonka, a compound name which he inherited from his father, the principal chief in the Ogillallah band. One of his brothers and two other young men accompanied him. We shook hands with the visitors, and when we had finished our meal — for this is the approved manner of entertaining Indians, even the best of them — we handed to each a tin cup of coffee and a biscuit, at which they ejaculated from the bottom of their throats, "How! how!" a monosyllable by which a Dakota contrives to express half the emotions of which he is capable. Then we lighted the pipe, and passed it to them as they squatted on the ground.

"Where is the village?"

"There," said Mahto-Tatonka, pointing southward; "it will come in two days."

"Will they go to the war?"

"Yes."

No man is a philanthropist on the prairie. We welcomed this news cordially, and congratulated ourselves that Bordeaux's interested efforts to divert The Whirlwind from his congenial vocation of bloodshed had failed of success, and that no further obstacles would interpose between us and our plan of repairing to the rendezvous at La Bonté's camp.

For that and several succeeding days Mahto-Tatonka and his friends remained our guests. They devoured the relics of our meals; they filled the pipe for us, and also helped us to smoke it. Sometimes they stretched themselves side by side in the shade, indulging in raillery and equivocal jokes, ill becoming the dignity of brave and aspiring warriors, such as two of them in reality were. 5

Two days dragged away, and on the morning of the third we hoped confidently to see the Indian village. It did not come; so we rode out to look for it. In place of the eight hundred Indians we expected, we met one solitary 6 savage riding towards us over the prairie, who told us that the Indians had changed their plan, and would not come within three days. Taking along with us this messenger of evil tidings, we retraced our footsteps to the camp, amusing ourselves by the way with execrating Indian inconstancy. When we came in sight of our little white tent under the big tree, we saw that it no longer stood alone. A huge old lodge was erected by its side, discolored by rain and storms, rotten with age, with the uncouth figures of horses and men and outstretched hands that were painted upon it well-nigh obliterated. The long poles which supported this squalid habitation thrust themselves rakishly out from its pointed top, and over its entrance were suspended a "medicine-pipe" and various other implements of the magic art. While we were yet at a distance we observed a greatly increased population, of various colors and dimensions, swarming about our quiet encampment. Morin, the trapper, having been absent for a day or two, had returned, it seemed, bringing all his family with him. He had taken to himself a wife, for whom he had paid the established price of one horse. This looks cheap at first sight, but in truth the purchase of a squaw is a transaction which no man should enter into without mature deliberation, since it involves not only the payment of the price, but the burden of feeding and supporting a rapacious horde of the bride's relatives, who hold themselves entitled to feed upon the indiscreet white man. They gather about him like leeches, and drain him of all he has.

Morin had not made a distinguished match. His bride's relatives occupied but a contemptible position in Ogillallah society; for among these democrats of the prairie, as among others more civilized, there are virtual distinctions of rank and place. Morin's partner was not the most beautiful of

her sex, and he had the bad taste to array her in an old
calico gown, bought from an emigrant woman, instead of
the neat tunic of whitened deer-skin usually worn by the
squaws. The moving spirit of the establishment was an
old hag of eighty. Human imagination never conceived
hobgoblin or witch more ugly than she. You could count
all her ribs through the wrinkles of her leathery skin.
Her withered face more resembled an old skull than the
countenance of a living being, even to the hollow, darkened sockets, at the bottom of which glittered her little
black eyes. Her arms had dwindled into nothing but
whip-cord and wire. Her hair, half black, half gray, hung
in total neglect nearly to the ground, and her sole garment consisted of the remnant of a discarded buffalo-robe
tied round her waist with a string of hide. Yet the old
squaw's meagre anatomy was wonderfully strong. She
pitched the lodge, packed the horses, and did the hardest
labor of the camp. From morning till night she bustled
about the lodge, screaming like a screech-owl when anything displeased her. Her brother, a "medicine-man," or
magician, was as gaunt and sinewy as herself. His mouth
spread from ear to ear, and his appetite, as we had
occasion to learn, was ravenous in proportion. The other
inmates of the lodge were a young bride and bridegroom,
the latter one of those idle, good-for-nothing fellows who
infest an Indian village as well as more civilized com-
munities. He was fit neither for hunting nor war, as one
might see from the stolid, unmeaning expression of his
face. The happy pair had just entered upon the honey-
moon. They would stretch a buffalo-robe upon poles to
protect them from the sun, and spreading under it a
couch of furs, would sit affectionately side by side for
half the day, though I could not discover that any conver-

sation passed between them.   Probably they had nothing to
say; for an Indian's supply of topics for conversation is far
from being copious.   There were half a dozen children,
too, playing and whooping about the camp, shooting birds
with little bows and arrows, or making miniature lodges
of sticks, as children of a different complexion build houses
of blocks.

A day passed, and Indians began rapidly to come in.
Parties of two, three, or more would ride up and silently
seat themselves on the grass.   The fourth day came at
last, when about noon horsemen appeared in view on the
top of the neighboring ridge.   Behind followed a wild
procession, hurrying in disorder down the hill and over
the plain below; horses, mules, and dogs, heavily-burdened
travois, mounted warriors, squaws walking amid the throng,
and a host of children.   For a full half-hour they continued to pour down; and keeping directly to the bend
of the stream, within a furlong of us, they soon assembled there, a dark and confused throng, until, as if by
magic, a hundred and fifty tall lodges sprang up.   The
lonely plain was transformed into the site of a swarming
encampment.   Countless horses were soon grazing over
the meadows around us, and the prairie was animated by
restless figures careering on horseback, or sedately stalking in their long white robes.   The Whirlwind was come
at last.   One question yet remained to be answered: "Will
he go to the war in order that we, with so respectable an
escort, may pass over to the somewhat perilous rendezvous
at La Bonté's camp?"

This still remained in doubt.   Characteristic indecision
perplexed their councils.   Indians cannot act in large
bodies.   Though their object be of the highest importance, they cannot combine to attain it by a series of con-

nected efforts. King Philip, Pontiac, and Tecumseh, all 8
felt this to their cost. The Ogillallah once had a war-
chief who could control them; but he was dead, and now
they were left to the sway of their own unsteady impulses.

As this Indian village and its inhabitants will hold a
prominent place in the rest of the story, perhaps it may
not be amiss to glance for an instant at the savage people
of which they form a part. The Dakota, or Sioux, range
over a vast territory, from the river St. Peter to the
Rocky Mountains. They are divided into independent
bands, united under no central government, and acknowledging no common head. The same language, usages, and
superstitions form the sole bond between them. They do
not unite even in their wars. The bands of the east fight
the Ojibwas on the Upper Lakes; those of the west make 9
incessant war upon the Snake Indians in the Rocky Mountains. As the whole people is divided into bands, so each
band is divided into villages. Each village has a chief, 10
who is honored and obeyed only so far as his personal
qualities may command respect and fear. Sometimes he is
a mere nominal chief; sometimes his authority is little
short of absolute, and his fame and influence reach beyond
his own village, so that the whole band to which he belongs is ready to acknowledge him as their head. This 11
was, a few years since, the case with the Ogillallah.
Courage, address, and enterprise may raise any warrior
to the highest honor, especially if he be the son of a
former chief, or a member of a numerous family, to support him and avenge his quarrels; but when he has reached
the dignity of chief, and the old men and warriors, by a
peculiar ceremony, have formally installed him, let it not be
imagined that he assumes any of the outward signs of rank
and honor. He knows too well on how frail a tenure he 12

holds his station.   He must conciliate his uncertain subjects.   Many a man in the village lives better, owns more
squaws and more horses, and goes better clad than he.
13   Like the Teutonic chiefs of old, he ingratiates himself
with his young men by making them presents, thereby
often impoverishing himself.   If he fails to gain their
favor they will set his authority at naught, and may
desert him at any moment; for the usages of his people
have provided no means of enforcing his authority.   Very
seldom does it happen, at least among these western bands,
that a chief attains to much power, unless he is the head
of a numerous family.   Frequently the village is principally made up of his relatives and descendants, and the
wandering community assumes much of the patriarchal
14   character.
      The western Dakota have no fixed habitations.   Hunt-
ing and fighting, they wander incessantly, through summer
and winter.   Some follow the herds of buffalo over the
waste of prairie; others traverse the Black Hills, thronging, on horseback and on foot, through the dark gulfs and
15   sombre gorges, and emerging at last upon the "Parks," —
those beautiful but most perilous hunting grounds.   The
buffalo supplies them with the necessaries of life; with
habitations, food, clothing, beds, and fuel, strings for
their bows, glue, thread, cordage, trail-ropes for their
horses, coverings for their saddles, vessels to hold water,
boats to cross streams, and the means of purchasing all
that they want from the traders.   When the buffalo are
16   extinct, they too must dwindle away.
      War is the breath of their nostrils.   Against most of the
neighboring tribes they cherish a rancorous hatred, trans-
mitted from father to son, and inflamed by constant aggres-
sion and retaliation.   Many times a year, in every village,

the Great Spirit is called upon, fasts are made, the war-parade is celebrated, and the warriors go out by handfuls at a time against the enemy. This fierce spirit awakens their most eager aspirations, and calls forth their greatest energies. It is chiefly this that saves them from lethargy and utter abasement. Without its powerful stimulus they would be like the unwarlike tribes beyond the mountains, scattered among the caves and rocks like beasts, and living on roots and reptiles. These latter have little of humanity except the form; but the proud and ambitious Dakota warrior can sometimes boast heroic virtues. It is seldom that distinction and influence are attained among them by any other course than that of arms. Their superstition, however, sometimes gives great power to those among them who pretend to the character of magicians; and their orators, such as they are, have their share of honor.

But to return. Look into our tent, or enter, if you can bear the stifling smoke and the close air. There, wedged close together, you will see a circle of stout warriors, passing the pipe around, joking, telling stories, and making themselves merry after their fashion. We were also infested by little copper-colored naked boys and snake-eyed girls. They would come up to us muttering certain words, which being interpreted conveyed the concise invitation, "Come and eat." Then we would rise, cursing the pertinacity of Dakota hospitality, which allowed scarcely an hour of rest between sun and sun, and to which we were bound to do honor, unless we would offend our entertainers. This necessity was particularly burdensome to me, as I was scarcely able to walk from the effects of illness, and was poorly qualified to dispose of twenty meals a day. So bounteous an entertainment looks like an outgushing

17

of good-will; but, doubtless, half at least of our kind hosts, had they met us alone and unarmed on the prairie, would have robbed us of our horses, and perhaps have bestowed 18 an arrow upon us besides.

One morning we were summoned to the lodge of an old 19 man, the Nestor of his tribe. We found him half sitting, half reclining, on a pile of buffalo-robes; his long hair, jet-black, though he had seen some eighty winters, hung on either side of his thin features. His gaunt but symmetrical frame did not more clearly exhibit the wreck of by-gone strength, than did his dark, wasted features, still prom- 20 inent and commanding, bear the stamp of mental energies. Opposite the patriarch was his nephew, the young aspirant Mahto-Tatonka; and besides these, there were one or two women in the lodge.

The old man's story is peculiar, and illustrative of a superstition that prevails in full force among many of the Indian tribes. He was one of a powerful family, re-nowned for warlike exploits. When a very young man he submitted to the singular rite to which most of the tribe subject themselves before entering upon life. He painted his face black; then seeking out a cavern in a sequestered part of the Black Hills, he lay for several days, fasting, and praying to the spirits. In the dreams and visions produced by his weakened and excited state he fancied, like all Indians, that he saw supernatural reve-lations. Again and again the form of an antelope appeared before him. The antelope is the graceful peace-spirit of the Ogillallah; but seldom is it that such a gentle visitor presents itself during the initiatory fasts of their young men. The terrible grizzly bear, the divinity of war, usu-ally appears, to fire them with martial ardor and thirst for renown. At length the antelope spoke. It told the young dreamer that he was not to follow the path of war; that a life of peace and tranquillity was marked out for him; that thenceforward he was to guide the people oy his counsels and protect them from the evils of their own feuds and dissensions. Others were to gain renown by fighting the enemy; but greatness of a different kind was in store for him. 21

The visions beheld during the period of this fast usually determine the whole course of the dreamer's life. From that time, Le Borgne, which was the only name by which we knew him, abandoned all thoughts of war, and devoted himself to the labors of peace. He told his vision to the people. They honored his commission and respected him in his novel capacity.

A far different man was his brother, Mahto-Tatonka, who had left his name, his features, and many of his qualities, to his son. He was the father of Henry Chatillon's squaw, a circumstance which proved of some advantage to us, as it secured the friendship of a family perhaps the most noted and influential in the whole Ogillallah band. Mahto-Tatonka, in his way, was a hero. No chief could vie with 22 him in warlike renown, or in power over his people. He had a fearless spirit, and an impetuous and inflexible resolution. His will was law. He was politic and sagacious, and with true Indian craft, always befriended the whites, knowing that he might thus reap great advantages for himself and his adherents. When he had resolved on any course of conduct, he would pay to the warriors the compliment of calling them together to deliberate upon it, and when their debates were over, quietly state his own opinion, which no one ever disputed. It fared hard with those who incurred his displeasure. He would strike them or stab them on the spot; and this act, which if attempted by any other chief would have cost him his life, the awe inspired by his name enabled him to repeat again and again with impunity. In a community where, from immemorial time, no man has acknowledged any law but his own will, Mahto-Tatonka raised himself to power little short of despotic.

His career came at last to an end. He had a host of enemies patiently biding their time; and our old friend Smoke in particular, together with all his kinsmen, hated him cordially. Smoke sat one day in his lodge, in the midst of his own village, when Mahto-Tatonka entered it alone, and approaching the dwelling of his enemy, challenged him in a loud voice to come out and fight. Smoke would not move. At this, Mahto-Tatonka proclaimed him a coward and an old woman, and striding to the entrance of the lodge, stabbed the chief's best horse, which was picketed there. Smoke was daunted, and even this insult failed to bring him out. Mahto-Tatonka moved haughtily away; all made way for him; but his hour of reckoning was near.

One hot day, five or six years ago, numerous lodges of Smoke's kinsmen were gathered about some of the Fur Company's men, who were trading in various articles with them, whiskey among the rest. Mahto-Tatonka was also there with a few of his people. As he lay in his own lodge, a fray arose between his adherents and the kinsmen of his enemy. The war-whoop was raised, bullets and arrows began to fly, and the camp was in confusion. The chief sprang up, and rushing in a fury from the lodge shouted to the combatants on both sides to cease. Instantly — for the attack was preconcerted — came the reports of two or three guns, and the twanging of a dozen bows, and the savage hero, mortally wounded, pitched forward headlong to the ground. Rouleau was present, and told me the particulars. The tumult became general, and was not quelled until several had fallen on both sides. When we were in the country the feud between the two families was still rankling.

Thus died Mahto-Tatonka; but he left behind him a goodly army of descendants, to perpetuate his renown and avenge his fate. Besides daughters, he had thirty sons, a number which need not stagger the credulity of those acquainted with Indian usages and practices. We saw 23 many of them, all marked by the same dark complexion, and the same peculiar cast of features. Of these, our visitor, young Mahto-Tatonka, was the eldest, and some reported him as likely to succeed to his father's honors. Though he appeared not more than twenty-one years old, he had oftener struck the enemy, and stolen more horses and more squaws, than any other young man in the village. Horse-stealing is well known as an avenue to distinction on the prairies, and the other kind of depredation is esteemed equally meritorious. Not that the act can confer 24 fame from its own intrinsic merits. Any one can steal a squaw, and if he chooses afterwards to make an adequate present to her rightful proprietor, the easy husband for the most part rests content, his vengeance falls asleep, and all danger from that quarter is averted. Yet this is regarded as a pitiful and mean-spirited transaction. The danger is averted, but the glory of the achievement also is lost. Mahto-Tatonka proceeded after a more dashing fashion. Out of several dozen squaws whom he had stolen he could boast that he had never paid for one, but snapping his fingers in the face of the injured husband, had defied the extremity of his indignation, and no one yet had dared to lay the finger of violence upon him. He was following close in the footsteps of his father. The young men and the young squaws, each in their way, admired him. The former would always follow him to war, and he was esteemed to have an unrivalled charm in the eyes of the latter. Perhaps his impunity may excite some wonder. An arrow shot from a ravine, or a stab given in the dark require no great valor, and are especially suited to the Indian genius; but Mahto-Tatonka had a strong protection. It was not alone his courage and audacious will that enabled him to career so dashingly among his compeers. His enemies did not forget that he was one of thirty warlike brethren, all growing up to manhood. Should they wreak their anger upon him many keen eyes would be ever upon them and many fierce hearts thirst for their blood. The avenger would dog their footsteps everywhere. To kill Mahto-Tatonka would be an act of suicide.

Though he found such favor in the eyes of the fair, he was no dandy. He was indifferent to the gaudy trappings and ornaments of his companions, and was content to rest his chances of success upon his own warlike merits. He never arrayed himself in gaudy blanket and glittering necklaces, but left his statue-like form, limbed like an Apollo of bronze, to win its way to favor. His voice was singularly deep and strong, and sounded from his chest like the deep notes of an organ. Yet after all, he was but an Indian. See him as he lies there in the sun

before our tent, kicking his heels in the air and cracking jokes with his brother. Does he look like a hero? See him now in the hour of his glory, when at sunset the whole village empties itself to behold him; for to-morrow their favorite young partisan goes out against the enemy. His head-dress is adorned with a crest of the war-eagle's feathers, rising in a waving ridge above his brow, and sweeping far behind him. His round white shield hangs at his breast, with feathers radiating from the centre like a star. His quiver is at his back; his tall lance in his hand, the iron point flashing against the declining sun, while the long scalplocks of his enemies flutter from the shaft. Thus, gorgeous as a champion in panoply, he rides round and round within the great circle of lodges, balancing with a graceful buoyancy to the free movements of his war-horse, while with a sedate brow he sings his song to the Great Spirit. Young rival warriors look askance at him; vermilion-cheeked girls gaze in admiration; boys whoop and scream in a thrill of delight; and old women yell forth his name and proclaim his praises from lodge to lodge. 26

Mahto-Tatonka was the best of all our Indian friends. Hour after hour, and day after day, when swarms of savages of every age, sex, and degree beset our camp, he would lie in our tent, his lynx-eye ever open to guard our property from pillage.

The Whirlwind invited us one day to his lodge. The feast was finished and the pipe began to circulate. It was a remarkably large and fine one, and I expressed admiration of it.

"If the Meneaska likes the pipe," asked The Whirlwind, "why does he not keep it?"

Such a pipe among the Ogillallah is valued at the price of a horse. The gift seemed worthy of a chieftain and a

11

warrior; but The Whirlwind's generosity rose to no such pitch. He gave me the pipe, confidently expecting that I in return would make him a present of equal or superior value. This is the implied condition of every gift among the Indians, and should it not be complied with, the present is usually reclaimed. So I arranged upon a gaudy calico handkerchief an assortment of vermilion, tobacco, knives, and gunpowder, and summoning the chief to camp, assured him of my friendship, and begged his acceptance of a slight token of it. Ejaculating "How! how!" he

27   folded up the offerings and withdrew to his lodge.

Late one afternoon a party of Indians on horseback came suddenly in sight from behind some clumps of bushes that lined the bank of the stream, leading with them a mule, on whose back was a wretched negro, sustained in his seat by the high pommel and cantle of the Indian saddle. His cheeks were shrunken in the hollow of his jaws; his eyes were unnaturally dilated, and his lips shrivelled and drawn back from his teeth like those of a corpse. When they brought him before our tent, and lifted him from the saddle, he could not walk or stand, but crawled a short distance,

28   and with a look of utter misery sat down on the grass. All the children and women came pouring out of the lodges, and with screams and cries made a circle about him, while he sat supporting himself with his hands, and looking from side to side with a vacant stare. The wretch was starving to death. For thirty-three days he had wandered alone on the prairie, without weapon of any kind; without shoes, moccasins, or any other clothing than an old jacket and trousers; without intelligence to guide his course, or any knowledge of the productions of the prairie. All this time he had subsisted on crickets and lizards, wild onions,

29   and three eggs which he found in the nest of a prairie-

dove. He had not seen a human being. Bewildered in the boundless, hopeless desert that stretched around him, he had walked on in despair, till he could walk no longer, and then crawled on his knees, till the bone was laid bare. He chose the night for travelling, lying down by day to sleep in the glaring sun, always dreaming as he said, of the broth and corncake he used to eat under his old master's shed in Missouri. Every man in the camp, both white and red, was astonished at his escape not only from starvation, but from the grizzly bears, which abound in that neighborhood, and the wolves which howled around him every night.

Reynal recognized him the moment the Indians brought him in. He had run away from his master about a year before and joined the party of Richard, who was then leaving the frontier for the mountains. He had lived with Richard until, at the end of May, he with Reynal and several other men went out in search of some stray horses, when he was separated from the rest in a storm, and had never been heard of to this time. Knowing his inexperience and helplessness, no one dreamed that he could still be living. The Indians had found him lying exhausted on the ground.

As he sat there, with the Indians gazing silently on him, his haggard face and glazed eye were disgusting to look upon. Deslauriers made him a bowl of gruel, but he suffered it to remain untasted before him. At length he languidly raised the spoon to his lips; again he did so, and again; and then his appetite seemed suddenly inflamed into madness, for he seized the bowl, swallowed all its contents in a few seconds, and eagerly demanded meat. This we refused, telling him to wait until morning; but he begged so eagerly that we gave him a small piece, which he devoured, tearing it like a dog. He said he must have more. We told him that his life was in danger if he ate so immoderately at first. He assented, and said he knew he was a fool to do so, but he must have meat. This we absolutely refused, to the great indignation of the senseless squaws, who, when we were not watching him, would slyly bring dried meat and *pommes blanches*, and place them on the ground by his side. Still this was not enough for him. When it grew dark he contrived to creep away between the legs of the horses and crawl over to the Indian camp. Here he fed to his heart's content, and was brought back again in the morning, when Gingras, the trapper, put him on horseback and carried him to the fort. He managed to survive the effects of his greediness. Though slightly deranged when we left this part of the country, he was otherwise in tolerable health, and expressed his firm conviction that nothing could ever kill him.

When the sun was yet an hour high it was a gay scene in the village. The warriors stalked sedately among the lodges, or along the margin of the stream, or walked out to visit the bands of horses that were feeding over the prairie. Half the population deserted the close and heated lodges and betook themselves to the water; and here you might see boys and girls, and young squaws, splashing, swimming, and diving, beneath the afternoon sun, with merry screams and laughter. But when the sun was resting above the broken peaks, and the purple mountains threw their shadows for miles over the prairie; when our old tree basked peacefully in the horizontal rays, and the swelling plains and scattered groves were softened into a tranquil beauty,— then the scene around our tent was worthy of a Salvator. Savage figures, with quivers at their backs, and guns, lances, or tomahawks in their hands, sat on horseback, motionless as statues, their arms crossed on their breasts and their eyes fixed in a steady, unwavering gaze upon us. Others stood erect, wrapped from head to foot in their long white robes of buffalo-hide. Others sat together on the grass, holding their shaggy horses by a rope, with their dark busts exposed to view as they suffered their robes to fall from their shoulders. Others again stood carelessly among the throng, with nothing to conceal the matchless symmetry of their forms. There was one in particular, a ferocious fellow, named The Mad Wolf, who, with the bow in his hand and the quiver at his back, might have seemed, but for his face, the Pythian Apollo himself. Such a figure rose before the imagination of West, when on first seeing the Belvedere in the Vatican, he exclaimed, "By God, a Mohawk!"

When the prairie grew dark the horses were driven in and secured near the camp, and the crowd began to melt away. Fires gleamed around, duskily revealing the rough trappers and the graceful Indians. One of the families near us was always gathered about a bright fire that lighted up the interior of their lodge. Withered, witch-like hags flitted around the blaze; and here for hour after hour sat a circle of children and young girls, laughing and talking, their round, merry faces glowing in the ruddy light. We could hear the monotonous notes of the drum from the Indian camp, with the chant of the war-song, deadened in the distance, and the long chorus of quavering yells, where the war-dance was going on in the largest lodge. For several nights, too, we heard wild and mournful cries, rising and dying away like the melancholy voice of a wolf. They came from the sisters and other female relatives of Mahto-Tatonka, who were gashing their limbs with knives, and bewailing the death of Henry Chatillon's squaw. The hour would grow late before all went to rest in our camp. Then, while the embers of the fires glowed dimly, the men lay stretched in their blankets on the ground, and nothing could be heard but the restless motions of the crowded horses.

I recall these scenes with a mixed feeling of pleasure and pain. At this time I was so reduced by illness that I could seldom walk without reeling like a drunken man; and when I rose from my seat upon the ground the landscape suddenly grew dim before my eyes, the trees and lodges seemed to sway to and fro, and the prairie to rise and fall like the swells of the ocean. Such a state of things is not enviable anywhere. In a country where a man's life may at any moment depend on the strength of his arm, or it may be on the activity of his legs, it is more particularly inconvenient. Nor is sleeping on damp ground, with an occasional drenching from a shower, very beneficial in such cases. I sometimes suffered the extremity of exhaustion, and was in a tolerably fair way of atoning for my love of the prairie, by resting there forever.

I tried repose and a very sparing diet. For a long time, with exemplary patience, I lounged about the camp, or at the utmost staggered over to the Indian village, and walked faint and dizzy among the lodges. It would not do; and I bethought me of starvation. During five days I sustained life on one small biscuit a day At the end of that time I was weaker than before, but the disorder seemed shaken in its stronghold, and very gradually I began to resume a less rigid diet.

I used to lie languid and dreamy before our tent, musing on the past and the future, and when most overcome with lassitude, my eyes turned always towards the distant Black

Hills. There is a spirit of energy in mountains, and they impart it to all who approach them.   At that time I did not know how many dark superstitions and gloomy legends are associated with the Black Hills in the minds of the Indians, but I felt an eager desire to penetrate their hidden recesses, and explore the chasms and precipices, black torrents, and silent forests that I fancied were concealed there.

CHAPTER XII.

ILL–LUCK.

A CANADIAN came from Fort Laramie, and brought a curious piece of intelligence. A trapper, fresh from the mountains, had become enamoured of a Missouri damsel belonging to a family who with other emigrants had been for some days encamped in the neighborhood of the fort. If bravery be the most potent charm to win the favor of the fair, then no wooer could be more irresistible than a Rocky Mountain trapper. In the present instance, the suit was not urged in vain. The lovers concerted a scheme, which they proceeded to carry into effect with all possible despatch. The emigrant party left the fort, and on the next night but one encamped as usual, and placed a guard. A little after midnight the enamoured trapper drew near, mounted on a strong horse, and leading another by the bridle. Fastening both animals to a tree, he stealthily moved towards the wagons, as if he were approaching a band of buffalo. Eluding the vigilance of the guard, who were probably half asleep, he met his mistress by appointment at the outskirts of the camp, mounted her on his spare horse, and made off with her through the darkness. The sequel of the adventure did not reach our ears, and we never learned how the imprudent fair one liked an Indian lodge for a dwelling, and a reckless trapper for a bridegroom.

At length The Whirlwind and his warriors determined to move. They had resolved, after all their preparations, not to go to the rendezvous at La Bonté's camp, but to pass through the Black Hills and spend a few weeks in hunting the buffalo on the other side, until they had killed enough to furnish them with a stock of provisions and with hides to make their lodges for the next season. This 3 done, they were to send out a small independent war-party against the enemy. Their final determination placed us in some embarrassment. Should we go to La Bonté's camp, it was not impossible that the other villages would prove as vacillating as The Whirlwind's, and that no assembly whatever would take place. Our old companion Reynal had conceived a liking for us, or rather for our biscuit and coffee, and for the occasional small presents which we made him. He was very anxious that we should go with the village, which he himself intended to follow. He was certain that no Indians would meet at the rendez-vous, and said, moreover, that it would be easy to convey our cart and baggage through the Black Hills. He knew, however, nothing of the matter. Neither he nor any white man with us had ever seen the difficult and obscure defiles through which the Indians intended to make their way. I passed them afterwards, and had much ado to force my distressed horse along the narrow ravines, and through chasms where daylight could scarcely penetrate. Our cart might as easily have been driven over the summit of Pike's Peak. But of this we were ignorant; and in view of the difficulties and uncertainties of an attempt to visit the rendezvous, we recalled the old proverb about "a bird in the hand," and decided to follow the village.

Both camps, the Indians' and our own, broke up on the morning of the first of July. I was so weak that the aid

of a spoonful of whiskey, swallowed at short intervals, alone enabled me to sit my horse through the short journey of that day. For half a mile before us and half a mile behind, the prairie was covered far and wide with the moving throng of savages. The barren, broken plain

stretched away to the right and left, and far in front rose
the precipitous ridge of the Black Hills. We pushed forward to the head of the scattered column, passing burdened
traineaux, heavily laden pack-horses, gaunt old women on
foot, gay young squaws on horseback, restless children
running among the crowd, old men striding along in their
white buffalo-robes, and groups of young warriors mounted
on their best horses. Henry Chatillon, looking backward
over the distant prairie, exclaimed suddenly that a horseman was coming; and in truth we could just discern
a small black speck slowly moving over the face of a distant swell, like a fly creeping on a wall. It rapidly grew
larger as it approached.

"White man, I b'lieve," said Henry; "look how he
ride. Indian never ride that way. Yes; he got rifle on
the saddle before him."

The horseman disappeared in a hollow of the prairie,
but we soon saw him again, and as he came riding at a
gallop towards us through the crowd of Indians, his long
hair streaming in the wind behind him, we recognized
the ruddy face and old buckskin frock of Gingras the
trapper. He was just arrived from Fort Laramie, and said
he had a message for us. A trader named Bisonette, one 5
of Henry's friends, had lately come from the settlements,
and intended to go with a party of men to La Bonté's
camp, where, as Gingras assured us, ten or twelve villages
of Indians would certainly assemble. Bisonette desired
that we would cross over and meet him there, and promised that his men should protect our horses and baggage
while we went among the Indians. Shaw and I stopped our
horses, held a council, and in an evil hour resolved to go.

For the rest of that day our course and that of the
Indians was the same. In less than an hour we came to

where the high barren prairie terminated, sinking down abruptly in steep descent; and standing on the verge we saw below us a great meadow. Laramie Creek bounded it on the left sweeping along in the shadow of the heights, and passing with its shallow and rapid current just beneath us. We sat on horseback, waiting and looking on, while the whole savage array went pouring by, hurrying down the declivity and spreading over the meadow below. In a few moments the plain was swarming with the moving multitude, some just visible, like specks in the distance, others still hastening by and fording the stream in bustle and confusion. On the edge of the heights sat a group of the elder warriors, gravely smoking and looking with unmoved faces on the wild and striking spectacle.

Up went the lodges in a circle on the margin of the stream. For the sake of quiet we pitched our tent among some trees half a mile distant. In the afternoon we were in the village. The day was a glorious one, and the whole camp seemed lively and animated in sympathy. Groups of children and young girls were laughing gayly outside the lodges. The shields, the lances, and the bows were removed from the tall tripods on which they usually hung, before the dwellings of their owners. The warriors were mounting their horses, and one by one riding away over the prairie toward the neighboring hills.

Shaw and I sat on the grass near the lodge of Reynal. An old woman, with true Indian hospitality, brought a bowl of boiled venison and placed it before us. We amused ourselves with watching a few young squaws who were playing together and chasing each other in and out of one of the lodges. Suddenly the wild yell of the war-whoop came pealing from the hills. A crowd of horsemen appeared, rushing down their sides, and riding at full speed towards

the village, each warrior's long hair flying behind him in the wind like a ship's streamer. As they approached, the confused throng assumed a regular order, and entering two by two, they circled round the area at full gallop, each

warrior singing his war-song as he rode.   Some of their
dresses were superb.   They wore crests of feathers, and
close tunics of antelope skins, fringed with the scalplocks of their enemies; many of their shields, too, fluttered with the war-eagle's feathers.   All had bows and
arrows at their backs; some carried long lances, and a few
were armed with guns.   The White Shield, their partisan,
rode in gorgeous attire at their head, mounted on a black-
6   and-white horse.   Mahto-Tatonka and his brothers took no
part in this parade, for they were in mourning for their
sister, and were all sitting in their lodges, their bodies
bedaubed from head to foot with white clay, and a lock
7   of hair cut from the forehead of each.

The warriors rode three times round the village; and as
each noted champion passed, the old women would scream
out his name to honor his bravery and excite the emulation of the younger warriors.   Little urchins, not two
years old, followed the warlike pageant with glittering
eyes, and gazed with eager admiration at the heroes of
8   their tribe.

The procession rode out of the village as it had entered
it, and in half an hour all the warriors had returned again,
dropping quietly in, singly or in parties of two or three.

The parade over, we were entertained with an episode of
Indian domestic life.   A vicious-looking squaw, beside her
self with rage, was berating her spouse, who, with a look
of total unconcern, sat cross-legged in the middle of his
lodge, smoking his pipe in silence.   At length, maddened
by his coolness, she made a rush at the lodge, seized the
poles which supported it, and tugged at them, one after
the other, till she brought down the whole structure, poles,
hides, and all, clattering on his head, burying him in the
wreck of his habitation.   He pushed aside the hides with

his hand, and presently his head emerged, like a turtle's
from its shell. Still he sat smoking sedately as before,
a wicked glitter in his eyes alone betraying the pent-up
storm within. The squaw, scolding all the while, proceeded to saddle her horse, bestride him, and canter out
of the camp, intending, as it seemed, to return to her
father's lodge, wherever that
might be. The warrior, who
had not deigned even to look
at her, now coolly rose, disengaged himself from the
ruins, tied a cord of hair by
way of bridle round the jaw
of his buffalo-horse, broke a
stout cudgel, about four feet
long from the but-end of a
lodge pole, mounted, and galloped majestically over the
prairie to discipline his offending helpmeet.

9

As the sun rose next morning we looked across the
meadow, and could see the lodges levelled and the Indians
gathering together in preparation to leave the camp. Their
course lay to the westward. We turned towards the north
with our three men, the four trappers following us, with
the Indian family of Morin. We travelled until night, and
encamped among some trees by the side of a little brook,
where during the whole of the next day we lay waiting for
Bisonette; but no Bisonette appeared. Here two of our
trapper friends left us, and set out for the Rocky Mountains. On the second morning, despairing of Bisonette's
arrival, we resumed our journey, traversing a forlorn and
dreary monotony of sun-scorched plains, where no living

thing appeared save here and there an antelope flying before us like the wind. When noon came we saw an unwonted and welcome sight,—a fine growth of trees, marking the course of a little stream called Horseshoe Creek. They stood wide asunder, spreading a thick canopy of leaves above a surface of rich, tall grass. The stream ran swiftly, as clear as crystal, through the bosom of the wood, sparkling over its bed of white sand, and darkening again as it entered a

deep cavern of foliage. I was thoroughly exhausted, and flung myself on the ground, scarcely able to move.

11

In the morning, as glorious a sun rose upon us as ever animated that wilderness. We advanced, and soon were surrounded by tall bare hills, overspread from top to bottom with prickly pears and other cacti, that seemed like clinging reptiles. A plain, flat and hard, with scarcely the vestige of grass, lay before us, and a line of tall, misshapen trees bounded the onward view. There was no sight or sound of man or beast, or any living thing, although behind those trees was the long-looked-for place of rendezvous, where we hoped to have found the Indians congregated by thousands. We looked and listened anxiously. We pushed forward with our best speed, and forced our horses through the trees. There were copses of some extent beyond, with a scanty stream creeping among them; and as we pressed through the yielding branches, deer sprang up to the right and left. At length we caught a glimpse of the prairie beyond, emerged upon it, and saw, not a plain covered with encampments and swarming with life, but a vast unbroken desert stretching away before us league upon league, without bush or tree, or any living thing. We drew rein and gave to the winds our sentiments concerning the whole aboriginal race of America. Our journey was worse than vain. For myself, I was vexed beyond measure; as I well knew that a slight aggravation of my disorder would render this false step irrevocable, and make it impossible to accomplish effectually the object which had led me an arduous journey of between three and four thousand miles. 12

And where were the Indians? They were mustered in great numbers at a spot about twenty miles distant, where at that very moment they were dancing their war dances. 13 The scarcity of buffalo in the vicinity of La Bonté's camp, which would render their supply of provisions scanty and precarious, had probably prevented them from assembling there; but of all this we knew nothing until some weeks after.

Shaw lashed his horse and galloped forward. I, though much more vexed than he, was not strong enough to adopt this convenient vent to my feelings; so I followed at a quiet pace. We rode up to a solitary old tree, which seemed the only place fit for encampment. Half its branches were dead, and the rest were so scantily furnished with leaves that they cast but a meagre and wretched shade. We threw down our saddles in the strip of shadow cast by the old twisted trunk, and sat down upon them. In silent indignation we remained smoking for an hour or more, shifting our saddles with the shifting shadow, for the sun was intolerably hot.

CHAPTER XIII.

A T last we had reached La Bonté's camp, towards which our eyes had turned so long. Of all weary hours, those that passed between noon and sunset of that day may bear away the palm of exquisite discomfort. I lay under the tree reflecting on what course to pursue, watching the shadows which seemed never to move, and the sun which seemed fixed in the sky, and hoping every moment to see the men and horses of Bisonette emerging from the woods. Shaw and Henry had ridden out on a scouting expedition, and did not return till the sun was setting. There was nothing very cheering in their faces or in the news they brought.

"We have been ten miles from here," said Shaw. "We climbed the highest butte we could find, and could not see a buffalo or an Indian; nothing but prairie for twenty miles around us." Henry's horse was disabled by clambering up and down the sides of ravines, and Shaw's was greatly fatigued.

After supper that evening, as we sat round the fire, I proposed to Shaw to wait one day longer, in hopes of

Bisonette's arrival, and if he should not come, to send Deslauriers with the cart and baggage back to Fort Laramie, while we ourselves followed The Whirlwind's village, and attempted to overtake it as it passed the mountains. Shaw, not having the same motive for hunting Indians that I had, was averse to the plan; I therefore resolved to go alone. This design I adopted very unwillingly, for I knew that in the present state of my health the attempt would be painful and hazardous. I hoped that Bisonette would appear in the course of the following day, and bring us some information by which to direct our course, thus enabling me to accomplish my purpose by means less objectionable. 1

The rifle of Henry Chatillon was necessary for the subsistence of the party in my absence; so I called Raymond, 2 and ordered him to prepare to set out with me. Raymond rolled his eyes vacantly about, but at length, having succeeded in grappling with the idea, he withdrew to his bed under the cart. He was a heavy-moulded fellow, with a broad face expressing impenetrable stupidity and entire self-confidence. As for his good qualities, he had a sort of stubborn fidelity, an insensibility to danger, and a kind of instinct or sagacity, which sometimes led him right where better heads than his were at a loss. Besides this, he knew very well how to handle a rifle and picket a horse.

Through the following day the sun glared down upon us with a pitiless, penetrating heat. The distant blue prairie seemed quivering under it. The lodge of our Indian associates parched in the burning rays, and our rifles as they leaned against the tree were too hot for the touch. There was a dead silence through our camp, broken only by the hum of gnats and mosquitoes. The men, resting their foreheads on their arms, were sleeping under the cart. The Indians kept close within their lodge, except the newly married pair, who were seated together under an awning of buffalo-robes, and the old conjurer, who, with his hard, emaciated face and gaunt ribs, was perched aloft like a turkey-buzzard, among the dead branches of an old tree, constantly on the lookout for enemies. We dined, and then Shaw saddled his horse.

"I will ride back," said he, "to Horseshoe Creek, and see if Bisonette is there."

"I would go with you," I answered, "but I must reserve all the strength I have."

The afternoon dragged away at last. I occupied myself in cleaning my rifle and pistols, and making other preparations for the journey. It was late before I wrapped myself in my blanket, and lay down for the night, with my head on my saddle. Shaw had not returned, but this gave us no uneasiness, for we supposed that he had fallen in with Bisonette and was spending the night with him. For a day or two past I had gained in strength and health, but about midnight an attack of pain awoke me, and for some hours I could not sleep. The moon was quivering on the broad breast of the Platte; nothing could be heard except those low, inexplicable sounds, like whisperings and footsteps, which no one who has spent the night alone amid deserts and forests will be at a loss to understand. As I was falling asleep a familiar voice, shouting from the distance, awoke me again. A rapid step approached the camp, and Shaw, on foot, with his gun in his hand, hastily entered.

"Where's your horse?" said I, raising myself on my elbow.

"Lost!" said Shaw. "Where's Deslauriers?"

"There," I replied, pointing to a confused mass of blankets and buffalo-robes.

Shaw touched them with the butt of his gun, and up sprang our faithful Canadian.

"Come, Deslauriers; stir up the fire and get me something to eat."

"Where's Bisonette?" asked I.

"The Lord knows; there's nobody at Horseshoe Creek."

Shaw had gone back to the spot where we had encamped two days before, and finding nothing there but the ashes of our fires, he had tied his horse to the tree while he bathed in the stream. Something startled his horse, which broke loose, and for two hours Shaw tried in vain to catch him. Sunset approached, and it was twelve miles to camp. So he abandoned the attempt, and set out on foot to join us. The greater part of his solitary and perilous walk was in darkness. His moccasins were worn to tatters, and his feet severely lacerated. He sat down to eat, however, the usual equanimity of his temper not at all disturbed by his misfortune; and my last recollection before falling asleep was of Shaw, seated cross-legged before the fire, smoking his pipe.

When I awoke again there was a fresh, damp smell in the air, a gray twilight involved the prairie, and above its eastern verge was a streak of cold, red sky. I called to the men, and in a moment a fire was blazing brightly in the dim morning light, and breakfast was getting ready. We sat down together on the grass, to the last civilized meal which Raymond and I were destined to enjoy for some time.

"Now bring in the horses."

My little mare Pauline was soon standing by the fire. She was a fleet, hardy, and gentle animal, christened after Paul Dorion, from whom I had procured her in exchange for Pontiac. She did not look as if equipped for a morning pleasure-ride. In front of the black, high-bowed mountain-saddle were fastened holsters, with heavy pistols. A pair of saddle-bags, a blanket tightly rolled, a small parcel of Indian presents tied up in buffalo-skin, a leather bag of flour, and a smaller one of tea, were all secured behind, and a long trail-rope was wound round her neck. Raymond had a strong black mule, equipped in a similar manner. We crammed our powder-horns to the throat, and mounted.

"I will meet you at Fort Laramie on the first of August," said I to Shaw.

"That is," he replied, "if we don't meet before that. I think I shall follow you in a day or two."

This in fact he attempted, and would have succeeded if he had not encountered obstacles against which his resolute spirit was of no avail. Two days after I left him he sent Deslauriers to the fort with the cart and baggage, and set out for the mountains with Henry Chatillon; but a violent thunder-storm had deluged the prairie, and obliterated not only our trail but that of the Indians themselves. They encamped at the base of the mountains, at a loss in what direction to go. In the morning Shaw found himself poisoned by the plant popularly known in New England as "poison ivy," in such a manner that it was impossible for him to travel. So they turned back reluctantly toward Fort Laramie. Shaw lay seriously ill for a week, and remained at the fort till I rejoined him some time after.

To return to my own story. Raymond and I shook hands with our friends, rode out upon the prairie, and clambering the sandy hollows channelled in the sides of the hills, gained the high plains above. If a curse had been pronounced upon the land, it could not have worn an aspect more forlorn. There were abrupt broken hills, deep hollows, and wide plains; but all alike glared with an insupportable whiteness under the burning sun. The country, as if parched by the heat, was cracked into innumerable fissures and ravines, that not a little impeded our progress. Their steep sides were white and raw, and along the bottom we several times discovered the broad tracks of the grizzly bear, nowhere more abundant than in this region. The ridges of the hills were hard as rock, and strewn with pebbles of flint and coarse red jasper; looking from them, there was nothing to relieve the desert uniformity, save here and there a pine-tree clinging at the edge of a ravine, and stretching its rough, shaggy arms into the scorching air. Its resinous odors recalled the pine-clad mountains of New England, and, goaded as I was with a morbid thirst, I thought with a longing desire on the crystal treasure poured in such wasteful profusion from our thousand hills. I heard, in fancy, the plunging and gurgling of waters among the shaded rocks, and saw them gleaming dark and still far down amid the crevices, the cold drops trickling from the long green mosses. 7

When noon came we found a little stream, with a few 8 trees and bushes; and here we rested for an hour. Then we travelled on, guided by the sun, until, just before sunset, we reached another stream called Bitter Cottonwood Creek. A thick growth of bushes and old, storm-beaten 9 trees grew at intervals along its bank. Near the foot of one of the trees we flung down our saddles, and hobbling our horses, turned them loose to feed. The little stream was clear and swift and ran musically over its white sands. Small water-birds were splashing in the shallows and filling the air with cries and flutterings. The sun was just sinking among gold and crimson clouds behind Mount Laramie. I lay upon a log by the margin of the water, and watched the restless motions of the little fish in a deep still nook below. Strange to say, I seemed to have gained strength since the morning, and almost felt a sense of returning health.

We built our fire. Night came, and the wolves began to howl. One deep voice began, answered in awful responses from hills, plains, and woods. Such sounds do not disturb one's sleep upon the prairie. We picketed the mare and the mule and did not awake until daylight. Then we turned them loose, still hobbled, to feed for an hour before starting. We were getting ready our breakfast when Raymond saw an antelope half a mile distant and said he would go and shoot it.

"Your business," said I, "is to look after the animals. I am too weak to do much if anything happens to them, and you must keep within sight of the camp."

Raymond promised, and set out with his rifle in his hand. The mare and the mule had crossed the stream, and were feeding among the long grass on the other side, much tormented by the attacks of large, green-headed flies. As I watched them I saw them go down into a hollow, and as several minutes elapsed without their reappearing, I waded through the stream to look after them. To my vexation and alarm I discovered them at a great distance, galloping away at full speed, Pauline in advance, with her hobbles broken, and the mule, still fettered, following with awkward leaps. I fired my rifle and shouted to recall Raymond. In a moment he came running through the stream, with a red handkerchief bound round his head. I pointed to the fugitives, and ordered him to pursue them. Muttering a "Sacré," between his teeth, he set out at full speed, still swinging his rifle in his hand. I walked up to the top of a hill, and, looking away over the prairie, could distinguish the runaways, still at full gallop. Returning to the fire, I sat down at the foot of a tree. Wearily and anxiously hour after hour passed away. The loose bark dangling from the trunk behind me flapped to and fro in the wind, and the mosquitoes kept up their drowsy hum; but other than this there was no sight nor sound of life throughout the burning landscape. The sun rose higher and higher, until I knew that it must be noon. It seemed scarcely possible that the animals could be recovered. If they were not, my situation was one of serious difficulty. Shaw, when I left him, had decided to move that morning, but whither he had not determined. To look for him would be a vain attempt. Fort Laramie was forty miles distant, and I could not walk a mile without great effort. Not then having learned the philosophy of yielding to disproportionate obstacles, I resolved, come what would, to continue the pursuit of the Indians. Only one plan occurred to me; this was, to send Raymond to the fort with an order for more horses, while I remained on the spot, awaiting his return, which might take place within three days. But to remain stationary and alone for three days, in a country full of dangerous Indians, was not the most flattering of prospects; and, protracted as my Indian hunt must be by such delay, it was not easy to foretell its result. Revolving these matters, I grew hungry; and as our stock of provisions, except four or five pounds of flour, was by this time exhausted, I left the camp to see what game I could find. Nothing could be seen except four or five large curlews wheeling over my head, and now and then alighting upon the prairie. I shot two of them, and was about returning, when a startling sight caught my eye. A small dark object, like a human head, suddenly appeared, and vanished among the thick bushes along the stream below.   In that country every stranger is a suspected enemy; and I threw forward the muzzle of my rifle.   In a moment the bushes were violently shaken; two heads, but not human heads, protruded; and to my great joy I recognized the downcast, disconsolate countenance of the black mule, and the yellow visage of Pauline.   Raymond came upon the mule, pale and haggard, complaining of a fiery pain in his chest.   I took charge of the animals while he kneeled down by the side of the stream to drink.   He had kept the runaways in sight as far as the Side Fork of Laramie Creek, a distance of more than ten miles; and here with great difficulty he had succeeded in catching them.   I saw that he was unarmed, and asked him what he had done with his rifle.   It had encumbered him in his pursuit, and he had dropped it on the prairie, thinking that he could find it on his return; but in this he had failed. The loss might prove a very serious one.   I was too much rejoiced, however, at the recovery of the animals, and at the fidelity of Raymond, who might easily have deserted with them, to think much about it; and having made some tea for him in a tin vessel which we had brought with us, I told him that I would give him two hours for resting before we set out again.   He had eaten nothing that day; but having no appetite, he lay down immediately to sleep.   I picketed the animals among the best grass that I could find, and made fires of green wood to protect them from the flies; then sitting down again by the tree, I watched the slow movements of the sun, grudging every moment that passed.

The time I had mentioned expired, and I awoke Raymond.   We saddled and set out again, but first we went in search of the lost rifle, and in the course of an hour

were fortunate enough to find it. Then we turned westward, and moved over the hills and hollows at a slow pace
towards Mount Laramie. The heat no longer tormented
us, for a cloud was before the sun. The air grew fresh
and cool, the distant mountains frowned more gloomily,
there was a low muttering of thunder, and dense, black
masses of cloud rose heavily behind the broken peaks.
At first they were fringed with silver by the afternoon
sun; but soon thick blackness overspread the sky, and
the desert around us was wrapped in gloom. There was
an awful sublimity in the hoarse murmuring of the thunder, and the sombre shadows that involved the mountains
and the plain. The storm broke with a zigzag blinding
flash, a terrific crash of thunder, and a hurricane that
howled over the prairie, dashing floods of water against
us. Raymond looked about him and cursed the merciless
elements. There seemed no shelter near, but we discerned at length a deep ravine gashed in the level prairie,
and saw half-way down its side an old pine-tree, whose
rough horizontal boughs formed a sort of pent-house against
the tempest. We found a practicable passage, led our animals down, and fastened them to large loose stones at the
bottom; then climbing up, we drew our blankets over our
heads, and crouched close beneath the old tree. Perhaps
I was no competent judge of time, but it seemed to me
that we were sitting there a full hour, while around us
poured a deluge of rain, through which the rocks on the
opposite side of the gulf were barely visible. The first
burst of the tempest soon subsided, but the rain poured in
steady torrents. At length Raymond grew impatient, and
scrambling out of the ravine, gained the level prairie above.

"What does the weather look like?" asked I from my
seat under the tree.

"It looks bad," he answered,—"dark all round;" and again he descended and sat down by my side. Some ten minutes elapsed.

"Go up again," said I, "and take another look;" and he clambered up the precipice. "Well, how is it?"

"Just the same, only I see one little bright spot over the top of the mountain."

The rain by this time had begun to abate; and going down to the bottom of the ravine we loosened the animals, who were standing up to their knees in water. Leading them up the rocky throat of the ravine, we reached the plain above. All around us was obscurity; 15 but the bright spot above the mountains grew wider and ruddier, until at length the clouds drew apart, and a flood of sunbeams poured down, streaming along the precipices, and involving them in a thin blue haze, as soft as that which wraps the Apennines on an evening in spring. 16 Rapidly the clouds were broken and scattered, like routed legions of evil spirits. The plain lay basking in sunbeams around us; a rainbow arched the desert from north to south, and far in front a line of woods seemed inviting us to refreshment and repose. When we reached them, they were glistening with prismatic dew-drops, and enlivened by the songs and flutterings of birds. Strange winged insects, benumbed by the rain, were clinging to the leaves and the bark of the trees.

Raymond kindled a fire with great difficulty. The animals turned eagerly to feed on the soft rich grass, while I, wrapping myself in my blanket, lay down and gazed on the evening landscape. The mountains, whose stern features had frowned upon us so gloomily, seemed lighted up with a benignant smile, and the green, waving undulations 17 of the plain were gladdened with warm sunshine. Wet, ill, and wearied as I was, my heart grew lighter at the view, and I drew from it an augury of good.

When morning came Raymond awoke coughing violently, though I had apparently received no injury. We mounted, crossed the little stream, pushed through the trees, and began our journey over the plain beyond. And now, as we rode slowly along, we looked anxiously on every hand for traces of the Indians, not doubting that the village had passed somewhere in that vicinity; but the scanty, shrivelled grass was not more than three or four inches high, and the ground was so hard that a host might have marched over it and left scarcely a trace of its passage.

Up hill and down hill, and clambering through ravines, we continued our journey. As we were passing the foot of a hill I saw Raymond, who was some rods in advance, suddenly jerk the reins of his mule, slide from his seat, and run in a crouching posture up a hollow; then in an instant I heard the sharp crack of his rifle. A wounded antelope came running on three legs over the hill. I lashed Pauline and made after him. My fleet little mare soon brought me by his side, and, after leaping and bounding for a few moments in vain, he stood still, as if despairing of escape. His glistening eyes turned up towards my face with so piteous a look that it was with feelings of infinite compunction that I shot him through the head with a pistol. Raymond skinned and cut him up, and we hung the fore-quarters to our saddles, much rejoiced that our exhausted stock of provisions was renewed in such good time.

Gaining the top of a hill we could see along the cloudy verge of the prairie before us the lines of trees and shadowy groves, that marked the course of Laramie Creek. Before

noon we reached its banks, and began anxiously to search
them for footprints of the Indians. We followed the stream
for several miles, now on the shore and now wading in the
water, scrutinizing every sand-bar and every muddy bank.
So long was the search that we began to fear that we had
left the trail undiscovered behind us. At length I heard
Raymond shouting, and saw him jump from his mule to
examine some object under the bank. I rode up to his
side. It was the impression of an Indian moccasin. Encouraged by this, we continued our search, till at last
some appearances on a soft surface of earth not far from
the shore attracted my eye; and going to examine them,
I found half a dozen tracks, some made by men and
some by children. Just then Raymond observed across
the stream the mouth of a brook entering it from the   20
south. He forded the water, rode in at the opening, and
in a moment I heard him shouting again; so I passed over
and joined him. The brook had a broad sandy bed, along
which the water trickled in a scanty stream; and on either
bank the bushes were so close that the view was completely intercepted. I found Raymond stooping over the
footprints of three or four horses. Proceeding, we found
those of a man, then those of a child, then those of more
horses; till at last the bushes on each bank were beaten
down and broken, and the sand ploughed up with a multitude of footsteps, and scored across with the furrows made
by the lodge-poles that had been dragged through. It was
now certain that we had found the trail. I pushed through
the bushes, and at a little distance on the prairie beyond
found the ashes of a hundred and fifty lodge-fires, with
bones and pieces of buffalo-robes scattered about, and the
pickets to which horses had been tied, still standing
in the ground. Elated by our success, we selected a con-

venient tree, and, turning the animals loose, prepared to
make a meal from the haunch of the antelope.

Hardship and exposure had thriven with me wonderfully. I had gained both health and strength since leaving La Bonté's camp. Raymond and I dined together
in high spirits; for we rashly presumed that having found
one end of the trail we should have little difficulty in
reaching the other. But when the animals were led in
we found that our ill-luck had not ceased to follow us.
As I was saddling Pauline, I saw that her eye was dull
as lead, and the hue of her yellow coat visibly darkened.
I placed my foot in the stirrup to mount, when she staggered and fell flat on her side. Gaining her feet with an
effort, she stood by the fire with a drooping head. Whether
she had been bitten by a snake, or poisoned by some nox-
ious plant, or attacked by a sudden disorder, it was hard
to say; but at all events, her sickness was sufficiently ill-
timed and unfortunate. I succeeded in a second attempt to
mount her, and with a slow pace we moved forward on the
trail of the Indians. It led us up a hill and over a dreary
plain; and here, to our great mortification, the traces
almost disappeared, for the ground was hard as adamant;
and if its flinty surface had ever retained the dint of a
hoof, the marks had been washed away by the deluge of yesterday. An Indian village, in its disorderly march, is
scattered over the prairie often to the width of half a
mile; so that its trail is nowhere clearly marked, and the
task of following it is made doubly wearisome and difficult.
By good fortune, many large ant-hills, a yard or more in
diameter, were scattered over the plain, and these were
frequently broken by the footprints of men and horses,
and marked by traces of the lodge-poles. The succulent
leaves of the prickly-pear, bruised from the same causes,

also helped to guide us; so inch by inch we moved along. Often we lost the trail altogether, and then found it again; but late in the afternoon we were totally at fault. We stood alone, without a clew to guide us. The broken plain expanded for league after league around us, and in front the long, dark ridge of mountains stretched from north to south. Mount Laramie, a little on our right, towered high above the rest, and from a dark valley just beyond one of its lower declivities, we discerned volumes of white smoke rising slowly.

21

"I think," said Raymond, "some Indians must be there. Perhaps we had better go." But this plan was not lightly to be adopted, and we determined still to continue our search after the lost trail. Our good stars prompted us to this decision, for we afterward had reason to believe, from information given us by the Indians, that the smoke was raised as a decoy by a Crow war-party.

Evening was coming on, and there was neither wood nor water nearer than the foot of the mountains. So thither we turned, directing our course towards the point where Laramie Creek issues upon the prairie. When we reached it, the bare tops of the mountains were still bright with sunshine. The little river was breaking, with an angry current, from its dark prison. There was something in the close vicinity of the mountains and the loud surging of the rapids wonderfully cheering and exhilarating. There was a grass-plot by the river bank, surrounded by low ridges, which would effectually screen us and our fire from the sight of wandering Indians. Here among the grass, I observed numerous circles of large stones, traces of a Dakota winter encampment. We lay down, and did not awake till the sun was up. A large rock projected from the shore, and behind it the deep water

22

was slowly eddying round and round. The temptation was irresistible. I threw off my clothes, leaped in, suffered myself to be borne once round with the current, and then, seizing the strong root of a water-plant, drew myself to the shore. The effect was so refreshing that I mistook it for returning health. But scarcely were we mounted and on our way, before the momentary glow passed. Again I hung as usual in my seat, scarcely able to hold myself erect.

"Look yonder," said Raymond; "you see that big hollow there; the Indians must have gone that way, if they went anywhere about here."

We reached the gap, which was like a deep notch cut into the mountain-ridge, and here we soon found an ant-hill furrowed with the mark of a lodge-pole. This was quite enough; there could be no doubt now. As we rode on, the opening growing narrower, the Indians had been compelled to march in closer order, and the traces became numerous and distinct. The gap terminated in a rocky gateway, leading into a rough and steep defile, between two precipitous mountains. Here grass and weeds were bruised to fragments by the throng that had passed through. We moved slowly over the rocks, up the passage; and in this toilsome manner advanced for an hour or two, bare precipices, hundreds of feet high, shooting up on either hand. Raymond, with his hardy mule, was a few rods before me when we came to the foot of an ascent steeper than the rest, and which I trusted might prove the highest point of the defile. Pauline strained upward for a few yards, moaning and stumbling, and then came to a dead stop, unable to proceed further. I dismounted, and attempted to lead her; but my own exhausted strength soon gave out; so I loosened the trail-rope from her neck, and tying it round my arm, crawled up on my hands and knees. I gained the top, totally spent, the sweat-drops trickling from my forehead. Pauline stood like a statue by my side, her shadow falling upon the scorching rock; and in this shade, for there was no other, I lay for some time, scarcely able to move a limb. All around, the black crags, sharp as needles at the top, stood baking in the sun, without tree or bush or blade of grass to cover their nakedness. The whole scene seemed parched with a pitiless, insufferable heat.

After a while I could mount again, and we moved on, descending the defile on its western side. There was something ridiculous in the situation. Man and horse were helpless alike. Pauline and I could neither fight nor run. 24

Raymond's saddle-girth slipped; and while I proceeded he stopped to repair the mischief. I came to the top of a little declivity, where a welcome sight greeted my eye; a nook of fresh green grass nestled among the cliffs, sunny clumps of bushes on one side, and shaggy old pine-trees leaning from the rocks on the other. A shrill, familiar voice saluted me, and recalled me to days of boyhood,—that of the insect called the "locust" by New 25 England schoolboys, which was clinging among the heated boughs of the old pine-trees. Then, too, as I passed the bushes, the low sound of falling water reached my ear. Pauline turned of her own accord, and pushing through the boughs we found a black rock overarched by the cool green canopy. An icy stream was pouring from its side into a wide basin of white sand, whence it had no visible outlet, but filtered through into the soil below. While I filled a tin cup at the spring, Pauline was eagerly plunging her head deep in the pool. Other visitors had been there before us. All around in the soft soil were the footprints of elk,

26   deer, and the Rocky Mountain sheep; and the grizzly bear too
had left the recent prints of his broad foot, with its frightful
array of claws.   Among these mountains was his home.

Soon after leaving the spring we found a little grassy
plain, encircled by the mountains, and marked, to our
great joy, with all the traces of an Indian camp.   Raymond's practised eye detected certain signs, by which he
recognized the spot where Reynal's lodge had been pitched
and his horses picketed.   I approached, and stood looking
at the place.   Reynal and I had, I believe, hardly a feeling in common, and it perplexed me a good deal to understand why I should look with so much interest on the ashes
of his fire, when between him and me there was no other
bond of sympathy than the slender and precarious one of
27   a kindred race.

In half an hour from this we were free of the mountains.   There was a plain before us totally barren and
thickly peopled in many parts with prairie-dogs, who sat
at the mouths of their burrows and yelped at us as we
passed.   The plain, as we thought, was about six miles
wide, but it cost us two hours to cross it.   Then another
mountain-range rose before us.   From the dense bushes
that clothed the steeps for a thousand feet shot up black
28   crags, all leaning one way, and shattered by storms and
thunder into grim and threatening shapes.   As we entered
a narrow passage on the trail of the Indians, they im-
pended frightfully above our heads.

Our course was through thick woods, in the shade and
sunlight of overhanging boughs.   As we wound from side
to side of the passage to avoid its obstructions, we could
see at intervals, through the foliage, the awful forms of
the gigantic cliffs, that seemed to hem us in on the right
29   and on the left, before and behind.

In an open space, fenced in by high rocks, stood two Indian forts, of a square form, rudely built of logs and branches. They were somewhat ruinous, having probably been constructed the year before. Each might have contained about twenty men. Perhaps in this gloomy spot some party had been beset by enemies, and those scowling rocks and blasted trees might not long since have looked down on a conflict, unchronicled and unknown. Yet if any traces of bloodshed remained they were hidden by the bushes and tall, rank weeds.

Gradually the mountains drew apart, and the passage expanded into a plain, where again we found traces of an Indian encampment. There were trees and bushes just before us, and we stopped here for an hour's rest and refreshment. When we had finished our meal Raymond struck fire, and lighting his pipe, sat down at the foot of a tree to smoke. For some time I observed him puffing away with a face of unusual solemnity. Then slowly taking the pipe from his lips, he looked up and remarked that we had better not go any farther.

"Why not?" asked I.

He said that the country was become very dangerous, that we were entering the range of the Snakes, Arapahoes, and Gros-ventre Blackfeet, and that if any of their wandering parties should meet us, it would cost us our lives; but he added, with blunt fidelity, that he would go anywhere I wished. I told him to bring up the animals, and mounting them we proceeded again. I confess that, as we moved forward, the prospect seemed but a doubtful one. I would have given the world for my ordinary elasticity of body and mind, and for a horse of such strength and spirit as the journey required.

Closer and closer the rocks gathered round us, growing

taller and steeper, and pressing more and more upon our path. We entered at length a defile which, in its way, I never have seen rivalled. The mountain was cracked from top to bottom, and we were creeping along the bottom of the fissure, in dampness and gloom, with the clink of hoofs on the loose shingly rocks, and the hoarse murmuring of a petulant brook which kept us company. Sometimes the water, foaming among the stones, overspread the whole narrow passage; sometimes, withdrawing to one side, it gave us room to pass dry shod. Looking up, we could see a narrow ribbon of bright blue sky between the dark edges of the opposing cliffs. This did not last long. The passage soon widened, and sunbeams found their way down, flashing upon the black waters. The defile would spread to many rods in width; bushes, trees, and flowers would spring by the side of the brook; the cliffs would be feathered with shrubbery that clung in every crevice, and fringed with trees that grew along their sunny edges. Then we would be moving again in darkness. The passage seemed about four miles long, and before we reached the end of it the unshod hoofs of our animals were broken, and their legs cut by the sharp stones. Issuing from the mountain we found another plain. All around it stood a circle of precipices, that seemed the impersonation of Silence and Solitude. Here again the Indians had encamped, as well they might after passing with their women, children, and horses, through the gulf behind us. In one day we had made a journey which it had cost them three to accomplish.

The only outlet to this amphitheatre lay over a hill some two hundred feet high, up which we moved with difficulty. Looking from the top we saw that at last we were free of the mountains. The prairie spread before

us, but so wild and broken that the view was everywhere
obstructed.   Far on our left one tall hill swelled up against
the sky, on the smooth, pale-green surface of which four
slowly moving black specks were discernible.   They were
evidently buffalo, and we hailed the sight as a good augury;   31
for where the buffalo were, there the Indians would probably
be found. We hoped on that very night to reach the village.   We were anxious to do so for a double reason, wishing to bring our journey to an end, and knowing moreover
that though to enter the village in broad daylight would be
perfectly safe, yet to encamp in its vicinity would be dangerous.   But as we rode on, the sun was sinking, and soon
was within half an hour of the horizon.   We ascended a hill
and looked about us for a spot for our encampment.   The
prairie was like a turbulent ocean suddenly congealed when
its waves were at the highest, and it lay half in light and
half in shadow, as the rich sunshine, yellow as gold, was
pouring over it.   The rough bushes of the wild sage were
growing everywhere, its dull pale-green overspreading hill
and hollow.   Yet a little way before us a bright green
belt of grass was winding along the plain, and here and
there throughout its course glistened pools of water.   We
went down to it, kindled a fire, and turned our horses loose
to feed.   It was a little trickling brook, that for some yards
on either side turned the barren prairie into fertility, and
here and there it spread into deep pools, where the beavers
had dammed it up.

We placed our last remaining piece of antelope before
a scanty fire, mournfully reflecting on our exhausted stock
of provisions.   Just then a large gray hare, peculiar to
these prairies, came jumping along, and seated himself
within fifty yards to look at us.   I thoughtlessly raised
my rifle to shoot him, but Raymond called out to me not

to fire, for fear the report should reach the ears of the Indians. That night for the first time we considered that the danger to which we were exposed was of a somewhat serious character; and to those who are unacquainted with Indians, it may seem strange that our chief apprehensions arose from the supposed proximity of the people whom we intended to visit. Had any straggling party of these faithful friends caught sight of us from the hill-top, they would probably have returned in the night to plunder us of our horses, and perhaps of our scalps. But the prairie is unfavorable to nervousness; and I presume that neither Raymond nor I thought twice of the matter that evening.

For eight hours, pillowed on our saddles, we lay insensible as logs. Pauline's yellow head was stretched over me when I awoke. I rose and examined her. Her feet were bruised and swollen by the accidents of yesterday, but her eye was brighter, her motions livelier, and her mysterious malady had visibly abated. We moved on, hoping within an hour to come in sight of the Indian village; but again disappointment awaited us. The trail disappeared upon a hard and stony plain. Raymond and I rode from side to side, scrutinizing every yard of ground, until at length I found traces of the lodge-poles, by the side of a ridge of rocks. We began again to follow them.

"What is that black spot out there on the prairie?"

"It looks like a dead buffalo," answered Raymond.

We rode to it, and found it to be the huge carcass of a bull killed by the hunters as they had passed. Tangled hair and scraps of hide were scattered on all sides, for the wolves had made merry over it, and hollowed out the entire carcass. It was covered with myriads of large black crickets, and from its appearance must have lain there four or five days. The sight was a disheartening one, and I observed to Raymond that the Indians might still be fifty or sixty miles off. But he shook his head, and replied that they dared not go so far for fear of their enemies the Snakes.

Soon after this we lost the trail again, and ascended a neighboring ridge, totally at a loss. Before us lay a plain perfectly flat, spreading on the right and left, without apparent limit, and bounded in front by a long, broken line of hills, ten or twelve miles distant. All was open and exposed to view, yet not a buffalo nor an Indian was visible.

"Do you see that?" said Raymond; "now we had better turn round."

But as Raymond's *bourgeois* thought otherwise, we descended the hill and began to cross the plain. We had come so far that neither Pauline's limbs nor my own could carry me back to Fort Laramie. I considered that the lines of expediency and inclination tallied exactly, and that the most prudent course was to keep forward. The ground immediately around us was thickly strewn with the skulls and bones of buffalo, for here, a year or two before, the Indians had made a "surround;" yet no living game was in sight. At length an antelope sprang up and gazed at us. We fired together, and both missed, although the animal stood, a fair mark, within eighty yards. This ill-success might perhaps be charged to our own eagerness, for by this time we had no provisions left except a little flour. We could see several pools of water, glistening in the distance. As we approached, wolves and antelopes bounded away through the tall grass around them, and flocks of large white plover flew screaming over their surface. Having failed of the antelope Raymond tried his hand at the birds, with the same ill-success. The water also disappointed us. Its margin was so mired by the crowd of buffalo that our timorous animals were afraid to approach. So we turned away and moved towards the hills. The rank grass, where it was not trampled down by the buffalo, fairly swept our horses' necks.

Again we found the same execrable barren prairie, offering no clew by which to guide our way. As we drew near the hills an opening appeared, through which the Indians must have gone if they had passed that way at all. Slowly we began to ascend it. I felt the most dreary forebodings of ill-success when on looking round I could discover neither dent of hoof, nor footprint, nor trace of lodge-pole, though the passage was encumbered by the skulls of buffalo. We heard thunder muttering; another storm was coming on.

As we gained the top of the gap the prospect beyond began to disclose itself. First, we saw a long dark line of ragged clouds upon the horizon, while above them rose the peaks of the Medicine-Bow range, the vanguard of the Rocky Mountains; then little by little the plain came into view, a vast green uniformity, forlorn and tenant-less, though Laramie Creek glistened in a waving line over its surface, without a bush or a tree upon its banks. As yet, the round projecting shoulder of a hill inter-cepted a part of the view. I rode in advance, when suddenly I could distinguish a few dark spots on the prairie, along the bank of the stream.

"Buffalo!" said I.

"Horses, by God!" exclaimed Raymond, lashing his mule forward as he spoke. More and more of the plain disclosed itself, and more and more horses appeared scat-tered along the river bank, or feeding in bands over the

prairie. Then, standing in a circle by the stream, swarming with their savage inhabitants, we saw, a mile or more
off, the tall lodges of the Ogillallah. Never did the heart
of wanderer more gladden at the sight of home than did
mine at the sight of that Indian camp. 37

CHAPTER XIV.

THE OGILLALLAH VILLAGE.

THIS is hardly the place for portraying the mental features of the Indians. The same picture, slightly changed in shade and coloring, would serve with very few exceptions for all the tribes north of the Mexican territories. But with this similarity in their modes of thought, the tribes of the lake and ocean shores, of the forests and of the plains, differ greatly in their manner of life. Having been domesticated for several weeks among one of the wildest of the hordes that roam over the remote prairies, I had unusual opportunities of observing them, and flatter myself that a sketch of the scenes that passed daily before my eyes may not be without interest. They were thorough savages. Neither their manners nor their ideas

were in the slightest degree modified by contact with civilization.   They knew nothing of the power and real character of the white men, and their children would scream in
terror when they saw me.   Their religion, superstitions,
and prejudices were those handed down to them from
immemorial time.   They fought with the weapons that
their fathers fought with, and wore the same garments of
skins.   They were living representatives of the "stone
age;" for though their lances and arrows were tipped
with iron procured from the traders, they still used the
rude stone mallet of the primeval world.

Great changes are at hand in that region.   With the
stream of emigration to Oregon and California, the buffalo will dwindle away, and the large wandering com-
munities who depend on them for support must be broken
and scattered.   The Indians will soon be abased by whiskey and overawed by military posts; so that within a few
years the traveller may pass in tolerable security through
their country.   Its danger and its charm will have disappeared together.

As soon as Raymond and I discovered the village from
the gap in the hills, we were seen in our turn; keen eyes
were constantly on the watch.   As we rode down upon
the plain, the side of the village nearest us was darkened
with a crowd of naked figures.   Several men came forward
to meet us.   I could distinguish among them the green
blanket of the Frenchman Reynal.   When we came up
the ceremony of shaking hands had to be gone through
in due form, and then all were eager to know what had
become of the rest of my party.   I satisfied them on this
point, and we all moved together towards the village.

"You 've missed it," said Reynal; "if you 'd been here
day before yesterday, you 'd have found the whole prairie

over yonder black with buffalo as far as you could see. There were no cows, though,—nothing but bulls. We made a 'surround' every day till yesterday. See the village there; don't that look like good living?"

In fact I could see, even at that distance, long cords stretched from lodge to lodge, over which the meat, cut by the squaws into thin sheets, was hanging to dry in the sun. I noticed too that the village was somewhat smaller than when I had last seen it, and I asked Reynal the cause. He said that old Le Borgne had felt too weak to pass over the mountains, and so had remained behind with all his relations, including Mahto-Tatonka and his brothers. The Whirlwind too had been unwilling to come so far, because, as Reynal said, he was afraid. Only half a dozen lodges had adhered to him, the main body of the village setting their chief's authority at naught, and taking the course most agreeable to their inclinations.

"What chiefs are there in the village now?" asked I.

"Well," said Reynal, "there's old Red-Water, and the Eagle-Feather, and the Big Crow, and the Mad Wolf, and The Panther, and the White-Shield, and — what's his name? — the half-breed Cheyenne."

By this time we were close to the village, and I observed that while the greater part of the lodges were very large and neat in their appearance, there was at one side a cluster of squalid, miserable huts. I looked towards them and made some remark about their wretched appearance. But I was touching upon delicate ground.

"My squaw's relations live in those lodges," said Reynal, very warmly; "and there isn't a better set in the whole village."

"Are there any chiefs among them?"

"Chiefs?" said Reynal; "yes, plenty!"

"What are their names?"

"Their names? Why, there's the Arrow-Head. If he isn't a chief he ought to be one. And there's the Hail-Storm. He's nothing but a boy, to be sure; but he's bound to be a chief one of these days."

Just then we passed between two of the lodges, and entered the great area of the village. Superb naked figures stood silently gazing on us.

"Where's the Bad Wound's lodge?" said I to Reynal.

"There you've missed it again! The Bad Wound is away with The Whirlwind. If you could have found him here, and gone to live in his lodge, he would have treated you better than any man in the village. But there's the Big Crow's lodge yonder, next to old Red-Water's. He's a good Indian for the whites, and I advise you to go and live with him."

"Are there many squaws and children in his lodge?" said I.

"No, only one squaw and two or three children. He keeps the rest in a separate lodge by themselves."

So, still followed by a crowd of Indians, Raymond and I rode up to the entrance of the Big Crow's lodge. A squaw came out immediately and took our horses. I put aside the leather flap that covered the low opening, and stooping, entered the Big Crow's dwelling. There I could see the chief in the dim light, seated at one side, on a pile of buffalo robes. He greeted me with a guttural "How, colà!" I requested Reynal to tell him that Raymond and I were come to live with him. The Big Crow gave another low exclamation. The announcement may seem intrusive, but, in fact, every Indian in the village would have deemed himself honored that white men should give such preference to his hospitality.

The squaw spread a buffalo-robe for us in the guest's place at the head of the lodge. Our saddles were brought in, and scarcely were we seated upon them before the place was thronged with Indians, crowding in to see us. The Big Crow produced his pipe and filled it with the mixture of tobacco and *shongsasha*, or red willow bark. Round and round it passed, and a lively conversation went forward. Meanwhile a squaw placed before the two guests a wooden bowl of boiled buffalo-meat; but unhappily this was not the only banquet destined to be inflicted on us. One after another, boys and young squaws thrust their heads in at the opening, to invite us to various feasts in different parts of the village. For half an hour or more we were actively engaged in passing from lodge to lodge, tasting in each of the bowl of meat set before us, and inhaling a whiff or two from our entertainer's pipe. A thunderstorm that had been threatening for some time now began in good earnest. We crossed over to Reynal's lodge, though it hardly deserved the name, for it consisted only of a few old buffalo-robes, supported on poles, and was quite open on one side. Here we sat down, and the Indians gathered round us.

"What is it?" said I, "that makes the thunder?"

"It's my belief," said Reynal, "that it's a big stone rolling over the sky."

"Very likely," I replied; "but I want to know what the Indians think about it."

So he interpreted my question, which produced some debate. There was a difference of opinion. At last old Mene-Seela, or Red-Water, who sat by himself at one side, looked up with his withered face, and said he had always known what the thunder was. It was a great black bird; and once he had seen it, in a dream, swooping

FREDERIC REMINGTON-

down from the Black Hills, with its loud-roaring wings; and when it flapped them over a lake, they struck lightning from the water.　　　　　　　　　　　　　　8

"The thunder is bad," said another old man, who sat muffled in his buffalo-robe; "he killed my brother last summer."

Reynal, at my request, asked for an explanation; but the old man remained doggedly silent and would not look up. Some time after, I learned how the accident occurred. The man who was killed belonged to an association which, among other mystic functions, claimed the exclusive power and privilege of fighting the thunder. Whenever a storm which they wished to avert was threatening, the thunder-fighters would take their bows and arrows, their guns, their magic drum, and a sort of whistle made out of the wing-bone of the war-eagle, and, thus equipped, run out and fire at the rising cloud, whooping, yelling, whistling, and beating their drum to frighten it down again. One afternoon a heavy black cloud was coming up, and they repaired to the top of a hill, where they brought all their magic artillery into play against it. But the undaunted　9 thunder, refusing to be terrified, darted out a bright flash, which struck one of the party dead as he was in the very act of shaking his long iron-pointed lance against it. The rest scattered and ran, yelling in an ecstasy of superstitious terror, back to their lodges.

The lodge of my host Kongra Tonga, or the Big Crow, presented a picturesque spectacle that evening. A score or more of Indians were seated round it in a circle, their dark naked forms just visible by the dull light of the smouldering fire in the middle. The pipe glowed brightly in the gloom as it passed from hand to hand. Then a squaw would drop a piece of buffalo-fat on the dull embers. Instantly a bright flame would leap up, darting its light to the very apex of the tall, conical structure, where the tops of the slender poles that supported the covering of hide were gathered together. It gilded the features of the Indians, as with animated gestures they sat, telling their endless stories of war and hunting, and displayed rude garments of skins that hung round the lodge, — the bow, quiver, and lance, suspended over the resting-place of the chief, and the rifles and powder-horns of the two white guests. For a moment all would be bright as day; then the flames would die out; fitful flashes from the embers would illumine the lodge, and then leave it in darkness. Then the light would wholly fade, and the lodge and all within it be involved again in obscurity.

As I left the lodge next morning I was saluted by howling and yelping all around the village, and half its canine population rushed forth to the attack. Being as cowardly as they were clamorous, they kept jumping about me at the distance of a few yards, only one little cur, about ten inches long, having spirit enough to make a direct assault. He dashed valiantly at the leather tassel which in the Dakota fashion was trailing behind the heel of my moccasin, and kept his hold, growling and snarling all the while, though every step I made almost jerked him over on his back. As I knew that the eyes of the whole village were on the watch to see if I showed any sign of fear, I walked forward without looking to the right or left, surrounded wherever I went by this magic circle of dogs. When I came to Reynal's lodge I sat down by it; on which the dogs dispersed growling to their respective quarters. Only one large white one remained, running about before me and showing his teeth. I called him,

but he only growled the more. I looked at him well.
He was fat and sleek; just such a dog as I wanted. "My
friend," thought I, "you shall pay for this! I will have
you eaten this very morning!"   10

I intended that day to give the Indians a feast, by way
of conveying a favorable impression of my character and
dignity; and a white dog is the dish which the customs
of the Dakota prescribe for all occasions of formality and
importance. I consulted Reynal: he soon discovered that
an old woman in the next lodge was owner of the white
dog. I took a gaudy cotton handkerchief, and, laying it
on the ground, arranged some vermilion, beads, and other
trinkets upon it. Then the old squaw was summoned.
I pointed to the dog and to the handkerchief. She gave
a scream of delight, snatched up the prize, and vanished
with it into her lodge. For a few more trifles, I engaged the services of two other squaws, each of whom
took the white dog by one of his paws, and led him away
behind the lodges. Having killed him they threw him
into a fire to singe; then chopped him up and put him
into two large kettles to boil. Meanwhile I told Ray-   11
mond to fry in buffalo-fat what little flour we had left,
and also to make a kettle of tea as an additional luxury.

The Big Crow's squaw was briskly at work sweeping
out the lodge for the approaching festivity. I confided
to my host himself the task of inviting the guests, thinking that I might thereby shift from my own shoulders
the odium of neglect and oversight.

When feasting is in question one hour of the day serves
an Indian as well as another. My entertainment came off
at about eleven o'clock. At that hour Reynal and Raymond walked across the area of the village, to the admiration of the inhabitants, carrying the two kettles of dog

meat slung on a pole between them. These they placed in the centre of the lodge, and then went back for the bread and the tea. Meanwhile I had put on a pair of brilliant moccasins, and substituted for my old buck-skin frock a coat which I had brought with me in view of such public occasions. I also made careful use of the razor, an operation which no man will neglect who desires to gain the good opinion of Indians. Thus attired, I seated myself between Reynal and Raymond at the head of the lodge. Only a few minutes elapsed before all the guests had come in and were seated on the ground, wedged together in a close circle. Each brought with him a wooden bowl to hold his share of the repast. When all were assembled, two of the officials, called "soldiers" by the white men, came forward with ladles made of the horn of the Rocky Mountain sheep, and began to distribute the feast, assigning a double share to the old men and chiefs. The dog vanished with astonishing celerity, and each guest turned his dish bottom upward to show that all was gone. Then the bread was distributed in its turn, and finally the tea. As the "soldiers" poured it out into the same wooden bowls that had served for the substantial part of the meal, I thought it had a particularly curious and uninviting color.

Oh," said Reynal, "there was not tea enough, so I stirred some soot in the kettle, to make it look strong."

Fortunately an Indian's palate is not very discriminating. The tea was well sweetened, and that was all they cared for.

Now the feast being over, the time for speech-making was come. The Big Crow produced a flat piece of wood, on which he cut up tobacco and *shongsasha*, and mixed them in due proportions. The pipes were filled and

passed from hand to hand around the company. Then I
began my speech, each sentence being interpreted by
Reynal as I went on, and echoed by the whole audience
with the usual exclamations of assent and approval. As
nearly as I can recollect, it was as follows : —

"I had come," I told them, "from a country so far distant that at the rate they travel, they could not reach it
in a year."

"How! how!"

"There the Meneaska were more numerous than the
blades of grass on the prairie. The squaws were far
more beautiful than any they had ever seen, and all the
men were brave warriors."

"How! how! how!"

I was assailed by twinges of conscience as I uttered these
last words. But I recovered myself and began again.   14

"While I was living in the Meneaska lodges, I had
heard of the Ogillallah, how great and brave a nation
they were, how they loved the whites, and how well they
could hunt the buffalo and strike their enemies. I resolved to come and see if all that I heard was true."

"How! how! how! how!"

"As I had come on horseback through the mountains,
I had been able to bring them only a very few presents."

"How!"

"But I had enough tobacco to give them all a small
piece. They might smoke it and see how much better it
was than the tobacco which they got from the traders."   15

"How! how! how!"

"I had plenty of powder, lead, knives, and tobacco at
Fort Laramie. These I was anxious to give them, and if
any of them should come to the fort before I went away,
I would make them handsome presents."

"How! how! how! how!"

Raymond then cut up and distributed among them two or three pounds of tobacco, and old Mene-Seela began to make a reply. It was long, but the following was the pith of it.

"He had always loved the whites. They were the wisest people on earth. He believed they could do anything, and he was always glad when any of them came to live in the Ogillallah lodges. It was true I had not made them many presents, but the reason of it was plain. It was clear that I liked them, or I never should have come so far to find their village."

Several other speeches of similar import followed, and then, this more serious matter being disposed of, there was an interval of smoking, laughing, and conversation. Old Mene-Seela suddenly interrupted it with a loud voice: —

"Now is a good time," he said, "when all the old men and chiefs are here together, to decide what the people shall do. We came over the mountains to make our lodges for next year. Our old ones are good for nothing; they are rotten and worn out. But we have been disappointed. We have killed buffalo-bulls enough, but we have found no herds of cows, and the skins of bulls are too thick and heavy for our squaws to make lodges of. There must be plenty of cows about the Medicine-Bow Mountain. We ought to go there. To be sure it is farther westward than we have ever been before, and perhaps the Snakes will attack us, for those hunting-grounds belong to them. But we must have new lodges at any rate; our old ones will not serve for another year. We ought not to be afraid of the Snakes. Our warriors are brave, and they are all ready for war. Besides, we have three white men with their rifles to help us."

This speech produced a good deal of debate. As Reynal 17 did not interpret what was said, I could only judge of the meaning by the features and gestures of the speakers. At the end of it however the greater number seemed to have fallen in with Mene-Seela's opinion. A short silence followed, and then the old man struck up a discordant chant, which I was told was a song of thanks for the entertainment I had given them.

"Now, said he, "let us go, and give the white men a chance to breathe."

So the company all dispersed into the open air, and for some time the old chief was walking round the village, singing his song in praise of the feast, after the custom of the nation. 18

At last the day drew to a close, and as the sun went down the horses came trooping from the surrounding plains to be picketed before the dwellings of their respective masters. Soon within the great circle of lodges appeared another concentric circle of restless horses; and here and there fires glowed and flickered amid the gloom, on the dusky figures around them. I went over and sat by the lodge of Reynal. The Eagle-Feather, who was a son of Mene-Seela, and brother of my host the Big Crow, was seated there already, and I asked him if the village would move in the morning. He shook his head, and said that nobody could tell, for since old Mahto-Tatonka had died, the people had been like children that did not know their own minds. They were no better than a body without a head. So I, as well as the Indians themselves, fell asleep that night without knowing whether we should set out in the morning towards the country of the Snakes.

At daybreak, however, as I was coming up from the river after my morning's ablutions, I saw that a movement was

contemplated. Some of the lodges were reduced to nothing but bare skeletons of poles; the leather covering of
others was flapping in the wind as the squaws pulled it
off. One or two chiefs of note had resolved, it seemed,
on moving; and they having set their squaws to work, the
example was followed by the rest of the village. One by
one the lodges were sinking down in rapid succession,
and where the great circle of the village had been only a
few moments before, nothing now remained but a ring of
horses and Indians, crowded in confusion together. The
ruins of the lodges were spread over the ground, together
with kettles, stone mallets, great ladles of horn, buffalo-
robes, and cases of painted hide, filled with dried meat.
Squaws bustled about in busy preparation, the old hags
screaming to one another at the stretch of their leathern
lungs. The shaggy horses were patiently standing while
the lodge-poles were lashed to their sides, and the baggage piled upon their backs. The dogs, with tongues lolling out, lay lazily panting, and waiting for the time of
departure. Each warrior sat on the ground by the decay-
ing embers of his fire, unmoved amid the confusion, holding in his hand the long trail-rope of his horse.

As their preparations were completed, each family moved
off the ground. The crowd was rapidly melting away. I
could see them crossing the river, and passing in quick
succession along the profile of the hill on the farther
side. When all were gone I mounted and set out after
them, followed by Raymond, and, as we gained the summit, the whole village came in view at once, straggling
away for a mile or more over the barren plains before us.
Everywhere glittered the iron points of lances. The sun
never shone upon a more strange array. Here were the
heavy-laden pack-horses, some wretched old woman leading

them,
and two or
three children
clinging to their backs.
Here were mules or ponies covered
from head to tail with gaudy trappings, and mounted by
some gay young squaw, grinning bashfulness and pleasure as the Meneaska looked at her. Boys with miniature
bows and arrows wandered over the plains, little naked children ran along on foot, and numberless dogs scampered
among the feet of the horses. The young braves, gaudy with
paint and feathers, rode in groups among the crowd, often
galloping, two or three at once along the line, to try the
speed of their horses. Here and there you might see a rank
of sturdy pedestrians stalking along in their white buffalo-

robes. These were the dignitaries of the village, the old men and warriors, to whose age and experience that wandering democracy yielded a silent deference. With the rough prairie and the broken hills for its background, the restless scene was striking and picturesque beyond description. Days and weeks made me familiar with it, but never impaired its effect upon my fancy.

As we moved on, the broken column grew yet more scattered and disorderly, until, as we approached the foot of a hill, I saw the old men before mentioned seating themselves in a line upon the ground, in advance of the whole. They lighted a pipe and sat smoking, laughing, and telling stories, while the people, stopping as they successively came up, were soon gathered in a crowd behind them. Then the old men rose, drew their buffalo-robes over their shoulders, and strode on as before. Gaining the top of the hill, we found a steep declivity before us. There was not a minute's pause. The whole descended in a mass, amid dust and confusion. The horses braced their feet as they slid down, women and children screamed, dogs yelped as they were trodden upon, while stones and earth went rolling to the bottom. In a few moments I could see the village from the summit, spreading again far and wide over the plain below.

At our encampment that afternoon I was attacked anew by my old disorder. In half an hour the strength that I had been gaining for a week past had vanished again, and I became like a man in a dream. But at sunset I lay down in the Big Crow's lodge and slept, totally unconscious till the morning. The first thing that awakened me was a hoarse flapping over my head, and a sudden light that poured in upon me. The camp was breaking up, and the squaws were moving the covering from the lodge. I arose and shook off my blanket with the feeling of perfect health; but scarcely had I gained my feet when a sense of my helpless condition was once more forced upon me, and I found myself scarcely able to stand. Raymond had brought up Pauline and the mule, and I stooped to raise my saddle from the ground. My strength was unequal to the task. "You must saddle her," said I to Raymond as I sat down again on a pile of buffalo-robes. He did so, 22 and with a painful effort I mounted. As we were passing over a great plain, surrounded by long broken ridges, I rode slowly in advance of the Indians, with thoughts that wandered far from the time and the place. Suddenly the sky darkened, and thunder began to mutter. Clouds were rising over the hills, as dark as the first forebodings of an approaching calamity; and in a moment all around was wrapped in shadow. I looked behind. The Indians had stopped to prepare for the approaching storm, and the dense mass of savages stretched far to the right and left. Since the first attack of my disorder the effects of rain upon me had usually been injurious in the extreme. I had no strength to spare, having at that moment scarcely enough to keep my seat on horseback. Then, for the first time, it pressed upon me as a strong probability that I might never leave those deserts. "Well," thought I to myself, "the prairie makes quick and sharp work. Better to die here, in the saddle to the last, than to stifle in the hot air of a sick chamber; and a thousand times better than to drag out life, as many have done, in the helpless inaction of lingering disease." So, drawing the 23 buffalo-robe on which I sat, over my head, I waited till the storm should come. It broke at last with a sudden burst of fury, and passing away as rapidly as it came, left the sky clear again. My reflections served me no

other purpose than to look back upon as a piece of curious experience; for the rain did not produce the ill effects
that I had expected. We encamped within an hour. Having no change of clothes, I contrived to borrow a curious
24 kind of substitute from Reynal; and this done, I went
home, that is, to the Big Crow's lodge, to make the entire transfer that was necessary. Half a dozen squaws were
in the lodge, and one of them taking my arm held it against
her own, while a general laugh and scream of admiration
was raised at the contrast in the color of the skin.

Our encampment that afternoon was not far from a spur
of the Black Hills, whose ridges, bristling with fir-trees,
25 rose from the plains a mile or two on our right. That
they might move more rapidly towards their proposed
hunting-grounds, the Indians determined to leave at this
place their stock of dried meat and other superfluous articles. Some left even their lodges, and contented themselves with carrying a few hides to make a shelter from
the sun and rain. Half the inhabitants set out in the
afternoon, with loaded pack-horses, towards the mountains.
Here they suspended the dried meat upon trees, where the
26 wolves and grizzly bears could not get at it. All returned
at evening. Some of the young men declared that they
had heard the reports of guns among the mountains to
the eastward, and many surmises were thrown out as to
the origin of these sounds. For my part, I was in hopes
27 that Shaw and Henry Chatillon were coming to join us.
I little suspected that at that very moment my unlucky
comrade was lying on a buffalo-robe at Fort Laramie,
fevered with ivy poison, and solacing his woes with tobacco and Shakspeare.

As we moved over the plains on the next morning,
several young men rode about the country as scouts; and

at length we began to see them occasionally on the tops
of the hills, shaking their robes as a signal that they saw
buffalo.   Soon after, some bulls came in sight.   Horsemen darted away in pursuit, and we could see from the
distance that one or two of the buffalo were killed.   Raymond suddenly became inspired.   28

"This is the country for me!" he said; "if I could only
carry the buffalo that are killed here every month down to
St. Louis, I'd make my fortune in one winter.   I'd grow
as rich as old Papin, or Mackenzie either.   I call this the   29
poor man's market.   When I'm hungry, I've only got to
take my rifle and go out and get better meat than the
rich folks down below can get, with all their money.
You won't catch me living in St. Louis another winter.   30

"No," said Reynal, "you had better say that, after you
and your Spanish woman almost starved to death there.
What a fool you were ever to take her to the settlements!"

"Your Spanish woman?" said I; "I never heard of her
before.   Are you married to her?"

"No," answered Raymond; "the priests don't marry their
women, and why should I marry mine?"

This honorable mention of the Mexican clergy introduced the subject of religion, and I found that my two
associates, in common with other white men in that country, were as indifferent to their future welfare as men
whose lives are in constant peril are apt to be.   Raymond had never heard of the Pope.   A certain bishop,
who lived at Taos or at Santa Fé, embodied his loftiest   31
idea of an ecclesiastical dignitary.   Reynal observed that
a priest had been at Fort Laramie two years ago, on his
way to the Nez Percé mission, and that he had confessed
all the men there, and given them absolution.   "I got a   32
good clearing out myself that time," said Reynal, "and

I reckon that will do for me till I go down to the settlements again."

Here he interrupted himself with an oath, and exclaimed: "Look! look! The Panther is running an antelope!"

The Panther, on his black-and-white horse, one of the best in the village, came at full speed over the hill in hot pursuit of an antelope, that darted away like lightning before him. The attempt was made in mere sport and bravado, for very few are the horses that can for a moment compete in swiftness with this little animal. The antelope ran down the hill towards the main body of the Indians, who were moving over the plain below. Sharp yells were given, and horsemen galloped out to intercept his flight. At this he turned sharply to the left, and scoured away with such speed that he distanced all his pursuers, even the vaunted horse of the Panther himself. A few moments after, we witnessed a more serious sport. A shaggy buffalo-bull bounded out from a neighboring hollow, and close behind him came a slender Indian boy, riding without stirrups or saddle, and lashing his eager little horse to full speed. Yard after yard he drew closer to his gigantic victim, though the bull, with his short tail erect and his tongue lolling out a foot from his foaming jaws, was straining his unwieldy strength to the utmost. A moment more, and the boy was close alongside. It was our friend the Hail-Storm. He dropped the rein on his horse's neck and jerked an arrow from the quiver at his shoulder.

"I tell you," said Reynal, "that in a year's time that boy will match the best hunter in the village. There, he has given it to him! and there goes another! You feel well now, old bull, don't you, with two arrows stuck in your lights! There, he has given him another! Hear how the Hail-Storm yells when he shoots! Yes, jump at him; try it again, old fellow! You may jump all day before you get your horns into that pony!"

The bull sprang again and again at his assailant, but the horse kept dodging with wonderful celerity. At length the bull followed up his attack with a furious rush, and the Hail-Storm was put to flight, the shaggy monster following close behind. The boy clung in his seat like a leech, and secure in the speed of his little pony, looked round towards us and laughed. In a moment he was again alongside the bull, who was now driven to desperation. His eyeballs glared through his tangled mane, and the blood flew from his mouth and nostrils. Thus still battling with each other, the two enemies disappeared over the hill.

Many of the Indians rode at full gallop towards the spot. We followed at a more moderate pace, and soon saw the bull lying dead on the side of the hill. The Indians were gathered around him, and several knives were already at work. These little instruments were plied with such wonderful address that the twisted sinews were cut apart, the ponderous bones fell asunder as if by magic, and in a moment the vast carcass was reduced to a heap of bloody ruins. The surrounding group of savages offered no very attractive spectacle to a civilized eye. Some were cracking the huge thigh-bones and devouring the marrow within; others were cutting away pieces of the liver and other approved morsels, and swallowing them on the spot with the appetite of wolves. The faces of most of them, besmeared with blood from ear to ear, looked grim and horrible enough. My friend the White Shield proffered me a marrow-bone, so skilfully laid open that all the rich substance within was exposed to view at once. Another Indian held out a large piece of the delicate lining of the paunch; but these

courteous offerings I begged leave to decline. I noticed
one little boy who was very busy with his knife about the
jaws and throat of the buffalo, from which he extracted
some morsel of peculiar delicacy. It is but fair to say
that only certain parts of the animal are considered eligible in these extempore banquets.

We encamped that night, and marched westward through
the greater part of the following day. On the next morning we again resumed our journey. It was the seventeenth
of July, unless my note-book misleads me. At noon we
stopped by some pools of rain-water, and in the afternoon
again set forward. This double movement was contrary
to the usual practice of the Indians, but all were very
anxious to reach the hunting-ground, kill the necessary
number of buffalo, and retreat as soon as possible from
the dangerous neighborhood. I pass by for the present
some curious incidents that occurred during these marches
and encampments. Late in the afternoon of the last-men-
tioned day we came upon the banks of a little sandy
stream, of which the Indians could not tell the name; for
they were very ill acquainted with that part of the country. So parched and arid were the prairies around that
they could not supply grass enough for the horses to
feed upon, and we were compelled to move farther and
farther up the stream in search of ground for encampment. The country was much wilder than before. The
plains were gashed with ravines and broken into hollows
and steep declivities, which flanked our course, as, in
long scattered array, the Indians advanced up the side of
the stream. Mene-Seela consulted an extraordinary oracle
to instruct him where the buffalo were to be found. When
he with the other chiefs sat down on the grass to smoke and
converse, as they often did during the march, the old man

picked up one of those enormous black-and-green crickets, 37
which the Dakota call by a name that signifies "They who
point out the buffalo." The "Root-Diggers," a wretched 38
tribe beyond the mountains, turn them to good account by
making them into a sort of soup, pronounced by certain
unscrupulous trappers to be extremely rich. Holding the
bloated insect respectfully between his fingers and thumb,
the old Indian looked attentively at him and inquired,
"Tell me, my father, where must we go to-morrow to
find the buffalo?" The cricket twisted about his long
horns in evident embarrassment. At last he pointed, or
seemed to point, them westward. Mene-Seela, dropping
him gently on the grass, laughed with great glee, and
said that if we went that way in the morning we should
be sure to kill plenty of game.

Towards evening we came upon a fresh, green meadow,
traversed by the stream, and deep-set among tall, sterile
bluffs. The Indians descended its steep bank; and as I
was at the rear, I was one of the last to reach this point.
Lances were glittering, feathers fluttering, and the water
below me was crowded with men and horses passing
through, while the meadow beyond swarmed with the
restless crowd of Indians. The sun was just setting, and
poured its softened light upon them through an opening in
the hills.

I remarked to Reynal that at last we had found a good
'camping-ground.

"Oh, it's very good," replied he, ironically, "especially
if there is a Snake war-party about, and they take it into
their heads to shoot down at us from the top of these hills.
It's no plan of mine, 'camping in such a hole as this."

The Indians also seemed anxious. High up on the top
of the tallest bluff, conspicuous in the bright evening sun-

light, sat a naked
warrior on horseback, looking around
over the neighboring country; and Raymond told me that
many of the young men had gone out in different directions as scouts.

The shadows had reached to the very summit of the
bluffs before the lodges were erected, and the village reduced again to quiet and order.   A cry was suddenly raised,
and men, women, and children came running out with

animated faces, and looked eagerly through the opening in the hills by which the stream entered from the westward. I could discern afar off some dark, heavy masses, passing over the sides of a low hill. They disappeared and then others followed. These were bands of buffalo cows. The hunting-ground was reached at last, and everything promised well for the morrow's chase. Being fatigued and exhausted, I lay down in Kongra-Tonga's lodge, when Raymond thrust in his head, and called upon me to come and see some sport. A number of Indians were gathered, laughing, along the line of lodges on the western side of the village, and at some distance I could plainly see in the twilight two huge black monsters stalking, heavily and solemnly, directly towards us. They were buffalo-bulls. The wind blew from them to the village, and such was their blindness and stupidity, that they were advancing upon the enemy without the least consciousness of his presence. Raymond told me that two young men had hidden themselves with guns in a ravine about twenty yards in front of us. The two bulls walked slowly on, heavily swinging from side to side in their peculiar gait of stupid dignity. They approached within four or five rods of the ravine where the Indians lay in ambush. Here at last they seemed conscious that something was wrong, for they both stopped and stood perfectly still, without looking either to the right or to the left. Nothing of them was to be seen but two black masses of shaggy mane, with horns, eyes, and nose in the centre, and a pair of hoofs visible at the bottom. At last the more intelligent of them seemed to have concluded that it was time to retire. Very slowly, and with an air of the gravest and most majestic deliberation, he began to turn round, as if he were revolving on a pivot. Little by little his ugly brown side was exposed to view. A white smoke sprang out, as it were from the ground; a sharp report came with it. The old bull gave a very undignified jump, and galloped off. At this his comrade wheeled about with considerable expedition. The other Indian shot at him from the ravine, and then both the bulls ran away at full speed, while half the juvenile population of the village raised a yell and ran after them. The first bull soon stopped, and while the crowd stood looking at him at a respectful distance he reeled and rolled over on his side. The other, wounded in a less vital part, galloped away to the hills and escaped.

In half an hour it was totally dark. I lay down to sleep, and ill as I was, there was something very animating in the prospect of the general hunt that was to take place on the morrow.

CHAPTER XV.

THE HUNTING CAMP.

LONG before daybreak the Indians broke up their camp. The women of Mene-Seela's lodge were as usual among the first that were ready for departure, and I found the old man himself sitting by the embers of the decayed fire, over which he was warming his withered fingers, as the morning was chill and damp. The preparations for moving were even more confused and disorderly than usual. While some families were leaving the ground the lodges of others were still standing untouched. At this old Mene-Seela grew impatient, and walking out to the middle of the village, he stood with his robe wrapped close around him, and harangued the people in a loud, sharp voice. Now, he said, when they were on an enemy's hunting-grounds, was not the time to behave like children; they ought to be more

1   active and united than ever. His speech had some effect.
The delinquents took down their lodges and loaded their
pack-horses; and when the sun rose, the last of the men,
women, and children had left the deserted camp.

This movement was made merely for the purpose of
finding a better and safer position. So we advanced only
three or four miles up the little stream, when each family
assumed its relative place in the great ring of the village,
and the squaws set actively at work in preparing the camp.
But not a single warrior dismounted from his horse. All
the men that morning were mounted on inferior animals,
leading their best horses by a cord, or confiding them to
the care of boys. In small parties they began to leave
the ground and ride rapidly away over the plains to the
westward. I had taken no food, and not being at all ambitious of farther abstinence, I went into my host's lodge,
which his squaws had set up with wonderful despatch,
and sat down in the centre, as a gentle hint that I was
hungry. A wooden bowl was soon set before me, filled
with the nutritious preparation of dried meat called *pem-*
2   *mican* by the northern voyagers, and *wasna* by the Dakota.
Taking a handful to break my fast upon, I left the lodge
just in time to see the last band of hunters disappear over
the ridge of the neighboring hill. I mounted Pauline and
galloped in pursuit, riding rather by the balance than by
any muscular strength that remained to me. From the
top of the hill I could overlook a wide extent of desolate
prairie, over which, far and near, little parties of naked
horsemen were rapidly passing. I soon came up to the
nearest, and we had not ridden a mile before all were
united into one large and compact body. All was haste
and eagerness. Each hunter whipped on his horse as if anxious to be the first to reach the game. In such move-

ments among the Indians this is always more or less the case; but it was especially so in the present instance, because the head chief of the village was absent, and there 3 were but few "soldiers," a sort of Indian police, who among their other functions usually assume the direction of a buffalo hunt. No man turned to the right hand or to the left. We rode at a swift canter straight forward, up hill and down hill, and through the stiff, obstinate growth of the endless wild-sage bushes. For an hour and a half the same red shoulders, the same long black hair rose and fell with the motion of the horses before me. Very little was said, though once I observed an old man severely reproving Raymond for having left his rifle behind him, when there was some probability of encountering an enemy before the day was over. As we galloped across a plain thickly set with sage bushes, the foremost riders vanished suddenly from sight, as if diving into the earth. The arid soil was cracked into a deep ravine. Down we all went in succession and galloped in a line along the bottom, until we found a point where, one by one, the horses could scramble out. Soon after, we came upon a wide, shallow stream, 4 and as we rode swiftly over the hard sand-beds and through the thin sheets of rippling water, many of the savage horsemen threw themselves to the ground, knelt on the sand, snatched a hasty draught, and leaping back again to their seats, galloped on as before.

Meanwhile scouts kept in advance of the party; and now we began to see them on the ridges of the hills, waving their robes in token that buffalo were visible. These however proved to be nothing more than old straggling bulls, feeding upon the neighboring plains, who would stare for a moment at the hostile array and then gallop clumsily off. At length we could discern several of these scouts making their signals to us at once,—no longer waving their robes boldly from the top of the hill, but standing lower down, so that they could not be seen from the plains beyond. Game worth pursuing had evidently been discovered. The excited Indians now urged forward their tired horses even more rapidly than before. Pauline, who was still sick and jaded, began to groan heavily; and her yellow sides were darkened with sweat. As we were crowding together over a lower intervening hill, I heard Reynal and Raymond shouting to me from the left; and, looking in that direction, I saw them riding away behind a party of about twenty mean-looking Indians. These were the relatives of Reynal's squaw, Margot, who, not wishing to take part in the general hunt, were riding towards a distant hollow, where they saw a small band of buffalo which they meant to appropriate to themselves. I answered to the call by ordering Raymond to turn back and follow me. He reluctantly obeyed, though Reynal, who had relied on his assistance in skinning, cutting up, and carrying to camp the buffalo that he and his party should kill, loudly protested, and declared that we should see no sport if we went with the rest of the Indians. Followed by Raymond, I pursued the main body of hunters, while Reynal, in a great rage, whipped his horse over the hill after his ragamuffin relatives. The Indians, still about a hundred in number, galloped in a dense body at some distance in advance, a cloud of dust flying in the wind behind them. I could not overtake them until they had stopped on the side of the hill where the scouts were standing. Here each hunter sprang in haste from the tired animal he had ridden, and leaped upon the fresh horse he had brought with him. There was not a saddle or a bridle in the whole party. A piece of buffalo-robe,

girthed over the horse's back, served in the place of the
one, and a cord of twisted hair, lashed round his lower
jaw, answered for the other. Eagle feathers dangled from
every mane and tail, as marks of courage and speed. As
for the rider, he wore no other clothing than a light cinc-

ture at his waist, and a pair of moccasins. He had a heavy whip, with a handle of solid elk-horn, and a lash of knotted bull-hide fastened to his wrist by a band. His bow was in his hand and his quiver of otter or panther skin hung at his shoulder. Thus equipped, some thirty of the hunters galloped away towards the left, in order to make a circuit under cover of the hills, that the buffalo might be assailed on both sides at once. The rest impatiently waited until time enough had elapsed for their companions to reach the required position. Then riding upward in a body, we gained the ridge of the hill, and for the first time came in sight of the buffalo on the plain beyond.

6   They were a band of cows, four or five hundred in number, crowded together near the bank of a wide stream that was soaking across the sand-beds of the valley. This valley was a large circular basin, sun-scorched and broken, scantily covered with herbage and surrounded with high, barren hills, from an opening in which we could see our allies galloping out upon the plain. The wind blew from that direction. The buffalo, aware of their approach, had begun to move, though very slowly and in a compact mass. I have no farther recollection of seeing the game until we were in the midst of them, for as we rode down the hill other objects engrossed my attention. Numerous old bulls were scattered over the plain, and ungallantly deserting their charge at our approach began to wade and plunge through the quicksands of the stream, and gallop away towards the hills. One old veteran was straggling behind the rest, with one of his fore-legs, which had been broken by some accident, dangling about uselessly. His appearance, as he went shambling along on three legs, was so ludicrous that I could not help pausing for a moment to look at him. As I came near he would try to

rush upon me, nearly throwing himself down at every awkward attempt. Looking up, I saw the whole body of Indians full a hundred yards in advance. I lashed Pauline in pursuit, and reached them just in time; for at that moment each hunter, as if by a common impulse, violently struck his horse, each horse sprang forward, and, scattering in the charge in order to assail the entire herd at once, we all rushed headlong upon the buffalo. We were among them in an instant. Amid the trampling and the yells I could see their dark figures running hither and thither through clouds of dust, and the horsemen darting in pursuit. While we were charging on one side, our companions attacked the bewildered and panic-stricken herd on the other. The uproar and confusion lasted but a moment. The dust cleared away, and the buffalo could be seen scattering as from a common centre, flying over the plain singly, or in long files and small compact bodies, while behind them followed the Indians riding at furious speed, and yelling as they launched arrow after arrow into their sides. The carcasses were strewn thickly over the ground. Here and there stood wounded buffalo, their bleeding sides feathered with arrows; and as I rode by them their eyes would glare, they would bristle like gigantic cats, and feebly attempt to rush up and gore my horse. Others, less disabled, were feebly staggering away, destined to the maws of wolves.

7

I left camp that morning with a philosophic resolution. Neither I nor my horse were at that time fit for such sport, and I had determined to remain a quiet spectator; but amid the rush of horses and buffalo, the uproar and the dust, I found it impossible to sit still; and as four or five buffalo ran past me in a line, I lashed Pauline in pursuit. We went plunging through the water and the quicksands, and clambering the bank, chased them through the wild-sage bushes that covered the rising ground beyond. But neither her native spirit nor the blows of the knotted bull-hide could supply the place of poor Pauline's exhausted strength. We could not gain an inch upon the fugitives. At last, however, they came full upon a ravine too wide to leap over; and as this compelled them to turn abruptly to the left, I contrived to get within ten or twelve yards of the hindmost. At this she faced about, bristled angrily, and made a show of charging. I shot at her, and hit her in the neck. Down she tumbled into the ravine whither her companions had descended before her. I saw their dark backs appearing and disappearing as they galloped along the bottom; then, one by one, they scrambled out on the other side, and ran off as before, the wounded animal following with the rest.

Turning back, I saw Raymond coming on his black mule to meet me; and as we rode over the field together, we counted scores of carcasses lying on the plain, in the ravines, and on the sandy bed of the stream. Far away in the distance, horsemen and buffalo were still scouring along, with clouds of dust rising behind them; and over the sides of the hills long files of the frightened animals were rapidly ascending. The hunters began to return. The boys, who had held the horses behind the hill, made their appearance, and the work of flaying and cutting up began in earnest all over the field. I noticed my host Kongra-Tonga beyond the stream, just alighting by the side of a cow which he had killed. Riding up to him, I found him in the act of drawing out an arrow, which, with the exception of the notch at the end, had entirely disappeared in the animal. I asked him to give it to me, and I still retain it as a proof, though by no means

the most striking one that could be offered, of the force and
dexterity with which the Indians shoot their arrows.   9

The hides and meat were piled upon the horses, and
the hunters began to leave the ground. Raymond and I,
too, getting tired of the scene, set out for the village,
riding straight across the intervening desert. There was
no path, and as far as I could see, no landmark sufficient
to guide us; but Raymond seemed to have an instinctive
perception of the point on the horizon towards which we
ought to direct our course. Antelope were bounding on
all sides, and as is always the case in the presence of
buffalo, they seemed to have lost their natural shyness.
Bands of them would run lightly up the rocky declivities,
and stand gazing down upon us from the summit. At
length we could distinguish the tall white rocks and the
old pine-trees that, as we well remembered, were just
above the site of the encampment. Still we could see
nothing of the camp itself, until, mounting a grassy hill,
we saw the circle of lodges, dingy with storms and smoke,
standing on the plain at our feet.

I entered the lodge of my host. His squaw instantly
brought me food and water, and spread a buffalo-robe
for me to lie upon; and being much fatigued I lay down
and fell asleep. In about an hour the entrance of Kongra-
Tonga, with his arms smeared with blood to the elbows,
awoke me; he sat down in his usual seat, on the left side
of the lodge. His squaw gave him a vessel of water for
washing, set before him a bowl of boiled meat, and, as he
was eating, pulled off his bloody moccasins and placed
fresh ones on his feet; then outstretching his limbs, my
host composed himself to sleep.   10

And now the hunters, two or three at a time, came
rapidly in, and each consigning his horses to the squaws,

entered his lodge with the air of a man whose day's work was done. The squaws flung down the load from the burdened horses, and vast piles of meat and hides were soon gathered before every lodge. By this time it was darkening fast, and the whole village was illumined by the glare of fires. All the squaws and children were gathered about the piles of meat, exploring them in search of the daintiest portions. Some of these they roasted on sticks before the fires, but often they dispensed with this superfluous operation. Late into the night the fires were still glowing upon the groups of feasters engaged in this savage banquet around them.

Several hunters sat down by the fire in Kongra-Tonga's lodge to talk over the day's exploits. Among the rest, Mene-Seela came in. Though he must have seen full eighty winters, he had taken an active share in the day's sport. He boasted that he had killed two cows that morning, and would have killed a third if the dust had not blinded him so that he had to drop his bow and arrows and press both hands against his eyes to stop the pain. The fire-light fell upon his wrinkled face and shrivelled figure as he sat telling his story, with such inimitable gesticulation that every man in the lodge broke into a laugh.

Old Mene-Seela was one of the few Indians in the village with whom I would have trusted myself alone without suspicion, and the only one from whom I should have received a gift or a service without the certainty that it proceeded from an interested motive. He was a great friend to the whites. He liked to be in their company, and was very vain of the favors he had received from them. He told me one afternoon, as we were sitting together in his son's lodge, that he considered the beaver and the whites the wisest people on earth; indeed, he was convinced they were the same; and an incident which had happened to him long before had assured him of this. So he began the following story, and as the pipe passed in turn to him, Reynal availed himself of these interruptions to translate what had preceded. But the old man accompanied his words with such admirable pantomime that translation was hardly necessary.

He said that when he was very young, and had never yet seen a white man, he and three or four of his companions were out on a beaver hunt, and he crawled into a large beaver-lodge, to see what was there. Sometimes he crept on his hands and knees, sometimes he was obliged to swim, and sometimes to lie flat on his face and drag himself along. In this way he crawled a great distance under ground. It was very dark, cold, and close, so that at last he was almost suffocated, and fell into a swoon. When he began to recover, he could just distinguish the voices of his companions outside, who had given him up for lost, and were singing his death-song. At first he could see nothing, but soon discerned something white before him, and at length plainly distinguished three people, entirely white, one man and two women, sitting at the edge of a black pool of water. He became alarmed, and thought it high time to retreat. Having succeeded, after great trouble, in reaching daylight again, he went to the spot directly above the pool of water where he had seen the three mysterious beings. Here he beat a hole with his war-club in the ground, and sat down to watch. In a moment the nose of an old male beaver appeared at the opening. Mene-Seela instantly seized him and dragged him up, when two other beavers, both females, thrust out their heads, and these he served in the same way. "These," said the old man, concluding his story, for which he was probably indebted

to a dream, "must have been the three white people whom
I saw sitting at the edge of the water."

13

Mene-Seela was the grand depository of the legends and
traditions of the village. I succeeded, however, in getting
from him only a few fragments. Like all Indians, he was
excessively superstitious, and continually saw some reason
for withholding his stories. "It is a bad thing," he would
say, "to tell the tales in summer. Stay with us till next
winter, and I will tell you everything I know; but now our
war-parties are going out, and our young men will be killed
if I sit down to tell stories before the frost begins."

14

But to leave this digression. We remained encamped
on this spot five days, during three of which the hunters
were at work incessantly, and immense quantities of meat
and hides were brought in. Great alarm, however, prevailed in the village. All were on the alert. The young
men ranged the country as scouts, and the old men paid
careful attention to omens and prodigies, and especially to
their dreams. In order to convey to the enemy (who, if
they were in the neighborhood, must inevitably have known
of our presence) the impression that we were constantly on
the watch, piles of sticks and stones were erected on all
the surrounding hills, in such a manner as to appear at a
distance like sentinels. Often, even to this hour, that
scene will rise before my mind like a visible reality, —
the tall white rocks; the old pine-trees on their summits;
the sandy stream that ran along their bases and half encircled the village; and the wild-sage bushes, with their
dull green hue and their medicinal odor, that covered all
the neighboring declivities. Hour after hour the squaws
would pass and repass with their vessels of water between
the stream and the lodges. For the most part, no one was
to be seen in the camp but women and children, two or

15

three superannuated old men, and a few lazy and worth-less young ones. These, together with the dogs, now grown fat and good-natured with the abundance in the camp, were its only tenants. Still it presented a busy and bustling scene. In all quarters the meat, hung on cords of hide, was drying in the sun, and around the lodges the squaws, young and old, were laboring on the fresh hides stretched upon the ground, scraping the hair from one side and the still adhering flesh from the other, and rubbing into them the brains of the buffalo, in order to render them soft and pliant.

In mercy to myself and my horse I did not go out with the hunters after the first day. Of late, however, I had been gaining strength rapidly, as was always the case upon every respite of my disorder. I was soon able to walk with ease. Raymond and I would go out upon the neighboring prairies to shoot antelope, or sometimes to assail straggling buffalo, on foot; an attempt in which we met with rather indifferent success. As I came out of Kongra-Tonga's lodge one morning, Reynal called to me from the opposite side of the village, and asked me over to breakfast. The breakfast was a substantial one. It consisted of the rich, juicy hump-ribs of a fat cow; a re-past unrivalled in its way. It was roasting before the fire, impaled upon a stout stick, which Reynal took up and planted in the ground before his lodge, when he, with Raymond and myself, taking our seats around it, un-sheathed our knives and assailed it with good will. In spite of all medical experience, this solid fare, without bread or salt, seemed to agree with me admirably.

"We shall have strangers here before night," said Reynal.

"How do you know that?" I asked.

"I dreamed so. I am as good at dreaming as an Indian. There's the Hail-Storm; he dreamed the same thing, and 19 he and his crony, the Rabbit, have gone out on discovery."

I laughed at Reynal for his credulity, went over to my host's lodge, took down my rifle, walked out a mile or two on the prairie, saw an old bull standing alone, crawled up a ravine, shot him, and saw him escape. Then, exhausted and rather ill-humored, I walked back to the village. By a strange coincidence, Reynal's prediction had been verified; for the first persons whom I saw were the two trap- 20 pers, Rouleau and Saraphin, coming to meet me. These men, as the reader may possibly recollect, had left our party about a fortnight before. They had been trapping among the Black Hills, and were now on their way to the Rocky Mountains, intending in a day or two to set out for the neighboring Medicine Bow. They were not the most elegant or refined of companions, yet they made a very welcome addition to the limited society of the village. For the rest of that day we lay smoking and talking in Reynal's lodge. This indeed was no better than a hut, made of hides stretched on poles, and entirely open in front. It was well carpeted with soft buffalo-robes, and here we remained, sheltered from the sun, surrounded by the domes- 21 tic utensils of Madame Margot's household. All was quiet in the village. Though the hunters had not gone out that day, they lay sleeping in their lodges, and most of the women were silently engaged in their heavy tasks. A few young men were playing at a lazy game of ball in the area of the village; and when they became tired, some girls supplied their place with a more boisterous sport. At a little distance, among the lodges, some children and half-grown squaws were playfully tossing one of their number in a buffalo-robe, an exact counterpart of the ancient pas-

time from which Sancho Panza suffered so much. Farther 22
out on the prairie, a host of little naked boys were roaming
about, engaged in various rough games, or pursuing birds
and ground-squirrels with their bows and arrows; and woe
to the unhappy little animals that fell into their merciless, torture-loving hands. A squaw from the next lodge,
a notable housewife, named Weah Wash-
tay, or the Good Woman, brought us a
large bowl of *wasna*, and went into an
ecstasy of delight when I presented her
with a green glass ring, such as I usually
wore with a view to similar occasions.

The sun went down, and half the sky
was glowing fiery red, reflected on the
little stream as it wound away among the
sage-bushes. Some young men left the
village, and soon returned, driving in
before them all the horses, hundreds
in number, and of every size, age, and color. The hunters came out and each securing those that belonged to
him, examined their condition, and tied them fast by
long cords to stakes driven in front of his lodge. It was
half an hour before the bustle subsided and tranquillity
was restored again. By this time it was nearly dark.
Kettles were hung over the fires, around which the squaws
were gathered with their children, laughing and talking
merrily. A circle of a different kind was formed in the
centre of the village. This was composed of the old men
and warriors of repute, who sat together with their white
buffalo-robes drawn close around their shoulders; and as
the pipe passed from hand to hand, their conversation had
not a particle of the gravity and reserve usually ascribed 23
to Indians. I sat down with them as usual. I had in my

hand half a dozen squibs and serpents, which I had made
one day when encamped upon Laramie Creek, with gunpowder and charcoal, and the leaves of "Fremont's Expedition," rolled round a stout lead-pencil. I waited till I
could get hold of the large piece of burning *bois-de-vache*
which the Indians kept by them on the ground for lighting their pipes. With this I lighted all the fireworks at
once, and tossed them whizzing and sputtering into the
air, over the heads of the company. They all jumped up
and ran off with yelps of astonishment and consternation.
After a moment or two they ventured to come back one
by one, and some of the boldest, picking up the cases of
burnt paper, examined them with eager curiosity to discover their mysterious secret. From that time forward I
enjoyed great repute as a "fire-medicine."

The camp was filled with the low hum of cheerful voices.
There were other sounds, however, of a different kind; for
from a large lodge, lighted up like a gigantic lantern by
the blazing fire within, came a chorus of dismal cries and
wailings, long drawn out, like the howling of wolves, and
a woman almost naked, was crouching close outside, crying violently, and gashing her legs with a knife till they
were covered with blood. Just a year before, a young man
belonging to this family had been slain by the enemy, and
his relatives were thus lamenting his loss. Still other
sounds might be heard; loud earnest cries often repeated
from amid the gloom, at a distance beyond the village.
They proceeded from some young men, who, being about
to set out in a few days on a war-party, were standing at
the top of a hill, calling on the Great Spirit to aid them
in their enterprise. While I was listening Rouleau, with
a laugh on his careless face, called to me and directed
my attention to another quarter. In front of the lodge

where Weah Washtay lived, another squaw was standing, angrily scolding an old yellow dog, who lay on the ground with his nose resting between his paws, and his eyes turned sleepily up to her face, as if pretending to give

respectful attention, but resolved to fall asleep as soon as it was all over.

"You ought to be ashamed of yourself!" said the old woman. "I have fed you well, and taken care of you ever since you were small and blind, and could only crawl about and squeal a little, instead of howling as you do now. When you grew old I said you were a good dog.

You were strong and gentle when the load was put on your back, and you never ran among the feet of the horses when we were all travelling together over the prairie. But you had a bad heart! Whenever a rabbit jumped out of the bushes you were always the first to run after him and lead away all the other dogs behind you. You ought to have known that it was very dangerous to act so. When you had got far out on the prairie, and no one was near to help you, perhaps a wolf would jump out of the ravine; and then what could you do? You would certainly have been killed, for no dog can fight well with a load on his back. Only three days ago you ran off in that way, and turned over the bag of wooden pins with which I used to fasten up the front of the lodge. Look up there, and you will see that it is all flapping open. And now to-night you have stolen a great piece of fat meat which was roasting before the fire for my children. I tell you, you have a bad heart, and you must die!"

So saying, the squaw went into the lodge, and coming out with a large stone mallet, killed the unfortunate dog at one blow. This speech is worthy of notice, as illustrating a curious characteristic of the Indians, who ascribe intelligence and a power of understanding speech to the inferior animals; to whom, indeed, according to many of their traditions, they are linked in close affinity; and they even claim the honor of a lineal descent from bears, wolves, deer, or tortoises.

25   As it grew late, I walked across the village to the lodge of my host, Kongra-Tonga. As I entered I saw him, by the blaze of the fire in the middle, reclining half asleep in his usual place. His couch was by no means an uncomfortable one. It consisted of buffalo-robes, laid to-

gether on the ground, and a pillow made of whitened
deer-skin, stuffed with feathers and ornamented with beads.
At his back was a light frame-work of poles and slender
reeds, against which he could lean with ease when in a
sitting posture; and at the top of it, just above his head,
hung his bow and quiver. His squaw, a laughing, broad-
faced woman, apparently had not yet completed her domestic arrangements, for she was bustling about the lodge,
pulling over the utensils and the bales of dried meat that
were ranged carefully around it. Unhappily, she and her
partner were not the only tenants of the dwelling; for half
a dozen children were scattered about, sleeping in every
imaginable posture. My saddle was in its place at the head
of the lodge, and a buffalo-robe was spread on the ground
before it. Wrapping myself in my blanket, I lay down;
but had I not been extremely fatigued, the noise in the
next lodge would have prevented my sleeping. There was
the monotonous thumping of the Indian drum, mixed with
occasional sharp yells, and a chorus chanted by twenty
voices. A grand scene of gambling was going forward,
with all the appropriate formalities. The players were
staking on the chances of the game, their ornaments, their
horses, and as the excitement rose, their garments, and
even their weapons; for desperate gambling is not con- 26
fined to the hells of Paris. The men of the plains and
forests no less resort to it as a relief to the tedious
monotony of their lives, which alternate between fierce
excitement and listless inaction. I fell asleep with the
dull notes of the drum still sounding on my ear; but
these orgies lasted without intermission till daylight. I 27
was soon awakened by one of the children crawling over
me, while another larger one was tugging at my blanket
and nestling himself in a very disagreeable proximity. I

immediately repelled these advances by punching the heads of these miniature savages with a short stick which I always kept by me for the purpose; and as sleeping half the day and eating much more than is good for them makes them extremely restless, this operation usually had to be repeated four or five times in the course of the night. My host himself was the author of another formidable annoyance. All these Indians, and he among the rest, think themselves bound to the constant performance of certain acts as the condition on which their success in life depends, whether in war, love, hunting, or any other employment. These "medicines," as they are called, which are usually communicated in dreams, are often absurd enough. Some Indians will strike the butt of the pipe against the ground every time they smoke; others will insist that everything they say shall be interpreted by contraries; and Shaw once met an old man who conceived that all would be lost unless he compelled every white man he met to drink a bowl of cold water. My host was particularly unfortunate in his allotment. The spirits had told him in a dream that he must sing a certain song in the middle of every night; and regularly at about twelve o'clock his dismal monotonous chanting would awaken me, and I would see him seated bolt upright on his couch, going through his dolorous performance with a most business-like air. There were other voices of the night, still more inharmonious. Twice or thrice, between sunset and dawn, all the dogs in the village, and there were hundreds of them, would bay and yelp in chorus; a horrible clamor, resembling no sound that I have ever heard, except perhaps the frightful howling of wolves that we used sometimes to hear, long afterward, when descending the Arkansas on the trail of General Kearney's army.

This canine uproar is, if possible, more discordant than that of the wolves. Heard at a distance slowly rising on the night, it has a strange, unearthly effect, and would fearfully haunt the dreams of a nervous man; but when you are sleeping in the midst of it the din is outrageous. One long, loud howl begins it, and voice after voice takes up the sound, till it passes around the whole circumference of the village, and the air is filled with confused and discordant cries, at once fierce and mournful. It lasts a few moments, and then dies away into silence.

Morning came, and Kongra-Tonga, mounting his horse, rode out with the hunters. It may not be amiss to glance at him for an instant in his character of husband and father. Both he and his squaw, like most other Indians, were very fond of their children, whom they indulged to excess, and never punished, except in extreme cases, when they would throw a bowl of cold water over them. Their offspring became sufficiently undutiful and disobedient under this system of education, which tends not a little to foster that wild idea of liberty and utter intolerance of restraint which lie at the foundation of the Indian character. It would be hard to find a fonder father than Kongra-Tonga. There was one urchin in particular, rather less than two feet high, to whom he was exceedingly attached; and sometimes spreading a buffalo-robe in the lodge, he would seat himself upon it, place his small favorite upright before him and chant in a low tone some of the words used as an accompaniment to the war-dance. The little fellow, who could just manage to balance himself by stretching out both arms, would lift his feet and turn slowly round and round in time to his father's music, while my host would laugh with delight, and look smiling up into

29

my face to see if I were admiring this precocious performance of his offspring. In his capacity of husband he was
less tender. The squaw who lived in the lodge with him
had been his partner for many years. She took good care
of his children and his household concerns. He liked her

well enough, and as far as I could see, they never quarrelled;
but his warmer affections were reserved for younger and
more recent favorites. Of these he had at present only
one, who lived in a lodge apart from his own. One day
while in this camp, he became displeased with her, pushed
her out, threw after her her ornaments, dresses, and everything she had, and told her to go home to her father. Having
consummated this summary divorce, for which he could show

good reasons, he came back, seated himself in his usual place, and began to smoke with an air of the utmost tranquillity and self-satisfaction.

30

I was sitting in the lodge with him on that very afternoon, when I felt some curiosity to learn the history of the numerous scars that appeared on his naked body. Of some of them, however, I did not venture to inquire, for I already understood their origin. Each of his arms was marked as if deeply gashed with a knife at regular intervals, and there were other scars also, of a different character, on his back and on either breast. They were the traces of the tortures which these Indians, in common with a few other tribes, inflict upon themselves at certain seasons; in part, it may be, to gain the glory of courage and endurance, but chiefly as an act of self-sacrifice to secure the favor of the spirits. The scars upon the breast and back were produced by running through the flesh strong splints of wood, to which heavy buffalo-skulls are fastened by cords of hide, and the wretch runs forward with all his strength, assisted by two companions, who take hold of each arm, until the flesh tears apart and the skulls are left behind. Others of Kongra-Tonga's scars were the result of accidents; but he had many received in war. He was one of the most noted warriors in the village. In the course of his life he had slain, as he boasted to me, fourteen men; and though, like other Indians, he was a braggart and liar, yet in this statement common report bore him out. Being flattered by my inquiries, he told me tale after tale, true or false, of his warlike exploits; and there was one among the rest illustrating the worst features of Indian character too well for me to omit it. Pointing out of the opening of the lodge towards the Medicine Bow Mountain, not many miles distant, he said

31

32

that he was there a few summers ago with a war-party of his young men. Here they found two Snake Indians hunting. They shot one of them with arrows, and chased the other up the side of the mountain till they surrounded him, and Kongra-Tonga himself, jumping forward among the trees, seized him by the arm. Two of his young men then ran up and held him fast while he scalped him alive. They then built a great fire, and cutting the tendons of their captive's wrists and feet, threw him in, and held him down with long poles until he was burnt to death. He garnished his story with descriptive particulars much too revolting to mention. His features were remarkably mild and open, without the fierceness of expression common among these Indians; and as he detailed these devilish cruelties, he looked up into my face with the air of earnest simplicity which a little child would wear in relating to its mother some anecdote of its youthful experience.

33

Old Mene-Seela's lodge could offer another illustration of the ferocity of Indian warfare. A bright-eyed, active little boy was living there who had belonged to a village of the Gros-Ventre Blackfeet, a small but bloody and treacherous band, in close alliance with the Arapahoes. About a year before, Kongra-Tonga and a party of warriors had found about twenty lodges of these Indians upon the plains a little to the eastward of our present camp; and surrounding them in the night, they butchered men, women, and children, preserving only this little boy alive. He was adopted into the old man's family, and was now fast becoming identified with the Ogillallah children, among whom he mingled on equal terms. There was also a Crow warrior in the village, a man of gigantic stature and most symmetrical proportions. Having been taken prisoner many years before and adopted by a squaw in place of a son whom she

34

had lost, he had forgotten his old nationality, and was now both in act and inclination an Ogillallah.

It will be remembered that the scheme of the grand war-party against the Snake and Crow Indians originated in this village; and though this plan had fallen to the ground, the embers of martial ardor continued to glow. Eleven young men had prepared to go out against the enemy, and the fourth day of our stay in this camp was fixed upon for their departure. At the head of this party was a well-built, active little Indian, called the White Shield, whom I had always noticed for the neatness of his dress and appearance. His lodge too, though not a large one, was the best in the village, his squaw was one of the prettiest, and altogether his dwelling was the model of an Ogillallah domestic establishment. I was often a visitor there, for the White Shield, being rather partial to white men, used to invite me to continual feasts at all hours of the day. Once, when the substantial part of the entertainment was over, and he and I were seated cross legged on a buffalo-robe smoking together very amicably, he took down his warlike equipments, which were hanging round the lodge, and displayed them with great pride and self-importance. Among the rest was a superb head-dress of feathers. Taking this from its case, he put it on 35 and stood before me, perfectly conscious of the gallant air which it gave to his dark face and his vigorous, graceful figure. He told me that upon it were the feathers of three war-eagles, equal in value to the same number of good horses. He took up also a shield gayly painted and hung with feathers. The effect of these barbaric ornaments was admirable. His quiver was made of the spotted skin of a small panther, common among the Black Hills, 36 from which the tail and distended claws were still allowed to hang. The White Shield concluded his entertainment in a manner characteristic of an Indian. He begged of me a little powder and ball, for he had a gun as well as a bow and arrows; but this I was obliged to refuse, because I had scarcely enough for my own use. Making him however a parting present of a paper of vermilion, I left him quite contented.

On the next morning the White Shield took cold, and was attacked with an inflammation of the throat. Immediately he seemed to lose all spirit, and though before no warrior in the village had borne himself more proudly, he now moped about from lodge to lodge with a forlorn and dejected air. At length he sat down, close wrapped in his robe, before the lodge of Reynal, but when he found that neither he nor I knew how to relieve him, he arose and stalked over to one of the medicine-men of the village. This old imposter thumped him for some time with both fists, howled and yelped over him, and beat a drum close to his ear to expel the evil spirit. This treatment failing of the desired effect, the White Shield withdrew to his own lodge, where he lay disconsolate for some hours. Making his appearance once more in the afternoon, he again took his seat on the ground before Reynal's lodge, holding his throat with his hand. For some time he sat silent, with his eyes fixed mournfully on the ground. At last he began to speak in a low tone.

"I am a brave man," he said; "all the young men think me a great warrior and ten of them are ready to go with me to the war. I will go and show them the enemy. Last summer the Snakes killed my brother. I cannot live unless I revenge his death. To-morrow we will set out and I will take their scalps."

The White Shield, as he expressed this resolution,

seemed to have lost all the accustomed fire and spirit of his look, and hung his head as if in a fit of despondency.

As I was sitting that evening at one of the fires, I saw him arrayed in his splendid war-dress, his cheeks painted with vermilion, leading his favorite war-horse to the front of his lodge. He mounted and rode round the village, singing his war-song in a loud, hoarse voice amid the shrill acclamations of the women. Then dismounting, he remained for some minutes prostrate upon the ground, as if in an act of supplication. On the following morning I looked in vain for the departure of the warriors.

38

All was quiet in the village until late in the forenoon, when the White Shield came and seated himself in his old place before us. Reynal asked him why he had not gone out to find the enemy.

" I cannot go," he answered in a dejected voice.   " I have given my war-arrows to the Meneaska " (the American).

"You have only given him two of your arrows," said Reynal.   "If you ask him he will give them back again."

For some time the White Shield said nothing.   At last he spoke in a gloomy tone, —

" One of my young men has had bad dreams.   The spirits of the dead came and threw stones at him in his sleep."

If such a dream had actually taken place it might have broken up this or any other war-party, but both Reynal and I were convinced at the time that it was a mere fabrication to excuse his remaining at home.

The White Shield was a warrior of noted prowess.   Very probably he would have received a mortal wound without the show of pain, and endured without flinching the worst tortures that an enemy could inflict upon him.   The whole power of an Indian's nature would be summoned to encounter such a trial; every influence of his education from childhood would have prepared him for it; the cause of his suffering would have been visibly and palpably before him, and his spirit would rise to set his enemy at defiance, and gain the highest glory of a warrior by meeting death with fortitude.   But when he feels himself attacked by a mysterious evil, before whose assaults his manhood is wasted, and his strength drained away, when he can see no enemy to resist and defy, the boldest warrior falls prostrate at once.   He believes that a bad spirit has taken possession of him, or that he is the victim of some charm. When suffering from a protracted disorder, an Indian will often abandon himself to his supposed destiny, pine away and die, the victim of his own imagination.   The same effect will often follow a series of calamities, or a long run of ill-luck, and Indians have been known to ride into the midst of an enemy's camp, or attack a grizzly bear single-handed, to get rid of a life supposed to lie under the doom of fate.

Thus, after all his fasting, dreaming, and calling upon the Great Spirit, the White Shield's war-party came to nought.

CHAPTER XVI.

THE TRAPPERS.

IN speaking of the Indians, I have almost forgotten two bold adventurers of another race, the trappers Rouleau and Saraphin. These men were bent on a hazardous enterprise. They were on their way to the country ranged by the Arapahoes, a day's journey west of our camp. These Arapahoes, of whom Shaw and I afterwards fell in with a large number, are ferocious savages, who of late had declared themselves enemies to the whites, and threatened death to the first who should venture within their territory. The occasion of the declaration was as follows: —

In the preceding spring, 1845, Colonel Kearney left Fort Leavenworth with several companies of dragoons, marched to Fort Laramie, passed along the foot of the mountains to Bent's Fort, and then, turning eastward again, returned to the point whence he set out. While at Fort Laramie, he sent a part of his command as far westward as Sweetwater, while he himself remained at the fort, and despatched messages to the surrounding Indians to meet him there in council. Then for the first time the tribes of that vicinity saw the white warriors, and, as might have been expected, they were lost in astonishment at their regular order, their gay attire, the completeness of their martial equipment, and the size and strength of their horses. Among the rest, the Arapahoes came in considerable numbers to the Fort. They had lately committed numerous murders, and Colonel

Kearney threatened that if they killed any more white men
he would turn loose his dragoons upon them and annihilate
their nation. In the evening, to add effect to his speech,
he ordered a howitzer to be fired and a rocket to be thrown
up. Many of the Arapahoes fell flat on the ground, while
others ran away screaming with amazement and
terror. On the following day they withdrew
to their mountains, confounded at the appearance of the dragoons, at their big gun
which went off twice at one shot
and the fiery messenger which
they had sent up to the
Great Spirit. For
many months they remained
quiet, and did no farther
mischief. At length, just
before we came into the
country, one of them,
by an act of the basest
treachery, killed two white
men, Boot and May, who were
trapping among the mountains.
For this act it was impossible to discover a motive. It seemed to spring from
one of those inexplicable impulses which
often possess Indians, and which appear to be
mere outbreaks of native ferocity. No sooner was the murder committed than the whole tribe were in consternation.
They expected every day that the avenging dragoons would
come, little thinking that a desert of nine hundred miles
lay between them and their enemy. A large deputation of them came to Fort Laramie, bringing a valuable
present of horses, in atonement. These Bordeaux refused

to accept. They then asked if he would be satisfied with their delivering up the murderer himself; but he declined

7   this offer also. The Arapahoes went back more terrified than ever. Weeks passed away, and still no dragoons appeared. A result followed which those best acquainted with Indians had predicted. They imagined that fear had prevented Bordeaux from accepting their gifts, and that they had nothing to apprehend from the vengeance of the whites. From terror they rose to the height of insolence. They called the white men cowards and old women; and a friendly Dakota came to Fort Laramie with the report that they were determined to kill the first white dog they could lay hands on.

8   Had a military officer, with suitable powers, been stationed at Fort Laramie; had he accepted the offer of the Arapahoes to deliver up the murderer, and ordered him to be led out and shot, in presence of his tribe, they would have been awed into tranquillity, and much danger averted; but now the neighborhood of the Medicine-Bow Mountain was perilous in the extreme. Old Mene-Seela, a true friend of the whites, and many other of the Indians, gathered about the two trappers, and vainly endeavored to turn them from their purpose; but Rouleau and Saraphin only laughed at the danger. On the morning preceding that on which they were to leave the camp, we could all see faint white columns of smoke rising against the dark base of the Medicine Bow. Scouts were sent out immediately, and reported that these proceeded from an Arapahoe camp, abandoned only a few hours before. Still the two trappers continued their preparations for departure.

Saraphin was a tall, powerful fellow, with a sullen and sinister countenance. His rifle had very probably drawn other blood than that of buffalo or Indians. Rouleau had

a broad, ruddy face, marked with as few traces of thought
or care as a child's. His figure was square and strong,
but the first joints of both his feet were frozen off, and
his horse had lately thrown and trampled upon him, by
which he had been severely injured in the chest. But
nothing could subdue his gayety. He went all day rolling about the camp on his stumps of feet, talking, singing,
and frolicking with the Indian women. Rouleau had an 9
unlucky partiality for squaws. He always had one, whom
he must needs bedizen with beads, ribbons, and all the
finery of an Indian wardrobe; and though he was obliged
to leave her behind him during his expeditions, this hazardous necessity did not at all trouble him, for his disposition was the reverse of jealous. If at any time he had
not lavished the whole of the precarious profits of his vocation upon his dark favorite, he devoted the rest to feasting
his comrades. If liquor was not to be had — and this was 10
usually the case — strong coffee would be substituted. As
the men of that region are by no means remarkable for
providence or self-restraint, whatever was set before them
on these occasions, however extravagant in price or enormous in quantity, was sure to be disposed of at one sitting. Like other trappers, Rouleau's life was one of
contrast and variety. It was only at certain seasons, and
for a limited time, that he was absent on his expeditions.
For the rest of the year he would lounge about the fort, or
encamp with his friends in its vicinity, hunting, or enjoying all the luxury of inaction; but when once in pursuit
of the beaver, he was involved in extreme privations and
perils. Hand and foot, eye and ear must be always alert.
Frequently he must content himself with devouring his
evening meal uncooked, lest the light of his fire should
attract the eyes of some wandering Indian; and some-

times, having made his rude repast, he must leave his fire still blazing, and withdraw to a distance under cover of the darkness, that his disappointed enemy, drawn thither by the light, may find his victim gone, and be unable to trace his footsteps in the gloom. This is the life led by scores of men among the Rocky Mountains. I once met a trapper whose breast was marked with the scars of six bullets and arrows, one of his arms broken by a shot, and one of his knees shattered; yet still, with the mettle of New England, whence he had come, he continued to follow his perilous calling.

On the last day of our stay in this camp the trappers were ready for departure. When in the Black Hills they had caught seven beavers, and they now left their skins in charge of Reynal, to be kept until their return. Their strong, gaunt horses were equipped with rusty Spanish bits, and rude Mexican saddles, to which wooden stirrups were attached, while a buffalo-robe was rolled up behind, and a bundle of beaver-traps slung at the pommel. These, together with their rifles, knives, powder-horns and bullet-pouches, flint and steel, and a tin cup, composed their whole travelling equipment. They shook hands with us, and rode away; Saraphin, with his grim countenance, was in advance; but

Rouleau, clambering gayly into his seat, kicked his horse's sides, flourished his whip, and trotted briskly over the prairie, trolling forth a Canadian song at the top of his voice. Reynal looked after them, with his face of brutal selfishness.

"Well," he said, "if they are killed, I shall have the beaver. They'll fetch me fifty dollars at the fort, anyhow."

This was the last I saw of them.

We had been five days in the hunting-camp, and the meat, which all this time had hung drying in the sun, was now fit for transportation. Buffalo-hides also had been procured in sufficient quantities for making the next season's lodges; but it remained to provide the long poles on which they were to be supported. These were only to be had among the tall pine woods of the Black Hills, and in that direction therefore our next move was to be made. Amid the general abundance which during this time had prevailed in the camp, there were no instances of individual privation, for although the hide and the tongue of the buffalo belong by exclusive right to the hunter who has killed it, yet any one else is equally entitled to help himself from the rest of the carcass. Thus the weak, the aged, and even the indolent come in for a share of the spoils, and many a helpless old woman, who would otherwise perish from starvation, is sustained in abundance.

On the twenty-fifth of July, late in the afternoon, the camp broke up, with the usual tumult and confusion, and we all moved once more, on horseback and on foot, over the plains. We advanced, however, but a few miles. The old men, who during the whole march had been stoutly striding along on foot in front of the people, now seated themselves in a circle on the ground, while the families, erecting their lodges in the prescribed order around them, formed the usual great circle of the camp; meanwhile these village patriarchs sat smoking and talking. I threw my bridle to Raymond, and sat down as usual along with them. There was none of that reserve and apparent dignity which an Indian always assumes when in council, or in the presence of white men whom he distrusts. The party, on the contrary, was an extremely merry one, and as in a social circle of a quite different character, "if there was not much wit, there was at least a great deal of laughter."

When the first pipe was smoked out, I rose and withdrew to the lodge of my host. Here I was stooping, in the act of taking off my powder-horn and bullet-pouch, when suddenly, and close at hand, pealing loud and shrill, and in right good earnest, came the terrific yell of the war-whoop. Kongra-Tonga's squaw snatched up her youngest child and ran out of the lodge. I followed, and found the whole village in confusion, resounding with cries and yells. The circle of old men in the centre had vanished. The warriors, with glittering eyes, came darting, weapons in hand, out of the low openings of the lodges, and running with wild yells towards the farther end of the village. Advancing a few rods in that direction, I saw a crowd in furious agitation. Just then I distinguished the voices of Raymond and Reynal, shouting to me from a distance, and looking back, I saw the latter with his rifle in his hand, standing on the farther bank of a little stream that ran along the outskirts of the camp. He was calling to Raymond and me to come over and join him, and Raymond, with his usual deliberate gait and stolid countenance, was already moving in that direction.

This was clearly the wisest course, unless we wished to

involve ourselves in the fray; so I turned to go, but just then a pair of eyes, gleaming like a snake's, and an aged familiar countenance was thrust from the opening of a neighboring lodge, and out bolted old Mene-Seela, full of fight, clutching his bow and arrows in one hand and his knife in the other. At that instant he tripped and fell sprawling on his face, while his weapons flew scattering in every direction. The women with loud screams were hurrying with their children in their arms to place them out of danger, and I observed some hastening to prevent mischief by carrying away all the weapons they could lay hands on. On a rising ground close to the camp stood a line of old women singing a medicine-song to allay the tumult. As I approached the side of the brook, I heard gun-shots behind me, and turning back saw that the crowd had separated into two long lines of naked warriors confronting each other at a respectful distance, and yelling and jumping about to dodge the shot of their adversaries, while they discharged bullets and arrows against each other. At the same time certain sharp, humming sounds in the air over my head, like the flight of beetles on a summer evening, warned me that the danger was not wholly confined to the immediate scene of the fray. So, wading through the brook, I joined Reynal and Raymond, and we sat down on the grass, in the posture of an armed neutrality, to watch the result.

Happily it may be for ourselves, though contrary to our expectation, the disturbance was quelled almost as soon as it began. When I looked again, the combatants were once more mingled together in a mass. Though yells sounded occasionally from the throng, the firing had entirely ceased, and I observed five or six persons moving busily about, as if acting the part of peace-makers. One of the village heralds or criers proclaimed in a loud voice something which my two companions were too much engrossed in their own observations to translate for me. The crowd began to disperse, though many a deep-set black eye still glittered with an unnatural lustre, as the warriors slowly withdrew to their lodges. This fortunate suppression of the disturbance was owing to a few of the old men, less pugnacious than Mene-Seela, who boldly ran in between the combatants, and aided by some of the "soldiers," or Indian police, succeeded in effecting their object.

It seemed very strange to me that although many arrows and bullets were discharged, no one was mortally hurt, and I could only account for this by the fact that both the marksman and the object of his aim were leaping about incessantly. By far the greater part of the villagers had joined in the fray, for although there were not more than a dozen guns in the whole camp, I heard at least eight or ten shots fired.

19

In a quarter of an hour all was comparatively quiet. A group of warriors was again seated in the middle of the village, but this time I did not venture to join them, because I could see that the pipe, contrary to the usual order, was passing from the left hand to the right around the circle; a sure sign that a "medicine-smoke" of reconciliation was going forward, and that a white man would be an intruder. When I again entered the still agitated camp it was nearly dark, and mournful cries, howls, and wailings resounded from many female voices. Whether these had any connection with the late disturbance, or were merely lamentations for relatives slain in some former war expeditions, I could not distinctly ascertain.

To inquire too closely into the cause of the quarrel was by no means prudent, and it was not until some time after

that I discovered what had given rise to it. Among the 20
Dakota there are many associations or fraternities, superstitious, warlike, or social. Among them was one called
"The Arrow-Breakers," now in great measure disbanded 21
and dispersed. In the village there were, however, four men
belonging to it, distinguished by the peculiar arrangement of their hair, which rose in a high, bristling mass
above their foreheads, adding greatly to their apparent
height, and giving them a most ferocious appearance. The
principal among them was the Mad Wolf, a warrior of remarkable size and strength, great courage, and the fierceness of a demon. I had always looked upon him as the
most dangerous man in the village; and though he often
invited me to feasts, I never entered his lodge unarmed.
The Mad Wolf had taken a fancy to a fine horse belonging to another Indian, called the Tall Bear; and anxious 22
to get the animal into his possession, he made the owner
a present of another horse nearly equal in value. According to the customs of the Dakota, the acceptance of this
gift involved a sort of obligation to make a return; and
the Tall Bear well understood that the other had his
favorite buffalo-horse in view. He however accepted the
present without a word of thanks, and having picketed
the horse before his lodge, suffered day after day to pass
without making the expected return. The Mad Wolf grew
impatient; and at last, seeing that his bounty was not
likely to produce the desired result, he resolved to reclaim
it. So this evening, as soon as the village was encamped,
he went to the lodge of the Tall Bear, seized upon the
horse he had given him, and led him away. At this the
Tall Bear broke into one of those fits of sullen rage not
uncommon among Indians, ran up to the unfortunate horse,
and gave him three mortal stabs with his knife. Quick as

lightning the Mad Wolf drew his bow to its utmost tension and held the arrow quivering close to the breast of his adversary. The Tall Bear, as the Indians who were near him said, stood with his bloody knife in his hand facing the assailant with the utmost calmness. Some of his friends and relatives, seeing his danger, ran hastily to his assistance. The remaining three Arrow-Breakers on the other hand, came to the aid of their associate. Their friends joined them, the war-cry was raised, and the tumult became general.

The "soldiers," who lent their timely aid in putting it down, are the most important executive functionaries in an Indian village. The office is one of considerable honor, being confided only to men of courage and repute. They derive their authority from the old men and chief warriors of the village, who elect them in councils occasionally convened for the purpose, and thus they can exercise a degree of authority which no one else in the village would dare to assume. While very few Ogillallah chiefs could venture without risk of their lives to strike or lay hands upon the meanest of their people, the "soldiers," in the discharge of their appropriate functions, have full license to make use of these and similar acts of coercion.

CHAPTER XVII.

THE BLACK HILLS.

WE travelled eastward for two days, and then the gloomy ridges of the Black Hills rose before us. The village passed along for some miles beneath their declivities, trailing out to a great length over the arid prairie, or winding among small detached hills of distorted shapes. Turning sharply to the left, we entered a wide defile of the mountains, down the bottom of which a brook came winding, lined with tall grass and dense copses, amid which were hidden many beaver dams and lodges. We passed along between two lines of high precipices and rocks piled in disorder one upon another, with scarcely a tree, a bush, or a clump of grass. The restless Indian boys wandered along their edges and clambered up and down their rugged sides, and sometimes a group of them would stand on the verge of a cliff and look down on the procession as it passed beneath. As we advanced, the passage grew more narrow; then it suddenly expanded into a round grassy meadow, completely encompassed by mountains; and here the families stopped as they came up in turn, and the camp rose like magic.

The lodges were hardly pitched when, with their usual precipitation, the Indians set about accomplishing the object that had brought them there; that is, obtaining poles for their new lodges. Half the population, men, women, and boys, mounted their horses and set out for the depths of

1

the mountains.   It was a strange cavalcade, as they rode at full gallop over the shingly rocks and into the dark open-
2   ing of the defile beyond.   We passed between precipices, sharp and splintering at the tops, their sides beetling over the defile or descending in abrupt declivities, bristling with fir-trees.   On our left they rose close to us like a wall,
3   but on the right a winding brook with a narrow strip of marshy soil intervened.   The stream was clogged with old beaver-dams and spread frequently into wide pools.   There were thick bushes and many dead and blasted trees along its course, though frequently nothing remained but stumps cut close to the ground by the beaver, and marked with the sharp chisel-like teeth of those indefatigable laborers. Sometimes we dived among trees, and then emerged upon open spots, over which, Indian-like, all galloped at full speed.   As Pauline bounded over the rocks I felt her saddle-girth slipping, and alighted to draw it tighter; when the whole cavalcade swept by me in a moment, the women with their gaudy ornaments tinkling as they rode, the men whooping, laughing, and lashing forward their horses.
4   Two black-tailed deer bounded away among the rocks; Raymond shot at them from horseback; the sharp report of his rifle was answered by another equally sharp from the opposing cliffs, and then the echoes, leaping in rapid succession from side to side died away rattling far amid the mountains.

After having ridden in this manner six or eight miles the scene changed, and all the declivities were covered with forests of tall, slender spruce and pine trees.   The Indians began to fall off to the right and left, dispersing with their hatchets and knives to cut the poles which they had come to seek.   I was soon left almost alone; but in the stillness of those lonely mountains, the stroke of hatchets and the sound of voices might be heard from far and near.

Reynal, who imitated the Indians in their habits as well as the worst features of their character, had killed buffalo enough to make a lodge for himself and his squaw, and now he was eager to get the poles necessary to complete it. He asked me to let Raymond go with him, and assist in the work. I assented, and the two men immediately entered the thickest part of the wood. Having left my horse in Raymond's keeping, I began to climb the mountain. I was weak and weary, and made slow progress, often pausing to rest; but after an hour I gained a height whence the little valley out of which I had climbed seemed like a deep, dark gulf, though the inaccessible peak of the mountain was still towering to a much greater distance above. Objects familiar from childhood surrounded me, — crags and rocks, a black and sullen brook that gurgled with a hollow voice deep among the crevices, a wood of mossy, distorted trees and prostrate trunks flung down by age and storms, scattered among the rocks, or damming the foaming waters of the brook.

Wild as they were, these mountains were thickly peopled. As I climbed farther, I found the broad, dusty paths made by the elk, as they filed across the mountain side. The grass on all the terraces was trampled down by deer; there were numerous tracks of wolves, and in some of the

5

rougher and more precipitous parts of the ascent I found footprints different from any that I had ever seen, and which I took to be those of the Rocky Mountain sheep. I sat down on a rock; there was a perfect stillness. No wind was stirring, and not even an insect could be heard. I remembered the danger of becoming lost in such a place, and fixed my eye upon one of the tallest pinnacles of the opposite mountain. It rose sheer upright from the woods below, and, by an extraordinary freak of nature, sustained aloft on its very summit a large, loose rock. Such a landmark could never be mistaken, and feeling once more secure, I began again to move forward. A white wolf jumped up from among some bushes and leaped clumsily away; but he stopped for a moment and turned back his keen eye and grim, bristling muzzle. I longed to take his scalp and carry it back with me as a trophy of the Black Hills, but before I could fire, he was gone among the rocks. Soon after I heard a rustling sound, with a cracking of twigs at a little distance, and saw moving above the tall bushes the branching antlers of an elk. I was in a hunter's paradise.

Such are the Black Hills, as I found them in July; but they wear a different garb when winter sets in, when the broad boughs of the fir-trees are bent to the ground by the load of snow, and the dark mountains are white with it. At that season the trappers, returned from their autumn expeditions, often build their cabins in the midst of these solitudes, and live in abundance and luxury on the game that harbors there. I have heard them tell how, with their tawny mistresses, and perhaps a few young Indian companions, they had spent months in total seclusion. They would dig pitfalls, and set traps for the white wolves, sables, and martens, and though through

the whole night the awful chorus of the wolves would re-
sound from the frozen mountains around them, yet within
their massive walls of logs they would lie in careless
ease before the blazing fire, and in the morning shoot
the elk and deer from their very door. 6

18

CHAPTER XVIII.

A MOUNTAIN HUNT.

THE camp was full of the newly cut lodge-poles; some, already prepared, were stacked together, white and glistening, to dry and harden in the sun; others were lying on the ground, and the squaws, the boys, and even some of the warriors were busily at work peeling off the bark and paring them with their knives to the proper dimensions. Most of the hides obtained at the last camp were dressed and scraped thin enough for use, and many of the squaws were engaged in fitting them together and sewing them with sinews, to form the coverings for the lodges. Men were wandering among the bushes that lined the brook along the margin of the camp, cutting sticks of red willow, or *shongsasha*, the bark of which, mixed with tobacco, they use for smoking. Reynal's squaw was hard at work with her awl and buffalo sinews upon her lodge, while her proprietor, having just finished an enormous breakfast of meat, was smoking a social pipe with Raymond and myself. He proposed at length that we should go out on a hunt. "Go to the Big Crow's lodge," said he, "and get your rifle. I'll bet the gray Wyandot pony against your mare that we start an elk or a black-tailed deer, or likely as not a big-horn, before we are two miles out of camp. I'll take my squaw's old yellow horse; you can't whip him more than four miles an hour, but he is as good for the mountains as a mule."

I mounted the black mule which Raymond usually rode. She was a powerful animal, gentle and manageable enough by nature; but of late her temper had been soured by misfortune. About a week before, I had chanced to offend some one of the Indians, who out of revenge went secretly into the meadow and gave her a severe stab in the haunch with his knife. The wound, though partially healed, still galled her extremely, and made her even more perverse and obstinate than the rest of her species.

The morning was a glorious one, and I was in better health than I had been at any time for the last two months. We left the little valley and ascended a rocky hollow in the mountain. Very soon we were out of sight of the camp, and of every living thing, man, beast, bird, or insect. I had never before, except on foot, passed over such execrable ground, and I desire never to repeat the experiment. The black mule grew indignant, and even the redoubtable yellow horse stumbled every moment, and kept groaning to himself as he cut his feet and legs among the sharp rocks.

It was a scene of silence and desolation. Little was visible except beetling crags and the bare shingly sides of the mountains, relieved by scarcely a trace of vegetation. At length, however, we came upon a forest tract, and had no sooner done so than we heartily wished ourselves back among the rocks again; for we were on a steep descent, among trees so thick that we could see scarcely a rod in any direction.

If one is anxious to place himself in a situation where the hazardous and the ludicrous are combined in about equal proportions, let him get upon a vicious mule, with a snaffle bit, and try to drive her through the woods down a slope of forty-five degrees. Let him have a long rifle, a buckskin frock with long fringes, and a head of long hair. These latter appendages will be caught every moment and twitched away in small portions by the twigs, which will also whip him smartly across the face, while the large branches above thump him on the head. His mule, if she be a true one, will alternately stop short and dive violently forward, and his positions upon her back will be somewhat diversified. At one time he will clasp her affectionately, to avoid the blow of a bough overhead; at another, he will throw himself back and fling his knee forward against her neck, to keep it from being crushed between the rough bark of a tree and the ribs of the animal. Reynal was cursing incessantly during the whole way down. Neither of us had the remotest idea where we were going; and though I have seen rough riding, I shall always retain an evil recollection of that five minutes' scramble.

At last we left our troubles behind us, emerging into the channel of a brook that circled along the foot of the descent; and here, turning joyfully to the left, we rode at ease over the white pebbles and the rippling water, shaded from the glaring sun by an overarching green transparency. These halcyon moments were of short duration. The friendly brook, turning sharply to one side, went brawling and foaming down the rocky hill into an abyss, which, as far as we could see, had no bottom; so once more we betook ourselves to the detested woods. When next we came out from their shadow we found ourselves standing in the broad glare of day, on a high jutting point of the mountain. Before us stretched a long, wide, desert valley, winding away far amid the mountains. Reynal gazed intently; he began to speak at last: —

"Many a time, when I was with the Indians, I have been hunting for gold all through the Black Hills. There 's plenty of it here; you may be certain of that. I have dreamed about it fifty times, and I never dreamed yet but what it came out true. Look over yonder at those black rocks piled up against that other big rock. Don't it look as if there might be something there? It won't do for a white man to be rummaging too much about these mountains; the Indians say they are full of bad spirits; and I believe myself that it's no good luck to be hunting about here after gold. Well, for all that, I would like to have one of those fellows up here, from down below, to go about with his witch-hazel rod, and I'll guarantee that it would not be long before he would light on a gold-mine. Never mind; we'll let the gold alone for to-day. Look at those trees down below us in the hollow; we'll go down there, and I reckon we'll get a black-tailed deer."

But Reynal's predictions were not verified. We passed mountain after mountain, and valley after valley; we explored deep ravines; yet still, to my companion's vexation and evident surprise, no game could be found. So, in the absence of better, we resolved to go out on the plains and look for an antelope. With this view we began to pass down a narrow valley, the bottom of which was covered with the stiff wild-sage bushes and marked with deep paths, made by the buffalo, who, for some inexplicable reason, are accustomed to penetrate, in their long grave processions, deep among the gorges of these sterile mountains.

Reynal's eye ranged incessantly among the rocks and along the edges of the precipices, in hopes of discovering the mountain-sheep peering down upon us from that giddy height. Nothing was visible for some time. At length we both detected something in motion near the foot of one of the mountains, and a moment afterward a black-tailed deer stood gazing at us from the top of a rock, and then, slowly turning away, disppeared behind it. In an instant

Reynal was out of his saddle, and running towards the spot. I, being too weak to follow, sat holding his horse and waiting the result. I lost sight of him; then heard the report of his rifle, deadened among the rocks, and finally saw him reappear, with a surly look, that plainly betrayed his ill-success. Again we moved forward down the long valley, till we came full upon what seemed a wide and very shallow ditch, incrusted at the bottom with white clay, dried and cracked in the sun. Under this fair outside Reynal's eye detected the signs of lurking mischief. He called to me to stop, and then alighting, picked up a stone and threw it into the ditch. To my amazement it fell with a dull splash, breaking at once through the thin crust, and spattering round the hole a yellowish, creamy fluid, into which it sank and disappeared. A stick five or six feet long lay on the ground, and with this we sounded the insidious abyss close to its edge. It was just possible to touch the bottom. Places like this are numerous among the Rocky Mountains. The buffalo, in his blind and heedless walk, often plunges into them unawares. Down he sinks; one snort of terror, one convulsive struggle, and the slime calmly flows above his shaggy head, the languid undulations of its sleek and placid surface alone betraying how the powerful monster writhes in his death-throes below.

We found after some trouble a point where we could pass the abyss, and now the valley began to open upon plains which spread to the horizon before us. On one of their distant swells we discerned three or four black specks, which Reynal pronounced to be buffalo.

"Come," said he, "we must get one of them. My squaw wants more sinews to finish her lodge with, and I want some glue myself."

He immediately put the yellow horse to such a gallop as he was capable of executing, while I set spurs to the mule, who soon far outran her plebeian rival. When we had galloped a mile or more, a large rabbit, by ill-luck, sprang up just under the feet of the mule, which bounded violently aside in full career. Weakened as I was, I was flung forcibly to the ground, and my rifle, falling close to my head, went off with the shock. Its sharp, spiteful report rang for some moments in my ear. Being slightly stunned, I lay for an instant motionless, and Reynal, supposing me to be shot, rode up and began to curse the mule. Soon recovering myself, I rose, picked up the rifle, and anxiously examined it. It was badly injured. The stock was cracked, and the main screw broken, so that the lock had to be tied in its place with a string; yet happily it was not rendered totally unserviceable. I wiped it out, reloaded it, and handing it to Reynal, who meanwhile had caught the mule and led her up to me, I mounted again. No sooner had I done so than the brute began to rear and plunge with extreme violence; but being now well prepared for her, and free from incumbrance, I soon reduced her to submission. Then, taking the rifle again from Reynal, we galloped forward as before.

We were now free of the mountains and riding far out on the broad prairie. The buffalo were still some two miles in advance of us. When we came near them, we stopped where a gentle swell of the plain concealed us, and while I held his horse Reynal ran forward with his rifle, till I lost sight of him beyond the rising ground. A few minutes elapsed: I heard the report of his piece, and saw the buffalo running away at full speed on the right; immediately after, the hunter himself, unsuccessful as before, came up and mounted his horse in excessive ill-humor. He cursed the Black Hills and the buffalo, swore that he was a good hunter, which indeed was true, and that he had never been out before among those mountains without killing two or three deer at least.

We now turned towards the distant encampment. As we rode along, antelope in considerable numbers were flying lightly in all directions over the plain, but not one of them would stand and be shot at. When we reached the foot of the mountain-ridge that lay between us and the village, we were too impatient to take the smooth and circuitous route; so turning short to the left we drove our wearied animals upward among the rocks. Still more antelope were leaping about among these flinty hillsides. Each of us shot at one, though from a great distance, and each missed his mark. At length we reached the summit of the last ridge. Looking down we saw the bustling camp in the valley at our feet, and ingloriously descended to it. As we rode among the lodges, the Indians looked in vain for the fresh meat that should have hung behind our saddles, and the squaws uttered various suppressed ejaculations, to the great indignation of Reynal. Our mortification was increased when we rode up to his lodge. Here he saw his young Indian relative, the Hail-Storm, his light, graceful figure reclining on the ground in an easy attitude, while with his friend the Rabbit, who sat by his side, he was making an abundant meal from a wooden bowl of *wasna*, which the squaw had placed between them. Near him lay the fresh skin of a female elk, which he had just killed among the mountains, only a mile or two from the camp. No doubt the boy's heart was elated with triumph, but he betrayed no sign of it. He even seemed totally unconscious of our approach, and his handsome face had all the tranquillity of Indian self-control, — a self-

control which prevents the exhibition of emotion without restraining the emotion itself. It was about two months since I had known the Hail-Storm, and within that time his character had remarkably developed. When I first saw him he was just emerging from the habits and feelings of the boy into the ambition of the hunter and warrior. He had lately killed his first deer, and this had excited his aspirations for distinction. Since that time he had been continually in search of game, and no young hunter in the village had been so active or so fortunate as he. All this success had produced a marked change in his character. As I first remembered him he always shunned the society of the young squaws, and was extremely bashful and sheepish in their presence; but now, in the confidence of his new reputation he began to assume the air and arts of a man of gallantry. He wore his red blanket dashingly over his left shoulder, painted his cheeks every day with vermilion, and hung pendants of shells in his ears. If I observed aright, he met with very good success in his new pursuits; still the Hail-Storm had much to accomplish before he attained the full standing of a warrior. Gallantly as he began to bear himself among the women and girls, he was still timid and abashed in the presence of the chiefs and old men; for he had never yet killed a man, or stricken the dead body of an enemy in battle. I have no doubt that the handsome, smooth-faced boy burned with desire to flesh his maiden scalping-knife, and I would not have encamped alone with him without watching his movements with a suspicious eye.

His elder brother, the Horse, was of a different character. He was nothing but a lazy dandy. He knew very well how to hunt, but preferred to live by the hunting of others. He had no appetite for distinction, and the Hail-

Storm already surpassed him in reputation. He had a dark and ugly face, and passed a great part of his time in adorning it with vermilion, and contemplating it by means of a little pocket looking-glass which I had given him. As for the rest of the day, he divided it between eating, sleeping, and sitting in the sun on the outside of a lodge. Here he would remain for hour after hour arrayed in all his finery, with an old dragoon's sword in his hand, evidently flattering himself that he was the centre of attraction to the eyes of the surrounding squaws. Yet he sat looking straight forward with a face of the utmost gravity, as if wrapped in profound meditation, and it was only by the occasional sidelong glances which he shot at his supposed admirers that one could detect the true course of his thoughts.

Both he and his brother may represent classes in the Indian community; neither should the Hail-Storm's friend the Rabbit, be passed by without notice. The Hail-Storm and he were inseparable; they ate, slept, and hunted together, and shared with one another almost all that they possessed. If there be anything that deserves to be called romantic in the Indian character, it is to be sought for in friendships such as this, which are common among many of the prairie tribes.

Slowly, hour after hour, that weary afternoon dragged away. I lay in Reynal's lodge, overcome by the listless torpor that pervaded the encampment. The day's work was finished, or if it were not, the inhabitants had resolved not to finish it at all, and were dozing quietly within the shelter of the lodges. A profound lethargy, the very spirit of indolence, seemed to have sunk upon the village. Now and then I could hear the low laughter of some girl from within a neighboring lodge, or the small

shrill voices of a few restless children who alone were
moving in the deserted area.   The spirit of the place infected me; I could not think consecutively; I was fit only
for musing and revery, when at last, like the rest, I fell
asleep.

8

When evening came, and the fires were lighted round
the lodges, a select family circle convened in the neighborhood of Reynal's domicile.   It was composed entirely
of his squaw's relatives, a mean and ignoble clan, among
whom none but the Hail-Storm held forth any promise of
future distinction.   Even his prospects were rendered not
a little dubious by the character of the family, less however from any principle of aristocratic distinction than
from the want of powerful supporters to assist him in his
undertakings and help to avenge his quarrels.   Raymond
and I sat down along with them.   There were eight or
ten men gathered round the fire, together with about as
many women, old and young, some of whom were tolerably good-looking.   As the pipe passed round among the
men, a lively conversation went forward, more merry than
delicate, and at length two or three of the elder women
(for the girls were somewhat diffident and bashful) began
to assail Raymond with various pungent witticisms.   Some
of the men took part, and an old squaw concluded by be-

9

stowing on him a ludicrous and indecent nickname, at
which a general laugh followed at his expense.   Raymond
grinned and giggled and made several futile attempts at
repartee.   Knowing the impolicy and even danger of suffering myself to be placed in a ludicrous light among the
Indians, I maintained a rigid, inflexible countenance, and
wholly escaped their sallies.

In the morning I found, to my great disgust, that the
camp was to remain where it was for another day.   I dreaded

its languor and monotony, and, to escape it, set out to explore the surrounding mountains. I was accompanied by a faithful friend, my rifle, the only friend indeed on whose prompt assistance in time of trouble I could wholly rely. Most of the Indians in the village, it is true, professed good-will towards the whites, but the experience of others and my own observation had taught me the extreme folly of confidence, and the utter impossibility of foreseeing to what sudden acts the strange, unbridled impulses of an Indian may urge him. When among this people danger is never so near as when you are unprepared for it, never so remote as when you are armed and on the alert to meet it at any moment. Nothing offers so strong a temptation to their ferocious instincts as the appearance of timidity, weakness, or security.

Many deep and gloomy gorges, choked with trees and bushes, opened from the sides of the hills, which were shaggy with forests wherever the rocks permitted vegetation to spring. A great number of Indians were stalking along the edges of the woods, and boys were whooping and laughing on the mountains, practising eye and hand, and indulging their destructive propensities by killing birds and small animals with their little bows and arrows. There was one glen, stretching up between steep cliffs far into the bosom of the mountain. I began to ascend along its bottom, pushing my way onward among the rocks, trees, and bushes that obstructed it. A slender thread of water trickled through it, which since issuing from the heart of its native rock could scarcely have been warmed or gladdened by a ray of sunshine. After advancing for some time, I conceived myself to be entirely alone; but coming to a part of the glen in a great measure free of trees and undergrowth, I saw at some distance the black head and red shoulders of an Indian among the bushes above. The reader need not prepare himself for a startling adventure, for I have none to relate. The head and shoulders belonged to Mene-Seela, my best friend in the village. As I had approached noiselessly with my moccasined feet, the old man was quite unaware of my presence; and turning to a point where I could gain an unobstructed view of him, I saw him seated alone, immovable as a statue, among the rocks and trees. His face was turned upward, and his eyes seemed riveted on a pine-tree springing from a cleft in the precipice above. The crest of the pine was swaying to and fro in the wind, and its long limbs waved slowly up and down, as if the tree had life. Looking for a while at the old man, I was satisfied that he was engaged in an act of worship, or prayer, or communion of some kind with a supernatural being. I longed to penetrate his thoughts, but I could do nothing more than conjecture and speculate. I knew that though the intellect of an Indian can embrace the idea of an all-wise, all-powerful Spirit, the supreme Ruler of the universe, yet his mind will not always ascend into communion with a being that seems to him so vast, remote, and incomprehensible; and when danger threatens, when his hopes are broken, and trouble overshadows him, he is prone to turn for relief to some inferior agency, less removed from the ordinary scope of his faculties. He has a guardian spirit, on whom he relies for succor and guidance. To him all nature is instinct with mystic influence. Among those mountains not a wild beast was prowling, a bird singing, or a leaf fluttering, that might not tend to direct his destiny, or give warning of what was in store for him; and he watches the world of nature around him as the astrologer watches the stars. So closely is he linked with it that his guardian spirit, no unsubstantial creation of the fancy, is usually embodied in the form of some living thing, — a bear, a wolf, an eagle, or a serpent; and Mene-Seela, as he gazed intently on the old pine-tree, might believe it to inshrine the fancied guide and protector of his life.

Whatever was passing in the mind of the old man, it was no part of good sense to disturb him. Silently retracing my footsteps, I descended the glen till I came to a point where I could climb the precipices that shut it in, and gain the side of the mountain. Looking up, I saw a tall peak rising among the woods. Something impelled me to climb; I had not felt for many a day such strength and elasticity of limb. An hour and a half of slow and often intermitted labor brought me to the summit; and emerging from the dark shadows of the rocks and pines, I stepped out into the light, and walking along the sunny verge of a precipice, seated myself on its extreme point. Looking between the mountain-peaks to the westward, the pale-blue prairie was stretching to the farthest horizon, like a serene and tranquil ocean. The surrounding mountains were in themselves sufficiently striking and impressive, but this contrast gave redoubled effect to their stern features.

CHAPTER XIX.

PASSAGE OF THE MOUNTAINS.

WHEN I took leave of Shaw at La Bonté's camp, I promised to meet him at Fort Laramie on the first of August. The Indians, too, intended to pass the mountains and move towards the fort. To do so at this point was impossible, because there was no passage; and in order to find one we were obliged to go twelve or fourteen miles southward. Late in the afternoon the camp broke up. I rode in company with three or four young Indians at the rear, and the moving swarm stretched before me, in the ruddy light of sunset, or the deep shadow of the mountains, far beyond my sight. It was an ill-omened spot they chose to encamp upon. When they were there just a year before, a war-party of ten men, led by the Whirlwind's son, had gone out against the enemy, and not one had ever returned. This was the immediate cause of this season's warlike preparations. I was not a little astonished, when I came to the camp, at the confusion of horrible sounds with which it was filled; howls, shrieks, and wailings rose from all the women present, many of whom, not content with this exhibition of grief for the loss of their friends and relatives, were gashing their legs deeply with knives. A warrior in the village, who had lost a brother in the expedition, chose another mode of displaying his sorrow. The Indians, who though often rapacious, are devoid of avarice, will some-

19

times, when in mourning, or on other solemn occasions, give away the whole of their possessions, and reduce themselves to nakedness and want. The warrior in question led his two best horses into the middle of the village, and gave them away to his friends; upon which songs and acclamations in praise of his generosity mingled with the cries of the women.

3 On the next morning we entered again among the mountains. There was nothing in their appearance either grand or picturesque, though they were desolate to the last degree, being mere piles of black and broken rocks, without trees or vegetation of any kind. As we passed among them along a wide valley, I noticed Raymond riding by the side of a young squaw, to whom he was addressing various compliments. All the old squaws in the neighborhood watched his proceedings in great admiration, and the girl herself would turn aside her head and laugh. Just then his mule thought proper to display her vicious pranks, and began to rear and plunge furiously. Raymond was an excellent rider, and at first he stuck fast in his seat; but the moment after, I saw the mule's hind-legs flourishing in the air and my unlucky follower pitching head foremost over her ears. There was a burst of screams and laughter from all the women, in which his mistress herself took part, and Raymond was assailed by such a shower of witticisms that he was glad to ride forward out of hearing.

Not long after, as I rode near him, I heard him shouting to me. He was pointing towards a detached rocky hill that stood in the middle of the valley before us, and from behind it a long file of elk came out at full speed and entered an opening in the mountain. They had scarcely disappeared, when whoops and exclamations came from fifty voices around me. The young men leaped from their horses, flung down their heavy buffalo robes and ran at full speed towards the foot of the nearest mountain. Reynal also broke away at a gallop in the same direction. "Come on! come on!" he called to us. "Do you see that band of big-horn up yonder? If there's one of them, there's a hundred!"

In fact, near the summit of the mountain I could see a large number of small white objects, moving rapidly upwards among the precipices, while others were filing along its rocky profile. Anxious to see the sport, I galloped forward, and entering a passage in the side of the mountain, ascended among the loose rocks as far as my horse could carry me. Here I fastened her to an old pine-tree. At that moment Raymond called to me from the right that another band of sheep was close at hand in that direction. I ran up to the top of the opening, which gave me a full view into the rocky gorge beyond; and here I plainly saw some fifty or sixty sheep, almost within rifle-shot, clattering upwards among the rocks, and endeavoring, after their usual custom, to reach the highest point. The naked Indians bounded up lightly in pursuit. In a moment the game and hunters disappeared. Nothing could be seen or heard but the occasional report of a gun, more and more distant, reverberating among the rocks.

I turned to descend, and as I did so, could see the valley below alive with Indians passing rapidly through it, on horseback and on foot. A little farther on, all were stopping as they came up; the camp was preparing and the lodges rising. I descended to this spot, and soon after Reynal and Raymond returned. They bore between them a sheep which they had pelted to death with stones from the edge of a ravine, along the bottom of which

it was attempting to escape. One by one the hunters came dropping in; yet such is the activity of the Rocky Mountain sheep, that although sixty or seventy men were out in pursuit, not more than half a dozen animals were killed. Of these only one was a full-grown male. He had a pair of horns, the size of which was almost beyond belief. I have seen among the Indians ladles with long handles, capable of containing more than a quart, cut out
4   from such horns.

Through the whole of the next morning we were moving forward among the hills. On the following day the heights closed around us, and the passage of the mountains began in earnest. Before the village left its 'camping-ground, I set forward in company with the Eagle-Feather, a man of powerful frame, but with a bad and sinister face. His son, a light-limbed boy, rode with us, and another Indian, named the Panther, was also of the party. Leaving the village out of sight behind us, we rode together up a rocky defile. After a while, however, the Eagle-Feather discovered in the distance some appearance of game, and set off with his son in pursuit of it, while I went forward with the Panther. This was a mere *nom de guerre;* for, like many Indians, he concealed his real name out of some
5   superstitious notion. He was a noble-looking fellow. As he suffered his ornamented buffalo-robe to fall in folds about his loins, his stately and graceful figure was fully displayed; and while he sat his horse in an easy attitude the long feathers of the prairie-cock fluttering from the crown of his head, he seemed the very model of a wild prairie-rider. He had not the same features with those of other Indians. Unless his face greatly belied him, he was free from the jealousy, suspicion, and malignant cunning of his people. For the most part, a civilized white

man can discover very few points of sympathy between his own nature and that of an Indian. With every disposition to do justice to their good qualities, he must be conscious that an impassable gulf lies between him and his red brethren. Nay, so alien to himself do they appear that, after breathing the air of the prairie for a few months or weeks, he begins to look upon them as a troublesome and dangerous species of wild beast. Yet, in the countenance of the Panther, I gladly read that there were at least some points of sympathy between him and me. We were excellent friends, and as we rode forward together through rocky passages, deep dells, and little barren plains, he occupied himself very zealously in teaching me the Dakota language. After a while we came to a grassy recess, where some gooseberry-bushes were growing at the foot of a rock; and these offered such temptation to my companion that he gave over his instructions, and stopped so long to gather the fruit that before we were in motion again the van of the village came in view. An old woman appeared, leading down her pack-horse among the rocks above. Savage after savage followed, and the little dell was soon crowded with the throng.

That morning's march was one not to be forgotten. It led us through a sublime waste, a wilderness of mountains and pine-forests, over which the spirit of loneliness and silence seemed brooding. Above and below, little could be seen but the same dark, green foliage. It overspread the valleys, and enveloped the mountains, from the black rocks that crowned their summits to the streams that circled round their bases. I rode to the top of a hill whence I could look down on the savage procession as it passed beneath my feet, and, far on the left, could see its thin and broken line, visible only at intervals, stretching away for miles among the mountains. On the farthest ridge, horsemen were still descending like mere specks in the distance.

I remained on the hill till all had passed, and then descending followed after them. A little farther on I found a very small meadow, set deeply among steep mountains; and here the whole village had encamped. The little spot was crowded with the confused and disorderly host. Some of the lodges were already set up, or the squaws perhaps were busy in drawing the heavy coverings of skin over the bare poles. Others were as yet mere skeletons, while others still, poles, covering, and all, lay scattered in disorder on the ground among buffalo-robes, bales of meat, domestic utensils, harness, and weapons. Squaws were screaming to one another, horses rearing and plunging, dogs yelping, eager to be disburdened of their loads, while the fluttering of feathers and the gleam of savage ornaments added liveliness to the scene. The small children ran about amid the crowd, while many of the boys were scrambling among the overhanging rocks, and standing with their little bows in their hands, looking down upon the restless throng. In contrast with the general confusion, a circle of old men and warriors sat in the midst, smoking in profound indifference and tranquillity. The disorder at length subsided. The horses were driven away to feed along the adjacent valley, and the camp assumed an air of listless repose. It was scarcely past noon; a vast white canopy of smoke from a burning forest to the eastward overhung the place, and partially obscured the rays of the sun; yet the heat was almost insupportable. The lodges stood crowded together without order in the narrow space. Each was a hot-house, within which the lazy proprietor lay sleeping. The camp was silent as

death. Nothing stirred except now and then an old woman
passing from lodge to lodge. The girls and young men
sat together in groups, under the pine-trees upon the surrounding heights. The dogs lay panting on the ground,
too languid even to growl at the white man. At the entrance of the meadow, there was a cold spring among the
rocks, completely overshadowed by tall trees and dense
undergrowth. In this cool and shady retreat a number of
girls were assembled, sitting together on rocks and fallen
logs, discussing the latest gossip of the village, or laughing and throwing water with their hands at the intruding
Meneaska. The minutes seemed lengthened into hours.
I lay for a long time under a tree studying the Ogillallah
tongue, with the aid of my friend the Panther. When we
were both tired of this, I lay down by the side of a deep,
clear pool, formed by the water of the spring. A shoal of
little fishes of about a pin's length were playing in it,
sporting together, as it seemed, very amicably; but on
closer observation I saw that they were engaged in cannibal
warfare among themselves. Now and then one of the smallest would fall a victim, and immediately disappear down the
maw of his conqueror. Every moment, however, the tyrant
of the pool, a goggle-eyed monster about three inches long,
would slowly emerge with quivering fins and tail from under
the shelving bank. The small fry at this would suspend
their hostilities, and scatter in a panic at the appearance
of overwhelming force.

"Soft-hearted philanthropists," thought I, "may sigh long
for their peaceful millennium; for, from minnows to men,
life is incessant war."

11

Evening approached at last; the crests of the mountains
were still bright in sunshine, while our deep glen was
completely shadowed. I left the camp, and climbed a

neighboring hill. The sun was still glaring through the stiff pines on the ridge of the western mountain. In a moment he was gone, and, as the landscape darkened, I turned again towards the village. As I descended, the howling of wolves and the barking of foxes came up out of the dim woods from far and near. The camp was glow ing with a multitude of fires, and alive with dusky naked figures, whose tall shadows flitted, weird and ghost-like, among the surrounding crags.

I found a circle of smokers seated in their usual place; that is, on the ground before the lodge of a certain warrior who seemed to be generally known for his social qualities. I sat down to smoke a parting pipe with my savage friends. That day was the first of August on which I had promised to meet Shaw at Fort Laramie. The fort was less than two days' journey distant, and that my friend need not suffer anxiety on my account, I resolved to push forward as rapidly as possible to the place of meeting. I went to look after the Hail-Storm, and having found him I offered him a handful of hawks'-bells and a paper of vermilion, on condition that he would guide me in the morning through the mountains.

The Hail-Storm ejaculated "How!" and accepted the gift. Nothing more was said on either side; the matter was settled, and I lay down to sleep in Kongra-Tonga's lodge.

Long before daylight, Raymond shook me by the shoulder.

"Everything is ready," he said.

I went out. The morning was chill, damp, and dark; and the whole camp seemed asleep. The Hail-Storm sat on horseback before the lodge, and my mare Pauline and the mule which Raymond rode were picketed near it. We saddled and made our other arrangements for the journey, but before these were completed the camp began to stir, and the lodge-coverings fluttered and rustled as the squaws pulled them down in preparation for departure. Just as the light began to appear we left the ground, passing up through a narrow opening among the rocks which led eastward out of the meadow. Gaining the top of this passage, I turned and sat looking back upon the camp, dimly visible in the gray light of morning. All was alive with the bustle of preparation. I turned away, half unwilling to take a final leave of my savage associates. We passed among rocks and pine-trees so dark that for a while we could scarcely see our way. The country in front was wild and broken, half hill, half plain, partly open and partly covered with woods of pine and oak. Barriers of lofty mountains encompassed it; the woods were fresh and cool in the early morning, the peaks of the mountains were wreathed with mist, and sluggish vapors were entangled among the forests upon their sides. At length the black pinnacle of the tallest mountain was tipped with gold by the rising sun. The Hail-Storm, who rode in front, gave a low exclamation. Some large animal leaped up from among the bushes, and an elk, as I thought, his horns thrown back over his neck, darted past us across the open space, and bounded like a mad thing away among the adjoining pines. Raymond was soon out of his saddle, but before he could fire the animal was full two hundred yards distant. The ball struck its mark, though much too low for mortal effect. The elk, however, wheeled in his flight, and ran at full speed among the trees, nearly at right angles to his former course. I fired and broke his shoulder; still he moved on, limping down into a neighboring woody hollow, whither the young Indian followed, and killed him. When

13 we reached the spot we discovered him to be no elk, but
a black-tailed deer, an animal nearly twice as large as the
common deer, and quite unknown in the East.   The reports
of the rifles had reached the ears of the Indians, and
several of them came to the spot.   Leaving the hide of
the deer to the Hail-Storm, we hung as much of the meat
as we wanted behind our saddles, left the rest to the Indians, and resumed our journey.   Meanwhile the village
was on its way, and had gone so far that to get in advance
of it was impossible.   We directed our course so as to
strike its line of march at the nearest point.   In a short
time, through the dark trunks of the pines, we could see
the figures of the Indians as they passed.   Once more we
were among them.   They were moving with even more
than their usual precipitation, crowded together in a nar-
14 row pass between rocks and old pine-trees.   We were on
the eastern descent of the mountain, and soon came to a
rough and difficult defile, leading down a steep declivity.
The whole swarm poured down together, filling the rocky
passage-way like some turbulent mountain-stream.   The
mountains before us were on fire, and had been so for weeks.
The view in front was obscured by a vast, dim sea of smoke,
while on either hand rose the tall cliffs, bearing aloft their
crests of pines, and the sharp pinnacles and broken ridges
of the mountains beyond were faintly traceable as through
a veil.   The scene in itself was grand and imposing, but
with the savage multitude, the armed warriors, the naked
children, the gayly apparelled girls, pouring impetuously
down the heights, it would have formed a noble subject
for a painter, and only the pen of a Scott could have done
it justice in description.

We passed over a burnt tract where the ground was hot
beneath the horses' feet, and between the blazing sides of

two mountains. Before long we had descended to a softer region, where we found a succession of little valleys watered by a stream, along the borders of which grew abundance of wild gooseberries and currants, and the children and many of the men straggled from the line of march to gather them as we passed along. Descending still farther, the view changed rapidly. The burning mountains were behind us, and through the open valleys in front we could see the prairie, stretching like an ocean beyond the sight. After passing through a line of trees that skirted the brook, the Indians filed out upon the plains. I was thirsty and knelt down by the little stream to drink. As I mounted again, I very carelessly left my rifle among the grass, and my thoughts being otherwise absorbed, I rode for some distance before discovering its absence. I lost no time in turning about and galloping back in search of it. Passing the line of Indians, I watched every warrior as he rode by me at a canter, and at length discovered my rifle in the hands of one of them, who, on my approaching to claim it, immediately gave it up. Having no other means of acknowledging the obligation, I took off one of my spurs and gave it to him. He was greatly delighted, looking upon it as a distinguished mark of favor, and immediately held out his foot for me to buckle it on. As soon as I had done so, he struck it with all his force into the side of his horse, which gave a violent leap. The Indian laughed and spurred harder than before. At this the horse shot away like an arrow, amid the screams and laughter of the squaws, and the ejaculations of the men, who exclaimed: "Washtay! — Good!" at the potent effect of my gift. The Indian had no saddle, and nothing in place of a bridle except a leather string tied round the horse's jaw. The animal was of course wholly uncontrollable, and stretched away at full speed over the prairie,

15

till he and his rider vanished behind a distant swell. I never saw the man again, but I presume no harm came to him. An Indian on horseback has more lives than a cat.

The village encamped on the scorching prairie, close to the foot of the mountains. The heat was intense and penetrating. The coverings of the lodges were raised a foot or more from the ground, in order to procure some circulation of air; and Reynal thought proper to lay aside his trapper's dress of buckskin and assume the very scanty costume of an Indian. Thus elegantly attired, he stretched himself in his lodge on a buffalo-robe, alternately cursing the heat and puffing at the pipe which he and I passed beween us. There was present also a select circle of Indian friends and relatives. A small boiled puppy was served up as a parting feast, to which was added, by way of dessert, a wooden bowl of gooseberries from the mountains.

"Look there," said Reynal, pointing out of the opening of his lodge; "do you see that line of buttes about fifteen miles off? Well, now do you see that farthest one, with the white speck on the face of it? Do you think you ever saw it before?"

"It looks to me," said I, "like the hill that we were 'camped under when we were on Laramie Creek, six or eight weeks ago."

"You've hit it," answered Reynal.

"Go and bring in the animals, Raymond," said I; "we'll camp there to-night, and start for the fort in the morning."

The mare and the mule were soon before the lodge. We saddled them, and in the mean time a number of Indians collected about us. The virtues of Pauline, my strong, fleet, and hardy little mare, were well known in camp, and

several of the visitors were mounted upon good horses
which they had brought me as presents.   I promptly
declined their offers, since accepting them would have
involved the necessity of transferring Pauline into their
barbarous hands.   We took leave of Reynal, but not of
the Indians, who are accustomed to dispense with such
superfluous ceremonies.   Leaving the camp we rode straight
over the prairie towards the white-faced bluff, whose pale
ridges swelled gently against the horizon, like a cloud.
An Indian went with us, whose name I forget, though
the ugliness of his face and the ghastly width of his
mouth dwell vividly in my recollection.   The antelope
were numerous, but we did not heed them.   We rode
directly towards our destination, over the arid plains and
barren hills; until, late in the afternoon, half spent with
heat, thirst, and fatigue, we saw a gladdening sight, — the
long line of trees and the deep gulf that mark the course
of Laramie Creek.   Passing through the growth of huge,
dilapidated old cotton-wood trees that bordered the creek,
we rode across to the other side.   The rapid and foam-   18
ing waters were filled with fish playing and splashing
in the shallows.   As we gained the farther bank, our
horses turned eagerly to drink, and we, kneeling on the
sand, followed their example.   We had not gone far before the scene began to grow familiar.

"We are getting near home, Raymond," said I.

There stood the big tree under which we had encamped
so long; there were the white cliffs that used to look down
upon our tent when it stood at the bend of the creek; there
was the meadow in which our horses had grazed for weeks,
and a little farther on, the prairie-dog village where I had
beguiled many a languid hour in shooting the unfortunate
inhabitants.   19

"We are going to catch it now," said Raymond, turning his broad face up towards the sky.

In truth the cliffs and the meadow, the stream and the groves, were darkening fast. Black masses of cloud were swelling up in the south, and the thunder was growling ominously.

"We will 'camp there," I said, pointing to a grove of trees lower down the stream. Raymond and I turned towards it, but the Indian stopped and called earnestly after us. When we demanded what was the matter he said that the ghosts of two warriors were always among those trees, and that if we slept there they would scream and throw stones at us all night, and perhaps steal our horses before morning. Thinking it as well to humor him, we left behind us the haunt of these extraordinary ghosts, and passed on towards Chugwater, riding at full gallop, for the big drops began to patter down. Soon we came in sight of the poplar saplings that grew about the mouth of the little stream. We leaped to the ground, threw off our saddles, turned our horses loose, and drawing our knives began to slash among the bushes to cut twigs and branches for making a shelter against the rain. Bending down the taller saplings as they grew, we piled the young shoots upon them, and thus made a convenient pent-house; but our labor was needless. The storm scarcely touched us. Half a mile on our right the rain was pouring down like a cataract, and the thunder roared over the prairie like a battery of cannon; while we by good fortune received only a few heavy drops from the skirt of the passing cloud. The weather cleared and the sun set gloriously. Sitting close under our leafy canopy we proceeded to discuss a substantial meal of *wasna* which Weah-Washtay had given me. The Indian had brought with him his pipe and a bag of *shong-*

sasha; so before lying down to sleep we sat for some time smoking together. First, however, our wide-mouthed friend had taken the precaution of carefully examining the neighborhood. He reported that eight men, counting them on his fingers, had been encamped there not long before,— Bisonette, Paul Dorion, Antoine Le Rouge, Richardson, and four others, whose names he could not tell. All this proved strictly correct. By what instinct he had arrived at such accurate conclusions, I am utterly at a loss to divine.

It was still quite dark when I awoke and called Raymond. The Indian was already gone, having chosen to go on before us to the fort. Setting out after him, we rode for some time in complete darkness and when the sun at length rose, glowing like a fiery ball of copper, we were within ten miles of the fort. At length, from the summit of a sandy bluff we could see Fort Laramie, miles before us, standing by the side of the stream like a little gray speck, in the midst of the boundless desolation. I stopped my horse, and sat for a moment looking down upon it. It seemed to me the very centre of comfort and civilization. We were not long in approaching it, for we rode at speed the greater part of the way. Laramie Creek still intervened between us and the friendly walls. Entering the water at the point where we had struck upon the bank, we raised our feet to the saddle behind us, and thus kneeling as it were on horseback, passed dry-shod through the swift current. As we rode up the bank a number of men appeared in the gateway. Three of them came forward to meet us. In a moment I distinguished Shaw; Henry Chatillon followed, with his face of manly simplicity and frankness, and Deslauriers came last, with a broad grin of welcome. The meeting was not on either side one of mere ceremony. For my own part, the change was a most agreeable one, from the society of savages and men little better than savages, to that of my gallant and high-minded companion, and our noble-hearted guide. My appearance was equally welcome to Shaw, who was beginning to entertain some uncomfortable surmises concerning me.

Bordeaux greeted me cordially, and shouted to the cook. This functionary was a new acquisition, having lately come from Fort Pierre with the trading wagons. Whatever skill he might have boasted, he had not the most promising materials to exercise it upon. He set before me, however, a breakfast of biscuit, coffee, and salt pork. It seemed like a new phase of existence to be seated once more on a bench with a knife and fork, a plate and teacup, and something resembling a table before me. The coffee seemed delicious, and the bread was a most welcome novelty, since for three weeks I had tasted scarcely anything but meat, and that for the most part without salt. The meal also had the relish of good company, for opposite to me sat Shaw in elegant dishabille. If one is anxious thoroughly to appreciate the value of a congenial companion, he has only to spend a few weeks by himself in an Ogillallah village. And if he can contrive to add to his seclusion a debilitating and somewhat critical illness, his perceptions upon this subject will be rendered considerably more vivid.

Shaw had been two or three weeks at the fort. I found him established in his old quarters, a large apartment usually occupied by the absent *bourgeois*. In one corner was a soft pile of excellent buffalo-robes, and here I lay down. Shaw brought me three books.

"Here," said he, "is your Shakspeare and Byron, and here is the Old Testament, which has as much poetry in it as the other two put together."

I chose the worst of the three, and for the greater part of that day I lay on the buffalo-robes, fairly revelling in the creations of that resplendent genius which has achieved no more signal triumph than that of half beguiling us to forget the unmanly character of its possessor.

25

CHAPTER XX.

THE LONELY JOURNEY.

ON the day of my arrival at Fort Laramie, Shaw and I were lounging on two buffalo-robes in the large apartment hospitably assigned to us; Henry Chatillon also was present, busy about the harness and weapons, which had been brought into the room, and two or three Indians were crouching on the floor, eying us with their fixed, unwavering gaze.

"I have been well off here," said Shaw, "in all respects but one; there is no good *shongsasha* to be had for love or money."

I gave him a small leather bag containing some of excellent quality which I had brought from the Black Hills. "Now, Henry," said he, "hand me Papin's chopping-board, or give it to that Indian, and let him cut the mixture; they understand it better than any white man."

The Indian, without saying a word, mixed the bark and the tobacco in due proportions, filled the pipe, and lighted

it. This done, my companion and I proceeded to deliberate on our future course of proceeding; first, however, Shaw
acquainted me with some incidents which had occurred at
the fort during my absence.

About a week before, four men had arrived from beyond
the mountains: Sublette, Reddick, and two others. Just 1
before reaching the fort they had met a large party of Indians, chiefly young men. All of them belonged to the
village of our old friend Smoke, who, with his whole band 2
of adherents, professed the greatest friendship for the
whites. The travellers therefore approached and began to
converse without the least suspicion. Suddenly, however,
their bridles were seized, and they were ordered to dismount. Instead of complying, they lashed their horses,
and broke away from the Indians. As they galloped off
they heard a yell behind them, with a burst of derisive
laughter, and the reports of several guns. None of them
were hurt, though Reddick's bridle-rein was cut by a bullet
within an inch of his hand. After this taste of Indian man- 3
ners, they felt for the moment no disposition to encounter
farther risks. They intended to pursue the route southward along the foot of the mountains to Bent's Fort; and
as our plans coincided with theirs, they proposed to join
forces. Finding, however, that I did not return, they
grew impatient of inaction, forgot their late danger, and
set out without us, promising to wait our arrival at
Bent's Fort. From thence we were to make the long
journey to the settlements in company, as the path was not
a little dangerous, being infested by hostile Pawnees and
Camanches. 4

We expected, on reaching Bent's Fort, to find there still
another reinforcement. A young Kentuckian had come out 5
to the mountains with Russel's party of California emi-

grants. One of his chief objects, as he gave out, was to kill an Indian; an exploit which he afterwards succeeded in achieving, much to the jeopardy of ourselves, and others who had to pass through the country of the dead Pawnee's 6 enraged relatives. Having become disgusted with his emigrant associates, he left them, and had some time before set out with a party of companions for the head of the Arkansas. He left us a letter, to say that he would wait until we arrived at Bent's Fort, and accompany us thence to the settlements. When however he came to the fort, he found there a party of forty men about to make the homeward journey, and wisely preferred to avail himself of so strong an escort. Sublette and his companions also joined this company; so that on reaching Bent's Fort, some six weeks after, we found ourselves deserted by our allies 7 and thrown once more upon our own resources.

On the fourth of August, early in the afternoon, we bade a final adieu to the hospitable gateway of Fort Laramie. Again Shaw and I were riding side by side on the prairie. For the first fifty miles we had companions with us: 8 Troché, a trapper, and Rouville, a nondescript in the employ of the Fur Company, who were going to join the trader Bisonette at his encampment near the head of Horse Creek. We rode only six or eight miles that after- 9 noon before we came to a little brook traversing the barren prairie. All along its course grew copses of young wild-cherry trees, loaded with ripe fruit, and almost concealing the gliding thread of water with their dense growth. Here we encamped; and being too indolent to pitch our tent, we flung our saddles on the ground, spread a pair of buffalo-robes, lay down upon them, and began to smoke. Meanwhile Deslauriers busied himself with his frying-pan, and Raymond stood guard over the band of grazing horses.

Deslauriers had an active assistant in Rouville, who professed great skill in the culinary art, and seizing upon a fork, began to lend his aid in cooking supper. Indeed, according to his own belief, Rouville was a man of universal knowledge, and he lost no opportunity to display his manifold accomplishments. He had been a circus-rider at St. Louis, and once he rode round Fort Laramie on his head, to the utter bewilderment of the Indians. He was also noted as the wit of the fort, and as he had considerable humor and abundant vivacity, he contributed more that night to the liveliness of the camp than all the rest of the party put together. At one instant he would kneel by Deslauriers, instructing him in the true method of frying antelope-steaks, then he would come and seat himself at our side, dilating upon the correct fashion of braiding up a horse's tail, telling apocryphal stories how he had killed a buffalo-bull with a knife, having first cut off his tail when at full speed, or relating whimsical anecdotes of the *bourgeois* Papin. At last he snatched up a volume of Shakspeare that was lying on the grass, and halted and stumbled through a line or two to prove that he could read. He went gambolling about the camp, chattering like some frolicsome ape; and whatever he was doing at one moment, the presumption was a sure one that he would not be doing it the next. His companion Troché sat silently on the grass, not speaking a word, but keeping a vigilant eye on a very ugly little Utah squaw, of whom he was extremely jealous.

On the next day we travelled farther, crossing the wide, sterile basin called "Goché's Hole." Towards night we became involved among ravines; and being unable to find water, our journey was protracted to a very late hour. On the next morning we had to pass a long line of bluffs, whose raw sides, wrought upon by rains and storms, were of a ghastly whiteness most oppressive to the sight. As we ascended a gap in these hills, the way was marked by huge footprints, like those of a human giant. They were the tracks of the grizzly bear, of which we had also seen abundance on the day before. Immediately after this we were crossing a barren plain, spreading in long and gentle undulations to the horizon. Though the sun was bright, there was a light haze in the atmosphere. The distant hills assumed strange, distorted forms in the mirage, and the edge of the horizon was continually changing its aspect. Shaw and I were riding together, and Henry Chatillon was a few rods before us, when he stopped his horse suddenly, and turning round with the peculiar earnest expression which he always wore when excited, called us to come forward. We galloped to his side. Henry pointed towards a black speck on the gray swell of the prairie, apparently about a mile off. "It must be a bear," said he; "come, now we shall all have some sport. Better fun to fight him than to fight an old buffalo-bull; grizzly bear so strong and smart."

So we all galloped forward together, prepared for a hard fight; for these bears, though clumsy in appearance, are incredibly fierce and active. The swell of the prairie concealed the black object from our view. Immediately after, it appeared again. But now it seemed very near to us; and as we looked at it in astonishment, it suddenly separated into two parts, each of which took wing and flew away. We stopped our horses and looked at Henry, whose face exhibited a curious mixture of mirth and mortification. His eye had been so completely deceived by the peculiar atmosphere that he had mistaken two large crows at the distance of fifty rods for a grizzly bear a mile off.

To the journey's end Henry never heard the last of the grizzly bear with wings.

In the afternoon we came to the foot of a considerable hill. As we ascended it Rouville began to ask questions concerning our condition and prospects at home, and Shaw was edifying him with an account of an imaginary wife and child, to which he listened with implicit faith. Reaching the top of the hill, we saw the windings of Horse Creek 12 on the plains below us, and a little on the left we could distinguish the camp of Bisonette among the trees and copses along the course of the stream. Rouville's face assumed just then a ludicrously blank expression. We inquired what was the matter; when it appeared that Bisonette had sent him from this place to Fort Laramie with the sole object of bringing back a supply of tobacco. Our rattlebrain friend, from the time of his reaching the fort up to the present moment, had entirely forgotten the object of his journey, and had ridden a dangerous hundred miles for nothing. Descending to Horse Creek we forded it, and on the opposite bank a solitary Indian sat on horseback under a tree. He said nothing, but turned and led the way towards the camp. Bisonette had made choice of an admirable position. The stream, with its thick growth of trees, inclosed on three sides a wide green meadow, where about forty Dakota lodges were pitched in a circle, and beyond them a few lodges of the friendly Cheyennes. 13 Bisonette himself lived in the Indian manner. Riding up to his lodge, we found him seated at the head of it, 14 surrounded by various appliances of comfort not common on the prairie. His squaw was near him, and rosy children were scrambling about in printed calico gowns; Paul Dorion, also, with his leathery face and old white capote, was seated in the lodge, together with Antoine Le Rouge, 15

16 a half-breed Pawnee, Sibille, a trader, and several other white men.

"It will do you no harm," said Bisonette, "to stay here
17 with us for a day or two, before you start for the Pueblo."

We accepted the invitation, and pitched our tent on a rising ground above the camp and close to the trees. Bisonette soon invited us to a feast, and we suffered abundance of the same sort of attention from his Indian associates. The reader may possibly recollect that when I joined the Indian village, beyond the Black Hills, I found that a few families were absent, having declined to pass the mountains along with the rest. The Indians in Bisonette's camp consisted of these very families, and many of them came to me that evening to inquire after their relatives and friends. They were not a little mortified to learn that while they, from their own timidity and indolence, were almost in a starving condition, the rest of the village had provided their lodges for the next season, laid in a great
18 stock of provisions, and were living in abundance. Bisonette's companions had been sustaining themselves for some time on wild cherries, which the squaws pounded, stones and all, and spread on buffalo-robes to dry in the

sun; they were then eaten without further preparation, or used as an ingredient in various delectable compounds.

On the next day the camp was in commotion with a new arrival. A single Indian had come with his family from the Arkansas. As he passed among the lodges he put on an expression of unusual dignity and importance, and gave out that he had brought great news to tell the whites. Soon after the squaws had pitched his lodge, he sent his little son to invite all the white men, and all the more distinguished Indians to a feast. The guests arrived and sat wedged together, shoulder to shoulder, within the hot and suffocating lodge. The Stabber, for that was our entertainer's name, had killed an old buffalo-bull on his way. This veteran's boiled tripe, tougher than leather, formed the main item of the repast. For the rest, it consisted of wild cherries and grease boiled together in a large copper kettle. The feast was distributed, and for a moment all was silent, strenuous exertion; then each guest, though with one or two exceptions, turned his wooden dish bottom upwards to prove that he had done full justice to his entertainer's hospitality. The Stabber next produced his chopping-board, on which he prepared the mixture for smoking, and filled several pipes, which circulated among the company. This done, he seated himself upright on his couch, and began with much gesticulation to tell his story. I will not repeat his childish jargon. It was so entangled, like the greater part of an Indian's stories, with absurd and contradictory details, that it was almost impossible to disengage from it a single particle of truth. All that we could gather was the following: —

He had been on the Arkansas, and there he had seen six great war-parties of whites. He had never believed before that the whole world contained half so many white

men. They all had large horses, long knives, and short
rifles, and some of them were dressed alike, in the most splendid war-dresses he had ever seen.   From this account it was
clear that bodies of dragoons and perhaps also of volunteer
cavalry had passed up the Arkansas. The Stabber had
also seen a great many of the white lodges of the Mene
aska, drawn by their long-horned buffalo. These could
be nothing else than covered ox-wagons used no doubt in
transporting stores for the troops. Soon after seeing this,
our host had met an Indian who had lately come from
among the Camanches, who had told him that all the
Mexicans had gone out to a great buffalo hunt; that the
Americans had hid themselves in a ravine; and that when
the Mexicans had shot away all their arrows, the Americans fired their guns, raised their war-whoop, rushed out,
and killed them all. We could only infer from this that
war had been declared with Mexico, and a battle fought
in which the Americans were victorious. When, some
weeks after, we arrived at the Pueblo, we heard of General Kearney's march up the Arkansas, and of General
20 Taylor's victories at Matamoras.

As the sun was setting that evening a crowd gathered on
the plain by the side of our tent, to try the speed of their
horses.   These were of every shape, size, and color. Some
came from California, some from the States, some from
among the mountains, and some from the wild bands of the
prairie. They were of every hue, white, black, red, and
gray, or mottled and clouded with a strange variety of colors.
They all had a wild and startled look, very different from
the sober aspect of a well-bred city steed. Those most
noted for swiftness and spirit were decorated with eagle
feathers dangling from their manes and tails. Fifty or
sixty Dakota were present, wrapped from head to foot in

their heavy robes of whitened hide. There was also a considerable number of the Cheyennes, many of whom wore gaudy Mexican ponchos, swathed around their shoulders, but leaving the right arm bare. Mingled among the crowd of Indians was a number of Canadians, chiefly in the employ of Bisonette, — men whose home is the wilderness, and who love the camp-fire better than the domestic hearth. They are contented and happy in the midst of hardship, privation, and danger. Their cheerfulness and gayety is irrepressible, and no people on earth understand better how "to daff the world aside and bid it pass." Besides t h e s e, were two or three half-breeds, a race of rather extraordinary composition, being, according to the

21

common saying, half Indian, half white man, and half devil. 22 Antoine Le Rouge was the most conspicuous among them, with his loose trousers and fluttering calico shirt. A handkerchief was bound round his head to confine his black, snaky hair, and his small eyes twinkled beneath it with a mischievous lustre. He had a fine cream-colored horse, whose speed he must needs try along with the rest. So he threw off the rude high-peaked saddle, and substituting a piece of buffalo-robe, leaped lightly into his seat. The space was cleared, the word was given, and he and his Indian rival darted out like lightning from among the crowd, each stretching forward over his horse's neck and plying his heavy Indian whip with might and main. A moment, and both were lost in the gloom; but Antoine soon came riding back victorious, exultingly patting the neck of his quivering and panting horse.

About midnight, as I lay asleep, wrapped in a buffalo-robe on the ground by the side of our cart, Raymond came and woke me. Something, he said, was going forward which I would like to see. Looking down into the camp, I saw on the farther side of it a great number of Indians gathered about a fire, the bright glare of which made them visible through the thick darkness; while from the midst proceeded a loud, measured chant, which would have killed Paganini outright, broken occasionally by a burst of sharp yells. I gathered the robe around me, for the night was cold, and walked down to the spot. The dark throng of Indians was so dense that they almost intercepted the light of the flame. As I was pushing among them with little ceremony, a chief interposed himself, and I was given to understand that a white man must not approach the scene of their solemnities too closely. By passing round to the other side, where there was a little opening in the crowd, I could see clearly what was going forward, without intruding my unhallowed presence into the inner circle. The society of the "Strong Hearts" were engaged in one of their dances. The "Strong Hearts" are a war-like association, comprising men of both the Dakota and Cheyenne nations, and entirely composed, or supposed to be so, of young braves of the highest mettle. Its fundamental principle is the admirable one of never retreating from any enterprise once begun. All these Indian associations have a tutelary spirit. That of the "Strong Hearts" is embodied in the fox, an animal which white men would hardly have selected for a similar purpose, though his subtle character agrees well enough with an Indian's notions of what is honorable in warfare. The dancers were circling round and round the fire, each figure brightly illumined at one moment by the yellow light, and at the next drawn in blackest shadow as it passed between the flame and the spectator. They would imitate with the most ludicrous exactness the motions and voice of their sly patron the fox. Then a startling yell would be given. Many other 24 warriors would leap into the ring, and with faces upturned towards the starless sky, they would all stamp and whoop, and brandish their weapons like so many frantic devils.

We remained here till the next afternoon. My com- 25 panion and I with our three attendants then set out for the Pueblo, a distance of three hundred miles, and we supposed the journey would occupy about a fortnight. During this time we all hoped that we might not meet a single human being, for should we encounter any, they would in all probability be enemies, in whose eyes our rifles would be our only passports. For the first two days nothing worth mentioning took place. On the third morning, however, an untoward incident occurred. We were encamped by the side of a little brook in an extensive 26 hollow of the plain. Deslauriers was up long before daylight, and before he began to prepare breakfast he turned loose all the horses, as in duty bound. There was a cold mist clinging close to the ground, and by the time the rest of us were awake the animals were invisible. It was only after a long and anxious search that we could discover by their tracks the direction they had taken. They had all set off for Fort Laramie, following the guidance of a mutinous old mule; and though many of them were hobbled, they travelled three miles before they could be overtaken and driven back.

For two or three days we were passing over an arid
desert. The only vegetation was a few tufts of short
grass, dried and shrivelled by the heat. There was abundance of strange insects and reptiles. Huge crickets,

27 black and bottle-green, and wingless grasshoppers of the
most extravagant dimensions, were tumbling about our
horses' feet, and lizards without number darting like lightning among the tufts of grass. The most curious animal,

28 however, was that commonly called the horned-frog. I caught
one of them and consigned him to the care of Deslauriers,
who tied him up in a moccasin. About a month after this
I examined the prisoner's condition, and finding him still
lively and active, I provided him with a cage of buffalo-
hide, which was hung up in the cart. In this manner he
arrived safely at the settlements. From thence he travelled the whole way to Boston, packed closely in a trunk,
being regaled with fresh air regularly every night. When

29 he reached his designation he was deposited under a glass
case, where he sat for some months in great tranquillity,
alternately dilating and contracting his white throat to the
admiration of his visitors. At length, one morning about
the middle of winter, he gave up the ghost, and he now
occupies a bottle of alcohol in the Agassiz Museum. His
death was attributed to starvation, — a very probable conclusion, since for six months he had taken no food whatever, though the sympathy of his juvenile admirers had

30 tempted his palate with a great variety of delicacies. We
found also animals of a somewhat larger growth. The
number of prairie-dogs was astounding. Frequently the
hard and dry plain was thickly covered, for miles together,
with the little mounds which they make at the mouth of
their burrows, and small squeaking voices yelped at us
as we passed along. The noses of the inhabitants were

just visible at the mouth of their holes, but no sooner
was their curiosity satisfied than they would instantly van-
ish.   Some of the bolder dogs — though in fact they are
no dogs at all, but little marmots rather smaller than   31
a rabbit — would sit yelping at us on the top of their
mounds, jerking their tails emphatically with every shrill
cry they uttered.   As the danger drew nearer they would
wheel about, toss their heels into the air, and dive in a
twinkling into their burrows.   Towards sunset, and especially if rain was threatening, the whole community made
their appearance above ground.   We saw them gathered in large knots around the burrow of some favorite
citizen.   There they would all sit erect, their tails spread
out on the ground, and their paws hanging down before
their white breasts, chattering and squeaking with the utmost vivacity upon some topic of common interest, while
the proprietor of the burrow sat on the top of his mound,
looking down with a complacent countenance on the enjoyment of his guests.   Meanwhile others ran about from
burrow to burrow, as if on some errand of the last importance to their subterranean commonwealth.   The snakes are
apparently the prairie-dog's worst enemies; at least I think
too well of the latter to suppose that they associate on
friendly terms with these slimy intruders, which may be
seen at all times basking among their holes, into which
they always retreat when disturbed.   Small owls, with
wise and grave countenances, also make their abode with
the prairie-dogs, though on what terms they live together
I could never ascertain.   32

On the fifth day after leaving Bisonette's camp, we saw,
late in the afternoon, what we supposed to be a considerable stream, but on approaching it, we found to our disappointment, nothing but a dry bed of sand, into which the

water had sunk and disappeared. We separated, some riding in one direction and some in another, along its course. Still we found no traces of water, not even so much as a wet spot in the sand. The old cotton-wood trees that grew along the bank, lamentably abused by lightning and tempest, were withering with the drought, and on the dead limbs, at the summit of the tallest, half a dozen crows were hoarsely cawing, like birds of evil omen. We had no alternative but to keep on. There was no water nearer than the South Fork of the Platte, about ten miles distant. We moved forward, angry and silent, over a desert as flat as the outspread ocean.

33

The sky had been obscured since the morning by thin mists and vapors, but now vast piles of clouds were gathered together in the west. They rose to a great height above the horizon, and looking up at them I distinguished one mass darker than the rest, and of a peculiar conical form. I happened to look again, and still could see it as before. At some moments it was dimly visible, at others its outline was sharp and distinct; but while the clouds around it were shifting, changing, and dissolving away, it still towered aloft in the midst of them, fixed and immovable. It must, thought I, be the summit of a mountain; and yet its height staggered me. My conclusion was right, however. It was Long's Peak, once believed to be one of the highest of the Rocky Mountain chain, though more recent discoveries have proved the contrary. The thickening gloom soon hid it from view, and we never saw it again, for on the following day, and for some time after, the air was so full of mist that the view of distant objects was entirely cut off.

34

It grew very late. Turning from our direct course, we made for the river at its nearest point, though in the utter

darkness it was not easy to direct our way with much precision.   Raymond rode on one side and Henry on the other.
We heard each of them shouting that he had come upon a
deep ravine.   We steered at random between Scylla and
Charybdis, and soon after became as it seemed inextri-
cably involved, with deep chasms all around us, while the
darkness was such that we could not see a rod in any
direction.   We partially extricated ourselves by scrambling,
cart and all, through a shallow ravine.   We came next to
a steep descent, down which we plunged without well
knowing what was at the bottom.   There was a great
crackling of sticks and dry twigs.   Over our heads were
certain large shadowy objects; and in front something
like the faint gleaming of a dark sheet of water.   Raymond ran his horse against a tree; Henry alighted, and,
feeling on the ground, declared that there was grass enough
for the horses.   Before taking off his saddle, each man led
his own horses down to the water in the best way he could.
Then picketing two or three of the evil-disposed, we turned
the rest loose, and lay down among the dry sticks to sleep.
In the morning we found ourselves close to the South Fork   35
of the Platte, on a spot surrounded by bushes and rank
grass.   Compensating ourselves with a hearty breakfast for
the ill-fare of the previous night, we set forward again on
our journey.   When only two or three rods from the camp
I saw Shaw stop his mule, level his gun, and fire at some
object in the grass.   Deslauriers next jumped forward, and
began to dance about, belaboring the unseen enemy with
a whip.   Then he stooped down, and drew out of the grass
by the neck a large rattlesnake, with his head completely
shattered by Shaw's bullet.   As Deslauriers held him out
at arm's length with an exulting grin, his tail, which still
kept slowly writhing about, almost touched the ground;

and his body in the largest part was as thick as a stout man's arm. He had fourteen rattles, but the end of his tail was blunted, as if he could once have boasted of many more. From this time till we reached the Pueblo, we killed at least four or five of these snakes every day, as they lay coiled and rattling on the hot sand. Shaw was the Saint Patrick of the party, and whenever he killed a snake he pulled off his tail and stored it away in his bullet-pouch, which was soon crammed with an edifying collection of rattles, great and small. Deslauriers with his whip also came in for a share of praise. A day or two after this, he triumphantly produced a small snake about a span and a half long, with one infant rattle at the end of his tail.

We forded the South Fork of the Platte. On its farther bank were the traces of a very large camp of Arapahoes. The ashes of some three hundred fires were visible among the scattered trees, together with the remains of sweating lodges, and all the other appurtenances of a permanent camp. The place, however, had been for some months deserted. A few miles farther on we found more recent signs of Indians, — the trail of two or three lodges which had evidently passed the day before; every footprint was perfectly distinct in the dry, dusty soil. We noticed in particular the track of one moccasin, upon the sole of which its economical proprietor had placed a large patch. These signs gave us but little uneasiness, as the number of the warriors scarcely exceeded that of our own party. At noon we rested under the walls of a large fort, built in these solitudes some years since by M. St. Vrain. It was now abandoned and fast falling into ruin. The walls of unbaked bricks were cracked from top to bottom. Our horses recoiled in terror from the neglected entrance, where the

heavy gates were torn from their hinges and flung down.
The area within was overgrown with weeds, and the long
ranges of apartments once occupied by the motley concourse of traders, Canadians, and squaws, were now miserably dilapidated.   Twelve miles farther on, near the
spot where we encamped, were the remains of another
fort, standing in melancholy desertion and neglect.   40

Early on the following morning we made a startling discovery. We passed close by a large deserted encampment of
Arapahoes.   There were about fifty fires still smouldering on   41
the ground, and it was evident from numerous signs that the
Indians must have left the place within two hours of our
reaching it.   Their trail crossed our own, at right angles,
and led in the direction of a line of hills, half a mile
on our left.   There were women and children in the
party, which would have greatly diminished the danger
of encountering them.   Henry Chatillon examined the
encampment and the trail with a very professional and
business-like air.

"Supposing we had met them, Henry?" said I.

"Why," said he, "we hold out our hands to them, and
give them all we 've got; they take away everything and
then I believe they no kill us. Perhaps," added he, looking up with a quiet, unchanged face, "perhaps we no let
them rob us.   Maybe before they come near, we have a
chance to get into a ravine, or under the bank of the
river; then, you know, we fight them."

About noon on that day we reached Cherry Creek.   Here   42
was a great abundance of wild-cherries, plums, gooseberries,
and currants.   The stream, however, like most of the others
which we passed, was dried up with the heat, and we had
to dig holes in the sand to find water for ourselves and our
horses.   Two days after, we left the banks of the creek,   43

which we had been following for some time, and began to cross the high dividing ridge which separates the waters of the Platte from those of the Arkansas. The scenery was altogether changed. In place of the burning plains, we passed through rough and savage glens, and among hills crowned with a dreary growth of pines. We encamped among these solitudes on the night of the sixteenth of August. A tempest was threatening. The sun went down among volumes of jet-black cloud, edged with a bloody red. But in spite of these portentous signs we neglected to put up the tent, and being extremely fatigued, lay down on the ground and fell asleep. The storm broke about midnight, and we pitched the tent amid darkness and confusion. In the morning all was fair again, and Pike's Peak, white with snow, was towering above the wilderness afar off.

We pushed through an extensive tract of pine woods. Large black-squirrels were leaping among the branches. From the farther edge of this forest we saw the prairie again, hollowed out before us into a vast basin, and about a mile in front we could discern a little black speck moving upon its surface. It could be nothing but a buffalo. Henry primed his rifle afresh and galloped forward. To the left of the animal was a low rocky mound, of which Henry availed himself in making his approach. After a short time we heard the faint report of the rifle. The bull, mortally wounded from a distance of nearly three hundred yards, ran wildly round and round in a circle. Shaw and I then galloped forward, and passing him as he ran, foaming with rage and pain, discharged our pistols into his side. Once or twice he rushed furiously upon us, but his strength was rapidly exhausted. Down he fell on his knees. For one instant he glared up at his enemies, with burning eyes, through his black, tangled mane, and then rolled over on his side. Though gaunt and thin, he was larger and heavier than the largest ox. Foam and blood flew together from his nostrils as he lay bellowing and pawing the ground, tearing up grass and earth with his hoofs. His sides rose and fell like a vast pair of bellows, the blood spouting up in jets from the bullet-holes. Suddenly his glaring eyes became like a lifeless jelly. He lay motionless on the ground. Henry stooped over him, and making an incision with his knife, pronounced the meat too rank and tough for use; so, disappointed in our hopes of an addition to our stock of provisions, we rode away and left the carcass to the wolves.

In the afternoon we saw the mountains rising like a gigantic wall at no great distance on our right. "*Des sauvages! des sauvages!*" exclaimed Deslauriers, looking round with a frightened face, and pointing with his whip towards the foot of the mountains. In fact, we could see at a distance a number of little black specks, like horsemen in rapid motion. Henry Chatillon, with Shaw and myself galloped towards them to reconnoitre, when to our amusement we saw the supposed Arapahoes resolved into the black tops of some pine-trees which grew along a ravine. The summits of these pines, just visible above the verge of the prairie, and seeming to move as we ourselves were advancing, looked exactly like a line of horsemen. 47

We encamped among ravines and hollows, through which a little brook was foaming angrily. Before sunrise in the morning the snow-covered mountains were beautifully tinged with a delicate rose color. A noble spectacle awaited us as we moved forward. Six or eight miles on our right, Pike's Peak and his giant brethren rose out of the level prairie, as 48 49 if springing from the bed of the ocean. From their summits down to the plain below they were involved in a mantle of clouds, in restless motion, as if urged by strong winds. For one instant some snowy peak, towering in awful solitude, would be disclosed to view. As the clouds broke along the mountain, we could see the dreary forests, the tremendous precipices, the white patches of snow, the gulfs and chasms as black as night, all revealed for an instant, and then disappearing from the view.

On the day after, we had left the mountains at some distance. A black cloud descended upon them, and a tremendous explosion of thunder followed, reverberating among the precipices. In a few moments everything grew black, and the rain poured down like a cataract. We got under an old cotton-wood tree, which stood by the side of a stream, and waited there till the rage of the torrent had passed.

The clouds opened at the point where they first had gathered, and the whole sublime congregation of mountains was bathed at once in warm sunshine. They seemed more like some vision of eastern romance than like a reality of that wilderness; all were melted together into a soft delicious blue, as voluptuous as the sky of Naples or the transparent sea that washes the sunny cliffs of Capri. On the left the sky was still of an inky blackness; but two concentric rainbows stood in bright relief against it, while far in front the ragged clouds still streamed before the wind, and the retreating thunder muttered angrily.

Through that afternoon and the next morning we were passing down the banks of the stream, called "Boiling Spring Creek," from the boiling spring whose waters flow into it. When we stopped at noon, we were within six or eight miles of the Pueblo. Setting out again, we found by the fresh tracks that a horseman had just been out to reconnoitre us; he had circled half round the camp, and then galloped back at full speed for the Pueblo. What made him so shy of us we could not conceive. After an hour's ride we reached the edge of a hill, from which a welcome sight greeted us. The Arkansas ran along the valley below, among woods and groves, and closely nestled in the midst of wide corn-fields and green meadows, where cattle were grazing, rose the low mud walls of the Pueblo.

CHAPTER XXI.

THE PUEBLO AND BENT'S FORT.

WE approached the gate of the Pueblo. It was a wretched species of fort, of most primitive construction, being nothing more than a large square inclosure, surrounded by a wall of adobe, miserably cracked and dilapidated. The slender pickets that surmounted it were half broken down, and the gate dangled on its wooden hinges so loosely that to open or shut it seemed likely to fling it down altogether. Two or three squalid Mexicans, with their broad hats, and their vile faces overgrown with hair, were lounging about the bank of the river in front of it. They disappeared as they saw us approach; and as we rode up to the gate, a light, active little figure came out to meet us. It was our old friend Richard. He had come from Fort Laramie on a trading expedition to Taos; but finding when he reached the Pueblo that the war would prevent his going farther, he was quietly waiting till the conquest of the country should allow him to proceed. He seemed to feel bound to do the honors of the place. Shaking us warmly by the hand, he led the way into the area.

Here we saw his large Santa Fé wagons standing together. A few squaws and Spanish women, and a few Mexicans, as mean and miserable as the place itself, were lazily sauntering about. Richard conducted us to the state apartment of the Pueblo, a small mud room, very neatly finished, considering the material, and garnished with a crucifix, a looking-glass, a picture of the Virgin, and a rusty horse-pistol. There were no chairs, but instead of them a number of chests and boxes ranged about the room. There was another room beyond, less sumptuously decorated, and here three or four Spanish girls, one of them very pretty, were baking cakes at a mud fireplace 3 in the corner. They brought out a poncho, which they spread upon the floor by way of table-cloth. A supper, which seemed to us luxurious, was soon laid out upon it, and folded buffalo-robes were placed around it to receive the guests. Two or three Americans besides ourselves were present. We sat down in Turkish fashion, and began to ask the news. Richard told us that, about three weeks before, General Kearney's army had left Bent's Fort to march against Santa Fé; that when last heard from they were approaching the defiles that led to the city. One of the Americans produced a dingy newspaper, containing an account of the battles of Palo Alto and Resaca de 4 la Palma. While we were discussing these matters the doorway was darkened by a tall, shambling fellow, who stood with his hands in his pockets taking a leisurely survey of the premises before he entered. He wore brown homespun trousers, much too short for his legs, and a pistol and bowie-knife stuck in his belt. His head and one eye were enveloped in a huge bandage of linen. Having completed his observations, he came slouching in, and sat down on a chest. Eight or ten more of the same stamp followed, and very coolly arranging themselves about the

room began to stare at the company. We were forcibly reminded of the Oregon emigrants, though these unwelcome visitors had a certain glitter of the eye, and a compression of the lips which distinguished them from our old acquaintances of the prairie. They began to catechise us at once, inquiring whence we had come, what we meant to do next, and what were our prospects in life.

The man with the bandaged head had met with an untoward accident a few days before. He was going down to the river to bring water, and was pushing through the young willows which covered the low ground, when he came unawares upon a grizzly bear, which, having just eaten a buffalo-bull, had lain down to sleep off the meal. The bear rose on his hind legs, and gave the intruder such a blow with his paw that he laid his forehead entirely bare, clawed off the front of his scalp, and narrowly missed one of his eyes. Fortunately he was not in a very pugnacious mood, being surfeited with his late meal. The man's companions, who were close behind, raised a shout, and the bear walked away, crushing down the willows in his leisurely retreat.

These men belonged to a party of Mormons, who, out of a well-grounded fear of the other emigrants, had postponed leaving the settlements until all the rest were gone.   On account of this delay, they did not reach Fort Laramie until it was too late to continue their journey to California. Hearing that there was good land at the head of the Arkansas, they crossed over under the guidance of Richard, and were now preparing to spend the winter at a spot about half a mile from the Pueblo.

5

When we took leave of Richard it was near sunset. Passing out of the gate, we could look down the little valley of the Arkansas; a beautiful scene, and doubly so to our eyes, so long accustomed to deserts and mountains. Tall woods lined the river, with green meadows on either hand; and high bluffs, quietly basking in the sunlight, flanked the narrow valley.   A Mexican on horseback was driving a herd of cattle towards the gate, and our little white tent, which the men had pitched under a tree in the meadow, made a pleasing feature in the scene.   When we reached it we found that Richard had sent a Mexican to bring us an abundant supply of green corn and vegetables and invite us to help ourselves to whatever we wanted from the fields around the Pueblo.

The inhabitants were in daily apprehension of an inroad from more formidable consumers than we.   Every year, at the time when the corn begins to ripen, the Arapahoes, to the number of several thousands, come and encamp around the Pueblo.   The handful of white men, who are entirely at the mercy of this swarm of barbarians, choose to make a merit of necessity; they come forward very cordially, shake them by the hand, and tell them that the harvest

is entirely at their disposal.   The Arapahoes take them at
their word, help themselves most liberally, and usually
turn their horses into the cornfields afterwards.   They
have the foresight, however, to leave enough of the crops
untouched to serve as an inducement for planting the fields
again for their benefit in the next spring.

The human race in this part of the world is separated
into three divisions, arranged in the order of their merits:
white men, Indians, and Mexicans; to the latter of whom
the honorable title of "whites" is by no means conceded.

In spite of the warm sunset of that evening, the next
morning was a dreary and cheerless one.   It rained steadily,
clouds resting upon the very tree-tops.   We crossed the
6 river to visit the Mormon settlement.   As we passed through
the water several trappers on horseback entered it from the
other side.   Their buckskin frocks were soaked through
by the rain, and clung fast to their limbs with a most
clammy and uncomfortable look.   The water was trickling down their faces, and dropping from the ends of their
rifles and from the traps which each carried at the pommel of his saddle.   Horses and all, they had a disconsolate and woe-begone appearance, which we could not help
laughing at, forgetting how often we ourselves had been
in a similar plight.

After half an hour's riding we saw the white wagons of
the Mormons drawn up among the trees.   Axes were sounding, trees falling, and log-huts rising along the edge of the
woods and upon the adjoining meadow.   As we came up
the Mormons left their work, seated themselves on the timber around us, and began earnestly to discuss points of the-
ology, complain of the ill-usage they had received from the
"Gentiles," and sound a lamentation over the loss of their
7 great temple of Nauvoo.   After remaining with them an hour

we rode back to our camp, happy that the settlements had
been delivered from the presence of such blind and desperate
fanatics.

On the following morning we left the Pueblo for Bent's   8
Fort. The conduct of Raymond had lately been less
satisfactory than before, and we had discharged him as
soon as we arrived at the former place, so that the party,
ourselves included, was now reduced to four. There was   9
some uncertainty as to our future course. The trail between Bent's Fort and the settlements, a distance com-
puted at six hundred miles, was at this time in a dangerous
state; for since the passage of General Kearney's army,
great numbers of hostile Indians, chiefly Pawnees and
Camanches, had gathered about some parts of it. They
became soon after so numerous and audacious that scarcely
a single party, however large, passed between the fort and
the frontier without some token of their hostility. The   10
newspapers of the time sufficiently display this state of
things. Many men were killed, and great numbers of horses
and mules carried off. Not long since I met with a young
man, who, during the autumn came from Santa Fé to Bent's
Fort, where he found a party of seventy men, who thought
themselves too weak to go down to the settlements alone,
and were waiting there for a reinforcement. Though this   11
excessive timidity proves the ignorance of the men, it may
also evince the state of alarm which prevailed in the country. When we were there in the month of August, the
danger had not become so great. There was nothing very
attractive in the neighborhood. We supposed, moreover,
that we might wait there half the winter without finding
any party to go down with us; for Sublette and the others
whom we had relied upon had, as Richard told us, already
left Bent's Fort. Thus far on our journey Fortune had

kindly befriended us.   We resolved therefore to take advantage of her gracious mood, and trusting for a continuance of her favors, to set out with Henry and Deslauriers, and

12   run the gauntlet of the Indians in the best way we could.

Bent's Fort stands on the river, about seventy-five miles below the Pueblo.   At noon of the third day we

13   arrived within three or four miles of it, pitched our tent under a tree, hung our looking-glasses against its trunk, and having made our primitive toilet, rode towards the fort.   We soon came in sight of it, for it is visible from a considerable distance, standing with its high clay walls

14   in the midst of the scorching plains.   It seemed as if a swarm of locusts had invaded the country.   The grass for miles around was cropped close by the horses of General Kearney's soldiery.   When we came to the fort we found that not only had the horses eaten up the grass, but their owners had made way with the stores of the little trading post; so that we had great difficulty in procuring the few articles which we required for our homeward journey.   The

15   army was gone, the life and bustle passed away, and the fort was a scene of dull and lazy tranquillity.   A few invalid officers and soldiers sauntered about the area, which was oppressively hot; for the glaring sun was reflected down upon it from the high white walls around.   The proprietors were absent, and we were received by Mr.

16   Holt, who had been left in charge of the fort.   He invited us to dinner, where to our admiration, we found a table laid with a white cloth, with casters in the middle, and chairs placed around it.   This unwonted repast concluded, we rode back to our camp.

Here, as we lay smoking round the fire after supper, we saw through the dusk three men approaching from the direction of the fort.   They rode up and seated themselves near us on the ground.   The foremost was a tall, well-formed man, with a face and manner such as inspire confidence at once.   He wore a broad hat of felt, slouching and tattered, and the rest of his attire consisted of a frock and leggings of buckskin, rubbed with the yellow clay found among the mountains.   At the heel of one of his moccasins was buckled a huge iron spur, with a rowel five or six inches in diameter.   His horse, which stood quietly looking over his head, had a rude Mexican saddle, covered with a shaggy bear-skin, and furnished with a pair of wooden stirrups of preposterous size.   The next man was a sprightly, active little fellow, about five feet and a quarter high, but very strong and compact.   His face was swarthy as a Mexican's, and covered with a close, curly, black beard.   An old, greasy, calico handkerchief was tied round his head, and his close buckskin dress was blackened and polished by grease and hard service.   The last who came up was a large, strong man, dressed in the coarse homespun of the frontiers, who dragged his long limbs over the ground as if he were too lazy for the effort.   He had a sleepy gray eye, a retreating chin, an open mouth, and a protruding upper lip, which gave him an air of exquisite indolence and helplessness.   He was armed with an old United States yager, which redoubtable weapon, though he 17 could never hit his mark with it, he was accustomed to cherish as the very sovereign of firearms.

The first two men belonged to a party who had just come from California, with a large band of horses, which they had sold at Bent's Fort.   Munroe, the taller of the two, was from Iowa.   He was an excellent fellow, open, warm-hearted, and intelligent.   Jim Gurney, the short man, was a Boston sailor, who had come in a trading vessel to California, and taken the fancy to return across the continent.   The jour- 18 ney had already made him an expert "mountain-man" and he presented the extraordinary phenomenon of a sailor who understood how to manage a horse. The third of our visitors, named Ellis, was a Missourian, who had come out with a party of Oregon emigrants; but having got as far as Bridger's Fort, he had fallen homesick, or as Jim averred, lovesick. He thought proper, therefore, to join the California men, and return homeward in their company.

They now requested that they might unite with our party, and make the journey to the settlements in company with us. We readily assented, for we liked the appearance of the first two men, and were very glad to gain so efficient a reinforcement. We told them to meet us on the next evening at a spot on the riverside, about six miles below the fort. After we had smoked a pipe together, our new allies left us, and we lay down to sleep.

CHAPTER XXII.

TÊTE ROUGE, THE VOLUNTEER.

THE next morning, having directed Deslauriers to repair with his cart to the place of meeting, we came again to the fort to make some arrangements for the journey. After completing these we sat down under a sort of porch, to smoke with some Cheyenne Indians whom we found there. In a few minutes we saw an extraordinary little figure approach us in a military dress. He had a small, round countenance, garnished about the eyes with the kind of wrinkles commonly known as crow's feet, and surmounted by an abundant crop of red curls, with a little cap resting on the top of them. Altogether, he had the look of a man more conversant with mint-juleps and oyster suppers than with the hardships of prairie service. He came up to us and entreated that we would take him home to the settlements, saying that unless he went with us he should have to stay all winter at the fort. We liked our peti-

tioner's appearance so little that we excused ourselves
from complying with his request. At this he begged us
so hard to take pity on him, looked so disconsolate, and
told so lamentable a story, that at last we consented,
though not without many misgivings.

The rugged Anglo-Saxon of our new recruit's real name
proved utterly unmanageable on the lips of our French
attendants; and Henry Chatillon, after various abortive
attempts to pronounce it, one day coolly christened him
2 Tête Rouge, in honor of his red curls. He had at different times been clerk of a Mississippi steamboat, and
agent in a trading establishment at Nauvoo, besides filling various other capacities, in all of which he had seen
much more of "life" than was good for him. In the
spring, thinking that a summer's campaign would be an
agreeable recreation, he had joined a company of St. Louis
volunteers.

"There were three of us," said Tête Rouge, "me and Bill
3 Stevens and John Hopkins. We thought we would just go
out with the army, and when we had conquered the country, we would get discharged and take our pay, you know,
and go down to Mexico. They say there's plenty of fun
going on there. Then we could go back to New Orleans
by way of Vera Cruz."

But Tête Rouge, like many a stouter volunteer, had
reckoned without his host. Fighting Mexicans was a less
amusing occupation than he had supposed, and his pleasure
4 trip was disagreeably interrupted by brain fever, which attacked him when about half-way to Bent's Fort. He jolted
along through the rest of the journey in a baggage wagon.
When they came to the fort he was taken out and left there,
with the rest of the sick. Bent's Fort does not supply the
best accommodations for an invalid. Tête Rouge's sick-

chamber was a little mud room, where he and a companion, attacked by the same disease, were laid together, with
nothing but a buffalo-robe between them and the ground.
The assistant-surgeon's deputy visited them once a day and
brought them each a huge dose of calomel, the only medi-   5
cine, according to his surviving victim, with which he was
acquainted.

Tête Rouge woke one morning, and turning to his companion saw his eyes fixed upon the beams above with the
glassy stare of a dead man.   At this the unfortunate vol-   6
unteer lost his senses outright.   In spite of the doctor,
however, he eventually recovered; though between the brain
fever and the calomel, his mind, originally none of the
strongest, was so much shaken that it had not quite recovered its balance when we came to the fort.   In spite of the
poor fellow's tragic story, there was something so ludicrous
in his appearance, and the whimsical contrast between his
military dress and his most unmilitary demeanor, that we   7
could not help smiling at them.   We asked him if he had a
gun.   He said they had taken it from him during his illness,
and he had not seen it since; but "perhaps," he observed,
looking at me with a beseeching air, "you will lend me one
of your big pistols if we should meet with any Indians."
I next inquired if he had a horse; he declared he had a magnificent one, and at Shaw's request, a Mexican led him in for
inspection.   He exhibited the outline of a good horse, but
his eyes were sunk in the sockets, and every one of his
ribs could be counted.   There were certain marks too about
his shoulders, which could be accounted for by the circumstance that, during Tête Rouge's illness, his companions
had seized upon the insulted charger, and harnessed him
to a cannon along with the draft horses.   To Tête Rouge's
astonishment we recommended him by all means to ex-

change the horse, if he could, for a mule. Fortunately the people at the fort were so anxious to get rid of him that they were willing to make some sacrifice to effect the object, and he succeeded in getting a tolerable mule in exchange for the broken-down steed.

A man soon appeared at the gate, leading in the mule by a cord, which he placed in the hands of Tête Rouge, who, being somewhat afraid of his new acquisition, tried various flatteries and blandishments to induce her to come forward. The mule, knowing that she was expected to advance, stopped short in consequence, and stood fast as a rock, looking straight forward with immovable composure. Being stimulated by a blow from behind, she consented to move, and walked nearly to the other side of the fort before she stopped again. Hearing the bystanders laugh, Tête Rouge plucked up spirit and tugged hard at the rope. The mule jerked backward, spun herself round, and made a dash for the gate. Tête Rouge, who clung manfully to the rope, went whisking through the air for a few rods, when he let go and stood with his mouth open, staring after the mule, which galloped away over the prairie. She was soon caught and brought back by a Mexican, who mounted a horse and went in pursuit of her with his lasso.

Having thus displayed his capacities for prairie travelling, Tête Rouge proceeded to supply himself with provisions for the journey, and with this view applied to a quartermaster's assistant, who was in the fort. This official had a face as sour as vinegar, being in a state of chronic indignation because he had been left behind the army. He was as anxious as the rest to get rid of Tête Rouge. So, producing a rusty key, he opened a low door which led to a half-subterranean apartment, into which the two disappeared together. After some time they came out again, Tête Rouge greatly embarrassed by a multiplicity of paper parcels containing the different articles of his forty days' rations. They were consigned to the care of Deslauriers, who about that time passed by with the cart, on his way to the appointed place of meeting with Munroe and his companions.

We next urged Tête Rouge to provide himself, if he could, with a gun. He accordingly made earnest appeals to the charity of various persons in the fort, but totally without success, — a circumstance which did not greatly disturb us, since, in the event of a skirmish, he would be more apt to do mischief to himself or his friends than to the enemy. When all these arrangements were completed we saddled our horses, and were preparing to leave the fort, when, looking round, we discovered that our new associate was in fresh trouble. A man was holding the mule for him in the middle of the fort, while he tried to put the saddle on her back, but she kept stepping sideways and moving round and round in a circle until he was almost in despair. It required some assistance before all his difficulties could be overcome. At length he clambered into the black war-saddle on which he was to have carried terror into the ranks of the Mexicans.

"Get up," said Tête Rouge; "come now, go along, will you?"

The mule walked deliberately forward out of the gate. Her recent conduct had inspired him with so much awe that he never dared to touch her with his whip. We trotted forward toward the place of meeting, but before we had gone far, we saw that Tête Rouge's mule, who perfectly understood her rider, had stopped and was quietly grazing, in spite of his protestations, at some distance behind. So getting behind him, we drove him and the contumacious mule before us, until we could see through the twilight the gleaming of a distant fire. Munroe, Jim, and Ellis were lying around it; their saddles, packs, and weapons were scattered about, and their horses picketed near them. Deslauriers was there too with our little cart. Another fire was soon blazing. We invited our new allies to take a cup of coffee with us. When both the others had gone over to their side of the camp, Jim Gurney still stood by the blaze, puffing hard at his little black pipe, as short and weather-beaten as himself.

"Well," he said, "here are eight of us; we'll call it six — for them two boobies, Ellis over yonder and that new man of yours, won't count for anything. We'll get through well enough, never fear for that, unless the Camanches
10   happen to get foul of us."

CHAPTER XXIII.

INDIAN ALARMS.

WE began our journey for the settlements on the twenty-seventh of August, and a more ragamuffin cavalcade never was seen on the banks of the Upper Arkansas. Of the large and fine horses with which we had left the frontier in the spring, not one remained: we had supplied their place with the rough breed of the prairie, as hardy as mules and almost as ugly; we had also with us a number of the latter detestable animals. In spite of their strength and hardihood, several of the band were already worn down by hard service and hard fare, and as none of them were shod, they were fast becoming footsore. Every horse and mule had a çord of twisted bullhide coiled about his neck, which by no means added to

the beauty of his appearance. Our saddles and all our equipments were worn and battered, and our weapons had become dull and rusty. The dress of the riders corresponded with the dilapidated furniture of our horses, and of the whole party none made a more disreputable appearance than my friend and I. Shaw had for an upper garment an old red flannel shirt, flying open in front, and belted round him like a frock; while I, in absence of other clothing, was attired in a time-worn suit of buck-
1 skin.

Thus, happy and careless as so many beggars, we crept slowly from day to day along the monotonous banks of the Arkansas. Tête Rouge gave constant trouble, for he could never catch his mule, saddle her, or indeed do anything else without assistance. Every day he had some new ailment, real or imaginary, to complain of. At one moment he would be woe-begone and disconsolate, and at the next he would be visited with a violent flow of spirits, to which he could only give vent by incessant laughing, whistling, and telling stories. When other resources failed, we used to amuse ourselves by tormenting him; a fair compensation for the trouble he cost us. Tête Rouge rather enjoyed being laughed at, for he was an odd compound of
2 weakness, eccentricity, and good-nature. He made a fig-ure worthy of a painter as he paced along before us, perched on the back of his mule, and enveloped in a huge buffalo-robe coat, which some charitable person had given him at the fort. This extraordinary garment, which would have contained two men of his size, he chose, for some reason best known to himself, to wear inside out, and he never took it off even in the hottest weather. It was fluttering all over with seams and tatters, and the hide was so old and rotten that it broke out every day in a new place.

Just at the top of it a large pile of red curls was visible, with his little cap set jauntily upon one side, to give him a military air. His seat in the saddle was no less remark-

3

able than his person and equipment. He pressed one leg close against his mule's side, and thrust the other out at an angle of forty-five degrees. His trousers were decorated with a military red stripe, of which he was extremely vain; but being much too short, the whole length of his boots was usually visible below them. His blanket, loosely rolled up into a large bundle, dangled at the back of his saddle, where he carried it tied with a string. Four or five times a day it would fall to the ground. Every few minutes he would drop his pipe, his knife, his flint and steel, or a piece of tobacco, and scramble down to pick them up. In doing this he would contrive to get in everybody's way; and as most of the party were by no means remarkable for a fastidious choice of language, a storm of anathemas would be showered upon him, half in earnest and half in jest, until Tête Rouge would declare that there was no comfort in life, and that he never saw such fellows before.

Only a day or two after leaving Bent's Fort Henry Chatillon rode forward to hunt, and took Ellis along with him. After they had been some time absent we saw them coming down the hill driving three dragoon horses, which 4 had escaped from their owners on the march, or perhaps had given out and been abandoned. One of them was in tolerable condition, but the others were much emaciated and severely bitten by the wolves. Reduced as they were, we carried two of them to the settlements, and Henry exchanged the third with the Arapahoes for an excellent mule.

On the day after, when we had stopped to rest at noon, a long train of Santa Fé wagons came up and trailed slowly past us in their picturesque procession. They belonged to 5 a trader named Magoffin, whose brother, with a number of other men, came and sat down with us on the grass. The news they brought was not of the most pleasing complexion. According to their accounts, the trail below was in a very dangerous state. They had repeatedly detected Indians prowling at night around their camps; and the large party which had left Bent's Fort a few weeks before us had

been attacked, and a man named Swan, from Massachusetts, had been killed. His companions had buried the
body; but when Magoffin found his grave, which was near
a place called "The Caches," the Indians had dug up and 6
scalped him, and the wolves had shockingly mangled his
remains. As an offset to this intelligence, they gave us
the welcome information that the buffalo were numerous
at a few days' journey below.

On the next afternoon, as we moved along the bank of the
river, we saw the white tops of wagons on the horizon. It
was some hours before we met them, when they proved to
be a train of clumsy ox-wagons, quite different from the
rakish vehicles of the Santa Fé traders, and loaded with
government stores for the troops. They all stopped, and
the drivers gathered around us in a crowd. Many of them 7
were mere boys, fresh from the plough. In respect to the
state of the trail, they confirmed all that the Santa Fé
men had told us. In passing between the Pawnee Fork
and the Caches, their sentinels had fired every night at 8
real or imaginary Indians. They said also that Ewing, a
young Kentuckian in the party that had gone down before
us, had shot an Indian who was prowling at evening about 9
the camp. Some of them advised us to turn back, and
others to hasten forward as fast as we could; but they all
seemed in such a state of feverish anxiety, and so little
capable of cool judgment, that we attached slight weight
to what they said. They next gave us a more definite
piece of intelligence: a large village of Arapahoes was
encamped on the river below. They represented them to
be friendly; but some distinction was to be made between
a party of thirty men, travelling with oxen, which are of
no value in an Indian's eyes, and a mere handful like
ourselves, with a tempting band of mules and horses. 10

Early in the afternoon of the next day, looking along the horizon before us, we saw that at one point it was faintly marked with pale indentations like the teeth of a saw. The distant lodges of the Arapahoes, rising between us and the sky, caused this singular appearance. It wanted still two or three hours of sunset when we came opposite their camp. There were full two hundred lodges standing in the midst of a grassy meadow at some distance beyond the river, while for a mile around on both banks of the Arkansas were scattered some fifteen hundred horses and mules, grazing together in bands, or wandering singly about the prairie. The whole were visible at once, for the vast expanse was unbroken by hills, and there was not 11 a tree or a bush to intercept the view.

Here and there walked an Indian, engaged in watching the horses. No sooner did we see them than Tête Rouge begged Deslauriers to stop the cart and hand him his military jacket, which was stowed away there. In this he invested himself, having for once laid the old buffalo-coat aside, assumed a martial posture in the saddle, set his cap over his left eye with an air of defiance, and earnestly entreated that somebody would lend him a gun or a pistol only for half an hour. Being called upon to explain these proceedings, Tête Rouge observed that he knew from experience what effect the presence of a military man in his uniform always has upon the mind of an Indian, and he thought the Arapahoes ought to know that there was a 12 soldier in the party.

Meeting Arapahoes here on the Arkansas was a very different thing from meeting the same Indians among their native mountains. There was another circumstance in our favor. General Kearney had seen them a few weeks 13 before as he came up the river with his army, and, renew-

ing his threats of the previous year he told them that if
they ever again touched the hair of a white man's head he
would exterminate their nation. This placed them for the
time in an admirable frame of mind, and the effect of his
menaces had not yet disappeared. I wished to see the
village and its inhabitants. We thought it also our best
policy to visit them openly, as if unsuspicious of any hostile design; and Shaw and I, with Henry Chatillon, prepared to cross the river. The rest of the party meanwhile
moved forward as fast as they could, in order to get as
far as possible from our suspicious neighbors before night
came on.

The Arkansas at this point, and for several hundred miles 14
below, is in August nothing but a broad sand-bed over which
glide a few scanty threads of water, now and then expanding into wide shallows. At several places, during the
autumn the water sinks into the sand and disappears
altogether. At this season, were it not for the numerous
quicksands, the river might be forded almost anywhere
without difficulty, though its channel is often a quarter
of a mile wide. Our horses jumped down the bank, and
wading through the water, or galloping freely over the
hard sand-beds, soon reached the other side. Here, as
we were pushing through the tall grass, we saw several
Indians not far off; one of them waited until we came
up, and stood for some moments in perfect silence before
us, looking at us askance with his little snake-like eyes.
Henry explained by signs what we wanted, and the Indian, gathering his buffalo-robe about his shoulders, led
the way towards the village without speaking a word.

The language of the Arapahoes is so difficult, and its
pronunciation so harsh and guttural, that no white man,
it is said, has ever been able to master it. Even Max-

15 well, the trader who has been most among them, is compelled to resort to the curious sign-language common to
most of the prairie tribes. With this sign-language Henry
16 Chatillon was perfectly acquainted.

Approaching the village, we found the ground strewn
with piles of waste buffalo-meat in incredible quantities.
The lodges were pitched in a circle. They resembled
those of the Dakota in everything but cleanliness. Passing between two of them, we entered the great circular
area of the camp, and instantly hundreds of Indians, men,
women, and children, came flocking out of their habitations to look at us; at the same time the dogs all around
the village set up a discordant baying. Our Indian guide
walked towards the lodge of the chief. Here we dismounted; and loosening the trail-ropes from our horses'
necks, held them fast as we sat down before the entrance,
with our rifles laid across our laps. The chief came out
and shook us by the hand. He was a mean-looking fellow,
very tall, thin-visaged, and sinewy, like the rest of the
nation, and with scarcely a vestige of clothing. We had
not been seated a moment before a multitude of Indians
came crowding around us from every part of the village,
and we were shut in by a dense wall of savage faces.
Some of our visitors crouched about us on the ground;
others sat behind them; others, stooping, looked over their
heads; while many more stood behind, peering over one another's shoulders, to get a view of us. I looked in vain
among this throng of faces to discover one manly or generous expression; all were wolfish, sinister, and malignant,
and their complexions, as well as their features, unlike
17 those of the Dakota, were exceedingly bad. The chief,
who sat close to the entrance, called to a squaw within
the lodge, who soon came out and placed a wooden bowl

of meat before us. To our surprise, however, no pipe was offered. Having tasted of the meat as a matter of form, I began to open a bundle of presents, — tobacco, knives, vermilion, and other articles which I had brought with me. At this there was a grin on every countenance in the rapacious crowd; their eyes began to glitter, and long thin arms were eagerly stretched towards us on all sides to receive the gifts.

The Arapahoes set great value upon their shields, which they transmit carefully from father to son. I wished to get one of them; and displaying a large piece of scarlet cloth, together with some tobacco, and a knife, I offered them to any one who would bring me what I wanted. After some delay a tolerable shield was produced. They were very anxious to know what we meant to do with it, and Henry told them that we were going to fight their enemies the Pawnees. This instantly produced a visible impression in our favor, which was increased by the distribution of the presents. Among these was a large paper of awls, a gift appropriate to the women; and as we were anxious to see the beauties of the Arapahoe village, Henry requested that they might be called to receive them. A warrior gave a shout, as if he were calling a pack of dogs together. The squaws, young and old, hags of eighty and girls of sixteen, came running with screams and laughter out of the lodges; and as the men gave way for them, they gathered round us and stretched out their arms, grinning with delight, their native ugliness considerably enhanced by the excitement of the moment.

Mounting our horses, which during the whole interview we had held close to us, we prepared to leave the Arapahoes. The crowd fell back on each side, and stood looking on. When we were half across the camp an idea occurred to us. The Pawnees were probably in the neighborhood of the Caches; we might tell the Arapahoes of this, and instigate them to send down a war-party and cut them off, while we ourselves could remain behind for a while and hunt the buffalo. At first thought, this plan of setting our enemies to destroy one another seemed to us a masterpiece of policy; but we immediately recollected that should we meet the Arapahoe warriors on the river below, they might prove quite as dangerous as the Pawnees themselves. So rejecting our plan as soon as it presented itself, we passed out of the village on the farther side. We urged our horses rapidly through the tall grass, which rose to their necks. Several Indians were walking through it at a distance, their heads just visible above its waving surface. It bore a kind of seed, as sweet and nutritious as oats; and our hungry horses, in spite of whip and rein, could not resist the temptation of snatching at this unwonted luxury as we passed along. When about a mile from the village, I turned and looked back over the undulating ocean of grass. The sun was just set; the western sky was all in a glow, and sharply defined against it, on the extreme verge of the plain, stood the clustered lodges of the Arapahoe camp.

Reaching the bank of the river, we followed it for some distance farther, until we discerned through the twilight the white covering of our little cart on the opposite bank. When we reached it we found a considerable number of Indians there before us. Four or five of them were seated in a row upon the ground, looking like so many half-starved vultures. Tête Rouge, in his uniform, was holding a close colloquy with another by the side of the cart. Finding his signs and gesticulation of no avail, he tried to make the Indian understand him by repeating English words very loudly and distinctly again and again. The Indian sat with his eye fixed steadily upon him, and in spite of the rigid immobility of his features, it was clear at a glance that he perfectly understood and despised his military companion. The exhibition was more amusing than politic, and Tête Rouge was directed to finish what he had to say as soon as possible. Thus rebuked, he crept under the cart and sat down there; Henry Chatillon stooped to look at him in his retirement, and remarked in his quiet manner that an Indian would kill ten such men and laugh all the time. 19

One by one our visitors arose and stalked away. As the darkness thickened we were saluted by dismal sounds. The wolves are incredibly numerous in this part of the country, and the offal around the Arapahoe camp had drawn such multitudes of them together that several hundreds were howling in concert in our immediate neighborhood. There was an island in the river, or rather an oasis in the midst of the sands, at about the distance of a gunshot, and here they seemed to be gathered in the greatest numbers. A horrible discord of low, mournful wailings, mingled with ferocious howls, arose from it incessantly for several hours after sunset. We could distinctly see the wolves running about the prairie within a few rods of our fire, or bounding over the sand-beds of the river and splashing through the water. There was not the slightest danger from them, for they are the greatest cowards on the prairie.

In respect to the human wolves in our neighborhood, we felt much less at our ease. That night each man spread his buffalo-robe upon the ground with his loaded rifle laid at his side or clasped in his arms. Our horses were picketed so close around us that one of them repeatedly stepped over me as I lay. We were not in the habit of placing a guard, but every man was anxious and watchful: there was little sound sleeping in camp, and some one of the party was on his feet during the greater part of the night. For myself, I lay alternately waking and dozing until midnight. Tête Rouge was reposing close to the river bank, and about this time, when half asleep and half awake, I was conscious that he shifted his position and crept on all-fours under the cart. Soon after I fell into a sound sleep, from which I was roused by a hand shaking me by the shoulder. Looking up, I saw Tête Rouge stooping over me with a pale face and dilated eyes.

"What's the matter?" said I.

Tête Rouge declared that as he lay on the river bank something caught his eye which excited his suspicions. So creeping under the cart for safety's sake, he sat there and watched, when he saw two Indians, wrapped in white robes, creep up the bank, seize upon two horses, and lead them off. He looked so frightened and told his story in such a disconnected manner that I did not believe him, and was unwilling to alarm the party. Still it might be true, and in that case the matter required instant atten-tion. So directing Tête Rouge to show me which way the Indians had gone, I took my rifle, in obedience to a thoughtless impulse, and left the camp. I followed the river bank for two or three hundred yards, listening and looking anxiously on every side. In the dark prairie on the right I could discern nothing to excite alarm; and in the dusky bed of the river, a wolf was bounding along in a manner which no Indian could imitate. I returned to the camp, and when within sight of it, saw that the whole party was aroused. Shaw called out to me that he had counted the horses, and that every one of them was in his place. Tête Rouge, being examined as to what he had seen, only repeated his former story with many asseverations, and insisted that two horses were certainly carried off. At this Jim Gurney declared that he was crazy; Tête Rouge indignantly denied the charge, on which Jim appealed to us. As we declined to give our judgment on so delicate a matter, the dispute grew hot between Tête Rouge and his accuser, until he was directed to go to bed, and not alarm the camp again if he saw the whole Arapahoe village coming.

21

CHAPTER XXIV.

THE CHASE.

1

THE country before us was now thronged with buffalo, and a sketch of the manner of hunting them will not be out of place. There are two methods commonly practised, — "running" and "approaching." The chase on horseback, which goes by the name of "running," is the more violent and dashing mode of the two, that is to say, when the buffalo are in one of their wild moods;

2 for otherwise it is tame enough. A practised and skilful hunter, well mounted, will sometimes kill five or six cows in a single chase, loading his gun again and

3 again as his horse rushes through the tumult. In attacking a small band of buffalo, or in separating a single animal from the herd and assailing it apart from the rest, there is less excitement and less danger. In fact, the animals are at times so stupid and lethargic that there

4 is little sport in killing them. With a bold and well-trained horse the hunter may ride so close to the buffalo that as they gallop side by side he may touch him with his hand; nor is there much danger in this as long as the buffalo's strength and breath continue unabated; but when he becomes tired and can no longer run with ease, when his tongue lolls out and the foam flies from his jaws, then the hunter had better keep a more respectful distance; the distressed brute may turn upon him at any instant, and especially at the moment when he fires his

gun. The horse then leaps aside, and the hunter has need of a tenacious seat in the saddle, for if he is thrown to the ground there is no hope for him. When he sees his attack defeated the buffalo resumes his flight, but if the shot is well directed he soon stops; for a few moments he stands still, then totters and falls heavily upon the prairie.

The chief difficulty in running buffalo, as it seems to me, is that of loading the gun or pistol at full gallop. Many hunters, for convenience' sake, carry three or four bullets in the mouth; the powder is poured down the muzzle of the piece, the bullet dropped in after it, or spit from the mouth into the barrel, the stock struck hard upon the pommel of the saddle, and the work is done. The danger of this is obvious. Should the blow on the pommel fail to send the bullet home, or should the bullet, in the act of aiming, start from its place and roll towards the muzzle, the gun would probably burst in discharging. Many a shattered hand and worse casualties besides have been the result of such an accident. To obviate it, some hunters make use of a ramrod, usually hung by a string from the neck, but this materially increases the difficulty of loading. The bows and arrows which the Indians use in running buffalo have many advantages over firearms, and even white men occasionally employ them.

The danger of the chase arises not so much from the onset of the wounded animal as from the nature of the ground which the hunter must ride over. The prairie does not always present a smooth, level, and uniform surface; very often it is broken with hills and hollows, intersected by ravines, and in the remoter parts studded by the stiff wild-sage bushes. The most formidable obstructions, however, are the burrows of wild animals, — wolves, badgers, and particularly prairie-dogs, with whose holes the ground for a great extent is frequently honey-combed. In the blindness of the chase the hunter rushes over it

unconscious of danger; his horse, at full career, thrusts his leg deep into one of the burrows; the bone snaps, the rider is hurled forward to the ground and probably killed. Yet accidents in buffalo running happen less frequently than one would suppose; in the recklessness of the chase, the hunter enjoys all the impunity of a drunken man, and may ride in safety over gullies and declivities, where, should he attempt to pass in his sober senses he would infallibly break his neck.

The method of "approaching," being practised on foot, has many advantages over that of "running;" in the former one neither breaks down his horse nor endangers his own life; he must be cool, collected, and watchful; must understand the buffalo, observe the features of the country and the course of the wind, and be well skilled in using the rifle. The buffalo are strange animals; sometimes they are so stupid and infatuated that a man may walk up to them in full sight on the open prairie, and even shoot several of their number before the rest will think it necessary to retreat. At another moment they will be so shy and wary that in order to approach them the utmost skill, experience, and judgment are necessary. Kit Carson, I believe, stands pre-eminent in running buffalo; in approaching, no man living can bear away the palm from Henry Chatillon.

After Tête Rouge had alarmed the camp, no farther disturbance occurred during the night. The Arapahoes did not attempt mischief, or if they did the wakefulness of the party deterred them from effecting their purpose. The next day was one of activity and excitement, for about ten o'clock the man in advance shouted the gladdening cry of "Buffalo! buffalo!" and in the hollow of the prairie just below us, a band of bulls were grazing. The temptation was irresistible, and Shaw and I rode down upon them. We were badly mounted on our travelling horses, but by hard lashing we overtook them, and Shaw, running alongside a bull, shot into him both balls of his double-barrelled gun. Looking round as I galloped by, I saw the bull in his mortal fury rushing again and again upon his antagonist, whose horse constantly leaped aside, and avoided the onset. My chase was more protracted, but at length I ran close to the bull and killed him with my pistols. Cutting off the tails of our victims by way of trophy, we rejoined the party in about a quarter of an hour after we had left it. Again and again that morning rang out the same welcome cry of "Buffalo! buffalo!" Every few moments, in the broad meadows along the river, we saw bands of bulls, who raising their shaggy heads would gaze in stupid amazement at the approaching horsemen, and then breaking into a clumsy gallop, file off in a long line across the trail in front, towards the rising prairie on the left. At noon, the plain before us was alive with thousands of buffalo, bulls, cows, and calves, all moving rapidly as we drew near; and far off beyond the river the swelling prairie was darkened with them to the very horizon. The party was in gayer spirits than ever. We stopped for a nooning near a grove of trees by the river.

"Tongues and hump-ribs to-morrow," said Shaw, looking with contempt at the venison steaks which Deslauriers placed before us. Our meal finished, we lay down to sleep. A shout from Henry Chatillon aroused us, and we saw him standing on the cart-wheel, stretching his tall figure to its full height while he looked towards the prairie beyond the river. Following the direction of his eyes, we could clearly distinguish a large dark object, like the black shadow of a cloud, passing rapidly over swell after swell of the distant plain; behind it followed another of similar appearance though smaller, moving more rapidly, and drawing closer and closer to the first. It was the hunters of the Arapahoe camp chasing a band of buffalo. Shaw and I caught and saddled our best horses, and went plunging through sand and water to the farther bank. We were too late. The hunters had already mingled with the herd, and the work of slaughter was nearly over. When we reached the ground we found it strewn far and near with numberless carcasses, while the remnants of the herd, scattered in all directions, were flying away in terror, and the Indians still rushing in pursuit. Many of the hunters, however, remained upon the spot, and among the rest was our yesterday's acquaintance, the chief of the village. He had alighted by the side of a cow, into which he had shot five or six arrows, and his squaw, who had followed him on horseback to the hunt, was giving him a draught of water from a canteen purchased or plundered from some volunteer soldier. Recrossing the river, we overtook the party, who were already on their way.

We had gone scarcely a mile when we saw an imposing spectacle. From the river bank on the right, away over the swelling prairie on the left, and in front as far as the eye could reach, was one vast host of buffalo. The outskirts of the herd were within a quarter of a mile. In many parts they were crowded so densely together that in the distance their rounded backs presented a surface of uniform blackness; but elsewhere they were more scattered, and from amid the multitude rose little columns of dust where some of them were rolling on the ground. Here and there a battle was going forward among the bulls. We could distinctly see them rushing against each other, and hear the clattering of their horns and their hoarse bellowing. Shaw was riding at some distance in advance, with Henry Chatillon; I saw him stop and draw the leather covering from his gun. With such a sight before us, but one thing could be thought of. That morning I had used pistols in the chase. I had now a

9   mind to try the virtue of a gun. Deslauriers had one,
and I rode up to the side of the cart; there he sat under
the white covering, biting his pipe between his teeth and
grinning with excitement.

"Lend me your gun, Deslauriers."

"Oui, Monsieur, oui," said Deslauriers, tugging with
might and main to stop the mule, which seemed obstinately bent on going forward. Then everything but his
moccasins disappeared as he crawled into the cart and
pulled at the gun to extricate it.

"Is it loaded?" I asked.

"Oui, bien chargé; you'll kill, mon bourgeois; yes,
you'll kill — c'est un bon fusil."

I handed him my rifle and rode forward to Shaw.

"Are you ready?" he asked.

"Come on," said I.

"Keep down that hollow," said Henry, "and then they
won't see you till you get close to them."

The hollow was a kind of wide ravine; it ran obliquely
towards the buffalo, and we rode at a canter along the
bottom until it became too shallow; then we bent close
to our horses' necks, and, at last, finding that it could no
longer conceal us, came out of it and rode directly towards
the herd. It was within gunshot; before its outskirts numerous grizzly old bulls were scattered, holding guard over
their females. They glared at us in anger and astonishment, walked towards us a few yards, and then turning
slowly round retreated at a trot which afterwards broke
into a clumsy gallop. In an instant the main body caught
the alarm. The buffalo began to crowd away from the
point towards which we were approaching, and a gap was
opened in the side of the herd. We entered it, still restraining our excited horses. Every instant the tumult

was thickening. The buffalo, pressing together in large bodies, crowded away from us on every hand. In front and on either side we could see dark columns and masses, half hidden by clouds of dust, rushing along in terror and confusion, and hear the tramp and clattering of ten thousand hoofs. That countless multitude of powerful brutes, ignorant of their own strength, were flying in a panic from the approach of two feeble horsemen. To remain quiet longer was impossible.

"Take that band on the left," said Shaw; "I'll take these in front."

He sprang off, and I saw no more of him. A heavy Indian whip, or "quirt," was fastened by a band to my wrist; I swung it into the air and lashed my horse's flank with all the strength of my arm. Away she darted, stretching close to the ground. I could see nothing but a cloud of dust before me, but I knew that it concealed a band of many hundreds of buffalo. In a moment I was in the midst of the cloud, half suffocated by the dust and stunned by the trampling of the flying herd; but I was drunk with the chase and cared for nothing but the buffalo. Very soon a long dark mass became visible, looming through the dust; then I could distinguish each bulky carcass, the hoofs flying out beneath, the short tails held rigidly erect. In a moment I was so close that I could have touched them with my gun. Suddenly, to my amazement, the hoofs were jerked upwards, the tails flourished in the air, and amid a cloud of dust the buffalo seemed to sink into the earth before me. One vivid impression of that instant remains upon my mind. I remember looking down upon the backs of several buffalo dimly visible through the dust. We had run unawares upon a ravine. At that moment I was not the most accurate judge of depth and width, but when I passed it on my return, I found it about twelve feet deep and not quite twice as wide at the bottom. It was impossible to stop; I would have done so gladly if I could; so, half sliding, half plunging, down went the little mare. She came down on her knees in the loose sand at the bottom; I was pitched forward against her neck and nearly thrown over her head among the buffalo, who amid dust and confusion came tumbling in all around. The mare was on her feet in an instant and scrambling like a cat up the opposite side. I thought for a moment that she would have fallen back and crushed me, but with a violent effort she clambered out and gained the hard prairie above. Glancing back I saw the huge head of a bull clinging as it were by the forefeet at the edge of the dusty gulf. At length I was fairly among the buffalo. They were less densely crowded than before, and I could see nothing but bulls, who always run at the rear of a herd to protect their females. As I passed among them they would lower their heads, and turning as they ran, try to gore my horse; but as they were already at full speed there was no force in their onset, and as Pauline ran faster than they, they were always thrown behind her in the effort. I soon began to distinguish cows amid the throng. One just in front of me seemed to my liking, and I pushed close to her side. Dropping the reins I fired, holding the muzzle of the gun within a foot of her shoulder. Quick as lightning she sprang at Pauline; the little mare dodged the attack, and I lost sight of the wounded animal amid the tumult. Immediately after, I selected another, and urging forward Pauline, shot into her both pistols in succession. For a while I kept her in view, but in attempting to load my gun lost sight of her also in the confusion. Believing her to be

mortally wounded and unable to keep up with the herd, I checked my horse. The crowd rushed onwards. The dust and tumult passed away, and on the prairie, far behind the rest, I saw a solitary buffalo galloping heavily. In a moment I and my victim were running side by side. My firearms were all empty, and I had in my pouch nothing but rifle bullets, too large for the pistols and too small for the gun. I loaded the gun, however, but as often as I levelled it to fire, the bullets would roll out of the muzzle and the gun returned only a report like a squib as the powder harmlessly exploded. I rode in front of the buffalo and tried to turn her back; but her eyes glared, her mane bristled, and, lowering her head, she rushed at me with the utmost fierceness and activity. Again and again I rode before her, and again and again she repeated her furious charge. But little Pauline was in her element. She dodged her enemy at every rush, until at length the buffalo stood still, exhausted with her own efforts, her tongue lolling from her jaws.

Riding to a little distance, I dismounted, thinking to gather a handful of dry grass to serve the purpose of wadding, and load the gun at my leisure. No sooner were my feet on the ground than the buffalo came bounding in such a rage towards me that I jumped back again into the saddle with all possible despatch. After waiting a few minutes more, I made an attempt to ride up and stab her with my knife; but Pauline was near being gored in the attempt. At length, bethinking me of the fringes at the seams of my buckskin trousers, I jerked off a few of them and, reloading the gun, forced them down the barrel to keep the bullet in its place; then approaching, I shot the wounded buffalo through the heart. Sinking to her knees, she rolled over lifeless on the prairie. To my astonishment, I found that, instead of a cow, I had been slaughtering a stout young bull. No longer wondering at his fierceness, I opened his throat, and cutting out his tongue tied it at the back of my saddle. My mistake was one which a more experienced eye than mine might easily make in the dust and confusion of such a chase.

Then for the first time I had leisure to look at the scene around me. The prairie in front was darkened with the retreating multitude, and on either hand the buffalo came filing up in endless columns from the low plains upon the river. The Arkansas was three or four miles distant. I turned and moved slowly towards it. A long time passed before, far in the distance, I distinguished the white covering of the cart and the little black specks of horsemen before and behind it. Drawing near, I recognized Shaw's elegant tunic, the red flannel shirt, conspicuous far off. I overtook the party, and asked him what success he had had. He had assailed a fat cow, shot her with two bullets, and mortally wounded her. But neither of us was prepared for the chase that afternoon, and Shaw, like myself, had no spare bullets in his pouch; so he abandoned the disabled animal to Henry Chatillon, who followed, despatched her with his rifle, and loaded his horse with the meat.

We encamped close to the river. The night was dark, and as we lay down we could hear, mingled with the howlings of wolves, the hoarse bellowing of the buffalo, like the ocean beating upon a distant coast.

CHAPTER XXV.

THE BUFFALO CAMP.

NOBODY in the camp was more active than Jim Gurney, and nobody half so lazy as Ellis. Between these two there was a great antipathy. Ellis never stirred in the morning until he was compelled, but Jim was always on his feet before daybreak; and this morning as usual the sound of his voice awakened the party.

"Get up, you booby! up with you now, you're fit for nothing but eating and sleeping. Stop your grumbling and come out of that buffalo-robe, or I'll pull it off for you."

Jim's words were interspersed with numerous expletives, which gave them great additional effect. Ellis drawled out something in a nasal tone from among the folds of his buffalo-robe; then slowly disengaged himself, rose into a sitting posture, stretched his long arms, yawned hideously, and, finally raising his tall person erect, stood staring about him to all the four quarters of the horizon. Deslauriers's fire was soon blazing, and the horses and mules, loosened from their pickets, were feeding on the neighboring meadow. When we sat down to breakfast the prairie was still in the dusky light of morning; and as the sun rose we were mounted and on our way again.

"A white buffalo!" exclaimed Munroe.

"I'll have that fellow," said Shaw, "if I run my horse to death after him."

1

He threw the cover of his gun to Deslauriers and galloped out upon the prairie.

"Stop, Mr. Shaw, stop!" called out Henry Chatillon, "you'll run down your horse for nothing; it's only a white ox."

But Shaw was already out of hearing. The ox, which had no doubt strayed away from some of the government wagon trains, was standing beneath some low hills which bounded the plain in the distance. Not far from him a band of veritable buffalo bulls were grazing; and startled at Shaw's approach, they all broke into a run and went scrambling up the hillsides to gain the high prairie above. One of them in his haste and terror involved himself in a fatal catastrophe. Along the foot of the hills was a narrow strip of deep marshy soil, into which the bull plunged and hopelessly entangled himself. We all rode to the spot. The huge carcass was half sunk in the mud, which flowed to his very chin, and his shaggy mane was outspread upon the surface. As we came near, the bull began to struggle with convulsive strength; he writhed to and fro, and in the energy of his fright and desperation would lift himself for a moment half out of the slough, while the reluctant mire returned a sucking sound as he strained to drag his limbs from its tenacious depths. We stimulated his exertions by getting behind him and twisting his tail; nothing would do. There was clearly no hope for him. After every effort his heaving sides were more deeply imbedded and the mire almost overflowed his nostrils; he lay still at length, and looking round at us with a furious eye, seemed to resign himself to his fate. Ellis slowly dismounted, and, levelling his boasted yager, shot the old bull through the heart; then lazily climbed back again to his seat, pluming himself no doubt on having actually killed a buffalo. That day the redoubtable yager drew blood for the first and last time during the whole journey.

The morning was a bright and gay one, and the air so clear that on the farthest horizon the outline of the pale blue prairie was sharply drawn against the sky. Shaw was in the mood for hunting; he rode in advance of the party, and before long we saw a file of bulls galloping at full speed upon a green swell of the prairie at some distance in front. Shaw came scouring along behind them, arrayed in his red shirt, which looked very well in the distance; he gained fast on the fugitives, and as the foremost bull was disappearing behind the summit of the swell, we saw him in the act of assailing the hindmost; a smoke sprang from the muzzle of his gun and floated away before the wind like a little white cloud; the bull turned upon him, and just then the rising ground concealed them both from view.

We were moving forward until about noon, when we stopped by the side of the Arkansas. At that moment Shaw appeared riding slowly down the side of a distant hill; his horse was tired and jaded, and when he threw his saddle upon the ground, I observed that the tails of two bulls were dangling behind it. No sooner were the horses turned loose to feed than Henry, asking Munroe to go with him, took his rifle and walked quietly away. Shaw, Tête Rouge, and I sat down by the side of the cart to discuss the dinner which Deslauriers placed before us, and we had scarcely finished when we saw Munroe walking towards us along the river bank. Henry, he said, had killed four fat cows and had sent him back for horses to bring in the meat. Shaw took a horse for himself and another for Henry, and he and Munroe left the camp together. After a short absence all three of them came back, their horses loaded with the choicest parts of the meat. We kept two of the cows for ourselves, and gave the others to Munroe and his companions. Deslauriers seated himself on the grass before the pile of meat and worked industriously for some time to cut it into thin broad sheets for drying, an art in which he had all the skill of an Indian squaw. Long before night, cords of raw hide were stretched around the camp, and the meat was hung upon them to dry in the sunshine and pure air of the prairie. Our California companions were less successful at the work; but they accomplished it after their own fashion, and their side of the camp was soon garnished in the same manner as our own.

We meant to remain at this place long enough to prepare provisions for our journey to the frontier, which, as we supposed, might occupy about a month. Had the distance been twice as great and the party ten times as large, the rifle of Henry Chatillon would have supplied meat enough for the whole within two days; we were obliged to remain, however, until it should be dry enough for transportation; so we pitched our tent and made other arrangements for a permanent camp. The California men who had no such shelter, contented themselves with arranging their packs on the grass around their fire. In the meantime we had nothing to do but amuse ourselves. Our tent was within a rod of the river, if the broad sand-beds, with a scanty stream of water coursing here and there along their surface, deserve to be dignified with the name of river. The vast flat plains on either side were almost on a level with the sand-beds, and they were bounded in the distance by low, monotonous hills, parallel to the course of the stream. All was one expanse of grass;

there was no wood in view, except some trees and stunted bushes upon two islands which rose from the wet sands of the river. Yet, far from being dull and tame, the scene was often a wild and animated one; for twice a day, at sunrise and at noon, the buffalo came issuing from the hills, slowly advancing in their grave processions to drink at the river. All our amusements were to be at their expense. An old buffalo-bull is a brute of unparalleled ugliness. At first sight of him every feeling of pity vanishes. The cows are much smaller and of a gentler appearance, as becomes their sex. While in this camp we forbore to attack them, leaving to Henry Chatillon, who could better judge their quality, the task of killing such as we wanted for use; but against the bulls we waged an unrelenting war. Thousands of them might be slaughtered without causing any detriment to the species, for their numbers greatly exceed those of the cows; it is the hides of the latter alone which are used for the purposes of commerce and for making the lodges of the Indians; and the destruction among them is therefore greatly disproportionate.

Our horses were tired and we now usually hunted on foot. While we were lying on the grass after dinner, smoking, talking, or laughing at Tête Rouge, one of us would look up and observe, far out on the plains beyond the river, certain black objects slowly approaching. He would inhale a parting whiff from the pipe, then rising lazily, take his rifle, which leaned against the cart, throw over his shoulder the strap of his pouch and powder-horn, and with his moccasins in his hand walk across the sand towards the opposite side of the river. This was easy; for though the sands were about a quarter of a mile wide, the water was nowhere more than two feet deep. The farther bank was about four or five feet high and quite perpendicular, being cut away by the water in spring. Tall grass grew along its edge. Putting it aside with his hand, and cautiously looking through it, the hunter can discern the huge shaggy back of the bull slowly swaying to and fro, as, with his clumsy swinging gait, he advances towards the water. The buffalo have regular paths by which they come down to drink. Seeing at a glance along which of these his intended victim is moving, the hunter crouches under the bank within fifteen or twenty yards, it may be, of the point where the path enters the river. Here he sits down quietly on the sand. Listening intently, he hears the heavy monotonous tread of the approaching bull. The moment after, he sees a motion among the long weeds and grass just at the spot where the path is channelled through the bank. An enormous black head is thrust out, the horns just visible amid the mass of tangled mane. Half sliding, half plunging, down comes the buffalo upon the river-bed below. He steps out in full sight upon the sands. Just before him a runnel of water is gliding, and he bends his head to drink. You may hear the water as it gurgles down his capacious throat. He raises his head, and the drops trickle from his wet beard. He stands with an air of stupid abstraction, unconscious of the lurking danger. Noiselessly the hunter cocks his rifle. As he sits upon the sand, his knee is raised, and his elbow rests upon it, that he may level his heavy weapon with a steadier aim. The stock is at his shoulder; his eye ranges along the barrel. Still he is in no haste to fire. The bull, with slow deliberation, begins his march over the sands to the other side. He advances his foreleg, and exposes to view a small spot, denuded of hair, just behind the point of his shoulder; upon this the hunter brings the sight of his rifle to bear;

lightly and delicately his finger presses the hair-trigger. The spiteful crack of the rifle responds to his touch, and instantly in the middle of the bare spot appears a small red dot. The buffalo shivers; death has overtaken him, he cannot tell from whence; still he does not fall, but walks heavily forward, as if nothing had happened. Yet before he has gone far out upon the sand, you see him stop; he totters; his knees bend under him, and his head sinks forward to the ground. Then his whole vast bulk sways to one side; he rolls over on the sand, and dies with a scarcely perceptible struggle.

8

Waylaying the buffalo in this manner, and shooting them as they come to water, is the easiest method of hunting them. They may also be approached by crawling up ravines, or behind hills, or even over the open prairie. This is often surprisingly easy; but at other times it requires the utmost skill of the most experienced hunter. Henry Chatillon was a man of extraordinary strength and hardihood; but I have seen him return to camp quite exhausted with his efforts, his limbs scratched and wounded, and his buckskin dress stuck full of the thorns of the prickly-pear, among which he had been crawling. Sometimes he would lie flat upon his face, and drag himself along in this position for many rods together.

On the second day of our stay at this place, Henry went out for an afternoon hunt. Shaw and I remained in camp until, observing some bulls approaching the water upon the other side of the river, we crossed over to attack them. They were so near, however, that before we could get under cover of the bank our appearance as we walked over the sands alarmed them. Turning round before coming within gun-shot, they began to move off to the right in a direction parallel to the river. I climbed up the bank and ran after them. They were walking swiftly, and before I could come within gun-shot distance they slowly wheeled about and faced me. Before they had turned far enough to see me I had fallen flat on my face. For a moment they stood and stared at the strange object upon the grass; then, turning away again, they walked on as before; and I, rising immediately, ran once more in pursuit. Again they wheeled about, and again I fell prostrate. Repeating this three or four times, I came at length within a hundred yards of the fugitives, and as I saw them turning again I sat down and levelled my rifle. The one in the centre was the largest I had ever seen. I shot him behind the shoulder. His two companions ran off. He attempted to follow, but soon came to a stand, and at length lay down as quietly as an ox chewing the cud. Cautiously approaching him, I saw by his dull and jelly-like eye that he was dead.

When I began the chase, the prairie was almost tenantless; but a great multitude of buffalo had suddenly thronged upon it, and, looking up, I saw within fifty rods a heavy, dark column stretching to the right and left as far as I could see. I walked towards them. My approach did not alarm them in the least. The column itself consisted almost entirely of cows and calves, but a great many old bulls were ranging about the prairie on its flank, and as I drew near they faced towards me with such a grim and ferocious look that I thought it best to proceed no farther. Indeed I was already within close rifle-shot of the column, and I sat down on the ground to watch their movements. Sometimes the whole would stand still, their heads all one way; then they would trot forward, as if by a common impulse, their hoofs and horns clattering together as they moved. I soon began to hear at a distance on the left the sharp reports of a rifle, again and again repeated; and not long after, dull and heavy sounds succeeded, which I recognized as the familiar voice of Shaw's double-barrelled gun. When Henry's rifle was at work there was always meat to be brought in. I went back across the river for a horse, and, returning, reached the spot where the hunters were standing. The buffalo were visible on the distant prairie. The living had retreated from the ground, but ten or twelve carcasses were scattered in various directions. Henry, knife in hand, was stooping over a dead cow, cutting away the best and fattest of the meat.

When Shaw left me he had walked down for some distance under the river-bank to find another bull. At length he saw the plains covered with the host of buffalo, and soon after heard the crack of Henry's rifle. Ascending the bank, he crawled through the grass, which for a rod or two from the river was very high and rank. He had not crawled far before to his astonishment he saw Henry standing erect upon the prairie, almost surrounded by the buffalo. Henry was in his element. Quite unconscious that any one was looking at him, he stood at the full height of his tall figure, one hand resting upon his side, and the other arm leaning carelessly on the muzzle of his rifle. His eye was ranging over the singular assemblage around him. Now and then he would select such a cow as suited him, level his rifle, and shoot her dead; then quietly reloading, he would resume his former position. The buffalo seemed no more to regard his presence than if he were one of themselves; the bulls were bellowing and butting at each other, or rolling about in the dust. A group of buffalo would gather about the carcass of a dead cow, snuffing at her wounds; and sometimes they would come behind those that had not yet fallen and endeavor to push them from the spot. Now and then some old bull would face towards Henry with an air of stupid amazement, but none seemed inclined to attack or fly from him. For some time Shaw lay among the grass, looking in surprise at this extraordinary sight; at length he crawled cautiously forward, and spoke in a low voice to Henry, who told him to rise and come on. Still the buffalo showed no sign of fear; they remained gathered about their dead companions. Henry had already killed as many cows as we wanted for use, and Shaw, kneeling behind one of the carcasses, shot five bulls before the rest thought it necessary to disperse.

The frequent stupidity and infatuation of the buffalo seems the more remarkable from the contrast it offers to their wildness and wariness at other times. Henry knew all their peculiarities; he had studied them as a scholar studies his books, and derived quite as much pleasure from the occupation. The buffalo were companions to him, and, as he said, he never felt alone when they were about him. He took great pride in his skill in hunting. He was one of the most modest of men; yet in the simplicity and frankness of his character, it was clear that he looked upon his pre-eminence in this respect as a thing too palpable and well established to be disputed. But whatever may have been his estimate of his own skill, it was rather below than above that which others placed upon it. The only time that I ever saw a shade of scorn darken his face was when two volunteer soldiers, who had just killed a buffalo for the first time, undertook to instruct him as to the best method of "approaching." Henry always seemed to think that he had a sort of pre-scriptive right to the buffalo, and to look upon them as something belonging to himself. Nothing excited his in-dignation so much as any wanton destruction committed among the cows, and in his view shooting a calf was a cardinal sin.

Henry Chatillon and Tête Rouge were of the same age; that is, about thirty. Henry was twice as large, and about six times as strong as Tête Rouge. Henry's face was roughened by winds and storms; Tête Rouge's was bloated by sherry-cobblers and brandy-toddy. Henry talked of Indians and buffalo; Tête Rouge of theatres and oyster-cellars. Henry had led a life of hardship and privation; Tête Rouge never had a whim which he would not gratify at the first moment he was able. Henry moreover was the most disinterested man I ever saw; while Tête Rouge, though equally good-natured in his way, cared for nobody but himself. Yet we would not have lost him on any account; he served the purpose of a jester in a feudal castle; our camp would have been lifeless without him. For the past week he had fattened in a most amazing manner; and, indeed this was not at all surprising, since his appetite was inordinate. He was eating from morning till night; half the time he would be at work cooking some private mess for himself, and he paid a visit to the coffee-pot eight or ten times a day. His rueful and disconsolate face became jovial and rubicund, his eyes stood out like a lobster's, and his spirits, which before were sunk to the depths of despondency, were now elated in proportion; all day he was singing, whistling, laughing, and telling stories. Being mortally afraid of Jim Gurney, he kept close in the neighborhood of our tent. As he had seen an abundance of low fast life, and had a considerable fund of humor, his anecdotes were extremely amusing, especially since he never hesitated to place himself in a ludicrous point of view, provided he could raise a laugh by doing so. Tête Rouge, however, was sometimes rather troublesome; he had an inveterate habit of pilfering provisions at all times of the day. He set ridicule at defiance; and would never have given over his tricks, even if they had drawn upon him the scorn of the whole party. Now and then, indeed, something worse than laughter fell to his share; on these occasions he would exhibit much contrition, but half an hour after we would generally observe him stealing round to the box at the back of the cart, and slyly making off with the provisions which Deslauriers had laid by for supper. He was fond of smoking; but having no tobacco of his own, we used to provide him with as much as he wanted, a small piece at a time. At first we gave him half a pound together; but this experiment proved an entire failure, for he invariably lost not only the tobacco, but the knife intrusted to him for cutting it, and a few minutes after he would come to us with many apologies and beg for more.

We had been two days at this camp, and some of the meat was nearly fit for transportation, when a storm came suddenly upon us. About sunset the whole sky grew as black as ink, and the long grass at the edge of the river bent and rose mournfully with the first gusts of the approaching hurricane. Munroe and his two companions brought their guns and placed them under cover of our tent. Having no shelter for themselves, they built a fire of driftwood that might have defied a cataract, and, wrapped in their buffalo-robes, sat on the ground around it to bide the fury of the storm. Deslauriers ensconced himself under the cover of the cart. Shaw and I, together with Henry and Tête Rouge, crowded into the little tent; but first of all the dried meat was piled together, and well protected by buffalo-robes pinned firmly to the ground. About nine o'clock the storm broke amid absolute darkness; it blew

a gale, and torrents of rain roared over the boundless expanse of open prairie. Our tent was filled with mist and
spray beating through the canvas, and saturating everything within. We could only distinguish each other at
short intervals by the dazzling flashes of lightning, which
displayed the whole waste around us with its momentary
glare. We had our fears for the tent; but for an hour or
two it stood fast, until at length the cap gave way before
a furious blast; the pole tore through the top, and in an
instant we were half suffocated by the cold and dripping
folds of the canvas, which fell down upon us. Seizing
upon our guns we placed them erect, in order to lift the
saturated cloth above our heads. In this agreeable situation, involved among wet blankets and buffalo-robes,
we spent several hours of the night, during which the
storm would not abate for a moment, but pelted down with
merciless fury. Before long the water gathered beneath us
in a pool two or three inches deep; so that for a considerable part of the night we were partially immersed in
a cold bath. In spite of all this, Tête Rouge's flow of
spirits did not fail him; he laughed, whistled, and sang
in defiance of the storm, and that night paid off the long
arrears of ridicule which he owed us. While we lay in   13
silence, enduring the infliction with what philosophy we
could muster, Tête Rouge, who was intoxicated with animal spirits, cracked jokes at our expense by the hour
together.

At about three o'clock in the morning, preferring "the
tyranny of the open night" to such a wretched shelter, we   14
crawled out from beneath the fallen canvas. The wind
had abated, but the rain fell steadily. The fire of the
California men still blazed amid the darkness, and we
joined them as they sat around it. We made ready some

hot coffee by way of refreshment; but when some of the party sought to replenish their cups, it was found that Tête Rouge, having disposed of his own share, had privately abstracted the coffee-pot and drunk the rest of the contents out of the spout.

In the morning, to our great joy, an unclouded sun rose upon the prairie. We presented a rather laughable appearance; for the cold and clammy buckskin, saturated with water, clung fast to our limbs. The light wind and warm sunshine soon dried it again, and then we were all encased in armor of intolerable stiffness. Roaming all day over the prairie and shooting two or three bulls were scarcely enough to restore the stiffened leather to its usual pliancy.

Besides Henry Chatillon, Shaw and I were the only hunters in the party. Munroe this morning made an attempt to run a buffalo, but his horse could not come up to the game. Shaw went out with him, and being better mounted soon found himself in the midst of the herd. Seeing nothing but cows and calves around him, he checked his horse. An old bull came galloping on the open prairie at some distance behind; and turning, Shaw rode across his path, levelling his gun as he passed, and shooting him through the shoulder into the heart.

A great flock of buzzards was usually soaring about a few trees that stood on the island just below our camp. Throughout the whole of yesterday we had noticed an eagle among them; to-day he was still there; and Tête Rouge, declaring that he would kill the bird of America, borrowed Deslauriers's gun and set out on his unpatriotic errand. As might have been expected, the eagle suffered no harm at his hands. He soon returned, saying that he could not find him, but had shot a buzzard instead. Being required to produce the bird in proof of his assertion, he said he believed that he was not quite dead, but he must be hurt from the swiftness with which he flew off.

"If you want," said Tête Rouge, "I'll go and get one of his feathers; I knocked off plenty of them when I shot him."

Just opposite our camp was another island covered with bushes, and behind it was a deep pool of water, while two or three considerable streams coursed over the sand not far off. I was bathing at this place in the afternoon when a white wolf, larger than the largest Newfoundland dog, ran out from behind the point of the island, and galloped leisurely over the sand not half a stone's-throw distant. I could plainly see his red eyes and the bristles about his snout; he was an ugly scoundrel, with a bushy tail, a large head, and a most repulsive countenance. Having neither rifle to shoot nor stone to pelt him with, I was looking after some missile for his benefit, when the report of a gun came from the camp, and the ball threw up the sand just beyond him; at this he gave a slight jump, and stretched away so swiftly that he soon dwindled into a mere speck on the distant sand-beds. The number of carcasses that by this time were lying about the neighboring prairie summoned the wolves from every quarter; the spot where Shaw and Henry had hunted together soon became their favorite resort, for here about a dozen dead buffalo were fermenting under the hot sun. I used often to go over the river and watch them at their meal. By lying under the bank it was easy to get a full view of them. There were three different kinds: the white wolves and the gray wolves, both very large, and besides these the small prairie wolves, not much bigger than spaniels. They would howl and fight in a crowd around a single carcass, yet they were so watchful, and their senses so acute, that I never was able to crawl within a fair shooting distance;

whenever I attempted it, they would all scatter at once and glide silently away through the tall grass. The air above this spot was always full of turkey-buzzards or black vultures; whenever the wolves left a carcass they would descend upon it, and cover it so densely that a rifle bullet shot at random among the gormandizing crowd would generally strike down two or three of them. These birds would often sail by scores just above our camp, their broad black wings seeming half transparent, as they expanded them against the bright sky. The wolves and the buzzards thickened about us every hour, and two or three eagles also came to the feast. I killed a bull within rifle-shot of the camp; that night the wolves made a fearful howling close at hand, and in the morning the carcass was completely hollowed out by these voracious feeders.

After remaining four days at this camp we prepared to leave it. We had for our own part about five hundred pounds of dried meat, and the California men had prepared some three hundred more; this consisted of the fattest and choicest parts of eight or nine cows, a small quantity only being taken from each, and the rest abandoned to the wolves. The pack animals were laden, the horses saddled, and the mules harnessed to the cart. Even Tête Rouge was ready at last, and slowly moving from the ground, we resumed our journey eastward. When we had advanced about a mile, Shaw missed a valuable hunting-knife, and turned back in search of it, thinking that he had left it at the camp. The day was dark and gloomy. The ashes of the fires were still smoking by the river-side; the grass around them was trampled down by men and horses, and strewn with all the litter of a camp. Our departure had been a gathering signal to the birds and beasts of prey. Scores of wolves were prowling about the smouldering fires, while multitudes were roaming over the neighboring prairie; they all fled as Shaw approached, some running over the sand-beds and some over the grassy plains. The vultures in great clouds were soaring overhead, and the dead bull near the camp was completely blackened by the flock that had alighted upon it; they flapped their broad wings, and stretched upward their crested head and long skinny necks, fearing to remain, yet reluctant to leave their disgusting feast. As he searched about the fires he saw the wolves seated on the hills waiting for his departure. Having looked in vain for his knife, he mounted again, and left the wolves and the vultures to banquet undisturbed.

17

CHAPTER XXVI.

DOWN THE ARKANSAS.

IN the summer of 1846 the wild and lonely banks of the Upper Arkansas beheld for the first time the passage of an army. General Kearney, on his march to Santa Fé, adopted this route in preference to the old trail of the Cimarron. When we were on the Arkansas the main body of the troops had already passed on; Price's Missouri regiment, however, was still on its way, having left the frontier much later than the rest; and about this time we began to meet one or two companies at a time moving along the trail. No men ever embarked upon a military expedition with a greater love for the work before them than the Missourians; but if discipline and subordination are the criterion of merit, they were worthless soldiers indeed. Yet when their exploits have rung through all America, it would be absurd to deny that they were excellent irregular troops. Their victories were gained in the teeth of every established precedent of warfare; and were owing to a combination of military qualities in the men themselves. Doniphan's regiment marched through New Mexico more like a band of free companions than like the paid soldiers of a modern government. When General Taylor complimented him on his success at Sacramento and elsewhere, the Colonel's reply very well illustrates the relations which subsisted between the officers and men of his command.

"I don't know anything of the manœuvres. The boys kept coming to me to let them charge; and when I saw a good opportunity, I told them they might go. They were off like a shot, and that's all I know about it." 6

The backwoods lawyer was better fitted to conciliate the good-will than to command the obedience of his men. There were many serving under him, who both from character and education could better have held command than he. 7

At the battle of Sacramento his frontiersmen fought under every disadvantage. The Mexicans had chosen their position ; they were drawn up across the valley that led to their native city of Chihuahua; their whole front was covered by intrenchments and defended by batteries, and they outnumbered the invaders five to one. An eagle 8 flew over the Americans, and a deep murmur rose along their lines. The enemy's batteries opened; long they re- 9 mained under fire, but when at length the word was given, they shouted and ran forward. In one of the divisions, when mid-way to the enemy, a drunken officer ordered a 10 halt; the exasperated men hesitated to obey.

"Forward, boys!" cried a private from the ranks; and 11 the Americans rushed like tigers upon the enemy. Four hundred Mexicans were slain upon the spot and the rest fled, scattering over the plain like sheep. The standards, cannon, and baggage were taken, and among the rest a wagon laden with cords, which the Mexicans, in the ful- 12 ness of their confidence, had made ready for tying the American prisoners.

Doniphan's volunteers, who gained this victory, passed up with the main army; but Price's soldiers, whom we now met were men from the same neighborhood, precisely similar in character, manners, and appearance. One morning, as we were descending upon a wide meadow, where we meant to rest for an hour or two, we saw a body of horsemen approaching at a distance. In order to find water, we were obliged to turn aside to the river bank, a full half-mile from the trail. Here we put up a kind of awning, and spreading buffalo-robes on the ground Shaw and I sat down to smoke.

"We are going to catch it, now," said Shaw; "look at those fellows; there'll be no peace for us here."

And in truth about half the volunteers had straggled away from the line of march, and were riding over the meadow towards us.

"How are you?" said the first who came up, alighting from his horse and throwing himself upon the ground. The rest followed close, and a score of them soon gathered about us, some lying at full length and some sitting on horseback. They all belonged to a company raised in St. Louis. There were some ruffian faces among them, and some haggard with debauchery; but on the whole they were extremely good-looking men, superior beyond measure to the ordinary rank and file of an army. Except that they were booted to the knees, they wore their belts and military trappings over the ordinary dress of citizens. Besides their swords and holster pistols, they carried slung from their saddles the excellent Springfield carbines, loaded at the breech. They inquired the character of our party, and were anxious to know the prospect of killing buffalo, and the chance that their horses would stand the journey to Santa Fé. All this was well enough, but a moment after a worse visitation came upon us.

"How are you, strangers? whar are you going, and whar are you from?" said a fellow who came trotting up with an old straw hat on his head. He was dressed in the coarsest brown homespun cloth. His face was rather sallow from fever-and-ague, and his tall figure, though strong and sinewy, had a lean angular look, which, together with his boorish seat on horseback, gave him an appearance anything but graceful. More of the same stamp were close behind him.

Their company was raised in one of the frontier counties, and we soon had abundant evidences of their rustic breeding; they came crowding round by scores, pushing between our first visitors, and staring at us with unabashed faces.

"Are you the captain?" asked one fellow.

"What's your business out here?" asked another.

"Whar do you live when you're to home?" said a third.

"I reckon you're traders," surmised a fourth; and to crown the whole, one of them came confidentially to my side and inquired in a low voice, "What's your partner's name?"

As each new-comer repeated the same questions, the nuisance became intolerable. Our military visitors were soon disgusted at the concise nature of our replies, and we could overhear them muttering curses. While we sat smoking, not in the best imaginable humor, Tête Rouge's tongue was not idle. He never forgot his military character, and during the whole interview he was incessantly busy among his fellow-soldiers. At length we placed him on the ground before us, and told him that he might play the part of spokesman. Tête Rouge was delighted, and we soon had the satisfaction of seeing him gabble at such a rate that the torrent of questions was in a great measure diverted from us. A little while after, a cannon with four horses came lumbering up behind the crowd; and the driver, who was perched on one of the animals, stretching his neck so as to look over the rest of the men, called out,—

"Whar are you from, and what's your business?"

The captain of one of the companies was among our visitors, drawn by the same curiosity that had attracted his men. Unless their faces belied them, not a few in the crowd might with great advantage have changed places with their commander.

"Well, men," said he, lazily rising from the ground where he had been lounging, "it's getting late; I reckon we'd better be moving."

"I sha'n't start yet anyhow," said one fellow, who was lying half asleep with his head resting on his arm.

"Don't be in a hurry, Captain," added the lieutenant.

"Well, have it your own way, we'll wait a while longer," replied the obsequious commander.

At length, however, our visitors went straggling away as they had come, and we, to our great relief, were left alone again.

No one was more relieved than Deslauriers by the departure of the volunteers; for dinner was getting colder every moment. He spread a well-whitened buffalo-hide upon the grass, placed in the middle the juicy hump of a fat cow, ranged around it the tin plates and cups, and then announced that all was ready. Tête Rouge, with his usual alacrity on such occasions, was the first to take his seat. In his former capacity of steamboat clerk, he had learned to prefix the honorary *Mister* to everybody's name, whether of high or low degree; so Jim Gurney was Mr. Gurney, Henry was Mr. Henry, and even Deslauriers, for the first time in his life, heard himself addressed as Mr. Deslauriers. This did not prevent his conceiving a violent enmity against Tête Rouge, who, in his futile though praiseworthy attempts to make himself useful, always intermeddled with cooking the dinners. Deslauriers's disposition knew no medium between smiles and sunshine and a downright tornado of wrath; he said nothing to Tête Rouge, but his wrongs rankled in his breast. Tête Rouge had taken his place at dinner; it was his happiest moment; he sat enveloped in the old buffalo-coat, sleeves turned up in preparation for the work, and his short legs crossed on the grass before him; he had a cup of coffee by his side and his knife ready in his hand, and while he looked upon the fat hump ribs, his eyes dilated with anticipation. Deslauriers sat opposite to him, and the rest of us by this time had taken our seats.

"How is this, Deslauriers? You haven't given us bread enough."

At this Deslauriers's placid face flew into a paroxysm of contortions. He grinned with wrath, chattered, gesticulated, and hurled forth a volley of incoherent words in broken English at the astonished Tête Rouge. It was just possible to make out that he was accusing him of having stolen and eaten four large cakes which had been laid by for dinner. Tête Rouge, confounded at this sudden attack, stared at his assailant for a moment in dumb amazement, with mouth and eyes wide open.   At last he found speech, and protested that the accusation was false; and that he could not conceive how he had offended Mr. Deslauriers, or provoked him to use such ungentlemanly expressions.   The tempest of words raged with such fury that nothing else could be heard.   But Tête Rouge, from his greater command of English, had a manifest advantage over Deslauriers, who, after sputtering and grimacing for a while, found his words quite inadequate to the expression of his wrath.   He jumped up and vanished, jerking out between his teeth one furious *Sacré enfant de garce!* a Canadian title of honor, made doubly emphatic by being usually applied, together with a cut of the whip, to refractory mules and horses.

The next morning we saw an old buffalo-bull escorting his cow with two small calves over the prairie.   Close behind came four or five large white wolves, sneaking stealthily through the long meadow-grass, and watching for the moment when one of the children should chance to lag behind his parents.   The old bull kept well on his guard, and faced about now and then to keep the prowling ruffians at a distance.

As we approached our nooning-place we saw five or six buffalo standing at the summit of a tall bluff.   Trotting forward to the spot where we meant to stop, I flung off my saddle and turned my horse loose.   By making a circuit under cover of some rising ground I reached the foot of the bluff unnoticed, and climbed up its steep side.   Lying under the brow of the declivity, I prepared to fire at the buffalo, who stood on the flat surface above, not five yards distant.   The gleaming rifle-barrel levelled over the edge caught their notice, and they turned and ran.   Close as they were, it was impossible to kill them when in that position, and stepping upon the summit, I pursued them over the high, arid table-land. It was extremely rugged and broken; a great sandy ravine was channelled through it, with smaller ravines entering on each side like tributary streams. The buffalo scattered, and I soon lost sight of most of them as they scuttled away through the sandy chasms; a bull and a cow alone kept in view. For a while they ran along the edge of the great ravine, appearing and disappearing as they dived into some chasm and again emerged from it. At last they stretched out upon the broad prairie, a plain nearly flat and almost devoid of verdure, for every short grass-blade was dried and shrivelled by the glaring sun. Now and then the old bull would face towards me; whenever he did so I fell to the ground and lay motionless. In this manner I chased them for about two miles, until at length I heard in front a deep hoarse bellowing. A moment after, a band of about a hundred bulls, before hidden by a slight swell of the plain, came at once into view. The fugitives ran towards them. Instead of mingling with the band, as I expected, they passed directly through, and continued their flight. At this I gave up the chase, crawled to within gun-shot of the bulls, and sat down on the ground to watch them. My presence did not disturb them in the least. They were not feeding, for there was nothing to eat; but they seemed to have chosen the parched and scorching desert as their play-ground. Some were rolling on the ground amid a cloud of dust; others, with a hoarse rumbling bellow, were butting their large heads together, while many stood motionless, as if quite inanimate. Except their monstrous growth of tangled, grizzly mane, they had no hair; for their old coat had fallen off in the spring, and their new one had not as yet appeared. Sometimes an old bull would step forward, and gaze at me with a grim and stupid countenance; then he would turn and butt his next neighbor; then he would lie down and roll over in the dust, kicking his hoofs in the air. When satisfied with this amusement, he would jerk his head and shoulders upward, and resting on his forelegs, stare at me in this position, half blinded by his mane, and his face covered with dirt; then up he would spring upon all fours, shake his dusty sides, turn half round, and stand with his beard touching the ground, in an attitude of profound abstraction, as if reflecting on his puerile conduct.

"You are too ugly to live," thought I; and aiming at the ugliest, I shot three of them in succession. The rest were not at all discomposed at this; they kept on bellowing, butting, and rolling on the ground as before. Henry Chatillon always cautioned us to keep perfectly quiet in the presence of a wounded buffalo, for any movement is apt to excite him to make an attack; so I sat still upon the ground, loading and firing with as little motion as possible. While I was thus employed a spectator made his appearance: a little antelope came running up to within fifty yards; and there it stood, its slender neck arched, its small horns thrown back, and its large dark eyes gazing on me with a look of eager curiosity. By the side of the shaggy and brutish monsters before me, it seemed like some lovely young girl in a den of robbers or a nest of bearded pirates. The buffalo looked uglier than ever. "Here goes for another of you," thought I, feeling in my pouch for a percussion-cap. Not a percussion-cap was there. My good rifle was useless as an old iron bar. One of the wounded bulls had not yet fallen, and I waited for some time, hoping every moment that his strength would fail him. He still stood firm, looking grimly at me; and disregarding Henry's advice, I rose and walked away. Many of the bulls turned and looked at me, but the wounded brute made no attack. I soon came upon a deep ravine which would give me shelter in case of emergency; so I turned around and threw a stone at the bulls. They received it with the utmost indifference. Feeling myself insulted at their refusal to be frightened, I swung my hat, shouted, and made a show of running towards them; at this they crowded together and galloped off, leaving their dead and wounded upon the field. As I moved towards the camp I saw the last survivor totter and fall dead. My speed in returning was wonderfully quickened by the reflection that the Pawnees were abroad, and that I was defenceless in case of meeting with an enemy. I saw no living thing, however, except two or three squalid old bulls scrambling among the sandhills that flanked the great ravine. When I reached camp the party were nearly ready for the afternoon move.

We encamped that evening at a short distance from the river bank. About midnight, as we all lay asleep on the ground, the man nearest me, gently reaching out his hand, touched my shoulder, and cautioned me at the same time not to move. It was bright starlight. Opening my eyes and slightly turning, I saw a large white wolf moving stealthily around the embers of our fire, with his nose close to the ground. Disengaging my hand from the blanket, I drew the cover from my rifle, which lay close at my side; the motion alarmed the wolf, and with long leaps he bounded out of the camp. Jumping up, I fired after him, when he was about thirty yards distant; the melancholy hum of the bullet sounded far away through the night. At the sharp report, so suddenly breaking upon the stillness, all the men sprang up.

"You 've killed him!" said one of them.

"No I have n't," said I; "there he goes, running along the river."

"Then there's two of them. Don't you see that one lying out yonder?"

We went out to it, and instead of a dead white wolf, found the bleached skull of a buffalo. I had missed my mark, and what was worse had grossly violated a standing law of the prairie. When in a dangerous part of the country, it is considered highly imprudent to fire a gun after encamping, lest the report should reach the ears of Indians.

The horses were saddled in the morning, and the last man had lighted his pipe at the dying ashes of the fire. The beauty of the day enlivened us all. Even Ellis felt its influence, and occasionally made a remark as we rode along; and Jim Gurney told endless stories of his cruisings in the United States service. The buffalo were abundant, and at length a large band of them went running up the hills on the left.

"Too good a chance to lose!" said Shaw. We lashed our horses and galloped after them. Shaw killed one with each barrel of his gun. I separated another from the herd and shot him. The small bullet of the rifle-pistol striking too far back did not immediately take effect, and the bull ran on with unabated speed. Again and again I snapped the remaining pistol at him. I primed it afresh three or four times, and each time it missed fire, for the touch-hole was clogged up. Returning it to the holster, I began to load the empty pistol, still galloping by the side of the bull. By this time he had grown desperate. The foam flew from his jaws and his tongue lolled out. Before the pistol was loaded he sprang upon me, and followed up his attack with a furious rush. The only alternative was to run away or be killed. I took to flight, and the bull, bristling with fury, pursued me closely. The pistol was soon ready, and then looking back I saw his head five or six yards behind my horse's tail. To fire at it would be useless, for a bullet flattens against the adamantine skull of a buffalo 18 bull. Inclining my body to the left, I turned my horse in that direction as sharply as his speed would permit. The bull, rushing blindly on with great force and weight, did not turn so quickly. As I looked back, his neck and shoulder were exposed to view; and turning in the saddle, I shot a bullet through them obliquely into his vitals. He gave over the chase and soon fell to the ground. An English tourist represents a situation like this as one of 19 imminent danger. This is a mistake; the bull never pursues long, and the horse must be wretched indeed that cannot keep out of his way for two or three minutes.

We were now come to a part of the country where we were bound in common prudence to use every possible precaution. We mounted guard at night, each man standing in his turn; and no one ever slept without drawing his rifle close to his side or folding it with him in his blanket. One morning our vigilance was stimulated by finding traces of a large Camanche encampment. Fortu- 20 nately for us, however, it had been abandoned nearly a week. On the next evening we found the ashes of a recent fire, which gave us at the time some uneasiness. At length we reached the Caches, a place of dangerous re- 21 pute; and it had a most dangerous appearance, consisting of sand-hills everywhere broken by ravines and deep chasms. Here we found the grave of Swan, killed at this place, 22 probably by the Pawnees, two or three weeks before. His remains, more than once violated by the Indians and the wolves, were suffered at length to remain undisturbed in their wild burial-place. 23

For several days we met detached companies of Price's regiment. Horses would often break loose at night from their camps. One afternoon we picked up three of these stragglers quietly grazing along the river. After we came to camp that evening, Jim Gurney brought news that more of them were in sight. It was nearly dark, and a cold, drizzling rain had set in; but we all turned out, and after an hour's chase nine horses were caught and brought in. One of them was equipped with saddle and bridle; pistols were hanging at the pommel of the saddle, a carbine was slung at its side, and a blanket rolled up behind it. In the morning, as we resumed our journey, our cavalcade presented a much more imposing appearance than ever before. We kept on till the afternoon, when, far behind, three horsemen appeared on the horizon. Coming on at a hand-gallop, they soon overtook us, and claimed all the horses as belonging to themselves and others of their company. Proof of ownership being shown, they were of course given up, very much to the mortification of Ellis and Jim Gurney.

Our own horses now showed signs of fatigue, and we resolved to give them half a day's rest. We stopped at noon at a grassy spot by the river. After dinner Shaw and Henry went out to hunt; and while the men lounged about the camp, I lay down to read in the shadow of the cart. Looking up, I saw a bull grazing alone on the prairie more than a mile distant, and taking my rifle I walked towards him. As I came near, I crawled upon the ground until I approached to within a hundred yards; here I sat down upon the grass and waited till he should turn himself into a proper position to receive his death-wound. He was a grim old veteran. His loves and his battles were over for that season, and now, gaunt and war-worn, he had withdrawn from the herd to graze by himself and recruit his exhausted strength. He was miserably emaciated; his mane was all in tatters; his hide was bare and rough as an elephant's, and covered with dried patches of the mud in which he had been wallowing. He showed all his ribs whenever he moved. He looked like some grizzly old ruffian grown gray in blood and violence, and scowling on all the world from his misanthropic seclusion. The old savage looked up when I first approached and gave me a fierce stare; then he fell to grazing again with an air of contemptuous indifference. The moment after, as if suddenly recollecting himself, he threw up his head, faced quickly about, and to my amazement came at a rapid trot directly towards me. I was strongly impelled to get up and run, but this would have been very dangerous. Sitting quite still, I aimed, as he came on, at the thin part of the skull above the nose, hoping that the shot might have the effect of turning him. After he had passed over about three quarters of the distance between us, I was on the point of firing, when, to my great satisfaction, he stopped short. I had full opportunity of studying his countenance; his whole front was covered with a huge mass of coarse, matted hair, which hung so low that nothing but his two forefeet were visible beneath it; his short, thick horns were blunted and split to the roots in his various battles, and across his nose and forehead were two or three large white scars, which gave him a grim, and at the same time a whimsical appearance. It seemed to me that he stood there motionless for a full quarter of an hour staring at me through the tangled locks of his mane. For my part I remained as quiet as he, and looked quite as hard. I felt greatly inclined to come to terms with him. "My friend," thought I, "if you'll let me off, I'll let you off." At length he seemed to have abandoned any hostile design. Very slowly and deliberately he began to turn about; little by little his side came into view, all beplastered with mud. It was a tempting sight. I forgot my prudent intentions, and fired my rifle; a pistol would have served at that distance. The old bull spun round like a top, and galloped away over the prairie. He ran some distance, and even ascended a considerable hill, before he lay down and died. After shooting another bull among the hills, I went back to camp.

26   At noon, on the fourteenth of September, a very large Santa Fé caravan came up. The plain was covered with the long files of their white-topped wagons, the close
27   black carriages in which the traders travel and sleep, large droves of mules and horses, and men on horseback and on foot. They all stopped on the meadow near us. Our diminutive cart and handful of men made but an insignificant figure by the side of their wide and bustling camp. Tête Rouge went to visit them, and soon came back with half a dozen biscuit in one hand, and a bottle of brandy in the other. I inquired where he got them. "Oh," said
28   Tête Rouge, "I know some of the traders. Dr. Dobbs is there besides." I asked who Dr. Dobbs might be. "One of our St. Louis doctors," replied Tête Rouge. For two days past I had been severely attacked by the same disorder which had so greatly reduced my strength when at the mountains; at this time I was suffering not a little from pain and weakness. Tête Rouge, in answer to my inquiries, declared that Dr. Dobbs was a physician of the first standing. Without at all believing him, I resolved to consult this eminent practitioner. Walking over to the camp, I found him lying sound asleep under one of the wagons. He offered in his own person but indifferent evi-

dence of his skill, for it was five months since I had seen so cadaverous a face. His hat had fallen off, and his yellow hair was all in disorder; one of his arms supplied the place of a pillow; his trousers were wrinkled half-way up to his knees, and he was covered with little bits of grass and straw upon which he had rolled in his uneasy slumber. A Mexican stood near, and I made him a sign to touch the doctor. Up sprang the learned Dobbs, and sitting upright rubbed his eyes and looked about him in bewilderment. I regretted the necessity of disturbing him, and said I had come to ask professional advice.

"Your system, sir, is in a disordered state," said he, solemnly, after a short examination.

I inquired what might be the particular species of disorder.

"Evidently a morbid action of the liver," replied the medical man; "I will give you a prescription."

Repairing to the back of one of the covered wagons, he scrambled in; for a moment I could see nothing of him but his boots. At length he produced a box which he had extracted from some dark recess within, and, opening it, presented me with a folded paper. "What is it?" said I. "Calomel," said the doctor.

Under the circumstances I would have taken almost anything. There was not enough to do me much harm, and it might possibly do good; so at camp that night I took the poison instead of supper. 29

That camp is worthy of notice. The traders warned us not to follow the main trail along the river, "unless," as one of them observed, "you want to have your throats cut!" The river at this place makes a bend; and a smaller trail, known as "the Ridge path," leads directly 30 across the prairie from point to point, a distance of sixty or seventy miles.

We followed this trail, and after travelling seven or eight miles came to a small stream, where we encamped. Our position was not chosen with much forethought or military skill. The water was in a deep hollow, with steep, high banks; on the grassy bottom of this hollow we picketed our horses, while we ourselves encamped upon the barren prairie just above. The opportunity was admirable either for driving off our horses or attacking us. After dark, as Tête Rouge was sitting at supper, we observed him pointing, with a face of speechless horror, over the shoulder of Henry, who was opposite to him. Aloof amid the darkness appeared a gigantic black apparition solemnly swaying to and fro as it advanced steadily upon us. Henry, half-vexed and half-amused, jumped up, spread out his arms, and shouted. The invader was an old buffalo-bull, who, with characteristic stupidity, was walking directly into camp. It cost some shouting and swinging of hats before we could bring him first to a halt and then to a rapid retreat.

The moon was full and bright, but as the black clouds chased rapidly over it, we were at one moment in light and at the next in darkness. As the evening advanced, a thunder-storm came up and struck us with such violence that the tent would have been blown over if we had not interposed the cart to break the force of the wind. At length it subsided to a steady rain. I lay awake through nearly the whole night, listening to its dull patter upon the canvas above. The moisture, which filled the tent and trickled from everything in it, did not add to the comfort of the situation. About twelve o'clock Shaw went out to stand guard amid the rain and pitchy darkness. Munroe was also on the alert. When about two hours had passed, Shaw came silently in, and, touching Henry, called to him in a low, quick voice to come out. "What is it?" I asked. "Indians, I believe," whispered Shaw; "but lie still; I 'll call you if there 's going to be a fight."

He and Henry went out together. I took the cover from my rifle, put a fresh percussion-cap upon it, and then, being in much pain, lay down again. In about five minutes Shaw returned. "All right," he said, as he lay down to sleep. Henry was now standing guard in his place. He told me in the morning the particulars of the alarm. Munroe's watchful eye had discovered some dark objects down in the hollow, among the horses, like men creeping on all fours. Lying flat on their faces, he and Shaw crawled to the edge of the bank, and were soon convinced that these dark objects were Indians. Shaw silently withdrew to call Henry, and they all lay watching in the same position. Henry's eye is one of the best on the prairie. He detected after a while the true nature of the intruders; they were nothing but wolves creeping among the horses.

It is very singular that, when picketed near a camp, horses seldom show any fear of such an intrusion. The wolves appear to have no other object than that of gnawing the trail-ropes of raw hide by which the animals are secured. Several times in the course of the journey my horse's trail-rope was bitten in two by these nocturnal visitors.

26

CHAPTER XXVII.

THE SETTLEMENTS.

1 THE next day was extremely hot, and we rode from morning till night without seeing a tree, a bush, or a drop of water. Our horses and mules suffered much more than we, but as sunset approached, they pricked up their ears and mended their pace. Water was not far off. When we came to the descent of the broad, shallow valley where it lay, an unlooked-for sight awaited us. The stream glistened at the bottom, and along its banks were pitched a multitude of tents, while hundreds of cattle were feed-
2 ing over the meadows. Bodies of troops, both horse and foot, and long trains of wagons, with men, women, and children, were moving over the opposite ridge and descending the broad declivity before us. These were the
3 Mormon battalion in the service of government, together with a considerable number of Missouri volunteers. The Mormons were to be paid off in California, and they were allowed to bring with them their families and property. There was something very striking in the half-military, half-patriarchal appearance of these armed fanatics, thus on their way, with their wives and children, to found, it might be, a Mormon empire in California. We were much more astonished than pleased at the sight before us. In order to find an unoccupied camping ground, we were obliged to pass a quarter of a mile up the stream, and here we were soon beset by a swarm of Mormons and Missourians. The

United States officer in command of the whole came also 4
to visit us, and remained some time at our camp.

In the morning the country was covered with mist. We
were always early risers, but before we were ready, the
voices of men driving in the cattle sounded all around
us. As we passed above their camp, we saw through the
obscurity that the tents were falling, and the ranks rapidly
forming; and, mingled with the cries of women and children, the rolling of the Mormon drums and the clear blast
of their trumpets sounded through the mist.

From that time to the journey's end, we met almost
every day long trains of government wagons laden with
stores for the troops, crawling at a snail's pace towards
Santa Fé.

Tête Rouge had a mortal antipathy to danger, but one
evening he achieved an adventure more perilous than had
befallen any man in the party. The day after we left the
Ridge-path we encamped close to the river, and at sunset
saw a train of wagons encamping on the trail, about three
miles off. Though we saw them distinctly, we and our little cart, as it afterward proved, entirely escaped their notice.
For some days Tête Rouge had been longing for a dram of
whiskey. So, resolving to improve the present opportunity, he mounted his horse "James," which he had obtained from the volunteers in exchange for his mule, slung
his canteen over his shoulder, and set out in search of his
favorite liquor. Some hours passed without his returning.
We thought that he was lost, or perhaps that some stray
Indian had snapped him up. While the rest fell asleep
I remained on guard. Late at night a tremulous voice
saluted me from the darkness, and Tête Rouge and James
soon became visible, advancing towards the camp. Tête
Rouge was in much agitation and big with important tid-

ings. Sitting down on the shaft of the cart, he told the following story: —

When he left the camp he had no idea, he said, how late it was. By the time he approached the wagoners it was perfectly dark; and as he saw them all sitting around their fires within the circle of wagons, their guns laid by their sides, he thought he might as well give warning of his approach, in order to prevent a disagreeable mistake. Raising his voice to the highest pitch, he screamed out in prolonged accents, "Camp ahoy!" This eccentric salutation produced anything but the desired effect. Hearing such hideous sounds proceeding from the outer darkness, the wagoners thought that the whole Pawnee nation was upon them. Up they sprang, wild with terror. Each man snatched his gun; some stood behind the wagons; some threw themselves flat on the ground, and in an instant twenty cocked muskets were levelled full at the horrified Tête Rouge, who just then began to be visible through the gloom.

"Thar they come!" cried the master wagoner. "Fire! fire! shoot that feller!"

"No, no!" screamed Tête Rouge, in an ecstasy of fright; "don't fire, don't; I'm a friend, I'm an American citizen!"

"You're a friend, be you?" cried a gruff voice from the wagons; "then what are you yellin' out thar for like a wild Injun. Come along up here if you're a man."

"Keep your guns p'inted at him," added the master wagoner; "maybe he's a decoy, like."

Tête Rouge in utter bewilderment made his approach, with the gaping muzzles of the muskets still before his eyes. He succeeded at last in explaining his true character, and the Missourians admitted him into camp. He got no whiskey; but as he represented himself as a great invalid, and suffering much from coarse fare, they made up a contribution for him of rice, biscuit, and sugar from their own rations. 5

In the morning at breakfast Tête Rouge once more related this story. We hardly knew how much of it to believe, though after some cross-questioning we failed to discover any flaw in the narrative. Passing by the wagoner's camp, they confirmed Tête Rouge's account in every particular.

"I would n't have been in that feller's place," said one of them, "for the biggest heap of money in Missouri." 6

A day or two after, we had an adventure of another sort with a party of wagoners. Henry and I rode forward to hunt. After that day there was no probability that we should meet with buffalo, and we were anxious to kill one, for a supply of fresh meat. They were so wild that we hunted all the morning in vain, but at noon as we approached Cow Creek we saw a large band feeding near 7 its margin. Cow Creek is densely lined with trees which intercept the view beyond, and it runs, as we afterwards found, at the bottom of a deep trench. We approached by riding along the bottom of a ravine. When we were near enough, I held the horses while Henry crept towards the buffalo. I saw him take his seat within shooting distance, prepare his rifle, and look about to select his victim. The death of a fat cow seemed certain, when suddenly a great smoke and a rattling volley of musketry rose from the bed of the creek. A score of long-legged Missourians leaped out from among the trees and ran after the buffalo, who one and all took to their heels and vanished. These fellows had crawled up the bed of the creek to within a hundred yards of the game. Never was there a fairer chance for a shot. They were good marksmen; all cracked away at once, and yet not a buffalo fell. In fact the animal is so tenacious of life that it requires no little knowledge of anatomy to kill it, and it is very seldom that a novice succeeds in his first attempt at

8 approaching. The balked Missourians were excessively mortified, especially when Henry told them that if they had kept quiet he would have killed meat enough in ten minutes to feed their whole party. Our friends, who were at no great distance, hearing the fusillade, thought that the Indians had fired the volley for our benefit. Shaw came galloping on to reconnoitre and learn if we were yet among the living.

At Cow Creek we found the welcome novelty of ripe grapes and plums, which grew there in abundance. At

9 the Little Arkansas, not much farther on, we saw the last buffalo, a miserable old bull, roaming over the prairie melancholy and alone.

From this time forward the character of the country was changing every day. We had left behind us the great arid deserts, meagrely covered by the tufted buffalo-

10 grass, with its pale-green hue, and its short, shrivelled blades. The plains before us were carpeted with rich herbage sprinkled with flowers. In place of buffalo we found plenty of prairie-hens, and bagged them by dozens without leaving the trail. In three or four days we saw

11 before us the forests and meadows of Council Grove. It seemed like a new sensation as we rode beneath the resounding arches of these noble woods, — ash, oak, elm, maple, and hickory, festooned with enormous grape-vines, purple with fruit. The shouts of our scattered party, and now and then the report of a rifle, rang through the breathless stillness of the forest. We rode out again with

regret into the broad light of the open prairie. Little more than a hundred miles now separated us from the frontier settlements. The whole intervening country was a succession of green prairies, rising in broad swells, and relieved by trees clustering like an oasis around some spring, or following the course of a stream along some fertile hollow. These are the prairies of the poet and the novelist. We had left danger behind us. Nothing was to be feared from the Indians of this region, the Sacs and Foxes, Kanzas and Osages. We had met with rare good fortune. Although for five months we had been travelling with an insufficient force through a country where we were at any moment liable to depredation, not a single animal had been stolen from us, and our only loss had been one old mule bitten to death by a rattlesnake. Three weeks after we reached the frontier the Pawnees and the Camanches began a regular series of hostilities on the Arkansas trail, killing men and driving off horses. They attacked, without exception, every party, large or small, that passed during the next six months.

Diamond Spring, Rock Creek, Elder Grove, and other 'camping places besides, were passed in quick succession. At Rock Creek we found a train of government provision-wagons under the charge of an emaciated old man in his seventy-first year. Some restless American devil had driven him into the wilderness at a time of life when he should have been seated at his fireside with his grandchildren on his knees. I am convinced that he never returned; he was complaining that night of a disease the wasting effects of which upon a younger and stronger man I myself had proved from severe experience. Long before this no doubt the wolves have howled their moonlight carnival over the old man's attenuated remains.

Not long after we came to a small trail leading to Fort Leavenworth, distant but one day's journey. Tête Rouge 17 here took leave of us. He was anxious to go to the fort in order to receive payment for his valuable military services. So he and his horse James, after an affectionate farewell, set out together, with what provisions they could conveniently carry, including a large quantity of brown sugar. On a cheerless rainy evening we came to our last 18 'camping ground.

In the morning we mounted once more. In spite of the dreary rain of yesterday, there never was a brighter autumnal morning than that on which we returned to the settlements. We were passing through the country of the half-civilized Shawanoes. It was a beautiful alternation of fertile plains and groves just tinged with the hues of autumn, while close beneath them nestled the log-houses of the Indian farmers. Every field and meadow bespoke the exuberant fertility of the soil. The maize stood rustling in the wind, ripe and dry, its shining yellow ears thrust out between the gaping husks. Squashes and huge yellow pumpkins lay basking in the sun in the midst of their brown and shrivelled leaves. Robins and blackbirds flew about the fences, and everything betokened our near approach to home and civilization. The forests that border the Missouri soon rose before us, and we entered the wide tract of bushes which forms their outskirts. We had passed the same road on our outward journey in the spring, but its aspect was now totally changed. The young wild apple-trees then flushed with their fragrant blossoms, were hung thickly with ruddy fruit. Tall grass grew by the roadside in place of tender shoots just peeping from the warm and oozy soil. The vines were laden with purple grapes, and 19 the slender twigs of the swamp maple, then tasselled with their clusters of small red flowers, now hung out a gorgeous display of leaves stained by the frost with burning crimson. On every side we saw tokens of maturity and decay where all had before been fresh with opening life. We entered 20 the forest, checkered, as we passed along, by the bright spots of sunlight that fell between the opening boughs. On either side rich masses of foliage almost excluded the sun, though here and there its rays could find their way down, striking through the broad leaves and lighting them with a pure transparent green. Squirrels barked at us from the trees; coveys of young partridges ran rustling 21 over the fallen leaves, and the golden oriole, the blue-jay, and the flaming red-bird darted among the shadowy branches. We hailed these sights and sounds of beauty by no means with unmingled pleasure. Many and power-ful as were the attractions of the settlements, we looked back regretfully to the wilderness behind us. 22

At length we saw the roof of a white man's dwelling 23 between the opening trees. A few moments after, we were riding over the miserable log-bridge that led into Westport. Westport had beheld strange scenes, but a rougher-looking troop than ours, with our worn equip-ments and broken-down horses, was never seen even there. We passed the well-remembered tavern, Boone's grocery, 24 and old Vogel's dram-shop, and encamped on a meadow be-yond. Here we were soon visited by a number of people who came to purchase our horses and equipments. This matter disposed of, we hired a wagon and drove to Kanzas landing. Here we were again received under the hospitable roof of our old friend Colonel Chick, and seated under his porch 25 we looked down once more on the eddies of the Missouri.

Deslauriers made his appearance in the morning strangely transformed by a hat, a coat, and a razor. His little log-house was among the woods not far off. It seems he had meditated giving a ball in honor of his return, and had consulted Henry Chatillon as to whether it would do to invite his *bourgeois*. Henry expressed his entire conviction that we would not take it amiss, and the invitation was now proffered accordingly, Deslauriers adding as a special

26 inducement that Antoine Lajeunesse was to play the fiddle. We told him we would certainly come, but before evening the arrival of a steamboat from Fort Leavenworth prevented

27 our being present at the expected festivities. Deslauriers was on the rock at the landing-place, waiting to take leave of us.

"Adieu! mes bourgeois, adieu! adieu!" he cried as the boat put off; "when you go another time to de Rocky Montagnes I will go with you; yes, I will go!"

He accompanied this assurance by jumping about, swinging his hat, and grinning from ear to ear. As the boat rounded a distant point the last object that met our eyes was Deslauriers still lifting his hat and skipping about the

28 rock. We had taken leave of Munroe and Jim Gurney at

29 Westport, and Henry Chatillon went down in the boat with us.

The passage to St. Louis occupied eight days, during about a third of which time we were fast aground on sand-

30 bars. We passed the steamer "Amelia" crowded with a roaring crew of disbanded volunteers, swearing, drinking,

31 gambling, and fighting. At length one evening we reached the crowded levee of St. Louis. Repairing to the Planters'

32 House, we caused diligent search to be made for our trunks, which were at length discovered stowed away in the farthest corner of the store-room. In the morning, transformed by the magic of the tailor's art, we hardly

33 recognized each other.

On the evening before our departure Henry Chatillon came to our rooms at the Planters' House to take leave of us. No one who met him in the streets of St. Louis would have taken him for a hunter fresh from the Rocky Mountains. He was very neatly and simply dressed in a suit of dark cloth; for although since his sixteenth year he had scarcely been for a month together among the abodes of men, he had a native good taste which always led him to pay great attention to his personal appearance. His tall, athletic figure with its easy, flexible motions appeared to advantage in his present dress; and his fine face, though roughened by a thousand storms, was not at all out of keeping with it. He had served us with a fidelity and zeal beyond all praise. We took leave of him with regret; and unless his changing features, as he shook us by the hand, belied him, the feeling on his part was no less than on ours. Shaw had given him a horse at Westport. My rifle, an excellent piece, which he had always been fond of using, is now in his hands, and perhaps at this moment its sharp voice is startling the echoes of the Rocky Mountains. On the next morning we left town, and after a fortnight of railroads, coaches, and steamboats, saw once more the familiar features of home.

THE END.

NOTES

The following notes restore almost all the significant passages which Parkman excised from the various versions of *The Oregon Trail* from its first serial publication in the *Knickerbocker Magazine* (K), the two Putnam "editions" of 1849–1852 (49–52), the five Little, Brown "editions" of 1872–1883 (72–83), and the "Illustrated Edition" of 1892 (92). The "Illustrated Edition" is my text; all substantive variants are set against it. I list, for example, 49–52 variant readings against 92, and K variants against 49–52. Other possible combinations include K–52 against 92, or K–83 against 92. Significant K variants against a passage canceled after 49–52 are usually printed within brackets in the restored passage from 49–52, but in a few instances I have given the K reading first and then the 49–52 revision, which in turn is set against the 92 text, simply to show how a given passage has changed through two revisions.

Considerations of typography and design dictate that short passages containing significant variant readings be run into the body of these notes within quotation marks and not set in reduced type.

Notes

1 The dedication to Shaw does not appear in K–52. Shaw (1824–1908), Parkman's first cousin and the bearer of three of the most distinguished names in Massachusetts history, originated the plan of the Oregon Trail trip, as a canceled passage shows, in an attempt to shake off the "effects of a disorder" perhaps brought on by overwork during his last year at Harvard. As Parkman noted in a letter to Frederic Remington on January 7, 1892, in *Letters*, II, 252–253, Shaw was "one of the handsomest men in Boston, though he seemed quite unconscious of being so, having no vanity whatever. He was tall, lithe, and active, and even in the roughest dress, had an air of distinction." Shaw's later career was remarkably successful. In 1860 he married Pauline Agassiz, the youngest daughter of Harvard's famous naturalist, Louis Agassiz; the couple had five children. As one of the founders and president of the great Calumet and Hecla Mining Company, Shaw became one of the richest men in New England, and his growing fortune allowed him an early and successful patronage of French landscape painters, particularly Millet. See *s.v.* "Shaw, Pauline Agassiz" in the *Dictionary of American Biography* (hereafter cited as *DAB*). Despite Parkman's occasionally patronizing tone toward Shaw in *The Oregon Trail*, the two men seem to have remained on good terms during their later lives.

2 The "Preface to the Illustrated Edition" does not appear in K–83. The following introductory note appears only in 49–52:

The journey which the following narrative describes was undertaken on the writer's part with a view of studying the manners and characters of Indians in their primitive state. Although in the chapters which relate to them, he has only attempted to sketch those features of their wild and picturesque life which fell, in the present instance, under his own eye, yet in doing so he has constantly aimed to leave an impression of their character correct as far as it goes. In justifying his claim to accuracy on this point, it is hardly necessary to advert to the representations given by poets and novelists, which, for the most part, are mere creations of fancy. The Indian is certainly entitled to a high rank among savages, but his good qualities are not those of an Uncas or an Outalissi.

The sketches were originally published in the Knickerbocker Magazine, commencing in February, 1847.

Boston, *February* 15, 1849.

Uncas, to whom Parkman refers in this note, is the young Indian hero of James Fenimore Cooper's *The Last of the Mohicans*; "Outalissi" is probably Outacity, or Outaissi, the famous Cherokee chief who visited England in 1762 and whose portrait was painted by Sir Joshua Reynolds. On the night before he sailed for England, he made a farewell speech to his tribesmen with a moving eloquence that was remembered half a century later by Thomas Jefferson. See *DAB, s.v.* "Outacity."

The following introductory note appears only in 72–83:

The "Oregon Trail" is the title under which this book first appeared. It was afterwards changed by the publisher, and is now restored to the form in which it originally stood in the Knickerbocker Magazine. As the early editions were printed in my absence, I did not correct the proofs, a process doubly necessary, since the book was written from dictation. The necessary corrections have been made in the present edition.

The following preface appears only in 52:

PREFACE TO THE THIRD EDITION.

"*This, too, shall pass away,*" were the words graven on the ring of the Persian despot, Nadir Shah, to remind him of the evanescence of all things earthly. *This, too, shall pass away,* was the doom long ago pronounced on all that is primitive in life or scenery within the limits of our national domain; but no one could have dreamed that the decree would find so swift an execution. Less than six years have passed since the incidents related in this volume took place, but that short interval has been the witness of changes almost incredible. The herds of buffalo which blackened the prairies of the Arkansas and the Platte have vanished before the increasing stream of emigrant caravans. Fort Laramie, which then was a mere trading post, occupied by a handful of Canadians, and overawed by surrounding savages, is now a military station of the United States, controlling and regulating the humbled tribes of the adjacent regions. The waste and lonely valley of the Great Salt Lake has become, as if by magic, the seat of a populous city, the hive of a fanatical multitude, whose movements are an object of national importance, and whose character and fortunes form a theme of the highest philosophic interest. Remote and barbarous California, rich in nothing but tallow and cow-hides, is transformed into a modern Ophir, swarming with eager life, and threatening to revolutionize the financial system of the world with the outpourings of its wealth.

Primeval barbarism is assailed at last in front and rear, from the Mississippi and from the Pacific; and, thus brought between two fires, it cannot long sustain itself. With all respect to civilization, I cannot help regretting this final consummation; and such regret will not be misconstrued by any one who has tried the prairie and mountain life, who has learned to look with an affectionate interest on the rifle that was once his companion and protector, the belt that sustained his knife and pistol, and the pipe which beguiled the tedious hours of his midnight watch, while men and horses lay sunk in sleep around him.

The following narrative was written in great measure with the view of preserving, in my own mind, a clear memory of the scenes and adventures which it records. It therefore takes the form of a simple relation of facts, free, for the most part, from reflections or digressions of any kind; and in this circumstance of its origin, the reader will find good assurance of its entire authenticity.

February 1st, 1852.

Nadir Shah (1688–1747), King of Persia from 1737 to 1747, was famous for his extensive conquests in India as well as for his extreme cruelty. With the identification of Salt Lake City as "the hive of a fanatical multitude," Parkman may be referring to Mormonism's symbol of industry and success, the beehive. The allusion to "tallow and cow-hides" may be explained by the fact that New England traded extensively in California leather during the 1830's and 1840's, a commerce which Richard Henry Dana described in *Two Years Before the Mast*.

3 By 1892 the American buffalo (*Bison bison*) was indeed almost extinct within the continental United States; only the determined efforts of conservationists and the establishment of the first of the national parks in the West in 1872 averted the extinction of America's best-known game animal. During the late 1860's and early 1870's buffalo were slaughtered in incredible numbers on their normal grazing ranges in the Dakotas, Nebraska, Kansas, Oklahoma, and Texas; professional hunters killed hundreds a day for their hides and, less often, for their meat, and during the 1890's bleached skeletons in enormous quantities were gathered on the western plains for fertilizer.

Before the period of white settlement the buffalo ranged throughout the temperate regions of North America from northwestern Canada to Texas and as far eastward as

Pennsylvania, Virginia, the Carolinas, and Georgia. They were gregarious animals, often gathering in great herds which wandered erratically and unpredictably. Full-grown bulls often reached a length of more than 11 feet and sometimes weighed more than a ton; the cows were considerably smaller, rarely more than 7 feet long or more than a thousand pounds in weight. Almost all early western travelers agree in their descriptions of buffalo meat as the richest and fattest game they had ever eaten. See E. Lendell Cockrum, *Mammals of Kansas* (Lawrence, Kans., 1952), pp. 276–278.

4 Parkman's reference to arsenic suggests the practice, widespread even during the 1870's and 1880's, of poisoning predators on grazing lands.

The wolf (*Canis lupus*) was formerly to be found almost everywhere within the temperate zones of North America and even within the land areas north of the Arctic Circle. Agriculture and white settlement on the Great Plains drove off the herbivores on which wolves normally subsisted, and between 1850 and 1890 hunters killed thousands of them for their pelts and for the bounties paid for their scalps. As Parkman frequently notes in *The Oregon Trail*, the wolf population of present Kansas and Nebraska depended to a large extent on the buffalo; Cockrum, *Mammals of Kansas*, p. 228, quotes an early Kansas trapper and hunter, J. R. Mead, on the ecological balance which the wolves helped to maintain by their attacks on the buffalo: "Lobo, the mountain wolf, locally known as 'big gray,' were congeners and associates of the buffalo, and lived almost exclusively upon them. Each wolf would kill in the course of the year, it is fair to assume, a dozen buffalo, many of them calves; but they, with equal facility, could kill the strongest bull, and did whenever appetite or circumstances made it most convenient."

The wolf has been extinct in Kansas for more than 60 years and is either extinct or nearly so in Nebraska, eastern Wyoming, and eastern Colorado, the regions Parkman traversed on his Oregon Trail trip.

5 To this day the rattlesnake has never been particularly "bashful and retiring."

6 "Old Ephraim" seems to have been a more common nickname for the grizzly bear than "Old Caleb" or "Old Enoch." On the evidence of *The Oregon Trail* itself and of the notebooks, Parkman never saw a grizzly during his trip to the West. The grizzly bear (*Ursus horribilis*) was for Americans of Parkman's generation and background almost a mythical creature, the fantastic "white bear" of the Lewis and Clark Expedition, of Edwin James's account of the Long Expedition, and of James Fenimore Cooper's *The Prairie*. Scarcely credible stories of single combats between trappers and grizzlies had appeared in popular accounts of western travel and adventure during the 1830's and 1840's, and the grizzly and the Indian became for many Easterners parallel metaphors of the savage mystery of the Far West.

Parkman's description of the grizzly in this paragraph, however, is quite consciously a demonstration of the destruction of "wildness" before encroaching civilization rather than a representation of the real nature of the grizzly bear and its habits. Though the grizzly was the largest bear found within the limits of the continental United States and the only truly omnivorous member of the Ursidae, it was never the bloodthirsty monster of popular imagination. The grizzly could and did pull down and devour a buffalo bull, but it was also usually "diffident" before human beings and scarcely ever showed fight unless it was first persistently attacked. In the United States its range extended from the western edges of the Great Plains throughout the Rocky Mountains and most of the Pacific

Coast; by the end of the nineteenth century the grizzly was almost extinct in this country, and today only small numbers of them can still be found in western national parks and in the mountainous areas of northwestern Montana. See Cockrum, *Mammals of Kansas,* pp. 235–236.

7 Parkman's evident admiration for the mountain men in this passage does not reflect the contemptuous tone of other references to them in *The Oregon Trail.* Parkman is quite correct in suggesting that the great days of the cowboy's frontier were over by 1892.

8 Frederic Remington (1861–1909), perhaps the greatest painter and sculptor of western subjects in the history of American art, had been commissioned in late 1891 to do the illustrations for a new edition of *The Oregon Trail.* Remington knew the West from personal experience; his studio at New Rochelle, New York, was full of cowboy and Indian clothes and weapons and even a dummy horse. See Harold McCracken, *Frederic Remington: Artist of the Old West* (New York, 1947), pp. 60–70. Remington's commission to illustrate the present text of *The Oregon Trail* was of considerable advantage to him; most of his previous work had been done for magazines, though his reputation was on the rise after the wide public acclaim given his illustrations for an 1890 edition of Longfellow's *The Song of Hiawatha,* a book which Parkman might have seen. Remington took a good deal of trouble with the authenticity of the illustrations for the present edition; on several occasions he wrote Parkman to ask for contemporary photographs of him, Shaw, and Henry Chatillon and to secure Parkman's final approval of preliminary sketches of dress and armaments. See *Letters,* II, 252–255.

9 The "Preface to the Fourth Edition" was printed without change in the five editions of 72–83.

10 The serial version of *The Oregon Trail* was published in the *Knickerbocker Magazine* in monthly installments (ex-

cept March and November, 1847, and September and November, 1848) from February, 1847, through February, 1849.

11 Parkman's reference in this passage is to the famous Pike's Peak Gold Rush of 1858–59, the result of what was probably the most important discovery of gold in North America between that at Sutter's Fort in 1848 and the Klondike in 1896.

12 The only way to justify the contrasted ironies at the beginning and at the end of this paragraph is to assume that the "ardor of our rejoicing" at the mixed blessings of "tame cattle" and "farm-houses"—marks of progressive civilization, however destructive of wildness and romance—would have been tempered had they foreseen that civilized vulgarity would also come in the train of civilized virtues. But the passage is sufficiently obscure.

13 The great panorama of thousands of Sioux on the march could, of course, still be seen in 1872 and for years thereafter, especially in 1876 in the vicinity of the Little Big Horn River.

14 This statement might be dismissed as mere rhetoric but for the fact that the operative word is "conspicuous," especially in the sense of "obvious" or even "apparent." However grudgingly, Parkman demonstrates in his great histories a fairly sophisticated appreciation of some of the "merits" of American Indian cultures, and he seems to recognize the tragic displacements these cultures suffered under the increasing pressures of the technologically superior civilization of the whites.

15 By 1872 Parkman had finished four of the eight parts of *France and England in North America. The Conspiracy of Pontiac* had first appeared in 1851, *Pioneers of France in the New World* in 1865, *The Jesuits in North America in the Seventeenth Century* in 1867, and *The Discovery of the Great West* in 1869. The last 20 years of Parkman's life were to see the histories completed; *The Old Régime*

in Canada was published in 1874, *Count Frontenac and New France under Louis XIV* in 1877, *Montcalm and Wolfe* in 1884, and *A Half-Century of Conflict* in 1892, a year before his death.

16 For Henry Chatillon see p. 14 of the present edition and note 12 for that page.

17 For Deslauriers see p. 14 of the present edition and note 8 for that page. Additional information about Raymond will be found on p. 124 and note 12 for that page.

Chapter 1

1 This chapter first appeared in *K* in February, 1847—hence the reference to "Last spring." Parkman reached St. Louis about April 13, Shaw a few days later. See *Journals*, ii, 410–412.

2 Between the sentences "Not . . . Fé" and "The hotels . . . travellers" *K*–52 supply the following additional sentence: "Many of the immigrants, especially of those bound for California, were persons of wealth and standing." Compare also David H. Coyner, *The Lost Trappers* (Cincinnati, 1859), p. 248, on the emigration of 1846: "It may, therefore, be taken for granted, that the emigrants from our state who are seeking a home beyond the Rocky Mountains, belong to the most enterprising and patient and resolute portion of our population, and are very far from being the poorest people in the country." In the allusion to "persons of wealth and standing" bound for California in the emigration of 1846, Parkman might well have been thinking of parties like the George Donner family, who set out from Illinois with a train of splendidly equipped wagons, valuable household goods, and a large sum of cash. See George R. Stewart, *Ordeal by Hunger: The Story of the Donner Party* (New York, 1936), p. 15.

    The number of persons leaving the Missouri frontier for

the Pacific Coast in 1846 has been variously estimated; perhaps the largest figure is found in J. Quinn Thornton, *Oregon and California in 1848* . . . (New York, 1849), I, 80, in which the whole emigration is given at 3,000 people. Hubert Howe Bancroft, *History of Oregon* (San Francisco, 1886–1888), I, 552–553, supplies the smallest figure; he numbered the total emigration of 1846 at 2,500 persons, of whom some 1,500–1,700 went to Oregon and the rest to California. More recent evaluations suggest that California was the primary goal of the emigrant wagons of 1846, for the first time since 1841, and that "Altogether, the Oregon emigration of 1846 may have totalled 1,100 to 1,200 souls. The California emigration in the end may not have been very much larger, say 1,500 men, women, and children." See Dale L. Morgan, ed. *Overland in 1846: Diaries and Letters of the California-Oregon Trail* (Georgetown, Calif., 1963), I, 88, 116. With perhaps 1,000 or more men engaged in the various details of the business, the Santa Fe trade in 1846 was probably the largest yet directed toward Mexican territory. See Louise A. Barry, "Kansas before 1854: A Revised Annals," *Kansas Historical Quarterly* (hereafter cited as *KHQ*), xxx (Autumn, 1964), 394.

3 The *Radnor*, bound up the Missouri River with 60 tons of ammunition and provisions for Kearny's Army of the West, struck a stump and sank near Boonville, Missouri, a day or two before August 3, 1846, by which date news of her loss had reached Fort Leavenworth. The *Radnor* was a comparatively new vessel, having entered the Missouri River traffic in the autumn of 1845. See Barry, "Kansas before 1854," *KHQ*, xxx (Summer, 1964), 238, and xxx (Autumn, 1964), 386; and "The Diary of Henry Standage" reprinted in Frank A. Golder, *The March of the Mormon Battalion* (New York, 1928), p. 142.

4 Though recent authorities have differed on the exact de-

tails of the shape and dimensions of the common Santa Fe
freight wagon, most contemporary illustrations and the
greater part of the evidence in the literature of the Santa
Fe trade suggest that it resembled the familiar Conestoga
wagon. The wagons that Parkman saw might have carried
as much as two and one-half tons of cargo and been drawn
by as many as five yoke of oxen. See Bernard DeVoto, *The
Year of Decision 1846* (Boston, 1943), p. 504; and Henry
Inman, *The Old Santa Fé Trail* (New York, 1897), p. 59.

5 Parkman's "mule-killer" seems to have been what was
almost always known as a "Red River cart."

6 Among the "adventurers" on board the *Radnor* Parkman
noted on April 28 a "party of Baltimoreans—flash genteel
—very showily attired in 'genteel undress,' though bound
for California." See *Journals*, II, 415.

The Kansas, or Kaw, Indians, a tribe of southwestern
Siouan stock, had lived in what is now the state of Kansas,
particularly along the Kansas River, at least from the time
of their earliest contact with white men. By 1825 they had
begun to relinquish their titles to lands in northern Kansas
and northeastern Nebraska; from about 1829 to 1847 their
three permanent villages were located west of the present
site of Topeka, in what is now Shawnee County, Kansas,
close to the eastern and southern borders of their reservation. During the 1830's and 1840's the tribe lived in peace
with the encroaching whites and with most of their Indian
neighbors except the more warlike Pawnees, who frequently raided the Kaw villages. By 1846 the tribe may
have numbered as many as 1,600 persons, though increasing pressure from white settlers and other reservation Indians had forced them to cede another 2 million acres of the
eastern part of their lands in January of that year. See
Frederick Webb Hodge, ed. *Handbook of American Indians North of Mexico* (Washington, 1912), I, 653–656;
and Barry, "Kansas before 1854," *KHQ*, XXVIII (Spring,

1962), 58. The Kansas aboard the *Radnor* were the first true Plains Indians Parkman had met; they did not impress him: "The wretched Caw Indians on board were hired, for a pint of whiskey, to sing. . . . One of the others indulged in a little fooling with a fat Negro, who danced while the Indian sang." See *Journals*, II, 416.

7 Parkman left St. Louis on April 28 and arrived at "Kansas" on May 3; see *Journals*, II, 415–417; and note 13 for page 4 of the present edition. The "seven or eight days" mentioned in this passage would have been a somewhat longer upriver trip than usual.

8 The heavy sedimentation of the lower Missouri River, frequently noted by western travelers, was responsible for the Indian name of the river, the "Big Muddy."

9 Parkman arrived at Blue Mills Landing—the Missouri River *entrepôt* for Independence, six miles inland—on May 2; see *Journals*, II, 417. Independence, founded in 1827, soon became the second starting point for the Santa Fe Trail after the village of Old Franklin was washed away by the Missouri. By 1832, the probable date of the founding of Blue Mills Landing, Independence had become the main outfitting center for the Santa Fe trade, a position which it maintained until the middle 1840's; it was also the usual rendezvous for the California and Oregon emigrations. See Hiram M. Chittenden, *The American Fur Trade of the Far West*, ed. Stallo Vinton (New York, 1935), I, 463–464; and Dean Earl Wood, *The Old Santa Fe Trail from the Missouri River* (Kansas City, Mo., 1951), pp. 1–27. By 1846 the permanent population of Independence may have numbered as many as 800 or 900 persons.

10 Parkman's "Spaniards" were in fact Mexicans. Compare Edwin Bryant, *What I Saw in California . . .* (New York, 1848), p. 13, on similar scenes in Independence: "I noticed, among the busy multitudes moving to and fro

through the streets, a large number of New-Mexicans, and half-breed Indians, with their dusky complexions and ragged and dirty costumes. They were generally mounted on miserably poor mules and horses, and presented a most shabby appearance."

11 Parkman seems to use the terms "French" and "Canadian" indiscriminately to refer both to French-speaking Americans from St. Louis and the old settlements in Illinois and to Canadian French from Quebec, many of whom had gravitated to the American fur trade during the 1820's and 1830's.

12 Parkman's approving notice of these emigrants is sharply in contrast to the contemptuous tone of most of his other descriptions of the California and Oregon pioneers he met along the trail.

13 Parkman and Shaw reached "Kanzas" on May 3; see *Journals*, II, 417. "Kansas"—the usual spelling of the Missouri River beginnings of present Kansas City, Missouri—was organized in 1838 by a 14-member Town Company hurriedly organized to purchase the Gabriel Prudhomme estate, a 257-acre property fronting on the river and containing Westport Landing, a site occasionally used in the 1830's for steamer off-loading for Westport, four miles to the south. By 1839 a number of lots had been sold in "Kansas," and Thomas A. Smart had built a log warehouse at Westport Landing. But, except for seasonal trading, particularly with newly arrived bands of reservation Indians from the East, "Kansas" did not begin to flourish until after 1846, when the legality of the Prudhomme estate title sale was finally determined and the Town Company filed a new survey and town plat. During the early 1840's "Westport Landing" and "Kansas" seem to have been used more or less synonymously for the same place. See Barry, "Kansas before 1854," *KHQ*, XXIX (Summer, 1963), 161–162; and Wood, *Old Santa Fe Trail*, pp. 38–60.

The original "Kansas" was laid out just west of Chou-teau's Landing, where Francis G. Chouteau had located in 1826 for the Indian trade. By about the same date, a number of frontiersmen and retired mountain men seem to have built log cabins in the area, particularly at the "Kawsmouth," or "Kansasmouth," French settlement. See Barry, "Kansas before 1854," *KHQ*, xxviii (Spring, 1962), 25; and Wood, *Old Santa Fe Trail*, pp. 8–39.

14 William Miles Chick (1790–1847), born in Lynchburg, Virginia, came to Missouri as early as 1822. By 1836 he had settled at Westport, purchased a store, and become the town's second postmaster. He was one of the original members of the Town Company which purchased the site of "Kansas" in 1838 and he himself moved there in 1843. By 1846 he had a warehouse on the banks of the Missouri and had built the first house on the bluffs above the river. His title was perhaps derived from his postmastership at Westport. See Alfred S. Waugh, *Travels in Search of the Elephant; The Wanderings of Alfred S. Waugh, Artist, in Louisiana, Missouri, and Santa Fe, in 1845–46*, ed. John Francis McDermott (St. Louis, 1951), p. 20 n.; and Barry, "Kansas before 1854," *KHQ*, xxix (Spring, 1963), 42, and xxix (Summer, 1963), 161–162. In the years after 1842, Frémont outfitted his expeditions at Chick's warehouse at "Kansas"; see Wood, *Old Santa Fe Trail*, p. 52. Chick's hospitality drew generous comment from other prairie travelers; compare Lewis H. Garrard, *Wah-To-Yah and the Taos Trail*, ed. Ralph P. Bieber (Glendale, Calif., 1938), p. 52: "Colonel Chick, the principal man at Kan-sas, treated me kindly during my stay, and with his clever sons, the horse ferry, skiffs, and duck shooting, afforded entertainment."

15 Parkman seems to have made his first visit to Westport on May 4; see *Journals*, ii, 417–418. The nucleus of Westport, also a part of modern Kansas City, Missouri, was the post

office first established at "Shawnee," Jackson County, Missouri, in 1832 and later changed to "West Port" in 1834 by John C. McCoy, the first postmaster, whose log-cabin store stood at the intersection of the present Westport and Pennsylvania avenues. McCoy filed his town plat of "West Port" for record in 1835. The new town was 12 miles from Independence and five or six miles from Chouteau's Landing. By the late 1830's Westport's strategic position had gained it a commanding position in trade with the newly arrived reservation Indians from the East who had located just west of the Missouri state line. See Barry, "Kansas before 1854," *KHQ*, xxviii (Autumn, 1962), 351–352; and Wood, *Old Santa Fe Trail*, pp. 32–59.

Westport's increasing importance for the Santa Fe caravans and the fur trade during the late 1830's and early 1840's can be traced in part to the excellent pasturage available on the prairies around the village and to its excellent position on the westernmost Missouri frontier. As Irene D. Paden, *The Wake of the Prairie Schooner* (New York, 1943), p. 20, has pointed out, Westport and its landing were "the unbeatable geographical location. If the river freight intended for Santa Fe went farther up the Missouri, it had to be landed north of the Kansas [River]; this entailed a difficult river crossing and was not to be considered. If it remained farther downstream, a longer wagon haul was necessary, which took time and was costly." By 1846 Westport could show a number of brick buildings and a permanent population of as many as 700 people. See Federal Writers' Project, *The Oregon Trail: The Missouri River to the Pacific Ocean* (New York, 1939), pp. 44–45.

16 The Sauks, an Algonquin tribe, figured largely in the history of the Old Northwest, particularly in Wisconsin and Illinois, though they were first discovered by white men in northern Michigan. Perhaps the most important event in

their recorded history occurred about 1750, when they formally allied themselves with their Algonquin kinsmen, the Foxes; at about the same time the Sauks moved from their villages near the head of Green Bay and crossed the Mississippi River into territory claimed by the Iowa Indians. By 1804, a band of Sauks who wintered annually at St. Louis began negotiations which finally culminated in large land cessions in Illinois and southern Wisconsin. The Foxes, enraged at the folly of the Missouri River Sauks, gradually abandoned the alliance and over the course of the next 20 years moved to new hunting grounds in Iowa. In 1832, presumably over conflicting claims made to the terms of a series of land cessions along the Rock River in Illinois, the Sauks rose under Black Hawk in a futile war which was easily suppressed. The surviving Illinois and Wisconsin Sauks took refuge with the Iowa Foxes; some of them remained in Iowa until 1842, though the Missouri River Sauks had removed as early as 1837 to their new reservation in present Doniphan County, Kansas, close to the Iowa reserve and directly north of the Kickapoos' territory, where they were joined by a number of Foxes also from Missouri. In December, 1845, other bands of Sauks and Foxes from Iowa under Chief Keokuk were encamped on the Shawnee reservation, south of the Kansas River in present Douglas County, Kansas, where they remained until the autumn of 1846; these may have been the tribesmen Parkman saw in May. See John R. Swanton, *The Indian Tribes of North America* (Washington, 1952), pp. 256–260; Hodge, ed. *Handbook of American Indians,* I, 472–474, and II, 471–480; and Barry, "Kansas before 1854," *KHQ,* xxix (Spring, 1963), 67, xxx (Summer, 1964), 242, and xxx (Autumn, 1964), 348.

The Shawnees—as the tribal name is usually spelled— were an Algonquin tribe whose hunting grounds at the time of their first encounters with white men were to be found in the Cumberland Basin of Tennessee and on the middle Savannah River in South Carolina. Frequently allied with the Delawares, the Shawnees were an extremely powerful and warlike tribe. After a good deal of wandering in the eighteenth century, a large number of Shawnees located permanently on the upper Ohio River on land granted them by the Wyandots. For a period of about 40 years—from the beginning of the French and Indian War to the Treaty of Greenville in 1795—the Shawnees were almost constantly at war with the English or the Americans; they ravaged the advancing line of frontier settlements in Kentucky, and almost all the expeditions sent across the Ohio River during the Revolutionary period were directed against them. After 1783 the Ohio Shawnees found themselves without British assistance, and some members of the tribe moved south to join the hostile Creeks and Cherokees. Another and larger group accepted the invitation of the Spanish government to settle in what is now Missouri and moved there about 1793. These Missouri Shawnees were joined by other members of the tribe after the Battle of Greenville in 1795, but scattered bands of Shawnees still remained in Ohio and Indiana. The last great Shawnee outbreak, under the Prophet, was crushed at Tippecanoe in 1811, though the Prophet's brother, the famous Tecumseh, led parts of the tribe at the Battle of the Thames in 1813. See Hodge, ed. *Handbook of American Indians*, ii, 530–537; and Swanton, *Indian Tribes*, pp. 225–229.

By 1825 many of the Missouri Shawnees had been persuaded to move to a reservation in present Shawnee Township, Wyandotte County, Kansas, south of the Kansas River and close to its mouth. These reservation Shawnees received further accessions from Missouri in 1826 and from Ohio in 1832 and 1833. See Barry, "Kansas before 1854," *KHQ*, xxviii (Spring, 1962), 48, and xxviii (Autumn, 1962), 334–335. The Shawnees' reservation ran at least 120 miles west of the Missouri state line, and the tribe may have numbered as many as 1,600 persons in 1844. See Rufus B. Sage, *Scenes in the Rocky Mountains . . . ,* reprinted in *Rufus B. Sage, His Letters and Papers, 1836–1847,* eds. LeRoy R. Hafen and Ann W. Hafen (Glendale, Calif., 1956), I, 122.

The Delawares, Cooper's "Leni Lenape," were at one time in their history the most important eastern tribe of Algonquin stock; they figured largely in the histories of colonial New York and Pennsylvania. During the latter half of the eighteenth century they moved slowly westward through the present states of Ohio and Indiana; in the late colonial and post-Revolutionary Indian wars culminating in the Treaty of Greenville they showed themselves determined foes of the encroaching whites. A part of the tribe moved to Missouri about 1789, where some of them remained, though other Delawares found their way as far south as Arkansas and Texas. See Hodge, ed. *Handbook of American Indians,* I, 385–387; and Swanton, *Indian Tribes,* pp. 48–55.

By November, 1830, about 100 Delawares living on the James Fork of the White River in southwestern Missouri established a settlement in northern Wyandotte County, Kansas, on the north bank of the Kansas River a few miles above its mouth. These Missouri Delawares were soon joined by parties from Ohio and from the "Spanish country" to the south. By 1835 all the Delawares had reached their Kansas reservation, predominately a very long and very narrow strip of territory running nearly 300 miles west of the Missouri line and north of the Kansas Indians' reserve. See Barry, "Kansas before 1854," *KHQ,* XXVIII (Summer, 1962), 177–178.

The Delawares seem to have been one of the very few tribes to exchange successfully a forest culture for the radically different life of the plains; almost every fur brigade had at least one Delaware hunter or trapper with it. The Delawares' impetuous bravery was well known, as Parkman noted at Westport on May 7: "Everybody here is full of praises of the courage of the Delawares. They are by far greater wanderers and hunters than any of the other half-civilized tribes. In small parties they spend years among the most remote and hostile tribes—they will fight with a courage like desperation, and, it is said, completely awed the Spaniards at Santa Fe." See *Journals*, II, 420.

The Wyandots were an essentially Iroquoian tribe composed of the scattered fragments of that great Huron Nation almost completely dispersed and destroyed by the Five Nations of the Iroquois Confederacy in the seventeenth century. At about the beginning of the eighteenth century, remnants of the tribe moved from the vicinity of Mackinac Island, their place of refuge after the attacks of the Iroquois, and began to reestablish themselves in Ohio, particularly around the present sites of Detroit and Sandusky. During the late eighteenth and early nineteenth centuries the Wyandots exercised a paramount influence over the other tribes of that area and supported the British in the War of 1812. They began ceding their Ohio lands as early as 1819, and by 1843 they had settled on the eastern section of the Delawares' reserve in present Wyandotte County, Kansas. The Wyandots, numbering about 600 in 1843, were the last Indians to leave Ohio; they seem to have been distinctly more civilized than most of the other tribes on the Kansas reservations. See Swanton, *Indian Tribes*, pp. 233–236; Hodge, ed. *Handbook of American Indians*, I, 584–591; and Barry, "Kansas before 1854," *KHQ*, XXIX (Winter, 1963), 483.

Parkman has been meeting, in "Kansas" and Westport, many of the tribesmen whose histories would become a part of his *France and England in North America*.

17 Captain Bill Chandler and his brother Jack were Irishmen,
probably in their forties; Romaine, the leader of their party,
seems to have been both younger and better educated than
his companions. According to Parkman's letter of May 12,
1846, to his mother in *Letters*, I, 38–39, Romaine had
"been on this route before—in 1841." The date thus identifies him as the Romaine who traveled with Father De
Smet's mission party of that year, under the direction of
Tom Fitzpatrick and in company part of the way with the
Bartleson-Bidwell company of emigrants. See John Bid-
well, *A Journey to California in 1841: The Journal of John
Bidwell*, ed. Francis P. Farquhar (Berkeley, 1964), p. 19;
Pierre-Jean De Smet, S.J., *Letters and Sketches: With a
Narrative of a Year's Residence among the Indian Tribes
of the Rocky Mountains*, in R. G. Thwaites, ed. *Early
Western Travels* (Cleveland, 1906) XXVII, 198; and
Hiram M. Chittenden and Alfred Talbot Richardson, eds.
*Life, Letters, and Travels of Father Pierre-Jean De Smet,
S.J. . . .* (New York, 1905), I, 276–295. Romaine traveled
as far west as the Green River and turned back toward the
settlements on July 25, arriving in Missouri in September,
1841. De Smet characterized Romaine as "of good English
family, and like most of his countrymen, fond of travel."
Romaine was also "jealous of the honor of his nation," a
trait which particularly appears in Parkman's notebook
entries and in several canceled passages in *The Oregon
Trail* itself. Romaine was about 30 when he set out on his
second trip to the prairies, and his age makes it possible
that he was the William Govett Romaine (1815–1893), a
Templar and graduate of Trinity College, who later served
in the Crimean War and rose to high rank in the Indian
and Egyptian judiciaries. See *s.v.* "Romaine, William
Govett" in the *Dictionary of National Biography* (hereafter cited as *DNB*). A long-canceled passage (see p. 51 of
the present edition and note 13 for that page) shows that

Romaine was well acquainted with the popular authors of the day; he seems to have had a legal background sufficient to allow him to write commentaries on some of Justice Joseph Story's decisions. Parkman's picture of Romaine in the present edition is considerably softened from that in K–52, where Romaine is shown as both foolish and foppish, for "although he had the usual complement of eyes and ears, the avenues between these organs and his brain appeared remarkably narrow and untrodden."

The Chandlers, touring the West at Romaine's invitation, seemed to Parkman far more congenial than their arrogant leader, even though the Captain showed what Parkman considered an excessive timidity and Jack was simply dull-witted. Captain Bill Chandler had served in the British Army for some 20 years before retiring to his estate near Dublin, where he lived with Jack, formerly a sailor. The Captain had seen service in Canada and Jamaica, and the attractions of the big game of the prairies and mountains had led him to accept Romaine's invitation to a cross-continent excursion, by 1846 a fairly common adventure for well-heeled sportsmen. Romaine and the Chandlers were established in St. Louis as early as April 6, when they are mentioned in the columns of the St. Louis *Weekly Reveille* as "a party of English gentlemen . . . now in our city, preparing for a trip in the mountains and through the countries to the Pacific." They appear again in the St. Louis *Missouri Republican* eight days later, by which time Parkman had probably met them. See Morgan, ed. *Overland in 1846*, II, 495, 499. A canceled passage (see p. 120 of the present edition and note 32 for that page) shows that Romaine left the Chandlers when their party reached Oregon City, in 1846 the center of American settlement in Oregon. The Captain's reticence about Romaine's subsequent activities allows a reasonable inference that, like George Frederick Ruxton, Romaine was a secret agent for the British during the period of the Oregon Boundary Dispute and "54-40 or Fight." See Bernard DeVoto, *Across the Wide Missouri* (Boston, 1947), p. 417.

18 Neither Sorel nor the English party's muleteer, hereafter called "Wright," can be positively identified.

19 Parkman visited Independence on May 7; see *Journals*, II, 418–419. On that date several emigrant parties were encamped on the Santa Fe Trail south of the town, notably at "Russell's Encampment" 12 miles out and at "Harlan's Camp," yet another 12 miles down the Trail. See "Laon [George L. Curry] to the St. Louis *Reveille*, 'On the Trace,' May 6, 1846," reprinted in Morgan, ed. *Overland in 1846*, II, 513–515. On May 7, William H. Russell, now accompanied by Edwin Bryant, moved his wagon another four miles, but his party still seems to be the one Parkman refers to here. See Bryant, *What I Saw in California*, pp. 23–26. Parkman had heard of Russell's growing company from Passed Midshipman Selim E. Woodworth (see note 26 for page 8). Woodworth returned with Parkman to Westport on the evening of May 7 and told Parkman, quite correctly, that Russell's party would organize on May 11. See *Journals*, II, 419; Bryant, *What I Saw in California*, pp. 30–31; "R. [William H. Russell] to the *Missouri Republican*, 'Indian Country, 20 Miles West of Independence, May 10, 1846,'" reprinted in Morgan, ed. *Overland in 1846*, II, 519–520; and "Laon [George L. Curry] to the St. Louis *Reveille*, 'Camping Ground, Shawnee Country, May 11, 1846,'" reprinted *ibid.*, II, 520–523. Curry's letter to the *Reveille* reports that the organization of Russell's company did in fact occur at Indian Creek on May 11. On May 10 Russell estimated the number of persons in his party at about 500. There may have been as many as 1,000 people encamped around Independence and

Westport in the first week of May, 1846, but Parkman's figure seems rather high.

20 This party of emigrants cannot be positively identified; compare Parkman's notebook description of them in *Journals*, II, 419:

> While I was at the Noland House [in Independence], the last arrival of emigrants came down the street with about twenty waggons, having just broken up their camp near Independence and set out for the great rendezvous about 15 miles beyond Westport. What is remarkable, this body, as well as a very large portion of the emigrants, were from the extreme western states—N. England sends but a small proportion, but they are better furnished than the rest. Some of these ox-wagons contained large families of children, peeping from under the covering. One remarkably pretty little girl was seated on horseback, holding a parasol over her head to keep off the rain. All looked well—but what a journey before them! The men were hardy and good-looking. As I passed the waggons, I observed three old men, with their whips in their hands, discussing some point of theology—though this is hardly the disposition of the mass of the emigrants.

This party could *not* have been the Donners, who apparently did not reach Independence until May 10 and departed it on May 12. See "The Miller-Reed Diary" and "Mrs. George Donner to Eliza Poor, Independence, Missouri, May 11, 1846," reprinted in Morgan, ed. *Overland in 1846*, I, 256, and II, 526–527. The Thorntons also left Independence on May 12. See Thornton, *Oregon and California in 1848*, I, 13–17. Parkman may, however, be referring to the Pringle company of Missouri, which reached Independence on May 7 and passed four miles beyond it before encamping. See "The Diary of Virgil Pringle," reprinted in Morgan, ed. *Overland in 1846*, I, 166.

21 This passage has frequently been cited to illustrate Parkman's Brahmin ignorance of frontier democracy and his toplofty Bostonian prejudices, and the preponderance of evidence does indeed suggest that most members of the emigration of 1846 were no better or worse than other Americans who decided to stay at home. A good deal of contemporary evdence might be cited to prove Thornton's comment in *Oregon and California in 1848*, I, 27, that "The majority [of the emigrants] were plain, honest, substantial, intelligent, enterprising, and virtuous. They were indeed much superior to those who usually settle a new country." Parkman's own notebooks show that he was well aware of at least one important reason for the emigrations to California and Oregon, the fevers and agues of the Mississippi Valley; compare *Journals*, II, 442: "The bad climate seems to have been the motive that has induced many of them to set out."

Parkman's insensitivity to the promise of the next horizon and his indifference to the mystic call of Manifest Destiny were not peculiar to him alone; compare James Clyman's amazement at the emigration of 1846 in *James Clyman, Frontiersman: The Adventures of a Trapper and Covered-Wagon Emigrant as Told in His Own Reminiscences and Diaries*, ed. Charles L. Camp (Portland, 1960), p. 224: "It is remarkable how anxious thes people are to hear from the Pacific country and strange that so many of all kinds and classes of People should sell out comfortable homes in Missouri and Elsewhare pack up and start across an emmence Barren waste to settle in some new Place of which they have at most so uncertain information but this is the character of my countrymen[.]" Unlike Parkman, Clyman *had* seen Oregon and California and was on his way home to Wisconsin. To Thornton, *Oregon and California in 1848*, I, 26, the last word, however, belongs: "The motives which thus brought this multitude together were, in fact, almost as various as their features. They agreed in one general object —that of bettering their condition. . . ."

22 Boisverd, who must have been hired by Romaine and the Chandlers as another hunter and guide, remains unidentified.

23 Romaine's camp—seven miles from Westport—must thus have been on or very near the banks of the Kansas River, though Parkman does not make this point absolutely clear.

24 At this point the ascertainable chronology of *The Oregon Trail* differs from that of the notebooks. The "deluge" and Parkman's visit to "Kansas" occurred on May 6, the day before the scenes in Independence described on pp. 6–7 of the present text. See *Journals*, II, 418, and compare Edwin Bryant's account of the same storm in *What I Saw in California*, p. 24: "About five o'clock, P.M. a very black and threatening cloud, which had been gathering for some hours in the west, rose over us, and discharged rain with the copiousness of a water-spout, accompanied with brilliant and incessant flashes of lightning, and crashing peals of thunder. The scene, during the violence of the storm, was inexpressibly grand. I had never previously witnessed any meteoric displays comparable with it."

25 At this point *The Oregon Trail* and Parkman's notebooks entirely contradict one another, though it is clear from the latter that this passage simply telescopes the events of three separate days. On May 6 Parkman rode from his base, Chick's house at "Kansas," to Westport to pick up the pair of mules he had purchased from Louis Vogle [Parkman's "Vogel"] and then led them back to Chick's. On May 7 he visited Independence and returned the same day to "Kansas" by way of Westport. On May 8, probably in the afternoon, he and the rest of the party moved over the four miles from "Kansas" to Westport, where they

undoubtedly spent the night of May 8–9. Thus May 8 must have been "the next day" of this passage, and the Captain, riding back from his camp near the Kansas River crossing, had left Westport before Parkman and his party arrived. See *Journals*, II, 418–421.

26 Parkman's notebook entry for May 7 in *Journals*, II, 419, gives an even more vivid picture of Westport: "Woodworth parades a revolver in his belt, which he insists is necessary—and it may be a prudent precaution, for the place seems full of desperadoes—all arms are loaded, as I have had occasion to observe. Life is held in little esteem." Passed Midshipman Selim E. Woodworth, the son of the author of "The Old Oaken Bucket," joined the emigration of 1846 as a bearer of dispatches to Oregon announcing the termination of Joint Occupancy. Other and more sinister or exhilarating rumors, perhaps spread by Woodworth himself, hinted at an expedition against Santa Fe. See De-Voto, *Year of Decision*, pp. 425–426. Parkman had first met Woodworth in St. Louis on or about April 16 and would encounter him again on June 4 on the Platte. See *Journals*, II, 411, 434.

After his arrival at Oregon City, Woodworth moved down to California, where he appeared in time to be placed in command of the San Francisco contingent of volunteers fitting out for the rescue of the doomed Donner party. As DeVoto, *Year of Decision*, p. 442, remarks, "Passed Midshipman Woodworth was just no damned good," for his cowardice and sloth kept him well below the Sierra and thus out of danger while the survivors of the Donner disaster—those not already dead or dying at "Cannibal Camp"—were straggling over the frozen lake and down the agonizing western slopes of the mountains. Woodworth's feeble attempt to lead the Donner Relief was a fiasco, timid in execution and hopeless in result. See De-Voto, *Year of Decision*, pp. 425–443, and Stewart, *Ordeal by Hunger*, pp. 156–157. Compare also "The Miller-Reed Diary"; *Illinois Journal*, Springfield, December 9, 1847, 'Narrative of Sufferings of a Company of Emigrants in the Mountains of California, in the Winter of '46 and '7 by J. F. Reed, Late of Sangamon County, Illinois' "; "Diary of Patrick Breen"; and "Diaries of the Donner Relief," all reprinted in Morgan, ed. *Overland in 1846*, I, 245–368.

27 Compare the sentence "As . . . door" with its *K*–52 form: "As we passed this establishment, we saw Vogel's broad German face and knavish-looking eyes thrust from his door." Louis Vogle, or "Vogel," whose dramshop seems to have been located on Pennsylvania Avenue near Westport Road in modern Kansas City, Missouri, is fairly frequently mentioned in books of western travel and adventure. By 1848 he had become a considerable landholder in Westport. See Wood, *Old Santa Fe Trail*, pp. 65, 198.

28 Parkman's "dissatisfaction" seems rather ingenuous, for, had Romaine's party not meant to abandon "the course of the traders"—probably the combined Oregon and Santa Fe Trails which ran west together for about 30 miles, to the present site of Gardner, Kansas—they would hardly have prepared to cross the Kansas River so close to its mouth. The First Dragoons under Kearny had marched to South Pass in 1845.

29 Parkman, Shaw, Chatillon, and Deslauriers left Westport on May 9. See *Journals*, II, 420.

30 Parkman has forgotten that his party "jumped off" for the prairies from Westport, four miles south of the river; see p. 8 of the present edition and note 25 for that page. In fact, he is remembering an event that occurred before they left "Kansas" on May 8. See *Journals*, II, 420.

31 Albert Gallatin Boone (1806–1882), one of the younger children of Jesse Bryan Boone (a son of Daniel Boone) and Chloe Van Bibber Boone, arrived with his family in Westport in 1838 after an adventurous youth in the fur

trade, in which his name occurs at least as early as 1825. In 1846 his company, Boone and Hamilton, was one of the most important general outfitters in Westport, where he remained until the beginning of the Civil War. See Lilian Hays Oliver, *Some Boone Descendants and Kindred of the St. Charles District* (n.p., 1954), pp. 39–40; *The West of William H. Ashley* . . . , ed. Dale L. Morgan (Denver, 1964), p. 301; and Barry, "Kansas before 1854," *KHQ*, xxix (Summer, 1963), 153. Later in this Oregon Trail summer Parkman would meet or hear of two other members of A. G. Boone's family, his older brother, Alphonso Boone, and his older sister, Panthea Grant Boone Boggs, on the way to the Pacific Coast with their families. See p. 136 of the present edition and note 34 for that page.

CHAPTER II

1 Before the sentence "Emerging . . . Atlantic" K–52 supply the following additional paragraph at the beginning of Chapter ii.

Both Shaw and myself were tolerably inured to the vicissitudes of travelling. We had experienced them under various forms, and a birch canoe was as familiar to us as a steamboat. The restlessness, the love of wilds and hatred of cities, natural perhaps in early years to every unperverted son of Adam, was not our only motive for undertaking the present journey. My companion hoped to shake off the effects of a disorder that had impaired a constitution originally hardy and robust; and I was anxious to pursue some inquiries relative to the character and usages of the remote Indian nations, being already familiar with many of the border tribes.

2 Parkman's party was following the "Mission Road" running almost due west from Westport. See Wood, *Old Santa Fe Trail*, pp. 226–227.

3 I am indebted to Professor Hugh Iltis of the Department

of Botany of the University of Wisconsin for an identification of Parkman's "Indian apple" as probably *Malus ioensis,* or the Iowa crabapple.

4 Parkman's description of Chatillon would have fit any seasoned hunter or trapper from 1820 to 1860. His heavy blanket-coat was often a luxury item in the mountains and might have had a hood, like a Canadian capôte. Most mountain men carried a 10-inch "Green River" butcher knife, sometimes called a "common scalper" in the Indian trade. The ordinary trapper's rifle—the best was made by the Hawken brothers of St. Louis and cost about $40—was shorter and heavier in weight than the usual Kentucky rifle. See DeVoto, *Across the Wide Missouri,* pp. 418–419.

5 Shaw's outfit deserves further explanation. His "Spanish" saddle, resembling a Mexican *vaquero*'s, had a high pommel and cantle and was considerably stronger and heavier in frame and housing than the ordinary gentleman's riding saddle to which Parkman and Shaw were accustomed. The "trail-rope" was simply a long tether, probably of braided rawhide, which could easily be converted into what Parkman calls a "lariette," or lasso. Both young men carried rifled muzzle-loading percussion-cap pistols, apparently of a fairly large caliber. Shaw's "double-barrelled smoothbore" musket or "gun," in distinction to Parkman's rifle, may have fired an ounce ball; such a bullet was not uncommon in the 1830's and 1840's. See James Josiah Webb, *Adventures in the Santa Fé Trade 1844–1847,* ed. Ralph P. Bieber (Glendale, Calif., 1931), p. 73. Parkman's 15-pound Kentucky rifle must have been an uncommonly heavy one; either its weight is wrong, or it fired rather a larger ball than even the usual "half-ounce of Galena" of the trapper's rifle. See DeVoto, *Across the Wide Missouri,* pp. 418–419.

6 Parkman wore his red flannel shirt like a rifle frock or hunting shirt.

7 Though of French lineage and language, Deslauriers was still sufficiently a Missouri mule skinner to call a slow or stubborn mule a "Holy son of a bitch"—a surprisingly strong epithet even in untranslated French.

8 Antoine De Laurier ("Delorier" in K–52) appears, by the evidence of Father Nicholas Point, S.J., to have been one of the 23 squaw men at the "Kawsmouth" French settlement in 1840. See Barry, "Kansas before 1854," *KHQ*, xxix (Autumn, 1963), 337, and xxx (Autumn, 1964), 350–351. St. Jean Baptiste is the patron saint of French Canada.

9 *"Bourgeois"* was a title usually applied to the leader of a fur brigade or to the "boss" of a trading post.

10 Parkman received invaluable assistance in organizing his Oregon Trail trip from Pierre Chouteau, Jr., & Company, the successor to Astor's American Fur Company and in 1846 still a powerful force in the mountain fur trade.

11 For Simoneau see p. 102 of the present text and note 40 for that page.

12 The best and most complete account of Henry Chatillon's life and career will be found in an article by Mrs. James L. O'Leary, "Henry Chatillon," *Missouri Historical Society Bulletin*, xxii, 2, pt. 1 (January, 1966), 123–142, the primary source for much of the factual information given below. Chatillon was born about 1808 in Carondelet, the old French settlement near St. Louis which his grandfather had founded in 1767; at his death in 1873 Chatillon's age was given as 65, and so he may have been closer to 40 than to the age which Parkman gives him here. Of his earlier career in the mountains little is certainly known, though it seems probable that his connection with the American Fur Company and its successors considerably antedated his first meeting with Parkman in the offices of Pierre Chouteau, Jr., & Company. He may have been the "Henry Chaleon" who went west in 1843 as a hunter in Sir William Drummond Stewart's famous excursion to the

Wind River Mountains. See Matthew C. Field, *Prairie and Mountain Sketches*, eds. Kate L. Gregg and John Francis McDermott (Norman, 1957), p. xlviii.

Chatillon was in many ways the best best guide Parkman could have chosen, for he was married or at least connected with Bear Robe, the daughter of Bull Bear, the principal chief among the Oglala Sioux until his death in 1841; Chatillon was thus allied to the most powerful family in the Indian villages Parkman was to visit. As late as 1931 Chatillon was remembered as "Yellow Whiteman" among the reservation Sioux at Pine Ridge, South Dakota, where several of his descendants still lived. See George E. Hyde, *Red Cloud's Folk: A History of the Oglala Sioux Indians* (Norman, 1937), pp. 53–60.

Whether Chatillon was ever a trapper before 1846 cannot be determined, though in his Oregon Trail notebooks Parkman set down Chatillon's recollections of "his adventures at one of the *blows-out* given by the bourgeois at the Yellow Stone, where the traders come in the spring. It was very characteristic. This is the custom at all the forts." See *Journals*, II, 437. If the post at the "Yellow Stone" be read to mean Fort Union, Chatillon's early association with the American Fur Company is assured, and his activities in 1847 as a hunter for Captain Joseph La Barge in the upper Missouri River steamboat traffic take on a new significance: Chatillon had known that part of the wilderness before, perhaps as a trapper or hunter under the great Kenneth McKenzie, until 1834 the *bourgeois* of Fort Union. This post at one time possessed a surreptitious distillery for the Indian trade—hence Parkman's reference to Chatillon's peculiar "*blows-out.*" For Captain La Barge of the *Martha* Chatillon hunted along the Missouri, caching each day's supply of game at convenient places along the bank. In later years, according to Chittenden, La Barge remembered Chatillon as "a fine man, an excellent hunter, and sensible and gentlemanly in all his relations." See

Hiram M. Chittenden, *History of Early Steamboat Navigation on the Missouri River: Life and Adventures of Joseph La Barge* (New York, 1903), p. 126.

By the end of 1847 Chatillon was probably back in St. Louis. On October 5, 1848, he married Odile Delor Lux, a wealthy widow, and for the next few years led what seems to have been a fairly uneventful life, working as a housebuilder and conducting minor real-estate speculations in St. Louis. By February 17, 1853, the date of his third extant letter to Parkman, Chatillon was claiming a fortune of $50,000 or $60,000, but "I am in Trouble all the time." In 1854 he joined Sir George Gore's luxurious hunting excursion to the Rocky Mountains, but the titled sportsman and Chatillon did not agree and parted company at Fort Laramie, where Jim Bridger took Chatillon's place as the party's guide.

For the next dozen years of his life Chatillon apparently remained in St. Louis, where Parkman visited him in 1867 and received a daguerreotype of his old friend taken at the time of his wedding in 1848. Parkman reported the visit and Chatillon's appearance in a letter to his sister, Eliza Parkman: "He is much broken down & by no means so rich as reported." See *Letters*, II, 16. Chatillon died on August 7, 1873, and was buried in Mount Olive Catholic Cemetery in St. Louis. Chatillon's 1848 daguerreotype will be found facing p. 62 of vol. I of the *Letters*; his four dictated letters to Parkman will be found in Mrs. O'Leary's excellent article cited above.

In a letter to Frederic Remington on January 7, 1892, in *Letters*, II, 252–253, Parkman wrote that in 1846 Henry Chatillon was "the most striking combination of strength and symmetry I have ever seen," and canceled passages in K–52, especially one comparing Chatillon to Napoleon and Lord Nelson, show even more clearly than does the present text how greatly Parkman admired his guide and friend. Chatillon became for Parkman a white surrogate for the Indian "Noble Savage," that untutored child of innocent Nature, for whom he had searched in vain among the Sioux; a canceled passage at the end of the K–52 versions of *The Oregon Trail* might with considerable justice be called almost ecstatic in its praise of Henry Chatillon as a symbol of natural freedom, simplicity, and goodness. The strength of Parkman's generous response to Chatillon's life and character evoked a like response from Parkman's greater contemporary, Herman Melville, who had himself spent a season among the savages and had published an unsigned review of *The California and Oregon Trail* in the *Literary World*, iv, 113 (March 31, 1849), 292:

> There, too, he [the reader of *The California and Oregon Trail*] will make the acquaintance of Henry Chatillon, Esq., as gallant a gentleman, and hunter, and trapper, as ever shot buffalo. For this Henry Chatillon we feel a fresh and unbounded love. He belongs to a class of men, of whom Kit Carson is the model; a class, unique, and not to be transcended in interest by any personage introduced to us by Scott. Long live and hunt Henry Chatillon! May his good rifle never miss fire; and where he roves through the prairies, may the buffalo for ever abound!

13 Chatillon's "excess of easy generosity, not conducive to thriving in the world"—a properly Bostonian euphemism, perhaps, for Chatillon's *blows-out*—recalls George F. Ruxton's more detailed picture of trapper extravagance in *Adventures in Mexico and the Rocky Mountains*, reprinted in *Ruxton of the Rockies*, ed. LeRoy R. Hafen (Norman, 1950), p. 231: "An old trapper, a French Canadian, assured me that he had received fifteen thousand dollars for beaver during a sojourn of twenty years in the mountains. Every year he resolved in his mind to return to Canada, and, with this object, always converted his fur into cash;

but a fortnight at the rendezvous always cleaned him out, and, at the end of twenty years, he had not even credit sufficient to buy a pound of powder."

14 Chatillon's 30 dead grizzlies may not impress a modern reader as much as they did Parkman, who was of course well aware of the limited range and muzzle velocity of the ordinary single-shot trapper's rifle. The literature of the Rocky Mountain fur trade is full of accounts of disastrous encounters between mountain men and grizzlies; the sufferings of Hugh Glass after a grizzly's murderous attack were remembered around many a mountain campfire, and Chatillon's "intrepidity" might be taken as easily for sheer bravado.

15 A necklace of grizzly-bear claws was a mark of great valor, for the Indian had to kill the bear to get the claws—not an easy task with a bow and arrow, lance, or a cheaply made trade musket.

16 In 1846 the Pawnees, a tribe of Caddoan stock, lived in the valley of the Platte River and along the banks of its tributaries, almost entirely within the borders of the present state of Nebraska, though as late as 1803 their territory extended as far southward as the Kansas River and as far northward and westward as they could hold.

The Pawnees first encountered white men about the beginning of the eighteenth century; their Platte River hunting grounds were, however, sufficiently far enough away from civilization that the Pawnees were not much demoralized by their infrequent contacts with white men and so were able to keep up their traditional fighting spirit and their very elaborate tribal ceremonies far longer than were tribes farther to the east. By 1833 the Pawnees had surrendered their claims to all lands south of the Platte; they had also gained a dangerous reputation among the fur caravans moving along "Sublette's Trace," the eastern reaches of what became the Oregon Trail. As Hodge, ed.

Handbook of American Indians, II, 213–216, notes, though the Pawnees were frequently fatal to stragglers from trading wagons or emigrant trains, they never rose against the United States and later in the century served the cavalry as brave and resourceful scouts in the Indian Wars. The Pawnees were accomplished horse thieves and were not above running off a drove of oxen for the fun of it, as several emigrant parties learned in 1846. Numbering perhaps as many as 2,000 warriors in their best days, the Pawnees frequently raided the dispirited Kaws and wandered on their hunting and war parties as far southward as the Arkansas River, where they occasionally killed a careless herder or snapped up a few mules and horses from a Santa Fe caravan. Josiah Gregg, *Commerce of the Prairies,* in R. G. Thwaites, ed. *Early Western Travels* (Cleveland, 1905) XX, 337, called them "the Ishmaelites of the Prairies —their hands are against every man, and every man's hand is against them"—an unusually temperate description of the tribe.

17 Parkman's comments on the culturally degenerate Kaws are markedly restrained; compare Clyman's description of the tribe in *James Clyman, Frontiersman,* pp. 71–72: "saw a number of Kaw Iindians [*sic*] a misrable poor dirty Lazy Looking Tribe and disgusting in the extreme[.] To lazy to work and to cowardly to go to the boffaloe whare they frequently meet with their enemies get a few killed and return to dig roots[.] Beg and starve 2 or 3 months then make another effort which may or may not be more successfull[.]" Many other similar accounts of the Kaws's degraded condition might be quoted; they excited the disgust of almost every prairie traveler.

18 Wood, *Old Santa Fe Trail,* p. 231, locates the crossing of this tributary of Turkey Creek a quarter mile west of the Missouri state line, on Eaton Street between 45th and 46th streets in modern Kansas City, Kansas.

19 Parkman is referring to the Shawnee Methodist Mission and Indian manual-labor school first established in late 1830 or early 1831 at a site near the present Turner, Kansas, and in 1839 moved to a location in what is now Johnson County, Kansas, about six miles south of the Kansas River and a half mile west of the Missouri state line. See Barry, "Kansas before 1854," *KHQ*, xxviii (Summer, 1962), 178–179, and xxix (Summer, 1963), 171–172, 184. Parkman and his party had made three or four miles of westward progress along the Mission Road since leaving Westport.

20 Captain Joseph Parks would have repaid more of Parkman's attention. One-quarter Shawnee and three-quarters white, Parks had grown up with the Indians and knew little or nothing about his parentage; he had, however, received a fairly good education, and, as an interpreter, he had taken part in the negotiations by which the Shawnees had resigned their Ohio lands for their new Kansas reserve. By September 15, 1833, Parks and 67 other Shawnees from Wapakoneta, Ohio, had reached Kansas, where Parks was frequently employed by the Indian agencies as an interpreter. His title he had presumably earned as the leader of a band of Shawnees and Delawares recruited in 1837 for service in the Seminole War. Later, as head chief of the Shawnees, he did much to encourage his tribe to develop their reservation. He died in 1859, aged about 65. See Louis O. Honig, *Westport, Gateway to the Early West* (n.p., 1950), pp. 30–69; and Barry, "Kansas before 1854," *KHQ*, xxviii (Autumn, 1962), 334–335, and xxix (Spring, 1963), 74–75.

21 The Lower Delaware Crossing, more commonly known as the Military, or Grinter, Crossing, was located just west of the present site of Turner, Kansas, where in 1831 Moses Grinter of Kentucky had established a ferry on the north bank of the Kansas River. See Wood, *Old Santa Fe Trail,*

pp. 226–227; and Barry, "Kansas before 1854," *KHQ*, XXVIII (Summer, 1962), 180, and XXX (Autumn, 1964), 350–351. Parkman's party had made eight or nine miles on this day's journey; they crossed the Kansas River by the Grinter Ferry next day, May 10. See *Journals*, II, 421.

22 Parkman's horses were named for two famous Indian heroes. Hendrick, a chief of the Mohawks, fell at Lake George on September 8, 1755, in the "bloody morning scout" against the French under Baron Dieskau. See *Montcalm and Wolfe*, I, 312–315 (Vol. XI of *Works*).

Pontiac (*c.* 1720–1769) was the central figure in the first of Parkman's histories, *The Conspiracy of Pontiac* (Vol. XIV–XV of *Works*). Pontiac's mixed parentage—his father was an Ottawa and his mother a Chippewa—did not stand in the way of his swift rise to a position of power among the Ottawas and other tribes of the Old Northwest.

As early as 1746 he appeared as supporter of French interests among the Indians of the Great Lakes; evidence suggests that in that year he led a band of Ottawas to Detroit in support of the French garrison there under attack by other northern tribesmen. Again, in 1755, he led the Ottawas against the British at Braddock's Field; in 1760, after the collapse of New France had become obvious to most of the colony's Indian allies, Pontiac was disposed to come to terms with the British and even supervised the surrender of Detroit to the victors. Encouraged, however, by rumors of new French efforts to retake Canada and the Mississippi Valley and having been resupplied with arms and ammunition from other posts still in French hands, Pontiac prepared a confederacy of almost all the Northwest Indians in a "conspiracy" which broke out in 1763 with the capture of eight British forts on the Great Lakes and beyond the Alleghenies and the massacres of most of their garrisons. Detroit and Fort Pitt were both besieged, and only the final grudging admission by the French commander at Fort Chartres that the war had been totally lost and the consequent defection of many of his Indian allies induced Pontiac at last to treat for peace at Detroit in 1765.

In 1769 he died near the old French settlement at Cahokia, probably murdered by a Kaskaskia Indian after a drinking bout. "Thus basely perished," Parkman wrote in *Pontiac*, ii, 329–330 (Vol. xv of *Works*), "this champion of a ruined race. . . . Tradition has but faintly preserved the memory of the event; and its only annalists, men who held the intestine feuds of the savage tribes in no more account than the quarrels of panthers or wildcats, have left but a meagre record. Yet enough remains to tell us that over the grave of Pontiac more blood was poured out in atonement, than flowed from the veins of the slaughtered heroes on the corpse of Patroclus. . . ." See also Hodge, ed. *Handbook of American Indians*, ii, 280. During his weeks at St. Louis Parkman had questioned members of the old French families there and at Cahokia, across the river, about traditions of Pontiac's last years and death.

23 For the Oglalas see p. 117 of the present edition and note 24 for that page.

24 Parkman is probably referring to the Delaware Methodist Mission and school, founded in 1832 near the Grinter Crossing of the Kansas River in present Wyandotte County, Kansas. The "meeting-house" Parkman notes is undoubtedly the one built in 1840 a mile or two away from the original site of the Mission. See Barry, "Kansas before 1854," *KHQ*, xxviii (Summer, 1962), 191–192, and xxix (Autumn, 1963), 332.

25 For Fort Leavenworth see p. 25 of the present edition and note 2 for that page.

26 This sentence describes the party's movements on May 11; it had taken them the best part of two days to cover the 25

miles between the Grinter Crossing and Fort Leavenworth. See *Journals*, II, 421.

27 The heavy, underslung "Spanish" bit is well shown in
Remington's illustration on p. 22 of the present text.

28 Parkman's remark that the "distant prairie Indians" did
not carry rifles should not be read to mean that the Sioux,
for instance, did not have firearms; they did, as *The Oregon Trail* itself shows. Here Parkman is making the usual
distinction between the heavy rifle, almost universally the
white man's weapon, and the "gun" or smoothbore musket. Under their mountain and prairie names of "Nor'-
West fusil," "fusee," or "Northwest gun," lightweight
smoothbores were a staple commodity in the Indian trade.
See W. A. Ferris, *Life in the Rocky Mountains*, ed. Paul
C. Phillips (Denver, 1940), p. 301; and Garrard, *Wah-
To-Yah and the Taos Trail*, p. 69.

29 Compare Theodore Talbot, *The Journals of Theodore
Talbot, 1843 and 1849–1852*, ed. Charles H. Carey (Portland, 1931), p. 8, on the condition of the Delawares in
1843: "These Indians are remarkably brave and intelligent,
qualities which give them great influence over their allies
and render them the terror of their enemies. They are very
proud of their renowned ancestry and with some justice,
assert superiority over the whole red race."

CHAPTER III

1 Stephen Watts Kearny was born in 1794 and joined the
New York City and County Militia as early as 1810; in
March, 1812, he was commissioned a first lieutenant in the
regular Army and served with credit in the War of 1812.
He remained in the Army for the rest of his life, spending
much of his career on frontier service. In 1825 he was a
member of the second Yellowstone Expedition; in 1831 he
rebuilt Cantonment Towson on the Red River. On July 4,

1836, he was commissioned colonel of the First U.S. Dragoons quartered at Fort Leavenworth, where he was to remain for the next six years. He returned to Fort Leavenworth briefly in 1845, when he led part of the regiment to South Pass, and in 1846, when he organized and commanded the Army of the West on its march to Santa Fe, which he captured without firing a shot.

With Kit Carson as his guide, Kearny pushed on to California, which he took without serious opposition, though he himself was badly wounded in a cavalry skirmish at San Pascual on December 6, 1846. In California he and John Charles Frémont, the ineffable "Pathfinder," fell out over a conflict of authorities and jurisdictions, though Kearny ultimately succeeded in enforcing his orders and in pacifying and organizing the new conquest. After one of the most famous courts-martial in the Army before the Civil War, Frémont was convicted of insubordinate conduct and resigned the service; Kearny himself, discouraged by the rancors of the trial and weakened by war, died at Jefferson Barracks in St. Louis on October 31, 1848. Kearny had been made a brigadier in June, 1846, and in December of the same year was brevetted a major general, the rank he held at his death. For a good account of Kearny's life and service, see Dwight L. Clarke, *Stephen Watts Kearny: Soldier of the West* (Norman, 1961).

2 Fort Leavenworth was established on March 7, 1827, after it became clear to the War Department that Fort Atkinson, the first military post of importance on the Missouri River, was not close enough to provide protection to the growing settlements along the Missouri frontier. See Federal Writers' Project, *Oregon Trail*, p. 47. Barry, "Kansas before 1854," *KHQ*, xxx (Autumn, 1964), 376–377, reprints a description of the fort which appeared in the St. Louis *New Era* on July 10, 1846, only two months after Parkman visited it:

The nearest buildings and block-houses . . . are situated about 400 yards from the steamboat landing, on the summit of the first swell of land which gradually rises from the river. . . . The area of ground occupied by the buildings, lawns and streets, is but little short of 20 acres, in the form of a square. At each corner is planted a block-house, to be used by artillery-men or rifle-men.

On the east side the buildings are of brick, two stories high, with double porticoes running their whole length, used by the troops as quarters. On the north side, the buildings are principally of brick, two stories, and occupied by the principal officers of the Fort as offices and family residences. These buildings are also fronted by porticoes and piazzas. The west side is not so closely built up. The arsenal and two or three buildings near the southwest corner of the Fort, are of brick, and the balance are large frame houses, occupied as quarters for officers and privates. The south side is altogether occupied by a long line of stables, and yard for artillery. South of the arsenal about 100 yards, on a beautiful piece of ground, stands the hospital. . . .

Fort Leavenworth had achieved its greatest importance, as Parkman seems to suggest in this passage, when it served as the base for Kearny's Army of the West, composed of the First Dragoons and detachments of Missouri volunteer cavalry and artillery, which began assembling at Fort Leavenworth as early as June 6, 1846. See Barry, "Kansas before 1854," *KHQ*, xxx (Autumn, 1964), 361–362.

3 The Kickapoos, a central Algonquin tribe, were located in central and northern Wisconsin at the time of their first encounter with the French during the second half of the seventeenth century. After the destruction of the Illinois Confederacy about 1765, most of the Kickapoos moved south into Illinois, settling for a time near the present site of Peoria; later in the century a part of the tribe moved north to the Sangamon River at the same time that other

Kickapoos were moving eastward toward the Wabash River.

Their later history is typical of that of many prairie tribes facing the irresistible pressure of American westward expansion. In 1809 they ceded their Indiana lands; in the War of 1812 they rose under Tecumseh and were defeated with him; in 1819 they surrendered their territories in central Illinois; and in 1832 they fought again, under Black Hawk, and were again defeated. By 1833 Kickapoos from the Vermilion River in Illinois and other tribesmen from Missouri, some 540 men, women, and children in all, were settled on their reserve about five miles north of Fort Leavenworth; they were accompanied by a band of Illinois Pottawatomies. See Hodge, ed. *Handbook of American Indians*, I, 684–685; Swanton, *Indian Tribes*, p. 253; and Barry, "Kansas before 1854," *KHQ*, xxviii (Autumn, 1962), 326. Their village must have been located a mile or two south of the present site of Kickapoo, Kansas.

4 Parkman's "Kickapoo trader" was almost certainly William H. Hildreth, who had located on the Kickapoo reserve at least as early as 1842. See Barry, "Kansas before 1854," *KHQ*, xxix, (Winter, 1963), 445, and xxx (Autumn, 1964), 351.

5 So far as I can determine, Parkman's "little swift stream" must have been Plum Creek, two miles south of present Kickapoo, Kansas.

6 Compare Parkman's notebook description of the same Kickapoos in *Journals*, ii, 422: "Inds. [Indians] are most provoking beings. We addressed one who was lying at full length in the sun before his house—he would not give the least sign of recognising our presence. We got from the rest nothing but silence, hesitation, or false directions."

7 The Pottawatomies, an Algonquin tribe, were first discovered by the French in the early seventeenth century at their villages in northeastern Wisconsin, near Green Bay.

By the end of the century the tribe had moved south toward the foot of Lake Michigan, and by 1800 their territory extended from the Milwaukee River to southeastern Michigan. Like other tribes of the Old Northwest, the Pottawatomies supported French interests until 1763; they sided with the British during the Revolution and the War of 1812. As early as 1833 some members of the tribe had joined the Kickapoos moving to their new Kansas reservation; other Pottawatomies settled near Council Bluffs or along the Marais des Cygnes. The trans-Mississippi sections of the tribe were reunited in 1846–47 on the eastern section of the former Kansas reservation. See Hodge, ed. *Handbook of American Indians*, II, 289–291; and Barry, "Kansas before 1854," *KHQ*, XXVIII (Autumn, 1962), 326, and XXX (Autumn, 1964), 360–361. Their lodges were probably made of bark or reed mats.

8 By "capped" Parkman means that the pistol was fitted with a percussion cap below the hammer.

9 The notebooks show clearly that Hildreth's "friend" was his mistress, a word Parkman seems to have considered too frank even in 1892.

10 The events described in this chapter occurred on May 12. See *Journals*, II, 422.

CHAPTER IV

1 The reference to a caliber of "sixteen to the pound" means that the Englishmen's rifles each fired a one-ounce ball. Ballistics measurements in the early nineteenth century were often made by reference to the number of bullets a pound of lead would provide for any particular weapon.

2 The reference to the "twenty-third of May" appears throughout K–83. In fact, the combined parties left Fort Leavenworth on May 13. See *Journals*, II, 422.

3 Parkman is referring to the expedition of five companies of
   the First Dragoons under Kearny which left Fort Leavenworth on May 18, 1845, bound for Fort Laramie and
   South Pass. The expedition was made in part in an attempt to find a direct road from the fort to the Big Blue
   River and "the grand trail of the Oregon emigrants up the
   Platte," the Oregon Trail itself. Kearny's command
   marched west by northwestward across the prairies,
   crossed Stranger Creek and several branches of the Delaware River, forded the South Fork of the Nemaha River
   near the present Seneca, Kansas, and, after crossing the
   Big Blue River above Marysville, joined the Oregon Trail
   in the triangle of prairie between the Big and Little Blue
   rivers. During the last day or two of its march Kearny's
   command had been on or close to the St. Joseph Road,
   which Parkman himself would follow in 1846. See P. St.
   George Cooke, *Scenes and Adventures in the Army: Or,
   Romance of Military Life* (Philadelphia, 1857),
   pp. 282–432; and Barry, "Kansas before 1854," *KHQ*, xxx
   (Summer, 1964), 221–222. See p. 258 of the present edition and note 3 for that page for further information
   about Kearny's 1845 expedition.

4 Their "bee-line" is pointing Parkman and his party westward, the direction they will follow until they come upon
   the new trail described below.

5 See Byron's *Mazeppa* ll.657–661 for the source of this
   quotation.

6 Compare the sentence "Riding . . . along" with Parkman's notebook description of the cavalcade in *Journals*,
   II, 422–423: "Riding at the head of the line and looking
   back, our straggling line of horsemen and animals
   stretched over the plain for a mile or more, and on the
   horizon the white waggons were slowly moving along."

7 The "traces of a large body of horse" are further explained
   by Parkman's notebook entry for May 13 in *Journals*, II,

422: "Struck off on a bye road—wandered over wide prairies for a long time, and at last struck upon the trail of two companies of dragoons who went out yesterday to build a new fort up the Missouri." Parkman is here referring to an overland party of horsemen from Company C, First Dragoons, under Second Lieutenant Andrew J. Smith, who had left Fort Leavenworth on May 12 to build the first Fort Kearny at Table Creek, near the present site of Nebraska City, Nebraska. See Barry, "Kansas before 1854," *KHQ*, xxx (Autumn, 1964), 355–356. Parkman and his companions must now be riding almost directly northward.

8 At this point both *The Oregon Trail* itself and Parkman's notebooks show his utter confusion about the route he and his companions were following, so that topographical details in both book and journals are either contradictory or completely wrong. I have attempted to follow Parkman's route through eastern Kansas, and in the topographical notes to follow I can only submit my own educated guesses as to the party's probable itinerary. Parkman's "lazy stream" in this passage may be Owl Creek, some 15 miles northwest of Fort Leavenworth.

9 The thunderstorm occurred on the afternoon of May 13. See *Journals*, II, 422–423.

10 This "muddy and treacherous" stream may be Walnut Creek, four or five miles southwest of present Atchison, Kansas, and three miles from their campsite on Owl Creek.

11 Parkman's estimate of "six or seven miles" from their former campsite seems to indicate that the brook at which the party halted may have been Deer Creek, at a point some three miles northwest of Atchison, Kansas.

12 Parkman's estimate of the party's distance from Fort Leavenworth is almost certainly wrong, especially since his notebook entry for May 16 in *Journals*, II, 423–424, records

that "Up to this time, our progress has been very slow—about thirty miles in three days," and the "three days" were May 13–15. Pontiac bolted and was recaptured on the afternoon of May 14, probably on the banks of Walnut Creek, and thus the party was, by the most generous reckoning, only about 25 miles away from Fort Leavenworth.

13 In fact, the chronologies of *The Oregon Trail* and of Parkman's notebooks are identical for the events of the next several days' journey.

14 Parkman's "route of the Platte" is, of course, the Oregon Trail itself, particularly that section running from Grand Island to Fort Laramie.

15 The report of vast desert regions lying east of the Rocky Mountains had been made as early as 1810 by Zebulon Pike; the map in James's 1823 account of the Stephen H. Long expedition fitted the idea of a "Great American Desert," the title given to the central mountain area, firmly into the American consciousness even as it seemed to limit westward expansion and to provide an ultimate sanctuary for the Indians beyond the Mississippi. See *The Journals of Zebulon Montgomery Pike with Letters and Related Documents 1783–1854*, ed. Donald Jackson (Norman, 1966), II, 27–28 n.; Edwin James, *Account of an Expedition from Pittsburg to the Rocky Mountains, Performed in the Years 1819, 1820* in R. G. Thwaites, ed. *Early Western Travels* (Cleveland, 1905), XVII, 147–148, 191; and Washington Irving, *Astoria or Anecdotes of an Enterprise Beyond the Rocky Mountains*, ed. Edgeley W. Todd (Norman, 1964), pp. 210–211. See also Henry Nash Smith, *Virgin Land: The American West as Symbol and Myth* (Cambridge, Mass., 1950), pp. 174–183, for an important discussion of the "Great American Desert" as one of the central "myths" of the American West.

16 Both *The Oregon Trail* and the notebooks show Parkman's extensive knowledge of the popular literature deal-

ing with western exploration and adventure. There is every indication that he had read Prince Maximilian's *Travels* and Gregg's *Commerce of the Prairies;* distinct echoes of both books appear in *The Oregon Trail.* He may have seen Ferris' accounts of western life in *The Western Literary Messenger* before their collected appearance as *Life in the Rocky Mountains.* In 1844 Parkman saw and approved George Catlin's Indian pictures in London, though he later rated Karl Bodmer the better artist. He had read Irving's western books, of course, and he knew Cooper's Leatherstocking novels almost by heart. There are references to C. A. Murray's book of western travels in both *The Oregon Trail* and in the notebooks, and Frémont's *Report* swung in his saddlebags from Independence to the Laramie Basin. Finally, a number of chapters in K–52 have for epigraphs lines from William Cullen Bryant's western poems, apparently quoted from memory.

17 Since Parkman seems to have been only 10 miles west of the Missouri River and was riding along a well-traveled military road, it is not surprising that he should see few traces of game.

18 The elk, or wapiti (*Cervus canadensis*), the largest of the Cervidae found on the prairies of the West in the 1840's, originally ranged as far north as central Canada and as far south as northern Oklahoma. Elk were probably quite rare in eastern Kansas in 1846; they undoubtedly became extinct in the Great Plains before the turn of the century. See Cockrum, *Mammals of Kansas*, p. 270.

19 Parkman's "prairie-hen" is the prairie chicken (*Tympanuchus cupido*), originally found on the short-grass plains in an area extending from southern Canada to Texas. Parkman is now passing through a region where prairie chickens were undoubtedly numerous, but at a time when most of the hens would be incubating and inconspicuous.

20 After the sentence "Add . . . skin" K–52 supply the fol-

lowing two additional sentences: "Such being the charms of this favored region, the reader will easily conceive the extent of our gratification at learning that for a week we had been journeying on the wrong track! How this agreeable discovery was made I will presently explain." At this point Parkman resumes the daily narrative with events that occurred on May 15. See *Journals*, II, 423.

21 Conjecturally Parkman's "little dribbling brook" is Independence Creek or one of its tributaries, at a site about 10 or 12 miles northwest of Atchison, Kansas.

22 To "catch up" means to saddle or harness up.

23 Before the sentence "His . . . himself" K–52 supply the following four sentences at the beginning of the paragraph:

We intimated that perhaps it would be as well to postpone such burdensome precautions until there should be some actual need of them; but he shook his head dubiously. The Captain's sense of military propriety had been severely shocked by what he considered the irregular proceedings of the party; and this was not the first time he had expressed himself upon the subject. But his convictions [K: 'convictions'] seldom produced any practical results. In the present case, he contented himself, as usual, with enlarging on the importance of his suggestions, and wondering that they were not adopted.

Parkman might not have been so ready to ridicule the Captain's "convictions" had he known that they were simply standard precautions—even to "vedettes" or scouts —that every fur caravan and almost every emigrant party practiced along the trail, though passwords may not have been too common.

24 This stream may have been the North Branch of Independence Creek, at a site some five miles southwest of Bendena, Kansas.

25 Parkman's "village of the Iowa Indians" is properly the Great Nemaha Subagency, located in April, 1837, near the present site of Highland, Kansas, for the Iowas, Sauks, and Foxes of Missouri. See Barry, "Kansas before 1854" *KHQ*, xxix (Spring, 1963), 62. The Iowas had a reservation of their own, north of that held in common by the Sauks and Foxes.

26 St. Joseph, formerly known as Blacksnake Hills, was laid out in June, 1843, and named for the elder Joseph Roubidoux, the well-known fur trader, whose post had originally occupied the site. Emigrant parties broke a trail from St. Joseph to the Big Blue River in 1844, and in 1845 as many as 950 people followed the St. Joseph Road to its junction with the Oregon Trail. In 1846, as Barry notes, some 274 wagons and "probably not fewer than 1350 persons set out for California or Oregon . . ." from St. Joseph or other upriver locations. See "Kansas before 1854," *KHQ*, xxx (Summer, 1964), 214–216, and (Autumn, 1964), 344–346. As Paden, *Wake of the Prairie Schooner*, p. 54, suggests, St. Joseph had many advantages as a point of departure for the Pacific Coast: "It was only natural that it should be a favorite take-off for the overland trail, for it lay a full two-day steamer journey from Independence, up the Missouri toward the mouth of the Platte, every mile of which was an advantage. In addition it was considered to be seventy miles farther west—or about four days' steady travel by ox team." The St. Joseph Road ran from St. Joseph to quite near the present sites of Elwood, Troy, Horton, Seneca, and Marysville, Kansas, its junction with the Oregon Trail. See *ibid.*, pp. 58–62; and Margaret Long, *The Oregon Trail* (Denver, 1954), pp. 39–49.

27 Parkman and his party reached the St. Joseph Road at a point near modern Denton, Kansas, and turned west down it on the afternoon of May 16. See *Journals*, ii, 423–424.

CHAPTER V

1 Reports of the approaching Mormon hordes had been widespread in the camps around Independence and Westport, as Parkman notes, and contemporary evidence suggests that the only reliable source of information which the emigrants possessed, the military authorities at Fort Leavenworth, had helped to spread the alarm. Compare George L. Curry's account of the latest rumors among the assembled wagon trains in his letter of May 6 to the St. Louis *Reveille*, reprinted in Morgan, ed. *Overland in 1846*, II, 514:

> The emigrants appear to be much concerned about the Mormons. There was a "camp report" that six hundred wagons of them had crossed at St. Joseph's. This report, like all "camp reports," could be traced to no reliable source. Yet such anxiety was manifested about the matter, that Col. Russell was induced to send out an express to Col. Kearney, at Fort Leavenworth, to ascertain the truth. Col. Kearney reports some two thousand having crossed the river, with artillery, &c., but peaceably disposed towards us. Why should they be otherwise.

Corroborative evidence of Kearny's letter describing the Mormons at St. Joseph will be found in Colonel William H. Russell's report of May 10 to the *Missouri Republican*, reprinted in Morgan, ed. *Overland in 1846*, II, 520. Bryant, *What I Saw in California*, pp. 15–16, 26, also mentions Kearny's letter and recounts even more astonishing rumors of bloodthirsty Mormons: "One of these rumors was, that five thousand Mormons were crossing, or had crossed, the Kansas River; that they marched with ten brass fieldpieces, and that every man of the party was armed with a rifle, a bowie-knife, and a brace of large revolving pistols. It was declared that they were inveterately hostile to the emigrating parties; and when the latter came up to the Mormons, they intended to attack and murder them. . . ." Bryant had heard other reports almost equally bizarre: "A third [rumor] was that a party of five Englishmen, supposed to be emissaries of their government, had started in advance of us, bound for Oregon; and that their object was to stir up the Indian tribes along the route, and incite them to deeds of hostility. . . ." The only small party known to have left the Missouri frontier before Bryant himself included Parkman, Shaw, Romaine, and the Chandlers, and Bryant is unquestionably referring to them here.

The emigrants around Independence and Westport, of course, had no cause for worry; the Mormons had troubles enough of their own in 1846. After years of persecution and of violent counterstrokes against their enemies, the Mormons had finally begun to leave their last sanctuary at Nauvoo, Illinois, in February, 1846, suffering scarcely credible hardships in temporary encampments in Iowa while they prepared for the march to the promised land in the West which Brigham Young had perhaps already selected. The vanguard of their scattered parties did not reach the Missouri River at Council Bluffs until June, 1846, and the whole body of the Saints did not break up their camp at Winter Quarters there until April, 1847, only three months before Young and a pioneer party reached the Great Salt Lake on July 24. The history of the conflicts between Mormon and gentile in Missouri and Illinois might be epitomized in the fact that among those encamped near Independence in this lengthening spring of 1846 were Lillburn Boggs and his second wife, Panthea Grant Boone Boggs. It was Boggs who, as Governor of Missouri, had signed the notorious "Extermination Order" of October, 1838, against the Mormons of Carroll and Daviess counties, a strategy of murderous weakness which Alexander Doniphan, then of the Missouri militia, refused to obey and which the Mormons so resented that one of their "Sons of Dan," Porter O. Rockwell, tried to revenge it with a nearly fatal shotgun assault on Boggs in 1842. See DeVoto, *Year of Decision*, pp. 69–101; and Wallace Stegner, *The Gathering of Zion* (New York, 1964), pp. 35–248.

2 Parkman's reference in this passage is to the Brown-Crosby party of 43 Mississippi Mormons, whom he later encountered at the Pueblo. See p. 331 of the present edition and note 5 for that page.

3 Compare the sentence "It . . . interruption" with its K form: "It was evident, by the traces, that large parties were a few days in advance of us; and supposing them to be Mormons, we had some apprehension of interruption from this horde of fanatics."

4 I am indebted to Professor Orie L. Loucks of the University of Wisconsin Department of Botany and to Cockrum, *Mammals of Kansas*, pp. 7–9, for specific accounts of vegetation patterns before extensive settlement in the early 1850's—with the simultaneous advent of both cattle and plow—drastically altered the original ecological patterns of the prairies which Parkman crossed on his way to the Platte and on his return to the Missouri frontier along the Santa Fe Trail from Bent's Fort. In the 1840's the eastern part of the Great Plains presented an almost idyllic combination of scattered groves of deciduous trees (elms, oaks, sycamores, and cottonwoods, among other species) and gently swelling tall-grass prairies. As the prairie traveler rode farther west, however, the country became increasingly drier, the trees disappeared, and the tall grasses gave way entirely to short grasses variously known as bunch grass, blue grama, and buffalo grass. This region comprised the short-grass prairies, the forbiddingly treeless area that helped create the rhetoric of the "Great American Desert."

5 The American Ornithologists' Union's *Check-List of*

North American Birds (5th ed.), p. 378, notes that, before the period of extensive white settlement, the raven (*Corvus corax*) bred only *locally* on the Great Plains and only as far south as central Kansas. In 1846, then, the raven must have been a comparatively rare species in the region Parkman was then crossing. See p. 382 of the present edition and note 16 for that page for information about the "turkey-buzzard."

6 I am indebted to George J. Knudsen of the Conservation Division, Wisconsin Department of Natural Resources, for an identification of Parkman's snake, "gayly striped with black and yellow," as a garter snake (genus *Thamnophis*).

7 I am again indebted to George J. Knudsen for a confirmation of Parkman's identification of this reptile as a water snake (genus *Natrix*), though the snake was certainly not checkered but rather irregularly *blotched* with black.

8 The bath took place on May 17, probably on either Plum Creek or Grasshopper Creek, a few miles west of the present site of Powhattan, Kansas. See *Journals*, II, 424.

9 Parkman's "dor-bug" is more commonly known as the dorbeetle, dung beetle, or cockchafer, though in general usage the name means any beetle that flies with a buzzing sound.

10 The animals bolted on the morning of May 18. See *Journals*, II, 424.

11 "Charrette" is the correct French spelling for a cart of the kind Parkman had with him.

12 At this point *The Oregon Trail* and the notebooks diverge widely in their respective chronologies. This paragraph and the ones immediately following contain an account apparently compiled from notebook entries describing the *two* storms the party endured on May 20–21; in any case, the events of May 19, on which date they crossed the South Fork of the Nemaha River near the present site of

Seneca, Kansas, go unrecorded in *The Oregon Trail*. See *Journals*, II, 424–426. Almost every narrative of western travel and adventure contains similar descriptions of the severity of spring storms on the prairies. Compare Clyman's account of the "Tremendeous Shower" his party endured in May, 1844, in *James Clyman, Frontiersman*, p. 67.

13 After the sentence "He stalked . . . heels" K–52 supply the following additional 35 paragraphs:

'Good morning, Captain.'

'Good morning to your honors,' said the Captain, affecting the Hibernian accent; but at that instant, as he stooped to enter the tent, he tripped upon the cords at the entrance, and pitched forward against the guns which were strapped around the pole in the centre.

'You are nice men, you are!' said he, after an ejaculation not necessary to be recorded, 'to set a man-trap before your door every morning to catch your visitors.'

Then he sat down upon Henry Chatillon's saddle. We tossed a piece of Buffalo robe to Jack, who was looking about in some embarrassment. He spread it on the ground, and took his seat, with a stolid countenance, at his brother's side.

'Exhilarating weather, Captain.'

'Oh, delightful, delightful!' replied the Captain; 'I knew it would be so; so much for starting yesterday at noon! I knew how it would turn out; and I said so at the time.'

'You said just the contrary to us. We were in no hurry, and only moved because you insisted on it.'

'Gentlemen,' said the Captain, taking his pipe from his mouth with an air of extreme gravity, 'it was no plan of mine. There's a man among us who is determined to have every thing his own way. You may express your opinion; but don't expect him to listen. You may be as reasonable as you like; oh, it all goes for nothing! That man is resolved to rule the roast [*sic*], and he'll set his face against any plan that he didn't think of himself.'

The Captain puffed for awhile at his pipe, as if meditating upon his grievances; then he began again.

'For twenty years I have been in the British army; and in all that time I never had half so much dissension, and quarrelling, and nonsense, as since I have been on this cursed prairie. He's the most uncomfortable man I ever met.'

'Yes;' said Jack, 'and don't you know, Bill, how he drank up all the coffee last night, and put the rest by for himself till the morning!'

'He pretends to know every thing,' resumed the Captain; 'nobody must give orders but he! It's, oh! we must do this; and, oh! we must do that; and the tent must be pitched here, and the horses must be picketed there; for nobody knows as well as he does.'

We were a little surprised at this disclosure of domestic dissensions among our allies, for though we knew of their existence, we were not aware of their extent. The persecuted Captain seeming wholly at a loss as to the course of conduct that he should pursue, we recommended him to adopt prompt and energetic measures; but all his military experience had failed to teach him the indispensable lesson, to be 'hard' when the emergency requires it.

'For twenty years,' he repeated, 'I have been in the British army, and in that time I have been intimately acquainted with some two hundred officers, young and old, and I never yet quarrelled with any man. Oh, "any thing for a quiet life!" that's my maxim.'

We intimated that the prairie was hardly the place to enjoy a quiet life, but that, in the present circumstances, the best thing he could do toward securing his wished-for tranquility, was immediately to put a period to the nuisance that disturbed it. But again the Captain's easy good-nature recoiled from the task. The somewhat vigorous measures necessary to gain the desired result were utterly repugnant to him; he preferred to pocket his grievances, still retaining the privilege of grumbling about them. 'Oh, any thing for a quiet life!' he said again, circling back to his favorite maxim.

But to glance at the previous history of our transatlantic

confederates. The Captain had sold his commission, and was living in bachelor ease and dignity in his paternal halls, near Dublin. He hunted, fished, rode steeple-chases, ran races, and talked of his former exploits. He was surrounded with the trophies of his rod and gun; the walls were plentifully garnished, he told us, with moose-horns and deer-horns, bear-skins and fox-tails; for the Captain's double-barrelled rifle had seen service in Canada and Jamaica; he had killed salmon in Nova Scotia, and trout, by his own account, in all the streams of the three kingdoms. But in an evil hour a seductive stranger came from London; no less a person than R——; who, among other multitudinous wanderings, had once been upon the western prairies, and naturally enough, was anxious to visit them again. The Captain's imagination was inflamed by pictures of a hunter's paradise that his guest held forth; he conceived an ambition to add to his other trophies the horns of a buffalo, and the claws of a grizzly bear; so he and R—— struck a league to travel in company. Jack followed his brother, as a matter of course. Two weeks on board of the Atlantic steamer brought them to Boston; in two weeks more of hard travelling they reached St. Louis, from which a ride of six days carried them to the frontier; and here we found them, in the full tide of preparation for their journey.

We had been throughout on terms of intimacy with the Captain, but R——, the motive-power of our companions' branch of the expedition, was scarcely known to us. His voice, indeed, might be heard incessantly; but at camp he remained chiefly within the tent, and on the road he either rode by himself, or else remained in close conversation with his friend Wright, the muleteer. As the Captain left the tent that morning, I observed R—— standing by the fire, and having nothing else to do, I determined to ascertain, if possible, what manner of man he was. He had a book under his arm, but just at present he was engrossed in actively superintending the operations of Sorel, the hunter, who was cooking some corn-bread over the coals for breakfast. R—— was a well-formed and rather good-looking man, some thirty years old; considerably younger than the Captain. He wore a beard and moustache of the oakum complexion, and his attire was altogether more elegant than one ordinarily sees on the prairie. He wore his cap on one side of his head; his checked shirt, open in front, was in very neat order, considering the circumstances, and his blue pantaloons, of the John Bull cut, might once have figured in Bond-street.

'Turn over that cake, man! turn it over quick! Don't you see it burning?'

'It ain't half done,' growled Sorel, in the amiable tone of a whipped bull-dog.

'It is. Turn it over, I tell you!'

Sorel, a strong, sullen-looking Canadian, who, from having spent his life among the wildest and most remote of the Indian tribes, had imbibed much of their dark vindictive spirit, looked ferociously up, as if he longed to leap upon his *bourgeois* and throttle him; but he obeyed the order, coming from so experienced an artist.

'It was a good idea of yours,' said I, seating myself on the tongue of the wagon, 'to bring Indian meal with you.'

'Yes, yes,' said R——, 'it's good bread for the prairie—good bread for the prairie. I tell you that's burning again.'

Here he stooped down, and unsheathing the silver-mounted hunting-knife in his belt, began to perform the part of cook himself; at the same time requesting me to hold for a moment the book under his arm, which interfered with the exercise of these important functions. I opened it; it was 'Macaulay's Lays;' and I made some remark, expressing my admiration of the work.

'Yes, yes; a pretty good thing. Macaulay can do better than that, though. I know him very well. I have travelled with him. Where was it we met first—at Damascus? No, no; it was in Italy.'

'So,' said I, 'you have been over the same ground with your countryman, the author of 'Eothen?' There has been some discussion in America as to who he is. I have heard Milnes' name mentioned.'

'Milnes? Oh, no, no, no; not at all. It was Kinglake; Kinglake's the man. I know him very well; that is, I have seen him.'

Here Jack C——, who stood by, interposed a remark (a thing not common with him), observing that he thought the weather would become fair before twelve o'clock.

'It's going to rain all day,' said R——, 'and clear up in the middle of the night.'

Just then, the clouds began to dissipate in a very unequivocal manner; but Jack, not caring to defend his point against so authoritative a declaration, walked away whistling, and we resumed our conversation.

'Borrow, the author of "The Bible in Spain," I presume you know him, too?'

'Oh, certainly; I know all those men. By the way, they told me that one of your American writers, Judge Story, had died lately. I edited some of his works in London; not without faults, though.'

Here followed an erudite commentary on certain points of law, in which he particularly animadverted on the errors into which he considered that the Judge had been betrayed. At length, having touched [K: But not to weary the reader with any farther record of his interminable conversation, suffice it to say, that having touched] successively on an infinite number of topics, I found that I had the happiness of discovering a man equally competent to enlighten me upon them all, equally an authority on matters of science or literature, philosophy or fashion. The part I bore in the conversation was by no means a prominent one; it was only necessary to set him going, and when he had run long enough upon one topic, to divert him to another, and lead him to pour out his heaps of treasure in succession.

'What has that fellow been saying to you?' said Shaw, as I returned to the tent. 'I have heard nothing but his talking for the last half-hour.'

R——had none of the peculiar traits of the ordinary 'British snob;' his absurdities were all his own, belonging to no particular nation or clime. He was possessed with an active devil, that had driven him over land and sea, to no great purpose, as it seemed; for although he had the usual complement of eyes and ears, the avenues between these organs and his brain appeared remarkably narrow and untrodden. His energy was much more conspicuous than his wisdom; but his predominant characteristic was a magnanimous ambition to exercise on all occasions an awful rule and supremacy, and this propensity equally displayed itself, as the reader will have observed, whether the matter in question was the baking of a hoe-cake or a point of international law. When such diverse elements as he and the easy-going Captain came in contact, no wonder some commotion ensued; R—— rode rough-shod, from morning till night, over his military ally.

A number of allusions in this canceled passage require further explanation. Parkman's admonition to the Captain to be "hard" undoubtedly reflects his own definition of the meaning of "true philosophy of life" in *Journals*, II, 410: "The true philosophy of life is to seize with a ready and strong hand upon all the good in it, and to bear inevitable evils as calmly and carelessly as need be." Parkman and Romaine both seem to have shared a decided taste for the romantic aspects of contemporary literature.

Thomas Babington Macaulay (1800–1859) published *Lays of Ancient Rome* in 1842, to very considerable attention and praise; indeed, Parkman quotes from "Horatius," the first poem in the *Lays*, for the K epigraph to Chapter x.

A. W. Kinglake's long poem, *Eōthen*, first published in 1844, describes his travels in the Near East. Kinglake (1809–1891), a widely known romantic traveler, is today perhaps best remembered for his exhaustive history of the Crimean War.

Richard Monckton Milnes (1809–1885), poet and politician, wrote among other works the first biography of Keats vigorously asserting the poet's genius.

George Borrow (1803–1881), novelist and traveler, was well known in the nineteenth century for the varied—not to say eccentric—sides of his personality and career. He helped to edit *The Newgate Calendar* and served in Russia and Spain as a colporteur for the British and Foreign Bible Society. His *The Bible in Spain*, first published in 1843, is a curious potpourri of picaresque adventure and Christian moralizing. Romaine's patronizing attitude toward Justice Joseph Story (1779–1845), Associate Justice of the Supreme Court and Dane Professor of Law at Harvard, must particularly have annoyed Parkman, who had himself studied under Story at Harvard. See *Letters*, I, pp. xxxvii–xxxviii. After John Marshall, Story—whose most influential judgments and commentaries were written in civil and admiralty law—was considered the greatest legal authority in the United States during the first half of the nineteenth century.

14 In fact, it rained heavily on the afternoon and evening of May 20. See *Journals*, II, 425–426.

15 For this quotation see Sir Walter Scott's *Marmion* III.xiii.17.

16 Compare the sentence "Meanwhile . . . Captain" with its K–52 form: "Meanwhile, the cow, taking advantage of the tumult, ran off, to the great discomfiture of the Captain, who seemed to consider her as his own special prize, since she had been discovered by Jack."

17 The capture and butchering of the cow occurred on the afternoon of May 21. See *Journals*, II, 426. They discovered and killed *another* cow next day.

18 Parkman and his party reached the Big Blue River on May 23, at a point near the present site of Marysville, Kansas. See *Journals*, II, 427; and Paden, *Wake of the Prairie Schooner*, pp. 61–62.

19 Compare the sentence "R——'s . . . activity" with its K–52 form: "R——'s sharp brattling voice might have been heard incessantly; and he was leaping about with the utmost activity, multiplying himself, after the manner of great commanders, as if his universal presence and supervision were of the last necessity."

20 Having been on the plains before, Romaine of course felt qualified to direct the crossing; his manner, however, vastly annoyed Parkman, who noted in *Journals* II, 427, that "Romaine was, as usual, noisy and obtrusive, offending the men by assuming the direction of affairs of which he knew nothing. The fellow overboils with conceit."

CHAPTER VI

1 The pool mentioned in this sentence is probably to be identified with the creek near which Parkman and his party made camp on the afternoon of May 23, five miles beyond the crossing of the Big Blue River. See *Journals*, II, 427. If Parkman's estimate of distance is correct, they were on either Raemer Creek or on Mountain Creek, at a point some four or five miles northwest of present Marysville.

2 They had seen no one since May 15, the date of their encounter with the four deserters from Fort Leavenworth, as described on pp. 39–40 of the present text.

3 For an identification of this party, see p. 59 of the present edition and note 9 for that page.

4 After the sentence "Such . . . occurrence" K–52 supply the following additional sentence to conclude the paragraph: "Nothing could speak more for the hardihood, or rather infatuation, of the adventurers, or the sufferings that await them upon the journey."

I have been unable to verify the death of a "Mary Ellis" in the emigration of 1845, and Parkman's own notebook entry describing her grave in *Journals*, II, 430, is very vague: "Grave of a child 4 yrs. old—May, 1845." There seem, in fact, never to have been many deaths along the eastern sections of the combined Oregon and California trails, for both the emigrants and their stock were still comparatively fresh and strong when they reached the valley of the Platte.

5 Compare Parkman's notebook description of this scene in

Journals, II, 428: "We had advanced a few miles when we saw a long line of specks upon the level edge of the prairie; and when we approached, we discerned about twenty wagons, followed by a crowd of cattle."

6 George R. Stewart notes (and contemporary illustrations show) that a light, canvas-covered farm wagon—smaller than the "prairie schooner" of popular imagination—was the usual vehicle driven west in the California and Oregon emigrations, though occasionally larger and heavier wagons were used by wealthy families, and almost every emigrant made some effort to strengthen the box and running gear on his wagon for the plains and mountains ahead. See *The California Trail* (New York, 1962), p. 108.

7 The discontents of this party were in no way untypical of the quarrels among other emigrant companies in 1846, some of which were in a constant state of fragmentation and reorganization from the Missouri frontier to Fort Laramie and, in a few cases, all the way to the Pacific Coast. The Trail itself wore down tempers and exacerbated old quarrels, and there were a number of chronic malcontents, as Bryant, *What I Saw in California*, p. 62, noted: "There are, however, men in all emigrating parties, desperate and depraved characters, who are perpetually endeavoring to produce discord, disorganization, and collision; and after a proper organization of a party, as few public assemblages as possible should be convened for legislative purposes." Before his party had reached even the Big Blue River, J. Quinn Thornton, *Oregon and California in 1848*, I, 38, noted sadly that "This morning [i.e., May 22, 1846] thirteen wagons, near half of which belonged to Mr. Gordon, of Jackson county, Mo., separated from our party, assigning as a reason for so doing, that the company was too large to move with the necessary celerity. A restlessness of disposition, and dissatisfaction, produced by trifling causes, and a wish to rule rather than be ruled, to lead

rather than be led, are the sources of frequent divisions and subdivisions of companies."

8 This event is not specifically mentioned in Parkman's notebook entry for May 24, but he is perhaps recalling an incident which occurred on the upper reaches of Horseshoe Creek, at a point some 12 miles northwest of Marysville.

9 Compare this passage with Parkman's notebook account of these emigrants in *Journals*, II, 428–429:

We have struck upon the old Oregon Trail, just beyond the Big Blue, about seven days from the Platte. The waggons we saw [on the evening of May 23; see *Journals*, II, 427] were part of an emigrant party, under a man named Keatley. They encamped about a mile from us behind a swell of the prairie. The Capt. paid them a visit, and reported that the women were damned ugly. Kearsley and another man came to see us in the morning. We had advanced a few miles when we saw a long line of specks upon the level edge of the prairie; and when we approached, we discerned about twenty waggons, followed by a crowd of cattle. This was the advanced party—the rest were at the Big Blue, where they were delayed by a woman in child-bed. They stopped a few miles farther to breakfast, where we passed them. They were from the western states. Kearsley had complained of want of subordination among his party, who were not very amenable to discipline or the regulations they themselves had made. Romaine stayed behind to get his horse shod, and witnessed a grand break-up among them. The Capt. threw up his authority, such was the hurly-burly—women crying—men disputing—some for delay—some for hurry— some afraid of the Inds. Four waggons joined us—Romaine urged them, and thereby offended us. Kearsley is of the party.

Parkman's "Keatley," or "Kearsley," was William Keithly, who on May 11, at the crossing of the Wakarusa, had been elected captain of the emigrant party with which Virgil Pringle traveled, a company which then joined John

Robinson's wagon train and shared with that group the services of "O. Brown" as pilot. See "The Diary of Virgil Pringle," reprinted in Morgan, ed. *Overland in 1846*, I, 166–167. Keithly and 20 wagons of his company crossed the Big Blue on May 20, leaving Pringle and the other members of the combined parties behind; they did not get across until May 23, when Pringle's diary, *ibid.*, I, 168, substantiates and further explains Parkman's account of the separation:

Saturday, May 23—Occupied this day in crossing the Blue River by fording; raised our wagons by placing blocks between the beds and bolsters and went over dry. Camped on a beautiful spring branch on the right bank of the river. A child born in the camp this night, it being an addition to the family of Aaron Richardson. . . . Our company burst asunder this day, . . . the captain and others taking the lead, the sickness of Mrs. Richardson and the detention being the cause.

Sunday, May 24—Travelled this day 12 miles and camped on a handsome branch. Found 8 of our runaway wagons waiting to join us. Three went ahead, viz. Keithly and Barnard with a company of hunters, ten in number. Price and four families from Illinois going, they knew not how but headway was the word.

Though Parkman and Pringle do not precisely agree on the details of this separation, their accounts do share sufficiently broad areas of comparison. Pringle's reference to 'a company of hunters, ten in number" is one of the very few notices of Parkman and his party in the published accounts of the emigration of 1846.

10 Compare the sentence "At . . . one" with its K–52 form: "As may well be conceived, these repeated instances of high-handed dealing sufficiently exasperated us."

11 After the sentence "I . . . 'em" K–52 supply the following additional sentence to conclude the paragraph: "Having

also availed myself of what satisfaction could be derived from giving R—— to understand my opinion of his conduct, I returned to our own side of the camp."

12 The Englishmen's wagon broke down on May 25. See *Journals*, II, 429. Because Parkman's notebook entries are very vague about the terrain and distance covered in the next few days' travel, it is hard to say certainly just where this accident occurred; an informed guess would locate it on Elm Creek, five or six miles southeast of the present site of Fairbury, Nebraska, or on nearby Rock Creek.

13 Parkman met Keithly again on June 1. See *Journals*, II, 431–432.

14 The Blackfeet, an Algonquin confederacy, ranged most of western Montana and northwestern Wyoming, especially the region around the Three Forks of the Missouri, the richest trapping grounds in the mountains. The Blackfeet consisted of three subtribes, the Siksika, the Kainahs (or Bloods), and the Piegans; the Atsina, or Gros Ventres of the Mountains, an Arapaho band, and the Sarsi were also called Blackfeet, and altogether they were perhaps the most dangerous and unrelenting enemies the mountain men ever encountered. Prince Maximilian recorded that in 1832 the Blackfeet had killed 58 white men. See Maximilian, Prince of Wied-Neuwied, *Travels in the Interior of North America*, in R. G. Thwaites, ed. *Early Western Travels* (Cleveland, 1906), XXIII, 96; Hodge, ed. *Handbook of American Indians*, II, 570–571; Chittenden, *American Fur Trade*, II, 838–842; and John C. Ewers, *The Blackfeet: Raiders on the Northwestern Plains* (Norman, 1958), pp. 19–71.

15 Though the details of this attack cannot be specifically verified, the literature of the fur trade is full of similar accounts of Indian night raids.

16 After the sentence "Ah! . . . decisively" K–52 supply the following additional paragraph: "I did not doubt the fact,

but was a little surprised at the frankness of the confession."

17 I am indebted to Ronald W. Olsen of the University of Wisconsin Department of Zoology for an identification of Parkman's "prairie-wolf" as the coyote (*Canis latrans*). Compare Gregg, *Commerce of the Prairies*, in Thwaites, ed. *Early Western Travels*, xx, 274, for another very similar description of coyotes: "Like ventriloquists, a pair of these will represent a dozen distinct voices in such quick succession—will bark, chatter, yelp, whine, and howl in such a variety of notes, that one would fancy a score of them at hand."

The coyote was found almost everywhere in the prairie and mountain West before the period of settlement and extensive agricultural operations, and even today its natural intelligence enables the coyote to survive in considerable numbers even in settled areas from which the larger wolf has been entirely extirpated. The coyote has usually preyed on smaller animals like woodrats, prairie dogs, rabbits, and moles; one of its most useful functions was its role as a scavenger of the remains of larger animals like the buffalo killed by other carnivores. See Cockrum, *Mammals of Kansas*, pp. 220–226.

18 Compare Parkman's account of Turner's adventures in his notebook entry for May 30 in *Journals*, II, 431:

Made a very hard day's work—came more than thirty miles from the [Little] Blue to the Platte. We had all along mistaken our route, thinking that we were less advanced than in fact we were. Soon after leaving the Blue, saw two men, Turner and another, come back from the emigrants in search of an ox. They set us right, telling that we were 26 miles from the river. Just before seeing us, they had met six Pawnees, who wanted to change horses, and laid hand on the bridle of one of them, till threatened with a pistol—the only weapon they had. They told this to Sorel, and then foolishly continued their journey.

Turner may have been a member of the previously mentioned Robinson company.

19 T. H. Jefferson's contemporary map, reprinted in vol. 1 of Morgan, ed. *Overland in 1846,* shows "Pawnee Trails" running southward from Grand Island and crossing the Oregon Trail at a point near the present site of Hastings, Nebraska.

20 The details of this raid have apparently not survived, though it resembles episodes of Iroquois-Huron warfare like those related in Parkman's own histories. As has been suggested (see p. 17 and note 16 for that page), the Pawnees were not as bad as Parkman pictures them here and in other passages in *The Oregon Trail,* and in presenting this particular episode Parkman may have meant to draw a more realistic picture of the tribesmen—both Sioux and Pawnees—whom James Fenimore Cooper had transformed out of all recognition in *The Prairie.*

21 These conscience-stricken Pawnees must be unique among western books with any claim to substantive realism of description and attitude.

22 Parkman and his party reached the Platte on May 30, at a point about 20 miles northwest of the present site of Hastings, Nebraska. See *Journals,* II, 431.

23 After the sentence "No . . . feet" K–52 supply the following sentences to conclude the paragraph:

And yet stern and wild associations gave a singular interest to the view; for here each man lives by the strength of his arm and the valor of his heart. [Here K supplies the following additional sentence: Here the feeble succumb to the brave, with nothing to sustain them in their weakness.] Here society is reduced to its original elements, the whole fabric of art and conventionality is struck rudely to pieces, and men find themselves suddenly brought back to the wants and resources of their original natures.

The curious ambivalences of this canceled passage represent in part the conflicts in Parkman's own assessment of the values of his Oregon Trail summer. On the one hand, the desolate prairies bring out the latent strengths and weaknesses of every man's character; the wilderness teaches him to be "hard" to survive. On the other hand, both "art and conventionality"—in the sense, certainly, of established personal as well as social values—are destroyed by the desert and by the atavistic "wants and resources of [men's] original natures," by the passions and appetites of animal existence.

24 The "Coasts of the Platte," as the whole valley of the river from Grand Island westward at least as far as the forks of the Platte was generally known, provoked almost every western traveler to flights of rhetoric in which the region was described in terms of ruined castles, the landscapes of mythology, or the mountains of the moon. See Heinrich Lienhard, *From St. Louis to Sutter's Fort, 1846*, eds. and trans. Erwin G. Gudde and Elizabeth K. Gudde (Norman, 1961), p. 64, for representative metaphors. The country around Scott's Bluff was, before the introduction of extensive irrigation schemes in the present century, particularly barren and picturesquely desolate.

25 Parkman's general description of the Platte below the forks is accurate so far as it goes, though in 1846 as in other years the river varied a great deal in width and depth, depending upon the season.

26 Compare Gregg, *Commerce of the Prairies*, in Thwaites, ed. *Early Western Travels*, xx, 219, on the attractions of the wilderness:

Since that time I have striven in vain to reconcile myself to the even tenor of civilized life in the United States; and have sought in its amusements and its society a substitute for those high excitements which have attracted me so strongly to the Prairie life. Yet I am almost ashamed to confess that scarcely a day passes without my experiencing a pang of regret that I am not now roving at large upon those western plains. Nor do I find my taste peculiar; for I have hardly known a man, who has ever become familiar with the kind of life which I have led for so many years, that has not relinquished it with regret.

27 Parkman met these Pawnees on May 31. See *Journals*, II, 431.

28 See p. 87 of the present edition and note 2 for that page for further identification of this party—probably Elam Brown's—which Parkman has confused with Fabritus Smith's company, to which Edward Trimble, the dead man, belonged.

29 After the sentence "The panic-stricken . . . body" K–52 supply the following additional paragraph:

The reader will recollect Turner, the man whose narrow escape was mentioned not long since. We heard that the men whom the entreaties of his wife induced to go in search of him, found him leisurely driving along his recovered oxen, and whistling in utter contempt of the whole Pawnee nation. [K: The reader will recollect Turner, the man whose narrow escape was mentioned not long since; and expect perchance a tragic conclusion to his adventures; but happily none such took place; for a dozen men whom the entreaties of his wife induced to go in search of him, found him leisurely driving along his recovered oxen, and whistling in utter contempt of the whole Pawnee nation.] His party was encamped within two miles of us; but we passed them that morning, while the men were driving in the oxen, and the women packing their domestic utensils and their numerous offspring in the spacious patriarchal wagons. As we looked back, we saw their caravan, dragging its slow length along the plain; wearily toiling on its way, to found new empires in the West.

30 On the afternoon of May 31 Parkman and his party encamped some few miles west of the present location of Kearney, Nebraska. See *Journals*, ii, 432. The storm here described, however, seems to represent in detail that which occurred on the following day, June 1.

31 Ruxton, *Adventures in the Rocky Mountains*, reprinted in *Ruxton of the Rockies*, pp. 227–228, gives a similar account of the mountain men;

> Keen observers of nature, they rival the beasts of prey in discovering the haunts and habits of game, and in their skill and cunning in capturing it. Constantly exposed to perils of all kinds, they become callous to any feeling of danger, and destroy human as well as animal life with as little scruple and as freely as they expose their own. Of laws, human or divine, they neither know nor care to know. Their wish is their law, and to attain it they do not scruple as to ways and means. Firm friends and bitter enemies, with them it is "a word and a blow," and the blow often first. They may have good qualities, but they are those of the animal; and people fond of giving hard names will call them revengeful, bloodthirsty, drunkards (when the wherewithal is to be had), gamblers, regardless of the laws of *meum* and *tuum*—in fact, "White Indians." However, there are exceptions, and I *have* met honest mountain men. Their animal qualities, however, are undeniable. Strong, active, hardy as bears, daring, expert in the use of their weapons, they are just what uncivilized white man might be supposed to be in a brute state, depending upon his instinct for the support of life.

32 On June 1, the date on which they rejoined Keithly's (Parkman's "Kearsley") wagons, Parkman and his companions encamped near Plum Creek, some eight or nine

miles southeast of the present site of Lexington, Nebraska.
See *Journals*, II, 432.

CHAPTER VII

1 *Bois de vache* is better known as buffalo-chips or dried
dung.

2 I am unaware of a breed of horses specifically called
Wyandots, though in *Journals*, II, 433, Chatillon's "poney"
is named "Wyandot."

3 I am indebted to Professor Orie L. Loucks of the University of Wisconsin Department of Botany for the information that Parkman's "tall rank grass" could have been any
one of a number of indigenous tall grasses (including Indian grass, big blue stem, and several varieties of the panic
grasses) overspreading much of eastern Nebraska before
extensive agricultural operations destroyed the original
ecological systems of the region.

4 Parkman's "antelope" are pronghorns (*Antilocapra americana*), bands of which can occasionally still be seen along
the Platte in western Nebraska.

5 Parkman and his companions first encountered buffalo on
June 3, probably not far from the present site of Gothen-
burg, Nebraska. See *Journals*, II, 433. Six days later Virgil
Pringle's party saw buffalo for the first time near the forks
of the Platte. See "The Diary of Virgil Pringle," reprinted
in Morgan, ed. *Overland in 1846*, I, 171.

6 By "prickly-pear" Parkman in this passage and elsewhere
in *The Oregon Trail* means any one of a number of different flat-jointed cacti (genus *Opuntia*).

7 Compare Parkman's notebook account of this scene in
Journals, II, 433: "Henry's blood was up. We spurred
along through ravines, and getting to leeward, managed to
approach one little herd of cows. I held the horses—Henry
crept over the hill and fired. I saw the buffalo come run-

ning down the hollow, and soon perceived that we had
shot one. Skinned and cut her up, and then saw another
herd, at which Henry again fired and brought down another cow."

8 Parkman's account of this "dissection" does not at all
indicate the prodigal wastefulness of prairie butchering;
compare Howard Stansbury, *An Expedition to the Valley
of the Great Salt Lake of Utah* . . . (Philadelphia, 1852),
p. 247:

> Contrary to the custom among us, the skinning process
> commences by making an incision along the top of the back-
> bone, and separating the hide downward, so as to get the more
> quickly at what are considered the choice parts of the animal.
> These are the "bass," [i.e., the "boss"] a hump projecting from
> the back of the neck just before the shoulders, and which is
> generally removed with the skin attached: it is about the size
> of a man's head, and, when boiled, resembles marrow, being
> exceedingly tender, rich, and nutritious. Next comes the
> "hump," and the "hump ribs," projections of the vertebrae
> just behind the shoulders, some of which are a foot in length.
> These are generally broken off with a mallet made of the lower
> joint of one of the forelegs, cut off for the purpose. After these
> come the "fleece," the portion of flesh covering the ribs; the
> "depuis" [properly "depuille" in mountain French, or "the
> strip"], a broad, fat part extending from the shoulders to the
> tail; the "belly fleece;" some of the ribs, called "side ribs," to
> distinguish them from the hump ribs; the thigh or marrow-
> bones, and the tongue. Generally the animal is opened and the
> tenderloin and the tallow secured. All the rest, including the
> hams and shoulders—indeed, by far the greater portion of
> the animal—is left on the ground. When buffalo are plenty, the
> hump, bass, and tongue—very frequently only the latter—are
> taken, and occasionally a marrow-bone for a tit-bit.

9 Prairie dog towns—sometimes covering hundreds of acres
—were frequently noted by western travelers. As Parkman

suggests in this passage, prairie dogs preferred hard, compact ground for their burrows. See also p. 82 of the present edition and note 21 for that page.

10 After the sentence "The Captain . . . over" K–52 supply the following seven additional paragraphs:

Nothing unusual occurred on that day; but on the following morning, Henry Chatillon, looking over the ocean-like expanse, saw near the foot of the distant hills something that looked like a band of buffalo. He was not sure, he said, but at all events, if they were buffalo, there was a fine chance for a race. Shaw and I at once determined to try the speed of our horses.

'Come, Captain; we'll see which can ride hardest, a Yankee or an Irishman.'

But the Captain maintained a grave and austere countenance. He mounted his led horse, however, though very slowly; and we set out at a trot. The game appeared about three miles distant. As we proceeded, the Captain made various remarks of doubt and indecision; and at length declared he would have nothing to do with such a break neck business; protesting that he had ridden plenty of steeple-chases in his day, but he never knew what riding was till he found himself behind a band of buffalo day before yesterday. 'I am convinced,' said the Captain, 'that "running" is out of the question. [Here 49–52 supply the following footnote: The method of hunting called 'running,' consists in attacking the buffalo on horseback and shooting him with bullets or arrows when at full speed. In 'approaching' the hunter conceals himself, and crawls on the ground towards the game, or lies in wait to kill them.] Take my advice now, and don't attempt it. It's dangerous, and of no use at all.'

'Then why did you come out with us? What do you mean to do?'

'I shall "approach," ' replied the Captain.

'You don't mean to "approach" with your pistols, do you? We have all of us left our rifles in the wagons.'

The Captain seemed staggered at this suggestion. In his characteristic indecision, at setting out, pistols, rifles, 'running' and 'approaching' were mingled in an inextricable medley in his brain. He trotted on in silence between us for a while; but at length he dropped behind, and slowly walked his horse back to rejoin the party. Shaw and I kept on; when lo! as we advanced, the band of buffalo were transformed into certain clumps of tall bushes, dotting the prairie for a considerable distance. At this ludicrous termination of our chase, we followed the example of our late ally, and turned back toward the party. We were skirting the brink of a deep ravine, when we saw Henry and the broad-chested pony coming toward us at a gallop.

"Approaching" was often also known as "still hunting" on the prairies. This unsuccessful hunt and the meeting with Papin's boats, described in the next paragraph, occurred on June 4, probably not far eastward of the present site of North Platte, Nebraska. See *Journals*, II, 433–434.

11 Compare Parkman's notebook description of this scene in *Journals*, II, 433–434:

This morning rode off towards the hills with Q. [Shaw] and the Capt. to look for buffalo—no success. Returning, met Henry on his little poney Wyandot; he came to say that 11 boats were coming down the river from Laramie. Gave my letter to Q. to be delivered, and rode back two or three miles after the waggons to get a letter H. had given [i.e., dictated to?] me, intended for Papin, the *bourgeois* of the boats. On my return, found the boats lashed to the bank waiting—flat-bottomed—with 110 packs each—one month from Laramie—aground every day, for the Platte is now low, and is very shallow and swift at best. The crews were a wild-looking set—the oarsmen were Spaniards—with them were traders, F[rench] and American, some attired in buckskin, fancifully slashed and garnished, and with hair glued up in Ind. fashion. Papin a rough-looking fellow, reclining on the leather covering that was thrown over the packs.

I saw Woodworth here. . . .

Pierre Didier Papin (1798–1858), well known and long experienced in the fur trade, probably came to Fort Laramie in the early fall of 1845, assuming command of the post from Joseph Picotte, another famous mountain man. Papin's career in the fur trade began as early as the middle 1820's; before 1830, as senior partner in the "French Company," he was responsible for the erection of the short-lived Teton Post on the upper Missouri. Papin seems to have spent the last 13 years of his life in the fur trade, probably in the vicinity of Fort Laramie. See Paul Beckwith, *Creoles of St. Louis* (St. Louis, 1893), p. 145; and LeRoy R. Hafen and Francis Marion Young, *Fort Laramie and the Pageant of the West, 1834–1890* (Glendale, Calif., 1938), pp. 113–115. "Frederic" may be Frederick Laboue, or LaBoue, or Labone, occasionally mentioned in the literature of the fur trade as one of Papin's associates in the business, though this identification is far from certain. Papin left Fort Laramie on or about May 7, and his fur boats are frequently mentioned by other diarists in the emigration of 1846. Indeed, Papin seems to have functioned as a sort of floating postmaster, for a number of persons sent letters to the East by him; see, for instance, "Nathan J. Putnam to Joseph Putnam, 'Platt River 370 Miles From Independence,' June 10, 1846," and "Laon [George L. Curry] to the St. Louis *Reveille*, 'Platte River, June 12, 1846,'" reprinted in Morgan, ed. *Overland in 1846*, II, 552–554. Morgan, *Overland in 1846*, II, 587, also reprints the news of Papin's arrival at Fort Leavenworth on July 2 from the St. Louis *Missouri Republican* of July 7:

FROM FORT JOHN.—Eight Mackinaw boats, laden with buffalo robes, &c., with a company of thirty-six men, under the charge of Mr. P. D. Papin, arrived at Fort Leavenworth on the 2d from Fort John [Laramie], at the junction of the Laramie and Big Platte rivers. The crews and cargo were there transferred to the steamer *Tributary*, which arrived here yesterday morning. The cargo consists of 1100 packs [of] buffalo robes, 10 packs of beaver, and 3 packs of bear and wolf skins, and was consigned to P. Chouteau, Jr. & Co. We learn from Mr. Papin that he had great difficulty in descending the Platte on account of the low water, and was obliged to transfer the cargoes from three of his boats and leave them behind. Two boats which left the Fort before him, he thinks will be unable to get down, not having enough men to haul them over the shoals. . . .

Since the average pack of robes contained 10 skins and weighed 80 pounds, the sheer size of Papin's lading from Fort Laramie is sufficiently indicative of the decline of the beaver trade in the 1840's, a decline caused by the coincidence of the shift of taste and fashion from beaver hats to silk ones (a change that Astor clearly foresaw when he got out of the fur trade) and the virtual extinction of the beaver in the mountains trapped by the American fur companies. By 1846 Fort Laramie dealt almost entirely in robes, for it was located at the center of the best buffalo country in 500 miles.

Papin must have abandoned his three boats only shortly after Parkman met him, for Bryant, *What I Saw in California*, p. 81, reports that on June 10 he saw only eight boats struggling down the Platte:

We saw from our encampment this morning eight small boats, loaded, as we ascertained by the aid of a glass, with bales of furs. The boats were constructed of light plank, and were what are called "Mackinaw boats." The water of the river is so shallow, that the men navigating this fleet were frequently obliged to jump into the stream, and with their strength force the boats over the bars or push them into deeper water. We watched from sunrise until 8 o'clock in the morning, and in that time they did not advance down stream more than a mile.

12 This letter, perhaps to Parkman's parents, is not to be found among the Parkman Papers at the Massachusetts Historical Society. However, it may have been a letter that Parkman wrote for Henry Chatillon.

13 As the newspaper account of Papin's arrival at St. Louis on July 6 (quoted in note 11 for p. 75) suggests, these two boats, "the property of private traders," had apparently left Fort Laramie before Papin's own departure and were thus probably not a part of the flotilla of 11 boats (later reduced to eight) which Parkman here describes. I have found very little contemporary notice of these two fur boats and nothing to substantiate Parkman's account of their capture by the Pawnees, though Bryant, *What I Saw in California*, pp. 82–83, recounts a meeting with them on June 11, at a point some 60 miles west of Grand Island:

About 11 o'clock this morning, being considerably in advance of our train, I discovered a man at the distance of half a mile, standing in the trail leaning upon his rifle. . . . After the ordinary salutations, he informed me that his name was Bourdeau;—that he was from St. Charles, Mo., and was one of a party which left a small trading-post [Fort Bernard] on the Platte, a few miles below Fort Laramie, early in May. They were navigating two "Mackinaw boats" loaded with buffalo skins, and were bound for the nearest port on the Missouri. He stated that they had met with continual obstructions and difficulties on their voyage from its commencement, owing to the lowness of the water, although their boats, when loaded, drew but fifteen inches. They had at length found it impossible to proceed, and had drawn their boats to the shore of the river, and landed their furs. Their intention now was to procure wagons if they could, and wheel their cargo into the settlements.

To meet men speaking our own language, in this remote wilderness, was to us an interesting incident. Our train coming up, we determined to proceed as far as the place where the party of Mr. Bourdeau had landed their furs, (about four miles,) and there to noon, in order to give all interested an opportunity of making inquiries, and to write letters to their friends in the United States, to send by this conveyance. The company of *voyageurs* consisted of Mr. Bourdeau, Mr. Richard, Mr. Branham, formerly of Scott county, Ky., a half-breed Mexican, an Indian, and several Creole Frenchmen, of Missouri. . . .

We traded with them for their buffalo skins, giving in exchange flour, bacon, sugar, and coffee, which they needed. Sugar and coffee were rated at one dollar per pound, flour at fifty cents, and buffalo-robes at three dollars.

Bryant met these two boats at roughly the same place where Virgil Pringle saw "thirteen boats for St. Louis from Fort Laramie, all loaded with peltry and furs" on June 6. See "The Diary of Virgil Pringle," reprinted in Morgan, ed. *Overland in 1846*, I, 171. Bordeaux's and Richard's boats must thus have separated from Papin's flotilla some time between June 6 and June 11, when Bryant met them.

14 Compare the sentence "Then . . . emigrants" with its K form: "Then, R——, we reaped the fruits of your precious plan of travelling in company with emigrants!"

The emigrants' cattle were driven off on the morning of June 6, *two* days after the meeting with Papin's boats. See *Journals*, II, 434.

15 K–52 read "butt of a rifle," certainly the preferred spelling.

16 Compare Washington Irving, *The Adventures of Captain Bonneville*, ed. Edgeley W. Todd (Norman, 1961), p. 351: "The buffalo are sometimes tenacious of life, and must be wounded in particular parts." The preferred targets were the lungs or spine of the buffalo.

17 After the sentence "As . . . dust" K supplies the following

two additional sentences to conclude the paragraph: "One old bull seemed hanging behind the rest, struggling vainly to keep up with his comrades. As my horse ran past him, within about twelve yards, I fired my remaining pistol, by a thoughtless impulse, striking him in the rump, too high for mortal effect."

18 Before the sentence "At . . . leather" K supplies the following additional three sentences at the beginning of the paragraph:

But to glance back at my friend and his exploits. Being a bold and excellent rider, he had succeeded, after much difficulty, in forcing his active little horse within a reasonable distance of a buffalo, and firing again and again, he at length disabled him; for our pistols, unless aimed with extreme precision, were of too small calibre to kill at a single shot. This was the old bull at whom I fired, ignorant that he was already in extremity.

There seems to be no real reason for Parkman's excisions of this passage and the one in the note immediately above except, perhaps, to avoid an appearance of mere bloodthirstiness.

19 The snaffle is a light bit without the heavy underslung curb which pulls down the horse's jaw when the reins are tightened.

20 Compare Parkman's rather different account of this adventure in his notebook entry of June 6 in *Journals*, ii, 434–435:

Got separated from the others—rode for hours westwardly over the prairie—saw the hills dotted with thousands of buffalo. Antelopes—prairie-dogs—burrowing owls—wild geese—wolves, etc. Finding my course wrong, followed a buffalo-track northward, and about noon came out on the road. Awkward feeling, being lost on the prairie. Waggons not yet come—rode east eight miles and met them.

The topographical details in Parkman's notebooks and in this passage in *The Oregon Trail* differ rather noticeably, but, on the more reliable because more circumstantial evidence of the notebooks, it seems probable that this buffalo hunt occurred somewhere between the present locations of Sutherland and Paxton, Nebraska.

21 The name "prairie dog" is applied to two species of marmot-like rodents of the genus *Cynomys*. Parkman is encountering the blacktail prairie dog (*Cynomys ludovicianus*), commonly found on short-grass prairies as far west as east central Colorado. I am indebted to Professor Chauncey D. Wood of the University of Wisconsin Department of English for an identification of Parkman's "demure little gray owls" as burrowing owls (*Speotyto cunicularia*), found widely in the plains and unforested areas of the Western Hemisphere from Canada to Tierra del Fuego. The burrowing owl, 9–11 inches long, breeds in animal burrows or in holes which it digs itself. Many western travelers noted the phenomenon of snakes and burrowing owls nesting in or near prairie dog towns. See, for example, Bryant, *What I Saw in California*, p. 81; and Lienhard, *St. Louis to Sutter's Fort*, p. 50.

22 This is the first direct reference in *The Oregon Trail* to the dysentery which so weakened Parkman during his stay in The Whirlwind's village in the Laramie Basin. By the chronology of the book, Parkman had begun to feel ill on June 6, but as early as May 26 his notebooks have an entry showing that a diet of buffalo meat washed down with alkali water was already beginning to have an effect on his health and spirits; he had felt no better on May 28. See *Journals*, ii, 429–430.

23 Compare Parkman's notebook entry for June 7 in *Jour-

nals, II, 435: *"June 7ᵗʰ*. Nothing special occurred. Walked all day along South Fork—no wood in sight—all prairie, and distant hills. The lagging pace of the emigrants—the folly of Romaine—and the old womanism of the Capt. combine to disgust us. We are resolved to push on alone, as soon as we have crossed the South Fork, which will probably be tomorrow. Saw rattlesnakes and other curious snakes." In fact, Parkman first noted Romaine's absence on June 8: "Sorel, Romaine, and two of the emigrants went off yesterday morning for buffalo, and did not return at night." See *Journals*, II, 435.

24 After the sentence "Shaw . . . example" K–52 supply the following five additional paragraphs to conclude the chapter:

'It will be a bad thing for our plans,' said he as we entered, 'if these fellows don't get back safe. The Captain is as helpless on the prairie as a child. We shall have to take him and his brother in tow; they will hang on us like lead.'

'The prairie is a strange place,' said I. 'A month ago I should have thought it rather a startling affair to have an acquaintance ride out in the morning and lose his scalp before night, but here it seems the most natural thing in the world; not that I believe that R—— has lost his yet.'

If a man is constitutionally liable to nervous apprehensions, a tour on the distant prairies would prove the best prescription; for though when in the neighborhood of the Rocky Mountains he may at times find himself placed in circumstances of some danger, I believe that few ever breathe that reckless atmosphere without becoming almost indifferent to any evil chance that may befall themselves or their friends.

Shaw had a propensity for luxurious indulgence. He spread his blanket with the utmost accuracy on the ground, picked up the sticks and stones that he thought might interfere with his comfort, adjusted his saddle to serve as a pillow, and composed himself for his night's rest. I had the first guard that evening; so, taking my rifle, I went out of the tent. It was perfectly dark.

A brisk wind blew down from the hills, and the sparks from the fire were streaming over the prairie. One of the emigrants, named Morton, was my companion; and laying our rifles on the grass, we sat down together by the fire. Morton was a Kentuckian, an athletic fellow, with a fine intelligent face, and in his manners and conversation he showed the essential characteristics of a gentleman. [K: Morton was a Kentuckian, an athletic fellow, with a fine intelligent face, and in his manners and conversation he showed more of the essential characteristics of the gentleman than the vulgar and ignorant boors who float on the scum of fashion in some of our eastern cities.] Our conversation turned on the pioneers of his gallant native state. The three hours of our watch dragged away at last, and we went to call up the relief.

R——'s guard succeeded mine. He was absent; but the Captain, anxious lest the camp should be left defenceless, had volunteered to stand in his place; so I went to wake him up. There was no occasion for it, for the Captain had been awake since nightfall. A fire was blazing outside of the tent, and by the light which struck through the canvas, I saw him and Jack lying on their backs, with their eyes wide open. The Captain responded instantly to my call; he jumped up, seized the double-barrelled rifle, and came out of the tent with an air of solemn determination, as if about to devote himself to the safety of the party. I went and lay down, not doubting that for the next three hours our slumbers would be guarded with sufficient vigilance.

I have been unable to identify Morton.

CHAPTER VIII

1 Parkman forded the South Platte River at the Lower California Crossing, some four miles west of the present site of Brule, Nebraska. See Paden, *Wake of the Prairie Schooner*, pp. 106–107; and W. J. Ghent, *The Road to Oregon* (New York, 1929), p. 130.

2 This was Elam Brown's company of California emigrants, once a much larger party and now reduced to 30 or 33 wagons by several acrimonious defections. Their losses on the Platte and later misfortunes are frequently mentioned by the diarists of the emigration of 1846; Virgil Pringle's diary, reprinted in Morgan, ed. *Overland in 1846*, I, 172, records that the stampede occurred on Thursday, June 4, a date which almost agrees with Parkman's "three days since" in this passage. Their total loss is usually given at 120 head of stock, about half of which were draft oxen, probably driven off by buffalo. See Barry, "Kansas before 1854," *KHQ*, xxx (Autumn, 1964), 345; and Morgan, ed. *Overland in 1846*, I, 106, 390.

3 Parkman has in this passage apparently confused his first-hand observations of Elam Brown's party at the Lower California Crossing on June 8 with reports (which he may have heard later at Fort Laramie) of the misfortunes of Fabritus Smith's Oregon-bound company, which, like Elam Brown's, had also traveled the St. Joseph Road to the Oregon Trail and indeed was the last party to cross the Missouri River in the emigration of 1846. There is no evidence that at this stage of their journey westward anyone in Brown's wagon train (which left St. Joseph on May 1) had been killed by the Pawnees, but Parkman's reference here and on p. 67 of the present edition is undoubtedly to the murder of Edward Trimble of Smith's company, who was killed by Pawnees on June 18, near the "Platte Crossings," while out searching for the 150 head of cattle stampeded by the Indians a day or two before. Contemporary accounts of the Smith company's losses and of Trimble's murder are numerous and well detailed. See particularly Joel Palmer, *Journal of Travels over the Rocky Mountains, to the Mouth of the Columbia River; Made During the Years 1845 and 1846*, in R. G. Thwaites, ed. *Early Western Travels* (Cleveland, 1906), xxx, 251–

252; *James Clyman, Frontiersman,* pp. 225, 275–277; and contemporary newspaper accounts in Morgan, ed. *Overland in 1846,* II, 591–592, 597.

4 I have been unable to discover any contemporary evidence to substantiate Parkman's account of an Indian raid on the Brown company's horses.

5 Parkman's comparison of these Oregon emigrants with wandering Germanic tribes shows that he was well aware of the main outlines of the Marquis de Condorcet's theory of the progressive stages of civilization, a formulation which, in a somewhat simplified form, was often applied to the advance of the American frontier. Parkman had already encountered Condorcet's first stage of civilization, the nomadic hunters, and in the emigrant wagon trains he found a higher level of progressive development, that of a migratory and pastoral tribal life, at least to the extent that the American frontier experience could be made to fit Condorcet's theory. See Smith, *Virgin Land,* pp. 210–224, for an illuminating discussion of this almost metaphoric method of classifying the various levels of civilized life along the advancing frontier. Parkman of course knew Cooper's *The Prairie,* the first chapter of which introduces the "squatter" Ishmael Bush and describes him as one of those primitive herdsmen at war with civilization.

6 There is no specific reference in Parkman's notebooks to the appearance of Elam Brown's wagon train at Fort Laramie.

7 Parkman's remarks in this paragraph are representative of a great deal of contemporary comment in the literature of the Oregon and California emigrations. See Chester Ingersoll, *Overland to California in 1847 . . . ,* ed. Douglas C. McMurtrie (Chicago, 1937), p. 25: "At every stopping place, you can see something which has been thrown away. Over loading at the start, compels many to throw away things, which could be carried, if properly laid in on the

start." Besides the difficulties of "over loading," however, the emigrants struggled with the steadily worsening climate of the western part of the Platte Valley; lack of water and of adequate forage took a heavy toll on the teams, and the increasing dryness of the atmosphere shrunk wagon boxes and yokes and trees, wheels and spokes, so that some wagons were almost falling apart by the time they reached Fort Laramie. Not only furniture, then, but sometimes barrels of flour and bacon could be found scattered a few feet off the trail, and now and then a dead ox or a shattered wagon box.

But Parkman is referring here not only to the tremendous physical attrition of the westward journey; in its broader meanings the "cherished relic" is civilization itself, refinement and manners, the thin veneer of tradition and breeding which the inexorable severities of the trail, so it seemed to Parkman, stripped away from the emigrants and made them a prey to the nameless and unforeseen terrors of a hostile wilderness. He had felt the loss of the supports of civilization when he wandered, sick and alone, among the dark tents of the Sioux in the Laramie Basin; the accounts he later read of the Donner party's disaster must have confirmed his observations of the moral and spiritual as well as physical disintegrations which the experience of the wilderness worked on all those exposed to it.

8 Fifteen or 20 miles *was* a "sufficient day's journey" for the oxen drawing the emigrant wagons, as a good deal of contemporary evidence makes clear. See, for example, Lienhard, *St. Louis to Sutter's Fort*, p. 43. Parkman and his friends might easily have covered 30 or more miles a day with their light, mule-drawn cart, but Romaine simply did not want to outrun the emigrants, whose company, as Parkman shows, made the day's march easier and certainly safer.

9 Between the sentences "Travelling . . . separation" and

"We . . . days" K–52 supply the following additional sentence: "The connection with this party [K: with them] had cost us various delays and inconveniences; and the glaring want of courtesy and good sense displayed by their virtual leader [K: by the virtual leader of their party] did not dispose us to bear these annoyances with much patience." But Romaine probably had other reasons for being unwilling to travel much farther with a pair of reasonably acute and distrustful Yankees.

10 Between the sentences "A very . . . remarked" and "The most . . . journey" K–52 supply the following additional sentence: "Then he began to enlarge upon the enormity of the design."

11 Compare the sentence "We . . . us" with its K–52 form: "To palliate the atrocity of our conduct, we ventured to suggest that we were only four in number, while his party still included sixteen men; and as, moreover, we were to go forward and they were to follow, at least a full proportion of the perils he apprehended would fall on us." The "sixteen men" in this sentence were, of course, Romaine, the Chandlers, Wright, Boisverd, Sorel, and the 10 men from the emigrant wagons.

12 After the sentence "A very . . . principal" K–52 supply the following additional paragraph:

By good luck, we found a meadow of fresh grass, and a large pool of rain-water in the midst of it. We encamped here at sunset. Plenty of buffalo skulls were lying around, bleaching in the sun; and sprinkled thickly among the grass was a great variety of strange flowers. [K: of flowers, wholly unknown farther toward the east.] I had nothing else to do, and so gathering a handful, I sat down on a buffalo-skull to study them. Although the offspring of a wilderness, [K: of a savage wilderness,] their texture was frail and delicate, and their colors extremely rich: pure white, dark blue, and a transparent crimson. One travelling in this country seldom has leisure to think of any thing but the stern features of the scenery and its accompaniments, or the practical details of each day's journey. Like them, he and his thoughts grow hard and rough. But now these flowers suddenly awakened a train of associations as alien to the rude scene around me as they were themselves; and for the moment my thoughts went back to New England. A throng of fair and well-remembered faces rose, vividly as life, before me. 'There are good things,' thought I, 'in the savage life, but what can it offer to replace those powerful and ennobling influences that can reach unimpaired over more than three thousand miles of mountains, forests, and deserts?'

13 Compare the sentence "The Captain . . . success" with its K–52 form: "The Captain replied with a salutation of the utmost dignity, which Jack tried to imitate; but being little polished in the gestures of polite society, his effort was not a very successful one."

Despite Parkman's rather heavily jocular tone in this and the preceding paragraph (and especially in several of the canceled sentences), he and Shaw were violating one of the standing laws of the prairie when on June 10 they left Romaine and the Chandlers in what was, after all, a tight spot. As has been suggested, however (see note 17 for p. 5), Romaine may have been more relieved than not at their departure. Parkman's notebook account of this scene in *Journals*, II, 436, shows even more clearly how alarmed the Captain was: "Bade adieu this morning to him and the rest. He considers our leaving 'an extraordinary proceeding'—and seems to look on us as deserting them in a dangerous crisis. . . . They say their party ought to be *larger*." Despite Parkman's irony at the expense of the other party's desire to be "*larger*," it seems probable that Chatillon at least must have raised some objection to a dangerous division of forces which Parkman treats so off-handedly here.

14 The "main stream" is, of course, the North Platte River;

Parkman and his party would remain on its south bank until they reached Fort Laramie.

15 Ash Hollow was the point at which the Oregon Trail touched the North Platte after passing over the triangle of prairie separating the two forks of the river. The canyon, named for a grove of ash trees that once stood there, is almost directly across the North Platte from the present site of Lewellen, Nebraska. See Paden, *Wake of the Prairie Schooner*, pp. 120–122; and Long, *Oregon Trail*, pp. 106–107. Ash Hollow was always a particularly difficult obstacle for the wagon trains—one descent came down "Windlass Hill"—but Bryant, *What I Saw in California*, p. 98, noted its attraction as well:

We found near the mouth of "Ash Hollow" a small log-cabin, which had been erected last winter by some trappers, returning to the "settlements," who, on account of the snows, had been compelled to remain here until spring. This rude structure has, by the emigrants, been turned into a sort of general post-office. Numerous advertisements in manuscript are posted on its walls outside; descriptive of lost cattle, horses, etc., etc.; and inside, in a recess, there was a large number of letters deposited, addressed to persons in almost every quarter of the globe, with requests, that those who passed would convey them to the nearest post-office in the states. The place had something of the air of a cross-roads settlement; and we lingered around it some time, reading the advertisements and overlooking the letters.

16 Compare Parkman's notebook description of this party in *Journals*, II, 436: "Travelled late . . . came up with the emigrants camped in a circle—fires, tents, and waggons outside—horses within. The bottom covered with their cattle. They visited us at camp—a very good set of men, chiefly Missourians." Though the identification is not certain, these emigrants may have belonged to Captain Bur-

nett's party of 28 wagons and 16 families, which, like William J. Martin's wagon train, had once been a part of the larger company led by Elam Brown; John R. McBride, the chronicler of the Burnett party, had, like Elam Brown, also crossed the Missouri River at St. Joseph and had followed the St. Joseph Road to its junction with the Oregon Trail. Although Martin's and Burnett's companies had separated sometime in the first week of June, both trains were well in the forefront of the emigration of 1846. Parkman may here be referring, however, to another fragment of Brown's originally large party. See "The Diary of William E. Taylor" reprinted in Morgan, ed. *Overland in 1846*, I, 124–125, and also I, 90–95; and Barry, "Kansas before 1854," *KHQ*, xxx (Autumn, 1964), 345–346.

17 Parkman and his companions reached Scott's Bluff on the afternoon of June 13. Compare Journals, II, 437–438, for Parkman's more detailed description of the scene: "All these bluffs are singular and fantastic formations—abrupt, scored with wooded ravines, and wrought by storms into the semblance of lines of buildings. Midway on one of them gushes the spring, in the midst of wild roses, currants, cherries, and a hundred trees; and cuts for itself a devious and wooded ravine across the smooth plain below. Stood among the fresh wild roses and recalled old and delightful associations."

Scott's Bluff, now within the limits of Scott's Bluff National Monument near Gering, Nebraska, and almost directly across the river from the town of Scottsbluff, was the most impressive landmark on the North Platte east of Fort Laramie. Towering 800 feet above the river, it was, with Chimney Rock and the Courthouse (other formations which Parkman unaccountably fails to mention), in part responsible for the increasing sense of phantasmagoric wonder which most emigrants felt as they moved ever farther westward toward the heart of the wilderness.

Caused by millennia of wind and water erosion, these strange sandstone relic outcrops in the midst of barren badlands drew surprised and sometimes fearful comment from almost every western traveler. The "well-known spring" mentioned in this paragraph came to be known as Roubidoux, or Robidoux, Spring, after the younger Antoine Roubidoux, whom Parkman had first met on June 12. See *Journals*, II, 437; and Morgan, ed. *Overland in 1846*, I, 391.

Scott's Bluff itself commemorates the death of Hiram Scott (c. 1805–1828), one of the original hundred "enterprising young men" who answered William H. Ashley's advertisement for recruits for the mountain fur trade in 1822–1823. The story of Scott's "celebrated end" and of the discovery of his bleached bones at the foot of the Bluff appears in a number of contemporary accounts of western travel and adventure. See, for instance, Irving, *Adventures of Captain Bonneville*, p. 30. Merrill J. Mattes has attempted to reconcile the disparate and somewhat confused accounts of Scott's death; he concludes that Scott, returning with the Ashley-Chouteau caravan from the rendezvous of 1828 at Bear Lake on the modern Idaho-Utah border, sickened either at the rendezvous itself or on the homeward journey, perhaps not far from the future site of Fort Laramie. One version of the details of his death suggests that a pair of false friends basely abandoned him at the junction of the North Platte and Laramie rivers after the bullboat in which Scott was being carried downstream capsized and that Scott, utterly alone, crawled the 60 miles to the Bluff, where his bones were found and buried by William L. Sublette in the spring of 1829. As other accounts run, Scott had simply been left to die at the Bluff itself. See Merrill J. Mattes, "Hiram Scott," in LeRoy R. Hafen, ed. *The Mountain Men and the Fur Trade*

of the Far West (Glendale, Calif., 1965), I, 355–366;
and Paden, *Wake of the Prairie Schooner*, pp. 147–148.
18 Parkman and Chatillon were descending Roubidoux, or
Robidoux, Pass, so named because "a. Rubidue" in 1847
or 1848 set up a smithy near the "well-known spring"
mentioned above. See Paden, *Wake of the Prairie
Schooner*, pp. 148–149; and Paul C. Henderson, *Landmarks on the Oregon Trail* (New York, 1953), pp. 15–16.
Dale Morgan, however, argues that it was either Michel
(or Michael R.) Robidoux or Joseph E. Robidoux, the son
of the founder of St. Joseph, Missouri, who established the
Scott's Bluff blacksmith shop, probably in 1849. See James
A. Pritchard, *The Overland Diary of James A. Pritchard,
from Kentucky to California in 1849*, ed. Dale L. Morgan
(Denver, 1959), p. 151 n.
19 For further details of "Old Smoke's" village, see the general discussion of the Sioux on p. 117 of the present edition and note 24 for that page. Parkman met these Indians
on June 14. See *Journals*, II, 438.

The "various mystic figures" which Parkman notes here
are frequently mentioned in the literature of western
travel and adventure. They were apparently used to distinguish tribe from tribe and village from village as well as to
give signals before and during buffalo hunts and battles.
See Richard Irving Dodge, *Our Wild Indians: Thirty-
Three Years' Personal Experience among the Red Men of
the Great West* (Hartford, 1883), p. 430; and Hodge, ed.
Handbook of American Indians, II, 565–566.
20 Compare Parkman's more detailed description of the
"mystic whistle" in *Journals*, II, 470: "The War-Whistle,
not used by the chief as a signal, but blown by the young
men during the fight. It is a 'medicine' instrument, and is
blown by the Inds. when undergoing the penance of the
·buffalo skulls." This whistle was a part of the ceremonial

regalia among several Oglala "soldier" societies and was used for other rituals than the sun dance, Parkman's "penance of the buffalo skulls."

21 These ornaments, ranging in size from about 1½ to ½ inches or less in diameter, may be identical to the "rosettes" which Prince Maximilian saw adorning the Sioux of the upper Missouri. See Maximilian, *Travels in North America,* in Thwaites, ed. *Early Western Travels,* XXIV, 51–52.

22 Horse Creek enters the North Platte several miles east of Lyman, Nebraska.

23 Though this passage has the air of an accomplished set piece—picturesque Indians in the foreground, laboring ox wagons in the background—the scene actually occurred just as Parkman here describes it. See *Journals,* II, 438–439.

24 In his medicine bundle or "mystery sack" the Indian carried some hard part or feather of the sacred animal revealed to him through dreams during his initiatory fast or by the "war prophet" at the time of his induction into the ceremonies of the Mystery Dance. The medicine bag might also have contained paints, miniature weapons, or tokens of the Indian's clan or "soldier" society. In any case, the medicine bag was the Indian's most sacred possession, conferring upon him "medicine" powers and even a sense of spiritual identity. See J. Owen Dorsey, "A Study of Siouan Cults," *Eleventh Annual Report of the Bureau of Ethnology* (Washington, D.C., 1894), pp. 443–445; Royal B. Hassrick, *The Sioux: Life and Customs of a Warrior Society* (Norman, 1964), pp. 199–201; and Dodge, *Our Wild Indians,* pp. 106–107. Compare also Parkman's *Jesuits,* I, 66 n. (Vol. III of *Works*): "The author has seen a Dahcotah warrior open his medicine-bag, talk with an air of affectionate respect to the bone, feather, or horn within, and blow tobacco-smoke upon it as an offering."

25 This feast to the Indians, like the ones that Parkman later saw the emigrants giving at Fort Laramie, was at least partially offered in tribute to the Indians for permission to cross their hunting grounds. Compare "Laon [George L. Curry] to the St. Louis *Reveille*, 'Fort Bernard, June 25, 1846,'" reprinted in Morgan, ed. *Overland in 1846*, II, 574:

> The advance company of emigrants, which were for Oregon, under charge, I believe, of a Mr. Brown, comprising forty wagons, *were stopped in the road*, on arrival at Laramie, by the Sioux, *and not permitted to pass until tribute had been paid*. The Sioux say they must have tobacco, &c., for the privilege of travelling through their country. Their country, forsooth! Did they not steal it from the Cheyennes, and do they not hold possession of it because they are the more powerful? (*Naughty* savages, to be so *unchristian!*—EDS.) This may cause trouble, and Government should attend to it at once, lest the reply of the emigrants to this demand for the payment of a tax may be made through the medium of powder and lead, and so bring on fearful consequences.

Parkman's own very similar comments on the "dangerous spirit" of the Sioux and their high-handed treatment of the emigrants appear on pp. 116–117 of the present edition.

26 Otherwise known as "The Hog" in *The Oregon Trail*, this Indian cannot be identified except as the "Lamalalie" of Parkman's notebooks.

27 See p. 350 of the present edition and note 16 for that page for additional information about sign language. Although Parkman maintains in this passage that he did not *then* know sign language, internal evidence in *The Oregon Trail* itself seems to suggest that, before setting out on his Oregon Trail trip, Parkman had probably read Prince Maximilian's *Travels in the Interior of North America,*

which contains an extensive description of this system of intertribal communication. See Thwaites's edition of Maximilian's *Travels* in *Early Western Travels*, xxiv, 303–312.

28 Compare Parkman's notebook entry for June 26 in *Journals*, ii, 447: "A few lodges at the fort—Old Lamalalie's among them. He offered me his niece for a horse." It is doubtful that "The Hog" contemplated a permanent union between Parkman and his niece.

29 The reference in this passage to "an arm of the Platte" is not perfectly clear, but Parkman may be referring to Cherry Creek, which enters the North Platte near the present site of South Torrington, Wyoming. Parkman and his friends encamped there on the evening of June 14. See *Journals*, ii, 439.

30 Parkman means the Laramie Range in this reference and others to the "Black Hills" of Wyoming, so called because of their heavy covering of cedar and spruce. Charles Preuss's map in Frémont's *Report* also calls the Laramie Range the "Black Hills."

31 Parkman arrived at Pratte, Cabanne & Company's Fort Bernard on June 15. See *Journals*, ii, 439. This post, named either for the deceased Bernard Pratte, Sr., or for Bernard Pratte, Jr., was established in the late summer or fall of 1845 on a site occupied in 1837–1838 by a fort built by Peter L. Sarpy. The brisk trade carried on at Fort Bernard by the Richard brothers and Bissonette in the winter of 1845–1846 and the spring of 1846 caused considerable concern at Fort Laramie, eight miles west, a concern which may have shown itself unmistakably when Fort Bernard burned to the ground sometime during the summer of 1846, while John Richard was at the Pueblo with the Brown-Crosby party of Mississippi Mormons. See Hafen and Young, *Fort Laramie*, pp. 87–88; Morgan, ed. *Overland in 1846*, ii, 753; and John Dishon McDermott, "John Baptiste Richard," in LeRoy R. Hafen, ed. *The*

Mountain Men and the Fur Trade of the Far West (Glendale, Calif., 1965), II, 289–303. Compare Bryant, *What I Saw in California*, p. 107, on the appearance of Fort Bernard: "An inhabited house, although of the rudest construction and with accommodations far inferior to an ordinary stable, was nevertheless a cheering sight."

32 Parkman's description of John Richard in this passage is perhaps the fullest in the literature of western travel and adventure. John, or Jean Baptiste, Richard was born in St. Charles, Missouri, in 1810 and first went west in the late 1830's. In 1840 he entered into partnership with A. M. Metcalfe and began trading for furs in the mountains, and in 1842 he became an employee of Sybille, Adams & Company, whose adobe-walled Fort Platte, built in 1840 or 1841 by Lancaster P. Lupton, was located on the south bank of the North Platte River about a mile from Fort Laramie. In the spring of 1842 Richard followed Sybille and Adams to St. Louis to sell a year's accumulation of robes; in 1843 he himself led the fur caravan east. Besides taking part in the usual commerce in furs and buffalo robes, however, Richard seems early to have been involved in the illegal liquor traffic with the Indians at Fort Platte; he rapidly gained a very bad reputation for smuggling whiskey from Taos to the Laramie region, and, during the winter of 1842–1843, he used "Taos Lightning" in such quantities in his trade with the Sioux on the north forks of the Cheyenne River that the government, in the person of Andrew Drips, became seriously interested in Richard's operations, especially after a large loss of life among Richard's customers, given to quarreling in their cups.

During the summer of 1843, Bernard Pratte and John Cabanne, operating as Pratte, Cabanne & Company, took over Fort Platte, and for a time Richard found himself without a situation, until on November 5, 1843, he became an employee of the partners at Fort Platte. At about this same time he married Mary Gardiner, a half-breed girl living in Smoke's village; six children were born of this union. Richard's proficiency at hauling whiskey from Taos, while successfully evading Drips and his subagent, Joseph Hamilton, helped Pratte, Cabanne & Company's trade very considerably during the winter of 1843–1844, but the American Fur Company at Fort Laramie had felt the competition, and Drips finally took a very active interest in getting the liquor traffic at Fort Platte suppressed altogether; that post was abandoned in the summer of 1845 and Fort Bernard established shortly thereafter. Whether Pratte, Cabanne & Company were actively involved in Fort Bernard or simply allowed Richard, his brother Peter Richard, Joseph Bissonette, and Branham and one of the Bordeaux to trade under their license I have been unable to determine, but in the winter of 1845–1846 John Richard was very busy at the new post. The two boats that Edwin Bryant met on June 11 (see p. 76 of the present edition and note 13 for that page) give some indication of the success of Richard's winter trade.

The narratives of the emigration of 1846 mention Richard and Fort Bernard very frequently, almost invariably commenting, as "Laon" (George L. Curry) did on June 25 in a letter to the St. Louis *Reveille* reprinted in Morgan, ed. *Overland in 1846*, II, 573–575, on the free and easy hospitality of the proprietor: "We stopped but a few minutes on our arrival at this post, and, promising to return and partake of the hospitalities politely offered us by its commander, J. F. X. Richards, Esq., we hastened on. . . . I returned to Fort Bernard yesterday, and have received much attention from the gentlemen of the establishment. . . . Its proprietors and inmates are agreeable and courteous in the extreme, and among them a stranger feels himself at home." Similar comments might be cited at some length, with correspondingly extensive misspellings of Richard's name; it appears variously as Reshaw, Renshaw, Reshau, and even Rosseaux.

After the destruction of Fort Bernard, Richard remained briefly engaged in the fur trade, but during the 1850's he was reduced to operating a toll bridge over the North Platte near Fort Laramie. He was one of the first frontiersmen to bring news of the Pike's Peak gold discoveries to the Kansas-Nebraska settlements in 1858. During the early 1860's he had a store and a saloon in Denver, and in 1865 he was probably one of Jim Bridger's comrades-in-arms in the Powder River campaign. He was killed by Indians—perhaps Cheyennes—on the upper crossing of the Niobrara River in the winter of 1875–1876. See J. Cecil Alter, *Jim Bridger* (Norman, 1962), p. 311; and John Dishon McDermott, "John Baptiste Richard," in Hafen, ed. *Mountain Men and the Fur Trade,* II, 289–303.

33 The Navajos, an Athapaskan tribe who lived and still live in New Mexico, Arizona, and southern Utah, were in 1846 only just beginning to be known by large numbers of Americans, for until that year they had been at least technically under the control of the successive Spanish and Mexican governments. The American troops who, as members of Kearny's Army of the West, saw the Navajos for the first time were much impressed with the high level of Navajo civilization, at least in comparison with that of the Plains Indians.

34 One of these mountain men seems to have been Antoine Reynal, who traded for Richard·in the Sioux villages and whom Parkman would meet again at Chugwater Creek and at The Whirlwind's village in the Laramie Basin. See *Journals,* II, 439.

35 After the sentence "Not . . . him" K supplies the following additional sentence to conclude the paragraph: "This boy, who was called the 'Hail Storm,' I shall introduce again to the reader."

36 Parkman later (p. 274 of the present edition) defines
   shongsasha as powdered red-willow bark, sometimes
   smoked alone but more frequently mixed with tobacco.
   George Frederick Ruxton, *Life in the Far West*, ed.
   LeRoy R. Hafen (Norman, 1964), p. 105, notes that "the
   inner bark of the red willow [which he calls "kinnik-kin-
   nik"] has a highly narcotic effect on those not habituated
   to its use, and produces a heaviness sometimes approaching stupefaction, altogether different from the soothing
   effects of tobacco." However, "kinnikinnick" may also be
   used to describe either a compound of tobacco and various
   pulverized barks or the powdered red-willow bark itself.
   See Hodge, ed. *Handbook of American Indians*, I, 692.
   Parkman's use of the word *shongsasha* seems to be unique
   to him; I have been unable to trace it in any Sioux vocabu-
   lary available to me.

37 Compare the sentence "Being . . . could" with its K
   form: "Being averse to appearing in such a plight among
   any society that could approach an approximation to the
   civilized, (and at Fort Laramie the approximation was
   very remote,) we soon stopped by the river to make our
   toilet in the best way we could."

38 This post was Fort Platte, built in late 1840 or early 1841
   by Lancaster P. Lupton, which, after having passed
   through the hands of Sybille, Adams & Company and
   Pratte, Cabanne & Company, had been abandoned in
   1845. See Ann W. Hafen, "Lancaster P. Lupton," in
   LeRoy R. Hafen, ed. *The Mountain Men and the Fur
   Trade of the Far West* (Glendale, Calif., 1965), II,
   207–216; and Hafen and Young, *Fort Laramie*, pp. 69–94
   passim.

39 Fort Laramie and the river, plains, and mountains in its
   vicinity all took their names from a Jacques Laramé (also
   spelled Laramee, Loremy, LaRamee, and Laramie), who,
   according to various accounts, began trapping in this region about 1818 and was killed by Indians on the upper

Laramie River or the North Platte in 1821 or 1822 or was drowned in the Laramie River in 1828 or 1829. Some accounts have it that he built a wintering house near the mouth of the Laramie River, the small beginning of the posts which would come to be called Fort Laramie. The fort itself, located on the north bank of the Laramie River a mile or two above its mouth, was some 650 or 675 miles from Independence by the usual reckoning of travelers on the Oregon Trail; it had taken Parkman and his companions from May 8 to June 15, more than five weeks, to reach Fort Laramie, fairly good time considering their wanderings in eastern Kansas before they struck the St. Joseph Road.

Parkman saw the second post to be called Fort Laramie; the first, in existence from 1834 to 1841, had been built by Robert Campbell and William Sublette, two famous mountain men, who named their log-built trading post Fort William, probably in honor of Sublette. It was briefly owned and operated by Milton Sublette, Jim Bridger, and Tom Fitzpatrick, former partners in the Rocky Mountain Fur Company, who had merged with Lucien Fontenelle and Andrew Drips to form a new firm, Fontenelle, Fitzpatrick & Company, and then in 1836 it finally passed into the hands of Pratte, Chouteau & Company, Astor's successors as the American Fur Company. In 1841 the fort was rebuilt in adobe at a cost of $10,000 and renamed Fort John, presumably for John B. Sarpy. This was the fort Parkman saw, for the old name soon supplanted any other title given the post. In 1846 Fort Laramie was owned by Pierre Chouteau, Jr., & Company, then also known as the American Fur Company. See DeVoto, *Across the Wide Missouri*, pp. 190–191, and *Year of Decision*, pp. 173–174; Hafen and Young, *Fort Laramie*, pp. 20–134; Paden, *Wake of the Prairie Schooner*, p. 151; and Osborne Russell, *Journal of a Trapper*, ed. Aubrey L. Haines (Portland, 1950), p. 155.

40 Chatillon's friend Simoneau ("Cimoneau" in K–52) has left little trace in the history of the mountain fur trade. There is, however, a "Cimoneau" mentioned in William F. May's obituary, reprinted in Adrienne T. Christopher and LeRoy R. Hafen, "William F. May," in LeRoy R. Hafen, ed. *The Mountain Men and the Fur Trade of the Far West* (Glendale, Calif., 1966), IV, 216. Chittenden, *American Fur Trade*, I, 370, mentions a "Simoneau's Island" on the upper Missouri and Dale L. Morgan and Eleanor Towles Harris, eds. *The Rocky Mountain Journals of William Marshall Anderson: The West in 1834* (San Marino, 1967), p. 334, have discovered in the records of the Missouri Historical Society several references to "Lajeunesse, Charles dit [called] Simond (Simono)," who may have been Parkman's Simoneau. Like Chatillon, Lajeunesse spent his earliest years on the upper Missouri as an American Fur Company *engagé*; Morgan and Harris provide some account of his adventures near Fort Laramie in the early 1830's. Except for several brief references to him in the account books of the Upper Missouri Outfit in 1839 and 1841, Morgan and Harris find no further allusion to Charles Lajeunesse until Jim Bridger's statement in November, 1853, that Lajeunesse had settled near Fort Bridger, sometime after 1843.

For James Bordeaux see p. 104 of the present edition and note 5 for that page. For "Vaskiss" and May see p. 111 of the present edition and note 14 for that page. Tucker, from the evidence of Parkman's own notebooks, must have been one of the *engagés* at Fort Laramie. See *Journals*, II, 448.

CHAPTER IX

1 On February 20, 1847, the *Literary World* of New York City published in its third number (pp. 60–61) the follow-

ing version of Chapter IX, "Scenes at Fort Laramie." An expanded but not essentially *different* version of this chapter did not appear in *K* until October, 1847, some seven months after the initial publication of some of the same material in the *Literary World*. The *Literary World* version of Chapter IX seems clearly to be an abstraction from some longer manuscript: the "we" of this version is never clearly identified; "Smoke" is only vaguely presented as an Indian chieftain; and the editorial comment at the beginning of the *Literary World* installment suggests that the editors of the magazine might have had the refusal of other parts of Parkman's manuscript. In any case, Parkman had a version of Chapter IX *in print* less than six months after the end of his Oregon Trail trip, and it seems safe to assume on the basis of this evidence that he had begun work on what was to be *The Oregon Trail* almost immediately after his return to the East.

We have been favored by a gentleman of Boston, Mr. Francis Parkman, who has recently returned from an excursion to the Rocky Mountains, undertaken during the last season, with a volume of sketches of the journey, a few pages of which we are at liberty to lay before the reader. The objects of Mr. Parkman's tour were adventure and the prosecution of some scientific inquiries relative to Indian languages, usages, &c, in the course of which he met with incidents, the opportunity for which is every moment passing rapidly away. At an advanced stage of the journey we find the traveller at the trading post of Fort Laramie, the quiet of which is invaded by the eager bands of emigrants who are more numerous now than the Buffalo on the great Western plains.

Scenes at Fort Laramie

Fort Laramie is a post of the American Fur Company. The men who stood at the gate cast, at first, inquisitive and suspicious glances upon us. When however, we handed our letters

to the deputy *Bourgeois* and the Clerk had read them to him
—for the men of that region are not remarkable for their
literary attainments—they saw that we were not rival traders,
and welcomed us with courtesy. The apartment of the absent
Bourgeois was assigned to us; and in the absence of beds,
which are unknown at Fort Laramie, plenty of excellent Buffalo robes were spread upon the floor. A species of balcony, in
front of our room, was just opposite the main entrance. From
this high station we could conveniently look down into the
square area of the fort.

Indians were reclining in the sun, or stalking hither and
thither, enveloped in their whitened buffalo robes, while a
whole brood of smaller growth were running restlessly about,
and dodging in and out of the rooms which opened upon the
area. In some of these were lodged the squaws of the traders
and hunters. In others, the *engagés* of the company,—for the
most part hardy and light-hearted Canadians, who are indifferent to danger except when it is immediately present, careless of
hardship, and ready to live on the coarsest and most meagre
fare. A number of these men, sinewy and weather-beaten, in
half-Indian costume, were engaged in packing the wagons that
were soon to set out for a remote post in the mountains. A
gaunt, rawboned, old Frenchman, one of the "horse-guards,"
was sauntering about with a large pistol stuck, as a necessary
weapon of defense, in his belt.

We were scarcely established in our new quarters before all
the Indians came crowding in to see and smoke with us. They
were chiefly the fathers, brothers, and uncles of the squaws in
the fort, whose unfortunate owners were obliged to feed and
sustain this rapacious herd of relatives.

Soon after our arrival Smoke's village came up, and encamped close at hand. The white wagons of the Oregon emigrants soon followed. Appearing in slow procession on the
opposite bank, and plunging heavily through the stream, they
formed their usual circle about a quarter of a mile above; and
soon came crowding in at the gate, men, women, and children,
—staring, wondering, asking a thousand questions, and searching through every part of the fort with eager curiosity. They

invaded the apartments of the astonished squaws, the men, and even of the Deputy *Bourgeois* himself; at last our door was pushed open, and a swarm of raw, awkward-looking men, and lank pale-faced women, came crowding in, but were promptly expelled. Nothing could exceed their curiosity and wonderment; and being wholly guileless of anything like a perception of delicacy or propriety, they seemed resolved to explore every mystery to the bottom. In their perfect ignorance of the country and its inhabitants, they appeared to think that every one was combined to deceive and injure them: in particular, a notion was prevalent among them that the *French Indians*, as they called the trappers and traders, were instigating the Sioux to attack them and cut them off. In their attempts at bargain-making they were exceedingly astonished and indignant at Fort Laramie prices, where bad coffee and the worst tobacco are each sold at a dollar and half a pound.

The Indians of Smoke's village, in common with all the rest, seemed resolved to make the best of the swarms of *Meanaska* that of late had begun so mysteriously to pass through their country. Accordingly, the wagons were scarcely wheeled into the circle when the Indians demanded a feast, which the emigrants, full of doubts and apprehensions, did not dare to deny.

The feast was spread on the ground, in the open space surrounded by the wagons. It consisted chiefly of wheat bread and cups of coffee; and the whole village left their encampment to partake of it. Before it commenced, the squaws, by way of expressing their gratitude, joined in a dance, at which the emigrants stared open-mouthed. The guests then seated themselves in a semi-circle, Smoke in the centre, with his chiefs and warriors on either hand, while the extremities of the line were composed of the young men, squaws, and children. We met them all returning in the twilight, the squaws gaily painted and attired in their dancing dresses; and the men with great contentment on their faces, declaring that the whites had good hearts, and well encouraged to persevere for the future in their rapacious demands.

These demands grew daily more exorbitant with every successive band of emigrants that arrived at the fort; until at length the unprovoked insolence of the Indians rose to such a height, that one evening they broke to pieces, out of mere wantonness, the cups and dishes out of which they had been feasted. This so enraged the emigrants, that many of them caught up their rifles, and could scarcely be restrained from firing at their guests. We saw constant proofs of this dangerous and increasing spirit on the part of the Indians; which, taken in conjunction with various murders and outrages which they have perpetrated this summer, makes it absolutely necessary to the security of those who travel in that region that a body of troops should be permanently stationed there. The country will at best be a dangerous one, as long as its fickle and jealous inhabitants retain their present savage condition: but the presence of an armed power will materially diminish the peril, and save the lives of many brave and adventurous men. And it is the conviction of every one familiar with Indians, or in the slightest degree acquainted with their peculiar characters, that *military* law is the only law by which they can be effectually restrained. During the few days that we were at the fort, an Indian brought in the news, that two trappers in the mountains had just been treacherously killed by the Arapahoes.

2 This chapter was first published in K in October, 1847— hence the reference to "the expiration of a year," which may establish July or August, 1847, as the possible terminal dates for the composition of this chapter for K.

3 The *engagés* were the comparatively unskilled laborers of the fur posts, to be carefully distinguished from the trappers and hunters, whose rank and self-esteem were considerably higher.

4 Parkman and Shaw's "letter of introduction" seems to have been the letter of credit issued to them at St. Louis on April 25, 1846, by John Clapp for "P. Chouteau Son & Co." and addressed "To any person or persons in our employ in the Indian Country." This "Oregon Trail Passport," as Mason Wade calls it (see a reproduction of this

letter facing p. 438° of *Journals*, II), introduced "our friends Mr. F. Parkman and Mr. Quincy A. Shaw, who visit the interior of the country for their pleasure & amusement," and directed that "If these Gentlemen shall be in need of any thing in the way of supplies &c. you will oblige us by furnishing them to the extent of their wants, as also to render them any & every aid in your power, of which they may stand in need." Parkman and Shaw both countersigned this letter, a strong suggestion that it was meant to be used as an authorization for credit at Fort Laramie (where Parkman did, in fact, buy supplies) and other American Fur Company posts. The reverse of this document (in the Parkman Papers, Massachusetts Historical Society; not reproduced in Wade) shows Parkman's rough pencil-jottings of the daily log of distances which the party traveled on their eastward journey from Bent's Fort to the Missouri frontier.

5 So far as I am aware, Monthalon does not appear in any published account of Fort Laramie in 1846 except Parkman's notebooks and *The Oregon Trail* itself. The best and most complete account of the life of James Bordeaux (1814–1878) will be found in John Dishon McDermott, "James Bordeaux," in LeRoy R. Hafen, ed. *The Mountain Men and the Fur Trade of the Far West* (Glendale, Calif., 1968), V, 65–80.

James Bordeaux was born near St. Charles, Missouri, the son of a Canadian fur trader then comfortably established as a farmer and miller. Young Bordeaux apparently cared little for the life of the settlements, however, and McDermott notes that a James Bordeaux was employed by the American Fur Company on an expedition to the Kickapoos on the Niangua River in Missouri as early as 1826— when the boy was only 12 years old. There is also some evidence to suggest that Bordeaux was trading with the Sauks as early as 1829. On April 29, 1830, he signed a contract with Pierre Chouteau, Jr., to serve for a year as hunter and voyageur at Fort Union, in the employ of the Upper Missouri Outfit.

McDermott believes that Bordeaux spent the next six years—or the greater part of them—trapping and trading on the upper Missouri; his friendship with Henry Chatillon may date from this period. During the later 1830's Bordeaux, still in the service of the American Fur Company, apparently moved south—to Fort Laramie in 1836, to the Great Salt Lake in 1837, in 1838 probably again to Fort Laramie or the region nearby. In about 1840, after some time again spent on the upper Missouri, Bordeaux returned to Fort Laramie, where he took as his second wife Huntkalutawin, the daughter of Lone Dog of the Red Lodge band of the Brules; 10 children were born of this marriage. "Marie," as Parkman calls her on p. 113 of the present edition, "the very model of a squaw," was the sister of the famous warrior Swift Bear, whose increasing power among the Brules was of considerable advantage to Bordeaux in his later career as an independent Indian trader.

By 1842, when competition among the fur companies established on the North Platte had become more cutthroat than ever, Bordeaux had already established himself firmly in the Indian trade of the region, frequently acting as the *bourgeois* of Fort Laramie when the chief factor of the post was absent. Bordeaux materially assisted Frémont at the fort in 1842 with what McDermott calls "the latest Indian intelligence," perhaps gleaned from his Brule relatives. His rising influence among the Brules and other Sioux seems to have kept the tribesmen loyal to Fort Laramie, even though he occasionally handled them roughly enough to be nicknamed *Mato*—the "Bear."

Bordeaux continued to trade for the American Fur Company at Fort Laramie until 1849, when the post was sold to the government. Shortly thereafter, he formed a partnership with Joseph Bissonette and Charles Primeau for a trading venture in the Laramie region. Bordeaux and Bissonette located their new post some eight miles down the North Platte from Fort Laramie, probably very near the former site of Fort Bernard. This partnership did not prosper, and in 1850 Bordeaux himself established a new post a few miles farther up the river, where he seems to have engaged extensively in the illegal liquor trade with the Indians. In 1852 or perhaps earlier he joined John Richard in toll-bridge operations on the North Platte near Fort Laramie and Deer Creek, and for a time his various enterprises succeeded.

In 1854, however, he was involved in the most serious affair of his career as an Indian trader; in that year he played no very courageous part in attempting to dissuade Lieutenant Grattan and his men from attacking a Miniconjou village, by all accounts an act of senseless bravado founded on Grattan's miscalculation of the Indians' fighting spirit. McDermott's account (p. 73 of his article) of the Grattan Massacre is so well written as to deserve extensive quotation here:

On August 19 [1854] Lieutenant John Grattan, twenty-nine men, and an interpreter left the military post [Fort Laramie] to arrest a Miniconjou warrior, who had killed and feasted upon a stray cow from a passing Mormon caravan the day before. When Grattan stopped at Bordeaux' store on the way to the Indian village, the trader volunteered to act as intermediary, but the lieutenant chose to act alone. After Grattan entered the camp, an Oglala chief prevailed upon Bordeaux to ride with him to the village and reason with the young hotspur, but at midpoint the trader's courage failed him, and he returned to the safety of his home with the excuse that his stirrups were too long. Another plea stirred Bordeaux to make a second attempt, but before he reached the camp, fighting broke out. It was no contest. Only one private survived long enough to reach Fort Laramie, and he succumbed to wounds a few days later. The rest of the command blackened on the river bottom before Bordeaux received a request from the commanding officer at Fort Laramie to bury them.

The rest of Bordeaux's career is of comparably little interest. For at least the next 13 or 14 years Bordeaux continued to trade with emigrants and Indians on the North Platte; from 1868 to 1871 he kept a store at Whetstone Agency among the Brules, and off and on for the next several years he farmed and traded with the Sioux at several different locations in Nebraska. He spent his last years in poverty and discouragement and died of pneumonia, at 64, among the Brules at the Rosebud Agency.

In addition to McDermott's article, see also his "Joseph Bissonette," in Hafen, ed. *The Mountain Men and the Fur Trade of the Far West* (Glendale, Calif., 1966), IV, 55–56; Lloyd E. McCann, "The Grattan Massacre," *Nebraska History*, XXXVII (March, 1956), p. 5 n.; Paden, *Wake of the Prairie Schooner*, pp. 159–160; and George E. Hyde, *Spotted Tail's Folk: A History of the Brulé Sioux* (Norman, 1961), pp. 50–54.

Bordeaux is frequently mentioned by diarists of the emigration of 1846, almost always in terms flatly contradicting Parkman's rather ungenerous description in this passage. Thornton, *Oregon and California in 1848*, I, 113, noted that "I was received by Mr. Bodeau, the gentleman in charge of the post, with much kindness. . . ." Improving on the opportunity of Bordeaux's hospitality, Thornton presented the vice-*bourgeois* with a bundle of tracts, which, Thornton thought, Bordeaux "appeared to receive with pleasure." Parkman himself, writing to his mother on June 19, remarked that "As for us, we are well lodged in the fort itself, and though the fare is none of the most luxurious, the *bourgeois*, Mr. Bordeau, takes the greatest pains to make us comfortable." See *Letters*, I, 42.

6 This "dismal trophy" was really the cause of the great Sioux war parties planned and organized in 1846. See p. 121 of the present edition and note 2 for that page.

7 A plan of Fort Laramie appears in Henderson, *Landmarks on the Oregon Trail*, p. 20. An extended, contemporary description of the post is provided in a letter of D. P. Woodbury's written from Fort Laramie on November 15, 1849 (after the post had been purchased by the government), and reprinted in Lillian W. Willman, "The History of Fort Kearny," *Publications of the Nebraska State Historical Society*, xxi (1930), 263–264:

The old fort consists in the main of 19 rooms, varying in size from 12 feet square to 12 feet by 29 feet, and running around an open space 80 feet by 72 feet. Two of the nineteen rooms belong to a two-story building having two rooms in the second story, making 21 rooms in all.

The outside walls are 3 feet thick at bottom, and diminish, by two offsets on the inside to less than 2 feet at the top. The partition walls are generally 2 feet thick.

Adjacent to the open space above mentioned, and connected with it by a passage way 8 feet wide, is another open space about 80 feet by 45 feet, surrounded on one side by buildings already described, on another by a barn 25 feet square and a stable 12 feet by 18 feet, on the third by a 3-foot wall about 15 feet high, and on the fourth by a similar wall.

The rooms will average about 8 feet in height. . . . There are towers six feet square at two of the angles and another over the principal entrance.

A sketch of Fort Laramie as it appeared in 1842 will be found in the engraving facing p. 40 of Frémont's *Report*.

8 Many Plains Indians painted their faces black to signify joy at killing an enemy or striking a coup. See Garrard,

Wah-To-Yah and the Taos Trail, p. 139; and Ruxton, *Life in the Far West,* p. 36.

9 "Medicine" meant for the Sioux, as for other tribes, any means by which the visible and invisible worlds might be propitiated and controlled; indeed, everything to the Indian might be said to have been or to have had a "medicine," an inherent being and power. Bernard DeVoto, in the introduction to his edition of T. D. Bonner, *The Life and Adventures of James P. Beckwourth* (New York, 1931), p. xxxvi, supplies one of the best brief descriptions of the Indian's psychology, with its emphatic reliance upon "medicine" as a complexly structured world view:

> Every moment of the Indian's life was oppressed by the necessity of this system of magic. His world was full of demonic spirits and of natural forces whose malevolence was no less dreadful. By sacrifice, propitiation, and prophylaxis it was possible to keep this world in an equilibrium, precarious but tolerable. An incredibly complex ritual resulted and hedged about every act, individual or communal. For everything there was a ceremony, and to omit it was to disturb the equilibrium and let loose violence.

"Medicine," a very rough translation of the Sioux word *wakan,* "covers the whole field of their fear and worship. Many things that are neither feared nor worshipped, but are simply wonderful, come under this designation," which may indeed mean simply power, strength, or mystery, according to Stephen R. Riggs as quoted in Dorsey, "A Study of Siouan Cults," *Eleventh Annual Report,* pp. 432–433. The medicine man's principal power and authority are to be ascribed to his ability to make his "medicine," his chants, tricks with fire, sleights of hand, and visions, accord with the "medicine" of the person he was treating or with the "medicine" of the knife and herbs he used in his cures. The term itself seems to come from the French *médecin,* applied by the trappers first to the shamans and medicine men and by extension to their methods. Whole villages might even in time of danger prepare a communal "medicine" to propitiate evil spirits or to repair the breach of some tribal taboo. See Hodge, ed. *Handbook of American Indians,* 1, 836–838; Hassrick, *The Sioux,* pp. 249–255; and Dorsey's monograph cited above. Some tribes made a careful distinction between shamans or magicians, who originated curative spells and formulas, and the medicine men, who under a kind of internship learned the secrets of their trade from the specializing shamans.

10 This passage is mere rhetoric, for even by 1846 Parkman had encountered during his backwoods excursions a good many Indians who had profited, to a greater or lesser degree, from the "exertions of the missionaries" as well as from other less purely edifying aspects of white culture and civilization. This passage, however, represents about the only obviously intentional misrepresentation of Indian character and psychology in *The Oregon Trail* and may, at least in part, be set down as Parkman's contribution to contemporary celebrations of American progressive civilization, a kind of cultural Manifest Destiny.

11 Garrard, *Wah-To-Yah and the Taos Trail,* p. 89, gives a good description of this method of Indian sepulture: "Three of us . . . saw, on the horizontal limbs of a cottonwood, two Indian graves, thirty feet or more from the ground. Short poles were tied transversely, from one limb to another, and the deceased, wrapped in many folds of robes with a few ornaments, was tied on this scaffolding with thongs of rawhide." Dorsey, "A Study of Siouan Cults," *Eleventh Annual Report,* p. 486, learned that the scaffolds were used to protect the bodies from water and mud, from wolves and other carnivores, and from desecration by the footsteps of men and animals.

12 The Crows, a Siouan tribe, may have numbered as many
as 5,000 persons in 1846; their territory embraced the
Absaroka region, primarily the valley and watershed of the
Big Horn River in southern Montana and northern Wyoming, though they were also to be found along the Powder
and Wind rivers and occasionally as far eastward as Fort
Laramie itself. The Crows were among the handsomest
Indians; socially they seem to have had the best discipline,
refusing for years to permit alcohol in their fur trade with
the whites. Indeed, the Crows were rather partial to white
men: Chittenden, *American Fur Trade*, II, 842–844, notes
that there is scarcely an instance of a white man's death at
the hands of the Crows. Two mulattoes, Edward Rose and
Jim Beckwourth, even became war chiefs of the tribe. See
Hodge, ed. *Handbook of American Indians*, I, 367–369;
and Lowie, *Crow Indians*, pp. 3–17.

13 Parkman is probably correct in describing the ring of buffalo skulls as part of the Sioux funeral rituals, but other
contemporary sources suggest that these curious and of-
ten-mentioned rings were part of the buffalo-dance ceremonies.

14 Louis Vasquez (1798–1868) had long been a famous
figure in the fur trade when Parkman saw his wagons
fitting out for his "remote post in the mountains," Fort
Bridger itself. Born in St. Louis and descended from pioneers and fur traders, Vasquez himself went to the upper
Missouri in 1822 with one of the Ashley-Henry expeditions. He first went to the mountains in 1825–1826 with
Jedediah Smith and was near Great Salt Lake later in the
decade; a number of western historians have suggested
that it was Louis Vasquez who discovered the Great Salt
Lake and circumnavigated it in a bullboat in 1826, but
more recent evaluations of his career do not accept this
discovery. In 1833 he traveled west as chief assistant to
Robert Campbell, the leader of the supply train to the

trappers' summer rendezvous of that year. In partnership with Andrew Sublette he built Fort Vasquez on the South Platte in 1835, a post which the partners sold in 1840 or 1841 and evacuated in 1842, the same year that Vasquez and Jim Bridger went into business together and built rough trading cabins on a bluff near Blacks Fork of the Green River.

The site was soon abandoned, and Fort Bridger was built in the late spring of 1843 on a grassy bottomland where Blacks Fork spreads into several branches, not far from the present site of Fort Bridger, Wyoming. According to Chittenden, *American Fur Trade*, II, 945, the founding of Fort Bridger in 1843 at a site specifically chosen to supply the Oregon and California emigrant trains marks the end of the great days of the mountain fur trade.

Fort Bridger and its owners were reasonably successful for the next several years, but by 1846 many wagon trains were bypassing their post in favor of the more direct route of the Greenwood Cut-Off to the north. Vasquez and Bridger had both arrived at Fort Laramie on or about May 7, 1846, and may have returned to their post as early as July 17; they were certainly there on July 31, when they were visited by James Frazier Reed of the Donner party. On July 18, Bryant, *What I Saw in California*, p. 144, noted that on that date he had left letters at Fort Bridger warning emigrants behind him not to take Lansford W. Hastings' new route to California around the foot of the Great Salt Lake; "Hastings' Cut-Off," so it seemed to Bryant on the basis of reports he had received from Joseph Reddeford Walker, a famous mountain man, was a dangerous experiment, possible perhaps only for a fast party on muleback like Bryant's own. Reed later placed the blame for the Donner party's disaster squarely upon Vasquez, who had recommended Hastings' route (which would keep emigrants passing Fort Bridger) and who had withheld Bryant's letters of warning. See Stewart, *California Trail*, p. 167.

The rest of Vasquez' life is of considerably less importance to Parkman and *The Oregon Trail*. Fort Bridger was sold to the Mormons in 1855, and Vasquez died at the age of 70 in Kansas City in 1868.

In addition to the citations given above, see LeRoy R. Hafen, "Louis Vasquez," in LeRoy R. Hafen, ed. *The Mountain Men and the Fur Trade of the Far West* (Glendale, Calif., 1965), II, 321–338; LeRoy R. Hafen, *Fort Vasquez* (Denver, 1964), pp. 1–10; Doyce Blackman Nunis, Jr., *Andrew Sublette: Rocky Mountain Prince* (Los Angeles, 1960), p. 53; Alter, *Jim Bridger*, p. 218; and Morgan, ed. *Overland in 1846*, II, 757–758.

William F. May (c. 1797–1855) was born in Kentucky and had served in the War of 1812 before going west sometime before 1820. By 1822 he was in charge of a trading post among the Mandans in what is now North Dakota and later in the 1820's he was engaged in the Santa Fe trade. From 1830 until at least 1843 May trapped and traded on the upper Missouri River; his name appears frequently in contemporary journals and records of the area, and Chatillon may have known him there. In the spring of 1843 he was robbed of a cargo of furs by some of Ebbetts & Company's men at the Little Bend of the Missouri, near the mouth of the Cheyenne River; it seems probable that May moved down to the Fort Laramie region shortly thereafter, where he must have remained until as late as 1854, a year before his death in Salt Lake City. See Christopher and Hafen, "William F. May," in Hafen, ed. *Mountain Men and the Fur Trade*, IV, 207–216. In *Journals*, II, 447, Parkman noted May's "nervous fiery temper" and what must have been his unfavorable "acct. of the French in the country."

15 George Catlin (1796–1872) was the author of *Letters and Notes on the Manners, Customs, and Civilization of the North American Indians* (2 vols., 1841), *Catlin's North American Indian Portfolio* (1844), and *Life among the Indians* (1867), among other works. After early training in and practice of the law, he began to paint Indians in 1829, and in 1832 went west for the first time, traveling up the Missouri on the famous *Yellowstone* steamboat. For the next six years he spent at least part of every year among the Indians, in 1834 along the Arkansas River frontier, in 1835 and 1836 on the upper Mississippi, with side trips during these years and the following ones along the Gulf Coast and the Great Lakes. During his later years he exhibited his paintings widely in the United States and Europe and found time and energy for further rambles in Texas, the Pacific Northwest, and South America. Catlin received a good deal of popular attention and acclaim during his immensely productive career, and recent critical evaluations have placed him among the finest of the early illustrators of the West. See *DAB, s.v.* "Catlin, George"; De-Voto, *Across the Wide Missouri,* pp. 399–401; and Marvin C. Ross's introduction to Catlin's *Episodes from Life among the Indians and Last Rambles* (Norman, 1959), pp. xix–xxv.

The "curious story" which May related, doubtless a memory from his years of experience on the upper Missouri, may be the same one which Parkman later repeated in *Jesuits,* I, 224 n. (Vol. III of *Works*): "Catlin, the painter, once caused a fatal quarrel among a band of Sioux, by representing one of them in profile, whereupon he was jibed by a rival as being but *half a man.*"

16 The *travois* is well shown in the illustration on p. 112 of this edition, though Parkman, writing to Remington to give his approval of the artist's finished sketches, suggested that "In the picture of a mule harnessed to a 'travois,' the

poles are in the same line with the ears which, I think, might be changed with advantage." See *Letters*, II, 256; and note that the *travois*-poles and the mule's ears are nevertheless still in line.

17 This party, not easily identifiable, arrived at Fort Laramie on June 16. See *Journals*, II, 441.

18 The sentences "Resolved . . . *bourgeois*" and "At . . . remain" replace the following three sentences in *K*–52: "They explored the apartments of the men, and even that of Marie and the *bourgeois*. At last a numerous deputation appeared at our door, but were immediately expelled. Being totally devoid of any sense of delicacy or propriety, they seemed resolved to search every mystery to the bottom."

19 After the sentence "The men . . . own" *K* supplies the following three additional sentences to conclude the paragraph: "In these transactions, conducted under the auspices of the smooth Montalon [*sic*], a most base advantage was taken of the ignorance and necessities of the emigrants. They were plundered and cheated without mercy. In one bargain, concluded in my presence, I calculated the profits that accrued to the fort, and found that at the lowest estimate they exceeded *eighteen hundred per cent*."

Parkman's reasons for excising this passage do not seem clear, for his notebook entry for June 16 in *Journals*, II, 440, presents an even harsher indictment of American Fur Company prices at Fort Laramie: "Prices are most extortionate. Sugar, two dollars a cup—5-cent tobacco at $1.50—bullets at $.75 a pound, etc. American Fur Cmp'y exceedingly disliked in this country—it suppresses all opposition, and keeping up these enormous prices, pays its men in necessaries on these terms." A reasonably literate trapper estimated that the usual prices at the forts represented a markup of 2,000 percent over St. Louis costs, and thus Parkman's complaints are well founded. See Russell,

Journal of a Trapper, p. 60. Parkman's own expensive purchases at Fort Laramie might have had something to do with his resentment at having to deal in a seller's market, for, among total charges of $105.50, he had to pay 20 cents a pound for 12 pounds of flour. See "Oregon Trail Accounts" in *Journals,* ii, 494. At Fort Bernard, on the other hand, Parkman found the price of flour 40 percent cheaper, a good reason, perhaps, why Richard's post was destroyed later this same year.

20 Compare the sentence "The emigrants . . . traders" with its form in *K:* "This system of contemptible trickery did not tend to remove the prejudice which the emigrants entertained against the French Indians, as they called the trappers and traders." Parkman expressed himself even more forcefully about the Fort Laramie traders in his notebook entry for June 28 in *Journals,* ii, 448: "People at the fort a set of mean swindlers, as witness my purchase of the bacon, and their treatment of the emigrants."

21 Both battles were, of course, American victories in the Mexican War, and General Zachary Taylor commanded the American troops in both conflicts. The Battle of Monterrey was fought on September 21–23, 1846, and was one of the longest and bloodiest struggles of the war. The Battle of Buena Vista occurred on February 22–23, 1847, six months before the publication of the *K* version of this edition.

22 Parkman described the emigrants at Fort Laramie in very similar terms in a letter to his mother on June 19: "Here at the fort, they are very suspicious and mistrustful, and seem to think the traders their natural enemies. We are invariably taken for traders in disguise, and find the most effectual way to persuade them to any thing, is to advise them to something directly the contrary." See *Letters,* i, 44.

23 I have been unable to verify the details of this incident, though it is doubtful that Parkman is reporting it on the

basis of first-hand knowledge. The identifiable source for Parkman's description of this incident is to be found in his notebook entry for August 6, some six weeks after his arrival at Fort Laramie, in *Journals*, ii, 468–469:

> Sioux told Rouville that the Pawnees had been committing outrages for years and no dragoons had come, and now *they* meant to do the same. But few of them saw the dragoons [in 1845, apparently], being afraid to come, then dissatisfied at getting no presents. Never so turbulent as this year. Declare that if the emigrants continued to pass through, they would rob and kill them if they resisted. Broke up the pots and pans of the emigrants who feasted them. Robbed Sublette and Reddick, and fired upon them. Robbed Bonny. Robbed a party of eight wagons at Independence Creek in July.

The details of these events *all* came to Parkman, it appears, at least at second-hand from the trapper Rouville, and though some of these reports of Sioux outrages have some ascertainable basis in fact, it seems clear that neither Parkman nor, probably, Rouville himself had anything like reliable knowledge of them. Compare also the account of one emigrant-train's feast to the Sioux on June 23, in "The Diary of Virgil Pringle," reprinted in Morgan, ed. *Overland in 1846*, i, 174: "This morning all united in giving our Sioux brethren a feast with which they appeared highly pleased. It was conducted with considerable order and regularity on their part, smoking the pipe of peace and a friendly address from their chief, and a present of powder, lead and tobacco on our part."

24 Parkman uses "Dakota" and "Sioux" indiscriminately throughout *The Oregon Trail* to refer to the Tetons, the largest division of the Dakota Indians, and specifically to the Oglalas, the largest group among the Tetons. Strictly speaking, "Sioux" and "Siouan" are linguistic distinctions only, and tribes speaking Siouan languages were, after the

great Algonquin language group, the most populous in North America. Before their displacement by the whites, most of the Siouan tribes inhabited the region from the Mississippi as far westward as the Rocky Mountains and north of the Arkansas River, but other groups were to be found in the central parts of North and South Carolina and in the Virginia piedmont; still other Siouan tribes were located along the Gulf Coast and Yazoo River regions of Mississippi.

The Dakotas (a word meaning "friends" or "allies"), the largest division of the Siouan linguistic family, were divided into four dialect groups, the Santees, the Yanktons, the Tetons, and the Assiniboins. At the time of their first encounters with white men the Dakotas seem to have been located in the forest region of southern Minnesota, particularly around Mille Lacs and the upper Mississippi, where Hennepin met the Tetons in 1680 at a point about 70 miles above Minneapolis. Most of the Dakotas remained in what is now Minnesota until comparatively recently; very few of the tribesmen had crossed the Missouri River before 1750, driven westward toward the plains by the Chippewas (whom the French had supplied with guns) and toward the Black Hills of South Dakota, which some Dakotas must have reached by 1765. The Mdewakantons, Wahpekutes, Wahpetons, and Sissetons, collectively known as the Santees, remained in Minnesota; the Yanktons and Yanktonais, another distinct dialect group recognized together as the Yanktons, held all the territory east of the Missouri River in North and South Dakota, and the Tetons controlled much of the territory west and south of the Missouri River as far as Fort Laramie.

The Tetons themselves were divided into seven distinct bands, the Brules, the Sans Arcs, the Sihasapas (or Blackfeet), the Miniconques (or Miniconjous), the Two Kettles, the Hunkpapas, and the Oglalas (the "scattered" or "to scatter one's own"), the largest single group among the Tetons.

The first significant contact between the Oglalas and white men occurred in 1806 when Lewis and Clark found them living above the Brules on the Missouri River between the Cheyenne and Bad rivers in present South Dakota. In 1825 they lived along both banks of the Bad River from the Missouri to the Black Hills of South Dakota and numbered about 1,500 persons, 300 of whom were rated as warriors. It was during the period 1810–1825 that Bull Bear's Kiyuksas and Red Water's band of Brules joined the Oglalas. From 1825 to 1834 the Oglala camps were almost always in sight of the Black Hills, where many tribal ceremonies were held, including the initiatory fasts like that which Parkman describes on pp. 156–157 of the present edition.

The establishment of the first Fort Laramie in 1834 marks the date when the Oglalas first began to appear in strength along the North Platte; a good deal of contemporary evidence shows that in that year William Sublette and Robert Campbell, the founders of Fort Laramie, sent Galpin and one of the Sybilles to the Black Hills to draw the elder Bull Bear (Mahto-Tatonka in *The Oregon Trail*) and some hundred lodges of the Oglalas, fully half the band, down to the newly established post. From that time on the Oglalas dominated, if they did not entirely control, the North Platte west of the forks and especially the Laramie Plains, one of the great crossroads of the West—and rich buffalo country besides.

By 1841 the Oglalas were firmly in possession of their new home and had for several years been sending out war parties in all directions, dealing particularly heavy blows against the Pawnees and the Arikaras. During this same period the Oglalas under Bull Bear's leadership began to hunt westward of Fort Laramie, frequently colliding with the Snakes; other bands of Oglalas, tenuously under the command of Chief Smoke (so called, probably, because he had taught white trappers how to smoke buffalo meat) had taken over the rich hunting grounds at the forks of the Platte formerly held by the Bear People, Bull Bear's followers among the Oglalas.

If 1841 marked a high point of Oglala fortunes along the North Platte, it was the year that saw the tribe badly split when Smoke arranged the murder of the elder Bull Bear on Chugwater Creek. Bull Bear was less friendly to the traders and trappers than was Smoke; there is some reason to believe that the whites instigated his murder. After Bull Bear's death, the Oglalas split into two mutually distrustful groups, a division that lasted more than 40 years. The Bear People (comprising The Whirlwind's Kiyuksa band, the "True Oglalas," and Red Water's village) gradually moved southeast and finally occupied the region in Nebraska and Kansas between the Platte River and the Smoky Hill Fork; the Smoke People moved north toward the headwaters of the Powder River. It was the Bear People, or at least part of the band, whom Parkman visited in the Laramie Basin.

See Hyde, *Red Cloud's Folk*, pp. 40–68; Hassrick, *The Sioux*, pp. 1–8; and Hodge, ed. *Handbook of American Indians*, I, 376–380; II, 109–111, 577–579, 736–737. Most accounts of the Oglalas in the 1830's and 1840's agree in describing them as the Reverend Samuel Parker did in his *Journal of an Exploring Tour Beyond the Rocky Mountains* (New York, 1846), p. 67: "These are the finest looking Indians I have ever seen."

25 Parkman's reference to "a wise people . . . living in leather lodges, like their own" is not perfectly clear, but he may mean those free trappers and "outside" traders who

followed the villages and lived like the Indians themselves.

26 *Meneaska* (properly *Mí-na-han-ska*) means "Long Knife" and hence an American. See Stephen R. Riggs, A *Dakota-English Dictionary*, ed. James Owen Dorsey, *Contributions to American North Ethnology*, VII (Washington, D.C., 1890), 314.

27 Parkman's fears were shared by other travelers in 1846. Compare George L. Curry's comments on the Sioux in note 25 for p. 97 of this edition.

28 Parkman described this scene in his notebook entry for June 19 in *Journals*, II, 443: "The begging dance—monotonous enough—in the area of the fort. Led by three dandies, the young squaws moved round singing in a circle." The Prairie Cock cannot be identified except as one of the "dandies" mentioned above.

29 Father De Smet, *Letters and Sketches,* in Thwaites, ed. *Early Western Travels*, XXVII, 300, noted: "These Indians suffer much from ophthalmic infections. Scarcely a cabin is to be found on Clarke river, in which there is not a blind or one eyed person, or some one laboring under some disease of the eye." Bernard DeVoto, *Year of Decision,* p. 164, concluded that trachoma was endemic among most tribes of the plains and mountains, and there is plenty of evidence to suggest that, far from curing his own eyestrain during his tour of the prairies, Parkman only worsened a condition serious enough before he went west. Compare Robert Eccleston, *Overland to California on the Southwestern Trail 1849,* eds. George P. Hammond and Edward H. Howes (Berkeley, 1950), p. 96: "I suffered a good deal today from one of my eyes, which yesterday from the dust, sun & wind, I could hardly open it. This morning, it being inflamed from the eyebrow to the cheek bone, I was obliged to wear a bandage over it today."

30 On the general principle of "like cures like," homeopathic

medicine as it was understood in the 1840's attempted to cure a given illness by applying a small portion of a drug or ointment which, if given to a healthy person, would make him ill of the same disease the patient was suffering from. Thus, Shaw wished that he had a "counter-irritant" like Spanish flies for the woman with sore eyes.

31 Parkman devoured the puppy in Smoke's lodge on June 20; "It was excellent," he remarked in *Journals*, II, 443. Garrard, *Wah-To-Yah and the Taos Trail*, pp. 97–98, met a trapper who liked dog almost as well as buffalo: "Well, hos! I'll dock off buffler, and then if thar's any meat that 'runs' can take the shine outen 'dog,' you can slide." There are a good many other contemporary references to dog feasts as signal marks of Indian hospitality to white men. See De Smet, *Letters and Sketches*, in Thwaites, ed. *Early Western Travels*, XXVII, 136; and Sage, *Scenes in the Rocky Mountains*, I, 279.

32 After the sentence "This . . . admitted" K–52 supply the following additional paragraph to conclude the chapter:

[K supplies the following additional sentence at the beginning of the paragraph: The reader will not have forgotten our comrades whom we had so basely run away from on the south fork of the Platte.] One morning, about a week after reaching Fort Laramie, we were holding our customary Indian levee, when a bustle in the area below announced a new arrival; and looking down from our balcony, I saw a familiar red beard and moustache in the gateway. They belonged to the Captain, who with his party had just crossed the stream. We met him on the stairs as he came up, and congratulated him on the safe arrival of himself and his devoted companions. But he remembered our treachery, and was grave and dignified accordingly; a tendency which increased as he observed on our part a disposition to laugh at him. After remaining an hour or two at the fort, he rode away with his friends, and we have heard nothing of him

since. As for R——, he kept carefully aloof. It was but too
evident that we had the unhappiness to have forfeited the kind
regards of our London fellow-traveller.

The editions of 49–52 supply the following additional
"Note" to the canceled paragraph above:

NOTE.

Somewhat more than a year from this time Shaw happened
to be in New York, and coming one morning down the steps
of the Astor House, encountered a small newsboy with a
bundle of penny papers under his arm, who screamed in his
ear, "Another great battle in Mexico!" Shaw bought a paper,
and having perused the glorious intelligence, was looking over
the remaining columns, when the following paragraph attracted his notice:

ENGLISH TRAVELLING SPORTSMEN.—Among the notable arrivals in town are two English gentlemen, William and John
C.——, Esqrs., at the Clinton Hotel, on their return home
after an extended Buffalo hunting tour in Oregon and the wild
West. Their party crossed the continent in March, 1846, since
when our travellers have seen the wonders of our great West,
the Sandwich Islands, and the no less agreeable Coasts of
Western Mexico, California, and Peru. With the real zeal of
sportsmen they have pursued adventure whenever it has offered, and returned with not only a correct knowledge of the
West, but with many a trophy that shows they have found the
grand sport they sought. The account of "Oregon," given by
these observing travellers, is most glowing, and though upon a
pleasure trip, the advantages to be realized by commercial men
have not been overlooked, and they prophecy for that "Western State," a prosperity not exceeded at the east. The fisheries
are spoken of as the best in the country, and only equalled by
the rare facilities for agriculture. A trip like this now closed is a
rare undertaking, but as interesting as rare to those who are
capable of a full appreciation of all the wonders that met them
in the magnificent region they have traversed.

In some admiration at the heroic light in which Jack and the Captain were here set forth, Shaw pocketed the newspaper, and proceeded to make inquiry after his old fellow-travellers. Jack was out of town, but the Captain was quietly established at his hotel. Except that the red moustache was shorn away, he was in all respects the same man whom we have left upon the South Fork of the Platte. Every recollection of former differences had vanished from his mind, and he greeted his visitor most cordially. "Where is R——?" asked Shaw. "Gone to the devil," hastily replied the Captain, "that is, Jack and I parted from him at Oregon City, and haven't seen him since." He next proceeded to give an account of his journeyings after leaving us at Fort Laramie. No sooner, it seemed, had he done so, than he and Jack began to slaughter the buffalo with unrelenting fury, but when they reached the other side of South Pass their rifles were laid by as useless, since there were neither Indians nor game to exercise them upon. From this point the journey, as the Captain expressed it, was a great bore. When they reached the mouth of the Columbia, he and Jack sailed for the Sandwich Islands, whence they proceeded to Panama, across the Isthmus, and came by sea to New Orleans.

Shaw and our friend spent the evening together, and when they finally separated at two o'clock in the morning, the Captain's ruddy face was ruddier than ever.

Romaine and the Chandlers arrived at Fort Laramie on June 17. See *Journals*, II, 442. Romaine's disappearance at Oregon City—then the center of American settlement in Oregon—and Bill Chandler's curious reluctance to discuss Romaine's further adventures should not escape the careful reader's consideration. I have been unable to find the source of the newspaper paragraph quoted by Parkman.

Chapter x

1 The chapter was not printed in *K*; all references to canceled passages therefore begin with 49–52.

2 The Whirlwind, the leader of the Kiyuksa band of the Bear People after the death of the elder Bull Bear in 1841, frequently appears in books of western travel and adventure from 1832 onward. Theodore Talbot, for instance, met him at Horse Creek in 1843 and described "Tourbillion" as a "very great soldier"; see *Journals of Theodore Talbot*, p. 32. After the collapse of the war party organized to avenge the death of his son, Male Crow, in 1845, The Whirlwind's power among the Oglalas was somewhat shaken, even though in 1850 he was still recognized by the whites as the head chief of the tribe. See Hyde, *Red Cloud's Folk*, pp. 58–59, 67.

3 Parkman's "Snakes" were probably the Shoshonis, the most northern division of the great Shoshonean family, who normally ranged westward of the Continental Divide in what is now southern Idaho and northern Utah, although war and hunting parties frequently appeared farther to the east. They were frequently hostile to the whites, and a number of pitched battles occurred between trappers and roving bands of Shoshonis. See Hodge, ed. *Handbook of American Indians*, ii, 556–557; and Virginia Cole Trenholm and Maurine Carley, *The Shoshonis: Sentinels of the Rockies* (Norman, 1964), pp. 3–10.

4 Compare this account with *Pontiac*, i, 195 n. (Vol. xiv of *Works*): "In the summer of the year 1846, when the western bands of the Dahcotah were preparing to go in concert against their enemies the Crows, the chief who was at the head of the design, and of whose village the writer was an inmate, impoverished himself by sending most of his horses as presents to the chiefs of the surrounding villages. On this occasion, tobacco was the token borne by the messengers. . . ." Bryant, *What I Saw in California*, p. 107, noted on June 23 that "about three thousand Sioux Indians" were encamped near Fort Laramie, "organ-

izing a war-party to attack the Snakes and Crows," and on the same date George McKinstry, "The Diary of George McKinstry," reprinted in Morgan, ed. *Overland in 1846*, I, 214, saw "some 2500 Sius Indians at the Ft. making up a war party to fight the 'Crows'. . . ." From these accounts it would seem that the Crows were to be the principal victims of The Whirlwind's "grand combination," and it is doubtful that the confederated Teton bands at Fort Laramie could aggregate the "five or six thousand souls" Parkman mentions in the next sentence.

5 "La Bonté's Camp"—the site of a trapper's winter cabin built sometime before 1834— was located near the mouth of the present La Bonte Creek (frequently also called the La Bonte River) some seven or eight miles south-southwest of modern Douglas, Wyoming. Who La Bonté was it is impossible to ascertain, though Howard Louis Conrad, *"Uncle Dick" Wootton, the Pioneer Frontiersman of the Rocky Mountain Region* (Chicago, 1890), p. 80, cites "Uncle Dick's" account of a mountain man named Le Bonte, "a noted character among the early trappers," who was killed and eaten by "Pah-Utes" sometime in 1839 or 1840. David Lee and J. H. Frost, *Ten Years in Oregon* . . . (New York, 1844), p. 126, note a retired trapper named Le Bonté and his son Louis, both of whom were in Oregon during the 1830's and 1840's. Dale L. Morgan, ed. *The West of William H. Ashley* . . . (Denver, 1964), p. 291, has discovered that a David La Bonte figured in the American Fur Company's account books during the 1830's and 1840's and that "One LaBonte, first name not supplied, is mentioned by Alexander Barclay at the Hardscrabble fort on the upper Arkansas [on] May 28, 1846. . . ." The hero of Ruxton's *Life in the Far West* is a trapper named La Bonté, who, according to Ruxton's account, went west as an *engagé* for Ashley in the early

1820's, and, after a strenuous career in the mountains, initiates Ruxton in 1846 into the pleasures and perils of a trapper's life.

6 Between the sentences "I . . . character" and "To . . . them" 49–52 supply the following additional two sentences:

Having from childhood felt a curiosity on this subject, and having failed completely to gratify it by reading, I resolved to have recourse to observation. I wished to satisfy myself with regard to the position of the Indians among the races of men; the vices and the virtues that have sprung from their innate character and from their modes of life, their government, their superstitions, and their domestic situation.

7 Most of the tribesmen joining The Whirlwind's war party seem to have been members of other Teton Sioux bands, some from as far away as the upper Missouri. See p. 135 of this edition and note 31 for that page.

8 Parkman's "prairie-cock" was the sage grouse (*Centrocercus urophasianus*), originally found on all the sagebrush plains of the West.

9 Called "His Horses" in several entries in Parkman's Oregon Trail notebooks, "The Horse" may have belonged to the famous Man-Afraid-Of-His-Horse family, one of the most distinguished among the Oglalas. If this supposition is correct, "The Horse" may even be tentatively identified as "Young-Man-Afraid-Of-His-Horse," who married one of Henry Chatillon and Bear Robe's daughters and later rose to an important chieftainship in the tribe. See Hyde, *Red Cloud's Folk*, p. 60.

10 See p. 83 of the present edition and note 22 for that page for the beginning of Parkman's illness. He was suffering from the dysentery, cramps, and dizziness often called "mountain fever," a sometimes prolonged period of adjustment to the diminished supply of oxygen in the higher

altitudes of the western prairies and the Rocky Mountains. Mountain fever was nearly pandemic among emigrants and took a heavy toll among the troops of Kearny's Army of the West; its natural causes and effects were almost invariably made more severe by a sudden shift to a diet predominantly of fresh meat undercooked in dirty utensils and washed down with draughts of water from the alkali-rich springs of the plains, a regimen which, as Bernard DeVoto, *Year of Decision*, p. 161, remarked, meant "an endless physicking by drinking water impregnated with Epsom and Glauber's salts." Almost every narrative of western travel and adventure contains an account of the effects of mountain fever on the surprised greenhorn; Parker, *Journal of an Exploring Tour*, p. 118, recorded that "I could walk only a few rods without much fatigue. It seemed, that such was my loss of strength, and I was becoming so emaciated, that I could not endure the fatigue of traveling. . . ." Bryant, *What I Saw in California*, p. 123, gives similar testimony: "I was seized, during the night, with a violent and exhausting sickness. The soil and water of the country . . . are strongly impregnated with salt, alkali, and sulphur; rendering the use of the water, in large quantities, deleterious to health, if not dangerous. I was scarcely able to mount my mule when we commenced the day's march."

Parkman may be correct in assuming that his illness was "the same disorder" that Taylor's troops, "the army on the Rio Grande," suffered, but it seems more probable that that army's high mortality rate from sickness was the cumulative result of dirty food and bad water, primitive sanitation for men and horses, and malarial fevers—all of which the soldiers called "camp fever."

11 Compare the sentence "Having . . . me" with its 49–52 form: "Having within that time taken six grains of opium, without the least beneficial effect, and having no medical

adviser, nor any choice of diet, I resolved to throw myself on Providence for my recovery, using, without regard to the disorder, any portion of strength that might remain to me."

Opium was quite commonly used in the 1840's as a specific against dysentery. Compare Parkman's "1846 Account Book" in *Journals*, II, 489: "Opium and Brandy (Diarrhea)." Lieutenant Abert also dosed himself frequently with opium while suffering the effects of mountain fever on the Santa Fe Trail in 1846. See J. W. Abert, *Western America in 1846–1847: The Original Travel Diary of Lieutenant J. W. Abert . . .* , ed. John Galvin (San Francisco, 1966), p. 14.

12 Raymond remains unidentified, though from *The Oregon Trail* and Parkman's notebooks it would seem clear that he was one of the numerous "free trappers" left nearly without an occupation in 1846, a year in which the almost complete collapse of the beaver trade had become apparent to the whole Rocky Mountain fraternity. In the book and in his journals Parkman presents Raymond as a dull-witted fellow, but he kept Parkman alive and moving during their difficult crossing of the Laramie Range and was probably an expert mountain man.

He may have been the "Raimond" whom Theodore Talbot, *Journals of Theodore Talbot*, p. 35, met at Fort Laramie in 1843 and who wished "to go to Fort Hall, where he has a brother in the service of the H. [Hudson's] Bay Company." Lieutenant Abert, *Western America in 1846–1847*, p. 85, had a Raymond with him as a hunter in New Mexico in November, 1846, and since Abert had recuperated at Bent's Fort until September, 1846, when Parkman had reached the post and there discharged *his* Raymond, it seems quite probable that Abert was describing Parkman's guide and hunter in the following passage: "This morning Raymond went back; he seemed very reluctant to leave me, but he is entirely unfit to live in any civilized country and would ere long be obliged to beg. Here, all he wants is his rifle—lazy fellow—half Indian, half white man." Compare this quotation with Parkman's account of Raymond on p. 179 and Raymond's own description of the pleasures of the wilderness on p. 221 of the present edition.

There is no record of a "Raymond" among the 11 men dead of exhaustion or exposure in Frémont's Fourth Expedition, a foolhardy attempt to find an all-weather railroad route across the Rocky Mountains in the winter of 1848–1849. For an account of this debacle and the names of the victims, see Alpheus H. Favour, *Old Bill Williams: Mountain Man* (Chapel Hill, 1936), p. 168; LeRoy R. Hafen and Ann W. Hafen, eds. *Frémont's Fourth Expedition* (Glendale, Calif., 1960), pp. 22–25; and Charles Preuss, *Exploring with Frémont* . . . , eds. and trans., Erwin G. Gudde and Elizabeth K. Gudde (Norman, 1958), pp. 143–153.

13 Reynal seems to have been connected with the Richards and Bissonette at Fort Bernard, probably acting for the partners as "outside man" or resident trader among The Whirlwind's band. In 1854 "Antoine Reynall" was listed as one of the witnesses to James Bordeaux's report of the Grattan Massacre in the *Annual Report of the Commissioner of Indian Affairs* . . . *1854* (Washington, D.C., 1855), and he was probably the same Antoine Reynal, or Raynal, recorded as living on the South Platte in 1864, when his stock was run off in the Cheyenne rising of that year. See Donald J. Berthong, *The Southern Cheyennes* (Norman, 1963), p. 205.

14 Here, as in similar comments on Reynal and other squaw men elsewhere in *The Oregon Trail*, Parkman is probably wrong in assuming that mountain men went native completely by choice; many trappers and traders did, in fact,

become Indians in everything but color, but such inclinations often enough included a strong realization that the Indians would respect and protect white men who had willingly joined them, adopted their habits, and even "married" among them.

15 I am indebted to Professor A. W. Schorger of the University of Wisconsin Department of Wildlife Ecology for the information that Parkman's "wild sage," hereafter erroneously described as identical to absinthe (*Artemisia Absinthium*) is probably the common sagebrush (*Artemisia tridentata*) of the West.

16 On the evening of June 20 Parkman and his companions encamped some seven miles southwest of Fort Laramie, apparently on the south bank of Laramie River, as Parkman's "Laramie Creek" is now called. See *Journals*, II, 444.

17 So far as I am aware, Parkman is the only writer to note a "deserted wintering-house" near the mouth of Chugwater Creek. See *Journals*, II, 444.

18 I am indebted to Professor A. W. Schorger of the University of Wisconsin Department of Wildlife Ecology for the information that Parkman's "gray hare" was probably the white-tailed jackrabbit (*Lepus townsendii*), the largest of the hares and commonly found on the northern plains and in the western mountains. It weighs twice as much as the eastern cottontail (*Sylvilagus floridanus*), the rabbit with which Parkman was obviously familiar in New England.

19 These curlew were doubtless long-billed curlew (*Numenius americanus*), a species of shorebird with a down-curved bill five to seven inches long; their "screaming" suggests that the birds had nests or young nearby.

20 Parkman's "white wolf" was probably a gray or timber wolf (*Canis lupus*) and might easily have weighed as much as 125 pounds. The wolf is now extinct in Wyoming.

21 On the afternoon of June 21 Parkman and his companions

made camp near the Laramie River, just west of the mouth of Chugwater Creek and some five miles east of the present site of Uva, Wyoming. See *Journals*, II, 444.

22 Parkman and Chatillon apparently expected to meet The Whirlwind and his band moving north down the valley of Chugwater Creek.

23 In fairness to Reynal it should be noted that on p. 357 of the present edition Parkman himself remarks that a bow and arrows have "many advantages over firearms" in buffalo-running.

24 Parkman's notebook entry for June 21 (?) in *Journals*, II, 445–446, describes these "hieroglyphics" more exactly: "On a large tree near our camp, the bark is cut off for the space of a foot square, and marked with 14 pipes and 14 straight marks, to indicate that a band of Crows had come down and struck *coups*."

25 Parkman's notebooks show clearly how this episode was synthesized from two separate daily entries in *Journals*, II, 446, 452. On June 23 he noted briefly "Some danger from war-parties of Crows," and it was not until July 5, 12 days later, that he discovered that "We had, it seems, a narrow escape a few days ago. The tracks seen on Chug. [Chugwater] by Reynal and H. [Henry?] proved to be a party of Crows, as the Sioux have just found some bones and corpses flung down down from their scaffolds. They were some thirty in number, and probably missed our camp in the morning fog."

26 The sequence of events and dates in this passage is somewhat obscure, but Parkman's notebook entries for June 23–25 in *Journals*, II, 446–447, clearly show what happened during these several days. Young Bull Bear (Mahto-Tatonka in *The Oregon Trail*) and his friends had separated from the main body of The Whirlwind's village and were coming on ahead of it. Parkman had ridden to Fort Laramie on June 25 (where he may have seen the

Harlan party) and had returned the same evening to camp, where he "found His Horses with a young son of [the elder] Bull Bear—they say that Tunica's [The Whirlwind's] village is four days distant, and that the lodge of Henry's squaw will be here day after tomorrow."

27 Parkman's notebooks again flatly contradict the narrative of these events in *The Oregon Trail*. On June 26 Parkman rode over to Fort Laramie alone and there spent the night, probably returning to the Chugwater Creek campsite on the evening of June 27. While Parkman was absent at the fort, Shaw and Henry also left camp and rode South in search of Bear Robe's lodge, so that when Parkman returned on the evening of June 27 he found them both "gone to bury the . . . squaw, who is just dead." See *Journals*, II, 447–448.

28 Parkman's identification of Paul Dorion as a "reputed son" of Pierre Dorion, Jr., must be accepted until further conclusive evidence comes to light. Paul Dorion's grandfather was Pierre Dorion, Sr., a St. Louis trader who had joined the Yankton Sioux as early as the middle 1770's and married a woman of the tribe; for a short time he served as both guide and interpreter for Lewis and Clark on the upper Missouri. His son, Pierre Dorion, Jr., traveled with Wilson Hunt's party of overland Astorians, and Paul Dorion was probably the half brother (by a Yankton squaw?) of the child born to Marie Aioë, the younger Dorion's wife, on the cross-country march to the Columbia. Parkman's description of Paul Dorion in this passage suggests that he was old enough to be the "Paul Dorio" whom Dale Morgan has discovered listed in the account books of William H. Ashley & Company as early as 1827. See Meriwether Lewis and William Clark, *The Journals of Lewis and Clark*, ed. Bernard DeVoto (Boston, 1953), p. 8; Irving, *Astoria*, ed. Edgeley W. Todd, pp. 141–500 *passim*; J. Neilson Barry, "Madame Dorion of the Astorians," *Ore-*

gon Historical Quarterly, xxx (September, 1929), 272–277; and Morgan, ed. *West of William H. Ashley*, p. 172.

29 Parkman's "Hohays" (or Hohes: the Sioux word may be translated as "rebels") were probably a band of Assiniboins, a tribe that had once been a part of the Yanktonai Sioux but which had by 1640 separated from the larger group and allied itself with the northern Crees. During the 1830's and 1840's the Assiniboins lived along the upper Missouri and were almost constantly at war with other bands of Sioux. More than 4,000 members of the tribe died of smallpox in the terrible epidemic of 1837. See Hodge, ed. *Handbook of American Indians*, I, 103–105; and Swanton, *Indian Tribes*, p. 387.

30 James P. Beckwourth, or Beckwith (1798–1866), reputedly the son of Sir Jennings Beckwith and a slave woman, was born in Virginia and spent his earliest years there until his father moved to Missouri in 1810. Apprenticed early to a St. Louis firm of blacksmiths, Beckwourth by his own account soon tired of civilized life and after various adventures became one of William H. Ashley's mountain men in 1824. During the 1830's and 1840's he traded at different times with the Blackfeet, the Snakes, the Cheyennes, and the Crows. Like Edward Rose, another mulatto, Beckwourth was adopted by the Crows and became one of their war chiefs, an honor which, by his own account, the Crows paid to his bravery and cunning. Contemporary evidence shows that during this period Beckwourth occasionally operated as a free trapper during intervals of service to Astor's American Fur Company, Smith, Jackson, and Sublette, and Bent, St. Vrain & Company.

Parkman himself came very near meeting Beckwourth, for Alexander Barclay at the Hardscrabble post on the upper Arkansas recorded Beckwourth's visits there at intervals from May 28, 1846, when he and "five trusty Americans" arrived at Hardscrabble from a horse-stealing expedition to California, to August 4, when Parkman himself had nearly reached the Pueblo, where most of Beckwourth's California horses had been sold. See Morgan, ed. *Overland in 1846*, II, 769. Garrard, *Wah-To-Yah and the Taos Trail*, pp. 309–311, met Beckwourth in Santa Fe later in 1846 and described him as a "large, good-humored fellow," the proprietor of "the best furnished saloon in the place—the grand resort for liquor-imbibing, monte-playing, and fandango-disposed American officers and men." During the rest of the Mexican War, Beckwourth served as a guide for Colonel Willcock in New Mexico and as a dispatch-courier between Santa Fe and Fort Leavenworth for Sterling Price. Since there is no absolutely positive date for the composition of this chapter, Parkman's reference to "last summer" in this passage may refer to the summer of 1847, when Beckwourth was in the East on government business; a date of 1848 either for the first writing of this chapter (perhaps written out of sequence, since it was not printed in the K installments) or for its revision in manuscript thus seems probable.

Beckwourth's later career may be summarized briefly. In the late 1840's and early 1850's he was occasionally engaged in business at Santa Fe, and in the 10 or 12 years before his mysterious death in a Crow village he frequently served the government as a guide and interpreter. In 1854–1855, apparently, he dictated his autobiography to T. D. Bonner, an obscure journalist; the resultant volume, *The Life and Adventures of James P. Beckwourth, Mountaineer, Scout, and Pioneer, and Chief of the Crow Nation of Indians* (New York, 1856), is one of the most curious books to come out of the West. In it Beckwourth is shown slaughtering hecatombs of enemies, preserving virtue in distress, and in general bodying forth every gallant ideal of mountain chivalry. DeVoto, who edited Beckwourth's *Life and Adventures* in 1931, suggested that at least *some* of the events therein described might have a reasonably firm foundation in fact, and more recent evaluations of Beckwourth's life and his book suggest that he was not simply the bare-faced liar that earlier commentators (e.g., Chittenden, *American Fur Trade,* II, 679–681) had made him out to be. Inman, *Old Santa Fé Trail,* pp. 338–340, went to a good deal of trouble to disprove Parkman's aspersions of Beckwourth's character and remarked that "I never saw Beckwourth, but I have heard of him from those of my mountaineer friends who knew him intimately. . . . Colonel [A. G.] Boone, the Bents, Carson, Maxwell, and others ascribed to him no such traits as those given him by Parkman. . . ."

However, a good deal of contemporary evidence seems to support Parkman's characterization of Beckwourth here: particularly the *bourgeois* Tom Fitzpatrick's strongly held belief that Beckwourth was behind the Crows who robbed a brigade of Rocky Mountain Fur Company trappers in 1833; Joe Meek's somewhat suspect statement to his biographer, Mrs. Victor, that in 1837 Beckwourth had brought up from St. Louis "two infected articles"—probably blankets—in order to spread smallpox among the Blackfeet; and finally the inordinate amount of space Beckwourth spent in his own autobiography in defending himself against accusations of double-dealing, theft, and murder.

Parkman himself later owned a copy of Beckwourth's *Life and Adventures* (which DeVoto used as his text in 1931) and had undoubtedly read Frémont's account in his *Report,* p. 30, of his meeting with Beckwourth on the South Platte in 1842. Having also, no doubt, read Irving's *Adventures of Captain Bonneville,* Parkman must have been aware that Beckwourth's "forted-up" fight with the Blackfeet (described on pp. 134–135 of the present edition) had with probably better reason been ascribed by

Irving and others to Edward Rose. According to Chapter XIV of Beckwourth's *Life and Adventures*, however, the attack on the Blackfoot fort must, by the very uneven chronology of the book, have occurred in March, 1827; Beckwourth claimed that he and his Crow allies faced and defeated almost 160 Blackfeet; other details of his account differ in minor respects from Parkman's description of the battle in this passage. In addition to the above sources, see Frances Fuller Victor, *The River of the West* . . . (Hartford, 1870), p. 232; Stanley Vestal, *Joe Meek: The Merry Mountain Man* (Caldwell, Idaho, 1952), p. 221; Irving, *Adventures of Captain Bonneville*, ed. Edgeley W. Todd, pp. 166–167; and Nolie Mumey, *James Pierson Beckwourth, 1856–1866* (Denver, 1957), pp. 23–174 *passim*.

31 The Miniconques, or Miniconjous, belonged to the same Teton division of the Dakotas as the Oglalas and ranged along the upper Missouri River in South Dakota. See Swanton, *Indian Tribes*, pp. 280–284; and Hodge, ed. *Handbook of American Indians*, II, 868–869.

32 Compare Parkman's June 28th notebook account in *Journals*, II, 447, of his encounter with the emigrants at Fort Bernard on the morning of June 27:

June 28th. Yesterday rode down with Paul Dorion, who wished to swap a wild horse, to Richard's fort. Found there Russel's or Boggs' comp'y, engaged in drinking and refitting, and a host of Canadians besides. Russel drunk as a pigeon— some fine-looking Kentucky men—some of D. Boone's grandchildren—Ewing, Jacob(s), and others with them—altogether more educated men than any I have seen. A motley crew assembled in Richard's rooms—squaws, children, Spaniards, French, and emigrants. Emigrants mean to sell liquor to the Miniconques, who will be up here tomorrow, and after having come all the way from the Missouri to go to the war, will no doubt break up if this is done. Paul very much displeased. . . .

At Fort Laramie on June 26, the day before, Parkman had encountered another separated section of the large emigrant company organized near Independence by Colonel William H. Russell in early May, a party which, as has been noted (see p. 6 of the present edition and note 19 for that page), Parkman had heard about from Woodworth and doubtless others. Thornton, *Oregon and California in 1848*, I, 21, estimated the original size of Russell's company at some 72 wagons, 130 men, 65 women, 125 children, and more than 700 cattle and horses. But the inevitable quarrels over wood and water—and simple human contrariety—had taken their toll, and at Fort Bernard on the morning of June 27 Parkman now discovered not only the fragments of Russell's original party—and Russell himself had been superseded by Lillburn Boggs—but the beginnings of other and more serious divisions.

Now, on a late morning in June on the North Platte, Parkman leaned against a doorpost at Richard's fort and for an hour or so looked on at the drunken antics of the emigrants celebrating their first release from the hardships of the trail—a quick drunk at Fort Bernard and a chance to refit wagons and rest oxen and horses before the long miles to Fort Bridger or Fort Hall, before the Sierra or the gorges of the Columbia River. From the doorway of Fort Bernard Parkman could see, corralled on the prairie, the Donners' wagons, and even now their owners were thinking and even writing home about a newer and faster route to California. Jesse Quinn Thornton and his fragile, botanizing wife were there, once a part of Russell's party and now encamped with other members of Rice Dunbar's Oregon-bound company. Russell himself, "drunk as a pigeon," and Lillburn Boggs and his wife and children too were at Richard's, and Edwin Bryant and his friends Ewing and Jacobs. For an hour or two, then, at Richard's post on the North Platte, Parkman had seen and clasped hands with the dusky figures of fate and Manifest Destiny, with James Frazier Reed, perhaps, or with Alphonso Boone or George Donner or Edwin Bryant, and had then turned his horse's head westward toward Fort Laramie, disgusted with the noise and the sudden joyful release at Fort Bernard. See DeVoto, *Year of Decision*, pp. 181–186; Bryant, *What I Saw in California*, pp. 112–114; Thornton, *Oregon and California in 1848*, I, 109–114; "The Diary of George McKinstry," reprinted in Morgan, ed. *Overland in 1846*, I, 258; and "George Donner to a Friend, 'Fort Bernard, June 27, 1846,' " reprinted *ibid.*, II, 576–577.

33 William Henry Russell (1802–1873), "Colonel" by courtesy only, was born in Kentucky and in his earlier years practiced law in Nicholas County, which he represented in the stage legislature in 1830. He soon came to the attention of Henry Clay, who befriended him and may have made Russell briefly his secretary. His nickname, "Owl" Russell, illustrates his pride in his connection with Clay; according to a number of accounts, Russell was one evening saluted by the whooing of owls and is said to have thundered in return, "Colonel William H. Russell, sir, of Kentucky—a bosom friend of Henry Clay!" In 1831 he moved to Missouri and in 1832 served in the Black Hawk War. From 1841 to 1846 he was United States Marshall for the District of Missouri, a post which no doubt explains if it does not justify his claims to a colonelcy. In these notes he has already been seen at Independence in early May, writing letters to the newspapers (as he would continue to do on the trail), and organizing his originally large company.

Parkman may be correct in asserting that members of his much-fragmented party had "mutinied and deposed him," but Bryant, *What I Saw in California*, p. 96, wrote that Russell had resigned voluntarily on June 18, not far east of Fort Laramie, because he "had been suffering for several days from an attack of bilious fever"—probably mountain fever itself. Writing to the St. Louis *Missouri Republican* from "Sweet Water River, 80 Miles West of Independence Rock," on July 12 (reprinted in Morgan, ed. *Overland in 1846*, II, 609), Russell reported that "I resigned my command of about 150 wagons at North Platte, where I considered all safe. . . ." Lillburn Boggs assumed control of the party until it reached Fort Bernard and Fort Laramie, where the inevitable process of disintegration recurred. On June 28 Russell, Edwin Bryant, and seven others (later reduced to six) set off for California on muleback; they reached Sinclair's Ranch on September 1 after a swift but difficult journey south of the Great Salt Lake and along the Humboldt-Truckee route.

After reaching Monterrey, Russell served as a major in Frémont's California Battalion. As Acting Governor, Frémont appointed Russell Secretary of State in the provisional government briefly established after the conquest. Upon the conclusion of Frémont's administration, Russell set out for Missouri along the southern route, befriended Garrard at Fort Mann, and returned with him to Missouri in July, 1847. After another year or two, Russell went back to California in 1849 and practiced law in San Jose and elsewhere for the next 10 or 12 years. In 1861 he was appointed to a consulship at Trinidad, Cuba, and died 12 years later in Washington, D.C.

Russell appears frequently though not always heroically in the narratives and journals of the emigration of 1846; he was perhaps the most widely known person to travel to California in that year, and Parkman's account of his stump oratory at Fort Bernard may not be much exaggerated: he seems to have been very nearly the epitome of the flamboyant frontier politician. In addition to the authorities cited above, see *DAB, s.v.* "Russell, William Henry"; Morgan, ed. *Overland in 1846*, II, 460–461; Garrard,

Wah-To-Yah and the Taos Trail, pp. 356–377; and De-
Voto, *Year of Decision*, pp. 121–122.

34 Parkman's reference in this passage to "three tall young
men, grandsons of Daniel Boone," though clearly founded
on his June 28th notebook entry cited in note 32 for
p. 135, still remains unclear, for the only positively identifiable grandchildren of Daniel Boone in the emigration of
1846 were Panthea Grant Boone Boggs (1801–1880) and
Alphonso Boone (1796–?), themselves the children of
Jesse Bryan Boone and Chloe Van Bibber Boone, and, of
course, the brother and sister of that Albert Gallatin Boone
whom Parkman had already met at Westport. Panthea
Boggs was Lillburn H. Boggs's second wife; most of their
10 children (some of whom were certainly old enough to
fit Parkman's description here) traveled with their parents
to California along the safe and established Fort Hall–
Humboldt River route, arriving at Sutter's Fort on October
28. In the "Emigrant Register" in his *History of California*
(San Francisco, 1886), Hubert Howe Bancroft does not
list any Boones among the California emigrants of 1846,
and thus it may be that in this passage Parkman is referring
to some of the younger Boggses, Daniel Boone's great-
grandchildren.

Like his sister Panthea Boggs, Alphonso Boone appears
frequently in the published narratives and journals of the
emigration of 1846. His destination, however, was Oregon,
and during at least part of the journey he traveled in
company with J. Quinn Thornton, who recorded that by
August 21 young Jesse Boone, Daniel Boone's great-grand-
son, had helped to kill a prowling Indian near camp.
Other evidence seems to suggest that Alphonso Boone had
his whole family with him on the road to Oregon, and the
"Emigrant Register" in Bancroft, *History of Oregon*, I,
567, mentions both Alphonso and Jesse Boone as well as
an "A. Boon" among the Oregon emigrants of 1846. It is

thus possible but on the whole unlikely that Parkman's "three tall young men" were Alphonso Boone's sons; surviving genealogical data and Parkman's own encounter with the Boggses at Fort Bernard seem to assure an identification of the "grandsons of Daniel Boone" as Panthea and Lillburn Boggs's sons.

In addition to the citations given above, see Oliver, *Some Boone Descendants*, pp. 39–40; Stewart, *Ordeal by Hunger*, p. 95; W. M. Boggs, "The W. M. Boggs Manuscript about Bent's Fort, Kit Carson, the Far West, and Life among the Indians," ed. LeRoy R. Hafen, *Colorado Magazine*, vii (March, 1930), pp. 45–46; and Thornton, *Oregon and California in 1848*, i, 38, 171.

35 Taken in context, this brief reference to the Donner party seems to have been intended as additional proof of the moral squalor so evident among the drunken emigrants at Fort Bernard, and Parkman clearly meant that his contemporary readers should at this point recall the earliest sensational accounts of the deaths at "Cannibal Camp" just below the last ridge of the Sierra, near what is now Donner Pass and Donner Lake. As more recent research has shown, however, the Donner party contained men and women wealthier, better educated, and more widely cultured than was common among members of the various emigrant companies in 1846; and if there were despair, cowardice, and unmitigated bestiality to be found in the characters of those who survived the ghastly cabins at Donner Lake, there was even among the children a heaping measure of courage, faith, and saving charity. It is Keseberg and the mutilated bodies that are today most vivid in the popular imagination, that have made the horrors of the Donner party the best-known event in the history of the overland emigrations. There was greater loss of life in other and later companies, and cannibalism in "starving times" is a recurring fact in the scattered narra-

tives of the trappers' West, but everything went wrong for the Donners and their friends after the wagons rolled away from Fort Laramie on June 28.

Death came because the Donners and the Reeds, the Eddys and the Breens and the others had heard of a newer and faster route, a route glowingly though rather vaguely described in Lansford W. Hastings' *The Emigrants' Guide to Oregon and California*, published in 1845, a year before Hastings had seen the route which he would recommend so bravely in the summer of 1846 (and part of which Frémont had followed westward in 1845). When on July 20 the 20 wagons of the Donner party finally separated at the Little Sandy River from the rest of the emigration of 1846, when the Boggses and the Thorntons had turned right on the Greenwood Cut-Off toward the safe Fort Hall route to California and Oregon, then, strictly speaking, the Donner party first appears as a separate entity, now alone in the heart of the vast western wilderness and bound for California by "a nigher route" because Lansford W. Hastings had written a letter from Fort Bridger to the emigrants at South Pass, urging them to follow his lead to the Golden Shore. He would lead them, he wrote to the emigrants crossing South Pass on or about July 17, but when the Donners arrived at Fort Bridger on July 28, Hastings had already left with the Harlan-Young party, Edwin Bryant's letters advising against the new route were not delivered, and Captain Joseph R. Walker had not been encouraging about the Wasatch canyons and the deserts south and west of the Great Salt Lake.

The agony of the Donner party began when the wagons swung away from Fort Bridger on July 31. Edwin Bryant and the party on muleback, traveling light, had had the advantage of a guide on the first leg of their journey, and Hastings, with a company much larger than the Donner party, had cut and leveled a trace through the canyons of the Weber River. But now, in the ever-shorter days of a mountain summer, the Donner party rolled down Hastings' trail, and here, in George R. Stewart's forbidding phrase, "the trap clicks behind." With pauses for rest, with delays in awaiting the return of an advance party, with the agonizing labor of cutting a new road after learning from Hastings at last that *his* route was impractical for a party of their size, even murderous to tired animals and men, they had spent 21 days in traveling the 36 miles from their first campsite on the Weber River to the valley of the Great Salt Lake; they had beaten the Wasatch and sealed themselves to death in the Sierra.

Neither the history of the various relief parties organized to rescue the emigrants in their squalid cabins near the frozen lake nor the brutal rending of human bodies and spirits at the camps and along the trail down from the Sierra requires special consideration at this point. When Kearny, heading eastward, passed the cabins on June 21, 1847, the totals were in; Stewart, *Ordeal by Hunger*, p. 271, provides the bill of account:

With the escape of Keseberg [the most brutalized survivor] the actual story comes to an end. Of the eighty-seven emigrants who had pierced the Wahsatch and camped in the valley of the Great Salt Lake, five had died before reaching the mountain camps, thirty-four either at the camps or upon the mountains while attempting to cross, and one just after reaching the valley. To the number of dead may also be added Sutter's two Indian vaqueros, Luis and Salvador. The totals are therefore: dead, forty-two; survived, forty-seven.

In addition, many emigrants and men of the relief parties had lost toes from frostbite and were otherwise injured. The oxen and dogs had all perished, and the horses and mules, too, with the possible exception of three which Stanton, McCutcheon and Reed may have taken through to Sutter's. Most of the emigrants' property had been left scattered along the way, or had been ruined by exposure. . . .

Parkman had undoubtedly read the specific details of the Donner disaster sometime in early September, 1847; Kearny had arrived at Fort Leavenworth on August 22, 1847, and the names of the victims and a fairly trustworthy account of the catastrophe were published in a St. Louis newspaper as early as August 30, while a less factual narrative appeared in the New York *Herald* on September 3. The best account of the Donner party appears in the two editions (1936, rev. 1960) of George R. Stewart's *Ordeal by Hunger;* Dale Morgan reprints diaries and other documents relative to the Donner party in both volumes of his *Overland in 1846.* See also the second volume of J. Quinn Thornton's *Oregon and California in 1848* for an almost contemporaneous account—though not always a trustworthy one—of the disaster; Bryant, *What I Saw in California,* pp. 249–264; and DeVoto, *Year of Decision,* pp. 122–526 *passim.*

36 This description of the not otherwise identifiable trapper, Perrault, and the account of his departure from Fort Laramie again show how Parkman used the resources of his notebooks to create detailed scenes in *The Oregon Trail.* Parkman did not actually see this episode himself; it rather derives from part of a conversation which he had with Gingras and other trappers at the Chugwater Creek campsite and which he recorded in his notebooks on June 30, in *Journals,* II, 449: "They brought news of Bisonette's arrival, and we allowed Henry to go down and see him. They also said that Bordeaux and another man had quarreled at the fort, and B. had shown himself a coward—which I can easily believe."

37 If Parkman did, in fact, learn most of the important facts of this brawl, the "old Indian" may have been the famous Swift Bear himself.

38 The literature of the mountain fur trade shows that a

number of duels were indeed fought "in the white man's manner" under the walls of the forts.

39 Fort Pierre, built in 1831–1832 and named in honor of Pierre Chouteau, Jr., was located not far from the present site of Pierre, South Dakota. See DeVoto, *Across the Wide Missouri*, p. 15.

40 At this point the separate chronologies of *The Oregon Trail* and of Parkman's notebooks and an extant letter to his father cannot easily be reconciled. By the sequence of events in the book, "that night" in this passage would be that of June 27–28, and Parkman wrote to his father from "Fort Learamie, June 28ᵗʰ, 1846," and therein mentioned "a party of homesick emigrants on the return," to whom, apparently, this letter was given for posting in the States. The "homesick emigrants" were undoubtedly James Clyman and his companions eastbound from California, some of whom had arrived at Fort Laramie on June 27. See *James Clyman, Frontiersman*, p. 225. But Parkman's notebook entry for June 28 in *Journals*, II, 447–448, provides a retrospective account of events at Fort Laramie on June 27, mentions the arrival of Clyman's party at Fort Laramie on the afternoon of the same day and Parkman's own return to the Chugwater camp later that afternoon, and concludes laconically, "Today [i.e., June 28] lay at camp." Internal evidence in Parkman's "June 28ᵗʰ" letter to his father would seem to indicate that it was misdated and that it was written on the afternoon of June 27, in the few hours between his arrival at Fort Laramie and his departure for camp.

This letter is especially interesting as it shows how equivocally Parkman wrote to his family to persuade them that he was enjoying good health, that the Indians and the landscape around Fort Laramie were both ineffably picturesque, and that he and Shaw, despite all the attractions of the plains and mountains, were planning to return almost at once to the States by the comparatively safe route to Fort Pierre and thence down the Missouri River. Every evidence suggests that Clyman took this letter back to Missouri with him, but nowhere in *The Oregon Trail* or in the notebooks is there any indication that Parkman paid any attention to Clyman, one of the great men in the early history of the fur trade and western exploration.

Clyman had crossed South Pass with Jedediah Smith in the early spring of 1824 on that journey which first made the comparatively easy South Pass route over the mountains widely known to mountain men. After years of adventure as a trapper, pioneer in Wisconsin, and overland emigrant to Oregon in 1844, Clyman was now returning to Missouri on horseback after having traveled with Lansford Hastings a considerable distance over that new route which Hastings in his self-infatuated folly proposed as the nearest and fastest road to California. But, unlike Hastings, Clyman had an eye for country and knew where wagons could and could not go; on June 27 he set down in his own journal the effects of his warnings against Hastings' Cut-Off:

27 we met numerous squad of emigrants untill we reached fort Larrimie whare we met Ex govornor Boggs and party from Jackson county Mi[ss]ourie Bound for California and we camped with them[.] several of us continued the conversation untill a late hour.

And here I again obtained a cup of excellent coffee at Judge Morins camp the first I had tasted since in the early part of last winter[.] and I fear that during our long conversation I changed the purposes of Govornor and the Judge for next morning they both told me they inte[n]ded to go to Oregon.

The Donners and their companions did not listen to Clyman.

Parkman's letter to his father will be found in the Parkman Papers, Massachusetts Historical Society, and in *Letters*, I, 45–47. See also *James Clyman, Frontiersman*, pp. 5–230 *passim*. Taken together, Clyman's account of the events of June 27 and Parkman's own notebooks suggest strongly that Parkman did not remain at Fort Laramie on the evening of June 27–28 and that most of the events in the next several pages of *The Oregon Trail* rest rather casually on what Parkman saw at Fort Bernard and Fort Laramie on June 26–27.

41 McCluskey remains unidentified.

42 Parkman might well have been thinking of the collapse of the Miniconques' war party when he later wrote in *A Half-Century of Conflict*, I, 290 (Vol. IX in *Works*), that "If the wild Indian has the passions of a devil, he has also the instability of a child, and this is especially true when a number of incoherent tribes or bands are joined in a common enterprise."

43 So far as I am aware, Parkman is the only writer to identify the smith at Fort Laramie in 1846 as specifically one of the famous and numerous Robidoux family, though which Robidoux Parkman met remains in doubt. See note 17 for p. 93 of this edition for a possible identification of this man as the younger Antoine Roubidoux. The smith may have been the same "Roubideau" Parkman met on June 12, just east of Scott's Bluff. See *Journals*, II, 437–438.

44 Neither Gingras ("Jean Gras" in K–52) nor his companion, Rouleau, can be positively identified, though a "Rulo" does appear occasionally in the literature of the frontier West, invariably without biographical details. See, for example, Alter, *Jim Bridger*, p. 314, in which "Rulo" figures with Jim Bridger in the Powder River campaign of 1865.

45 A free trapper was not contractually bound to any of the fur companies operating in the mountains and could sell

his furs to the post which offered the highest prices for them. Formerly a significant force in the fur trade, the free trappers were beginning to disappear after the last rendezvous in 1840 and the general collapse of the beaver market, though of course solitary trappers still took a plew whenever they found beaver sign.

46 For a fuller description of the Arapahoes see p. 348 of the present edition and note 11 for that page. Bull Tail, or Bull's Tail, a famous Brule chief, was well known for his partiality for white men; Parkman might have read in Frémont's *Report*, pp. 44–45, how the old chief had visited Frémont at Fort Laramie in 1842 and warned him against pushing forward his explorations while a number of war parties were out and the braves were looking for scalps. P. St. George Cooke, *Scenes and Adventures in the Army: Or, Romance of Military Life* (Philadelphia, 1857), p. 337, described Bull Tail as the leader of the Brules at Fort Laramie at the time of Kearny's reconnaissance in 1845, and Bull Tail appears quite often in other comparatively early accounts of western travel and adventure. He died sometime in late 1846. See Ruxton, *Life in the Far West*, p. 69; Sage, *Scenes in the Rocky Mountains*, I, 203; and Hyde, *Spotted Tail's Folk*, p. 34.

Bull Tail's account of the deaths of the two trappers is supported by other contemporary evidence. On June 1, Clyman, *James Clyman, Frontiersman*, p. 218, noted in his journals that "These Ewtaws as well as we could understand informed us that the snakes and whites ware now at war and that the snakes had killed two white men[.] this news was not the most pleasant as we have to pass through a portion of the snake country[.]" Writing from Fort Bernard to the St. Louis *Reveille* on June 26, "Laon" reported that "Two trappers, named Leamai and Buck, or Burk, were murdered on Bear river recently, by an Arrapahoe Indian." See Morgan, ed. *Overland in 1846*, II,

575–576. Thomas J. Farnham, *Travels in the Great West-ern Plains, the Anahuac and Rocky Mountains and in the Oregon Country*, in R. G. Thwaites, ed. *Early Western Travels* (Cleveland, 1906), xxviii, 239, reports a similar instance of a trapper named "Redman" being surprised and murdered with his own rifle.

47 Parkman's trappers in this passage and elsewhere in *The Oregon Trail* are more genteel in their language than were the mountain men Garrard, *Wah-To-Yah and the Taos Trail*, p. 76, encountered: "Hyar's the doins, and hyar's the coon as *savys* 'poor bull' from 'fat cow;' freeze into it, boys!"

48 A positive identification of this party seems impossible, though most of the emigrants Parkman saw at Fort Ber-nard on the morning of June 27 had moved camp to Fort Laramie on the afternoon of the same day.

49 Parkman's description of the antelope's often fatal curios-ity is confirmed by many western travelers. Compare Rux-ton, *Adventures in the Rocky Mountains*, reprinted in *Ruxton of the Rockies*, p. 259:

They [the antelope] are exceedingly timid animals, but at the same time wonderfully curious; and their curiosity very often proves their death, for the hunter, taking advantage of this weakness, plants his wiping-stick [i.e., his ramrod] in the ground, with a cap or red handkerchief on the point, and, concealing himself in the long grass, waits, rifle in hand, the approach of the inquisitive antelope, who, seeing an unusual object in the plains, trots up to it, and, coming within range of the deadly tube, pays dearly for his temerity.

50 Shaw and Chatillon returned to the Chugwater Creek campsite on June 28. See *Journals*, ii, 448.

51 As the son of a prominent Unitarian minister, Parkman of course felt himself well qualified to comment on the "ab-surd notion," however widespread in the first half of the

nineteenth century, that the Lost Ten Tribes of Israel had somehow reached America after the Assyrian captivity. Books like Epaphoras Jones's *On the Ten Tribes of Israel, and the Aborigines of America* (New Albany, Indiana, 1831), as cited by Roy Harvey Pearce (*The Savages of America: A Study of the Indian and the Idea of Civilization* [Baltimore, 1965], p. 62), made more or less, far-fetched comparisons between the racial characteristics, customs, languages, and surviving monuments of the Jews of antiquity and the Indians of America, particularly the tribes of the Mississippi River valley. The Reverend Samuel Parker, who went west in 1835, later set down at considerable length what seemed to him the startling resemblances between the ancient Israelites and the Indians he himself saw along the Oregon Trail. See Parker, *Journal of an Exploring Tour*, pp. 192–198.

Parkman might also be alluding here to the story of the prophet Lehi, recounted at length in *The Book of Mormon*, who with his family left Jerusalem about 600 B.C. and sailed to America, like a second Noah, in a kind of ark.

52 This sequence of events does not agree with the account of the squaw's death in Parkman's notebooks. Summarizing on June 28 the incidents of that day and of the day before, Parkman noted that on June 27, when he returned to the Chugwater camp from Fort Laramie, he found Shaw and Chatillon already "gone to bury the latter's squaw, who is just dead." In the same entry Parkman noted Shaw and Chatillon's return to camp on June 28 and their account of the plans for Bear Robe's burial. See *Journals*, II, 448.

53 From Shaw and Chatillon, Parkman had heard a reasonably accurate account of what Dorsey, "A Study of Siouan Cults," *Eleventh Annual Report*, pp. 485–489, describes as one of the ceremonies of the "ghost lodge." Compare also his account of Sioux burial customs: "All the dead man's possessions are buried with him. The favorite horse is

decorated and saddled, and to this day various articles belonging to the deceased are fastened to him. The horse is shot and part of his tail is cut off and laid near the head of the burial scaffold, as it is thought that in such a case the ghost can ride the ghost of the horse and use all the articles carried by that animal."

CHAPTER XI

1 The trappers arrived at the Chugwater camp on June 30. See *Journals*, II, 449. Morin and Saraphin remain unidentified.

2 Compare Russell, *Journal of a Trapper*, p. 82, for an excellent description of a typical trapper's outfit:

A Trappers equipments in such cases is generally one Animal upon which is placed one or two Epishemores a riding Saddle and bridle a sack containing six Beaver traps a blanket with an extra pair of Mocasins his powder horn and bullet pouch with a belt to which is attached a butcher Knife a small wooden box containing bait for Beaver a Tobacco sack with a pipe and implements for making fire with sometimes a hatchet fastened to the Pommel of his saddle[.] his personal dress is a flannel or cotton shirt (if he is fortunate enough to obtain one, if not Antelope skin answers the purpose of over and under shirt) a pair of leather breeches with Blanket or smoked Buffaloe skin, leggings, a coat made of Blanket or Buffaloe robe a hat or Cap of wool, Buffaloe or Otter skin[.] his hose are pieces of Blanket lapped round his feet which are covered with a pair of Moccassins made of Dressed Deer Elk or Buffaloe skins with his long hair falling loosely over his shoulders complets his uniform. He then mounts and places his rifle before him on his Saddle.

3 So large a body of men and horses—and the primitive sanitation—made "camp fever" inevitable if they were to remain encamped too long in one place.

4 The younger Bull Bear, his brother The Mad Wolf, several other braves, and a number of women and children rode into Parkman's camp on the morning of July 2. See *Journals*, II, 449. Though Mahto-Tatonka is shown hereafter in *The Oregon Trail* as the very model of Oglala virtue and bravery, there is little, if any other, positive evidence substantiating Parkman's account of him, and I have been unable to discover any reliable facts about his later life. For the elder Bull Bear, a famous Oglala chieftain, see pp. 157–158 of the present edition and note 22 for those pages.

5 Compare Parkman's notebook description of this scene in *Journals*, II, 449: "The utter laziness of an Ind.'s life. It is scarce tolerable to us, and yet is theirs from year's end to year's end. Bull Bear, a young chief, famous for his intrepidity, ambition, and activity, lies kicking his heels by the fire like the rest."

6 Parkman's notebooks flatly contradict the sequence of events set down in this paragraph. On July 2 Parkman, Shaw, and Reynal rode out to look for The Whirlwind's village and met the "solitary savage" mentioned here. Mahto-Tatonka, The Mad Wolf, and a number of other Indians rode into camp later the same day, and the rest of the village appeared on July 3. See *Journals*, II, 449–450.

7 Compare the sentence "His . . . place" with its *K*–52 form: "His relatives occupied but a contemptible position in Ogillallah society; for among these wild democrats of the prairie, as among us, there are virtual distinctions of rank and place; though this great advantage they have over us, that wealth has no part in determining such distinctions."

8 King Philip, the great chief of the Wampanoags, led an Indian confederacy against New England in 1675–1676. See Hodge, ed. *Handbook of American Indians*, I, 690. Tecumseh (1768–1813), a Shawnee, planned and organ-

ized a union of all the frontier tribes against the United States in the War of 1812 and was killed at the Battle of the Thames in 1813. Parkman instances these Indians and Pontiac to show that no chieftain could long hold together a large band of tribesmen even temporarily united for a common purpose. He had learned that the Oglala's great "war-chief," apparently the elder Bull Bear, could not restrain his fellow tribesmen and the Cheyennes from attacking the *bourgeois* Henry Fraeb and his trappers in early August, 1841. See *Journals*, II, 429; and LeRoy R. Hafen, "Fraeb's Last Fight and How Battle Creek Got Its Name," *Colorado Magazine*, VII (May, 1930), 97–101.

9 The Ojibwas, or Chippewas, an Algonquin tribe, were found historically in Michigan, Wisconsin, and Minnesota. Their comparatively early possession of firearms gave them a distinct advantage in their wars with the Santee Sioux during the eighteenth century. See Hodge, ed. *Handbook of American Indians*, I, 277–281.

10 Parkman seems not to have clearly understood the distinctions between the major divisions of the Dakotas, like the Yanktons or Tetons, the subdivisions like the Oglalas or Miniconques among the Tetons, and the separate bands like the Kiyuksas among the Oglalas.

11 Compare Gregg, *Commerce of the Prairies*, in Thwaites, ed. *Early Western Travels*, xx, 319, for a very similar account of the power and influence of the chiefs among the Plains Indians: "These petty bands seldom unite under one general leader, except for the common defense, when threatened with danger. Occasionally there springs up a master spirit—a great brave and a great sage, who is able to unite his whole tribe in which he is generally aided by a sufficient knack at sorcerous tricks to give him the character of a great 'medicine man.' "

12 Parkman's description of the system of chieftainship among the Dakotas omits a number of qualifying details

and does not suggest the complexity of a kind of collective leadership which Wissler calls the "chiefs society . . . an organization comprising the efficient older men of forty years or more," who in turn delegated their powers to four younger men who were known as "shirt wearers." The "shirt wearers" were the supreme councillors and executives, but they in turn elected four *wakicun* for periods of a year or more to exercise daily authority in camp and on the march. The *wakicun* were assisted in the performance of their duties by the leaders of each "soldier" society. See Clark Wissler, "Societies and Ceremonial Associations in the Oglala Division of the Teton-Dakota," *Anthropological Papers of the American Museum of Natural History,* XI (New York, 1916), 7–12.

13 The comparison of the Oglala headman to "the Teutonic chiefs of old" shows again how completely Parkman had absorbed the nineteenth century's reformulations of the Marquis de Condorcet's theory of the stages of civilization.

14 After the sentence "Frequently . . . character" K–52 supply the following additional sentence to conclude the paragraph: "A people so loosely united, torn, too, with rankling feuds and jealousies, can have little power or efficiency."

15 The "Parks" were the three great mountain valleys in Colorado, usually known as North Park, Middle Park, and South Park—the trappers' favorite wintering grounds. On Charles Preuss's map published with Frémont's *Report,* North Park, or New Park, is located some 50 miles north of the present site of Denver, Middle Park, or Old Park, near Denver, and South Park, or the Bayou Salade, close to modern Colorado Springs. See Charles Preuss, *Exploring with Frémont,* pp. 136–137 n.

16 Parkman's recognition of the close dependence of the Sioux (and other Plains Indians) on the buffalo is of

course correct, even to the reference to "boats to cross streams," the "bullboat" often made of two or three green hides stretched over a framework of willow branches. Other western travelers did not view the tragic inevitability of the destruction of the great buffalo herds and the consequent collapse of tribal society with quite the apparent equanimity Parkman shows in this passage. Ferris, *Life in the Rocky Mountains*, p. 287, for example, also noted the growing scarcity of game in the early 1840's and recognized that the Indians themselves were not entirely to blame for the increasing wretchedness of their condition:

Beaver and other kinds of game become every year more rare; and both the hunters and Indians will ultimately be compelled to herd cattle, or cultivate the earth for a livelihood; or in default of these starve. Indeed the latter deserve the ruin that threatens their offspring, for their inexcusable conduct, in sacrificing the millions of buffalo which they kill in sport, or for their skins only. The robes they obtain in the latter case, are most frequently exchanged for WHISKEY. . . .

17 Compare this comment on the "unwarlike tribes beyond the mountains" with Parkman's notebook entry for April 22(?) in *Journals*, ii, 414, in which he recorded part of a conversation he had had with Tom Fitzpatrick, one of the very greatest mountain men: "He [Fitzpatrick] thinks that the warlike spirit is the stimulant that saves the Indian from utter abasement, and mentions, in proof, the wretches whom he met near the Great Salt Lake, who were without this motive." The "wretches" to whom Fitzpatrick referred were probably Paiutes; they and other transmontane tribes were frequently lumped together as "Diggers," whom Stansbury, *Expedition to the Great Salt Lake*, p. 148, called "the most degraded and the lowest in the scale of being of any I had ever seen." Originally the term "Diggers" meant almost any Indians who dug roots,

and thus included many other Shoshonean tribes besides the Paiutes. See Hodge, ed. *Handbook of American Indians*, I, 390. On p. 225 of the present edition Parkman uses "Root-Diggers" in its common pejorative sense.

18 After the sentence "So . . . besides" K–52 supply the following additional three sentences to conclude the paragraph: "Trust not an Indian. Let your rifle be ever in your hand. Wear next your heart the old chivalric motto, 'semper paratus.'" The "old chivalric motto" means "always prepared."

19 I have been unable to identify satisfactorily Le Borgne, or "One Eye," especially since the French nickname was borne by a number of Indians of the period. Le Borgne, otherwise known as "Old Burns," may be the same Oglala whom Theodore Talbot, *Journals of Theodore Talbot*, p. 32, met near Horse Creek in August, 1843.

20 Between the sentences "His . . . energies" and "Opposite . . . lodge" K–52 supply the following additional sentence: "I recalled, as I saw him, the eloquent metaphor of the Iroquois sachem: 'I am an aged hemlock; the winds of a hundred winters have whistled through my branches, and I am dead at the top!'" I have been unable to find the source of this quotation.

21 Parkman did not hear the account of Le Borgne's initiatory visions from the old man himself. As his notebook entry for August 5 in *Journals*, II, 467–468, shows, Parkman got the story from Rouville, a trapper:

> Rouville's acct. of old Borne's life—told him by the old man. Old B. was eighteen when he dreamed of an interview with a grizzly bear—the *war-spirit* of the Inds. as the *antelope* is the *peace-spirit*. He saw the bear eating; and, waiting till he had appeased his hunger, went up to him. The bear told him it was time for him to think of going to war, but he must not do as the other Inds. did—he must fight openly, and not commit useless barbarities.

Next day he set out, went to the Black Hills, and soon discovered a Crow, before the latter observed him. As he was on the point of firing, he recalled the white bear's injunction, refrained, and called out to his enemy to step forwards and fight. They grappled—the Crow fell wounded. B. was on the point of despatching him, when he begged to speak a few words—he told B. that too much ambition was the cause of his present fate—that he had killed thirty-six Sioux, and now fell a victim to his desire to kill more—that he (B.) was a brave and good young man—that he had better renounce ambition and be content with a peaceful life. So old Borne has led a peaceful though honored life, very different from that of his fierce and ambitious brother, Bull Bear.

This passage from Parkman's notebooks shows clearly how the extremely romantic—not to say sentimentalized —picture of Le Borgne in this passage in *The Oregon Trail* differs from what may very probably be a reliable account of the old Indian's initiatory fast and visions, although the repentant Crow, renouncing ambition and praising his enemy, may owe something to Parkman's desire to present for once a real Noble Savage to the fireside circle in Boston. These considerations aside, Parkman's description of Le Borgne's "supernatural revelations" in the book almost certainly echoes Prince Maximilian's very similar account of initiatory fasts among the Mandans in *Travels in North America*, in Thwaites, ed. *Early Western Travels*, XXIII, 318:

These Indians are full of prejudice and superstition, and connect all the natural phenomena with the before-mentioned silly creations of their own imaginations. They undertake nothing without first invoking their guardian spirit, or medicine, who mostly appears to them in a dream. When they wish to choose their medicine or guardian spirit, they fast for three or four days, and even longer, retire to a solitary spot, do penance, and even sacrifice joints of their fingers, howl and cry to the lord of life, or to the first man, beseeching him to point out their guardian spirit. They continue in this excited state until they dream, and the first animal or other object which appears to them is chosen for their guardian spirit or medicine. Every man has his guardian spirit.

Precisely how much credence is to be given to Parkman's account of Le Borgne's initiatory vision in this passage, an account already much qualified by Parkman's own revision of a story which reached him at least at second-hand, cannot easily be determined, though clearly the episode described in the book and Rouville's original narrative no doubt both rest upon some substratum of fact. It seems probable that both accounts confused the "Spirits of the Mystery Sacks" or medicine bags (see note 24 for p. 197), which are given as guardian spirits to each Indian at the time of his initiation into the order of the Mystery Dance, with what Dorsey, "A Study of Siouan Cults," *Eleventh Annual Report*, pp. 443–444, calls the "Armor Gods":

As each young man comes to maturity, a tutelar divinity . . . is sometimes assigned to him. It is supposed to reside in the consecrated armor then given to him, consisting of a spear, an arrow, and a small bundle of paint. It is the spirit of some bird or animal, as the wolf, beaver, loon, or eagle. He must not kill this animal, but hold it ever sacred, or at least until he has proved his manhood by killing an enemy. Frequently the young man forms an image of this sacred animal and carries it about with him, regarding it as having a direct influence upon his everyday life and ultimate destiny.

Dorsey also notes that Parkman's account of the appearance of the guardian spirit during the initiatory fast in this passage and in *Jesuits*, 1, 65 n. (Vol. III of *Works*), is probably not trustworthy: "If this is ever true among the

Dakota, it is not the rule. This knowledge [of the "Armor Gods"] is communicated by the 'war prophet.' " However, periods of fasting and solitary retirement, often in conjunction with puberty rites but also as a part of the Indian's ordinary religious life, are well established. See also Mari Sandoz, *These Were the Sioux* (New York, 1961), pp. 47–48, for a colorful account of these ceremonies by a writer who knew the Sioux during their early reservation years.

22 The history of the Oglalas during the 1820's and 1830's might almost be called identical with the leading facts of chief Bull Bear's biography. During the 16 years (1825–1841) when he appears most often in chronicles of western exploration and adventure, it was he and the calculating force of his leadership and example that were most responsible for the extremely important movements which the Oglalas made during this period, as well as for the rankling feuds which divided the tribe after his murder on Chugwater Creek in November, 1841. He first comes into prominence in a treaty signed in 1825, when the Oglalas were still living along the Bad and White rivers east of the Black Hills of what came to be South Dakota and when Bull Bear was the head warrior of the Kiyuksas, one of the four bands into which the Oglalas were then divided and which after 1835 were to be known collectively as the Bear People—the followers of Bull Bear.

As has been shown on p. 117 of the present edition and note 24 for that page, the appearance of Bull Bear and a hundred Oglala lodges at Fort Laramie in 1834 permanently altered the balance of Indian power on the North Platte and had a profound effect on subsequent Oglala history. From 1834 to 1841 Bull Bear appears often in the literature of the fur trade. His portrait, done by Alfred Jacob Miller in 1837, shows a man of heavy, prominent features, the inevitable hatchet cradled in his crossed forearms. Parkman's account in this passage of Bull Bear's influence and power among his tribesmen seems completely justified by the available facts, for so great was his authority that he was able not only to bring most of the remaining Oglalas down from their favorite hunting grounds near the Black Hills to the North Platte but also to lead his Kiyuksas and Red Water's band in increasingly deeper and more dangerous penetrations of the much-contested territory west of Fort Laramie and toward the headwaters of the North Platte. Bull Bear's death on the Chugwater in 1841 seems to have occurred much as Parkman describes it on p. 159 of the present edition, an account which Hyde credits in large part, although he maintains that the young Red Cloud was Bull Bear's murderer. See *Red Cloud's Folk*, pp. 40, 40–63 *passim*; and Sage, *Scenes in the Rocky Mountains*, I, 256–257. Miller's portrait of Bull Bear is conveniently reproduced in DeVoto, *Across the Wide Missouri*, Plate LXIX, and in Marvin C. Ross, *The West of Alfred Jacob Miller* (Norman, 1951), Plate 45.

Talbot, *Journals of Theodore Talbot*, p. 32, thought that in 1843, two years after old Bull Bear's death, the Oglalas still numbered some 1,500 persons, and, even though the Smoke People and the Bear People were not on good terms in 1846, the Oglalas were still a formidable power on the North Platte. Chief Smoke himself was still alive as late as 1854. See Henry Chatillon's letter of February 16, 1867, to Parkman in O'Leary, "Henry Chatillon," pp. 137–138.

23 Wislizenus, who met old Bull Bear on the South Platte in 1839, noted that the chief, "rather aged, and of a squat, thick figure," had seven wives. See F. A. Wislizenus, *A Journey to the Rocky Mountains in the Year 1839* (St. Louis, 1912), p. 58.

24 Parkman's notebook entry for July 2 in *Journals*, II,

449–450, clearly shows his disgust at wife-stealing among the Oglalas: "An Ind. becomes great by such exploits as stealing other men's wives, and refusing to make any present in compensation. The Mad Wolf, Bull Bear's brother, now with us, had often done this. It is a great proof of bravery, thus setting the husband at defiance. If the husband claims a present, and it is given, the merit of the thing is gone. So much for the regulation of Indian society."

25 The sentence "He . . . merits" replaces the following two sentences in K–52: "As among us, those of highest worth and breeding are most simple in manner and attire, so our aspiring young friend was indifferent to the gaudy trappings and ornaments of his companions. He was content to rest his chances of success upon his own warlike merits."

26 After the sentence "Young . . . lodge" K supplies the following additional paragraph:

Truly it is a poor thing, this life of an Indian. Few and mean are its pleasures. War without the inspiration of chivalry, gallantry with no sentiments to elevate it. Yet never have I seen in any Indian village on the remote prairies such depravity, such utter abasement and prostitution of every nobler part of humanity, as I have seen in great cities, the centres of the world's wisdom and refinement. The meanest savage in the Whirlwind's camp would seem noble and dignified compared with some of the lost children of civilization.

The recurrent rhetorical figures in this passage, particularly evident after the paragraph excised in K has been restored, show again Parkman's too facile contrasts between Indians and whites. The Oglalas are presented in imagery appropriate to an epic or chivalric tradition, however much that tradition may have been debased in the typical figure of a naked "partisan" riding at the head of his "soldier" society. The "lost children of civilization" *are* clearly lost because civilization—in the most oversimplified sense of that much-abused term—has torn them from a natural context and replaced the crude vigor of blood and soil with a spurious and destructive refinement. Parkman's "primitivism," especially in the canceled paragraph, was inspired by something more than the cult of the "Noble Savage." The description of arms and armor and the brave picture of a savage hero resoundingly named recall the Homeric poems, even as Parkman carefully distinguishes between mere ferocity "without the inspiration of chivalry" and the ideal "sentiments" of an epic or chivalric hero.

27 Parkman received the pipe from The Whirlwind on July 3. See *Journals*, II, 450.

28 "Jack," as he is called in K–52, was brought into camp on July 4. See *Journals*, II, 451. I have been unable to discover any other contemporary reference to him or to his sufferings.

29 Parkman's "prairie-dove" was almost certainly the mourning dove (*Zenaidura macroura*), the only breeding dove normally found in the area of "Jack's" wanderings.

30 I am indebted to Professor Hugh Iltis of the University of Wisconsin Department of Botany for the identification of "*pommes blanches*" as *Psoralea esculenta*, a legume otherwise known as *Pommes de Prairie*, or Indian breadroot.

31 Parkman's rather trite allusion is to Salvator Rosa (1615–1673), satiric poet, musician, and the great master of the Neapolitan school of painting in the seventeenth century, particularly noted for his romantic landscapes and vigorous genre scenes. Like Parkman and many another western traveler, George Gibbs, "The Diary of George E. Gibbs," reprinted in *The March of the Mounted Riflemen . . .* , ed. Raymond W. Settle (Glendale, Calif., 1940), pp. 287–288, also found suitable figures for a scene

after Salvator among the Indians: "As the firelight flashed on their faces, I could not but recall the pictures of Salvator and regret that the inspiration of such a pencil was wanting here."

32 Compare the sentence "Others again . . . forms" with its K–52 form: "Others again stood carelessly among the throng, with nothing to conceal the matchless symmetry of their forms; and I do not exaggerate when I say, that only on the prairie and in the Vatican have I seen such faultless models of the human figure."

33 The sentence "There was . . . himself" replaces the following three sentences in K–52: "See that warrior standing by the tree, towering six feet and a half in stature. Your eyes may trace the whole of his graceful and majestic height, and discover no defect or blemish. With his free and noble attitude, with the bow in his hand, and the quiver at his back, he might seem, but for his face, the Pythian Apollo himself."

34 Benjamin West (1738–1820), the first American painter to win widespread European recognition, rose ultimately to the presidency of the Royal Academy and to an appointment as court painter to George III. His famous exclamation on first seeing the Apollo Belvedere has often been quoted in illustration of that romantic primitivism which professed to see in the cold marble and the living Indian the same flawless grace of artless Nature. See *DAB*, s.v. "West, Benjamin."

After the sentence "Such . . . Mohawk!' " K supplies the following additional paragraph: "The Mad Wolf was the name of the lofty champion. Unless fame belied him, he was a bold, subtle, and cruel warrior, and his features bore the impress of such a character."

35 Scarification as a manifestation of grief at the death of a relative was a fairly common practice among western Indians. See Hodge, ed. *Handbook of American Indians*, II,

484–485, and compare Alexander Ross, *The Fur Hunters of the Far West*, ed. Kenneth A. Spaulding (Norman, 1956), p. 137:

To have seen those savages streaming all over with blood, one would suppose that they could not have suffered such acts of cruelty inflicted on themselves; but such wounds though bad are not dangerous. To inflict those wounds the person takes hold of any part of his skin between the forefinger and thumb, draws it out to the stretch, and then runs a knife through it between the hand and the flesh which leaves, when the skin resumes its former place, two unsightly gashes resembling ball holes out of which the blood issues freely. With such wounds and sometimes others of a more serious nature the near relatives of the deceased completely disfigure their bodies.

36 Compare the sentence "Nor . . . cases" with its K–52 form: "Medical assistance of course there was none; neither had I the means of pursuing a system of diet; and sleeping on damp ground, with an occasional drenching from a shower, would hardly be recommended as beneficial."

37 Compare the sentence "I . . . forever" with its K–52 form: "I sometimes suffered the extremity of languor and exhaustion, and was in a tolerably fair way of atoning for my love of the prairie by resting there forever, and though at the time I felt no apprehensions of the final result, I have since learned that my situation was a critical one."

38 Before the sentence "I tried . . . diet" K–52 supply the following additional sentence at the beginning of the paragraph: "Besides other formidable inconveniences, I owe it in a great measure to the remote effects of that unlucky disorder, that from deficient eyesight I am compelled to employ the pen of another in taking down this narrative from my lips; and I have learned very effectually that a

violent attack of dysentery on the prairie is a thing too serious for a joke."

39 After the sentence "At . . . diet" K–52 supply the following additional sentence to conclude the paragraph: "No sooner had I done so than the same detested symptoms revisited me; my old enemy resumed his pertinacious assaults, yet not with his former violence or constancy, and though before I regained any fair portion of my ordinary strength weeks had elapsed, and months passed before the disorder left me, yet thanks to old habits of activity, and a merciful providence, I was able to sustain myself against it."

The restoration of these *four* excised passages describing his illness shows how strongly Parkman's imagination as well as his body had been affected by the "pertinacious assaults" of his wilderness "enemy."

CHAPTER XII

1 The K version of this chapter was printed consecutively with the K version of Chapter XI, "Scenes at the Camp," in the same issue of the magazine, and does not contain the present opening paragraph describing the trapper's "elopement" with the emigrant belle. The addition of this paragraph in 49 would seem to provide a strong argument that Parkman was personally responsible for at least the revision of the K versions of these two chapters and probably for most of the other significant variants between K and 49–52.

2 The "imprudent fair one" first appears in Parkman's notebook entry for June 26 in *Journals*, II, 447: "One woman, of more than suspected chastity, is left at the Fort; and Bordeaux is fool enough to receive her." She is also mentioned as a "scandal" in Parkman's letter of June 28 (27?) to his father, and she may conjecturally be identified as

"the notorious widow" who, with her two children and a man "whom we considered to be the woman's husband," had traveled from Missouri in the same emigrant train with Heinrich Lienhard. Her demands soon sapped the energies of her "husband," who abandoned her east of Fort Laramie, and at last she disgusted the rest of the company, who left her at the fort on June 26. See Lienhard, *St. Louis to Sutter's Fort*, pp. 54–55, 68. Morgan, ed. *Overland in 1846*, I, 110, notes that "In all probability the widow was espoused by a prominent mountain man, but for lack of definite evidence, I forbear naming the husband"—a sufficiently tantalizing suggestion. However, Parkman's notebook entry for July 9 in *Journals*, II, 453–454, records that "Jeangras met a party of emigrants, from whom some trapper from the fort stole a woman, as they were encamped night before last [July 7?]. He approached with two horses—met the fair one at the edge of the camp—mounted her, and vanished." Clearly Parkman had not learned that Lienhard's "notorious widow" and the emigrant "fair one" were the same person, and perhaps the identification still remains in doubt.

3 The Whirlwind's band was apparently preparing to set out for their customary July, or summer, hunt. Compare Mari Sandoz, *These Were the Sioux*, p. 62: "In a July hunt the jerky hardened fast and sweet in a few hours of hot wind, and the hides were easily cleaned of their thin summer wool for lodge skins, saddle bags, shield and regalia boxes, travois skins, and other purposes. For these young cows were selected, the skins lighter, thinner, softer, and easier to tan and handle, the meat better, too. . . ."

4 Parkman and his party and the Indians left the Chugwater camp on July 5—*not* July 1—and rode three or four miles west to the forks of the Laramie River—"the short journey of that day." See *Journals*, II, 452.

5 For a full account of Joseph Bissonette (whom Parkman

was to meet on Horse Creek on August 6), see p. 311 of the present edition and note 14 for that page. Bissonette had arrived at Fort Bernard from Missouri on or about June 28, when Clyman met him and his wagons on the North Platte a few miles east of the post. See *James Clyman, Frontiersman*, p. 225. In his partnership with Richard at Fort Bernard, Bissonette seems to have been the "outside man," trading directly with the Indians in their camps.

6 The "war parade" of the "Strong Hearts" or *tokala* (Kit-Fox) "soldier" society occurred on the afternoon of July 5. See *Journals*, II, 452. The White Shield, hereafter (pp. 253–257 of the present edition) described as the leader of a war party against the Crows, is unidentified.

7 Compare Prince Maximilian's very similar description of Sioux mourning customs in *Travels in North America*, in Thwaites, ed. *Early Western Travels*, XXII, 311: "As a sign of mourning, they cut off their hair with the first knife that comes to hand, daub themselves with white clay, and give away all their best clothes and valuable effects. . . ."

8 Compare the sentence "Little . . . tribe" with its K–52 form: "Little urchins, not yet two years old, followed the warlike pageant with glittering eyes, and looked with eager wonder and admiration at those whose honors were proclaimed by the public voice of the village."

After this sentence K–52 supply the following additional sentence to conclude the paragraph: "Thus early is the lesson of war instilled into the mind of an Indian, and such are the stimulants which excite his thirst for martial renown."

9 This paragraph describing the "vicious-looking squaw" and her husband's revenge was first inserted in 72, apparently for comic relief. The episode, however, appears in Parkman's notebooks in *Journals*, II, 452, under date of July 5, and its appearance in 72 seems to suggest that

Parkman, in the process of revising *The Oregon Trail* for the new edition, returned to the original notebooks for some of the details of this scene from "Indian domestic life."

10 The sentence "We . . . appeared" replaces the following three sentences in *K*: "We travelled until night, and encamped. I suffered not a little from pain and weakness, the latter of which would have forced me to take an uncomfortable refuge in the cart, but for the aid of my former friend, the whiskey. We encamped among some trees by the side of a little brook and here during the whole of the next day we lay waiting for Bisonette, but no Bisonette appeared."

The clause "the latter . . . whiskey" in the *K* version of the passage above was excised in 49–52.

The chronology of Parkman's ride to La Bonte Creek is not readily apparent in *The Oregon Trail*. He and the rest of his party parted from the Indians at the camp near the forks of Laramie River on July 6 and camped the same night on Cottonwood Creek (the "little stream" of this passage), some four or five miles west of the present site of Wendover, Wyoming. They remained encamped on Cottonwood Creek through the morning of July 8, the trappers having in the meanwhile left for the mountains on July 7. On July 8, "the second morning" of this passage, Parkman and his companions rode over to Horseshoe Creek and camped on its bank at a point some 10 miles southwest of modern Glendo, Wyoming. They reached La Bonte Creek, probably close to its mouth, the next day and made camp at a site 10 miles south of the present Douglas, Wyoming. They were now some 55 miles north-northwest of Fort Laramie. See *Journals*, II, 452–454.

11 After the sentence "I . . . move" *K*–52 supply the following two sentences to conclude the paragraph: "All that afternoon I lay in the shade by the side of the stream, and

those bright woods and sparkling waters are associated in my mind with recollections of lassitude and utter prostration. When night came I sat down by the fire, longing, with an intensity of which at this moment I can hardly conceive, for some powerful stimulant."

12 After the sentence "For . . . miles" K–52 supply the following additional sentence to conclude the paragraph: "To fortify myself as well as I could against such a contingency, I resolved that I would not under any circumstances leave the country until my object was gained."

It is hard to explain Parkman's computation of his distance from Boston; while he was camped on La Bonte Creek he was perhaps 2,300 miles from the Atlantic Coast.

13 I have been unable to determine exactly where Parkman thought the Sioux were encamped, but the distance cited might allow a conjectural location of their campsite on or near Boxelder Creek, close to modern Careyhurst, Wyoming.

CHAPTER XIII

1 Parkman's determination to follow the Indians led him to take some extraordinarily dangerous—and therefore foolhardy—risks; the probability of his being plundered and even scalped was very strong, and it is surprising that Henry Chatillon, in a sense responsible for Parkman's safety, allowed him to set out with only Raymond for protector and guide. Shaw's refusal to accompany his friend is in these circumstances especially puzzling.

2 For more information about Raymond, see p. 124 of the present edition and note 12 for that page.

3 Between the sentences "The Indians . . . enemies" and "We . . . horse" K–52 supply the following three additional sentences: "He would have made a capital shot. A rifle bullet, skilfully planted, would have brought him

tumbling to the ground. Surely, I thought, there could be no more harm in shooting such a hideous old villain, to see how ugly he would look when he was dead, than in shooting the detestable vulture which he resembled."

4 Between the sentences "I . . . journey" and "It . . . saddle" K–52 supply the following additional sentence: "After supper, Henry Chatillon and I lay by the fire, discussing the properties of that admirable weapon, the rifle, in the use of which he could fairly out-rival Leatherstocking himself."

5 Shaw rode back to Horseshoe Creek on the afternoon of July 10 and returned to camp before daylight on July 11. See *Journals*, II, 454.

6 Between the sentences "So . . . Laramie" and "Shaw . . . after" K–52 supply the following additional two sentences: "Shaw's limbs were swollen to double their usual size, and he rode in great pain. They encamped again within twenty miles of the fort, and reached it early on the following morning."

7 The sentences "Its . . . hills" and "I . . . mosses" replace the following four sentences in K–52:

Under the scorching heat, these melancholy trees diffused their peculiar resinous odor through the sultry air. There was something in it, as I approached them, that recalled old associations: the pine-clad mountains of New-England, traversed in days of health and buoyancy, rose like a reality before my fancy. In passing that arid waste I was goaded with a morbid thirst produced by my disorder, and I thought with a longing desire on the crystal treasure poured in such wasteful profusion from our thousand hills. Shutting my eyes, I more than half believed that I heard the deep plunging and gurgling of waters in the bowels of the shaded rocks. I could see their dark icy glittering far down amid the crevices, and the cold drops trickling from the long green mosses.

8 The "little stream" was Horseshoe Creek.

9 Parkman and Raymond were retracing the route that they had followed from the camp near the forks of Laramie River over to La Bonte Creek. On the evening of July 11 they reached the same Cottonwood Creek campsite where the whole party had spent July 6–8. See *Journals*, II, 454.

10 The animals bolted on the morning of July 12. See *Journals*, II, 454.

11 The Cottonwood Creek campsite was located not more than 25 miles north-northwest of Fort Laramie and close to the Oregon Trail itself, so that Parkman in this passage seems consciously to have exaggerated the dangers of his position.

12 Compare the sentence "I . . . drink" with its *K* form: "I took charge of the animals while he kneeled down by the side of the stream to drink; but he was faint and dizzy, and the water was instantly rejected."

13 Parkman's "Side Fork," some 15 miles distant from the Cottonwood Creek campsite, is now known as North Laramie River.

14 Mount Laramie, or Laramie Peak (elev. 10,274 ft.), is located some four miles northwest of Fletcher Park, Wyoming.

15 Between the sentences "Leading . . . above" and "All . . . spring" *K*–52 supply the following additional sentence: " 'Am I,' I thought to myself, 'the same man, who a few months since, was seated, a quiet student of belles-lettres, in a cushioned arm-chair by a sea-coal fire?' "

16 Parkman saw the Apennines in March, 1844, during his European tour. See *Journals*, I, 184–185.

17 This paragraph presents a striking demonstration of Parkman's partiality for the pathetic fallacy in its imagery of frowning mountains "lighted up with a benignant smile."

18 This "little stream" must have been the North Laramie

River, where Parkman and Raymond passed the night of July 12–13. See *Journals*, II, 454–455.

19 Although specific details of distances and topographical features are at times vague and general in this section of the book and in the corresponding entries in Parkman's notebooks, it seems probable that he and Raymond reached the Laramie River at a point some 27 or 28 miles west-southwest of Fort Laramie.

20 The brook is probably Sybille Creek, though the Laramie River itself flows northward past the mouth of Sybille Creek a mile or two before its big bend to the east.

21 This passage follows closely part of Parkman's notebook entry for July 13 in *Journals*, II, 455: "Followed slowly all the afternoon, losing the trail repeatedly. Saw a heavy smoke rising from a valley this side [i.e., south of] Laramie Mt. Lost the trail at last, and encamped in a hollow bottom, where Laramie comes swiftly out of the hills, and where our fire would be invisible." If Parkman really *was* on Laramie River, he and Raymond had now crossed the triangle of country separating Sybille Creek and the river and were encamped on a site perhaps 14 or 15 miles west-southwest of present Wheatland, Wyoming.

22 These "circles of large stones," frequently noted by western travelers and sometimes described as ceremonial dancing rings, were indeed "traces of a Dakota winter encampment." Each circle marked the spot where a lodge had been pitched; the stones helped to hold down the lodge-coverings during winter storms.

23 This passage closely parallels part of Parkman's notebook entry for July 14 in *Journals*, II, 455–456:

Following a creek that flows from the south into Laramie, we found the traces of lodge-poles again, but soon lost them. Not long after, we found them again, and a camp, where by the number of fires we saw that we were on the trail of only part of the village. Traced it up a bare and scorching valley of the mts. where we led our animals. Descending, we came to a succession of little grassey and well watered nooks among these black and desolate hills, and presently came upon another camp. Not long after, with a dreary interval of hot and barren prairie, we came to a succession of defiles among fine abrupt mts. . . . Bare cliffs above—beautiful woods below—a clear stream glancing in their shadows over a bed of rock—and all alive with birds like Mt. Auburn. It was a place to repay a week's travel. After twelve miles' riding we found another camp and nooned there. Several rude little forts, some twelve feet square, of interlaced logs and branches, marked the war-like character of the region. In the afternoon we ascended a narrow and most romantic pass—the stream in its bed of rocks by our sides, a dense foliage around us, and lofty beetling cliffs above. Larkspur and a sort of aster were among the numberless flowers—pleasant mementos of civilization in such a wilderness.

Precisely what route Parkman used to get into the Medicine Bow Basin seems to me still in doubt, though Jacobs, *Letters*, I, xli, suggests that Parkman and Raymond followed Sybille Creek over the divide and presumably crossed Morton Pass (elev. 7,301 ft.), probably on the afternoon of July 14. But it is at least conceivable that the creek which flowed "from the south into Laramie" might have been another tributary of Laramie River, and perhaps Parkman and Raymond crossed the Laramie Range at a point on the Laramie River 10 or 15 miles northeast of the present Wheatland Reservoir and thus well to the north of Morton Pass.

24 The sentences "There . . . situation"; "Man . . . alike"; and "Pauline . . . run" replace the following two sentences in *K–52*: "Thinking of that morning's journey, it has sometimes seemed to me that there was something ridiculous in my position; a man, armed to the teeth, but

wholly unable to fight, and equally so to run away, traversing a dangerous wilderness, on a sick horse. But these
thoughts were retrospective, for at the time I was in too
grave a mood to entertain a very lively sense of the ludicrous."

25 Parkman's "locust" was probably one of the cicadas. The
Cicadidae are not true locusts, but Parkman's description
of both sound and habitat would suggest this insect.

26 Parkman's "Rocky Mountain sheep" are mountain sheep
(*Ovis canadensis*), which are now restricted to the rugged,
mountainous country of the West. Also known as big-
horns or bighorn sheep, they formerly descended to lower
altitudes where they often mingled with antelope and deer.

27 The effect of this passage—whether or not so intended—is
to present in the strongest possible terms Parkman's sense
of his own isolation from all familiar associations and,
perhaps, his compulsion to find in the ashes of Reynal's
campfire a tenuous "bond of sympathy" not merely with
another white man but with the very idea of civilization
itself.

28 I am indebted to Professor David Stephenson of the University of Wisconsin Department of Geology for the information that Parkman's "black crags . . . shattered by
storms and thunder" were probably granite outcroppings
or hogbacks in a fracture pattern bearing east or northeast.

29 The sentence "As . . . behind" replaces the following five
sentences in *K–52*:

I would I could recall to mind all the startling [K: the wild and
startling] combinations that presented themselves, as winding
from side to side of the passage, to avoid its obstructions, we
could see, glancing at intervals through the foliage, the awful
forms of the gigantic cliffs, that seemed at times to hem us in
on the right and on the left, before us and behind! Another
scene in a few moments greeted us; a tract of gay and sunny
woods, broken into knolls and hollows, enlivened by birds and

interspersed with flowers. Among the rest I recognized the mellow whistle of the robin, an old familiar friend, whom I had scarce expected to meet in such a place. Humble-bees [*sic*] too were buzzing heavily about the flowers; and of these a species of larkspur caught my eye, more appropriate, it should seem, to cultivated gardens than to a remote wilderness. Instantly it recalled a multitude of dormant and delightful associations.

After "Instantly . . . associations" in the passage above, K supplies the following additional three sentences to conclude the paragraph:

Civilization, with those that adorn and grace it, rose before me under an aspect more than ever attractive and engaging. Again looking around me, I was struck with the strong resemblance of the features of the scene to those of the cemetery of Mount Auburn. By a natural association, my thoughts recurred to quiet years spent in the neighboring university, and more especially to certain *Noctes Ambrosianae* convocations, where festivity and literature contended which should preside; until, as the hours moved on, the contest was no longer in doubt, and Bacchus drove Minerva from the field.

Parkman himself is buried in Mount Auburn Cemetery, near Cambridge, Massachusetts. The *Noctes Ambrosianae*, by John Wilson and other hands, was published in 71 installments in *Blackwood's Magazine* from 1822 to 1835; these papers presented the lively conversations of the waggish habitués of Ambrose's Tavern in London and depicted, under easily penetrable masks, the characters of a number of contemporary literary men.

30 Raymond's fears were well founded, for in 1846 the Medicine Bow Range and Basin and much of the country as far eastward as Fort Laramie was a contested area, a kind of no-man's-land which the Oglalas dominated but certainly

did not control. The Crows were present on Chugwater Creek in the summer of 1846 (see p. 130 of the present edition and note 25 for that page), and it is quite possible that the Gros Ventres, or Atsinas, a detached band of Arapahoes allied with the Blackfeet, might have been found near the Medicine Bows on a summer hunt, just as The White Shield confidently expected to encounter the Snakes with the war party he was organizing.

31 Compare the conclusion of Parkman's notebook entry for July 14 in *Journals*, ii, 456: "In a basin among rugged hills, at the head of a pass, the Inds. had encamped again, and a little farther on we did the same. (Absanth [i.e., sage-brush] everywhere.) Just emerging from the hills, saw several bulls on a distant butte."

32 After the sentence "But . . . evening" K–52 supply the following additional paragraph:

While he was looking after the animals, I sat by the fire engaged in the novel task of baking bread. The utensils were of the most simple and primitive kind, consisting of two sticks inclining over the bed of coals, one end thrust into the ground while the dough was twisted in a spiral form round the other. Under such circumstances all the epicurean in a man's nature is apt to awaken within him. I revisited in fancy the far distant abodes of good fare, not indeed Frascati's, or the Trois Frères Provençaux, for that were too extreme a flight; but no other than the homely table of my old friend and host, Tom Crawford, of the White Mountains. By a singular revulsion, Tom himself, whom I well remember to have looked upon as the impersonation of all that is wild and backwoodsman-like, now appeared before me as the ministering angel of comfort and good living. Being fatigued and drowsy, I began to doze, and my thoughts following the same line of association, assumed another form. Half-dreaming, I saw myself surrounded with the mountains [K: with the wild and noble forms of the mountains] of New England, alive with water-falls, their black crags cinctured with milk-white mists. For this reverie I paid a speedy penalty; for the bread was black on one side and soft on the other.

The references in this canceled paragraph to the very famous—even notorious—Parisian restaurants, Frascati's and the Trois Frères Provençaux, and to the Notch House in the White Mountains of New Hampshire, demonstrate again Parkman's almost obsessive contrasts between civilization and the wilderness. The Trois Frères Provençaux, opened shortly after the end of the Terror, was located on the Rue Valois and for more than 80 years was perhaps the most distinguished restaurant in Paris. Frascati's, situated between the Rue de Richelieu and the Boulevard Montmarte, began business as early as 1789 and lasted until 1838, though in its later years it was chiefly known as a splendid gambling hall which Emerson, in some trepidation, visited in 1833 and described as "the most noted of the gambling houses or hells of Paris . . . a very handsome house on the Rue Richelieu." See Pierre Andrieu, *Fine Bouche: A History of the Restaurant in France,* trans. Arthur L. Hayward (London, 1956), pp. 33–35, 70–71; and *The Journals and Miscellaneous Notebooks of Ralph Waldo Emerson, 1832–1834,* ed. Alfred R. Ferguson, IV (Cambridge, Mass., 1964), 203–204. Parkman had visited the White Mountains during three summer outings in 1841–1843 and had met Thomas J. Crawford, the resident guide and operator of the Notch House, built in 1828 by his father, Abel Crawford, and his brother, Ethan Allen Crawford, at the southern end of what came to be known as the Crawford Notch of the White Mountains. Tom Crawford was a local celebrity to visiting Bostonians; Emerson met him in August, 1829, and described him as "A man of *guiding* memory" whose house lay "two miles from the throat of the pass." See *Journals,* I, 12, 330–331; and *The Journals and Miscellaneous Notebooks of Ralph*

Waldo Emerson, 1826–1832, eds. William H. Gilman and Alfred R. Ferguson, III (Cambridge, Mass., 1963), 161–162.

33 Parkman's notebook entry for July 15 in *Journals*, II, 456, shows that the traces "pointed . . . towards the head of Laramie Creek," probably due west from the point where he and Raymond then stood. If Parkman's direction is correct, then it is probable that he and Raymond had crossed the mountains by way of Sybille Canyon and Morton Pass.

34 The "surround" or encirclement of a band of buffalo— described in detail on pp. 231–236 of the present text—was the commonest method by which Plains Indians pursued the buffalo during the communal summer hunts. Russell, *Journal of a Trapper*, p. 36, saw a "surround" in which 1,000 buffalo cows were killed without "burning one single grain of gun powder."

35 Parkman's "white plover" in this passage might quite possibly have been avocets (*Recurvirostra americana*), a large shorebird which nests near pools, marshes, ponds, and alkaline lakes in the so-called "transition zone" of the western United States. Avocets are extremely rare in the East, and so Parkman may here be simply making a guess at the birds' identity when he calls them "white plover."

36 Medicine Bow Peak (elev. 12,013 ft.), one of the highest summits in the range, is located 40 miles west of Laramie, Wyoming.

37 Compare Parkman's notebook account of his discovery of the Oglala village in *Journals*, II, 456: "Raymond advised return. Resolved to advance till night, and soon after, ascending a butte, saw the circle of lodges, with the bands of horse [*sic*], close by the bare banks of Laramie. Thanked God that my enterprise was not defeated. Groups stood in front of the lodges as we descended. . . ."

Chapter xiv

1 Parkman reached the village on July 15 and left it for Fort Laramie on August 2.

2 The sentence "They were . . . world" does not appear in K–52. Here and in the following paragraph Parkman has adopted most of the rhetoric appropriate to a consideration of the Indians in terms of "savagism," that set of complementary attitudes which regarded the Indians as the children of the human race, an expendable remnant of the past temporarily standing in the way of the triumphant progress of American civilization. Parkman's remarks here demonstrate quite clearly what Pearce, *Savages of America*, p. 64, has described as the crux of the "Indian Problem" in the first half of the nineteenth century: "Americans were thus of two minds about the Indians whom they were destroying. They pitied his state but saw it as inevitable; they hoped to bring him to civilization but saw that civilization would kill him." As Parker, *Journal of an Exploring Tour*, p. 50, expressed the problem: "The question is, by whom shall this region of country be inhabited? It is plain that the Indians, under their present circumstances, will never multiply and fill this land. They must be brought under the influence of civilization and Christianity, or they will continue to melt away, until nothing will remain of them but the relics found in the museums, and some historical records. Philanthropy and the mercy of God plead in their behalf."

3 Compare Joel Palmer on the preparation of "jerky" in *Travels over the Rocky Mountains*, in Thwaites, ed. *Early Western Travels*, xxx, 53: "We then commenced jerking it. This is a process resorted to for want of time or means to cure meat by salting. The meat is sliced thin, and a scaffold prepared, by setting forks in the ground, about

three feet high, and laying small poles or sticks crosswise upon them. The meat is laid upon these pieces, and a slow fire built beneath; the heat and smoke complete the process in half a day; and with an occasional sunning the meat will keep for months."

4 Most of the Indians Parkman mentions in this paragraph cannot be positively identified. The White Shield has already been shown as the leader of the "Strong Hearts" or *tokala* "soldier" society; The Mad Wolf was the younger Bull Bear's brother; nothing is certainly known of the Indian named The Panther; as Parkman notes on p. 292 of the present edition, "The Panther" may, however, have been a ceremonial title. The Big Crow, or Kongra-Tonga, Parkman's host during his stay in the village, may possibly be identified as the Miniconjou chieftain killed by the Crows in 1859. See Hassrick, *The Sioux*, p. 310. The Eagle-Feather appears to have been the Big Crow's son. Red Water, usually called Mene-Seela in *The Oregon Trail*, was a very famous Oglala leader whose band was numbered among the Brules by Lewis and Clark; at some time before 1825, however, Red Water's village joined Bull Bear and the Kiyuksas. Apparently Red Water's band soon followed the rest of the Bear People to the new Fort Laramie in 1834, and for years thereafter the two groups were seemingly identical, especially after Bull Bear's death in 1841 and the division of the Oglalas into two suspicious and often hostile factions, the Bear People and the Smoke People. It seems probable that Red Water himself died during or shortly after the great cholera epidemic of 1849–1850. See Hyde, *Red Cloud's Folk*, pp. 31–67 *passim*.

5 The Arrow-Head remains unidentified.

6 Hyde, *Red Cloud's Folk*, p. 30, notes that in 1856 General William S. Harney made Bad Wound of the True Oglalas band the head chief of all the Oglalas. The name itself

seems to have been an hereditary one, for in 1804 Lewis and Clark had met a Sioux chief named Owawicha, or Bad Wound.

7 According to Stephen R. Riggs, *Dakota-English Dictionary*, p. 293, "colà" or "kola" is Teton Sioux for *"the particular friend* of a Dakota man"—perhaps a warmer greeting than Parkman might have expected.

8 Red Water's description of the Thunderbird is remarkably similar to Prince Maximilian's account of that myth as he found it among the Mandans. Compare *Travels in North America*, in Thwaites, ed. *Early Western Travels*, xxiii, 304: "The Mandans believe that the thunder is produced by the motion of the wings of a gigantic bird. When this bird . . . flaps his wings violently, he occasions a roaring noise." See also Hodge, ed. *Handbook of American Indians*, ii, 747: "On the plains a thunderstorm was supposed to be due to a contest between the thunderbird and a huge rattlesnake, or an underground or subaqueous monster—called Unktéhi by the Dakota. . . ." Hodge's cited account of the Thunderbird is in part a summary of the extended discussion of the *Wakinyan*, or Thunder-Beings, in Dorsey, "A Study of Siouan Cults," *Eleventh Annual Report*, pp. 441–443.

9 Parkman seems to have heard a somewhat confused account of one of the ceremonies of the *Heyokas*, Thunder-Dreamers, or Contraries, as the same society is variously called. Wissler, "Societies and Ceremonial Associations," *Anthropological Papers*, xi, 82–85, reprints part of the narrative of Calico, an Oglala, who described his initiation into the *Heyoka* cult in a ceremony rather like the one Parkman had heard of: "When everything was in readiness, I came out and danced around through the camp with the other heyoka, sounding my rattles and dodging about. While this was going on a cloud came up and threatened rain, but after we stopped it broke away. Then

I took off my regalia in the ceremonial tipi and some old heyoka took the things out to a high hill and left them as an offering. . . . After this I did not feel uneasy and afraid because of a threatening storm." Calico's account agrees well enough with that of Sandoz, *These Were the Sioux*, p. 20, who had had first-hand experience with members of the *Heyoka* cult: "[A *Heyoka*] was one of those who had dreamed of thunder in his puberty fasting and to avoid this threat of lightning for himself, and for those about him, he must do all things in an unexpected, backward and foolish way, like the walking upside down, with the false face behind. The *heyoka* often dipped his supper out of the boiling kettle with his bare hands . . . and rode his horse facing the tail, his bow or gun drawn against himself."

10 Parkman gave his feast on July 16. See *Journals*, II, 457.

11 Compare the sentence "Having . . . boil" with its *K* form: "Having hammered him on the head with a stone mallet, they threw him into a fire to singe; then chopped him up and put him into two large kettles to boil." These details may represent some of the vividness which Wade finds in the *K* installments of *The Oregon Trail* and which Norton too squeamishly excised, but it may be that Parkman suppressed part of this passage as offensive to the wider audience which he hoped that the first edition of the book would finally reach.

12 As Parkman notes in *Jesuits*, I, 224 n., (Vol. III of *Works*), "The Indian dislike of a beard is well known."

13 Compare Wissler, "Societies and Ceremonial Associations," *Anthropological Papers*, XI, pp. 9–10:

The Indians define the word akicita as "those who see that there is general order in camp when traveling from one place to another; those who attend to the duties of overseeing the buffalo hunts so that no one may chase the buffalo singly; those who see that all can charge the buffalo at once or split up the party so that when one chases buffalo one way, the other band closes in; and those who supervise the chase to get better results. They also see that no one kills another, but in case one does, they either kill him or destroy all his property, kill his horses, destroy his tipi, etc." Thus, though in general literature the term akicita is rendered as "soldiers," its approximate equivalent seems to be police or marshalls.

There were a number of different "soldier" societies among the Oglalas as among other bands of the Tetons.

14 Compare the sentence "I . . . words" with its K–52 form: "Here I was assailed by sharp twinges of conscience, for I fancied I could perceive a fragrance of perfumery in the air, and a vision rose before me of white-kid gloves and silken moustaches with the mild and gentle countenances of numerous fair-haired young men."

Here again Parkman presents another pointed contrast between East and West, in this instance with the effete characteristics of civilization emphasized to the advantage of the robust wilderness.

15 It is doubtful that Reynal translated literally a remark so opposed to his own interests in the Oglala village.

16 Since each lodge might contain as many as 10 or 12 persons and thus required a dozen or more hides for its construction, the Indians naturally preferred the lighter, more easily worked skins of the buffalo cows. See Ruxton, *Life in the Far West*, p. 105.

17 Before the sentence "This . . . debate" K–52 supply the following additional sentence at the beginning of the paragraph: "I could not help thinking that the old man relied a little too much on the aid of allies, one of whom was a coward, another a blockhead, and the third an invalid." Parkman is in a manner congratulating himself, in this canceled passage, on being an invalid.

18 Compare the account of this feast in Parkman's notebooks in *Journals*, II, 457:

Today, gave them a feast—dog, tea, and bread. My host, the Big Crow, issued the invitations—a slender banquet for more than 20 guests, but nothing gratifies an Ind. like giving him a morsel of food, especially that which the whites use. Old Red Water, the fast friend and imitator of the whites, spoke at some length, expressing his gratitude. I answered, Reynal interpreting. Feast distributed by soldiers chosen for such purposes, whose awards, says R. [Reynal? Red Water?] never give dissatisfaction. R., on the instigation of the Eagle Feather, took the occasion of this meeting to enforce the expediency of moving tomorrow after the buffalo; Eagle Feather seconded him, and remarked that since Bull Bear's death, there had been nothing but divisions and separations among them—they were a body without a head. Others gave their opinion, but there was no decision—a completer democracy never subsisted. When all was eaten, Red Water sang his song of thanks, made another speech, and then intimated that the company ought to leave breathing room to the whites—on which they went out. This was a soldier feast.

With the exception of a few minor details, the account of Parkman's feast in *The Oregon Trail* follows the notebook description closely; Parkman's development of this scene in the book, however, indicates at least some of the art which went into its composition, for it seems obvious that the construction of this episode in *The Oregon Trail* shows a strong novelistic sense in the careful presentation of setting as Reynal and Raymond appear among the crowded lodges with the kettles of meat and tea; in Parkman's attempts to imitate the rhetoric of the Indians in his own address to them, their monosyllabic grunts at his fine phrases, and finally the "Noble Savage" rhetoric of old Red Water, with its careful balances and periodicity; and finally in the graceful *exeunt* of the Indians at the end of the feast, when Parkman is again alone in the deserted lodge. It is preeminently the sense of "effect" that one finds in this passage, a strong impression of scene carefully thought out in advance and constructed with a greater economy and wit than Parkman could have found in Cooper, probably his model for the composition of this episode.

19 The village began to move on July 17. See *Journals*, II, 458.

20 After the sentence "Days . . . fancy" *K* supplies the following additional sentence to conclude the paragraph: "I had never seen, and I do not believe that the world can show a spectacle more impressive than the march of a large Indian village over the prairies."

Compare Sandoz, *These Were the Sioux*, p. 74: "The gayest time for the boys and youths was usually when the village moved for fresh grass and water, or with the season. The four old pipe bearers always went ahead, deciding the stops for rest, for water and the sleeps, with scouts far out, the warriors riding in front, at the sides and behind the people, directed by the war society selected to guard this move."

21 "Mountain fever" seems often to have been accompanied by dizziness and even delirium. Compare J. W. Abert, "Report of Lieut. J. W. Abert of His Examination of New Mexico, in the Years 1846–'47," in W. H. Emory, *Notes of a Military Reconnoissance from Fort Leavenworth, in Missouri, to San Diego, in California* . . . (Washington, 1848), p. 419, for another account of the effects of mountain fever on one of the members of Kearny's Army of the West:

On the 22d of July I was taken ill, to such a degree that it was necessary to carry me in a wagon from that time until the 30th of July, on which day we arrived at Bent's Fort. At this time my disease had obtained such an influence over my senses, that days and nights were passed in delirium, and a mental struggle to ascertain whether the impressions my mind received were true or false. Even my sight was affected; and when I gazed on

Bent's fort, the buildings seemed completely metamorphosed; new towers had been erected, the walls heightened. . . .

Many similar accounts testify to the havoc mountain fever made among the troops of Kearny's army, including Parkman's own description, on pp. 338–339 of the present edition, of Tête Rouge's sufferings before his arrival at Bent's Fort.

22 The sentences "You . . . buffalo-robes" and "He . . . mounted" replace the following three sentences in *K*–52:

'You must saddle her,' said I to Raymond as I sat down again on a pile of buffalo-robes:
> 'Et haec etiam fortasse meminisse juvabit,'
I thought, while with a painful effort I raised myself into the saddle. Half an hour after, even the expectation that Virgil's line expressed seemed destined to disappointment.

For the line from Virgil see *Aeneid* 1.203. Parkman is evidently quoting from memory, for the Virgilian reading is "forsan et haec olim meminisse iuvabit," which may be translated as "We shall live to think with pleasure of this as past," or as "This too sometime we shall haply remember with delight."

23 When Parkman first wrote or dictated this passage, he himself may well have been stifling "in the hot air of a sick chamber" and recovering all too slowly, as Wade would have it, from the first dangerous assault of that "Enemy" with whom he struggled at agonizing intervals for the rest of his life.

24 The "curious . . . substitute" was probably a breechclout.

25 Though the evidence in Parkman's notebook entry for July 18 in *Journals*, II, 458–459, is not very clear, it seems possible that this campsite may have been located a few miles west of the present site of the Wheatland Reservoir.

26 The meat was cached apparently on July 18–19. See *Journals*, II, 459.

27 Between the sentences "For . . . us" and "I . . . Shakspeare" K–52 supply the following additional sentence: "I would have welcomed them gladly, for I had no other companions than two brutish white men and five hundred savages." There is a certain sense of bravado and even of smugness in Parkman's contrasting *his* dangerous situation with Shaw's uncomfortable safety at Fort Laramie.

28 After the sentence "Raymond . . . inspired" K–52 supply the following additional sentence to conclude the paragraph: "I looked at him as he rode by my side; his face had actually grown intelligent!"

29 Kenneth McKenzie was born in Scotland in 1797 and came to Canada in 1816, where he remained as an employee of the North West Company until 1821 or 1822; in the latter year he arrived at St. Louis and joined the Columbia Fur Company, of which he soon became president. In 1827 he became a part of the Western Department of Astor's great American Fur Company, though he operated his own division of the combine, the Upper Missouri Outfit, almost entirely on his own terms. Perhaps his most significant accomplishment was the construction of Fort Union on the north bank of the Missouri River a short distance above the mouth of the Yellowstone, where the scope, daring, and energy of his activities gained him the well-deserved titles of "Emperor of the West" and "King of the Missouri" and where he was both respected and feared by the hundreds of trappers and *engagés* under his control there and at Fort Cass, Fort McKenzie, and Fort Piegan. A number of contemporary accounts of his reign at Fort Union stress the almost feudal sovereignty he exercised as well as the pomp and circumstance of his personal household. The still he operated for a time at

Fort Union, however, seriously compromised his reputation, and in 1834 he retired with a fortune from the fur trade. During the 1840's he operated a wholesale grocery and commission company at St. Louis, apparently without notable success. He died in St. Louis in 1861. See Chittenden, *American Fur Trade*, I, 383–385; and Ray H. Mattison, "Kenneth McKenzie," in LeRoy R. Hafen, ed. *The Mountain Men and the Fur Trade of the Far West*, II (Glendale, Calif., 1965), 217–224.

30 Raymond's attitude toward civilization is very like that expressed by Killbuck, Ruxton's fictional trapper in *Life in the Far West*, p. 18: "No; darn the settlements, I say. It won't shine, and whar's the dollars?"

31 There is no evidence to suggest that either Santa Fe or Taos was ever an episcopal see before the period of American occupation in 1846. The bishopric embracing the scattered settlements in New Mexico and Arizona was located at Durango in Old Mexico, though Raymond might have been thinking of the pastoral visit of Bishop Zubiria to Santa Fe in 1845. See Ralph Emerson Twitchell, *The Leading Facts of New Mexico History* (Cedar Rapids, 1912), II, 187–188.

32 The possible identification of the priest at Fort Laramie "two years ago" depends upon whether Parkman means two years before Reynal told him about the priest or two years before the date (late 1847?) of the composition of this chapter, which appeared in *K* in February, 1848. In August, 1844, Andrew Sublette arrived at Fort Laramie from Westport with a "company of Catholicks" including a Jesuit priest and 20 other young men; the priest apparently went on to the Catholic missions in the Northwest. Again, in August, 1845, Father Soderena of Kalispell Mission, Montana, arrived at Fort Laramie with six other men returning to Missouri; and Father Ravalli reached the Flathead Mission at St. Mary's in the same year. See

Barry, "Kansas before 1854," *KHQ*, xxx (Spring, 1964), 72, and xxx (Summer, 1964), 236; and P. J. De Smet, S. J., *Oregon Missions and Travels over the Rocky Mountains in 1845–1846*, in R. G. Thwaites, ed. *Early Western Travels* (Cleveland, 1906), xxix, 321 n. It is even possible that Reynal might have been referring to two Jesuits, Father DeVos and Father Hoecken, who visited Fort Laramie in 1843 in company with Sir William Drummond Stewart's famous pleasure excursion to the Wind River Mountains. See Field, *Prairie and Mountain Sketches*, pp. xlv, xlix.

33 The little boy was after the tongue of the buffalo—an especial delicacy.

34 After the sentence "It . . . banquets" K–52 supply the following additional sentence to conclude the paragraph: "The Indians would look with abhorrence upon anyone who should partake indiscriminately of the newly-killed carcass." This incident seems to be based on part of Parkman's notebook entry for July 18 in *Journals*, ii, 459: "In the morning His Horses killed a bull, which was at once surrounded and butchered, and much of it eaten raw."

35 The "double movement" described in this passage must have occurred on July 18, for it is specifically mentioned in Parkman's notebooks on that date. See *Journals*, ii, 458–459.

36 Parkman's "little sandy stream" may be Rock Creek at a point northwest of the forks and some four or five miles northwest of the present site of Rock River, Wyoming. This identification is, however, only conjectural since Parkman's notebooks give the vaguest possible details of his and the village's whereabouts for the next several days.

37 Parkman had learned about the crickets from old Red Water on July 16. Compare *Journals*, ii, 457: "Old Red Water says that the large crickets so common about here, when taken in the hand, always twist their long horns,

when asked, in the direction of the buffalo. This was told them by their great grandfather, and the name by which they call crickets means: 'Those that show where the buffalo are.' " I am indebted to Professor Charles F. Koval of the University of Wisconsin Department of Entomology for an identification of these "enormous black-and-green" insects as Mormon crickets.

38 Parkman might have read in his copy of Frémont's *Report*, p. 154, how the *bourgeois* Joseph R. Walker had once made a meal of insect larvae, and many other contemporary accounts mention trappers reduced to devouring grasshopper *paté* or soup, as Joe Meek had to during Milton Sublette's Humboldt River expedition of 1832. See Victor, *River of the West*, p. 120; and Ross, *Fur Hunters of the Far West*, p. 269, for a description of grasshopper soup as "a common repast" among the Snakes. Compare also Joseph Williams' account of the "Diggers" in *Narrative of a Tour from the State of Indiana to the Oregon Territory in the Years 1841–42*, ed. James C. Bell, Jr. (New York, 1921), pp. 80–81: "These creatures have been known, when pressed with hunger, to kill their children and eat them! and to gather up crickets and ants; and dry them in the sun, and pound them into dust, and make bread of it to eat!" See also p. 155 of the present edition and note 17 for that page.

39 This event apparently occurred on the evening of July 18. See *Journals*, II, 458–459.

Chapter XV

1 Compare part of Parkman's notebook entry for July 17 in *Journals*, II, 458: "Moved camp, though very slowly and in disorder. Old Red Water in a loud voice upbraided the village for their want of promptitude and having *two hearts*."

2 Most Plains Indians made pemmican by drying strips of buffalo meat in the sun, pulverizing it, and mixing it with tallow and a flavoring like crushed wild cherries. It was then packed in rawhide bags or in buffalo intestines, like sausage. Pemmican was the best of all concentrated foods, a mainstay of Indians and trappers alike. See Hodge, ed. *Handbook of American Indians*, II, 223–224.

3 The Whirlwind and a part of the village had remained encamped near Fort Laramie, probably on Chugwater Creek.

4 The "wide, shallow stream" may possibly be Rock Creek southwest of the forks and five or six miles southwest of modern Rock River, Wyoming.

5 This defection from the organized procedure of the "surround" was under normal circumstances a grave offense, though, as Parkman notes on p. 231, there were few "soldiers" in camp to enforce the usual discipline of the hunt.

6 The "surround" occurred on the morning of July 20. See *Journals*, II, 459–460.

7 The sentence "Others . . . wolves" does not appear in K–83 and seems to have been added in 92 to conform to the illustration at the beginning of the chapter on p. 229.

8 Compare Parkman's notebook description of this scene in *Journals*, II, 460: "Came back to where Big Crow was butchering, and his son eating raw meat, in which I joined and found the liver excellent."

9 Talbot, *Journals of Theodore Talbot*, p. 31, provides a more detailed description of the force of the Indian bow: "Soon the swift steed brings him alongside, the arrow is drawn back to its very head, a moment more and it is buried in the ground on the opposite side of the huge buffalo. . . ."

10 This episode in *The Oregon Trail* has been very carefully developed according to narrative techniques quite common in nineteenth-century adventure fiction, particularly

the composition of scenic action in terms of a period of premonitory stasis, the greater and more intense involvement of the narrative *persona* in the "developing action" of the scene, and a concluding return to stasis. Compare Chapter xlviii, "The First Lowering," in Melville's *Moby-Dick*. I am unaware of a more dramatic, more carefully structured account of an Indian buffalo chase in all the literature of western travel and adventure than Parkman's in this chapter of *The Oregon Trail*.

11 Compare Parkman's particularly vivid notebook description of this scene in *Journals*, ii, 460: "The village was soon filled with meat. Groups were gorging themselves all around the lodges—eating was the engrossing occupation of the time, and the result was that all night vomitings and retchings could be heard among the children of the lodges around."

12 The account of the "surround" in *Journals*, ii, 460, gives Red Water's age as only "over sixty," but the old chief's long prominence in Oglala affairs may justify Parkman's estimate of "full eighty winters" as his correct age in 1846.

13 Variant forms of Red Water's story were common among western Indians, as Father De Smet noted in *Letters and Sketches*, in Thwaites, ed. *Early Western Travels*, xxvii, 260–261: "Some of the Indian tribes believe that the beavers are a degraded race of human beings, whose vices and crimes have induced the Great Spirit to punish them by changing them into their present form; and they think, after the lapse of a number of years, their punishment will cease, and they will be restored to their original shape." It seems possible that Red Water was playing on Parkman's ignorance and credulity by substituting white persons for the traditional wicked Indians in this campfire legend.

14 Compare Red Water's reluctance to "tell the tales in summer" with Parkman's subsequent account of Iroquois

and Algonquin mythologies in *Jesuits*, I, 85 (Vol. III of *Works*): "In respect to this wigwam lore, there is a curious superstition of very wide prevalence. The tales must not be told in summer; since at that season, when all Nature is full of life, the spirits are awake, and, hearing what is said of them, may take offence; whereas in winter they are fast sealed up in snow and ice, and no longer capable of listening." Parkman's footnote to this passage makes a specific reference to Red Water and to his refusal to tell his stories: "The prevalence of this fancy among the Algonquins in the remote parts of Canada is well established. The writer found it also among the extreme western bands of the Dahcotah. He tried, in the month of July, to persuade an old chief, a noted story-teller, to tell him some of the tales; but, though abundantly loquacious in respect to his own adventures, and even his dreams, the Indian obstinately refused, saying that winter was the time for the tales, and that it was bad to tell them in summer."

Dorsey, "A Study of Siouan Cults," *Eleventh Annual Report*, p. 369, notes, however, that "Though it has been said that the Indians feared to tell myths except on winter nights (and some Indians have told this to the author), the author has had no trouble in obtaining myths during the day at various seasons of the year." But Dorsey's informants were reservation Indians, for whom the legends may have lost much of their mystery and power.

15 The "five days" mentioned in this passage seem to have been July 20–24. See *Journals*, II, 460–462.

16 Between the sentences "Raymond . . . success" and "As . . . breakfast" K–52 supply the following sentence: "To kill a bull with a rifle-ball is a difficult art, in the secret of which I was as yet very imperfectly initiated."

17 Parkman was sitting down to the prime prairie delicacy: almost every western traveler of the period speaks of hump ribs as the finest and richest meat he had ever tasted.

18 Garrard, *Wah-To-Yah and the Taos Trail*, p. 77, makes a similar judgment on the benefits of a diet based almost entirely on the buffalo: "One remarkable peculiarity is there about buffalo meat—one can eat even beyond plenitude, without experiencing any ill effects." Such statements appear frequently in western literature, but, given Parkman's dysentery, cramps, and dizziness, a regimen consisting almost entirely of fat meat could not have been very beneficial.

19 The Rabbit remains unidentified. For almost all Indians, dreams, whether or not preceded or even induced by ritual and ceremony, were a revelation from the supernatural powers and thus more or less sacred in origin and character. See Hodge, ed. *Handbook of American Indians*, I, 400–401.

20 The trappers arrived on July 22. See *Journals*, II, 461.

21 Compare the sentence "It . . . household" with its K form: "It was well carpeted with soft buffalo-robes, and here we all remained, sheltered from the sun, but surrounded by the various domestic utensils of Madame Margot's household, her copper kettles and her horn spoons, her wooden dishes and bales of meat, together with the usual articles of her aboriginal wardrobe, well packed in cases of painted hide." There is no obvious reason why this interesting description of the interior of a lodge should have been excised.

22 For Sancho Panza's misadventures at the inn, see *Don Quixote*, Bk. III, Chap. iii.

23 Ferris, *Life in the Rocky Mountains*, p. 292, confirms Parkman's approving notice of Indian sociability: "In their lodges and domestic circles, they are loquacious as the whites, with the difference of good-breeding, that the person speaking is never interrupted; and in turn each speaks, and is listened to with profound attention."

24 Cited several times previously in these notes, Frémont's

Report was published in 1845 as the *Report of the Exploring Expedition to the Rocky Mountains in the Year 1842, and to Oregon and North California in the Years 1843–'44,* with the imprimatur of the Senate and in part through the influence of Senator Thomas Hart Benton, Frémont's father-in-law. Since Frémont's *Report* contained Charles Preuss's very large map of most of the valley of the Platte and of parts of the central mountain and Pacific Coast regions as well as smaller route maps, it was much in use as an emigrant's guide for the Oregon and California trails.

25 Parkman's description of clan relationships through totem animals is not very complete. Briefly, the totem animal distinguished individuals supposedly related by blood, often in maternal lines of descent; no Indian was allowed to marry within his own clan; and the totem animal itself was generally recognized as the guardian spirit of all members of the same clan. See Hodge, ed. *Handbook of American Indians,* ii, 787–795. Parkman seems in this passage to have been applying to the Oglalas his early-acquired and somewhat imprecise understanding of the totem systems of Iroquoian and Algonquin tribes.

26 Compare Garrard's description of the "game of hand," probably the most common form of Indian gambling, in *Wah-To-Yah and the Taos Trail,* p. 113:

Their game, however, is simple, though not the less injurious in its effects. It is played by the young men and women; who, sitting in a circle, and with a rocking to-and-fro motion of the body, accompanied by a low, quick chant, increased in vigor as the game progresses, hold a bit of wood, cherrystone, or any thing small in the hand; and, after a series of dexterous shiftings, so as to deceive, hold them out, while the singing stops, for the players to bet in which hand is the stone. So soon as they say, the object is shown; the fortunate ones sweep the stakes; the stone is given to the next in order of rotation, the chant again strikes up—other trinkets are put up, and the betting recommences. They laugh and get much excited over their primitive game; and, often, an unlucky maiden rises from her amusement without the numerous bracelets, rings, and beads, with which she came gayly decked to the meeting lodge.

27 Compare Irving's very similar account in *Adventures of Captain Bonneville*, p. 332: "These gambling games were kept up throughout the night; every fire glared upon a group that looked like a crew of maniacs at their frantic orgies. . . ."

28 Compare Garrard's very similar comment in *Wah-To-Yah and the Taos Trail*, pp. 83–84: "Some must have the pipe presented them stem downward; others with the bowl resting on the ground; and others, again, with the stem upward. All have their peculiar *medicine* or religion, and they are as punctilious, in this matter, as ever was a Hidalgo in politeness." Parkman himself would meet the "old man" at Fort Laramie on August 4. Compare *Journals*, II, 467: "There is an old Ind. at the fort, badly wounded, who is always singing to cure himself. His 'medicine,' which he always resorts to when in pain, is to hand some bystander a cup of water and let him drink it."

29 Much evidence exists to support Parkman's account of the leniency of child-rearing practices among the Dakotas; boys especially were rarely if ever punished, since blows and enforced authority were thought to weaken their spirits.

30 This episode is not recorded in Parkman's notebooks, and it is thus difficult to understand what the "good reasons" for this "summary divorce" were, especially since a number of authorities, including Parkman himself, attest that the usual punishment for adultery among the Dakotas was the mutilation of the offending woman. See *Jesuits*, I, 21 n. (Vol. III of *Works*), though other authorities (e.g., Hassrick) mention only banishment.

31 Parkman's account of part of the ceremonies of the Sun Dance may owe something to Prince Maximilian's description of these rites among the Mandans in *Travels in North America* in Thwaites, ed. *Early Western Travels*, xxiii, 332: "The tortures of the penitents now begin. In many of them strips of skin and flesh are cut from the breast, or the arms, and on the back, but in such a manner that they remain fast at both ends. A strap is then passed under them, and the sufferers are thrown over the declivity of the bank, where they remain suspended in the air; others have a strap drawn through the wound, to which the head of a buffalo is fastened, and they are obliged to drag this heavy weight about; others have themselves suspended by the muscles of the back. . . ." Most accounts of the Sun Dance among the Dakotas stress its propitiatory character for the Indians, who seem to have performed it primarily as a kind of tribal as well as personal catharsis, "the overcoming of certain cosmic elements" and the fulfillments of vows made in prayers. The buffalo-skull ordeal was only part of six or eight days of ritual fasting, dancing, and singing. See Hodge, ed. *Handbook of American Indians*, ii, 649–652; Dorsey, "A Study of Siouan Cults," *Eleventh Annual Report*, pp. 450–467; and Hassrick, *The Sioux*, pp. 230–248.

Most Plains Indians had ceremonies analogous to the Dakota Sun Dance although they appear in the literature under different names and with occasionally different ritual functions and purposes.

32 As in this passage, so in the histories Parkman often prefaces a description of Indian brutalities with a disclaimer of any intent to shock or titillate his readers by the barbarous scenes to follow. Compare *Jesuits*, ii, 65–68 (Vol. iv of *Works*).

33 Parkman heard the Big Crow's story of the death of a "Utah" on July 20. See *Journals*, ii, 460.

34 I have been unable to verify the details of this Oglala raid against the Gros Ventres.

35 The White Shield was wearing the familiar "war bonnet," a part of his ceremonial regalia.

36 Parkman's "small panther" seems almost a contradiction in terms, since "panther" in the West always meant the mountain lion (*Felis concolor*), which is neither small (adults may be more than six feet long) nor spotted. The White Shield's quiver may, however, have been made from the skin of a young mountain lion: kittens of this species are spotted between the ages of three and six months. Another possibility is the bobcat (*Lynx rufus*), which *is* small and spotted, though its short tail and small feet do not quite fit Parkman's description of the pelt here.

37 The account of the collapse of the White Shield's war party draws heavily on part of Parkman's notebook entry for July 23 in *Journals*, II, 462:

> The White Shield came and sat before Reynal's lodge. He had a bad sore throat, which he bore with anything but stoicism. He seemed depressed to the last degree.
>
> R. says that they bear *wounds* with the greatest fortitude, but yield at once to a stroke of sickness. The White Shield said he meant to have gone to war tomorrow—that his brother was killed last summer, and he must avenge him or die—that ten young men would follow him. His preparations are complete; and his sickness makes him very despondent. I hear the medicine drum at this moment—he is probably under medical treatment.

38 The White Shield's war parade occurred on the evening of July 24. See *Journals*, II, 462.

39 Parkman seems to have heard some form of the widespread Dakota belief that ghosts often appeared to those about to die. See Dorsey, "A Study of Siouan Cults," *Eleventh Annual Report*, pp. 485–486.

CHAPTER XVI

1 Compare the sentence "These Arapahoes . . . territory" with its K–52 form: "These Arapahoes, of whom Shaw and I afterwards fell in with a large village, are ferocious barbarians, of a most brutal and wolfish aspect; and of late they had declared themselves enemies to the whites, and threatened death to the first who should venture within their territory."

2 Bent's Fort was located near the present site of La Junta, Colorado, some 300 miles south-southwest of Fort Laramie. See p. 334 of the present edition and note 14 for that page.

3 Parkman's account of this part of Kearny's expedition is in error, for Kearny, who arrived at Fort Laramie on June 16, 1845, left Company A of the First Dragoons encamped near the fort and himself led four other companies to South Pass (Parkman's "Sweetwater") at the end of June. By July 13 Kearny had returned to Fort Laramie. Marching south along the foot of the mountains, his command passed Bent's Fort on July 29 and arrived at Fort Leavenworth on August 24, after 99 days and 2,200 miles of travel. See Cooke, *Scenes and Adventures*, pp. 335–432; and Barry, "Kansas before 1854," *KHQ*, xxx (Summer, 1964), 220–222. Edwin L. Sabin, *Kit Carson Days* (Chicago, 1913), p. 75, notes that Sweetwater River owes its name either to a sugar-laden mule which foundered in the stream or to some drunken trappers who poured a sack of sugar into the river and so christened it, but Morgan and Harris regard both explanations of the name as improbable and remark that the river was early known as *Eau Douce*—"Sweet [i.e., Pure] Water"—as well as *Eau Sucrée*—"Sugared Water." See *Rocky Mountain Journals of W. M. Anderson*, p. 119 n.

4 From Cooke's and other contemporary accounts it seems

clear that the rockets and cannon fire at Fort Laramie on June 16, 1845, were meant to overawe the 1,200 Sioux under Bull Tail and other chiefs encamped near the fort. See *Scenes and Adventures*, pp. 337–338; and Aurora Hunt, *Major General James Henry Carleton, 1814–1873, Western Frontier Dragoon* (Glendale, Calif., 1958), pp. 92–94.

5 For the murders of Buck, or Burk, and Leamai, see p. 141 of the present edition and note 46 for that page.

6 Parkman's "desert of nine hundred miles" must represent his rough estimate of the distance between Fort Leavenworth and the "Bear River" (the Yampa River in northwestern Colorado) where Buck, or Burk, and Leamai were killed "by an Arapahoe Indian." See Morgan, ed. *Overland in 1846*, II, 576, 754.

7 I have been unable to confirm the details of Parkman's account of the visit of the Arapahoes to Fort Laramie.

8 Frémont, *Report*, p. 47, made a very similar comment in 1842: "If it is in contemplation to keep open the communication with Oregon territory, a show of military force in this country is absolutely necessary; and a combination of advantages renders the neighborhood of Fort Laramie the most suitable place . . . for the establishment of a military post." A great many other western travelers of the period made similar observations.

9 Garrard, *Wah-To-Yah and the Taos Trail*, p. 114, gives a very similar account of the trappers he had met: "Yet these aliens from society, these strangers to the refinements of civilized life, who will tear off a bloody scalp with even grim smiles of satisfaction, are fine fellows, full of fun, and often kind and obliging."

10 The government had been trying for years—often in vain —to keep alcohol out of the fur trade.

11 Compare Irving's quite similar account of trapper life in *Adventures of Captain Bonneville*, pp. 11–12:

There is, perhaps, no class of men on the face of the earth, says Captain Bonneville, who lead a life of more continued exertion, peril, and excitement, and who are more enamored of their occupations, than the free trappers of the West. No toil, no danger, no privation can turn the trapper from his pursuit. His passionate excitement at times resembles a mania. In vain may the most vigilant and cruel savages beset his path; in vain may rocks and precipices and wintry torrents oppose his progress; let but a single track of a beaver meet his eye, and he forgets all dangers and defies all difficulties. At times, he may be seen with his traps on his shoulder, buffeting his way across rapid streams, amidst floating blocks of ice; at other times, he is to be found with his traps swung on his back clambering the most rugged mountains, scaling or descending the most frightful precipices, searching, by routes inaccessible to the horse, and never before trodden by white men, for springs and lakes unknown to his comrades, and where he may meet with his favorite game. Such is the mountaineer, the hardy trapper of the West; and such, as we have slightly sketched it, is the wild, Robin Hood kind of life, with all its strange and motley populace, now existing in full vigor among the Rocky Mountains.

12 Since this trapper is nowhere specifically named or described in Parkman's Oregon Trail notebooks, a positive identification of him is probably impossible.

13 After the sentence "I . . . calling" K–52 supply the following additional sentence to conclude the paragraph:

To some of the children [K: the spoiled children] of cities it may seem strange, that men with no object in view should continue to follow a life of such hardship and desperate adventure, yet there is a mysterious, resistless charm in the basilisk eye of danger, [K: fascinating that it may destroy,] and few men perhaps remain long in that wild region without learning to love peril for its own sake, and to laugh carelessly in the face of death.

This significantly excised passage is very reminiscent of Ferris' description of trapper life in *Life in the Rocky Mountains*, p. 41:

Strange, that people can find so strong and fascinating a charm in this rude nomadic, and hazardous mode of life, as to estrange themselves from home, country, friends, and all the comforts, elegances, and privileges of civilization; but so it is, the toil, the danger, the loneliness, the deprivation of this condition of living, fraught with all its disadvantages, and replete with peril, is, they think, more than compensated by the lawless freedom, and the stirring excitement, incident to their situation and pursuits. The very danger has its attraction, and the courage and cunning, and skill, and watchfulness made necessary by the difficulties they have to overcome, the privations they are forced to contend with, and the perils against which they must guard, become at once their pride and boast. A strange, wild, terrible, romantic, hard, and exciting life they lead, with alternate plenty and starvation, activity and repose, safety and alarm, and all the other adjuncts that belong to so vagrant a condition, in a harsh, barren, untamed, and fearful region of desert, plain, and mountain. Yet so attached to it do they become, that few ever leave it, and they deem themselves, nay are, with all these bars against them, far happier than the in-dwellers of towns and cities, with all the gay and giddy whirl of fashion's mad delusions in their train.

This description of mountain life appeared in the *Western Literary Messenger* as early as March 1, 1843, where Parkman could certainly have seen it.

14 Compare Osborne Russell's description of a trapper's outfit in note 2 for p. 148 of the present edition.

15 Rouleau and Saraphin left the Oglala camp on the morning of July 24. See *Journals*, ii, 462.

16 If Reynal expected $50 for seven beaver plews, he was bound to be disappointed, for, as Ruxton, *Adventures in the Rocky Mountains*, reprinted in Hafen, ed. *Ruxton of*

the Rockies, p. 225, noted in 1847: "Beaver has so depreciated in value within the last few years that trapping has been almost abandoned—the price paid for the skin of this valuable animal having fallen from six and eight dollars per pound to one dollar, which hardly pays the expenses of traps, animals, and equipment for the hunt. . . ."

17 As Parkman notes, the lodgepole pine (*Pinus contorta*), with its tall, straight bole, was only to be found in the mountains, and usually at elevations above 7,000 feet. According to Donald Culross Peattie, *A Natural History of Western Trees* (Boston, 1953), p. 106, it was the custom among western Indians to cut the trunks of the lodgepole pines into sections 10 or 15 feet long, peel off the bark, and stack the poles in some protected spot to dry. Lodgepoles were usually cut in the spring and allowed to season until the fall; after some five or six months of "curing," they weighed only six or eight pounds but almost never fractured or split. The methods of lodgepole preparation described on p. 274 of the present edition must have been unusually hasty.

18 For the source of this quotation compare Oliver Goldsmith's *The Vicar of Wakefield*, Chap. 32: "I can't say whether we have more wit amongst us now than usual; but I am certain we had more laughing, which answered the end as well." Dodge, *Our Wild Indians*, p. 59, confirms Parkman's description of Indian gaiety: "In his own camp, away from strangers, the Indian is a noisy, jolly, rollicking, mischief-loving braggadocio. . . ."

19 This outbreak seems to have occurred on July 25, though Parkman described it in his notebook under date of July 26 in *Journals*, II, 462–463:

Scarcely arrived—old men and warriors seated smoking in the middle—squaws unpacking horses and dogs—when a quarrel arose. There are in the village three of the broken and dispersed band of the Arrow Breakers—they undertook to sieze upon a horse belonging to a brave killed not long since. A brother of the deceased took the horse away from them, on which they shot him. There was a rush from all parts of the village—guns and arrows were siezed and discharged, some taking one side, some another. Some squaws set up a howling for the slaughtered horse—other[s] ran to a place of safety with their children—and other[s] siezed on the weapons. A fight was threatened, but it ended in smoke. . . .

20 Sometime during August 7–8, while he was encamped with Bisonnette on Horse Creek, Parkman heard from the younger Bull Bear an account of the origins of the quarrel substantially identical to that given in this passage. See *Journals*, II, 471.

21 I have been unable to identify Parkman's "Arrow-Breakers" in any of the standard accounts of Oglala "soldier" societies.

22 Tall Bear remains unidentified.

Chapter XVII

1 Parkman and the Indians encamped on the western slope of the Laramie Range, apparently not far from Morton Pass, on the afternoon of July 27. See *Journals*, II, 463.

2 Compare the sentence "It . . . beyond" with its K form: "As they rode scattering at full gallop over the shingly rocks and into the dark opening of the defile beyond, I thought I had never read or dreamed of a wilder or more picturesque cavalcade."

A somewhat revised version of the sentence above appears in 49–52: "As they rode at full gallop over the shingly rocks and into the dark opening of the defile beyond, I thought I had never read or dreamed of a more strange or picturesque cavalcade."

3 Possibly the "winding brook" is Sybille Creek, south of the divide.

4 Parkman's "black-tailed deer" are more commonly known as mule deer (*Odocoileus hemionus*).

5 After the sentence "Objects . . . brook" K–52 supply the following four additional sentences to conclude the paragraph:

The objects were the same, yet they were thrown into a wilder and more startling scene, for black crags and the savage trees assumed a grim and threatening aspect, and close across the valley the opposing mountain confronted me, rising from the gulf for thousands of feet, with its bare pinnacles and its ragged covering of pines. Yet the scene was not without its milder features. As I ascended, I found frequent little grassy terraces, and there was one of these close at hand, across which the brook was stealing, beneath the shade of scattered trees that seemed artificially planted. Here I made a welcome discovery, no other than a bed of strawberries, with their white flowers and their red fruit, close nestled among the grass by the side of the brook, and I sat down by them, hailing them as old acquaintances; for among those lonely and perilous mountains, they awakened delicious associations of the gardens and peaceful homes of far-distant New-England.

6 Russell, *Journal of a Trapper*, p. 51, presents a vivid account of the trapper's winter lodge:

We all had snug lodges made of dressed Buffaloe skins in the center of which we built a fire and generally comprised about six men to the lodge[.] The long winter evenings were passed away by collecting in some of the most spacious lodges and entering into debates arguments or spinning long yarns until midnight in perfect good humour and I for one will cheerfully confess that I have derived no little benefit from the frequent arguments and debates held in what we termed the Rocky Mountain College and I doubt not but some of my comrades who considered themselves Classical Scholars have had some little added to their wisdom in these assemblies however rude they might appear[.]

<h3 style="text-align:center">Chapter XVIII</h3>

1 Between the sentences "The morning . . . months" and "We . . . mountain" K–52 supply the following additional sentence: "Though a strong frame and well-compacted sinews had borne me through hitherto, it was long since I had been in a condition to feel the exhilaration of the fresh mountain-wind and the gay sunshine that brightened the crags and trees." Reynal and Parkman went hunting on July 28. See *Journals*, ii, 464.

2 Between the sentences "Before . . . mountains" and "Reynal . . . last" K supplies the following additional sentence: "My heart thrilled as I recollected that no civilized eye but mine had ever looked upon that savage waste."

This sentence has been somewhat curtailed in 49–52: "No civilized eye but mine had ever looked upon that virgin waste."

3 Sage, *Scenes in the Rocky Mountains*, i, 344, had also heard of the possibility of gold in the Laramie Range and along Chugwater Creek.

4 The main screw held the gunlock to the stock of the rifle.

5 That is, the Hail-Storm had never "counted coup" on a dead body, an act regarded by most Plains tribes as showing singular bravery and even as conferring warrior's status on a young brave, since he had to run on foot into the middle of a fight and touch the corpse or, even more daringly, a living enemy with his "coup stick" or his open hand. Coups might also be counted for killing or scalping a foe or sometimes even for stealing horses or attacking a grizzly bear. See Hodge, ed. *Handbook of American Indi-*

ans, I, 354; and compare Sandoz, *These Were the Sioux*, p. 45: "The first-class coup—striking an enemy with the hand, the bow, or the coup stick without harming him— was the highest war achievement, more important than any scalp."

6 Compare the sentence "If . . . tribes" with its K form: "If there be any thing that deserves to be called romantic in the Indian character, it is to be sought for in the friend- ships such as this, which are quite common among many of the prairie tribes, and perhaps the absence, or at least the infrequency, of any deep sentiment on the part of the men toward the fair partners of their toil may in some measure account for these permanent and devoted attach- ments."

7 Parkman's notebooks show that in this passage he has combined the events of two days. On July 28 he rode out hunting with Reynal, and on the evening of July 29 the Hail-Storm came in with his elk, the same day that Park- man lounged away the afternoon. See *Journals*, II, 464.

8 Compare part of Parkman's notebook entry for July 29 in *Journals*, II, 464: "Dozed away the afternoon in Reynal's lodge, thinking of things past and meditating on things to come. Here one feels overcome with an irresistable laziness —he cannot even muse consecutively."

9 Compare Parkman's description of this scene in *Journals*, II, 465: "As the pipe passed the circle around the fire in the evening, there was plenty of that obscene conversation that seems to make up the sum of Ind. wit, and which very much amuses the squaws. The Inds. are a very licentious set."

10 This passage seems surely overstated, for on the evidence of Parkman's own notebooks and *The Oregon Trail* itself he had been a very sick man during his two weeks in the Oglala village and yet had suffered no harm from the Indians.

11 Parkman's romantic ramble among the mountains seems to have occurred on the morning of July 29. Compare *Journals*, II, 464: "Climbed a high rocky Mt. a few miles from camp. On the way, in woody ravines where little streams came down, cold as ice, among the stones and moss, and everywhere about the rocks were scattered the Ind. boys, looking after berries or small game. They destroy all that comes to hand—young rabbits, ducks, prairie cocks—every thing; and this is their education. A savage prospect from the summit—lodges in the green valley like a circle of white specks."

The chronology of this chapter of *The Oregon Trail* is almost completely at variance with the dates for specific events in Parkman's notebooks.

12 This sudden and even dramatic discovery of old Red Water is not recorded in Parkman's notebooks.

13 This passage is clearly intended to complement the account of Le Borgne's initiatory vision of pp. 156–157 of the present edition. A very similar account of an Indian's "guardian spirit" will be found in *Jesuits*, I, 61 (Vol. III of *Works*):

To the Indian, the material world is sentient and intelligent. Birds, beasts, and reptiles have ears for human prayers, and are endowed with an influence on human destiny. A mysterious and inexplicable power resides in inanimate things. They, too, can listen to the voice of man, and influence his life for evil or for good. Lakes, rivers, and waterfalls are sometimes the dwelling-place of spirits, but more frequently they are themselves living beings, to be propitiated by prayers and offerings. The lake has a soul; so has the river, and the cataract. Each can hear the words of men, and each can be pleased or offended. In the silence of a forest, the gloom of a deep ravine, resides a living mystery, indefinite, but redoubtable. Through all the works of Nature or of man, nothing exists, however seemingly trivial, that may not be endowed with a secret power for blessing or for bane.

14 Between the sentences "An . . . point" and "Looking . . . ocean" *K* supplies the following additional three sentences:

A wilderness of mountains lay around me, their ridges bristling with rocky pinnacles, avalanches of rock thrown around their bases, and their sides thinly clothed with a tattered and squalid covering of stunted woods. There were black chasms, deep clefts and ravines, where the precipices had split asunder, and here and there, in the midst of the desolation, small green glens and valleys, deeply embosomed among the savage heights. In the largest of these I could discern, like small spots upon the meadow, the encampment of the wild and impetuous people with whom I was associated.

Parkman juxtaposes the Indian's veneration for Nature's spiritual power with the savagery of the landscape itself (particularly in this canceled passage) to undermine, however subtly, the image of the Noble Savage paying a devout if untutored reverence to a ·beneficent Nature. Both landscape *and* Indian are savage, and so by implication is the religion inspired by the one and reverenced by the other.

CHAPTER XIX

1 The Indians broke camp on July 30. See *Journals*, ii, 465. What "passage of the mountains" lay "twelve or fourteen miles southward" is not easy to determine. The distance is about right for a movement from Sybille Creek to South Sybille Creek or from Bluegrass Creek or one of its branches to Sybille Creek itself. Parkman's notebooks are

of no help in discovering his movements for the next several days.

2 Compare part of Parkman's notebook entry for July 30 in *Journals*, II, 465: "On the way passed the site of a camp, whence last year the war-party that was defeated set out. The relatives of the slain immediately raised the mourning song, and the half-breed Shienne, one of whose relations was killed, gave away on the spot two horses. He will receive their value back again. After camping, nothing was heard but shouts of praise and thanks."

3 In this passage and in the rest of the chapter *The Oregon Trail* is often at variance with Parkman's notebooks, which provide a different chronology of events. The great bighorn hunt occurred on July 30; on July 31—"the next morning"—Parkman moved into the mountains with the Indians and killed an antelope; on August 1 the village was still crossing the Laramie Range, perhaps by way of Morton Pass; and on August 2 Parkman and Raymond left the village and rode on ahead toward Fort Laramie. See *Journals*, II, 465–467. *The Oregon Trail* rearranges the sequence of these events and adds an extra day to the time it took Parkman and the Indians to cross the mountains.

4 After the sentence "I . . . horns" K–52 supply the following additional paragraph: "There is something peculiarly interesting in the character and habits of the mountain sheep, whose chosen retreats are above the region of vegetation and of storms, and who leap among the giddy precipices of their aerial home as actively as [K: as actively and carelessly as] the antelope skims over the prairies below."

Parkman's description of the size of a mature bighorn ram's horns is quite correct; a good-sized pair of horns might measure 36 inches around the outside curve from base to tip and as much as 15 inches around at the base.

5 Compare Hodge, ed. *Handbook of American Indians,* II, 17, for the real reasons behind this "superstitious notion":

> The possession of a name was everywhere jealously guarded, and it was considered discourteous or even insulting to address one directly by it. This reticence, on the part of some Indians, at least, appears to have been due to the fact that every man, and every thing as well, was supposed to have a real name which so perfectly expressed his inmost nature as to be practically identical with him. This name might long remain unknown to all, even to its owner, but at some critical period of life it was confidentially revealed to him. It was largely on account of this sacred character that an Indian commonly refused to give his proper designation, or, when pressed for an answer, asked someone else to speak it.

6 Compare the sentence "Nay . . . beast" with its K–52 form: "Nay, so alien to himself do they appear, that having breathed for a few months or a few weeks the air [K: the magic air] of this region, he begins to look upon them as a troublesome and dangerous species of wild beast, and if expedient, he could shoot them with as little compunction as they themselves would experience after performing the same office upon him."

This statement, of course, represents the final solution to the problem which Pearce, *Savages of America,* p. 49, sees as the crux of "savagism": "The Indian was the remnant of a savage past away from which civilized men had struggled to grow. To study him was to study the past. To civilize him was to triumph over the past. To kill him was to kill the past. History would thus be the key to the moral worth of cultures. . . ." Compare also Jim Clyman's statement of the problem in *James Clyman, Frontiersman,* p. 14: "But I will not tire you with details of the savage habits of Indians to their enimies but I will merely state that it is easy to make a savage of a civilised man but impossible to make a civilised man of a savage in one Generation[.]"

7 Parkman displays his own knowledge of the "Dakota language" in *La Salle*, pp. 248–249 n. (Vol. v of *Works*).

8 After the sentence "Savage . . . throng" K supplies the following additional paragraph: "That day my old ill-luck had again assailed me. A renewed attack of my disorder suddenly prostrated all my newly-gained strength. As I rode on, in any posture but an erect one, the squaws mistook my weakness and languor for drowsiness, and laughed at me for falling asleep on horseback. I repaid their raillery in kind, and they never suspected the truth."

9 Writing to Remington on February 25, 1892, Parkman described the scene of the "Indians coming down the mountain gorge" in this paragraph as "the most striking sight I ever saw anywhere." See *Letters*, II, 256.

10 The sentences "I . . . mountains" and "On . . . distance" replace the following two sentences and additional paragraph in K–52:

Scenery like this, it might seem, could have no very cheering effect on the mind of a sick man, (for today my disease had again assailed me,) [the parenthetical comment does not appear in K] in the midst of a horde of savages; but if the reader has ever wandered, with a true hunter's spirit, among the forests [K: the endless forests] of Maine, or the more picturesque solitudes of the Adirondack Mountains, he will understand how the sombre woods and mountains around me might have awakened any other feelings than those of gloom. In truth, they recalled gladdening recollections of similar scenes in a distant and far different land.

After we had been advancing for several hours, through passages always narrow, often obstructed and difficult, I saw at a little distance on our right a narrow opening between two high, wooded precipices. All within seemed darkness and mystery. In the mood in which I found myself, something strongly impelled me to enter. Passing over the intervening space, I guided my horse through the rocky portal, and as I did so, instinctively drew the covering from my rifle, half expecting that some unknown evil lay in ambush within those dreary recesses. The place was shut in among tall cliffs, and so deeply shadowed by a host of old pine-trees, that though the sun shone bright on the side of the mountain, nothing but a dim twilight could penetrate within. As far as I could see, it had no tenants except a few hawks and owls, who, dismayed at my intrusion, flapped hoarsely away among the shaggy branches. I moved forward, determined to explore the mystery to the bottom, and soon became involved among the pines. The genius of the place exercised a strange influence upon my mind. Its faculties were stimulated into extraordinary activity, and as I passed along, many half-forgotten incidents, and the images of persons and things far distant, rose rapidly before me, with surprising distinctness. In that perilous wilderness, eight hundred miles removed beyond the faintest vestige of civilization, the scenes of another hemisphere, the seat of ancient refinement passed before me, more like a succession of vivid paintings than any mere dreams of the fancy. I saw the church of St. Peter's illumined on the evening of Easter-Day, the whole majestic pile from the cross to the foundation-stone, pencilled in fire, and shedding a radiance [K: a calm radiance] like the serene light of the moon, on the sea of upturned faces below. I saw the peak [K: the blue peak] of Mount Etna towering above its inky mantle of clouds, and lightly curling its wreath of milk-white smoke against the soft sky, flushed with the Sicilian sunset. I saw also the gloomy vaulted passages and the narrow cells of the Passionist convent, where I once had sojourned for a few days with the fanatical monks, its pale stern inmates, in their robes of black; and the grated window from whence I could look out, a forbidden indulgence, upon the melancholy Coliseum and the crumbling ruins of the Eternal City. The mighty glaciers of the Splugen, too, rose before me, gleaming in the sun like polished silver, and those terrible solitudes, the birth-place of the Rhine, where bursting from the bowels of its native mountain it lashes and foams down the rocky abyss into the little valley of Andeer. These recollections, and many more crowded upon me, until remembering that it was hardly wise to remain long in such a place, I mounted again and retraced my steps. Issuing from between the rocks, I saw, a few rods before me, the men, women and children, dogs and horses, still filing slowly across the little glen. A bare round hill rose directly above them. I rode to the top, and from this point I could look down on the savage procession as it passed just beneath my feet, and far on the left I could see its thin and broken line, visible only at intervals, stretching away for miles among the mountains. On the farthest ridge, horsemen were still descending like mere specks in the distance. [K adds the following additional sentence to conclude the paragraph: The imagination might have tasked itself in vain, to have conceived a more striking spectacle than that wild scene, with the wilder men who animated it.]

Parkman had visited Maine during his three summer outings in 1841–1843, the northern Adirondacks during the summers of 1842 and 1843, and the Berkshires in 1844. See *Journals*, I, 3–98, 251–277. During his European tour Parkman spent four days in the Passionist monastery "beyond the Coliseum" in April, 1844; he left the "convent" on Palm Sunday, unable to surrender to the rigors of monastic asceticism or to the persuasions of the monks. He crossed the Alps at Splügen Pass and visited the Swiss village of Andeer in the Grisons in early May, 1844. See *Journals*, I, 190–195, 209–211.

11 Parkman's own often-stated creed of "hardness" and his ingrained distrust of the idealism of the "she-philosophers" of West Roxbury find clear expression in this rejection of the "philanthropists" so industriously reforming New England and the world during the 1830's and 1840's. See Wade, *Francis Parkman*, pp. 177, 293.

12 Compare Parkman's notebook description of this scene in *Journals*, II, 466:

Aug. 1". Fairly among the mts. Rich, grassy valley—plenty of gooseberries and currants—dark pine mts.—an opening dell that tempted me to ride up into it, and here in the cool pine woods I recalled old feelings, and old and well remembered poetry. Climbed a steep hill—on the left, the mts. and the black pine forests—far down, the bare hills, and threading the valley below came the long, straggling procession of Inds.

They soon camped in a grassy nook, where crowded together —dogs and horses, men, women, and children—the sight was most picturesque. The men sat smoking—the women worked at the lodges—the children and young men climbed the steep rocks, or straggled among the pine-covered hills around the place. Droves of horses were driven to water—girls with spoons and buffalo paunches went down to a deep dell for water. Heat intense—sat on a shady rock and watched the scene. Climbed at sunset a high hill and looked over the mts. and pine forests. All night, the Inds. were playing at a great gambling game.

13 Parkman's "black-tailed deer," or mule deer, were certainly larger than the common white-tailed deer of his own earlier eastern experience, but they were not "nearly twice as large." Mature mule deer often weighed as much as 400 pounds; the smaller full-grown white-tailed deer might have weighed up to 300 pounds.

14 Between the sentences "They . . . pine-trees" and "We . . . declivity" *K* supplies the following additional sentence: "The young girls and the children clambered upon the back of the horses or clung to the baskets of the *travaux*, while the multitudes of dogs not a little increased the confusion."

15 The stream may have been one of the tributaries of Sybille Creek some miles northeast of the divide, perhaps Muleshoe Creek or Sand Creek.

16 Compare the sentence "The coverings . . . Indian" with its *K* form: "The coverings of the lodges were raised a foot or more from the ground, in order to procure some circulation of air; and Reynal, who closely imitated the habits of

his red associates, thought proper to lay aside his trapper's dress of buck-skin and assume the costume of an Indian, which closely resembles that adopted by Father Adam."

17 Apparently Reynal is referring to the campsite near the mouth of Chugwater Creek, on the south bank of Laramie River, where Parkman and his companions had first established themselves on June 21. See *Journals*, II, 444. If Reynal's estimate of the distance is correct, the village made its nooning on August 2 a few miles southwest of the present site of Natwick, Wyoming.

18 Parkman's notebook entry for August 2 in *Journals*, II, 464–465, does not mention his crossing Laramie River to arrive at the old Chugwater Creek campsite, and this passage is thus particularly confusing. On p. 303 of the present text Parkman notes that he and Raymond crossed the river again (that is, from the south bank) to reach Fort Laramie, and in the present instance it would seem that he has reached the banks of the river from the northwest and has now crossed over to the *south* bank of the stream.

19 Compare the sentence "There . . . inhabitants" with its K form: "There stood the Big Tree under which we had encamped so long; there were the white cliffs that used to look down upon our tent when it stood at the bend of the creek; there was the meadow in which our horses had grazed for weeks, and a little farther on, the prairie-dog village where I had beguiled many a languid hour by scooping out the brains of the unfortunate inhabitants with rifle bullets."

20 "Noisy ghosts" appeared quite frequently among the Oglalas, as Dorsey notes in "A Study of Siouan Cults," *Eleventh Annual Report*, p. 486: "If a quiet and well-behaved person dies his ghost is apt to be restless and cause trouble, but the ghost of a bad person who dies a natural death is never feared. The ghost of a murdered person is always dangerous."

21 For Antoine Le Rouge see pp. 311–313 of the present edition and note 15 for that page. "Richardson" may have been Paul Richardson, born in Connecticut or Vermont about 1793 and a well-known figure in the mountains. He had penetrated to the headwaters of the Fraser River before 1834, when he served Nathaniel Wyeth as guide and hunter on the long overland march to that year's rendezvous. As "an experienced mountaineer" he guided Wislizenus and his companions in the West in 1839, and contemporary accounts of Richardson's adventures often emphasize his strange loneliness. Farnham, *Travels in the Plains*, in Thwaites, ed. *Early Western Travels*, xxviii, 274–275, who met Richardson in 1843, noted that "This old Yankee woodsman had been upon one of his favorite trips from St. Louis to the borders of Oregon," and Bancroft, *History of Oregon*, i, 76, summarizing Richardson's career, also remarked upon his lonely wanderings: "He crossed the continent a number of times and had countless adventures, which he seldom related. He died in California in 1857, poor and alone, as he had lived." In addition to the authorities cited above, see Wislizenus, *Journey to the Rocky Mountains*, p. 104; and John Kirk Townsend, *Narrative of a Journey Across the Rocky Mountains, to the Columbia River, and a Visit to the Sandwich Islands* . . . (Philadelphia, 1839), pp. 38–49 *passim*. Though he is nowhere mentioned in Parkman's notebooks, Richardson may have been the New England trapper described on p. 262 of the present edition.

22 Parkman described this episode again in *Pontiac*, i, 167–168 n. (Vol. xiv of *Works*):

A striking example of Indian acuteness once came under my observation. Travelling in company with a Canadian named Raymond, and an Ogillallah Indian, we came at nightfall to a small stream called Chugwater, a branch of Laramie Creek. As we prepared to encamp, we observed the ashes of a fire, the footprints of men and horses, and other indications that a party had been on the spot not many days before. Having secured our horses for the night, Raymond and I sat down and lighted our pipes, my companion, who had spent his whole life in the Indian country, hazarding various conjectures as to the number and character of our predecessors. Soon after, we were joined by the Indian, who, meantime, had been prowling about the place. Raymond asked what discovery he had made. He answered, that the party were friendly, and that they consisted of eight men, both whites and Indians, several of whom he named, affirming that he knew them well. To an enquiry how he gained his information, he would make no intelligible reply. On the next day, reaching Fort Laramie, a post of the American Fur Company, we found that he was correct in every particular, —a circumstance the more remarkable as he had been with us for three weeks, and could have had no other means of knowledge than we ourselves.

But Parkman surely knew how easily and well Indians could "read sign" of distinctive footprints and hoofprints, of particular campfire patterns, and even of the size and build of a man from the trampled grass where he had spread his robe.

23 Between the sentences "Setting . . . fort" and "At . . . desolation" K supplies the following additional two sentences: "That path which I had travelled so often was well known to me. I welcomed every familiar object like one returning to his home after a long absence."

24 Compare Parkman's notebook entry for August 3 in *Journals*, II, 467: "Setting out before daybreak, reached the fort early, and found all there, Shaw having been there a fortnight. A civilized breakfast not to be sneezed at!"

25 Parkman's ambivalent feelings at enjoying Byron typically reflect the nineteenth century's appreciation of the poet's genius and its equally characteristic detestation of what it considered his lurid personal life.

CHAPTER XX

1 Solomon P. Sublette, Charles Taplin, Walter Reddick, and a fourth unidentified man are frequently mentioned in the journals and newspaper accounts of the emigration of 1846. Sublette had traveled the California Trail in 1845; Charles Taplin was a member of Frémont's Third Expedition; and Walter Reddick, apparently a Kentuckian, seems to have told Edwin Bryant that he also was one of Frémont's men, though there is no evidence that he was in fact part of the expedition. Taplin had left Frémont's camp on March 31, 1846, and in company with Reddick, Sublette, and the fourth member of their party had at the end of May left Pueblo de Los Angeles en route to Fort Bridger, traveling at least part of the way with the *bourgeois* Joe Walker. Walker and at least five other men were driving a herd of horses and mules east to the Pueblo and Bent's Fort, and Sublette and his companions probably served as herders for Walker's big *remuda* at least part of the way east.

Sublette and his three friends left Fort Bridger sometime in the first week of July; Bryant met them near South Pass on the afternoon of July 11; and Parkman's date of "a week before" for their arrival at Fort Laramie suggests that they appeared at the post sometime in the last week of July—more than two weeks after Bryant had seen them, though Parkman's rough date for their arrival may after all be wrong. Sublette and the others reached Bent's Fort on August 17 and apparently left it next day on their eastward journey to the settlements. Though the evidence is not conclusive, it appears that the four men left Bent's Fort alone and made a comparatively rapid journey to the Missouri frontier, which they reached sometime before September 11, when Sublette and Reddick are definitely noticed as having arrived at St. Louis on board the steamboat

Little Missouri. See Morgan, ed. *Overland in 1846*, I,
372–373, and II, 769–771; " 'From California,' *Weekly
Tribune*, New York, September 26, 1846," and " 'From
Bent's Fort,' *Weekly Reveille*, St. Louis, September 14,
1846," reprinted in Morgan, ed. *Overland in 1846*, II,
646–648, 648–649; Bryant, *What I Saw in California*,
p. 131; and Barry, "Kansas before 1854," KHQ, xxx (Autumn, 1964), 395.

Solomon P. Sublette (c. 1816–1857), the youngest of
five brothers all at one time or another engaged in the
fur trade, went west to Santa Fe as early as 1839. After an
interval of trapping and trading in the mountains with his
brother Andrew and Louis Vasquez, Solomon Sublette
returned to Independence in 1842. With his famous
brother William L. Sublette he was a member of Sir
William Drummond Stewart's luxurious excursion to the
Wind River Mountains and the Green River valley in
1843. He is known to have spent at least part of 1844 at or
near Bent's Fort; by March, 1845, he turned up in Taos. In
October of the same year he arrived at Sutter's Fort, and
in May, 1846, he began his overland journey eastward with
Walker and his band of horses and mules. By December,
Solomon Sublette had become a government despatch
messenger to Santa Fe. His later career found him engaged
in the Santa Fe trade and in unsuccessful farming ventures in Missouri. See Nunis, *Andrew Sublette*, pp. 72–73,
76, 231–232; John E. Sunder, "Solomon P. Sublette," in
LeRoy R. Hafen, ed. *The Mountain Men and the Fur
Trade of the Far West* (Glendale, Calif., 1965), I,
377–389; and John E. Sunder, "Solomon Perry Sublette:
Mountain Man of the Forties," *New Mexico Historical
Society Review*, xxxvi (January, 1961), 49–61.

2 Smoke and his band seem to have remained hovering
along the Oregon Trail west of Fort Laramie until at least
the middle of October, when the missionary Dr. Elijah

White met Smoke himself and most of his village 20 miles west of the fort. See A. J. Allen, *Thrilling Adventures, Travels and Explorations of Doctor Elijah White among the Rocky Mountains and in the Far West* . . . (New York, 1859), pp. 294–296.

3 Parkman's account of the Sublette party's encounter with the Sioux west of Fort Laramie is substantially identical to the report of this episode in " 'From Bent's Fort,' *Weekly Reveille*, St. Louis, September 14, 1846," reprinted in Morgan, ed. *Overland in 1846*, II, 648: "A detached band of twenty-five [Indians] encountered Mr. S. [Sublette] and his men, and commenced cutting off the packs from the horses. The owners interfered, and the Indians commenced firing upon them; they, however, after a chase of five miles, succeeded in escaping without injury, and saved all their pack horses but two. The savages stole a great part of their provisions."

4 The Comanches, a Shoshonean tribe and the only branch of that stock living completely on the plains, have been called the finest cavalry in history. Their territory embraced Oklahoma, New Mexico, northern Texas, and southern Kansas, though they often raided north into Colorado and far south into Mexico. They were especially active along the Santa Fe Trail in late 1846 and 1847. See Hodge, ed. *Handbook of American Indians*, I, 327–328.

5 The identity of the "young Kentuckian" remains in doubt, but he was probably Robert M. Ewing of Louisville, whom Parkman had already met at St. Louis on April 25 and at Fort Bernard on June 27. See *Journals*, II, 415, 447. Ewing and his companion, R. T. Jacobs (or Jacob), had traveled with Edwin Bryant to the emigrants' rendezvous at Independence on May 1; all three apparently journeyed together in Russell's train as far as Ash Hollow, where Bryant, Ewing, and seven other men rode on ahead to make arrangements at Fort Bernard and Fort Laramie for

the planned fast party on muleback, which Jacobs, Bryant, and Russell among others finally joined. At some time during the journey from Independence to Ash Hollow, Ewing met an otherwise unidentified E. Hewett, who may also have ridden on ahead from Ash Hollow with Bryant and Ewing and the rest, though Bryant does not mention his name.

On June 28 Bryant learned that "Ewing had joined a party of traders, bound for Taos or the head-waters of the Arkansas." The leader of this party was John Conn; they all arrived at the Hardscrabble post on July 18, and Ewing and Hewett then pushed on, apparently alone, for Bent's Fort, which they reached on or about July 22. According to the account which they gave the St. Louis *Daily Union* in early September, "After remaining at the Fort seven days [until July 29?], they started, in company with some other gentlemen about to return to the United States, some wagoners, and eleven sick volunteers, in all about thirty men, with ten empty provision wagons." The whole party reached Council Grove on or about August 22 and Independence some five days or a week later. It seems very doubtful that Sublette and his three companions traveled in company with Ewing from Bent's Fort to the settlements, for other newspaper accounts specifically place Taplin and Sublette at Bent's Fort on August 17–18. See Bryant, *What I Saw in California*, pp. 13, 98, 115; Barry, "Kansas before 1854," *KHQ*, xxx (Autumn, 1964), 391; " 'From the Plains,' *The Gazette*, St. Joseph, September 18, 1846" and " 'News from Capt. Fremont and Bent's Fort,' *Daily Union*, St. Louis, September 21, 1846," reprinted and annotated in Morgan, ed. *Overland in 1846*, II, 651–654, 654, 770–771. Ewing had certainly quarreled with Russell on the trail in late May. See "The Diary of George McKinstry," reprinted *ibid.*, I, 208, 403–404.

6 Compare the sentence "One . . . relatives" with its K

form: "One of his chief objects, as he gave out, was to kill an Indian; an exploit which he afterward succeeded in achieving in his own defense, not a little to the jeopardy of ourselves and others who had to pass through the country of the dead Pawnee's enraged relatives."

The excision of "in his own defense" makes Ewing sound more bloodthirsty than does his own account of this adventure published as " 'From the Plains,' *The Gazette,* St. Joseph, September 18, 1846," reprinted in Morgan, ed. *Overland in 1846,* II, 653–654: "At Cow creek, the party were again attacked by a large party. The intentions of the assailants seemed to be the driving off of stock. In this attempt, one lost his life through the rifle of Mr. Ewing, and it was thought two others were killed. In this affair, three very fine mules belonging to a gentleman of the company, were stolen."

7 After the sentence "Sublette . . . resources" K–52 supply the following additional two paragraphs:

But I am anticipating. When, before leaving the settlement, we had made inquiries concerning this part of the country of General Kearney, Mr. Mackenzie, Captain Wyeth, and others well acquainted with it, they had all advised us by no means to attempt this southward journey with fewer than fifteen or twenty men. The danger consists in the chance of encountering Indian war-parties. Sometimes, throughout the whole length of the journey, (a distance of three hundred and fifty miles,) one does not meet a single human being; frequently, however, the route is beset by Arapahoes and other unfriendly tribes; in which case the scalp of the adventurer is in imminent peril. As to the escort of fifteen or twenty men, such a force of whites could at that time scarcely be collected in the whole country; and had the case been otherwise, the expense of securing them, together with the necessary number of horses, would have been extremely heavy. We had resolved, however, upon pursuing this southward course. There were, indeed, two other routes from Fort Laramie; but both of these were less interesting and neither was free from danger. Being unable therefore to procure the fifteen or twenty men recommended, we determined to set out with those we had already in our employ: Henry Chatillon, Delorier and Raymond. The men themselves made no objection, nor would they have made any had the journey been more dangerous; for Henry was without fear, and the other two without thought.

Shaw and I were much better fitted for this mode of travelling than we had been on betaking ourselves to the prairies for the first time a few months before. The daily routine had ceased to be a novelty. All the details of the journey and the camp had become familiar to us. We had seen life under a new aspect; the human biped had been reduced to his primitive condition. We had lived without law to protect, a roof to shelter, or garment of cloth to cover us. One of us at least had been without bread, and without salt to season his food. Our idea of what is indispensable to human existence and enjoyment had been wonderfully curtailed; and a horse, a rifle and a knife seemed to make up the whole of life's necessaries. For these once obtained, together with the skill to use them, all else that is essential would follow in their train, and a host of luxuries besides. One other lesson our short prairie experience had taught us; that of profound contentment in the present, and utter contempt for what the future might bring forth.

According to his letter of June 28 (27?) to his father in *Letters*, I, 45–47, Parkman had first thought of returning from Fort Laramie by way of Fort Pierre and the upper Missouri; what other route homeward he had in mind does not appear from his notebooks, unless of course he meant to retrace his steps eastward along the Platte.

Nathaniel Jarvis Wyeth (1802–1856), born in Cambridge, Massachusetts, began his career in the ice business at Fresh Pond in 1824. After falling under the influence of Hall Kelley, Wyeth began in 1831 to formulate plans for the colonization of Oregon; by 1832, however, he had changed the direction of his thinking and, heavily backed by Boston money, planned to reduce the chaotic beaver trade to order by establishing a series of fixed posts in the mountains and a Pacific Coast fishery, and thus to reduce the exorbitant overhead of the fur trade by transshipping furs and fish and trade goods by sea. His intelligent and on the whole well-organized plans were ruined by a number of acrimonious defections from his leadership (particularly that of his cousin, John B. Wyeth, who published a book ridiculing Wyeth's efforts), by vigorous and even unscrupulous opposition, and by a number of unforeseen disasters.

Wyeth left the West in 1836. His most important contribution to the history of the fur trade is doubtless the construction of Fort Hall in 1834. He was "Captain" Wyeth because, on setting out for the mountains in 1832, he had organized his party very much like a militia company and also because he himself had led fur brigades in the mountains. After 1836 he spent the rest of his life in the ice business at Fresh Pond and in the 1840's was very well known in and near Boston for the innovations he had introduced to that commerce, including early and successful experiments with frozen fruits and vegetables. See DeVoto, *Across the Wide Missouri*, pp. 61–261 *passism;* Morgan and Harris, eds. *Rocky Mountain Journals of W. M. Anderson*, pp. 388–391; and William R. Sampson, "Nathaniel Jarvis Wyeth," in LeRoy R. Hafen, ed. *The Mountain Men and the Fur Trade of the Far West* (Glendale, Calif., 1968), v, 381–391.

8 Troché and Rouville remain unidentified.

9 The "little brook" must have been Cherry Creek.

10 "Goché's Hole" is located in present Goshen County, Wyoming, south of Torrington.

11 Field, *Prairie and Mountain Sketches*, p. 99, reports a similar episode in which two low-flying crows were mistaken for a galloping buffalo.

12 Parkman's notebooks are not altogether clear about whether Bissonette was camped on Horse Creek or on Little Horse Creek; in his entry for August 6 in *Journals*, II, 468, Parkman has the party crossing Little Horse Creek first and then discovering Bissonette's camp on the main stream, though in reality Little Horse Creek west of the forks lies south of Horse Creek itself. If Bissonette was on Horse Creek, however, his camp was located some 50 miles south of Fort Laramie—two days' ride—and somewhere near the present site of Meriden, Wyoming. Parkman's "Little Horse Creek" may have been Bear Creek or one of its affluents.

13 Like the Sioux, the Cheyennes, an Algonquin tribe, had been moving steadily westward for almost 150 years and were discovered by Lewis and Clark on the Cheyenne River in modern South Dakota. Part of the tribe, the Southern Cheyennes, moved down to the upper Arkansas River at about the time of the building of Bent's Fort in the early 1830's; the rest of the tribe remained near the headwaters of the North Platte and the Yellowstone. Though the tribe had been driven out of the Dakotas by the Sioux, a peace between the two tribes was made sometime before 1840, and for the next 30 years both the Northern and Southern Cheyennes and the western bands of the Sioux were closely allied. See Hodge, ed. *Handbook of American Indians*, II, 251–257.

14 Joseph Bissonette (1818–1894) was born in St. Louis, the son of a family long involved in the Indian trade. An Antoine Bissonette was killed at the mouth of the Osage River in 1807, and Prince Maximilian had heard of another member of the family who had served as "chief trader" among the Mandans at the time of the Atkinson-

O'Fallon expedition to the upper Missouri in 1825. Joseph Bissonette himself went west for the first time about 1836 and thereafter spent his life in the plains and mountains. His ties to the wilderness were doubtless strengthened by the seven children born to him and his first wife, an Oglala, and the 14 children of his second marriage to a Brule.

Bissonette's success in the fur trade was apparently quite rapid; by 1842 he had become one of the principal Indian traders for Sybille, Adams & Company, the firm operating Fort Platte. Frémont met Bissonette at Fort Platte and there engaged him as guide and interpreter for that part of the First Expedition westward from Fort Laramie to the Red Buttes. Bernard Pratte and John Cabanne bought Fort Platte in the summer of 1843 and thereafter began to give Bissonette more responsibility: in 1844 he was sent back to St. Louis by the partners to purchase trade goods for the post, and he led the packtrain returning to Fort Platte. Bissonette acted as interpreter for Kearny at Fort Laramie in June, 1845, and shortly after Kearny's departure he supervised the abandonment of Fort Platte and the construction of the new Fort Bernard eight miles east of the deserted post.

Pratte and Cabanne, however, sold out to the American Fur Company in December, 1845, and now John Richard and Bissonette, both formerly and even now perhaps covertly working for Pratte, Cabanne & Company, laid out a careful campaign to undersell the American Fur Company's Fort Laramie, with the results already shown in note 31 for page 99. Richard now ran the day-to-day operations at Fort Bernard while Bissonette traded with the Indians in their camps as "outside man." After the destruction of Fort Bernard, Bissonette continued to trade in the Laramie area, often in partnership with James Bordeaux, and was long active in seeking a measure of justice for his dispossessed Indian relatives. See John Dishon McDermott, "Joseph Bissonette," in Hafen, ed. *Mountain Men and the Fur Trade*, IV, 49–60; Berthong, *Southern Cheyennes*, p. 169; Richard Edward Oglesby, *Manuel Lisa and the Opening of the Missouri Fur Trade* (Norman, 1963), p. 7; and Prince Maximilian, *Travels in North America*, in Thwaites, ed. *Early Western Travels*, XXIII, 227.

15 Antoine Le Rouge, identified on p. 312 of the present text as a "half-breed Pawnee," may have been Antoine Ledoux, Jr., nicknamed "Le Rouge," the son of the well-known trapper the trader Antoine Ledoux who is known to have been on the upper Arkansas in the spring of 1846. Janet Lecompte, "Antoine and Abraham Ledoux," in LeRoy R. Hafen, ed. *The Mountain Men and the Fur Trade of the Far West* (Glendale, Calif., 1966), III, 173–179, noted that the younger Ledoux claimed that he had been captured at the forks of the Platte River by the Sioux and that he had been raised among them. He lived at Fort Laramie for a number of years and there served as a guide for the cavalry until his death in 1881.

16 Identified as "N. Sibille" in *Journals*, II, 468, he may have been Nat Sibille, or Sybille (the name is variously spelled), a well-known Indian trader, but other contemporary evidence seems to suggest that this "Sibille" was probably the same John, or Jean, Sibille frequently mentioned in Bissonette's company throughout the spring of 1846. Toward the end of his life John Sibille claimed to have been one of the original builders of Fort Vasquez. See Barry, "Kansas before 1854," *KHQ*, XXX (Autumn, 1964), 351; " 'From Oregon. California Emigrants,' *Weekly Reveille*, St. Louis, July 20, 1846," reprinted in Morgan, ed. *Overland in 1846*, II, 592; and Hafen, *Fort Vasquez*, p. 6. The Sibilles were long established in the fur trade, and several place-names in Wyoming commemorate the family.

17 See p. 328 of the present edition and note 1 for that page for additional information about the Pueblo.

18 Parkman noted 40 Sioux lodges, "several Shienne," and The Whirlwind himself encamped with Bissonette. See *Journals*, ii, 468.

19 The Stabber, "a Missouri Ind.," arrived at the Horse Creek camp on August 7 or 8, the latter date being the more probable. See *Journals*, ii, 470. Hyde, *Red Cloud's Folk*, p. 30, notes, however, that the name "Stabber" was an hereditary title among the Oglalas and that in 1875 there was a Stabber Band among the Sioux, apparently named after an Oglala chieftain bearing that name.

20 The Stabber's narrative included the details of the march of Kearny's Army of the West from Fort Leavenworth to Bent's Fort along the Mountain Route of the Santa Fe Trail, as well as a garbled description of Zachary Taylor's victories at Palo Alto (May 8) and Resaca de la Palma (May 9), which together led to the American occupation of Matamoros, Mexico. Parkman doubtless had heard of the beginning of the Mexican War before he got very far from the Missouri frontier; news of the defeat and capture of Thornton's dragoons had reached both Edwin Bryant and Jesse Quinn Thornton between May 16 and May 18. See *What I Saw in California*, p. 39; and *Oregon and California in 1848*, i, 32. Parkman heard the Stabber's account of these events probably on August 8, some three months after Taylor's victories but only a week after Kearny's departure from Bent's Fort. See *Journals*, ii, 470.

21 For this quotation see 1 *Henry IV* iv.i.96. Parkman's account of these Canadians is reminiscent of a similar description in Irving's *Astoria*, p. 44: "No men are more submissive to their leaders and employers, more capable of enduring hardship, or more good-humored under privations. Never are they so happy as when on long and rough expeditions, toiling up rivers or coasting lakes; encamping

at night on the borders, gossipping round their fires, and bivouacking in the open air."

22 Parkman's evident contempt for these half-breeds is at least partially explainable by his century's fear and detestation of miscegenation. Ross, *Fur Hunters of the Far West*, p. 196, presents an even more damning account of the "half Indian, half white man, and half devil":

> Half-breeds, or as they are more generally styled, brules, from the peculiar color of their skin, being of a swarthy hue, as if sunburnt, as they grow up resemble, almost in every respect, the pure Indian. They are indolent, thoughtless, and improvident. Licentious in their habits, unbounded in their desires, sullen in their disposition. Proud, restless, and clannish, fond of flattery. They alternately associate with the white and the Indians. . . . They form a composition of all the bad qualities of both.

23 Niccolò Paganini (1782–1840), the Italian violinist, was famous in the nineteenth century for his extraordinary technical virtuosity and for the extremely sensitive effects which he achieved in his own violin concerti.

24 From Parkman's description of this scene it is clear that he was observing a ritual of the *tokala*, or Kit-Fox, "soldier" society, which, as Wissler, "Societies and Ceremonial Associations," *Anthropological Papers*, XI, p. 14, notes, was "so named because its members are supposed to be as active and wily on the warpath as the little animal is known to be in his native state. It is said that the kit-fox has great skill in finding things, as, for example, marrow-bones buried in the earth; hence the members of the tokala organization regarded themselves as foxes and their enemies as marrow-bones." Wissler observes that their motto *was* never to retire "from any enterprise once begun."

25 Parkman's party left Bissonette's camp on the afternoon of August 9. See *Journals*, II, 471.

26 On August 11, the day the animals bolted and ran back to Lodgepole Creek, Parkman and his companions were probably encamped on Muddy Creek, just south of the present site of Egbert, Wyoming. See *Journals*, II, 471.

27 I acknowledge with thanks the assistance of Professor Robert Dicke of the University of Wisconsin Department of Entomology in identifying these insects as Mormon crickets and young grasshoppers, the latter perhaps "wingless" because they were still in the nymphal stage, for there is properly no such insect as a wingless grasshopper.

28 Parkman's "horned-frog" was doubtless a horned toad (*Phrynosoma douglassi*).

29 K–52 supply "destination" as a better reading than "designation" in 72–92.

30 Gregg, *Commerce of the Prairies*, in Thwaites, ed. *Early Western Travels*, XX, 282, supplies a very similar account of the horned toad: "I once took a pair of them upon the far-western plains, which I shut up in a box and carried to one of the eastern cities, where they were kept for several months before they died—without having taken food or water, though repeatedly offered them." Parkman's reference to the Agassiz Museum ("and he now . . . Museum") was added in 72, some 13 years after the establishment of the museum at Harvard in 1859; the Agassiz Museum is now known as the Museum of Comparative Zoology.

31 Marmots, squirrels, and chipmunks all belong to the family *Sciuridae*.

32 After the sentence "Small . . . ascertain" K–52 supply the following additional sentence to conclude the paragraph: "The manners and customs, the political and domestic economy of these little marmots is worthy of closer attention than one is able to give when pushing by forced marches through their country, with his thoughts engrossed by objects of greater moment."

Parkman has already described similar scenes on pp. 73 and 82 of the present edition.

33 Parkman and his party camped at the mouth of the Cache à la Poudre River, some five miles east of the present site of Greeley, Colorado, on the evening of August 12. See *Journals*, II, 471. Thus, the reference on p. 319 of the present edition to the "fifth day after leaving Bisonette's camp" does not agree with the actual chronology of their southward journey from Horse Creek.

34 Long's Peak (elev. 14,255 ft.) was named for Major Stephen H. Long, who led an exploring expedition to the area in 1820. The mountain was some 50 or more miles west-southwest of Parkman's August 12–13 campsite at the mouth of the Cache à la Poudre.

35 Since they had encamped at or very close to the mouth of Cache à la Poudre, Parkman must mean here that he and his companions were still on the left, or western, bank of the South Platte River.

36 Since a span is nine inches, Deslauriers' "infant" rattler must have measured just over a foot in length.

37 The party crossed to the right, or east, bank of the South Platte on the morning of August 13. See *Journals*, II, 471.

38 Compare Parkman's description of a sweating lodge in *La Salle*, pp. 262–263 n. (Vol. V of *Works*): "These baths consist of a small hut, covered closely with buffalo-skins, into which the patient and his friends enter, carefully closing every aperture. A pile of heated stones is placed in the middle, and water is poured over them, raising a dense vapor. They are still (1868) in use among the Sioux and some other tribes." Like the sauna, the Indians' sweating lodges were often used therapeutically. They also served for ceremonial purifications, particularly before battle, and for puberty rites. See Hodge, ed. *Handbook of American Indians*, II, 660–662.

39 First named Fort Lookout, Fort George (or Fort St.

Vrain) was built by Bent, St. Vrain & Company in the summer or early fall of 1837 to take advantage of the rich beaver trade based on the hunting grounds of the nearby Parks, or mountain valleys. The post was located on the east bank of the South Platte River, a mile and a half below the mouth of St. Vrain Creek and some six miles northwest of modern Platteville, Colorado. See Hafen, *Fort Vasquez*, p. 8; LeRoy R. Hafen, "Fort St. Vrain," *Colorado Magazine*, xxix (October, 1952), 241–255; and David Lavender, *Bent's Fort* (Garden City, N.Y., 1954), pp. 177–185.

Compare Talbot's description of Fort St. Vrain in 1843 a year or two before it was finally abandoned, in *Journals of Theodore Talbot*, p. 23:

About noon we reached "Fort George" or as it is more commonly called "St. Vrain's Fort". . . . We encamped opposite the main entrance. The Fort is built on an elevated level near the river. It is built of "Adobes," or unburnt bricks, and is quadrangular, with bastions at the alternate angles so arranged as to sweep the four faces of the walls. The main entrance is guarded by heavy gates and above by a tower. . . . The interior or court is surrounded by houses one story high, on one side is the "Korall" or pen for cattle and horses. The wall is built sufficiently above the houses to make a good breastwork to their roofs.

40 Parkman and his party passed Fort Lupton or Fort Lancaster on the morning of August 14. See *Journals*, ii, 472. Fort Lupton was built in 1836 or 1837 at a site about a mile north of the present town of Fort Lupton, Colorado. Its founder, Lancaster P. Lupton (1807–1885), had resigned his commission in the First Dragoons in 1836 to enter the fur trade, in which he did not prosper; Fort Lancaster was apparently abandoned in late 1845 or early 1846, three years or more after Lupton's Fort Platte had passed into

the hands of Sybille, Adams & Company. See Ann W. Hafen, "Lancaster P. Lupton," in Hafen, ed. *Mountain Men and the Fur Trade*, II, 207–216; LeRoy R. Hafen, "Old Fort Lupton and Its Founder," *Colorado Magazine*, VI (November, 1929), 220–226; and LeRoy R. Hafen, "Fort Jackson and the Early Fur Trade on the South Platte," *Colorado Magazine*, V (February, 1928), 9–17.

On August 13–14 Parkman had passed the sites of two other posts, Fort Vasquez, a mile and a half south of present Platteville, Colorado, and Fort Jackson, near Ione. For the past several days and for several more to come Parkman and his companions would be following the route of Kearny's march with the First Dragoons in 1845 over part of the "Old Trapper's Trail" which ran north and south from the Pueblo to Fort Laramie and Taos. These four posts, located along less than 20 miles of the South Platte, show how important to the fur trade this region was in the late 1830's and early 1840's.

41 The Southern Arapahoes were frequently to be encountered along the upper reaches of the South Platte. See p. 348 of the present edition and note 11 for that page.

42 Parkman and his party reached Cherry Creek, apparently some miles southeast of its junction with the South Platte at the modern site of Denver, on the morning of August 15. See *Journals*, II, 472.

43 On August 16 the party nooned at a point well up the valley of Cherry Creek, probably not far from the modern Franktown, Colorado. See *Journals*, II, 472.

44 Parkman first glimpsed Pike's Peak (elev. 14,110 ft.) on the morning of August 17, before his party made a nooning "on the head of Kiowa" Creek, a campsite located a few miles south of modern Elbert, Colorado. See *Journals*, II, 472. The mountain was almost 40 miles southwest of the Kiowa Creek camp, where the party spent the rest of the day.

45 Parkman's "black squirrels . . . leaping among the branches" of a pine forest were probably melanistic Abert's squirrels (*Sciurus aberti*), largely restricted to ponderosa pine forests and especially common in Colorado.

46 On August 17 Parkman noted that "Henry killed a straggling bull, too rank and tough to eat," *before* the party reached the Kiowa Creek campsite. See *Journals*, II, 472.

47 In this passage Parkman seems to be combining the events of two days, August 17–18. On the afternoon of August 17, as has been noted, the party remained encamped on Kiowa Creek. On August 18 they moved south from Kiowa Creek and nooned on what was probably the West Fork of Black Squirrel Creek, west of present Ellicott, Colorado. See *Journals*, II, 472.

48 On the evening of August 18–19 they camped on Jimmy Camp Creek at a point some seven or eight miles east or southeast of modern Colorado Springs. See *Journals*, II, 472.

49 Pike's Peak was in fact more than 20 miles west of westsouthwest of their camp on Jimmy Camp Creek. The mountain was named for Zebulon M. Pike, whose second expedition of 1806–1807 was organized in part to explore the headwaters of the Arkansas River and the surrounding mountain region before tracing the Red River from its source to American territory. In the last week of November, 1806, Pike approached the mountain later to bear his name but did not succeed in climbing it or even in coming very near its base. As Donald Jackson shows in his edition of the *Journals of Z. M. Pike*, I, 352 n., the peak was even named by other explorers:

Pike made no effort to name the mountain after himself. He called it the Grand Peak. When the Long expedition came through in 1820, and Dr. Edwin James reached the summit [on July 14, 1820], he earned title to the mountain. Long named it James Peak, but the appellation failed to stick. A period of confusion followed, during which some travelers applied Pike's name to the Spanish Peaks—rising far to the south of Pike's Peak. As late as 1839, Thomas Farnham wrote of "Pike's Peak in the southwest, and James' Peak in the northwest," as he came up the Arkansas. . . . Edwin James was finally honored less signally by the naming of a lesser peak in the Front Range, near Berthoud Pass. . . . Perhaps the first geographer to give the name of "Pike's mountain" to the Peak was Dr. Robinson, when he published a map of the West in 1818.

50 After the sentence "As . . . view" K and 49–52 each supply an additional sentence: "Immediately the stanza of Childe Harold occurred to my memory:" [K]; "One could not but recall the stanza of Childe Harold:" [49–52].

Both K and 49–52 then supply a stanza of verse to conclude the paragraph and another additional paragraph thereafter:

'Morn dawns, and with stern Albania's hills,
Dark Suli's rocks, and Pindus' inland peak,
Robed half in mist, bedewed with snowy rills,
Array'd in many a dun and purple streak,
Arise; and, as the clouds along them break,
Disclose the dwelling of the mountaineer:
Here roams the wolf, the eagle whets his beak,
Birds, beasts of prey, and wilder men appear,
And gathering storms around convulse the closing year.'

Every line save one of this description was more than verified here. There were no 'dwellings of the mountaineer' among these heights. [K: these fearful heights.] Fierce savages, restlessly wandering through summer and winter, alone invade them. 'Their hand is against every man, and every man's hand against them.'

Compare this canceled passage with part of Parkman's notebook entry for August 19 in *Journals,* II, 473: "As we left camp, there was promise of a warm and clear day, but white wreaths of cloud soon gathered about the mts., reminding one of Bryon's description of Suli and Pargo. The white snow patches—the ravines and black forests were obscured and revealed by turns—it was a sublime and beautiful sight." The description of Suli and Pargo appears in Byron's *Childe Harold* ii.xlii.1–9. For "Their hand is against every man, and every man's hand against them," compare Genesis xvi.12.

51 The storm occurred on the afternoon of August 19. See *Journals*, ii, 473.

52 Parkman had visited Naples in February, 1844, during his European tour. See Wade, *Francis Parkman*, pp. 117–123.

53 During the afternoon of August 19 and most of the next day Parkman and his companions were descending Fountain Creek, often called "La Fontaine qui bouille," southward toward its mouth and the location of the Pueblo. They spent the night of August 19–20 encamped in the vicinity of modern Pinyon, Colorado, and reached the Pueblo on the afternoon of August 20. See *Journals*, ii, 473.

Chapter xxi

1 Ruxton, *Adventures in the Rocky Mountains*, reprinted in *Ruxton of the Rockies*, p. 211, visited and described the Pueblo in late 1846 or early 1847: "The Pueblo is a small square fort of adobe with circular bastions at the corners, no part of the walls being more than eight feet high, and round the inside of the yard or corral are built some half-dozen little rooms inhabited by as many Indian traders, *coureurs des bois*, and mountain men." The post had apparently not much improved when Richard Kern saw it as a member of Frémont's Fourth Expedition in 1848: "There is a fort built of Adobes—a miserable looking

place, the inside resembling a menagerie—a compound of Spaniards, Horses mules dogs chickens and bad stench." See Hafen and Hafen, eds. *Frémont's Fourth Expedition*, p. 118.

The site of the Pueblo (at modern Pueblo, Colorado) had been occupied by white men as early as November, 1806, when Pike built a stockade there. Jacob Fowler seems to have erected a log house and corral near Pike's old encampment in January, 1822, and there may have been trading houses located on the site in 1839. The post Parkman and Ruxton saw, however, was built in 1842 by Joe Doyle, George Simpson, and Alexander Barclay, though the ineffable Beckwourth also claimed most of the credit for its construction. See Jackson, ed. *Journals of Z. M. Pike*, I, 349–351; Nolie Mumey, *Old Forts and Trading Posts of the West: Bent's Old Fort and Bent's New Fort on the Arkansas River* (Denver, 1956), p. 13; Clarence A. Vandiveer, *The Fur-Trade and Early Western Exploration* (Cleveland, 1929), p. 163; Harvey L. Carter and Janet S. Lecompte, "George Semmes Simpson," in LeRoy R. Hafen, ed. *The Mountain Men and the Fur Trade of the Far West* (Glendale, Calif., 1966), III, 290; Harvey L. Carter, "Joe Doyle," *ibid.*, III, 89; and Bonner, *Life and Adventures of J. P. Beckwourth* (1856), p. 464.

2 Among its other attractions, Taos was famous for its potent and cheap "Taos Lightning" or *aguardiente de Taos* —a native whiskey much prized by mountain men. See Garrard, *Wah-To-Yah and the Taos Trail*, p. 246.

3 That is, the girls were making cakes of *bread*.

4 See p. 314 of the present edition and note 20 for that page for Palo Alto and Resaca de la Palma.

5 The Brown-Crosby party of Mississippi Mormons, unaware that the date for the Saints' final departure for their new sanctuary in the West had been set back a year,

arrived at Independence on May 26, several weeks after the greater part of the Oregon and California emigrants had left the frontier. The 43 members of the Mormon party under the command of William Crosby had wisely avoided most of the Illinois and Missouri companies, though they did not learn of Brigham Young's altered plans until late June, when they were well out on the plains. The Mississippi Mormons and their 19 wagons left Independence on May 27, in company with 13 or 14 gentiles and six wagons bound for Oregon. The Oregon emigrants separated from the Mormons when both parties reached the Platte; the Mormons arrived at Fort Bernard in early July and started south with John Richard on July 10, bound for the Pueblo, which they reached on August 7, some two weeks before Parkman met them on August 20. The man nearly scalped by the grizzly was named George Thirlkill. See LeRoy R. Hafen and Frank M. Young, "The Mormon Settlement at Pueblo, Colorado, During the Mexican War," *Colorado Magazine*, ix (July, 1932), 121–136; and Barry, "Kansas before 1854," *KHQ*, xxx (Autumn, 1964), 357–358.

Ruxton, *Life in the Far West*, p. 204, saw these Mormons later in 1846 or early in 1847 and gives a good description of their encampment near the Pueblo, where the original Brown-Crosby party had been joined by the "Sick Detachment" from the Mormon Battalion: "In the wide and well-timbered bottom of the Arkansas, the Mormons had erected a street of log shanties, in which to pass the inclement weather. These were built of rough logs of cottonwood, laid one above the other, the interstices filled with mud, and rendered impervious to wind or wet. At one end of the row of shanties was built the 'church' or temple —a long building of huge logs, in which the prayer-meetings and holdings-forth took place."

6 Parkman visited the Mormon camp on August 21. See *Journals*, II, 473–474.

7 See p. 41 of the present edition and note 1 for that page for an account of the Mormons' evacuation of Nauvoo. Ruxton, *Life in the Far West*, p. 205, recounts a fictional Mormon preacher's sermon, a discourse which combines the Saints' overwhelming sense of self-pity and their indestructible optimism: "As there are a many strange gentlemen now—a—present, it's about right to tell 'em—a—what our doctrine just is, and so I tells 'em right off what the Mormons is. They are the chosen of the Lord; they are the children of glory, persecuted by the hand of man: they flies here to the wilderness, and, amongst the *Injine* and the buffler, they lifts up their heads, and cries with a loud voice, Susannah, and hurray for the promised land! Do you believe it? I *know* it."

8 Parkman and his companions left the Pueblo on the morning of August 22. See *Journals*, II, 474.

9 The "1846 Account Book" in *Journals*, II, 494–495, shows that Parkman paid off Raymond at Bent's Fort, not at the Pueblo. Raymond's services were worth $38 and the price ($3) of a cotton shirt purchased for him at Fort Laramie.

10 The Pawnees began to be especially active along the eastern stretches of the Santa Fe Trail in late September and October, 1846; they killed a teamster and wounded the wagon master of a government supply train at Pawnee Fork on October 13; 20 miles below the Arkansas crossings they captured 19 teamsters and looted their wagons on or about October 15. On October 28, 25 or 30 miles below the Arkansas crossings, they stampeded almost all the animals of another government supply train, killed one man, wounded four others, and burned a wagon. See Barry, "Kansas before 1854," *KHQ*, xxx (Autumn, 1964), 401–403; and compare Webb, *Adventures in the Santa Fé Trade*, p. 287, on the state of the trail in 1847:

I think the first train we met was on the Cimarrón river. They had been much annoyed by the Indians and cautioned us to keep a good lookout, as they were in large numbers and unusually daring. From this on [*sic*], we met many trains, not one until we passed the Big Bend of Arkansas, but what had been attacked, and nearly all had lost one or more men.

Before reaching the Arkansas, we met F. X. Aubry, who warned us of the danger from Indians. He said he had one man killed a few rods ahead of the train. The man was walking along, not apprehending any danger, when an Indian shot an arrow from his ambush in the grass, ran and lanced and scalped him, and escaped before his men could recover from their surprise sufficient to shoot. . . .

11 Compare Ruxton, *Adventures in the Rocky Mountains,* reprinted in *Ruxton of the Rockies,* pp. 270–271:

On the thirtieth of April [1847], having the day before succeeded in collecting my truant *mulada,* I proceeded alone to the forks of the Arkansa and St. Charles . . . and here I remained two or three days, the animals faring well on the young grass, waiting for my two companions, who were to proceed with me across the grand prairies. As, however, the trail was infested by the Pawnees and Comanche, who had attacked every party which had attempted to cross from Santa Fé during the last six months, and carried off all their animals, it was deemed prudent to wait for the escort of [William] Tharpe [or Tharp], the Indian trader, who was about to proceed to St. Louis with the peltries, the produce of his winter trade; and as he would be accompanied by a large escort of mountain men, we resolved to remain and accompany his party for the security it offered. . . .

On the second of May, my two fellow travellers arrived with the intelligence that Tharpe could not leave until a trading party from the north fork of the Platte came in to Arkansa, and consequently we started the next day alone. I may here mention that Tharpe started two days after us, and was killed on Walnut Creek by the Pawnees. . . .

Barring the important difference in dates, Parkman's "young man" in this passage might have been Ruxton himself, who had come north to the upper Arkansas from Santa Fe and Taos in the late fall of 1846. Both Ruxton and Parkman were in New York City in early July, 1847, before Ruxton left the United States for England and when *The Oregon Trail* had been running in the *Knickerbocker Magazine* for some months. The probable date of the original composition of "The Pueblo and Bent's Fort" (first published in K in August, 1848) was probably "not long since" July, 1847, and these tentative correspondences lend partial support to an identification of Ruxton as Parkman's source of information about the state of the Santa Fe Trail after Parkman himself had returned to the East. Parkman's account of the "young man" in this passage suggests that Parkman might have combined Ruxton's oral account of his adventures in New Mexico and along the upper Arkansas in the fall and winter of 1846–1847 with Ruxton's narrative of Indian outrages along the Santa Fe Trail in the spring of 1847. See *ibid.*, p. 306; and Wade, *Francis Parkman*, pp. 291–300.

12 Parkman might well have hoped for a continuation of Fortune's favors in his needlessly dangerous journey eastward, although it was not absolutely unknown for very small parties to brave the wilderness alone. For example, Wislizenus, *Journey to the Rocky Mountains*, pp. 127–130, rambled among the Rockies with only five men in his party, and on November 3, 1846, while the danger of a Pawnee attack was still acute, Captain W. S. Murphy with only three men and a single wagon reached Westport from Santa Fe by the Desert Route without meeting any hostile Indians. See Barry, "Kansas before 1854," *KHQ*, xxx (Autumn, 1964), 405.

13 Parkman and his companions reached Bent's Fort on the afternoon of August 25. They had spent almost four days

—August 22–25—riding down from the Pueblo. See *Journals*, II, 474.

14 Compare Garrard's description of Bent's Fort in early November, 1846, in *Wah-To-Yah and the Taos Trail*, pp. 92–93:

The fort is a quadrangular structure, formed of *adobes*, or sun-dryed brick. It is thirty feet in hight [*sic*], and one hundred feet square; at the north-east corner, and its corresponding diagonal, are bastions of a hexagonal form in which are a few cannon. The fort walls serve as the back walls to the rooms, which front inward on a courtyard. In the center of the court is the "robe press;" and lying on the ground was a small brass cannon, burst in saluting General Kearney.

The roofs of the houses are made of poles, and a layer of mud, a foot or more thick, with a slight inclination, to run off the water. There was a billiard table, in a small house on top of the fort, where the *bourgeoise* [*sic*] and visitors amused themselves; and, in the clerk's office, contiguous, a first-rate spy-glass. . . . In the belfry, two eagles, of the American bald species, looked from their prison. . . .

Bent's Fort, or Fort William, was built in 1833–1834 by William (1809–1869) and Charles (1799–1847) Bent and Ceran St. Vrain (1802–1870), in partnership as Bent, St. Vrain & Company, at a site on the north bank of the Arkansas River seven miles east of modern La Junta, Colorado. Bent's Fort lay at the western end of the Mountain Route of the Santa Fe Trail and near the intersection of the Arkansas River and the Old Trapper's Trail from Taos to Fort Laramie. The post's Indian trade was based on the Southern Cheyennes and Arapahoes on the southern edge of the buffalo plains and the Kiowas and Comanches from the Canadian River; its own trappers hunted the beaver streams of the Parks and the central Rockies. Bent's Fort frequently had as many as 150 men in its employ and was probably the largest single trading establishment in the West.

Contemporary reports of Bent's Fort as well as more recent accounts of its history differ considerably in their descriptions of the post, but Mumey, *Old Forts and Trading Posts*, pp. 23–24, seems reliably precise when he suggests that the fort and its attached corral formed a trapezoid measuring approximately 137 feet on the east, 178 feet on the north, 180 feet on the west, and more than 200 feet on the south. A double gate opened into the area of the fort from the east wall, over which rose a sentry station with a belfry and the famous billiard room and bar. The larger eastern section of the post held the storerooms and living quarters, a blacksmith shop and a store, and a courtyard with a well; the considerably smaller western portion of the entire enclosure of the fort held the corral. The trading area of the fort was protected by walls 18 feet high, the height of the round towers, 27 feet in diameter, which stood at the northwest and southeast corners of the larger eastern trading area and enclosure. The corral was attached to the western wall of the trading area by a circumscribing wall of adobe bricks six feet high. Garrard's estimate of the size of Bent's Fort as "one hundred feet square" is doubtless his rough estimate of the interior dimensions of the eastern trading area of the post. Besides its bar and billiard table Bent's Fort had such other unlikely comforts as an icehouse and Charlotte, the black cook, famous for her pumpkin pies.

A number of contemporary pictures of Bent's Fort will be found collected in Mumey, *Old Forts and Trading Posts*. See also Frank McNitt, *The Indian Traders* (Norman, 1962), pp. 27–29; Lavender, *Bent's Fort*, pp. 123–271; and LeRoy R. Hafen "When Was Bent's Fort Built?" *Colorado Magazine*, XXXI (April, 1954), 105–119.

15 The Army of the West reached Bent's Fort in scattered detachments between July 21 and July 30. Kearny's troops left the post on August 1–2, more than three weeks before Parkman's arrival. See Barry, "Kansas before 1854," *KHQ*, xxx (Autumn, 1964), 361–363, 369–374; DeVoto, *Year of Decision*, pp. 263–274; Marcellus Ball Edwards, "Journal of Marcellus Ball Edwards, 1846–1847," in Ralph P. Bieber, ed. *Marching with the Army of the West 1846–1848* (Glendale, Calif., 1936), pp. 160–173; George Rutledge Gibson, *Journal of a Soldier under Kearny and Doniphan 1846–1847*, ed. Ralph P. Bieber (Glendale, Calif., 1935), pp. 121–170; and Frank S. Edwards, *A Campaign in New Mexico with Colonel Doniphan* (Philadelphia, 1847), pp. 17–44.

16 Garrard, *Wah-To-Yah and the Taos Trail*, pp. 126–127, identifies "Holt" as the storekeeper at Bent's Fort, a man noted for his generosity and good manners. Compare Parkman's notebook entry for August 26, his second day at the fort, in *Journals*, II, 474: "Holt and young [Marcellin] St. Vrain treated us very hospitably." William Bent was with Kearny's army on the march southward to Santa Fe, and Charles Bent, returning from St. Louis with a fast party on horseback, had arrived at his post on August 17 and had almost immediately thereafter pushed on in pursuit of the Army of the West. Parkman himself met Ceran St. Vrain and his caravan near Rock Creek in east-central Kansas on September 23–24. See *Journals*, II, 482. It was no doubt Marcellin St. Vrain, Ceran's younger brother, who gave Parkman additional information of Indian outrages along the Santa Fe Trail east of Bent's Fort, for the wagon train which the younger St. Vrain had led from the fort to Missouri in May and June had lost a man to the Pawnees on or about May 28, west of Pawnee Fork. See Barry, "Kansas before 1854," *KHQ*, xxx (Autumn, 1964), 358, 385–386; DeVoto, *Year of Decision*, pp. 272–273; F. A.

Wislizenus, *Memoir of a Tour to Northern Mexico, Connected with Col. Doniphan's Expedition, in 1846 and 1847* (Washington, 1848), pp. 8, 10; Harold H. Dunham, "Ceran St. Vrain," in LeRoy R. Hafen, ed. *The Mountain Men and the Fur Trade of the Far West* (Glendale, Calif., 1968) v, 297–316; and Harold H. Dunham, "Charles Bent," *ibid.*, ii (1965), 27–48.

17 The yager, or yaeger, was a government-issue carbine which fired a half-ounce ball.

18 Parkman met Munroe and Gurney on August 26. See *Journals*, ii, 474, and p. 307 of the present edition and note 1 for that page for Solomon P. Sublette's connection with Joseph R. Walker's "large band of horses." Munroe and Gurney must have been two of the six men in Walker's original party in California, before Sublette and his three companions joined up for the eastward journey to Fort Bridger. Walker, his herders, and the horses and mules reached Fort Bridger on July 4 and were still there on July 23–24 when Lienhard arrived at the post (more than two weeks after Sublette and his three companions had left for Fort Laramie). Alexander Barclay noted their appearance at the Hardscrabble fort on August 20 and their departure for the Pueblo two days later. Lieutenant Abert met Walker at Bent's Fort on August 26, the same day that Munroe and Gurney decided to travel eastward with Parkman and his friends and not more than a day or two after the arrival of the Walker party at Bent's Fort. Parkman mentions Abert as "Lt. Abbot, of the dragoons," in his notebook entry for August 25 in *Journals*, ii, 474. See also Morgan and Harris, eds. *Rocky Mountain Journals of W. M. Anderson*, p. 384; Lienhard, *St. Louis to Sutter's Fort*, pp. 94–95; Morgan, ed. *Overland in 1846*, i, 372–373; Mumey, *Old Forts and Trading Posts*, pp. 76–77; Abert, "Report," in Emory, *Notes of a Military Reconnoissance*, p. 420; and Bryant, *What I Saw in California*, p. 143.

19 "Ellis" cannot be positively identified, though he may have been the "mr. Ellis," of the California-bound Cooper party, whose cow ran off on June 7. See "The Diary of Nicholas Carriger," reprinted in Morgan, ed. *Overland in 1846*, I, 152. For Fort Bridger see note 14 for p. 111 of the present edition.

CHAPTER XXII

1 Parkman's notebooks provide a different chronology of events. The party reached Bent's Fort, as has been noted, on the afternoon of August 25 and spent the night of August 25–26 encamped a little distance from the post. Deslauriers moved the cart a few miles down the river on the morning of August 26, while Parkman dined at the fort and there met Munroe, Gurney, Ellis, and "Tête Rouge." Parkman spent the night of August 26–27 at a campsite six or seven miles east of Bent's Fort. See *Journals*, II, 474–475.

2 Called "Hodgman" in Parkman's notebook entry for August 26 in *Journals*, II, 474, Tête Rouge is probably to be identified as H. C. Hodgman, a private in "Artillery Company A (St. Louis)," otherwise known as Weightman's Battery, whose muster roll is printed in William E. Connelley, ed. *Doniphan's Expedition and the Conquest of New Mexico and California* (Topeka, 1907), pp. 374–377. Captain Richard H. Weightman's battery of light artillery marched from St. Louis on June 13 and arrived at Fort Leavenworth on June 18. It left Fort Leavenworth on June 30 in company with Kearny himself and his staff and reached Bent's Fort on July 28. Weightman's Battery included among its volunteers such distinguished Missourians as Sergeant William Clark Kennerly, the diarist, and Lieutenant Edmund F. Chouteau of the famous fur-trading family, as well as a noticeably rougher element repre-

sented by Antoine Clement, formerly Sir William Drummond Stewart's hunter. Company A suffered severely on the overland march to Bent's Fort; several of the artillerists were prostrated with mountain fever, and 60 of its "hundred fine cannon horses" foundered on the way. See Barry, "Kansas before 1854," *KHQ*, xxx (Autumn, 1964), 372–373; William Clark Kennerly, *Persimmon Hill: A Narrative of Old St. Louis and the Far West*, ed. Elizabeth Russell (Norman, 1948), pp. 184–188; Edwards, *Campaign with Colonel Doniphan*, pp. 17–44; and Valentine Mott Porter, "A History of Company 'A' of St. Louis," *Missouri Historical Society Collections*, ii (March, 1905), 1–10. Porter describes Hodgman's company as the *"corps d'elite"* of Doniphan's regiment.

3 These names do not appear in any of the muster rolls of Missouri volunteer companies contained in Connelley's reprint of John T. Hughes's *Doniphan's Expedition*, and it seems probable that they are simply Parkman's inventions.

4 Compare note 21 for p. 218 of the present edition for Abert's account of his bout of mountain fever during the march of the Army of the West. Even Kearny briefly succumbed to the disease, and Parkman's later patronizing references to the "disagreeable" aspects of Hodgman's illness do not come with a good grace from a man who had discussed his own ill health so often and so intensively in earlier chapters of *The Oregon Trail*.

5 Calomel, a strong cathartic, was very commonly used in the 1840's and later as a specific for undiagnosable ailments of the stomach and bowels, particularly diarrhea. One of the army physicians in 1846, Dr. George B. Sanderson, earned an enduring infamy in Mormon history as "Captain Death" because of the heapng doses of calomel he served out to the unwilling sufferers in the Mormon Battalion. See DeVoto, *Year of Decision*, pp. 325–327; and Golder, *March of the Mormon Battalion*, pp. 152, 163–164, 216.

Lieutenant Abert noted in his "Report," in Emory, *Notes of a Military Reconnoissance*, p. 421, that the resident physician at Bent's Fort was a Dr. Hempstead, but the man who dosed Hodgman so generously was probably Assistant Surgeon I. P. Vaughan, who had been left behind with some 60 or more sick troopers, infantrymen, and artillerists from both the First Dragoons and Doniphan's First Missouri Volunteers when Kearny's army moved south from Bent's Fort toward Taos and Santa Fe. John T. Hughes, *Doniphan's Expedition*, reprinted in Connelley, ed. *Doniphan's Expedition and the Conquest of New Mexico and California*, p. 245, remarked that "Whether Dr. Vaughan treated the men with that attention and kindness which the condition of the sick requires . . . was questioned by those who were under his direction," but Marcellus Ball Edwards, "Journal of Marcellus Ball Edwards," in Bieber, ed. *Marching with the Army of the West*, p. 172, noted that Vaughan had complained about being left at Bent's Fort with a totally inadequate supply of medicines for a large number of invalids.

6 Hodgman's "companion" cannot be identified, though a James W. Durrett is known to have died at Bent's Fort on August 12. See "Journal of Marcellus Ball Edwards," in Bieber, ed. *Marching with the Army of the West*, p. 172.

7 Kennerly, *Persimmon Hill*, p. 185, notes that each of his comrades in Weightman's Company A "furnished his own good horse, saddle, clothing, and everything but arms. Our uniform, similar to that of the regulars, included a blue jacket with red standing collar and trousers with red stripes. . . . We carried large knives in our belts, and some of us had revolvers." Kennerly's description of his outfit would seem to contradict Parkman's subsequent account of Hodgman as simply another backwoods conscript.

8 This scene no doubt explains Parkman's reference to Tête Rouge in *Journals*, II, 474, as "a very 'slow coach.'"

9 According to a number of contemporary accounts, the

acting quartermaster at Bent's Fort from August to December, 1846, was Second Lieutenant John O. Simpson of Hodgman's own Company A. Simpson also served as commander of the sick detachment and supply troops at the fort. See Barry, "Kansas before 1854," *KHQ*, xxx (Autumn, 1964), 410; " 'From California,' *Weekly Tribune*, New York, September 26, 1846," reprinted in Morgan, ed. *Overland in 1846*, II, 647; Mumey, *Old Forts and Trading Posts*, p. 83; and Connelley, ed. *Doniphan's Expedition and the Conquest of New Mexico and California*, p. 574.

10 This chapter concludes with the details of Parkman's departure from Bent's Fort on the afternoon of August 26. See *Journals*, II, 474–475.

CHAPTER XXIII

1 After the sentence "Shaw . . . buckskin" K supplies the following additional two sentences to conclude the paragraph: "If our cavalcade could have filed through the streets of our native city of Boston, it would have created a sensation not much in our favor in the breasts of its excellent though somewhat precise inhabitants. The charmed circle of good society would have been closed to us forever."

2 Parkman's description of Tête Rouge in this passage is very reminiscent of Irving's accounts of the vagaries and misadventures of "Tonish," or Antoine Deshetres, a halfbreed *engagé* with his party touring the West in 1832. See *A Tour on the Prairies*, ed. John Francis McDermott (Norman, 1956), especially Chapter XI.

3 In his letter to Remington of February 25, 1892, in *Letters*, II, 256, Parkman remarked of this illustration that "As for *Tête Rouge*, nothing could be better. The features may not be his—for the little vagabond hardly had any,—but attitude, dress and expression are given to the life."

4 Compare Parkman's notebook entry for August 27 in *Journals*, II, 475: "Afternoon, camped some eight miles below nooning place. Henry and Ellis, or rather H. alone, caught three stray dragoon horses, in very low condition, and bitten by the wolves. The worst of them was taken by Ellis, we retaining the others."

5 Parkman met William Magoffin, the younger brother of James and Samuel Magoffin, well-known Sante Fe traders, on August 29. See *Journals*, II, 475. William Magoffin reached Bent's Fort on September 2 with 25 wagons; he had been 35 days on the trail since leaving Independence in late July. See Barry, "Kansas before 1854," *KHQ*, xxx (Autumn, 1964), 389; Abert, "Report," in Emory, *Notes of a Military Reconnoissance*, p. 426; and Susan Shelby Magoffin, *Down the Santa Fe Trail and into Mexico: The Diary of Susan Shelby Magoffin*, ed. Stella M. Drumm (New Haven, 1926), p. 124.

6 William L. (or Z.) Swan, of Northampton, Massachusetts, had joined the same party of returning wagoners and invalids with which Robert M. Ewing and E. Hewett had left Bent's Fort on or about July 29. See p. 307 of the present edition and note 5 for that page. George R. Clark and the artist Albert S. Waugh, both of St. Louis, and one "Fay . . . an Italian" also belonged to this large and apparently slow-moving party. Compare this passage in *The Oregon Trail* with the account of Swan's death which Ewing and Hewett gave in an interview with the St. Louis *Daily Union* in mid-September and reprinted in Morgan, ed. *Overland in 1846*, II, 653:

When near Chouteau's Island, which lies in the Arkansas [near present Hartland, Kearny County, Kansas], Mr. Wm. L. Swan, a gentleman of the party, discovered that a horse belonging to him was missing. Taking a fine animal belonging to Mr. Geo. Clark, of this city, he mounted and went in pursuit. After returning on their trail some miles, he came up with the horse and returned with him to near where the main body was encamped. The shades of evening had closed in, and he had arrived within seventy yards of the camp, when the reports of two guns were heard. The persons in camp had no means of ascertaining the real state of affairs before morning, when Mr. Swan was found lying dead on his back, having been shot through the heart. The alarmed horse had apparently fled in the direction he had come, and there were the foot prints of four persons in pursuit. The horse eventually was taken by a wagon master, ninety miles distant, and returned to the party. Mr. Swan was buried in the plains. The persons who murdered him were believed to be Cheyennes, though they had attempted by signs to convey the impression that they were Camanches.

See also Barry, "Kansas before 1854," *KHQ*, xxx (Autumn, 1964), 391; and Waugh, *Travels in Search of the Elephant*, pp. xiii–xiv. Swan was killed on or about August 11.

7 Between the sentences "They . . . crowd" and "Many . . . plough" K–52 supply the following additional sentence: "I thought that the whole frontier might have been ransacked in vain to furnish men worse fitted to meet the dangers of the prairie."

Compare Parkman's description of this supply-train in his notebook entry for August 30 in *Journals*, II, 475: "Afternoon, met a train of government waggons. They say that the road ahead is dangerous. They themselves were alarmed, and had made a halt of some time, a few days back. Raw, smock-faced boys, and of a sickly appearance."

8 The Pawnee Fork, or Pawnee River, joins the Arkansas River at modern Larned, Kansas; the "Caches" were located five miles west of the present site of Dodge City, Kansas. See Margaret Long, *The Santa Fe Trail* (Denver, 1954), p. 267.

9 Compare Ewing and Hewett's account of this attack in note 6 for p. 308 of the present edition.

10 After the sentence "They . . . horses" K–52 supply the following additional sentence and two paragraphs:

This story of the Arapahoes therefore caused us some anxiety.

Just after leaving the government wagons, as Shaw and I were riding along a narrow passage between the river-bank and a rough hill that pressed close upon it, we heard Tête Rouge's voice behind us. 'Hallo!' he called out; 'I say, stop the cart just for a minute, will you?'

'What's the matter, Tête?' asked Shaw, as he came riding up to us with a grin of exultation. He had a bottle of molasses in one hand, and a large bundle of hides on the saddle before him, containing, as he triumphantly informed us, sugar, biscuits, coffee and rice. These supplies he had obtained by a stratagem on which he greatly plumed himself, and he was extremely vexed and astonished that we did not fall in with his views of the matter. He had told Coates, the master-wagoner, that the commissary at the fort had given him an order for sick-rations, directed to the master of any government train, which he might meet on the road. This order he had unfortunately lost, but he hoped that the rations would not be refused on that account, as he was suffering from coarse fare and needed them very much. As soon as he came to camp that night, Tête Rouge repaired to the box at the back of the cart, where Delorier used to keep his culinary apparatus, took possession of a saucepan, and after building a little fire of his own, set to work preparing a meal out of his ill-gotten booty. This done, he seized upon a tin plate and spoon, and sat down under the cart to regale himself. His preliminary repast did not at all prejudice his subsequent exertions at dinner; where, in spite of his miniature dimensions, he made a better figure than any of us. Indeed, about this time his appetite grew quite voracious. He began to thrive wonderfully. His small body visibly expanded, and his cheeks, which when we first took him were rather yellow and cadaverous, now dilated in a wonderful manner, and became ruddy in proportion. Tête Rouge, in short, began to appear like another man.

Compare these canceled paragraphs with part of Parkman's notebook entry for August 30 in *Journals*, II, 475: "By a ready lie Hodgman procured 'sick rations' from Coates, the master driver." I have been unable to identify Coates.

11 Parkman met the Arapaho village on August 31. See *Journals*, II, 475–476. The Arapahoes, an Algonquin tribe, separated into northern and southern branches at the time of their arrival on the western plains soon after 1800. The Northern Arapahoes lived on the edge of the mountains near the headwaters of the North Platte River; the Southern Arapahoes had been moving up the valley of the Arkansas River for several decades before 1846. While they waged almost constant warfare against the Shoshonis, Utes, and Pawnees, the Southern Arapahoes were generally on good terms with white men, and Parkman probably exaggerates the dangers of meeting them, especially when, as in the present instance, the tribe was out on a communal buffalo hunt. See Hodge, ed. *Handbook of American Indians*, I, 72–74.

12 Compare part of Parkman's notebook entry for August 31 in *Journals*, II, 475: "This afternoon, saw the Arapaho village on the other side of the river. Hodgman, thinking the whole party were going, was clamorous for my pistols, and wished to put on his cap and uniform coat, to strike terror."

13 I have been unable to discover any other reference to Kearny's encounter with the Arapahoes in July, 1846, though some members of the tribe were certainly at Bent's Fort while Kearny was there with the Army of the West. See Gibson, *Journal of a Soldier*, pp. 167–168.

14 Since Parkman's notebook entries from the date of his

departure from Bent's Fort are very vague and general in their references to specific topographical features, the location of the Arapaho village remains in doubt, though an educated guess would place it not far from the present Colorado-Kansas border, perhaps near modern Granada, Colorado.

15 "Maxwell, the trader who has been most among" the Arapahoes, may be identified as Lucien B. Maxwell (1818–1875), whom Frémont, *Report*, pp. 28, 31, met in 1842 and described as a trader among the tribe. Maxwell, as Frémont noted, had a fair command of the Arapaho language, which he had probably learned during 1840–1841 when he traded for Bent, St. Vrain & Company at Fort St. Vrain. He was born in Kaskaskia, Illinois, the son of Hugh B. and Marie Odille Menard Maxwell and a grandson of Pierre Menard, the first lieutenant governor of the state. Maxwell first went to Taos and Santa Fe in the 1830's; his early adventures in New Mexico marked the beginning of his lifelong friendship with Kit Carson, with whom he served as a hunter on Frémont's First Expedition. He joined Carson again on Frémont's Third Expedition in 1845–1846 and served the Pathfinder faithfully during the stormy days of the Bear Flag Republic in California in 1846. Maxwell later became a large landowner in New Mexico but passed his last years in obscurity and near poverty. See *DAB, s.v.* "Maxwell, Lucien B."

16 James Mooney notes in Hodge, ed. *Handbook of American Indians*, ii, 567–568, that sign language, the *lingua franca* of most of the trans-Mississippi tribes, represented "a highly developed system of gesture communication which, for all ordinary purposes, hardly fell short of the perfection of a spoken language," even though its nonverbal symbolism had scarcely advanced beyond pantomimic conventions. Mooney suggests that there were minor variants of sign symbols between tribes but that "even with

these slight dissimilarities a Sioux or a Blackfoot from the Upper Missouri has no difficulty in communicating with a visiting Kiowa or Comanche from the Texas border on any subject from the negotiating of a treaty to the recital of a mythic story or the telling of a hunting incident." Sign language among the Indians, Mooney asserts, combined comprehensiveness of meaning with rapidity and economy of gesture:

Thus the sign for *man* is made by throwing out the hand, back outward, with index finger extended upward, apparently having reference to an old root word in many Indian languages which defines *man* as the erect animal. *Woman* is indicated by a sweeping downward movement of the hand at the side of the head, with fingers extended toward the hair to denote long flowing hair or the combing of flowing locks. A *white man* is distinguished as the hat wearer, either by drawing the index finger across the forehead or by clasping the forehead with outstretched thumb and index finger. For *Indian* the speaker rubs the back of his left hand, or, perhaps, his cheek, with the palm of the right to indicate a person whose skin is of the same color. . . . A *tipi* is shown by bringing both index fingers together like an inverted V to indicate the conical shape and the crossing of the poles. An ordinary house would be distinguished by adding the sign for white man. The *buffalo,* and in later days a *cow,* is indicated by crooking the index finger at the side of the head to resemble a horn. A *dog* is indicated by drawing the hand, with first and second fingers spread apart, across in front of the body, typifying the old time travois dragged by the animal when used as a beast of burden.

Mooney concludes his article by demonstrating how easily and comprehensively sign language might be used to form complete sentences.

17 Compare Parkman's notebook description of this scene in *Journals,* ii, 476:

Village all in a stench with meat. Squaws busy with skins. Sat before one of the chief lodges, holding our horses fast, and the curious crowd soon gathered around. Bad faces—savage and sinister. In complexion form, size, and feature inferior to the Sioux. Their faces formed a complete wall around us. Distributed a few presents—traded a shield, trail-ropes, etc.—took out some awls, and had the women called to receive them. They came screaming with delight—very ugly and dirty, like the men. The whole village, lodges and all, were in keeping with the inhabitants.

Parkman's description of the Arapahoes in his notebooks and in the present passage in *The Oregon Trail* is corroborated by Talbot, *Journals of Theodore Talbot*, p. 25, who noted that "The Arapahoe nation is said to reckon 325 Lodges. They are generally of dark complexion, have a broad and rather flat face, large mouth and sunken eye. The woman of low stature and mostly ugly." On the other hand, Ruxton, *Adventures in the Rocky Mountains*, reprinted in *Ruxton of the Rockies*, p. 232, remarked that "Not one of this Arapahó band but could have sat as a model for an Apollo"—a conventional comparison recalling Parkman's description of the Mad Wolf on p. 165 of the present edition and somewhat qualifying Parkman's pointed contrast between the handsome Oglalas and the squalid Arapahoes.

18 I am indebted to Professor A. W. Schorger of the University of Wisconsin Department of Wildlife Ecology for an identification of this grass as switchgrass (*Panicum*), usually found in undisturbed sandy soil in river valleys.

19 Compare Parkman's description of this scene in *Journals*, ii, 476: "Near sunset, rode through the long grass and across the Arkansas to camp, where a few Inds. had arrived before us. Hodgman was engaged in trading a robe with them, and behaved so ridiculously, or rather insanely, that he amused us all. Jim [Gurney] made great fun of him."

20 Compare Parkman's account of this alarm in his notebook entry for August 31 in *Journals*, II, 476:

> At night the wolves set up a most mournful and discordant howling which lasted all night. There was little sleep in camp —the men were anxious for the horses—H. [Henry?] was sick —Hodgman was fidgetty and restless—and I was kept awake by the burning pain of my poison—the horses, too, tramped incessantly through the camp. Hodgman woke me out of a nap with a story that he had seen an Ind. in a white robe drive off three horses, which were just out of sight. Went out to see, and on the way he talked so vaguely and strangely that I perceived the fever had not left his brain. It was, I suppose, nothing but his fright.

21 After the sentence "As . . . coming" K supplies the following additional sentence to conclude the paragraph: "Tête Rouge's valor was not more conspicuous than his other martial qualities, and the story he told us was probably nothing more than an offspring of his imagination, excited no doubt by the remnants of fever which still lingered in his brain."

The K version of this chapter contains material which appears in the next chapter of the present edition at the beginning of the second new paragraph on p. 359 ("After . . . night") and which continues through the last paragraph on p. 366 of this text.

Chapter XXIV

1 The first four paragraphs of this chapter (from p. 356 through the end of the first new paragraph on p. 359, "Kit . . . Chatillon") first appeared in the K version of Chapter XXV, "The Buffalo Camp." Chapter XXIV is, in fact, composed of fragments of Chapters XXIII and XXV in their K versions and subsequently rearranged for 49.

2 Between the sentences "The chase . . . enough" and "A practised . . . tumult" K–52 supply the following additional three sentences:

Indeed, of all American wild sports this is the wildest. Once among the buffalo, the hunter, unless long use has made him familiar with the situation, dashes forward in utter recklessness and self-abandonment. He thinks of nothing, cares for nothing but the game; his mind is stimulated to the highest pitch, yet intensely concentrated on one object. In the midst of the flying herd, where the uproar and the dust are thickest, it never wavers for a moment; he drops the rein and abandons his horse to his furious career; he levels his gun, the report sounds faint amid the thunder of the buffalo; and when his wounded enemy leaps in vain fury upon him, his heart thrills with a feeling like the fierce delight of the battlefield.

3 Inman, *Old Santa Fé Trail*, p. 208, mentions that Kit Carson once killed five bulls from horseback with only four bullets. The famous scout paused only long enough in the chase to cut out the ball from one of his victims and then fired it into another galloping buffalo.

4 The sentence "In fact . . . them" was added in 72.

5 Stansbury, *Expedition to the Great Salt Lake*, pp. 249–250, describes an accident during a buffalo chase in which Lieutenant Gunnison shot his own horse through the neck and killed her; he himself was thrown and seriously injured. Similar accounts are very numerous in the chronicles of western adventure and exploration.

6 Compare Gregg, *Commerce of the Prairies*, in Thwaites, ed. *Early Western Travels*, xx, 269, on "still hunting" or "approaching":

If the hunter succeed in "bringing down" his first shot, he may frequently kill several out of the same herd; for, should the game neither see nor smell him, they may hear the rifle-cracks, and witness their companions fall one after another, without heeding, except to raise their heads, and perhaps start a little at each report. They would seem to fancy that the fallen are only lying down to rest, and they are loth to leave them. On one occasion, upon the Cimarron river, I saw some ten or a dozen buffaloes lying upon a few acres of ground, all of which had been shot from the same herd by a couple of our hunters. Had not the gang been frightened by the approaching caravan, perhaps a dozen more of them might have fallen.

Compare also Parkman's similar account of Chatillon's "still hunting" on pp. 375–376 of the present edition.

7 Christopher (Kit) Carson (1809–1868) was born in Kentucky and passed his earliest years in Howard County, Missouri. Apprenticed to a saddler, he ran off in 1826 to join a caravan bound for Santa Fe and spent the next several years in New Mexico as a teamster and cook before signing on one of Ewing Young's trapping parties bound west of the Rio Grande.

In the summer of 1831 he joined Thomas Fitzpatrick and the Rocky Mountain Fur Company, and for a number of years thereafter he was one of the principal figures in the mountain fur trade; various garbled accounts of his adventures (including his celebrated duel with "bully Shunar" at the rendezvous of 1835) had already gained currency in the East by the end of the 1830's. In 1840 Carson joined Bent, St. Vrain & Company and served as a hunter for Bent's Fort until the spring of 1842, when for the first time since 1826 he made a visit to Missouri to place his daughter (by an Arapaho squaw) with his relatives.

While in the East he fell in with Frémont, then setting out on his First Expedition, and guided the Pathfinder to South Pass and back to Fort Laramie. He also accompanied Frémont on the Second Expedition to Oregon and California in 1843–1844; Parkman might have heard of Carson's skill in buffalo-running from Henry Chatillon or from some of the *engagés* at Bent's Fort, but his own copy of Frémont's *Report* could have given him a number of anecdotes of Carson's skill, for it was Frémont above all who made Carson a nationwide symbol of heroic wilderness adventure.

Carson was a member of Frémont's Third Expedition to California in 1845–1846; after good service to the Bear Flag Republic, he left Los Angeles on September 15, 1846, with Frémont's dispatches for Washington. Traveling eastward, he met Kearny on the Rio Grande, who ordered him to turn over his messages to Tom Fitzpatrick and to return to California as Kearny's guide. After the skirmish at San Pascual, Carson crept through Mexican lines to seek reinforcements at San Diego—one of his most daring exploits. After the Mexican War, he spent almost all his later years in New Mexico, fighting Indians and Confederate invaders during the Civil War and rising at last to a colonelcy and a brevet rank of brigadier general of volunteers.

See Morgan and Harris, eds. *Rocky Mountain Journals of W. M. Anderson*, pp. 274–281; Edwin L. Sabin, *Kit Carson Days* (Chicago, 1914), pp. 32–503 *passim*; De-Voto, *Across the Wide Missouri*, pp. 38–439 *passim*; and Christopher Carson, *Kit Carson's Autobiography*, ed. Milo M. Quaife (Chicago, 1935). In his *Autobiography* Carson makes no particular mention of his skill in buffalo-running.

8 Parkman first began to meet the buffalo on September 1. See *Journals*, II, 476, in which Parkman describes the plains before them as "literally black with buffalo."

9 Parkman is again making the usual distinction between a musket or "gun" and his own rifled weapon.

10 A "squib" is a small firecracker.

11 Compare De Smet, *Letters and Sketches*, in Thwaites, ed. *Early Western Travels*, XXVII, 265: "A young American

had the imprudence to swim over a river and pursue a wounded buffalo with no other weapon but his knife."

12 Compare Parkman's account of this chase in *The Oregon Trail* with part of his notebook entry for September 1 in *Journals*, ii, 476–477:

> The mare brought me upon the rear of a large herd. In the clouds of dust I could scarcely see a yard, and dashed on almost blind, amidst the trampling of the fugitives. Their rumps became gradually visible, as they shouldered along, but I could not urge the mare amongst them. Suddenly down went buffalo after buffalo, in dust and confusion, into an invisible ravine some dozen feet deep, and down in the midst of them plunged the mare. I was almost thrown, but she scrambled up the opposite side. As the dust cleared, I fired—the wounded beast soon dropped behind—I plied him with shot after shot, and killed—not a cow—but a yearling bull!

13 After the sentence "The night . . . coast" K supplies the following additional sentence to conclude the paragraph: "There were two wearied men in camp that night, whose dreamless sleep the thunder of an avalanche would not have disturbed."

I consider Parkman's account of the buffalo chase in this and the following chapter of *The Oregon Trail* unsurpassed in the literature of western travel and adventure.

Chapter xxv

1 Kennerly, *Persimmon Hill*, p. 157, noted that white, or albino, buffalo were exceedingly rare and were much prized as trophies of the chase; the Indians regarded them as "great medicine."

2 Parkman and his companions discovered the "old bull stuck in a quagmire" on the morning of September 2. See *Journals*, ii, 477.

3 Precisely where this camp was located does not appear from Parkman's notebooks, although it seems safe to assume that it was located well upriver from the Middle Cimarron Crossing of the Arkansas River between modern Cimarron and Ingalls, Kansas. On September 2 Parkman met Captain Giddings' company of Price's Second Regiment of Missouri Mounted Volunteers and Captain Morin's "Extra Battalion" company, whom he described as "two companies of Munroe and Platte City mounted volunteers." See *Journals*, ii, 477; and Barry, "Kansas before 1854," *KHQ*, xxx (Autumn, 1964), 386. Giddings' and Morin's companies were the only parts of the reinforcements under Colonel Sterling Price's command to travel to New Mexico by way of the Mountain Route of the Santa Fe Trail and Bent's Fort; the rest of Price's regiment and of Willcock's "Extra Battalion" marched to Santa Fe down the Desert Route.

In any case, this camp was located well to the westward of the Santa Fe traders' usual hunting grounds. David Meriwether, *My Life in the Mountains and on the Plains*, ed. Robert A. Griffen (Norman, 1965), pp. 180–181, notes that "On reaching the Big Bend of the Arkansas River, where the road leaves that stream for the Missouri [near modern Great Bend, Kansas] . . . all Mexican trains were in the habit of camping before leaving the buffalo regions, killing and curing sufficient meat to last them to the Missouri River and back to the Arkansas again, and that this would require a detention of about a week."

4 The sentence "An . . . ugliness" replaces the following four sentences in *K*:

It may be that after the fashion of the day some one of our New-England reformers may incline to denounce such sport as repugnant to his notions of humanity. I need only beg him, if he knows how to ride and use a gun, to mount a good horse and place himself within sight of a band of buffalo. If he has red blood in his veins he will inevitably forget his principles and attack them no less eagerly than if they were human antagonists who had opposed his measures or called in question the truth of his theories; and when he has slain his shaggy enemy and has leisure to contemplate him, he will take credit to himself for having rid the earth of a hideous and brutish monster. Except an elephant, I have seen no animal that can surpass a buffalo bull in size and strength, and the world may be searched in vain to find any thing of a more ugly and ferocious aspect.

This passage is further reduced in 49–52: "Except an elephant, I have seen no animal that can surpass a buffalo bull in size and strength, and the world may be searched in vain to find any thing of a more ugly and ferocious aspect."

5 Compare the sentence "At . . . vanishes" with its *K*–52 form: "At first sight of him every feeling of sympathy vanishes; no man who has not experienced it, can understand with what keen relish one inflicts his death wound, with what profound contentment of mind [*K*: spirit] he [*K*: one] beholds him [*K*: the gigantic savage] fall.

6 Compare Anderson, *Rocky Mountain Journals of W. M. Anderson*, p. 178, on the declining numbers of the buffalo as early as 1834:

This evening a conversation was had upon the subject of the diminution of the buffaloe, which several of the oldest mountaineers pronounced to be very considerable. This lead to an inquirey as to the number of robes traded of the Indian Tribes by the American Fur Company, which seems to be enormous. Mr. Fontanelle [Lucien Fontenelle (1800–1840), famous brigade leader] lately of said company told me that three years ago there was traded from the Sioux [alone?] fifty thousand robes. From this an idea, of the immense numbers of these animals which are yearly destroyed, may be formed. The uninformed too are to be taught, that for the purposes of trade, & for no other purpose, save for the making of parflèches [i.e., rawhides?], are the bulls stripped of their hides. The season too of killing them is confined to about 2 months of winter; I mean for the making robes—for clothing, lodge making & eating they are destroyed throughout the year. In four days our hunter alone has butchered fourteen cows.

A great deal of other contemporary evidence—and the near extinction of the buffalo in the 1870's—shows how wrong Parkman was when he thought that thousands of bulls "might be slaughtered without causing any detriment to the species. . . ." For other early and representative accounts of the needless destruction of the buffalo herds and their rapidly decreasing numbers, see Gregg, *Commerce of the Prairies*, in Thwaites, ed. *Early Western Travels*, xx, 120; and Prince Maximilian, *Travels in North America*, in Thwaites, ed. *Early Western Travels*, xxiv, 130.

7 Compare Anderson's description of a bull in *Rocky Mountain Journals of W. M. Anderson*, p. 107: "Nothing can be more revolting, more terrific, than a front view of an old bull buffalo. His huge hump, covered with long wool, rising eighteen or twenty inches above his spine; a dense mat of black hair, padding a bullet-proof head; a dirty dunkard [*sic*] beard, almost sweeping the ground, and his thick, dark horns and sparkling eyes, give him, altogether, the appearance and expression of some four-legged devil. . . ."

8 After the sentence "Then . . . struggle" *K* supplies the following additional two sentences to conclude the paragraph: "The hunter steps forward and looks upon the inanimate pile of flesh and bones, hides, tendons and matted hair. At the slightest touch of his forefinger those gigantic limbs were paralyzed, that mountain of flesh reeled and fell prostrate."

Compare Parkman's description of the dying buffalo in this passage with Ruxton's somewhat more circumstantial account of a similar scene in *Adventures in the Rocky Mountains*, reprinted in *Ruxton of the Rockies*, p. 251:

No animal requires so much killing as a buffalo. Unless shot through the lungs or spine, they invariably escape, and, even when thus mortally wounded, or even struck through the very heart, they will frequently run a considerable distance before falling to the ground, particularly if they see the hunter after the wound is given. If, however, he keeps himself concealed after firing, the animal will remain still, if it does not immediately fall. It is a most painful sight to witness the dying struggles of the huge beast. The buffalo invariably evinces the greatest repugnance to lie down when mortally wounded, apparently conscious that, when once touching mother earth, there is no hope left him. A bull, shot through the heart or lungs, with blood streaming from his mouth, and protruding tongue, his eyes rolling, bloodshot, and glazed with death, braces himself on his legs, swaying from side to side, stamps impatiently at his growing weakness, or lifts his rugged and matted head and helplessly bellows out his conscious impotence. To the last, however, he endeavours to stand upright, and plants his limbs farther apart, but to no purpose. As the body rolls like a ship at sea, his head slowly turns from side to side, looking about, as it were, for the unseen and treacherous enemy who has brought him, the lord of the plains, to such a pass. Gouts of purple blood spurt from his mouth and nostrils, and gradually the failing limbs refuse longer to support the ponderous carcase [*sic*]; more heavily rolls the body from side to side, until suddenly, for a brief instant, it becomes rigid and still; a convulsive tremor seizes it, and, with a low, sobbing gasp, the huge animal falls over on his side, the limbs extended stark and stiff, and the mountain of flesh without life or motion.

9 Compare part of Parkman's notebook entry for September 3 in *Journals*, II, 477: "Shot an old bull in the back, as he

came up from the river—his death-agonies were terrific. Shot another in the afternoon."

10 Between the sentences "Henry . . . element" and "Quite . . . rifle" K supplies the following additional sentence: "Nelson on the deck of the 'Victory,' Bonaparte at the head of his army, hardly felt a prouder sense of mastery than he."

This sentence received slight revision in 49–52: "Nelson, on the deck of the 'Victory,' hardly felt a prouder sense of mastery than he."

11 Compare De Smet, *Letters and Sketches*, in Thwaites, ed. *Early Western Travels*, xxvii, 266: "The report of the gun, and the noise made by the fall of the wounded buffalo, astound, but do not drive away the rest. In the meantime, the hunter re-loads his gun, and shoots again, repeating the maneuvre, till five or six, and sometime more buffalos have fallen, before he finds it necessary to abandon his place of concealment."

12 In his descriptions of Tête Rouge and Henry Chatillon in this passage, Parkman is again and all too obviously and mechanically using his favorite rhetorical patterns of juxtaposition and contrast to represent the vices of civilization in the dissipated Hodgman and the manly vigor of the wilderness in Chatillon.

13 Compare part of Parkman's notebook entry for September 3 in *Journals*, ii, 477–478: "Very hot in the day, but cloudy at night. Put up the tent, but about 9 o'clock a furious tornado came up, with driving rain; down went the tent upon us all; we held it up as we could, and got completely drenched, bedding and all. Hodgman kept on singing and rattling away, but the predicament was uncomfortable enough."

14 For this quotation see *King Lear* iii.iv.2.

15 That is, timber wolves and coyotes.

16 Both the turkey buzzard, or turkey vulture (*Cathartes*

aura), and the black vulture (*Coragyps atratus*) have black plumage and bald heads; the slightly larger turkey vulture and the heavier black vulture are renowned scavengers.

17 Parkman and his companions left "the buffalo camp" on the morning of September 6. See *Journals*, II, 478.

CHAPTER XXVI

1 The Mountain Route of the Santa Fe Trail by way of Bent's Fort was a better road for a mass of raw and comparatively undisciplined troops than "the old trail of the Cimarron," since it had better water and more abundant grass than did the Desert Route from the Arkansas crossings (or the Cimarron crossings) southwestward to Santa Fe. The longer march to Bent's Fort made better soldiers of the green recruits in Doniphan's First Missouri; the fort itself gave them a brief opportunity to rest and refit before they marched on Taos and Santa Fe.

2 Parkman had already met two companies of horsemen from Colonel Sterling Price's Second Regiment of Missouri Mounted Volunteers and the "extra" battalion on September 2; see p. 370 of the present edition and note 3 for that page. On September 6 or 8 (Parkman's notebooks are not clear about the exact date), he encountered two more companies of Price's regiment, "a set of undisciplined ragamuffins," somewhere on the Arkansas River east of modern Ingalls, Kansas.

The Second Missouri was recruited largely from the frontier counties of the state and was inferior in discipline, if not in fighting ability, to Doniphan's First Missouri, which had been part of Kearny's Army of the West. Price (1809–1867), later to attain high rank in the Confederate Army, marched out of Fort Leavenworth on or about August 23; he was then well behind most of his regiment, which had been leaving the fort in scattered detachments since August 11. On September 10, however, he had caught up with the head of his command at a point "12 miles West of the crossing [Middle Cimarron Crossing, between Cimarron and Ingalls, Kansas] of the Arkansas."

By October 12 most of Price's regiment had reached Santa Fe, where, drunken and brawling, they did much to ruin the good impression left on the New Mexicans by Kearny and Doniphan. As Ruxton notes in *Adventures in the Rocky Mountains,* reprinted in *Ruxton of the Rockies,* p. 188, Price's troops were largely responsible for exciting "the most bitter feeling and most determined hostility . . . against the Americans, who certainly in Santa Fé and elsewhere have not been very anxious to conciliate the people, but by their bullying and overbearing demeanour towards them, have in a great measure been the cause of this hatred, which shortly after broke out in an organized rising of the northern part of the province, and occasioned great loss of life to both parties." The "organized rising" was the Taos Revolt of January 19, 1847, in which Charles Bent, the first United States civil governor of New Mexico, and other Americans were butchered by a mob of New Mexicans and Pueblo Indians. These deaths at Taos and others elsewhere in the territory were avenged by Price and Ceran St. Vrain at the battle of La Cañada on January 24 and by the destruction of the Pueblo of Taos on February 4.

See Barry, "Kansas before 1854," *KHQ,* xxx (Autumn, 1964), 382–384, 387–388; Garrard, *Wah-To-Yah and the Taos Trail,* pp. 233–258; Hughes, *Doniphan's Expedition,* reprinted in Connelley, ed. *Doniphan's Expedition and the Conquest of New Mexico and California,* pp. 40–45, 256–260; DeVoto, *Across the Wide Missouri,* pp. 321–408 *passim;* and Dunham, "Charles Bent," in Hafen, ed. *Mountain Men and the Fur Trade,* ii, 46–48.

3 Parkman's opinion of these "excellent irregular troops" might be more easily justified if the context made it clear that he was definitely referring to Doniphan's regiment rather than to Price's.

4 Between the sentences "Their . . . themselves" and "Doniphan's . . . government" K–52 supply the following additional sentence: "Without discipline or a spirit of subordination, they knew how to keep their ranks and act as one man."

5 Alexander W. Doniphan (1808–1887), one of the rare geniuses in American military history, was born in Kentucky. By 1830 he had moved to Missouri and been admitted to the bar in Lexington. In 1833 he settled in Liberty, Missouri, then a frontier town; in 1836 and 1840 he represented Clay County in the state legislature. In 1838, as the commander of a brigade of state militia, Doniphan refused obedience to Governor Lillburn Boggs's "Extermination Order" against Joseph Smith and other Mormon leaders at Far West, Missouri, and thus saved their lives; he had also protected Smith and the Mormons on several earlier occasions.

   In May, 1846, Doniphan enlisted as a private in a company of volunteers raised in Clay County; when the First Missouri began to organize at Fort Leavenworth in June he was elected colonel of the regiment. The First Regiment of Missouri Mounted Volunteers was composed of eight companies of light cavalry and numbered some 830 men; another mounted company, the Laclede Rangers of St. Louis, was attached to Kearny's First Dragoons, and there were two other companies of volunteer infantry (some 145 men) and two light artillery companies forming a battalion of 232 men—one of whom was Tête Rouge. These 13 companies of volunteers and about 430 troopers of the First Dragoons formed Kearny's Army of the West. Hughes, *Doniphan's Expedition*, reprinted in

Connelley, ed. *Doniphan's Expedition and the Conquest of New Mexico and California*, pp. 152–153, who marched out of Fort Leavenworth with Doniphan's regiment, "the elite of Missouri," later recalled:

"The Army of the West," was, perhaps, composed of as fine material as any other body of troops in the field. The volunteer corps consisted almost entirely of the young men of the country; generally of the very first families of the State. All parties were united in one common cause for the vindication of the national honor. Every calling and profession contributed its share. There might be seen under arms, in the ranks, the lawyer, the doctor, the professor, the student, the legislator, the farmer, the mechanic, and artisans of every description, all united as a band of brothers to defend the rights and honor of their country; to redress her wrongs and avenge her insults. . . . Their chivalry failed them not.

Gibson, *Journal of a Soldier*, p. 323, noted, however, that Doniphan's First Missouri "was composed of men of a restless and roving disposition, and the little discipline which prevailed was totally insufficient to prevent rioting and dissipation. . . ."

The Army of the West left Fort Leavenworth in detachments between June 22 and June 30; they were reunited at Bent's Fort at the end of July and almost immediately thereafter marched on Santa Fe, which they captured, without firing a shot, on August 13. While Kearny and most of the Dragoons turned westward toward California, the First Missouri stayed in New Mexico until December, establishing an American presence in the conquest and pacifying the Navahoes. Ordered south to link up with the army of General John Wool marching on Chihuahua, the 850 men of Doniphan's reinforced command fought the battle of El Brazito on Christmas Day and captured El Paso on December 27. Learning at last that Wool had not advanced on Chihuahua, Doniphan nevertheless decided to continue his southward march and left El Paso on February 8, 1847, fought the battle of Sacramento, just outside Chihuahua, on February 28, and occupied the city on March 1–2.

On April 25–28 Doniphan's column turned eastward from Chihuahua and arrived at Taylor's camp near Monterrey on May 26. When they stopped at Reynosa on the Gulf of Mexico to wait for steamers to carry them to New Orleans, they had reached the end of more than 3,500 miles of prairies, deserts, and mountains. They burned their saddles on the beach and went home to Missouri. As Hughes said, "Their chivalry failed them not."

See Connelley, ed. *Doniphan's Expedition and the Conquest of New Mexico and California*, pp. 3–524 *passim*, with special reference to Hughes, *Doniphan's Expedition*; Edwards, *Campaign with Colonel Doniphan*, pp. 18–165; "Journal of Marcellus Ball Edwards," in Bieber, ed. *Marching with the Army of the West*, pp. 108–280 *passim*; "Journal of Abraham Robinson Johnston, 1846," ibid., pp. 75–104 *passim*; Gibson, *Journal of a Soldier*, pp. 111–363 *passim*; DeVoto, *Year of Decision*, pp. 83–407 *passim*; and Barry, "Kansas before 1854," *KHQ*, xxx (Autumn, 1964), 361–363.

6 I have been unable to identify the source of this quotation, but it seems likely that Parkman is here paraphrasing a newspaper account of Doniphan's meeting with Taylor at the camp near Monterrey in late May, 1847.

7 As I have tried to show, and as almost all contemporary and more recent accounts agree, Parkman's offhand judgment of Doniphan's military ability *and* his apparent slur at the defects of Doniphan's "character" are both not to be taken seriously.

8 DeVoto, *Year of Decision*, pp. 408–409, estimates that at the battle of Sacramento Doniphan's command of "924

effectives" faced 3,000 regular Mexican troops and almost 1,000 peons armed mostly with machetes. Doniphan had been reinforced before the battle by Weightman's Battery and a makeshift battalion of Santa Fe traders and teamsters.

9 Hughes, *Doniphan's Expedition*, reprinted in Connelley, ed. *Doniphan's Expedition and the Conquest of New Mexico and California*, p. 407 n., recalled that, at the battle of Sacramento, "An eagle sometimes soaring aloft and sometimes swooping down amongst the fluttering [American] banners, followed along the lines all day, and seemed to herald the news of victory. The men regarded the omen as good."

10 The "drunken officer" was Lieutenant James A. De Courcy, Doniphan's adjutant. Hughes, *Doniphan's Expedition*, reprinted in Connelley, ed. *Doniphan's Expedition and the Conquest of New Mexico and California*, p. 410, thought that the charge of one of Doniphan's columns "was halted for a moment under a heavy cross-fire from the enemy, by the adjutant's misunderstanding the order," but Connelley notes that "The charge was stopped by De Courcy, who, it was believed, was drunk at the time."

11 Hughes, *Doniphan's Expedition*, in Connelley, ed. *Doniphan's Expedition and the Conquest of New Mexico and California*, pp. 410–411, noted that Captain John W. Reid, "either not hearing or disregarding the adjutant's order to halt, leading the way, waved his sword, and rising in his stirrups, exclaimed, '*will my men follow me?*' "

12 The "wagon laden with cords" is well attested in a number of accounts of the battle of Sacramento, although Kennerly, *Persimmon Hill*, p. 199, "learned that the *vaqueros* had been ready for us with their lariats, expecting to rope and drag us to death if firearms failed."

13 Parkman met these "St. Louis county" companies on September 8. See *Journals*, II, 478. They may have been Cap-

tain John C. Dent's St. Louis company and Captain
Thomas M. Horine's Ste. Genevieve company. See Barry,
"Kansas before 1854," *KHQ*, xxx (Autumn, 1964), 383,
387.

14 After the sentence "At . . . again" K–52 supply the following additional paragraph:

> No one can deny the intrepid bravery of these men, their
> intelligence and the bold frankness of their character, free
> from all that is mean and sordid. Yet for the moment the
> extreme roughness of their manners, half inclines one to forget
> their heroic qualities. Most of them seem without the least
> perception of delicacy or propriety, though among them indi-
> viduals may be found in whose manners there is a plain
> courtesy, while their features bespeak a gallant spirit equal to
> any enterprise.

> After the sentence "Most . . . enterprise" in the can-
> celed passage above, K supplies the following additional
> sentence to conclude the paragraph: "The bravery of the
> Missourians is not exclusively their own: the whole Ameri-
> can nation are as fearless as they; but in roughness of
> bearing and fierce impetuousity [*sic*] of spirit they may
> bear away the palm from almost any rival."

15 Compare part of Parkman's notebook entry for September
6(?) in *Journals*, II, 478: "I shot some bulls back upon
the prairie"—presumably the animals "too ugly to live."

16 This episode is not described in Parkman's notebooks.

17 After the sentence "The buffalo . . . left" K–52 supply the
following additional six paragraphs:

> 'Do you see them buffalo?' said Ellis, 'now I'll bet any man
> I'll go and kill one with my yager."
> And leaving his horse to follow on with the party, he strode
> up the hill after them. Henry looked at us with his peculiar
> humorous expression, and proposed that we should follow Ellis
> to see how he would kill a fat cow. As soon as he was out of

sight we rode up the hill after him, and waited behind a little ridge till we heard the report of the unfailing yager. Mounting to the top, we saw Ellis clutching his favorite weapon with both hands, and staring after the buffalo, who one and all were galloping off at full speed. As we descended the hill we saw the party straggling along the trail below. When we joined them, another scene of amateur hunting awaited us. I forgot to say that when we met the volunteers, Tête Rouge had obtained a horse from one of them, in exchange for his mule, whom he feared and detested. This horse he christened James. James, though not worth so much as the mule, was a large and strong animal. Tête Rouge was very proud of his new acquisition, and suddenly became ambitious to run a buffalo with him. At his request, I lent him my pistols, though not without great mis-givings, since when Tête Rouge hunted buffalo the pursuer was in more danger than the pursued. He hung the holsters at his saddle-bow; and now as we passed along, a band of bulls left their grazing in the meadow, and galloped in a long file across the trail in front.

'Now's your chance, Tête; come, let's see you kill a bull.'

Thus urged, the hunter cried, 'get up!' and James, obedient to the signal, cantered deliberately forward at an abominably uneasy gait. Tête Rouge, as we contemplated him from be-hind, made a most remarkable figure. He still wore the old buffalo-coat; his blanket which was tied in a loose bundle behind his saddle, went jolting from one side to the other, and a large tin canteen half full of water which hung from his pommel, was jerked about his leg in a manner which greatly embarrassed him.

'Let out your horse, man; lay on your whip!' we called out to him. The buffalo were getting farther off at every instant. James being ambitious to mend his pace, tugged hard at the rein, and one of his rider's boots escaped from the stirrup.

'Woh! I say, woh!' cried Tête Rouge, in great perturbation, and after much effort James' progress was arrested. The hunter came trotting back to the party, disgusted with buffalo-run-ning, and he was received with overwhelming congratula-tions.

Compare part of Parkman's notebook entry for September 7(?) in *Journals*, II, 478: "Fired at bulls as we rode along. Hodgman ran one at a slow lope!" The sequence of events in this chapter does not always coincide with the dates given for them in Parkman's notebooks.

18 Compare Townsend, *Narrative*, p. 97: "Upon examining the head, and cutting away the enormous mass of matted hair and skin which enveloped the skull, my large bullet of twenty to the pound, was found completely flattened against the bone . . . without producing the slightest fracture."

19 Parkman's "English tourist" may have been Charles Augustus Murray, whose two-volume *Travels in North America During the Years 1834, 1835, & 1836* (London, 1839) Parkman is known to have read. Murray's descriptions of buffalo-running are extremely vivid.

20 Parkman does not mention the "traces of a large Camanche encampment" in his notebooks, though on September 9 he "Saw several Pawnee forts, and passed a large Indian trail." See *Journals*, II, 479.

21 Parkman and his party reached the Caches (four or five miles west of modern Dodge City, Kansas) on the morning of September 9. See *Journals*, II, 479. In the early spring of 1823, Santa Fe traders James Baird and Samuel Chambers left almost all their merchandise in several deep pits—the Caches—dug on the north bank of the Arkansas River after losing most of their draft animals during three months of severe winter storms. See Long, *Old Santa Fe Trail*, p. 104; and Barry, "Kansas before 1854," *KHQ*, XXVII (Winter, 1961), 523.

22 For Swan see p. 347 of the present edition and note 6 for that page. At the Caches, however, Parkman was well east of Chouteau's Island, where Swan had been killed, and in this passage Parkman *may* be referring to the grave of a Bent and St. Vrain *engagé* killed by Comanches (?) near the Pawnee, or Pawnee Fork, River on or about May 28.

See Wislizenus, *Memoir of a Tour to Northern Mexico,* pp. 8, 10; Garrard, *Wah-To-Yah and the Taos Trail,* p. 76; and Barry, "Kansas before 1854," *KHQ,* xxx (Autumn, 1964), 358. Parkman does not mention Swan's grave in his notebooks.

23 After the sentence "His . . . burial-place" K supplies the following two sentences and additional paragraph:

Swan, it was said, was a native of Northampton, in Massachusetts. That day more than one execration was discharged against that debauched and faithless tribe who were the authors of his death, and who even now might be following like blood-hounds on our trail.

About this time a change came over the spirit of Tête Rouge; his jovial mood disappeared, and he relapsed into rueful despondency. Whenever we encamped, his complaints began. Sometimes he had a pain in the head; sometimes a racking in the joints; sometimes an aching in the side, and sometimes a heart-burn. His troubles did not excite much emotion, since they rose chiefly no doubt from his own greediness, and since no one could tell which were real and which were imaginary. He would often moan most dismally through the whole evening, and once in particular I remember that about mid-night he sat bolt upright and gave a loud scream. 'What's the matter now?' demanded the unsympathizing guard. Tête Rouge, rocking to and fro, and pressing his hands against his sides, declared that he suffered excruciating torment. 'I wish,' said he, 'that I was in the bar-room of the 'St. Charles' only just for five minutes!'

I have been unable to identify the *St. Charles* precisely; several Mississippi River packets, however, are known to have borne that name.

24 Compare part of Parkman's notebook entry for September 8 in *Journals,* ii, 478: "In the afternoon, picked up three stray horses of the volunteers, saddles and all!"

25 The sentence "After . . . sight" was added in 49.

26 In fact, Parkman met this caravan—perhaps R. Gentry's

train of 43 wagons—on September 9, somewhere in the vicinity of modern Dodge City, Kansas. See *Journals*, II, 479; and Barry, "Kansas before 1854," *KHQ*, XXX (Autumn, 1964), 391.

27 These "close black carriages," dearborns, or dearborn carriages, were usually the property of the owner or chief trader of a Santa Fe caravan. Most contemporary accounts agree that they were not much more comfortable than an ordinary ox wagon.

28 Neither "Dr. Dobbs" nor his prescription appears in Parkman's notebooks, and I have found no specific mention of a "Dr. Dobbs" in the Santa Fe trade in 1846. Gregg, *Commerce of the Prairies*, in Thwaites, ed. *Early Western Travels*, XIX, 164, mentions a Dr. Samuel B. Hobbs, "long and favorably associated with the Santa Fe Trade," and Hobbs *may* have been the man Parkman describes in this passage.

29 On the evening of September 9 Parkman and his companions encamped on upper Coon Creek, at a point a few miles southwest of modern Windthorst, Kansas. See *Journals*, II, 479.

30 Parkman and his party turned down the "Ridge-path" (otherwise known as the Ridge Road or Hill Trail) on the afternoon of September 9. The Ridge Road ran directly northeast across the prairies from a point on the Arkansas River a mile or two east of the present site of Fort Dodge, Kansas, to the Pawnee, or Pawnee Fork, River, seven miles west of modern Larned. The Ridge Road cut across the bottom of a bend of the Arkansas to the southeast and thus was considerably shorter than the River Trail, which ran along the banks of the Arkansas. The Ridge Road, however, was much drier than the River Trail, especially in the late summer. See Long, *Santa Fe Trail*, p. 94.

31 Between the sentences "At . . . rain" and "I . . . above" *K* supplies the following additional two sentences: "My

own situation was [*sic*] a pleasant one, having taken Dr. Dobbs' prescription long before there was any appearance of a storm. I now lay in the tent, wrapped in a buffalo-robe, and in great pain, from the combined effects of the disease and the remedy."

This storm occurred on the night of September 9–10. See *Journals*, II, 479.

CHAPTER XXVII

1 The "next day" was September 10. See *Journals*, II, 479.

2 Neither this passage nor the corresponding entry for September 10 in Parkman's notebooks shows very clearly where he and his companions met the Mormon Battalion; the stream Parkman mentions here, however, must have been one of the tributaries of Coon Creek, at a point some four or five miles north or northeast of modern Kinsley, Kansas. See *Journals*, II, 479; and "The Diary of Henry Standage," reprinted in Golder, *March of the Mormon Battalion*, p. 161, for Standage's description of the battalion's September 10th campsite 20 miles down the Ridge Road from the Pawnee River.

3 In many ways Parkman's meeting with the infantrymen of the Mormon Battalion—whom he characteristically calls "armed fanatics"—expresses much of the burden of disillusionment he undoubtedly felt in the West. Since early May he had been hearing rumors of Mormon hordes, and now he had finally met some of them, only to find in their "half-military, half-patriarchal appearance" merely another band of gaping rustics. Once again the commonplace had invaded the wilderness, "wildness" had been displaced by Mormon wives and children, and the Santa Fe Trail had repeated his experiences among the Oregon and California emigrants along the Platte.

The Mormon Battalion *was* a military curiosity, how-

ever; its organization and history reflected the long chronicle of the Mormons' struggles with authority—almost *any*
authority—and the convenient compromises which they
were willing to make in adversity. The origins of the battalion clearly reflect the flexibility and foresight of
Brigham Young's mind, for, even before the evacuation of
Nauvoo, he had begun to consider ways by which the
government might be persuaded to assist the Mormons on
their migration to the West.

On January 26, 1846, he had appointed Elder Jesse C.
Little, head of the Eastern States Mission, to approach
influential people in Washington on the Mormons' behalf. With letters to George Bancroft, Secretary of the
Navy, and to Vice President Dallas, Little arrived in
Washington on May 20 and on May 22 met President
Polk himself. From Little's own account of the subsequent proceedings (reprinted with other pertinent documents cited here in Golder, *March of the Mormon Battalion*, pp. 74–103), it seems clear that he was persuaded by
Amos Kendall, one of Polk's closest advisors, to make an
offer of a "thousand of our men" for the pacification and
defense of California. By May 26 Kendall had told Little
that "he had laid my case before the President, who determined to take possession of California, and also employ
our men, who would receive orders to push through and
fortify the country. . . ." After writing an impassioned
letter of loyalty to Polk and the United States on June 1,
Little learned from Polk on June 5 that the government
would accept his offer. On June 8 Little again saw Polk,
who "expressed his good feelings to our people, regarding
us as good citizens," though Polk's acceptance of what
became the Mormon Battalion was founded on the strategy which he set down in his diary on June 2: "Col.
Kearny was also authorized to receive into service as volunteers a few hundred of the Mormons who are now on their

way to California, with a view to conciliate them, attach them to our country, & prevent them from taking part against us." On June 3 Secretary of War Marcy wrote to Kearny and authorized him "to muster into service such [Mormons] as can be induced to volunteer not, however, to a number exceeding one third of your entire force."

By June 19 Kearny had ordered Captain James Allen of the First Dragoons to proceed to the Mormon encampments in Iowa and there enlist "four or five companies of volunteers" whom Allen would eventually command. On June 26 Allen was at the "Camp of the Mormons, at Mount Pisgah, one hundred and thirty-miles east of Council Bluffs. . . ." Allen's appearance at "Mount Pisgah" and his offer to enlist 500 Mormon infantrymen came most opportunely for Brigham Young, who had for some weeks been struggling with the combined problems of feeding the Mormons he had with him in Iowa and at the same time preparing for the Saints' departure for their new sanctuary in the West, though whether Zion was to be established in California or in the Great Basin perhaps even he did not then know absolutely. For a time he had thought of sending out an advance party of 500 men or of the same number of picked families; he had even considered an expedition by the Twelve Apostles of Mormonism themselves, but, as DeVoto, *Year of Decision,* pp. 244–245, believed, Allen's arrival and the government's firm offer to enlist as many as 500 Mormons for the conquest of California solved most of Young's immediate problems and promised large rewards in the future as well:

Brigham needed little time to understand the importance of the government's desire for volunteers and to readjust all his plans. He saw at once that the Mormon Battalion would both prohibit any large emigration this year and save Israel. . . .

The government Israel was fleeing from would take Israel to its sanctuary.

That, the free transportation for five hundred men and the sum in cash for their pay and allowances which would solve the financial problem of the main emigration, was undoubtedly the weightiest reason for Young's decision. Almost as important, however, was a basic reason of strategy and diplomatics. The outbreak of war made it certain that Zion, the land of Israel's inheritance, would be under American jurisdiction, not Mexican as it had been when the preparations for the exodus had been made. It would be of the greatest importance for the Church to locate there by the encouragement and permission of the United States and after answering a demand for patriotic service. The Mormons would not only be the "old settlers," the first arrivals, the ones who broke the wilderness and so could dictate to those who followed after, but they would have the United States considerably in their debt for the conquest of this very country.

Even so, Brigham Young had to resort to exhortations and threats before the Saints began to volunteer in significant numbers for the battalion, and it was not until August 1 that the more than 500 infantrymen of the five companies enlisted began to appear at Fort Leavenworth, accompanied by a number of aged relatives, some 30 wives disguised as "laundresses," and more than 30 children. A number of the Mormon volunteers were sick when they reached Fort Leavenworth, racked with fevers and agues from the rigors of the overland march from "Mount Pisgah," from the fatigues of the evacuation of Nauvoo, or, in several fatal cases, from sheer age and decrepitude.

It was not until August 16 that the Mormon Battalion crossed the Kansas River and turned down the Santa Fe Trail. The original commander of the column, Captain Allen, had fallen sick and had been left behind at Fort Leavenworth (where he died on August 23), and from Council Grove to Santa Fe they were commanded by

Lieutenant Andrew Jackson Smith of the First Dragoons, "our Tyrant," as Standage called him. They were also attended by Dr. Sanderson, "Captain Death," whom the Mormons suspected of thirsting for their blood and of poisoning them with calomel. On September 15 they crossed the Arkansas River and on October 12, making good time, three companies of the battalion arrived at Santa Fe, to be joined there three days later by the two other companies and most of the "laundresses" and children. On October 13 Captain Philip St. George Cooke took command of the battalion and on October 18 dispatched a "Sick Detachment" of 86 men, 20 wives, and the children to the Mormon settlement at the Pueblo. On October 19 the reduced companies of the battalion set out for San Diego, which they reached on January 30, 1847; they were mustered out of service at Los Angeles on July 16. Their active service was practically confined to a great deal of marching, repulsing a stampede of wild cattle in the desert, and carrying out a punitive expedition against the ferocious dogs of San Diego. They had made themselves into soldiers on their long walk across half the continent, chafing under discipline and groaning under Dr. Sanderson's doses, and their memory is still green in Brigham Young's Zion.

See Golder, *March of the Mormon Battalion*, pp. 75–233, especially "The Diary of Henry Standage"; P. St. George Cooke, "Cooke's Journal of the March of the Mormon Battalion, 1846–1847," in Ralph P. Bieber, ed. *Exploring Southwestern Trails 1846–1854* (Glendale, Calif., 1938), pp. 63–240; Cooke, *The Conquest of New Mexico and California*. . . (New York, 1878), pp. 83–197; Cooke, "Report of Lieut. Col. P. St. George Cooke of His March from Santa Fé, New Mexico, to San Diego, Upper California," in Emory, *Notes of a Military Reconnoissance*, pp. 549–563; Hafen and Young, "The Mormon

Settlement at Pueblo, Colorado," *Colorado Magazine*, ix (July, 1932), 128–133; DeVoto, *Year of Decision*, p. 240–387 *passim*; and Barry, "Kansas before 1854," *KHQ*, xxx (Autumn, 1964), 383–385.

4 Parkman mentions "Col. Smith" in his notebook entry for September 10 in *Journals*, ii, 479.

5 This adventure occurred on the evening of September 12, the same day that Parkman and his party crossed the Pawnee River. See *Journals*, ii, 479–480.

6 After the sentence " 'I . . . Missouri' " K–52 supply the following additional paragraph: "To Tête Rouge's great wrath they expressed a firm conviction that he was crazy. We left them after giving them the advice not to trouble themselves about war-whoops in future, since they would be apt to feel an Indian's arrow before they heard his voice."

7 Parkman reached Cow Creek, five or six miles west of modern Lyons, Kansas, on September 14. See *Journals*, ii, 480.

8 Compare Russell, *Journal of a Trapper*, p. 142, on "approaching":

It also requires a considerable degree of practice to approach on foot and kill Buffaloe with a Rifle[.] A person must be well acquainted with the shape and make of the animal and the manner which it is standing in order to direct his aim with certainty—And it also requires experience to enable him [to] choose a fat animal[;] the best looking Buffaloe is not always the fattest and a hunter by constant practice may lay down rules for selecting the fattest when on foot which would be no guide to him when running upon horseback for he is then placed in a different position and one which requires different rules for choosing.

9 Parkman and his companions camped on the Little Arkansas River, some six miles southeast of modern Little River,

Kansas, on the evening of September 15–16. See *Journals*, II, 480.

10 Blue grama (*Bouteloua gracilis*) and buffalo grass (*Buchloe dactyloides*) are the characteristic grasses of western Kansas, particularly west of the hundredth meridian. See Cockrum, *Mammals of Kansas*, p. 9.

11 Compare part of Parkman's notebook entry for September 20 in *Journals*, II, 481: "Came at noon to Council Grove —beautiful meadows and woods. Here was a blacksmith's shop, and a train of waggons repairing. Passing through the luxuriant woods at this place was a foretaste of the settlements."

Council Grove, at the present site of Council Grove, Kansas, was named for a meeting held in August, 1825, between the Osage Indians and three government agents surveying a road from western Missouri to New Mexico. See Long, *Santa Fe Trail*, p. 261; and Webb, *Adventures in the Santa Fé Trade*, p. 46 n. At Council Grove small separate parties of Santa Fe traders often gathered into one or more larger caravans for protection against the Indians; as Magoffin, *Down the Santa Fe Trail*, p. 16, noted, " 'Council Grove' may be considered the dividing ridge between the civilized and the savage, for we may now look out for hostile Indians."

12 The Osages, a powerful and important tribe of Siouan stock, had once owned most of Missouri and large tracts in Arkansas and Oklahoma before the land cessions which they made in 1808, 1825, and 1839. In 1846 many Osages lived along the Verdigris and Neosho rivers in southeastern Kansas. See Hodge, ed. *Handbook of American Indians*, II, 156–158.

13 For an account of some of these "hostilities," see p. 333 of the present edition and note 10 for that page.

14 Parkman nooned at Diamond Spring, some four miles north of the present location of Diamond Springs, Kansas,

on September 18. See *Journals*, II, 481. Which Rock Creek Parkman means here is not clear; the Santa Fe Trail crossed one Rock Creek about eight or nine miles east of Council Grove (or near the modern Morris-Lyons County line), but the trail also forded another Rock Creek six miles northeast of modern Overbrook, Kansas, at the Osage-Douglas County line.

I have been unable to discover the location of "Elder Grove"; Parkman's rough log of distances on the reverse of his "letter of introduction" from "P. Chouteau Son & Co." (in the Parkman Papers, Massachusetts Historical Society) shows that "Elder Grove" was 15 miles east or east-northeast of Rock Creek (near Overbrook) and 18 miles west of Hickory Point (located 10 or 12 miles south of modern Lawrence, Kansas). These distances cannot be reconciled, for Rock Creek and Hickory Point are, by the most generous reckoning, only about 20 miles apart.

15 Compare Parkman's account of a meeting with a party of wagoners on September 21 in *Journals*, II, 481: "Camped at Dragoon Creek [five miles west of modern Burlingame, Kansas]. Met waggons. 'Whar are ye from? Californy?' 'No.' 'Santy Fee?' 'No, the Mountains.' 'What yer been doing thar? Tradin'?,' 'No.' 'Trappin'?' 'No.' 'Huntin'?' 'No.' 'Emigratin'?' 'No.' 'What *have* ye been doing then, God damn ye?' (Very loud, as we were by this time almost out of hearing.)"

16 The "emaciated old man" does not appear in Parkman's notebooks, though in his entry for September 22 in *Journals*, II, 482, he records a meeting at Rock Creek (northeast of modern Overbrook, Kansas) with "Messrs. [Jared W.] Folger, [Elliott] Lee, and Upton [Lancaster P. Lupton], connected with Bent & St. Vrain, whose waggons were encamped a few miles behind." Next day Parkman met Ceran St. Vrain, "a brother [Edmund Chadwick] of Catlin's friend, Joe Chadwick," and, very probably, Lewis

H. Garrard, who was traveling west for the first time in this same Bent & St. Vrain caravan. See *Wah-To-Yah and the Taos Trail*, pp. 54–68.

17 Tête Rouge left the party on September 24, six days after Munroe, Jim Gurney, and Ellis had parted from Parkman and his friends at their Lost Spring campsite near modern Lost Springs, Kansas. See *Journals*, II, 481, 482.

18 After the sentence "On . . . ground" K–52 supply the following additional sentence and paragraph:

Some [K: A dozen] pigs belonging to a Shawanoe farmer, were grunting and rooting at the edge of the grove.

'I wonder how fresh pork tastes,' murmured one of the party, and more than one voiced murmured in response. The fiat went forth, 'That pig must die,' and a rifle was levelled forthwith at the countenance of the plumpest porker. Just then a wagon train, with some twenty Missourians, came out from among the trees. The marksman suspended his aim, deeming it inexpedient under the circumstances to consummate the deed of blood.

[K then supplies the following additional canceled paragraph: The reader should have seen us at our camp in the grove that night, every man standing before the tree against which he had hung his little looking-glass and grimacing horridly as he struggled to remove with a dull razor the stubble of a month's beard.]

19 The red, scarlet, or swamp maple (*Acer rubrum*) is frequently found in low, wet ground.

20 The values of Parkman's wilderness experience are clearly present in the carefully contrasted metaphors of "opening life" in the spring and the "maturity and decay" in the fall. He had seen the wilderness, and he carried its burdens upon his body and mind.

21 Parkman's "partridges" were ruffed grouse (*Bonasa umbellus*), frequently found along wooded riverbottoms in eastern Kansas before the settlement of the region.

22 Compare the sentence "Many . . . us" with its K–52 form: "Many and powerful as were the attractions which drew us toward the settlements, we looked back even at that moment with an eager longing toward the wilderness of prairies and mountains behind us."

After the sentence "Many . . . us" K–52 supply the following additional sentence to conclude the paragraph: "For myself I had suffered more that summer from illness than ever before in my life, and yet to this hour I cannot recall those savage scenes and savage men without a strong desire again to visit them."

Compare this canceled sentence with Ruxton's similar nostalgic reminiscences in *Adventures in the Rocky Mountains*, reprinted in *Ruxton of the Rockies*, p. 162:

Scarcely, however, did I ever wish to change such hours of freedom for all the luxuries of civilized life, and, unnatural as it may appear, yet such is the fascination of the life of the mountain hunter, that I believe not one instance could be adduced of even the most polished and civilized of men, who had once tasted the sweets of its attendant liberty and freedom from every worldly care, not regretting the moment when he exchanged it for the monotonous life of the settlements, nor sighing, and sighing again, once more to partake of its pleasures and allurements.

23 Wood, *Old Santa Fe Trail*, p. 230, identifies the "white man's dwelling" as Yoacham's tavern on the Mission Road, just west of the "miserable log bridge" over Mill Creek. Parkman arrived at Westport on the afternoon of September 26 and spent the evening of September 26–27 at Chick's house in "Kansas." See *Journals*, II, 482, and *Letters*, I, 47–49, for Parkman's letter of September 26 to his father in which he announces his arrival at Westport and assures his family that "I have enjoyed myself in spite of temporary illness (which, by the way, I am none the

worse for)—and the experience of one season on the prairies will teach a man more than half a dozen in the settlements. There is no place on earth where he is thrown more completely on his own resources."

24 For "Vogel's dram-shop" and "Boone's grocery" see pp. 8 and 9 of the present edition and notes 27 and 31 for those pages.

25 For Colonel Chick see p. 4 of the present edition and note 14 for that page.

26 I have been unable to identify Antoine Lajeunesse, though he must have belonged to that well-known Missouri family that included Charles Lajeunesse, or "Simono," Chatillon's old friend. See Morgan and Harris, eds. *Rocky Mountain Journals of W. M. Anderson*, p. 334.

27 The date of Parkman's departure from "Kansas" cannot be positively determined from his notebooks, though on September 28 he had ridden over to "Wyandot City," near modern Kansas City, Kansas, and on October 1 he recorded that his steamboat down the Missouri was "stuck on a sandbar in the river." See *Journals*, II, 482–483. On October 7 he wrote to his mother from St. Louis after "a vexatious voyage of seven days down the Missouri from Westport." See *Letters*, I, 50. He must therefore have left "Kansas" on September 29 or September 30, the latter date being more probable.

28 Compare the sentence "As . . . rock" with its form in K: "As the boat rounded a distant point, the last object that met our eyes was Delorier still lifting his hat and skipping like a monkey about the rock."

29 Parkman had met Gurney and Munroe again at Westport on September 26. See *Journals*, II, 482.

30 The *Amelia* had entered the Missouri River traffic on August 24, 1846. See Barry, "Kansas before 1854," *KHQ*, XXX (Autumn, 1964), 392.

31 These "disbanded volunteers," members of a regiment of

Missouri volunteers arriving at Fort Leavenworth between August 24 and September 14, had been discharged at the fort between September 29 and October 2. This "Third Missouri" regiment saw no active service. See Barry, "Kansas before 1854," *KHQ*, xxx (Autumn, 1964), 392.

32 The Planters' House was probably the leading hotel in St. Louis in the 1840's.

33 Compare the sentence "In . . . other" with its K–52 form: "In the morning we hardly recognized each other; a frock of broadcloth had supplanted the frock of buckskin; well-fitted pantaloons took the place of Indian leggins, and polished boots were substituted for the gaudy moccasins."

After "In . . . moccasins" K supplies the following additional 12 sentences to conclude the paragraph:

We sallied forth, our hands encased in kid gloves and made calls at the houses of our acquaintance. After we had been several days at St. Louis we heard news of Tête Rouge. He had contrived to reach Fort Leavenworth, where he had found the paymaster and received his money. As a boat was just ready to start for St. Louis, he went on board and engaged his passage. This done, he immediately got drunk on shore, and the boat went off without him. It was some days before another opportunity occurred, and meanwhile the settler's [*sic*; 49–52: sutler's] stores furnished him with abundant means of keeping up his spirits. Another steamboat came at last, the clerk of which happened to be a friend of his, and by the advice of some charitable person on shore he persuaded Tête Rouge to remain on board, intending to detain him there until the boat should leave the Fort. At first Tête Rouge was well contented with this arrangement, but on applying for a dram the bar-keeper at the clerk's instigation, refused to let him have it. Finding them both inflexible in spite of his entreaties, he became desperate and made his escape from the boat. The clerk found him after a long search in one of the barracks; a dozen dragoons stood contemplating him as he lay on the floor, maudlin drunk and crying dismally. With the help of one of them the clerk pushed him on board, and our informant who came down in the same boat, declared that he remained in great despondency during the whole passage. As we left St. Louis soon after his arrival we did not see the worthless, good-natured little vagabond again.

This passage is reprinted in 49–52 almost without change, except that in these two editions the sentence "We sallied . . . acquaintance" has been deleted and a new paragraph division made at "After we . . . Rouge."
34 At the sentence "We . . . ours" 49–52 supply the following footnote:

I cannot take leave of the reader without adding a word or two of the guide who had served us throughout with such zeal and fidelity. Indeed his services had far surpassed the terms of his engagement. Yet whoever had been his employers, or to whatever closeness of intercourse they might have thought fit to admit him, he would never have changed the bearing of quiet respect which he considered due to his *bourgeois*. If sincerity and honor, a boundless generosity of spirit, a delicate regard to the feelings of others, and a nice perception of what was due to them, are the essential characteristics of a gentleman, then Henry Chatillon deserves the title. He could not write his own name, and he had spent his life among savages. In him sprang up spontaneously those qualities which all the refinements of life and intercourse with the highest and best of the better part of mankind, fail to awaken in the brutish natures of some men. In spite of his bloody calling, Henry was always humane and merciful; he was gentle as a woman, though braver than a lion. He acted aright from the free impulses of his large and generous nature. A certain species of selfishness is essential to the sternness of spirit which bears down opposition and subjects the will of others to its own. Henry's character was of an opposite stamp. His easy good-nature almost amounted to weakness; yet while it unfitted him for any position of command, it secured the esteem and good-will of all those who were not jealous of his skill and reputation.

35 After the sentence "On . . . home" K supplies an additional paragraph which is substantially identical to the deleted footnote in 49–52 cited immediately above, except that the K version of this paragraph supplies, after the sentence "His . . . reputation" the following additional two sentences to conclude the canceled paragraph: "The polished fops of literature or fashion would laugh with disdain at the idea of comparing his merits with theirs. I deem them worthless by the side of that illiterate hunter."

REFERENCE MATTER

Bibliography

This bibliography contains a number of books and articles nowhere specifically cited in this edition of *The Oregon Trail*. I have included them because from these sources I have learned a great deal about the early history of western exploration and the fur trade—a necessary background for many of the historical judgments made in this book.

PRIMARY SOURCES

Manuscript Materials

Norton, Charles Eliot. Letterbooks, 1846–1850. Houghton Library at Harvard University.

Parkman, Francis. "Letters Received" Folders, 1846–1850. Parkman Papers, Massachusetts Historical Society, Boston.

———. "Oregon Trail" Journals. Parkman Papers, Massachusetts Historical Society, Boston.

Published Materials

Norton, Charles Eliot. *Letters of Charles Eliot Norton, with Biographical Comment*, eds. Sarah Norton and M. A. DeWolfe Howe. 2 vols. Boston: Houghton Mifflin Co., 1913.

Parkman, Francis. *The Journals of Francis Parkman*, ed. Mason Wade. 2 vols. New York: Harper and Bros., 1947.

———. *Letters from Francis Parkman to E. G. Squier*, ed. Don C. Seitz. Cedar Rapids: The Torch Press, 1911.

———. *Letters of Francis Parkman*, ed. Wilbur R. Jacobs. 2 vols. Norman: University of Oklahoma Press, 1960.

———. *The Parkman Reader*, ed. Samuel Eliot Morison. Boston: Little, Brown & Co., 1955.

————. "Scenes at Fort Laramie," *Literary World*, I, 3 (February 20, 1847), 60–61.

————. *Francis Parkman's Works*. Frontenac Edition. 17 vols. Boston: Little, Brown & Co., 1901.

————. "The Works of James Fenimore Cooper," *North American Review*, LXXIV (January, 1852), 147–161.

————, and Henry Stevens. "The Correspondence of Francis Parkman and Henry Stevens, 1845–1885," ed. John Buechler, *Transactions of the American Philosophical Society*, N.S., LVII, pt. 6 (August, 1967), 3–34.

SECONDARY SOURCES

Abert, J. W. "Report of Lieut. J. W. Abert, of His Examination of New Mexico, in the Years 1846–'47," in W. H. Emory, *Notes of a Military Reconnoissance from Ft. Leavenworth, in Missouri, to San Diego, in California* . . . , pp. 417–546. House Executive Document no. 41, 30th Congress, 1st session (serial 517). Washington, D.C., 1848.

————. *Western America in 1846–1847: The Original Travel Diary of Lieutenant J. W. Abert* . . . , ed. John Galvin. San Francisco: John Howell, 1966.

Allen, A. J. *Thrilling Adventures, Travels and Explorations of Doctor Elijah White among the Rocky Mountains and in the Far West.* . . . New York: J. W. Yale, 1859.

Alter, J. Cecil. *Jim Bridger*. Norman: University of Oklahoma Press, 1962.

American Ornithologists' Union. *Check-List of North American Birds*. 5th ed., 1957. [c/o Museum of Natural History, Smithsonian Institution, Washington, D.C.]

Anderson, William Marshall. *The Rocky Mountain Journals of William Marshall Anderson: The West in 1834*, eds. Dale L. Morgan and Eleanor Towles Harris. San Marino: The Huntington Library, 1967.

Andrieu, Pierre. *Fine Bouche: A History of the Restaurant in France*, trans. Arthur L. Hayward. London: Cassell and Co., 1956.

Annual Report of the Commissioner of Indian Affairs . . . *1854*. Washington, D.C.: A. O. P. Nicholson, 1855.

Ashley, William H. *The West of William H. Ashley* . . . , ed. Dale L. Morgan. Denver: Old West Publishing Co., 1964.

Bancroft, Hubert Howe. *History of California.* 7 vols. San Francisco: The History Co., 1886–1890.

———. *History of Nevada, Colorado, and Wyoming.* San Francisco: The History Co., 1890.

———. *History of Oregon.* 2 vols. San Francisco: The History Co., 1886–1888.

Barry, J. Neilson. "Madame Dorion of the Astorians," *Oregon Historical Quarterly,* xxx (September, 1929), 272–277.

Barry, Louise A. "Kansas before 1854: A Revised Annals," *Kansas Historical Quarterly,* xxvii (1961), 67–93, 201–219, 353–382, 497–543; xxviii (1962), 25–59, 167–204, 317–370, 497–514; xxix (1963), 41–81, 143–189, 324–359, 429–486; xxx (1964), 62–91, 209–244, 339–412, 492–559.

Beckwith, Paul. *Creoles of St. Louis.* St. Louis: Nixon-Jones Printing Co., 1893.

Bennett, Emerson. *Leni-Leoti.* Cincinnati: J. A. & U. P. James, 1853.

———. *The Prairie Flower.* Cincinnati: J. A. & U. P. James, 1851.

Berthong, Donald J. *The Southern Cheyennes.* Norman: University of Oklahoma Press, 1963.

Bidwell, John. *A Journey to California in 1841: The Journal of John Bidwell,* ed. Francis P. Farquhar. Berkeley: The Bancroft Library, 1964.

Billington, Ray Allen. *The Far Western Frontier, 1830–1860.* New York, Harper & Bros., 1956.

———. *Westward Expansion: A History of the American Frontier.* New York: Macmillan Co., 1967.

Boggs, W. M. "The W. M. Boggs Manuscript about Bent's Fort, Kit Carson, the Far West, and Life among the Indians," ed. LeRoy R. Hafen, *Colorado Magazine,* vii (March, 1930), 45–69.

Bonner, T. D. *The Life and Adventures of James P. Beckwourth, Mountaineer, Scout, and Pioneer, and Chief of the Crow Nation of Indians.* New York: Harper and Bros., 1856.

Bryant, Edwin. *What I Saw in California* . . . . New York: D. Appleton & Co., 1848.

Callahan, Edward W. *List of Officers of the Navy and of the Marine Corps from 1775 to 1900.* New York: L. R. Hamersly & Co., 1901.

Carleton, J. Henry. *The Prairie Logbooks,* ed. Louis Pelzer. Chicago: Caxton Club, 1943.

Carson, Christopher. *Kit Carson's Autobiography,* ed. Milo M. Quaife. Chicago: The Lakeside Press, 1935.

Carter, Harvey L. "Joe Doyle," in LeRoy R. Hafen, ed. *The Mountain Men and the Fur Trade of the Far West,* III, 89–98. Glendale, Calif.: The Arthur H. Clark Co., 1966.

———. "Marcellin St. Vrain," in LeRoy R. Hafen, ed. *The Mountain Men and the Fur Trade of the Far West,* III, 273–277. Glendale, Calif.: The Arthur H. Clark Co., 1966.

———, and Janet S. Lecompte. "George Semmes Simpson," in LeRoy R. Hafen, ed. *The Mountain Men and the Fur Trade of the Far West,* III, 285–299. Glendale, Calif.: The Arthur H. Clark Co., 1966.

Catlin, George. *Episodes from Life among the Indians and Last Rambles,* ed. Marvin C. Ross. Norman: University of Oklahoma Press, 1959.

Chittenden, Hiram M. *The American Fur Trade of the Far West,* ed. Stallo Vinton, 2 vols. New York: Press of the Pioneers, 1935.

———. *History of Early Steamboat Navigation on the Missouri River: Life and Adventures of Joseph La Barge.* New York: Francis P. Harper, 1903.

———, and Alfred Talbot Richardson. *Life, Letters, and Travels of Father Pierre-Jean De Smet, S. J.* . . . 4 vols. New York: Francis P. Harper, 1905.

Christopher, Adrienne T., and LeRoy R. Hafen, "William F. May," in LeRoy R. Hafen, ed. *The Mountain Men and the Fur Trade of the Far West,* IV, 207–216. Glendale, Calif.: The Arthur H. Clark Co., 1966.

Clarke, Dwight L. *Stephen Watts Kearny: Soldier of the West.* Norman: University of Oklahoma Press, 1961.

Clyman, James. *James Clyman, Frontiersman: The Adventures of a Trapper and Covered-Wagon Emigrant as Told in His Own*

Reminiscences and Diaries, ed. Charles L. Camp. Portland: Champoeg Press, 1960.

Cockrum, E. Lendell. *Mammals of Kansas.* University of Kansas Publications, Museum of Natural History, vol. vii, no. 1. Lawrence: University of Kansas, 1952.

Conard, Howard Louis. *"Uncle Dick" Wootton, the Pioneer Frontiersman of the Rocky Mountain Region.* Chicago: W. E. Dibble & Co., 1890.

Connelley, William E., ed. *Doniphan's Expedition and the Conquest of New Mexico and California.* Topeka: published by the editor, 1907.

Cooke, P. St. George. *The Conquest of New Mexico and California; An Historical and Personal Narrative.* New York: G. P. Putnam's Sons, 1878. (Reprint. Oakland: Biobooks, 1952.)

————. "Cooke's Journal of the March of the Mormon Battalion, 1846–1847," in Ralph P. Bieber, ed. *Exploring Southwestern Trails 1846–1854,* pp. 63–240. The Southwest Historical Series, vol. vii. Glendale, Calif.: The Arthur H. Clark Co., 1938.

————. "Report of Lieut. Col. P. St. George Cooke of His March from Santa Fé, New Mexico, to San Diego, Upper California," in W. H. Emory, *Notes of a Military Reconnoissance from Ft. Leavenworth, in Missouri, to San Diego, in California . . . ,* pp. 549–562. House Executive Document no. 41, 30th Congress, 1st session (serial 517). Washington, D.C., 1848.

————. *Scenes and Adventures in the Army: Or, Romance of Military Life.* Philadelphia: Lindsay and Blakiston, 1857.

Coyner, David H. *The Lost Trappers.* Cincinnati: Anderson, Gates & Wright, 1859.

Darton, N. H., et al. *Guidebook of the Western United States; Part C. The Santa Fe Route. . . .* U.S. Geological Survey Bulletin 613. Washington, D.C.: Government Printing Office, 1915.

De Smet, Pierre-Jean, S.J. *Letters and Sketches: With a Narrative of a Year's Residence among the Indian Tribes of the Rocky Mountains,* in Reuben Gold Thwaites, ed. *Early Western Travels,* xxvii, 127–402. Cleveland: The Arthur H. Clark Co., 1906.

————. *Oregon Missions and Travels over the Rocky Mountains in 1845–1846,* in Reuben Gold Thwaites, ed. *Early Western*

Travels, XXIX, 107–424. Cleveland: The Arthur H. Clark Co., 1906.

DeVoto, Bernard. *Across the Wide Missouri*. Boston: Houghton Mifflin Co., 1947.

———. *The Year of Decision 1846*. Boston: Little, Brown and Co., 1943.

———, ed. *The Life and Adventures of James P. Beckwourth*, by T. D. Bonner. New York: Alfred A. Knopf, 1931.

Dodge, Richard Irving. *Our Wild Indians: Thirty-Three Years' Personal Experience among the Red Men of the Great West*. Hartford: A. D. Worthington & Co., 1883.

Dorsey, J. Owen. "A Study of Siouan Cults," *Eleventh Annual Report of the Bureau of Ethnology*, pp. 361–554. Washington, D.C.: Smithsonian Institution, 1894.

Doughty, Howard. *Francis Parkman*. New York: Macmillan Co., 1962.

Dunham, Harold H. "Ceran St. Vrain," in LeRoy R. Hafen, ed. *The Mountain Men and the Fur Trade of the Far West*, V, 297–316. Glendale, Calif.: The Arthur H. Clark Co., 1968.

———. "Charles Bent," in LeRoy R. Hafen, ed. *The Mountain Men and the Fur Trade of the Far West*, II, 27–48. Glendale, Calif.: The Arthur H. Clark Co., 1965.

Eccleston, Robert. *Overland to California on the Southwestern Trail 1849*, eds. George P. Hammond and Edward H. Howes. Berkeley: University of California Press, 1950.

Edwards, Frank S. *A Campaign in New Mexico with Colonel Doniphan*. Philadelphia: Carey and Hart, 1847.

Edwards, Marcellus Ball. "Journal of Marcellus Ball Edwards, 1846–1847," in Ralph P. Bieber, ed. *Marching with the Army of the West 1846–1848*, pp. 107–282. The Southwest Historical Series, vol. IV. Glendale, Calif.: The Arthur H. Clark Co., 1936.

Emerson, Ralph Waldo. *The Journals and Miscellaneous Notebooks of Ralph Waldo Emerson, 1826–1832*, vol. III, eds. William H. Gilman and Alfred R. Ferguson. Cambridge: Harvard University Press, 1963.

———. *The Journals and Miscellaneous Notebooks of Ralph Waldo Emerson, 1832–1834*, vol. IV, ed. Alfred R. Ferguson. Cambridge: Harvard University Press, 1964.

Emory, W. H. *Notes of a Military Reconnoissance from Fort Leavenworth, in Missouri, to San Diego, in California, Including Part of the Arkansas, Del Norte, and Gila Rivers*, pp. 7–134. House Executive Document no. 41, 30th Congress, 1st session (serial 517). Washington, D.C., 1848.

Ewers, John C. *The Blackfeet: Raiders on the Northwestern Plains.* Norman: University of Oklahoma Press, 1958.

Farnham, Thomas J. *Travels in the Great Western Plains, the Anahuac and Rocky Mountains, and in the Oregon Country*, in Reuben Gold Thwaites, ed. *Early Western Travels*, xxviii–xxix. Cleveland: The Arthur H. Clark Co., 1906.

Favour, Alpheus H. *Old Bill Williams, Mountain Man.* Chapel Hill: University of North Carolina Press, 1936.

Federal Writers' Project of the Works Progress Administration. *The Oregon Trail: The Missouri River to the Pacific Ocean.* American Guide Series. New York: Hastings House, 1939.

Ferris, W. A. *Life in the Rocky Mountains*, ed. Paul C. Phillips. Denver: Old West Publishing Co., 1940.

Field, Matthew C. *Matt Field on the Santa Fe Trail*, ed. John E. Sunder. Norman: University of Oklahoma Press, 1960.

——. *Prairie and Mountain Sketches*, eds. Kate L. Gregg and John Francis McDermott. Norman: University of Oklahoma Press, 1957.

Fowler, Jacob. *The Journal of Jacob Fowler*, ed. Elliott Coues. American Explorers Series, vol. 1. New York: Francis P. Harper, 1898. (Reprint. Minneapolis: Ross & Haines, Inc., 1965.)

Frémont, John Charles. *Report of the Exploring Expedition to the Rocky Mountains in the Year 1842, and to Oregon and North California in the Years 1843–'44.* Senate Executive Document no. 174, 28th Congress, 2d session (serial 461). Washington, D.C., 1845.

Fussell, Edwin S. *Frontier: American Literature and the American West.* Princeton, N.J.: Princeton University Press, 1965.

Garrard, Lewis H. *Wah-To-Yah and the Taos Trail*, ed. Ralph P. Bieber. The Southwest Historical Series, vol. vi. Glendale, Calif.: The Arthur H. Clark Co., 1938.

Ghent, W. J. *The Road to Oregon.* New York: Longmans, Green and Co., 1929.

Gibbs, George E., "The Diary of George E. Gibbs," in Raymond W. Settle, ed. *The March of the Mounted Riflemen*. . . . pp. 273–327. Glendale, Calif.: The Arthur H. Clark Co., 1940.

Gibson, George Rutledge. *Journal of a Soldier under Kearny and Doniphan, 1846–1847*, ed. Ralph P. Bieber. The Southwest Historical Series, vol. III. Glendale, Calif.: The Arthur H. Clark Co., 1935.

Golder, Frank A. *The March of the Mormon Battalion.* New York: The Century Co., 1928.

Gould, G. M. *Biographic Clinics.* 6 vols. Philadelphia: P. Blakiston's Son, 1903–1909.

Gregg, Josiah. *Commerce of the Prairies*, in Reuben Gold Thwaites, ed. *Early Western Travels*, XIX–XX. Cleveland: The Arthur H. Clark Co., 1905.

Hafen, Ann W. "Jean Baptiste Charbonneau," in LeRoy R. Hafen, ed. *The Mountain Men and the Fur Trade of the Far West*, I, 205–224. Glendale, Calif.: The Arthur H. Clark Co., 1965.

——. "Lancaster P. Lupton," in LeRoy R. Hafen, ed. *The Mountain Men and the Fur Trade of the Far West*, II, 207–216. Glendale, Calif.: The Arthur H. Clark Co., 1965.

Hafen, LeRoy R. "Fort Jackson and the Early Fur Trade on the South Platte," *Colorado Magazine*, V (February, 1928), 9–17.

——. "Fort St. Vrain," *Colorado Magazine*, XXIX (October, 1952), 241–255.

——. *Fort Vasquez.* Denver: State Historical Society of Colorado, 1964.

——. "Fraeb's Last Fight and How Battle Creek Got Its Name," *Colorado Magazine*, VII (May, 1930), 97–101.

——. "Louis Vasquez," in LeRoy R. Hafen, ed. *The Mountain Men and the Fur Trade of the Far West*, II, 321–338. Glendale, Calif.: The Arthur H. Clark Co., 1965.

——. "Old Fort Lupton and Its Founder," *Colorado Magazine*, VI (November, 1929), 220–226.

——. "When Was Bent's Fort Built?" *Colorado Magazine*, XXXI (April, 1954), 105–119.

——, and W. J. Ghent. *Broken Hand: The Life Story of*

Thomas Fitzpatrick, Chief of the Mountain Men. Denver: Old West Publishing Co., 1931.

———, and Francis Marion Young. *Fort Laramie and the Pageant of the West, 1834–1890.* Glendale, Calif.: The Arthur H. Clark Co., 1938.

———, and Frank M. Young. "The Mormon Settlement at Pueblo, Colorado, During the Mexican War," *Colorado Magazine,* IX (July, 1932), 121–136.

———, ed. *The Mountain Men and the Fur Trade of the Far West.* 5 vols. to date. Glendale, Calif.: The Arthur H. Clark Co., 1965———.

———, ed. *Ruxton of the Rockies,* containing reprint of George Frederick Ruxton, *Adventures in Mexico and the Rocky Mountains* (London: J. Murray, 1847). Norman: University of Oklahoma Press, 1950.

———, and Ann W. Hafen, eds. *Frémont's Fourth Expedition.* . . . The Far West and the Rockies Historical Series 1820–1875, vol. XI. Glendale, Calif.: The Arthur H. Clark Co., 1960.

———, and ———, eds. *To the Rockies and Oregon 1839–1842.* The Far West and the Rockies Historical Series 1820–1875, vol. III. Glendale, Calif.: The Arthur H. Clark Co., 1955.

Hagan, William T. *The Sac and Fox Indians.* Norman: University of Oklahoma Press, 1958.

Hancock, Samuel. *The Narrative of Samuel Hancock, 1845–1860,* ed. A. D. Howden Smith. New York: R. M. McBride & Co., 1927.

Hassrick, Royal B. *The Sioux: Life and Customs of a Warrior Society.* Norman: University of Oklahoma Press, 1964.

Hastings, Lansford Warren. *A New History of Oregon and California.* . . . Cincinnati: G. Conclin, 1847. (First published as *The Emigrants' Guide to Oregon and California.* Cincinnati: G. Conclin, 1845.)

Henderson, Paul C. *Landmarks on the Oregon Trail.* New York: Peter Decker, 1953.

Hodge, Frederick Webb, ed. *Handbook of American Indians North of Mexico.* 2 vols. Bureau of American Ethnology Bulletin no. 30. Washington: Smithsonian Institution, 1912.

Honig, Louis O. *Westport, Gateway to the Early West*. N.p., 1950.

Hughes, John T. *Doniphan's Expedition*, reprinted in William E. Connelley, ed. *Doniphan's Expedition and the Conquest of New Mexico and California*. Topeka: published by the editor, 1907.

Hunt, Aurora. *Major General James Henry Carleton, 1814–1873, Western Frontier Dragoon*. Glendale, Calif.: The Arthur H. Clark Co., 1958.

Hunter, Louis C. *Steamboats on the Western Rivers*. Cambridge: Harvard University Press, 1949.

Hyde, George E. *Indians of the High Plains*. Norman: University of Oklahoma Press, 1959.

———. *Red Cloud's Folk: A History of the Oglala Sioux Indians*. Norman: University of Oklahoma Press, 1937.

———. *Spotted Tail's Folk: A History of the Brulé Sioux*. Norman: University of Oklahoma Press, 1961.

Ingersoll, Chester. *Overland to California in 1847 . . .* , ed. Douglas C. McMurtrie. Chicago: Black Cat Press, 1937.

Inman, Henry. *The Old Santa Fé Trail*. New York: Macmillan Co., 1897.

Irving, Washington. *The Adventures of Captain Bonneville*, ed. Edgeley W. Todd. Norman: University of Oklahoma Press, 1961.

———. *Astoria or Anecdotes of an Enterprise Beyond the Rocky Mountains*, ed. Edgeley W. Todd. Norman: University of Oklahoma Press, 1964.

———. *A Tour on the Prairies*, ed. John Francis McDermott. Norman: University of Oklahoma Press, 1956.

———. *The Western Journals of Washington Irving*, ed. John Francis McDermott. Norman: University of Oklahoma Press, 1944.

Jackson, Donald, ed. *The Journals of Zebulon Montgomery Pike with Letters and Related Documents*. 2 vols. Norman: University of Oklahoma Press, 1966.

———, ed. *Letters of the Lewis and Clark Expedition with Related Documents 1783–1854*. Urbana: University of Illinois Press, 1962.

Jacobs, Wilbur R. "Some of Parkman's Literary Devices," *New England Quarterly*, XXXI (June, 1958), 244–252.

James, Edwin. *Account of an Expedition from Pittsburg to the Rocky Mountains, Performed in the Years 1819, 1820*, in Reuben Gold Thwaites, ed. *Early Western Travels*, XIV–XVII. Cleveland: The Arthur H. Clark Co., 1905.

James, Thomas. *Three Years among the Indians and Mexicans*, ed. Milo M. Quaife. Chicago: The Lakeside Press, 1953.

Johnston, Abraham Robinson. "Journal of Abraham Robinson Johnston, 1846," in Ralph P. Bieber, ed. *Marching with the Army of the West 1846–1848*, pp. 73–106. The Southwest Historical Series, vol. IV. Glendale, Calif.: The Arthur H. Clark Co., 1936.

Kennerly, William Clark. *Persimmon Hill: A Narrative of Old St. Louis and the Far West*, ed. Elizabeth Russell. Norman: University of Oklahoma Press, 1948.

Kunetz, W. Vernon. *John Mix Stanley and His Indian Paintings.* Ann Arbor: University of Michigan Press, 1942.

Larpenteur, Charles. *Forty Years a Fur Trader on the Upper Missouri*, ed. Milo M. Quaife. Chicago: The Lakeside Press, 1933.

Lavender, David. *The American Heritage History of the Great West.* New York: American Heritage Publishing Co., 1965.

———. *Bent's Fort.* Garden City, N.Y.: Doubleday & Co., 1954.

———. *The Fist in the Wilderness.* Garden City, N.Y.: Doubleday & Co., 1964.

———. *Land of Giants: The Drive to the Pacific Northwest 1750–1950.* Garden City, N.Y.: Doubleday & Co., 1958.

———. *Westward Vision: The Story of the Oregon Trail.* New York: McGraw-Hill Book Co., 1963.

Lecompte, Janet. "Antoine and Abraham Ledoux," in LeRoy R. Hafen, ed. *The Mountain Men and the Fur Trade of the Far West*, III, 173–179. Glendale, Calif.: The Arthur H. Clark Co., 1966.

Lee, Daniel, and J. H. Frost. *Ten Years in Oregon . . . .* New York: J. Collord, 1844.

Lee, Robert Edson. *From West to East: Studies in the Literature of the American West*. Urbana: University of Illinois Press, 1966.

Lee, Willis T., Ralph W. Stone, Hoyt S. Gale, et. al. *Guidebook of the Western United States; Part B. The Overland Route*. U.S. Geological Survey Bulletin 612. Washington, D.C.: Government Printing Office, 1915.

Leonard, Zenas. *The Narrative of Zenas Leonard*, ed. W. F. Wagner. Cleveland: The Burrows Brothers Co., 1904.

Levin, David. *History as Romantic Art: Bancroft, Prescott, Motley, and Parkman*. Stanford: Stanford University Press, 1959.

Lewis, Meriwether, and William Clark. *The Journals of Lewis and Clark*, ed. Bernard DeVoto. Boston: Houghton Mifflin Co., 1953.

Lienhard, Heinrich. *From St. Louis to Sutter's Fort, 1846*, eds. and trans. Erwin G. Gudde and Elizabeth K. Gudde. Norman: University of Oklahoma Press, 1961.

Long, Margaret. *The Oregon Trail*. Denver: W. H. Kistler Co., 1954.

———. *The Santa Fe Trail*. Denver: W. H. Kistler Co., 1954.

Lowie, Robert H. *The Crow Indians*. New York: Farrar & Rinehart, 1935.

McCann, Lloyd E. "The Grattan Massacre," *Nebraska History*, xxxvii (March, 1956), 1–25.

McCracken, Harold. *Frederic Remington: Artist of the Old West*. New York: J. B. Lippincott Co., 1947.

McDermott, John Dishon. "James Bordeaux," in LeRoy R. Hafen, ed. *The Mountain Men and the Fur Trade of the Far West*, v, 65–80. Glendale, Calif.: The Arthur H. Clark Co., 1968.

———. "John Baptiste Richard," in LeRoy R. Hafen, ed. *The Mountain Men and the Fur Trade of the Far West*, ii, 289–303. Glendale, Calif.: The Arthur H. Clark Co., 1965.

———. "Joseph Bissonette," in LeRoy R. Hafen, ed. *The Mountain Men and the Fur Trade of the Far West*, iv, 46–60. Glendale, Calif.: The Arthur H. Clark Co., 1966.

McNitt, Frank. *The Indian Traders*. Norman: University of Oklahoma Press, 1962.

Magoffin, Susan Shelby. *Down the Santa Fe Trail and into Mexico: The Diary of Susan Shelby Magoffin*, ed. Stella M. Drumm. New Haven: Yale University Press, 1926.

Mattes, Merrill J. "Hiram Scott," in LeRoy R. Hafen, ed. *The Mountain Men and the Fur Trade of the Far West*, I, 355–366. Glendale, Calif.: The Arthur H. Clark Co., 1965.

Mattison, Ray H. "Kenneth McKenzie," in LeRoy R. Hafen, ed. *The Mountain Men and the Fur Trade of the Far West*, II, 217–224. Glendale, Calif.: The Arthur H. Clark Co., 1965.

Maximilian, Prince of Wied-Neuwied. *Travels in the Interior of North America*, in Reuben Gold Thwaites, ed. *Early Western Travels*, XXII–XXIV. Cleveland: The Arthur H. Clark Co., 1906.

Meek, Stephen H. *The Autobiography of a Mountain Man, 1805–1889*, ed. Arthur Woodward. Pasadena: G. Dawson, 1948.

[Melville, Herman]. "Mr. Parkman's Tour," *Literary World*, IV, 113 (March 31, 1849), 291–293.

Meriwether, David. *My Life in the Mountains and on the Plains*, ed. Robert A. Griffen. Norman: University of Oklahoma Press, 1965.

Miller, Alfred Jacob. *The West of Alfred Jacob Miller*, ed. Marvin C. Ross. Norman: University of Oklahoma Press, 1951.

Miller, Gerrit S., Jr., and Remington Kellogg. *List of North American Recent Mammals*. U.S. National Museum, Bulletin 205. Washington, D.C.: Smithsonian Institution, 1955.

Miller, Perry. *The Raven and the Whale: The War of Words and Wits in the Era of Poe and Melville*. New York: Harcourt, Brace and Co., 1956.

Morgan, Dale L., ed. *Overland in 1846: Diaries and Letters of the California-Oregon Trail*. 2 vols. Georgetown, Calif.: The Talisman Press, 1963.

——, ed. *The West of William H. Ashley* . . . . Denver: Old West Publishing Co., 1964.

——, and Eleanor Towles Harris, eds. *The Rocky Mountain Journals of William Marshall Anderson: The West in 1834*. San Marino: The Huntington Library, 1967. (The editors provide a number of important biographies of mountain men in their concluding section, "A Galaxy of Mountain Men.")

Mumey, Nolie. *James Pierson Beckwourth, 1856–1866*. Denver: Old West Publishing Co., 1957.

——. *Old Forts and Trading Posts of the West: Bent's Old Fort and Bent's New Fort on the Arkansas River*. Denver: Artcraft Press, 1956.

Murray, Charles Augustus. *Travels in North America During the Years 1834, 1835, & 1836.* 2 vols. London: R. Bentley, 1839.

Nadeau, Remi. *Fort Laramie and the Sioux Indians.* Englewood Cliffs, N.J.: Prentice-Hall, 1967.

Nelson, Bruce O. *Land of the Dahcotahs.* Minneapolis: University of Minnesota Press, 1946.

Newell, Robert. *Robert Newell's Memoranda . . . ,* ed. Dorothy O. Johansen. Portland: Champoeg Press, 1959.

Nunis, Doyce Blackman, Jr. *Andrew Sublette: Rocky Mountain Prince.* Los Angeles: Dawson's Book Shop, 1960.

Nye, Russel B. "Parkman, Red Fate, and White Civilization," in *Essays on American Literature in Honor of Jay B. Hubbell,* ed. Clarence Gohdes, pp. 152–163. Durham, N.C.: Duke University Press, 1967.

Oglesby, Richard Edward. *Manuel Lisa and the Opening of the Missouri Fur Trade.* Norman: University of Oklahoma Press, 1963.

O'Leary, Mrs. James L. "Henry Chatillon," *Missouri Historical Society Bulletin,* XXII, no. 2, pt. 1 (January, 1966), 123–142.

Oliver, Lilian Hays. *Some Boone Descendants and Kindred of the St. Charles District.* N.p., 1954.

Paden, Irene D. *The Wake of the Prairie Schooner.* New York: Macmillan Co., 1943.

Palmer, Joel. *Journal of Travels over the Rocky Mountains, to the Mouth of the Columbia River; Made During the Years 1845 and 1846,* in Reuben Gold Thwaites, ed. *Early Western Travels,* XXX. Cleveland: The Arthur H. Clark Co., 1906.

Parker, Rev. Samuel. *Journal of an Exploring Tour Beyond the Rocky Mountains. . . .* New York: M. H. Newman & Co., 1846.

Pattie, James O. *Personal Narrative,* ed. Milo M. Quaife. Chicago: The Lakeside Press, 1930.

Pearce, Roy Harvey. *The Savages of America: A Study of the Indian and the Idea of Civilization.* Baltimore: Johns Hopkins University Press, 1965.

Pease, Otis A. *Parkman's History: The Historian as Literary Artist.* New Haven: Yale University Press, 1953.

Peattie, Donald Culross. *A Natural History of Western Trees.* Boston: Houghton Mifflin Co., 1953.

Peckham, Howard H. "The Sources and Revisions of Parkman's *Pontiac*," *Papers of the Bibliographical Society of America*, XXXVII (1943), 1–15.

Pike, Zebulon Montgomery. *The Journals of Zebulon Montgomery Pike with Letters and Related Documents 1783–1854*, ed. Donald Jackson. 2 vols. Norman: University of Oklahoma Press, 1966.

Point, Nicholas, S.J. *Wilderness Kingdom; Indian Life in the Rocky Mountains: 1840–1847*, ed. and trans. Joseph P. Donnelly, S.J. New York: Holt, Rinehart and Winston, 1967.

Porter, Mae Reed, and Odessa Davenport. *Scotsman in Buckskin: Sir William Drummond Stewart and the Rocky Mountain Fur Trade*. New York: Hastings House, 1963.

Porter, Valentine Mott. "A History of Battery 'A' of St. Louis," *Missouri Historical Society Collections*, II (March, 1905), 1–48.

Preuss, Charles. *Exploring With Frémont . . .* , eds. and trans. Erwin G. Gudde and Elizabeth K. Gudde. Norman: University of Oklahoma Press, 1958.

Pritchard, James A. *The Overland Diary of James A. Pritchard from Kentucky to California in 1849*, ed. Dale L. Morgan. Denver: Old West Publishing Co., 1959.

Riggs, Stephen R. *A Dakota-English Dictionary*, ed. James Owen Dorsey. *Contributions to North American Ethnology*, VII; Department of the Interior, U.S. Geographical and Geological Survey of the Rocky Mountain Region. Washington, D.C.: Government Printing Office, 1890.

Robidoux, Olive Messmore. *Memorial to the Robidoux Brothers*. Kansas City: Smith-Grieves Co., 1924.

Ross, Alexander. *The Fur Hunters of the Far West*, ed. Kenneth A. Spaulding. Norman: University of Oklahoma Press, 1956.

Russell, Osborne. *Journal of a Trapper*, ed. Aubrey L. Haines. Portland: Oregon Historical Society, 1950.

Ruxton, George Frederick. *Adventures in Mexico and the Rocky Mountains*, reprinted in LeRoy R. Hafen, ed. *Ruxton of the Rockies*. Norman: University of Oklahoma Press, 1950.

———. *Life in the Far West*, ed. LeRoy R. Hafen. Norman: University of Oklahoma Press, 1964.

Sabin, Edwin L. *Kit Carson Days*. Chicago: A. C. McClurg & Co., 1914.

Sage, Rufus B. *Scenes in the Rocky Mountains* . . . , reprinted in *Rufus B. Sage, His Letters and Papers, 1836–1847*, eds. LeRoy R. Hafen and Ann W. Hafen. 2 vols. The Far West and the Rockies Historical Series 1820–1875, vols. IV–V. Glendale, Calif.: The Arthur H. Clark Co., 1956.

Sampson, William R. "Nathaniel Jarvis Wyeth," in LeRoy R. Hafen, ed. *The Mountain Men and the Fur Trade of the Far West*, V, 381–401. Glendale, Calif.: The Arthur H. Clark Co., 1968.

Sandoz, Mari. *These Were the Sioux*. New York: Hastings House, 1961.

Schramm, Wilbur L. "A New Englander on the Road to Oregon," *New England Quarterly*, XIII (March, 1940), 49–64.

Settle, Raymond W., ed. *The March of the Mounted Riflemen*. . . . Glendale, Calif.: The Arthur H. Clark Co., 1940.

Smith, Henry Nash. *Virgin Land: The American West as Symbol and Myth*. Cambridge: Harvard University Press, 1950.

Stansbury, Howard. *An Expedition to the Valley of the Great Salt Lake of Utah* . . . . Philadelphia: Lippincott, Grambo & Co., 1852.

Stegner, Wallace. *The Gathering of Zion*. New York: McGraw-Hill Book Co., 1964.

Stewart, George R. *The California Trail*. New York: McGraw-Hill Book Co., 1962.

———. *Ordeal by Hunger: The Story of the Donner Party*. New York: Henry Holt and Co., 1936. (Rev. ed. Boston: Houghton Mifflin Co., 1960.)

Stuart, Robert. *The Discovery of the Oregon Trail: Robert Stuart's Narratives of His Overland Trip Eastward from Astoria in 1812–1813*, ed. Philip Ashton Rollins. New York: Charles Scribner's Sons, 1935.

———. *On the Oregon Trail: Robert Stuart's Journey of Discovery*, ed. Kenneth A. Spaulding. Norman: University of Oklahoma Press, 1953.

Sunder, John E. *Bill Sublette: Mountain Man*. Norman: University of Oklahoma Press, 1959.

———. "Solomon P. Sublette," in LeRoy R. Hafen, ed. *The*

Mountain Men and the Fur Trade of the Far West, I, 377–389. Glendale, Calif.: The Arthur H. Clark Co., 1965.

———. "Solomon Perry Sublette: Mountain Man of the Forties," *New Mexico Historical Society Review*, XXXVI (January, 1961), 49–61.

Swanton, John R. *The Indian Tribes of North America*. Bureau of American Ethnology Bulletin no. 145. Washington, D.C.: Smithsonian Institution, 1952.

Talbot, Theodore. *The Journals of Theodore Talbot, 1843 and 1849–1852*, ed. Charles H. Carey. Portland: Metropolitan Press, 1931.

Thornton, J. Quinn. *Oregon and California in 1848 . . . .* 2 vols. New York: Harper and Bros., 1849.

Thwaites, Reuben Gold, ed. *Early Western Travels*. 32 vols. Cleveland: The Arthur H. Clark Co., 1904–1907.

Townsend, John Kirk. *Narrative of a Journey Across the Rocky Mountains, to the Columbia River, and a Visit to the Sandwich Islands . . . .* Philadelphia: Henry Perkins, 1839.

Trenholm, Virginia Cole, and Maurine Carley. *The Shoshonis: Sentinels of the Rockies*. Norman: University of Oklahoma Press, 1964.

Turner, Henry Smith. *The Original Journals of Henry Smith Turner: With Stephen Watts Kearny to New Mexico and California 1846–1847*, ed. Dwight L. Clarke. Norman: University of Oklahoma Press, 1966.

Twitchell, Ralph Emerson. *The Leading Facts of New Mexico History*. 2 vols. Cedar Rapids: The Torch Press, 1912.

Vandiveer, Clarence A. *The Fur-Trade and Early Western Exploration*. Cleveland: The Arthur H. Clark Co., 1929.

Vestal, Stanley. *Jim Bridger*. New York: W. Morrow & Co., 1946.

———. *Joe Meek: The Merry Mountain Man*. Caldwell, Idaho: Caxton Printers, 1952.

Victor, Frances Fuller. *The River of the West . . . .* Hartford: R. W. Bliss & Co., 1870.

Wade, Mason. *Francis Parkman: Heroic Historian*. New York: The Viking Press, 1942.

Walker, Ardis M. "Joseph R. Walker," in LeRoy R. Hafen, ed.

The Mountain Men and the Fur Trade of the Far West, v, 361–380. Glendale, Calif.: The Arthur H. Clark Co., 1968.

Walsh, James E. "*The California and Oregon Trail*: A Bibliographic Study," *New Colophon*, iii, 9 (December, 1950), 279–285.

Waugh, Alfred S. "Desultory Wanderings in the Years 1845–46," ed. John Francis McDermott, *Missouri Historical Society Bulletin*, vi (April, 1950), 288–322.

———. *Travels in Search of the Elephant: The Wanderings of Alfred S. Waugh, Artist, in Louisiana, Missouri, and Santa Fe, in 1845–46*, ed. John Francis McDermott. St. Louis: Missouri Historical Society, 1951.

Webb, James Josiah. *Adventures in the Santa Fé Trade 1844–1847*, ed. Ralph P. Bieber. The Southwest Historical Series, vol. i. Glendale, Calif.: The Arthur H. Clark Co., 1931.

Webb, Walter Prescott. *The Great Plains*. Boston: Ginn and Co., 1931.

Wells, Eugene T. "The Growth of Independence, Missouri, 1827–1850," *Missouri Historical Society Bulletin*, xvi (October, 1959), 33–46.

Williams, Joseph. *Narrative of a Tour from the State of Indiana to the Oregon Territory in the Years 1841–42*, ed. James C. Bell, Jr. New York: Cadmus Book Shop, 1921.

Willman, Lillian W. "The History of Fort Kearny," *Publications of the Nebraska State Historical Society*, xxi (1930), 213–326.

Wilson, Edmund. *Apologies to the Iroquois*. New York: Farrar, Straus and Cudahy, 1960.

Wislizenus, F. A. *A Journey to the Rocky Mountains in the Year 1839*. St. Louis: Missouri Historical Society, 1912.

———. *Memoir of a Tour to Northern Mexico, Connected with Col. Doniphan's Expedition, in 1846 and 1847*. Senate Miscellaneous Document no. 26, 30th Congress, 1st session (serial 517). Washington, D.C., 1848.

Wissler, Clark. "Societies and Ceremonial Associations in the Oglala Division of the Teton-Dakota," *Anthropological Papers of the American Museum of Natural History*, xi, 1–100. New York, 1916.

Wood, Dean Earl. *The Old Santa Fe Trail from the Missouri River.* Kansas City, Mo.: E. L. Mendenhall, 1951.

Work, John. *The Journal of John Work,* eds. William S. Lewis and Paul C. Phillips. Cleveland: The Arthur H. Clark Co., 1923.

Index

Abert, J. W.: and Fitzpatrick, 33*a* n; cited on Raymond, 544–45; suffers from "mountain fever," 601–2, 664; at Bent's Fort, 662; mentioned, 11*a*, 544, 665

Absaroka region, 526. *See also* Crow Indians

Absinthe. *See* Sagebrush

Adirondack Mountains: FP visits, 628, 630

Agassiz Museum (Museum of Comparative Zoology), 318, 647

Aioë, Marie, 548

Algonquin Indians, 533

Allen, James, 697–98

Amelia (steamboat), 410, 705

American Fur Company: Chatillon and, 14, 444–45; Fort Laramie and, 106, 513; owns other posts, 107, 117; Beckwourth and, 133; mentioned, 67*a*, 68, 158, 308, 444, 510, 515, 519, 520, 530, 541, 549, 603, 634, 643, 680. *See also* Astor, John Jacob; Pierre Chouteau, Jr., & Co.

American Society for Encouraging the Settlement of Oregon, 20*a*

Antelope (pronghorn): described, 71, 82, 126, 142–43, 222, 237, 392, 565; as Indian peace spirit, 156–57; discussed, 485; mentioned, 15*a*, 70, 125, 127–28, 176, 184, 190, 192, 201, 277, 280, 301, 493, 590

Arapaho Indians: kill trappers, 141, 259, 518, 616; and Gros Ventre

Blackfeet, 252; FP characterizes, 258; Kearny meets in 1845, 258–59, 616; menace whites, 260; deserted camp of, 322–23; at Pueblo, 331–32; FP describes village of, 348–52, 615, 670, 672–73; language of, 349–50; Maxwell and, 349–50; make a "surround," 360–61; history of, 670; mentioned, 25*a*, 35*a*, xii, 325, 346, 347, 355, 359, 564, 639, 650, 669

Arikara Indians, 534

Arkansas River: Pike explores, 23*a*, 651; FP follows, 327–400 *passim*; FP describes, 327, 331, 349, 370–71, 384, 391; mentioned, 23*a*, 24*a*, 248, 308, 313, 314, 324, 327–400 *passim*, 500–533 *passim*, 638–99 *passim*

"Armor Gods," 574. *See also* Medicine bags

Army of the West: occupies New Mexico, 25*a*; described, 35*a*–36*a*, 25, 384, 687; on Santa Fe Trail, 314–15; marches on Santa Fe, 334; at Bent's Fort, 334, 661, 670; at Fort Leavenworth, 455; sickness in, 543, 601–2; campaign of, 645; composition of, 686–87; mentioned, 11*a*, 248, 333, 454, 511, 684. *See also* Dragoons, First U.S.; Kearny, Stephen Watts; Volunteers, Missouri

Arrow-Head, the (Oglala Indian), 207, 596

Arsenic, vii, 419